MW01518091

And Only The Horses Wore No Uniforms

And Only The Horses Wore No Uniforms

✦

A Memoir

Hermann Moratz

iUniverse, Inc.
New York Lincoln Shanghai

And Only The Horses Wore No Uniforms
A Memoir

Copyright © 2007 by Hermann Moratz

iUniverse books may be ordered through booksellers or by contacting:

iUniverse
2021 Pine Lake Road, Suite 100
Lincoln, NE 68512
www.iuniverse.com
1-800-Authors (1-800-288-4677)

The views expressed in this work are solely those of the author and do not necessarily reflect the views of the publisher, and the publisher hereby disclaims any responsibility for them.

ISBN-13: 978-0-595-42849-6 (pbk)
ISBN-13: 978-0-595-68191-4 (cloth)
ISBN-13: 978-0-595-87187-2 (ebk)
ISBN-10: 0-595-42849-5 (pbk)
ISBN-10: 0-595-68191-3 (cloth)
ISBN-10: 0-595-87187-9 (ebk)

Printed in the United States of America

"Defeat is never permanent
Nor triumph everlasting
Only memory seals these moments
In unending grace."
(Ernestine Bradley)

Contents

ACKNOWLEDGMENT

I thank my children, William Christopher Moratz (referred to in this book as "Bill" while younger, or "Chris"), Karen Evans Moratz and George Evans for publishing this book. I am grateful to my wife Anna Lore for her encouragement and hard work in typing and editing it. Many thanks also to Joanne Button of the Cornell University Uris Library Computer Lab for her much-needed moral support and technical assistance.

SCOPE

My life's memories start in Germany. Among many places, they take me to the countries of Brazil, USA and Germany again. They conclude in my home country, the USA. See Table of Contents for details.

FOREWORD

I am happy to introduce what has been a story told to my sister Karen and me in small fragments around our dining room table or at holidays while we were growing up. Our small American family kept close together. All of our blood relatives remain in Europe. My father Hermann Moratz told some of his stories once, others more often. Growing up, I started pestering him to write them down. I even started putting them on paper myself as I remembered them. But my memories are not his memories. Some were not accurate, so he started writing. The end result is this book. It brings back our old family life. The aroma of the Brazilian cigars Dad sometimes smoked while talking about his life is a part of these memoirs. Sometimes Prussian marching music from the era of Frederick the Great would play on our family hi-fi. I feel lucky to have been born into this story. One can see from our family's adventures since my birth that Karen's and my lives have been exciting, too. Growing up, I perhaps felt more than a bit of awe at the circumstances of my parents' arrival in these United States and at how our family navigated the ups and downs many 1st generation immigrants undergo while finding their way in a new land. I always found Hermann's war experiences fascinating, but they never touched me as much as when I read his book. I had never fully understood some parts of these stories until then. Now, their astounding clarity has given me a new perspective on Hermann's life. Together with my mother's earlier writings about her background, they have resulted in new insights about my parents' history and origins. My father's description on learning to fly makes the reader feel like sitting in the airplane with him. It reminds me of two wonderful experiences he and I shared. In my early professional career I had an assignment in Germany. Visiting me, Dad showed me the cradle of the German sport. Here, at the "Wasserkuppe" near Fulda, some of the very early glider experiments took place after World War I. In the aviation museum, he pointed out the features of such models as the "Grunau Baby" and the "Kranich" two-seater, on which he learned to fly. Later, in the Mosel Valley, we sampled its extraordinary wines and viniculture. Some of the best Riesling wines are grown in what must be one of Germany's most beautiful areas.

My own life experiences will never compare to the struggles Hermann faced in the dark days as World War II was ending. I can only liken them to the grimmest situation mountain climbers might face, the only comparison that comes to mind from my experience. Naturally, in the mountains there is more control over the outcome of one's own fate than there is in war. I can only compare the onslaught of the Red Army to a massive avalanche coming to sweep away Hermann and his poor comrades in arms. The reader will agree that he was indeed a "lucky boy," as his mother often called him. Perhaps a bit of luck rubbed off on me—I never had to fight such a war. When I sometimes asked: "What did you do during the war?" Hermann was likely to answer: "I was on the wrong side," which he did not choose. I think Bertolt Brecht's poem comes close to what Hermann felt when he came home to Berlin in late 1945:

'HOMECOMING'

City of my fathers, how do I find thee?
I arrive at home
Following swarms of bombers.
Where is this city?
It is where the ominous black mountain of fire stands.
There it is, that thing in the fires.

City of my fathers, how will you receive me?
Ahead of me came the bombers.
Deadly swarms
Announce my return.
Fireballs
Precede the son.

(From Brecht: Gedichte 6 Gedichte im Exil/in Sammlungen nicht enthaltene Gedichte 1941–1947) published by Suhrkamp Verlag. Translated by William Christopher Moratz, May 2006, Gardiner, NY

These memoirs are significant since few men survived the German side of the war. Of his large 1938 all-male middle school class in Berlin-Spandau, he encountered only three who were left after the war. The few survivors in the East were further decimated after the incredibly hard and cruel years in Russian gulags. And few of those men would want to dredge up those dark memories. How or what German people then knew—or thought—of what was happening when Hitler came to power and about what was happening to the Jews and other victims of that regime can also be seen in these pages. Germans of the war generation rarely bring up such an uncomfortable topic, but the important questions it raises will never go away and would often be discussed in our family. Outsiders make their own assumptions about what it means to have German origins, but my father's memories provide a rare glimpse from inside one family's ethnic perspective. When I was younger, I had struggles with the meaning of my own ethnicity.

Germany's postwar rebuilding and economic successes were not on the horizon when my father left. Having lived in modern times on both sides of the Atlantic, I am thankful my parents took the course they did. Questions of immigration and ethnic groups' inclusion into society are valid everywhere today. With a high percentage of Turkish and other "foreigners" in Germany, the question remains: "What does it mean to be German?" There is no one answer. My family's answer is that we are not Germans, but proud to be Americans. The USA is a land of immigrants, except for the Native American people who, in the distant past, may also have arrived via the Bering Land Bridge. Later in life Hermann came out on the winning side more and more by making the right decisions. This is easier to do in a free society, such as the one in which we live. For this we are grateful.

I now live four hours away by car. My sister Karen and her husband George live an airplane ride away from our parents. All of us would get together more often if we could. Hermann gave us the first draft of his memoirs in time for our parents' fiftieth wedding anniversary, celebrated in grand style at a Midwestern family gathering in March of 2006. He had never considered publishing this work himself. Our gift to our parents was to celebrate their legacy by publishing this book. As we reflect on the past, Hermann's memoirs will accompany our lives, while the story continues to unfold in fulfillment, success and happiness.

William Christopher Moratz
(To my father: "Bill," to many of my friends: "Chris")

Gardiner, NY, July 2006

GERMANY

MY ROOTS IN KLEIN SABIN

The Moratz', that is, the father of Gustav Emil Moratz (my father), came from the village of Klein Sabin, County (Kreis) Dramburg, in the Prussian province of Eastern Pomerania (Hinterpommern). This province bordered the Baltic Sea to the North, the Oder River to the West, and West and East Prussia to the East. It is now entirely Polish. My grandparents were farmhands (Tageloehner). They also spoke some form of the Polish language that even some of their kids at times jokingly applied, especially the youngest, Wilhelm, who lived in Falkensee near Berlin. The other children besides father were Mila, Emilie, Minna and Hermann who was K.I.A. in World War I, after whom I was named. Grandpa Moratz had about the same face features as my father, who was born in 1888. They were typically "ostbaltisch", the kind of features that dominated Eastern Germany. In accordance with my documents he was totally German: no other origin is traceable as far back as about 1800. The joking in "Polish" may have been typical for people who worked together with Poles, who came to the large farms in the summer to help with the harvest, like Mexican farm workers in the U.S.

I don't remember father talking about his childhood in Klein Sabin, where he was born January 4, 1888, except for stories about amazing amounts of chanterelles (Pfifferlinge) he harvested in the woods, cutting them down with a sickle. I know his sole education took about four years and believe it occurred at a one-room village school-similar to those in the American Midwest around the 19th century or earlier. He could write, but hated it and always left it to mother. He could read; I remember him with the 'Spandauer Volksblatt,' a Socialist paper. Gustav wrote in awkward Gothic (Suetterlin) letters, which I also learned in school; he never used Latin letters. I don't remember him doing math. If he knew some, it couldn't have been much.

FROM KLEIN SABIN TO SPANDAU

As the German Reich underwent an intensive industrial expansion at the end of the 19th century after the Franco-German war in 1870/71, Grandpa Moratz must have made the decision to look for opportunities to better the family's life. I have never heard exactly in which year he left Pomerania and its poverty and dependence-almost serfdom-which had been his fate "back home." Of course he hit the road to Berlin where industries were sprouting and growing at the end of the 19th century. He must have arrived in Spandau around the turn of the century. I saw him during approximately 1924–25 when I was very young, in the Staakener Strasse, which starts where is now the new railway station Spandau (old Spandau West). I also vividly remember my Aunt Minna who was married to Hermann Dorow. They lived at the Klosterstrasse opposite the railway freight station (now gone, along with the house). More about this later.

FATHER'S FIRST MARRIAGE

Gustav, who must have done his active military duty around 1908–1910, served in the infantry and was trained to operate machine guns. Something new at the time! Shortly before World War I, he must have started working in one of the many armament factories in Spandau as a non-skilled laborer. He then found a job with the B.V.G. (Berliner Verkehrsgesellschaft) as a streetcar money collector (Strassenbahnschaffner): a somewhat more socially secure position, but it paid rather poorly—just enough for renting a place to sleep and food, but there must have been a bit left over to befriend girls! So, on April 3, 1913 Gustav Emil Moratz married Amanda Amalie Boehlke, born April 29, 1889 at Betckenhammer near Deutsch-Krone, West Prussia. Anyway, shortly thereafter my sister Elisabeth (Lisbeth to me, Lisa to her later husband) saw the lights of this universe, not realizing that rough times were ahead.

Gustav had to say "Goodbye" to his young family early in WWI (1914) and was shipped, flowers decorating the rifles, to the Western front. Later he rarely elaborated on his exploits during that war. I remember seeing only one or two group photos with his comrades, in which most were sporting two feet long porcelain pipes-I still wonder how these were transported along during that war! Later in life I remember one of those pipes—which he never used—hanging on the wall of the W.C. when we lived at Ulmenstrasse 6. I do recall him telling once that he was at the battle of Verdun, where I think 400,000 German soldiers died and a larger amount of French. The German (and French) military leaders tried to kill off more of the enemy than the opposite forces and thus "win" the war. What irony! Soon, his Regiment was transferred to the East-a much easier part of the conflict-at least for the Germans. In between, Gustav must have gotten furlough, which is the custom, and the result was Ursula (later known as Ulli to me). I believe she was born in February of 1917. During that time, the blockade of Germany by the British Empire finally resulted in acute food shortages, particularly for people in the large cities who had no countryside relations or garden plots. Amanda got sick and passed away in 1918 or 19 (some, for instance Marianne, say she died in childbirth with the third baby, to which the lack of food and care must have contributed). So, father returned from the war, settled with two small daughters. I simply do not know how he could have fed everyone or taken care of the other immediate and pressing need, not to speak about illnesses.

FATHER'S SECOND MARRIAGE, TO MY MOTHER

Perhaps father had already known Amanda's niece, Martha, who at 22 was seven years his junior at the end of WWI. She had left home in Nauen to become a domestic employee at Pastor Kneisel's in Spandau at the Nikolaikirche. Maybe she could sidetrack some food from the kitchen where she worked, and where she learned to make those good things like pork- or beef roast, goose, duck, Koenigsberger Klopse, etc. etc. Martha Boehlke, the later Mrs. Moratz, came from Nauen, County (Kreis) of Osthavelland where all of her ties were during her lifetime. My parents must have gotten married around 1920. I heard mother saying at the time that all girls were simply and foolishly looking for guys who returned from the war and still had all their limbs and guts. They were thought to be honest. I also learned somewhere that there was another interested gentleman who left for the USA, and I believe she sometimes thought she could have had an easier life. (Isn't everything easier in America? Snicker, snicker …). She was to visit the USA later.

MOTHER'S HOME IN NAUEN

Mother had grown up with her younger brother Fritz, later a mechanic, and the older Willy, who was trained and worked for the rest of his life as a land surveyor. The household might be described today as lower middle class. Grandpa had been a laborer without much education in West Prussia (an area east of Frankfurt/Oder), got employed by the Railway (Reichsbahn) in Nauen and later wrangled himself up to the title of "Oberladeschaffner". I assume he supervised the loading and unloading of freight cars at the railway. His wife Eline, nee Kuehl came from a "better" family. Her father was a master carpenter (Schreinermeister)-the best pedigree any of my ancestors could muster. All other men were laborers (Arbeiter) and women domestic help (Dienstmagd). Marriage- and other documents actually contain these same occupational descriptions. Grandma Kuehl passed away very early. Whenever I visited Grandpa (Opa) later together with mother, we would stop first at the cemetery, where Grandma (Oma) occupied a very nice plot with an impressive, large stone. The hillock and stone were overgrown with ivy. There, my mother would rest a long time on a bench, visibly immersed in thoughts about her past, which she did not tell me anything about. This was her way of doing things ... no malice or ill will ... just: this was how things were. By that time, Opa had remarried: Mrs. Milius, whose son was married to Aunt Frieda. They lived at the main highway Berlin-Hamburg, as one enters Nauen coming from Berlin. I remember excitedly observing fashionable sport cars racing by-part of the Deutschland Rallye, from East Prussia to Southern Germany. The drivers sported the kinds of goggles, caps and overalls one nowadays sees in the movies. I saw Mercedes, Bugattis, Alfa Romeos, Bentleys, Horchs, etc. These dust-covered men in their driving machines impressed me greatly. They seemed to belong to another unreachable, untouchable world. The thought of owning an automobile in the late 20's was about as futile as going on vacation to a fashionable place. I simply did not venture this kind of foolish musings. At that time I didn't believe I could ever own a car. It was only for others, period. Tall, blond and blue-eyed, Aunt Frieda had a wonderfully open, beaming expression. And-she cooked a turkey for one of our visits-which was unheard of and very avant-garde for that time. The bird was delicious and the dinner a huge success. One must consider that, in German households of our class, dinners were rarely offered-and especially not such super-extravagant affairs. This visit remains engraved in my mind until today, though I was in the dark about any special reason, nor did we ever visit Frieda again afterwards. Neither did I know why father never accompanied us on these Nauen visits, which struck me as strange. Since Amanda, his first wife, was Opa's sister, whom I now find out in writing this, I think there may have been problems at the occasion of Amanda's death. But this is speculation only, about 80 years later.

Opa visited us once or twice in Spandau during my life. It was strange seeing him one hour after arrival marching up and down in front of our wall-pendulum clock, comparing the time of his pocket watch with the wall clock and appearing anxious to leave. I also remember never receiving a present from him, and I was certainly not spoiled to expect it. I do remember him, though, visiting me at the Spandau Hospital at Lynarstrasse, when he brought me a huge Jaffa Orange. I had never had such an orange before. There I was recuperating from diphtheria-which was deadly then. After Opa left, I wolfed down the whole fruit and got terribly sick. Nothing stayed down and the entire sections came up whole. Soon thereafter, the disease came back with increased intensity and danger. I barely made it, because a relapse was usually deadly. Besides all this, I liked the Nauen visits with Opa. He, or better Oma (Mrs. Milius), had a wonderful glass jar filled with sweets which she always got at the grocery store as a come-on. And he had brown beer (no alcohol), which was brought by horse drawn carriage and had to ferment a little before we drank it. And in the evening that was served together with "Mettwurst" and rye bread on a wooden plate. You cut a piece of sausage and put it in your mouth together with a piece of the bread-delicious-something we didn't do at home. Opa had two fairly large garden plots, apparently leased from the railway, close to the railway dam. The railway coming from Berlin, became elevated shortly before Nauen, and so was the train station-so that the Nauen Street traffic would not get interrupted by the many trains passing through from Berlin to Hamburg. There was everything a gardener could dream of … very utilitarian! Strawberries, Loganberries, Gooseberries green and purple, cucumbers, lettuce, peas, beans, potatoes, beets, cabbage, dill, parsley, onions, everything! Mother always went home with a heavy load. Naturally we mostly visited in good weather when something was up for harvest. These plots were blessed with wonderful black earth … all wetland waste before Friedrich II (the Great) had canals dug throughout the Havelland to draw out the water: one of the great accomplishments of that kind. During those years mother's older brother Willy married Aunt Hanni. I faintly remember the great festivities. Her father ran a cattle trading outfit, so there was some substance for a proper celebration. Willy later settled in Koepenick South of Berlin and I never saw him again until I mustered the courage in 1939 or 1940 to visit them. Hanni fried filet of sole in pure butter for this occasion. Something we never had at home … what a waste, we thought, for valuable butter! Connections with the brothers were very scarce. The younger brother, Uncle Fritz-a hunk of a man and a competition swimmer—once visited when I was small. All of us visited our garden plot West of Spandau (Magistratsweg). Fritz had a little Kayak on the Canal in Nauen. Anyway, since he was over six feet tall, he knocked his head against the doorframe when entering the tool shed. Blood was flowing profusely; he never came again. He married in the late 30's and settled in Oranienburg North of Berlin.

EARLY CHILDHOOD

The first embarrassment I remember was during play in the Sprengelstrasse, which runs parallel to Ulmenstrasse. There was an exit from our courtyard also into that street. Because it was so tiny, kids couldn't play in the court below our apartment; it was paved in concrete. Suddenly, all kids were running away from me one day during play, shouting "hee-hee," a German child's expression of disgust, while I hastened to run after them, repeating: "hee-hee." But it soon dawned on me that they were trying to escape from me, because a big B.M. in form of a sausage was emerging from my pants. Mother, to the rescue!

A wedding was going on at Aunt Minna's. The whole family had to appear, except that I had to stay in bed with a terrible flu. No physician was called for just a simple flu! He would have prescribed the same thing: "good old Maehliss"-then young and making home visits by bike. At the age of three or four, a cold wet towel was wrapped around my chest, then some dry ones, followed by all the woolen blankets we had, and covered by a feather bed. Before that I had to drink lemonade. Thus I sweated alone in a dark room profusely for about two hours. The blankets all got wet, the fever receded—the horse cure always worked! Obviously no harm was done, neither did I feel shortchanged.

Decisions had to be made constantly by everyone. Sometimes one listens to one's peers, sometimes siblings, and at times parents. One day this pal Unne Reschke played with me at Ulmenstrasse around a street drain, which was solid iron with a movable lid fitting precisely into its counterpart. Said Unne, who lifted the lid and balanced it with one hand: "Sohni," (mother's nickname for me, perhaps derived from the American "Sonny." When it was no longer appreciated, she stopped-perhaps love changed to adoration?) "Why don't you place your finger here in the drain? I want to try something." I did, and Unne let the lid go. What a yell I gave off when he let it go, which squashed half of my finger when it fell. Thanks to Dr. Maehliss and luck, it grew back together. When I was five or six, I played in the Metzerstrasse on top of a deep utility ditch, slipped and landed on top of a sharp rock. My whole left thigh cracked open to the bone, so one could see it. Somehow they got me to Maehliss' office, and he stitched it all together again. I still have the large scar on the left thigh.

GROWING UP IN SPANDAU

I spent my early years in a very small apartment in the back court of the main building on the second floor of Ulmenstrasse 6 in Spandau: one living room, a very spartanic, narrow W.C., which contained a toilet bowl plus seat, with a tiny 12x12" window way up high. It was very dark, but I could see a porcelain pipe hanging on the wall; no facility to wash hands, shower or take a bath. The "Spandauer Volksblatt" (daily journal) was cut up in neat, handy pieces, which you had to crumble by hand to soften the impact on your you know what, as there was no toilet paper. The kitchen contained a wood and bituminous coal briquette-fired stove. In the early 20's, there was gas light only. Baths were taken once weekly in the kitchen. All five of us—one after the other—used heated water from an oversized bucket. We were very close, because there was hardly any room! The living room also served as bedroom for all of us-lots of beds, one table and one sofa, and a ceramic, wood/coal fired oven. The sun never made it into this room. Adjacent to Ulmenstrasse six, father kept two goats in a small corner of an empty plot with a very primitive shed. I don't remember who milked the goats but I must have gotten most of that milk. I do remember the harrowing occasion when father wanted, or had to, kill the goats-probably because he had to vacate the shed. He swung frantically with a large ax at the goat's head. It surely did not enjoy this treatment. It took an awful lot of swings and cursing until the poor thing finally succumbed. We used the goat's meat mostly in cabbage purees, etc. It was leathery and tasted horrible. I may have been the only one not affected by the shortage of living space, which was pathetic but not unusual for those of the same class. At least we had the apartment and food. Before joining the BVG, from the time he returned from the war in 1918, until about 1923–24, father had been a laborer in some kind of sweatshop near the Spandau Hauptbahnhof. Inflation was then so bad that mother came to the gate Fridays with a knapsack to get the pay-rushing the moneybag immediately to the nearest grocery store to exchange everything for food-if available. In the mid 20's, father was promoted to streetcar driver, which entitled him to a great sheepskin coat. Yes, it paid a few more pennies, but hardly sufficed to ever get a beer for him. To see him drink one at home would have been the ultimate luxury. The only time he did was when he went out to play "Skat" with his colleagues Piesker, Glaser and Maureschat, when a "Boenicke" cigar was also lit, and when I was four or five years old, I could kiebitz with him. In the winters, father sported the great coat for work-gray-green wool fabric outside, sheepskin inside—and felt boots and sheepskin cap. The streetcar drivers were exposed to the weather-some winters, particularly in 1927, had temperatures as low as -27deg.C (-17F).

Christmas brought a transformation of the great coat, which was turned inside out. Voila! With a man stuffed inside, Santa Claus emerged. A Christmas tree would be lit with real candles. We never had a cat, because there was no room!

After saying a little poem, each of us received a Christmas plate of apples, oranges, nuts and some cookies. Santa arrived with a bag and a bundle of birch twigs. The good kids got a little present-always of a practical nature, such as socks knit by mother. We did not know toys, except a self-made recorder, which father had made of wound willow skin, which really made sounds. Boys' wool socks were always long, since the pants were short; long boys' pants did not exist, so they had to wear a contraption: socks were fastened to an elastic, which ended in a halter, by a button at the end. In the summers we went barefoot; shoes were too expensive. Father had shoe repair tools; when a sole broke loose or wore thin, it was fastened again with tacks, or a leather patch was nailed to the thin sole portion. Often the results were quite imperfect, and I now believe mother and the girls must have hated it. But I believe this helped father to accumulate some pennies in a savings account, not heeding the warnings from sister Minna and her husband, Hermann Dorow, who had lost all they had during the 1923 inflation and started from zero, again!

Despite the extreme frugality, times were relatively good after the horrible 1923 inflation and before the thirties depression. The goats in the shed helped a lot; so did the garden plot on the Magistratsweg towards Staaken. The big crop there was potatoes, cabbage, onions, beans, peas, Kohlrabi, Kale … in short, things to fill the belly. The plot had to be worked intensely, so we needed a hand drawn cart. Father had one custom-made, to be pulled by two people with leather straps we put around the shoulder. About six feet long, with four very sturdy steel-ring wheels, it easily carried up to 600 lbs. It was used to bring in large amounts of manure from area farmers, with father and mother in leather straps, pulling, and the kids pushing the flavorful load from behind. This most valuable equipment was kept in the basement family partition, and I thought of it often after I had left for foreign shores-how it helped with gathering firewood and other necessities. There was an expensive, easy way, and there was a hard, inexpensive way to get firewood. Naturally, father scouted for timber harvesting spots in the summer and negotiated with the forester in charge for the right to dig up roots, which cost only a pittance, but required enormous muscle work to dig up and split. So, in the summer, the entire family would take the cart way out into the country behind Seeburg up to the army proving grounds Doeberitz. Father worked all day like a madman, and mother helped as much as she could, while the kids fooled around, sometimes collecting mushrooms or berries. In the evening the cart was loaded with firewood, and it took up to 1-1/2 hours to pull it home, the kids usually on top or pushing from behind. Few people could do this, because almost no one had the foresight to acquire the kind of cart we had-most people preferred spending their time joining political parties and root or demonstrate for a better life. All parties promised better conditions, salaries, etc., but father was not an activist, but conservative at heart. Though his sympathies were always cautiously with the Social Democratic Party (SPD), he never thought much of any politician. Actually, he would nicely fit into today's times. He felt a man has to provide for his family; also, he found his laboring enjoyable in a way. He loved nature, and to be in the fresh air, which may have reminded him of his childhood in the Pommerania countryside.

SCHOOL ... AND BUSINESS START-UP

Around 1927 I started school. All children had long-pinpointed conical containers filled with goodies. Everyone but me! I didn't think I had reason to complain-this whole school thing was so exciting that I forgot the silly ramifications. My class teacher was Mr. Schmeling, but not the boxer Max Schmeling! The school was only five minutes away at the Adamstrasse on Foelderichplatz. It is still there, never was modified, and still serves the same purpose: teach kids the basics; no play, no babysitting, just basics, which works well. I had no trouble learning the basics and did well in everything but religion. Somewhere in my second or third school year we moved to Weissenburger Strasse Ecke Woertherstrasse. Father seemed to have scrounged some money together during all these years, probably in a cigar box somewhere. I wonder if he ever knew enough about business to analyze his actions; I believe he just wanted to strike out and do what other merchants did: get a piece of the action, collect a percentage of cash flow: the <u>only</u> way to get somewhere. He moved into a small grocery store, which included living quarters. So now he had to run his streetcar and fetch fresh produce, which kept him very busy. Naturally there were already old, established stores around. My mother took care of sales, and Lisbeth was there quite a bit. It must have been on a full-time basis. There was no cash register; how anyone kept track of cash and sales is a mystery. I was then too little to understand and have only flashes of memory: Lisbeth's white coat, small sales of 1/4 lbs. of this and 1/8 lbs. of that ... no real volume. One morning tragedy struck: father tried to kill himself by opening the gas valve of the stove, which he could only do because living quarters were across the hallway. The entire family stood in horrible shock as our suffering, moaning father was carried out. And how were we to go on without him? Naturally I could not see through this, but mother must have been worried stiff. A few days later father returned, and we moved out-that's all I remember of this disaster. Father must have lost all of his savings and then some; I believe he also gave up that garden plot near the Magistratsweg. How long this grocery business lasted I don't recall … perhaps a year. This was a low, low point in the Moratz family life, and very depressing, particularly mother and the girls were so sad, and no one talked to me about this as long as they lived. It seems unreal-most of it was never explained to me.

A NEW BEGINNING AT THE ZIMMERSTRASSE

No. 13A, second floor, had a little balcony, two bedrooms, one living room, kitchen and a small food supply storage room (Speisekammer: refrigerators did not exist). The bathroom with a real tub was a huge improvement, but don't think one could just enter, open the hot water faucet and take a bath anytime! Tub usage was strictly controlled for this very old construction; one sat on bare, galvanized steel without porcelain enamel or paint finish, but what a celebration it was when the water heater got fired up with wood and bituminous coal, about once a month or less. After father, I went in (same water), and then the others-not necessarily in that order. No one received preferential treatment. It was an enormous improvement of family hygiene. The two girls were now fifteen and eleven. Lisbeth was no longer in school; Ulli and I still attended it daily. What about Lisbeth? I remember her as a saleslady at Woolworth's downtown Breit-estrasse store in the chocolate department. Hard-working and bright, she was later promoted to department manager, then to sidekick to the store manager. So, not much attention was given to the girls' educational needs. One can sympa-thize with them as long as one wishes, but father had just lost everything and had undergone a severe depression and suicide attempt. There was no taste for extrav-agance left, if there ever had even been a trace.

We were then slowly approaching the '29 depression. Luckily father had a secure, if meager, job, which carried reasonable health insurance, and the com-pany (owned by the municipality) had other benefits. For instance, when I almost succumbed to diphtheria, I spent eight weeks in a special children's recu-peration home in Bad Pyrmont, in the lovely hills of Lower Saxony. I lost several weeks of school, but Mr. Schmeling was confident I would catch up easily, which I did. Thus, I did not have to repeat a class, which often happens in German schools-about 3-4 out of a class of 25-30 in our case. When depression hit Ger-many (and the world), the family had somehow mentally recuperated from the devastating blow of the failed business. Father was the only breadwinner; Lisbeth contributed a smidgeon. The two girls occupied one bedroom; the parents and I the other. Of course, with an ever-changing schedule, father was often gone at night; often he would return at 1:00 or 2:00 a.m. to catch up on sleep. On other days he would leave at 4:00 a.m. There was a large scheduling board at the streetcar station on Pichelsdorfer South of Adamstrasse where we had to copy his starting time and streetcar numbers-all went from Spandau into Berlin Center. Then he coordinated with mother if he would take along a sandwich and a thermos (barley brew, not coffee), or if mother would have to wait for his streetcar at a certain time at the Zimmerstrasse stop and pass him a full dinner. The dinner would be packed in a wicker basket wrapped in blankets to keep it warm until father ate it at the Johannesstift final stop in the North of Spandau.

Father also did all necessary repairs around the apartment and saw to it that wood, kindling, bituminous coal, potatoes etc. were stored. We purchased huge amounts of potatoes in the fall when they were inexpensive. A farmer delivered them to the door. Our basement partition contained a special box which held 400-600 lbs. This lasted until the next harvest. We ate potatoes daily in any imaginary form as basis for our meals: the most delicious being crisp, brown fried potato pancakes, perhaps topped with home-made applesauce. Those we gathered in the city drainage (sewage) fields, where very sour apples grew, and made them into sauce. We also knew where to pick free plums or cherries-there was always something to be canned for the winter. Canned goods were something we never could afford. The only luxury was a little chocolate for birthdays, Easter, Christmas, etc.

Mother did all the chores in the house: upkeep, cleaning, cooking, shopping for supplies (never toilet paper or paper towels!), knitting, sewing of new dresses and repairs, and washing for the whole household. The "big wash" took place under the roof of the four-story apartment building, in a special washing kitchen and drying space. The "Waschkueche" contained a huge wood-coal fired copper kettle. The wash was boiled and transferred into a big galvanized container where each piece was individually washed, kneaded, rinsed and wrung dry, ready for the line. This was a three-day Herculean task in the drafty, cold, steamy "wash-kitchen," which was shared on a schedule by all tenants. Thereafter came the ironing, mending, folding and storing. Though exhausting, she did this alone. I do not recall the girls ever helping her much. Either they were too small, or later too devious, to be a real help, but I may be wrong. I confess I never took much interest in this, but I knew that the routine during those days was somewhat disturbed, with extra-simple meals such as peeled potatoes with matjes herring (very cheap then, today a delicacy)! Mother extensively used her foot operated sewing machine, which adorned a corner in the living room below the pendulum clock.

As I grew up, I started helping with the chores. One of the biweekly rituals was the cleaning of runners and carpets. The landlord set aside certain days and hours for these cleanings. Until perhaps the 1960's, vacuum cleaners were not known. To clean the carpets, they would be rolled up into a sausage and carried down to the courtyard-a 30-50 ft. space, solidly paved with concrete, surrounded by four-story buildings. At the end a divider fence of wood bordered the next lot, which was Bruederstrasse. Here, on a horizontal bar, supported by wooden uprights, the carpets were hung and beaten with the "Teppichklopfer," a sort of giant fly-swatter of woven cane, about the size of a tennis racquet. Hitting the carpet made a very loud noise, and dust clouds emanated from the rug to settle into the environs. Naturally, everyone had to close the apartment windows. For smaller pieces a 7-tailed cat was used-seven leather straps on a wooden handle. Both devices were sometimes also used to mete out punishment for very severe offenses. Once I got lashed with the cat-o-tails when I was about ten or twelve years old for wearing a new pair of very nice shoes during the week, although they must be worn "only on Sundays." Naturally this meant I would outgrow them while they were relatively new, and they would never receive a second sole. That's precisely what happened. I never enjoyed wearing them since.

On those rare Sunday mornings off when nothing else needed to be done, father, using a cane of hazel wood, took me down Pichelsdorfer Strasse and Heerstrasse into the Grunewald, in his best blue suit. He seldom took the girls, if at all. But when it came to mushroom picking in the fall, we went together. The girls never played or bothered with me, perhaps because they were so much older, or perhaps due to other interests. On the other hand, the family provided no incentives for this. There was little opportunity for play, and no toys. Not surprisingly, as soon as I could read, I was eager to hit the books-there was nothing more interesting to do! I have been an avid bookworm since.

EARLY POLITICAL OBSERVATIONS

As I became more aware of the surroundings around 1930/31, I observed such happenings in the streets as marches of communist, socialist, rightist and Nazi organizations-each column headed by a flag. All had storm troopers and sported some kind of uniforms and were usually accompanied by marching bands and placards with slogans. The papers would report street battles, especially around election time, sometimes with guns, but mostly fists, knives, and clubs. One day a socialist activist was shot in the entrance hallway of our building. I heard the shot and trampling of fleeing boots-they were Nazis; the victim a socialist trooper.

These incidents were frequent—not necessarily around our building entrance. Germany was in turmoil because of the dismal economical conditions. Large armies of unemployed, with no hope or social safety net, were desperately seeking some kind of solution. Many joined the storm troopers of the radical parties. There was no big daddy country handing out 40 Billion to jumpstart the economy like almost daily today. At election time, many flags were displayed in apartment windows or from balconies: black/white/red, black/red/gold, red with hammer and sickle, swastika, etc.… representing different parties, programs and supposedly outlook. There seemed to be little unifying consensus. Remember that people in the USA only display one flag-unless one counts state flags. Many Germans then seriously questioned the efficacy of the German constitution, foundation of the Weimar Republic. Most people actually never knew what it meant, or had ever read it.

In our circles no one ever talked or argued about constitutional questions, which means people were scarcely aware about their importance and how it related to them. All was overshadowed by the dire needs of a large part of the populace and the head bashing of the party propaganda machines. The most effective in this respect were the NSDAP (Nazi) and KPD (Communist), and it all came down to the wire between the two. Both extreme parties conspired in the Reichstag to destabilize the government, which was a very weak coalition and changed often. Through political destabilization these two extreme parties wanted to gain power. They were right on. In 1933, as another government was forced to resign under pressure, the largest party emerging from the last elections was the NSDAP. The president (von Hindenburg), in his mid 80's and somewhat senile, had the constitutional power to appoint the next chancellor. By advice of the rightist parties he then chose Hitler and the NSDAP, although this party never had been a majority. After this, things moved in one direction only.

LIFE IN THE 1930's

My sisters were then 20 and 16. Fortunately they both worked. Ulli had found a hat maker's apprenticeship, without much pride or enthusiasm. It paid very little (about RM10 or $2.50 weekly).

Reflecting on German schools in my time I should say that healthy, sound development of basic knowledge and skills took priority. Competition was strong; the best progressed to higher learning. Those who did not meet the goals of a grade had to repeat it. Money did not help much in any event, and there was little difference in educational quality and goals between schools located in different neighborhoods. There was also a secondary educational path for late bloomers, who could later attend the "Aufbauschule" to obtain "Mittelschule" finish. I had a buddy later at the Heereszeugamt (Heiner Herbold), who would do this and then volunteer for flight training. He was killed in action as fighter pilot. 1931 brought an opportunity for all elementary school kids of my age to transfer to schools of higher learning. This would lead to advanced career paths, but tuition and books were expensive, which gave our family something to scratch their heads about. The sisters had not attended those schools, finishing the elementary program at 14-so why should I? Last, but not least, no Boehlke or Moratz had ever attended advanced school, except Uncle Willy, who must have taken special surveying courses somewhere. It did dawn on mother what this school attendance could be worth during one's lifetime. And unfortunately there was my flawless school record, a superior grade with the entrance exam and teacher Schmeling who went to bat for little "Sohni" who had slowly turned into little Hermann. I would learn about this much later, but he talked extensively with father to convince him I should attend "Gymnasium" or "Oberrealschule," completion of which would make university attendance possible. The outcome was a compromise: that I would attend "Mittelschule," which stops at age 16. There was also an opportunity to continue to age 18 later, but this never happened. I could go on only because my superior record freed us from tuition payments. Without this most significant turn of events of my first 20 years, I would have lost many opportunities later in life. I owe Mr. Schmeling (and mother) a monument! Well, father also participated, didn't he? Each of us has a different perspective!

Much later I heard that my sisters never liked this. Most kids in the higher schools were then running around with their colorful velvet caps-another type for each school and year-except me. I can still see myself pressing my nose flat against the shop windows displaying these caps, but this was not for a Moratz, and it surely would have been an affront for the two girls. I don't mean that I was vain-but all the other kids had them! That did not keep me from producing more and more good grades, effortlessly. I never overworked or extended myself, but learned the teachers' systems. For example, when we had to learn a poem by heart, I figured when it would be my turn to recite it and then I studied it only on my walk from home to school in 20 minutes-otherwise never. This usually worked. But I studied interesting things thoroughly, since I was an avid reader. Books could be borrowed free from the city library. And I could borrow 52 Karl May books from this Westphal kid, which he let only his favorite pals borrow. An unattractive fellow, he lived downtown overlooking the "Markt," and we became fairly close for a time.

And there were sports: During the summer the family would go swimming along the Havel River. The closest was a beach called Stoessenseer Badewiese. One had to turn right shortly after crossing the river, about a 40 minute walk. In hot weather on weekends the meadows were packed; one blanket bordered the next, with little room to place your feet without invading someone's blanket. Everyone brought sandwiches and thermos bottles. To teach me the art of swimming, father engineered a life-saving vest from reed, gathered at the riverbank. It didn't look as fashionable as the other kids' and was less than appealing to me; they had store-bought swim vests made of cork. Poor father! I ran away when he good-naturedly wanted to wrap it around me. In utter despair I looked at the other people: how they did this swim thing. I had to do it before the contraption caught up with me, and in one afternoon I copied the movements, and from there learned it did not take much to become an accomplished swimmer-never a lesson! But later I passed the official 15 minutes test (Freischwimmen) and 45 minutes test (Fahrtenschwimmen), which was officiated by a swim instructor and was free. Otherwise there would have been no test. For each expenditure I had to ask permission, had to explain the reason, and then got the cash; checks were not known. I remember father also received his salary in a cash envelope. We did not need a bank.

Other sports were taught at school two or three times weekly for an hour. In summer there were outdoor athletics such as running, broad, and high jump, etc. In the mid-30's I made it into the school handball team (the only team sport there), since I was pretty good at sports. We always were a factor in the Berlin championship, but were usually beaten in the quarterfinals by some hunks from an affluent division of the city. But around 1937 we beat the NAPOLA-a special political school, which prepared carefully selected kids for future leadership of the "Reich," most of them hunks, with typical Nordic features. They just did not have the skills we had and were not as eager as we were to win. Sweet vengeance! We were proud, as we did not like those arrogant, privileged guys in their golden Hitler Youth uniforms sporting a special "NAPOLA" band (Nationalpolitische Erziehungsanstalt or National Political Education Institution). This was a federal program, free for the selected, with three or four institutions throughout Germany. In winter, sports occurred in our marvelous gymnasium (Turnhalle), which was exclusively used by my school in the daytime, and by a sports club in the evenings-probably the TSV Spandau 1860, the largest local general sports club (gymnastics, handball, track and field, but no soccer). That hall divided the men from the sissies! All of us had to perform the tasks on the high bar, parallel bars, horse, rings, ropes, etc.-all of which was highly body-building and required lots of guts, like climbing up a 25 foot vertical rope 1-1/2" thick. The star was a certain Schmidt, who whirled around the high bar, seemingly without gravity, and later joined the German gymnastic team. We marveled at him-he simply had the right body features and must have started as a small child. The town had many other sports clubs for swimming, soccer, track and field, hockey (land), rowing, sailing, etc. etc. I later joined a sports club in '37 or '38. I don't remember if there were any dues. It was KEMS (Kameradschaft ehemaliger Mittelschueler). Perhaps active team members did not have to pay. Werner Ehling, Lisbeth's husband since 1935, was a member of Spandau 04, a swim club with an excellent water polo team. He recalled that they often played against the Nauener Swim Club, where one of the outstanding team members was Fritz Boehlke. Both were mighty hunks, much over 6 feet tall. Spandau had a wide selection of sports activities, with many athletic fields and soccer/handball facilities. There were always some goings-on in the summer, and many spectators congregated to watch their preferred teams.

In the early thirties Lisbeth, approaching 20 years, was old enough to date boys. I was never part of knowing the kinds of agreements struck with her regarding dating. There must have been precious few rules and little advice. I guess in most families a gentleman caller would ring the doorbell and one had a little chat, which is now the rule and normal, but not in ours. There seemed to be a lack of communication and underlying thought processes. I later heard that Lisbeth often visited the Ehlings and perhaps felt more comfortable there than in her own home. I recall a peculiar event, when Lisbeth went out one night … I don't know if she indicated where she would be. While father was working, mother took me for a late summer evening walk toward Suedpark and Heerstrasse, where there was a garden restaurant nicknamed" BoeHue." (Boernicker Huette), with a nice indoor and outdoor dance floor and live music. I was about 11 years old. Through the lattice fence, to my embarrassment, mother then casually observed Lisbeth dancing elegantly with a handsome-looking, blond, blue-eyed young man. I knew what was going on but was too embarrassed to tell Lisbeth. With mother's poor communication skills, this must have been her only way possible to find out with whom Lisbeth was going out. I neither got involved nor did I think about it, but, looking back, I record this event now only because it is important to construct a baseline: where did I com from? I believe father might not have done this at all! This brings me to relations with other family members.

The relatives living closest to us were Aunt Minna, father's sister, with her husband Hermann Dorow. As mentioned, they lived in a comfortable wood frame house on Klosterstrasse, about 200 yards south of city hall opposite the railway freight yard. They had an ample courtyard; a large garden plot in the back stretched almost to the Havel River. Father visited there once in a great while and checked the status of the fruit wine Hermann made in a six-gallon glass crock. At times they would get quite animated! When there was another guy, they whipped out the cards and a cigar. It seemed to me always that they had a lot of fun. Hermann, who had no children, often let me ride on his knee during the games, while I marveled at his pocket watch and thick golden chain hanging over his tummy. He looked more like an Italian than a German, and rumors abounded how he got his good looks. But I cannot recall mother ever coming along; only once when I was very young to attend a wedding while I was home with the flu. Is my memory failing or was there a problem? Also, she never came along to visit Grandpa Moratz in the Staakener Strasse. When he later lived in Falkensee-probably after his wife Henriette passed away-we would go out alone, except once to greet a new baby at Uncle Wilhelm's. The two sisters Mila and Emilie, both seamstresses and quite gregarious-at least Mila, the youngest—took Grandpa in. Emilie, like father, had big trouble with her nose; I inherited that condition. Generally visiting was rare, because of—I'm sure—our never-ending chores. But I also don't recall father visiting his former brother-in-law and then his father-in-law even once in Nauen. Who knows what the reasons were. I was never told; neither did I ever hear anyone talk about possible reasons. It could have been just due to scheduling problems. For me it was an exciting adventure to ride the suburban train with its steam locomotive and see all the familiar stations come up and fall behind: Falkensee, Finkenkrug, Brieseland, and then Nauen, a 25 km ride. One day, going toward Spandau West station-mother in front of me and I looking strenuously back toward an onrushing fast train to Hamburg with its huge locomotive—I straightened the head suddenly and bumped head-on against a streetlight post. Stars were flying and I arrived in Nauen with an enormous, bruised bump on my forehead.

Thus, father maintained closest contact with sister Minna and husband Hermann Dorow, while mother stuck to the Boehlke family. Once, when I was eight or nine years old, mother and I visited Doeberitz, the first railway station on the way to Wustermark-Lehrte-Hannover. She had an uncle there, apparently Opa's brother, who had a pretty good position as railway loc operator. But this is the only contact I recall; there still must be Boehlkes in Dalgow or Doeberitz, unless they moved to the West at the right time. Meanwhile, father not only sampled

Hermann's fruit wine, but was also active there. The property held a comfortable one-story wood frame house for him and a second one for a colleague of the railway, and there was a large courtyard and utility shed, where one could drive in an automobile if one had it. Naturally, the working and middle classes in the end-twenties and thirties could not think about such luxuries-they were reserved for industrialists, doctors, artists, actors, top bureaucrats, wealthy landowners, etc. There was no Henry Ford in Germany-though Ford started a facility in Cologne. The courtyard served well for father's enormous pull cart, and, since the leased property on Magistratsweg was gone, Uncle Hermann gave father permission to cart timber onto the courtyard and deposit it there for processing, i.e. sawing and splitting. Here I learned to handle and to sharpen a saw and got introduced to using an ax. Although I liked to work out with father, sometimes I felt other activities would have been better. Uncle Hermann's garden plot had wonderful berries, plums and chestnuts. I just recalled that mother did help pick at harvest time. The berries were pressed to juice, which she made into jelly. In the summer mother canned strawberries and plums with our own pasteurization pot and dozens of jars, which was handy, since we could not afford to buy canned goods. There were so many chores in the summer and fall; it seemed mother's work never stopped.

But once in a great while mother would take me on the streetcar and subway to shop for such things as towels, linens, clothes, etc.-usually in the vicinity of Potsdamer Platz in downtown Berlin, which was to become "Checkpoint Charlie" later. In the late twenties and the thirties here were the large department stores "Tietz" and "Wertheim" on the Leipziger Strasse. Mother's purchases did not interest me, but I had learned that she would invariably terminate her shopping with "Windbeutel mit Schlagsahne" in the department store coffee shop. This looked like a large hamburger bun, but was of sweet dough and hollow inside, so that the product was like a large hole surrounded by a skin of delicious, soft pastry. Filled with whipped cream to the brim, it was quite a treat after a hard day's trampling around the department stores. These outings happened perhaps once a year. I do not recall father or the girls ever coming along. Why did mother prefer me? She did, because I was her only child, but at the time I did not use such rationale, just doing my things as they came along. Relationships or preferences to me were poppycock (or worse) which I did not think about.

As I entered "Mittelschule" in the spring of 1932, the depression had gotten gradually worse in Germany. Many millions lost their support completely, going hungry. The political agitation and fights took up grotesque proportions. In daily life I did not notice much, since we were pretty much protected by father's secure job with the BVG. We did not go hungry, because father got out and provided additional things: berries, mushrooms, fire wood, etc. The streets by and large were secure and a professional army (Reichswehr) of 100,000 men provided overall stability. We noticed signs of poverty as more and more people knocked at the doors of our apartment to ask for food. Sometimes mother handed out some. Street musicians in our courtyard sang or played street organs cranked up by a handle, some carrying little monkeys on their shoulders. Other people had simple business ideas; those offering kindling for potato peels seemed to have connections with someone fattening pigs or other animals. These guys went through the streets bellowing such offerings as "Brennolz fuea Kaatoffelschaln" (kindling for potato peels), which sounded like a town crier's sing-song. Others pulled carts through the streets offering prunes, chanting loudly into the street canyons: "Pflaum, Pflaum, zuckerseesse Pflaum, frishgeflickt vom Baum," etc. There was a melody to it. So daily there was coming and going and always something happening in the streets.

Spandau then had a garrison, with one battalion of infantry at Askanierring. There were particularly more soldiers in Potsdam—20 miles to the south in what was for the last 300 years the center of Prussian military training and stationing of the most prestigious regiments. Potsdam never had any other reason for being. Once King Frederick (the Great) lived there, at Sanssouci. Many other army units were located around Berlin. From Doeberitz, a 15x20 mile training ground, artillery fire could be heard in Spandau, which itself had developed large armament factories over the last 200 years. In later, more modern times this distinction fell more and more upon the Ruhr area as heavy weapons were becoming "useful." Once a year the Reichswehr had its day in Berlin. I don't recall any patriotic reason, but many units with their bands assembled at the Sports Stadium between Charlottenburg and Spandau (where five years later the new Olympic Stadium would be built). There was an evening of military display and old Prussian march music, ending with enormous fireworks, which I attended once, probably with father. I was kind of impressed and touched by all these patriotic-sounding things-somehow I associated solemn marching music with patriotism-a mistake many people made. But naturally different kinds of music arouse different types of emotions. Anyway, I walked away impressed for the moment.

Then, a bit later in 1933 there were big activities of brown NSDAP units-another change of government. Hitler had been entrusted to serve the Reich. A few months afterwards he took great pains to show the population and the world his supposed honest intentions to lead Germany to a better future. At a grand black/white tie affair at the Potsdam "Garnisonkirche" (Garrison Church), attended by the entire diplomatic corps, generals, industry leaders, church leaders, etc., Hitler bowed his head in deference to the very old, if not senile, von Hindenburg, for everyone to see. However, a few months later Von Hindenburg (president) died. As a result the army was sworn in to obey and follow the "Fuehrer" Hitler instead of defending the constitution. Hitler simply did not fill in the president's job and assumed all those responsibilities also, which included becoming supreme commander of all armed forces-one of the most tragic events in German/European history. Another event around that time ('33 or '34) was the fire in the Reichstag (German equivalent of the capitol) which burned out completely. It was attributed to a Bulgarian communist and thus the Bolsheviks. During the state of emergency which was declared, all other party leaders, activists and known Nazi enemies were rounded up and sent to concentration camps. No one knew how this condition suddenly came about. People disappeared. Nazi brown shirts knocked at the doors, usually at night, dragging people away without notice, which was called "Schutzhaft" (incarceration for protection). This became openly known to us only after World War II, since no one took us into custody and the newspapers reported nothing. By now they had to report what was promoted by the government, i.e. the Nazi Party. The multi-party system actually had terminated as a result of the fire, which was, of course, started by Hermann Goering and a gang of Nazi thugs. So, Germany had been inexorably moved into dictatorship without the populace knowing much about it and without organizations to oppose it. Very soon the NSDAP was omnipotent-undesired figures were removed from government, judiciary, army, media, etc. Only Hitler's and his henchmen's direction was left.

Rearmament of the armed forces followed soon. An air force and a navy were created. There were large purchases of equipment, military buildings started appearing all around, and near Doeberitz at Elstal a large airfield with huge buildings was constructed to house the Jagdgeschwader "Richthofen" No. 1. In Spandau several proper barracks went up in no time … everything built very well … for the next 1000 years! A large barrack complex was built for the air force in Kladow, South of us, and between Gatow and Kladow the Air Force academy also went up with a large airfield for cadet training. The draft was reinstituted soon to fill all those buildings. Able-bodied men had to serve for two years, plus one half year in the Arbeitsdienst (mandatory working service). Consequently, unemployment disappeared and now jobs went begging. The "Arbeitsdienst" was a totally new invention, supposedly to teach all Germans the value and ethic of work. Those battalions of manual laborers wore special uniform and learned basic military exercises like in the army. For these they carried their shovels like those in the armed services used their rifles. They worked on large national projects like the Autobahnen, digging drainage systems, dikes at the North Sea, and much later to build fortifications along the French border or the Atlantic Wall to protect against invasion. Massive manual labor was wasted; earth moving equipment should have done the job.

Regardless, in my early teens I saw these developments as positive, like other people: no unemployment, no more street fights. Most people did not know or imagine what kind of consequences the streamlining of everything along Nazi lines could have later. I never had any instructions or lesson at school about civics, how a government works or how foreign nations were governed, e.g. what the American constitution means. People never heard or read about their own constitution, which was gradually dismantled and substituted practically by decrees. The Reichstag was occupied by Nazis only, who approved everything their "Fuehrer" demanded. I noticed one day the fellow living in our house, who was a storm trooper for the socialist party in '31 and '32, and who had been shot in our apartment house entrance hall, coming by in an army uniform, and a little later he was corporal. He seemed to have successfully adjusted to the new winds, as did millions. Soon the spooky days of the Weimar Republic were swept under the rug, at least on the surface. I knew father was very concerned; millions of others must have felt likewise.

EARLY TEENS-GROUP ACTIVITIES

I naturally had school buddies and friendships in the neighborhood. There were Paschke, Herwig and others, and a group of kids who congregated around "Bonne" Bornschein's group. These were organized, met once weekly and sometimes went into the country on Sundays to do what boy scouts do in other countries. We did not have much of a uniform, except black shorts, a brown shirt with a black tie or shawl placed under the collar, similar to what the American cowhands wear. I believe the boy scouts wear this type of tie also, but not in black. In colder weather we wore dark blue or black jackets-mostly those from our "training suit" from sports activities. Mine was faded dark blue. We met in some obscure church's recreation building on Heerstrasse, about a 15 min. walk. I joined this group to experience some fellowship, after some of them-all guys from the neighborhood-had approached me once or twice. The "leader" Bonne Bornschein, lived next door, but I had not met him or his family before; people then did not become acquainted easily. Neither had I known Koepke next door, whose father was "Oberbaurat," i.e. someone with an architecture degree working for the municipal administration in a management capacity, where building permits, were issued, etc. The Koepke's were the first family I knew with a television, showing live pictures in 1939. The Moratz' then never even had a "people's radio" ("Volksempfaenger"), a small radio which began to be offered as the electronic equivalent of the Volkswagen. There were also Aze Koziol, Sossna, Gehrmann, Machmud Kasakoff, "Schwengel," who was the keeper of the books and a kind of song master. He preferred medieval soldiers' songs, which we learned and sang more or less enthusiastically. At the start of the evening, the troop assembled in front of the building, Schwengel took the roll call, and in front of the troop our emblem, a little flag, was fastened to a portable pole. Schwengel reported to leader "Bonne," who greeted us-all was done with a kind of military hoopla. I remember that we did not use the Nazi salute (we were not incorporated in the H.J.=Hitlerjugend=Hitler Youth), and that there was no political indoctrination. If there would have been, I think everyone would have split for good. There were no Nazi flags (Swastika) and no flag raising ceremony. So, what did we do during those evenings? First, we had left the house, so parents could have a few hours to themselves-that alone was a good reason. And once we entered the building, there was a large, primitive table with some chairs and candles burning, where we sang a few songs. Next, we intensely discussed the next Sunday outing, which usually took place around the Fort Hahneberg to Seeburg area West of Spandau. Saturday was then a workday for most people; as an apprentice in industry or trade, one worked Saturdays until 1 p.m. A lecture often followed, which could have been on the use of a magnetic compass or orientation without any assist, use of maps, etc. We had two different maps: that with the largest resolution (1:25,000), where details included large estates in the country and the exact topography via distinct elevation lines, and the so-called "Generalstabskarte" (1:100,000) with less resolution. The former was called "Messtischblatt." The latter was used extensively by the military and was helpful for outings and to reach any destination via roads. Black and white, these maps were also indispensable for exact surveying, including direction of artillery. I'm sure Uncle Willy worked with those "Messtischblaetter" all his life. In those days we enjoyed learning many of these outdoor things in theory and practice. Beyond those orientation lectures, we were active in limited sports, e.g. an instructor taught us the rudimentary aspects of boxing. Practicing with gloves and ropes, many of us got knocked out, but it did not hurt seriously. We marched in formation, our little flag flying toward the Hahneberg region where we tried to put our knowledge into practice, e.g. orientation, how to get a teepee together from regulation military canvas squares, how to keep the tent dry in rainy weather, etc. First we searched for a proper camping spot, preferably a little elevated, with water in the vicinity. We carried full field equipment: a regular German backpack, canvas square and blanket, a regular chow container and "Brotbeutel mit Feldflasche," (food bag and insulated water bottle). Canvas and blanket were rolled in a predetermined fashion to look like sausages, of the exact length needed for wrapping them around the backpack on three sides. The canvas could be used as a rain poncho, as a single lean to, open tent (2 canvasses) or a real teepee with three. Some or all of us had sticks, ropes and field shovels (Feldspaten), and almost everyone had a serious knife blade with sheath, for cutting tent poles or for firewood. Knives were handy, but one thing we never had or engaged in: firearms. These were neither talked about, nor was there any discussion or instruction in politics. We speculated about progress at school and what to do with our lives, as it started to dawn on some of us teens that we had to make choices soon. But deep, searching conversations were not the rule; mostly we were very busy with the tasks on hand—pretty much dictated by troop leader "Bonne" and his Lieutenants Schwengel and Machmud Kasakoff, who were three to five years older than the rest of us. They already had jobs, but I didn't know what they did; neither did it occur to the younger members to question why they were hanging out with us. One thing was certain: there was never any foul play, and I know in reminiscing that we never talked or expressed interest in girls. All of us were tucked away in boys' schools. Coeducation did not exist then, which worked fabulously. We were entirely unconcerned and, I might say, even oblivious and a bit contemptuous of girls. We did not call it sex; on average this interest developed much later than today. Our daily activities usually focused on domestic and school tasks, interaction with friends and the scout thing-with lots of reading in between. Though the scout activities appeared a bit like semi-military preparation, there was no organization beyond "Bonne" which would demand, prescribe or enforce those things. Where did we get the ideas of field training? First, it was tough, and it was challenging. We wanted to move beyond bourgeois comfort, expose ourselves to nature and live at its bosom, studying it. In those days there was much wartime (WWI) literature, describing the common soldier's exploits and suffering, but mostly focusing on individual heroism. It led to the conclusion that Germany had been forced to submit to an unjust, abominable "peace." Apparently very lopsided, it was peace only for the others. I believe we wanted to emulate what that literature showed us. There were no explicit lectures or directions along these lines, but in this literary climate we wanted to do manly things, similar to what scouts do today in the U.S. On weekends we sometimes camped overnight in the countryside west of Spandau, with many roads, villages, woods, rivers and lakes to explore. After meeting at the Spandau West train station opposite city hall, we boarded a train-sometimes a narrow rail train (Boetzow Bahn). That one left behind and below the station and was the kind which could have a sign: "Prohibited to pick flowers while train moves."

After arrival, we shouldered our gear. Unaware of our final destination, we headed for the blue yonder: first over a paved highway, then into unpaved roads, and then into the woods. Machmud Kasakoff was responsible for the maps and orientation. Schwengel gave the tune for the songs, as we marched through villages, with people stopping right and left to stare at us. We looked very trained and motivated. Before entering a town, we would get our act together to look and sound good. When reaching our destination after a three to four hours' march, it was already dark, with fog rising in the meadows. Some guys were assigned to collect firewood and kindling, and the rest started building one or more tents, or a large one of 12 canvasses, bringing in dry leaves for more comfort, if available. Others started to prepare soup in a hanging pot over a fire (usually "Erbswurst-a dried pea soup bought in sausage form): a simple, nourishing meal, and it was hot! Then guards were assigned: each one for two hours, waking up the next at the end of the shift, who then stumbled out to face the dark, his sleepiness and the night sounds. As the morning dawned, we sometimes heard sounds like hogs—the wild kind! The guard soon took refuge in the tent in horror-there wasn't much he could do otherwise! After some grunting around the tent, they trotted off, leaving us unscathed. We never saw such other large animals as deer. I believe the noise we made allowed them to flee in time.

Before field exercises started on the next day (usually Sunday) we brewed some barley coffee, breakfasting with rye bread, butter and jam. We then played several games. Sometimes each of us was assigned to find a spot defined on the map, or one party hid and the others had to find them-preferably without being noticed. When it rained, things got pretty miserable. There was no raingear, so we had to stay inside the tent until departing for the two or more hours march back. The canvass was not water repellant and kept rain out only when made taut in tent form. So, these overnighters were a joy when we could swim in rivers or lakes, but sometimes real misery. More than once we returned home exhausted and soaked-no wonder some guys did not show up again after a while. But types like Sossna (Tossi), Gehrmann (Osram), I (Jumbo) and Orje Herwig kept on going for a long time until later developments like working life, armed forces, or politization of the troop dispersed all. These kinds of nicknames (Schwengel was another) were given to all members as some kind of badge of acceptance.

Annually at vacation time the troop tried to take a big trip for about two weeks. One was to Thuringia forest-a wonderful, mountainous-forested area southwest of Berlin bordering Frankonia/Bavaria. We visited the town of Eisenach, where Luther had translated the Bible. Then we went up the hills and walked the length of the ridge. A wonderful experience—my best vacation in the thirties. Other kids also vacationed with their families, but I think not too many in my circles wasted any time thinking about this. Neither the Moratz', nor anyone in the entire Moratz/Boehlke family, ever spent time away from home on vacation. It would have been such an expense, and then-why leave an apartment we already occupied? Unheard of! I still wonder how I pried the money out of father that year for the Thuringia trip—the much reduced group train rate only, plus some basic food stuff. On the way home we just about ran out of money, with just enough left for "Schiebewurst" (slice of rye with one piece of salami, 1" diameter, that was pushed around the bread so as to get a tiny bite with each bite of the bread). Once finished, still with the salami aroma in the mouth, we did not realize we were preparing for the times ahead.

I remember another long trip in which I couldn't participate for lack of funds. When I was between twelve and 14 years old, the school organized a glorious trip to Kopenhagen. Only one out of thirty did not go: little Hermann. By then mother neither dared call me "Sohni" any more than she dared call me Hermann. I don't remember what father called me-he may never have addressed me by my name. Some guys in the street called me "Manius," the last syllable of Hermann plus the "ius"-designating a studious kid. Mother never knew the troop's nickname: "Jumbo," which I didn't like, but could not discourage its use. However, I did not want it used at home.

On our winter and fall outings, we did not sleep in tents. Sleeping bags were not known, and our blankets could not protect us from the weather. But opportunities to put our tired heads down offered themselves in the form of huge structures around Berlin where farmers stored their hay and straw. Farms existed in villages and even towns, but did not have space for this purpose, which necessitated these 30 ft. high structures. With roofs on stilts, they were ideal for housing a troop like ours. We especially liked sleeping in the hay, because it was loose and softer, while the compressed straw provided only a meager foundation for a night's sleep. Not knowing if any laws were violated, we usually did not contact the owner. We were very careful with fire and never saw a barn burn down. Sometimes we asked farmers in the villages to grant us a night in their barns, which gave us a chance to have water in the morning. Once a friendly farmer's wife prepared us hot cocoa from their fresh milk. Sometimes in fall we would make a camp fire and sit around it. Schwengel would give the tune to one or more of those old medieval songs, and we would sing, getting us into a pensive, moody and solemn frame of mind.

But we didn't much think about why-wasn't everything o.k. around us? The loud, wild propaganda efforts of communist or Nazi troopers were gone. All one could see now were SA troops (the original brownshirts), meeting on Sunday mornings at their favorite corner pubs. At times they marched singing through the streets with their large swastika flag in front. Meanwhile, all those troopers had work and nothing more to protest, complain or worry about, so they wallowed in their party's successes. So, they mainly met for companionship and perhaps an excuse to escape from domestic duties. (When arriving home, they expected the wife to be waiting with a nice meal.) Many picked up municipal or other government jobs vacated by former opposition party members, who, in turn, got assigned menial jobs if they did not immediately convert to the right (Nazi) "religion" of the day. Once, returning from an outing into the woods along Heerstrasse and the Havel River, father and I walked down Pichelsdorfer Str. just passing Adamstrasse. It was one of those rare, free Sundays. During the rest of the week I attended school, including Saturday. We were happily strolling along the left side of the street facing north, when a troop of S.A. (Nazi storm troopers) came toward us with a large swastika in front. About 20 steps after passing them, we heard trampling of boots behind us and were confronted by about six of those toughs: "Why did you not lift your right arm to the German salute to greet the (our) flag?" they demanded in a very threatening manner. "Return at once, run to the front of the column and greet it … properly, as is the custom now." Well, having never lifted his arm in his life to greet any flag, father saw no good reason to do it then. I sensed his blood boiling and felt embarrassed that these morons interrupted our good mood. There really were no laws or regulations demanding citizens to greet the swastika. But this was heavy intimidation. Luckily, father mustered enough survival sense to run up front with me to greet the flag, as demanded. I believe that I myself, at his age, would not have complied, as demonstrated much later in other examples of intimidation. I do shudder to think what would have happened, had he not complied. They would have dragged him forthwith to a concentration camp, leaving me standing there to inform mother that father had been led away—nobody would have known where to. I am sure this left a lasting impression on father and much deepened his hatred of the Nazis, if that was actually possible. Also, had he not complied, he might have lost his BVG job with years of seniority: a disaster for the entire family. It would have meant to start from the absolute bottom again at age 47. I would have had to forego further schooling at age 14 to help make money, etc. etc.

Many people must have experienced similar incidents. No one knew how to counteract this kind of directed despotism. On the other hand, it was all sugar coated in public by the economic successes: no more unemployment. One must now wonder about the state of mind of those brownshirts. Several months before our threatening experience, Hitler, with a gang of cronies like Goering and Hess, in one night (of the long knives) liquidated about 400 of the top S.A.leaders, claiming high treason-that they had wanted to get rid of him because he was not radical enough in introducing the Nazi Party program. Hitler accomplished this with the help and connivance of the military leadership. Germany became a cesspool of putsches and lawlessness. Now the military was solidly linked to Hitler's fate. They had already sworn a solemn oath to support him (the Fuehrer), but as ruthless a politician as he was, their influence was quickly counterbalanced by the SS (Schutzstaffel) with their black uniforms. Overnight, regular SS, fully motorized, military divisions were created out of nowhere and equipped with the best available hardware. SS boss Heinrich Himmler also headed the entire police and secret police (GESTAPO), the latter a Nazi era invention. Germany had never had a secret police before, and naturally the public was not told. All media were censored and controlled. As worrisome as all this development was, I simply did not get things together then, for lack of information, and because in my early teens I was more focused on my immediate surroundings. But, while it did not immediately result in total rejection of everything related to the Nazi movement, my father's and my treatment by the brownshirts must have left some subconscious imprint on me.

NAZIS TAKE OVER YOUTH ORGANIZATIONS

I remained skeptical about the "movement," which became more and more apparent as time went on. More Germans started worrying about Hitler's apparently successful methods. Other subtle changes also began taking place in my group's relation to its surroundings. As mentioned, no command structure linked us to the H.J. (Hitler Jugend), an arm of the Nazi organization. While not exactly rejecting anything "Nazi," we were apolitical with a nationalistic bias. We had introduced a new tradition: long-standing members with good performance and attendance received a braided cord and whistle, to be worn around the chest pocket. The colors: gold/green/black conformed to those worn by some independent scout groups on their uniforms and pennants (Wimpel). But little by little, the independent groups were prohibited-later by government directive. Some were loosely connected to former political parties. To equalize everything, any non-Nazi elements were staved off. Around 1936, H.J. leaders posted some posses in front of the train station, which made us remove our braided, colored cords. Once inside the train, we naturally put them back on-wondering what went on in these people's dirty minds, and where all this nonsense was coming from. We later realized that this was just the beginning of a thorough campaign. Soon, guards appeared around the train station to prevent non-Nazi troops from leaving for weekends. Bonne told us later: "we are now part of the H.J. As in the military, we report to a higher leader (Gefolgschaftsfuehrer)." That guy, named von der Goltz, strutted around in full H.J. regalia, cords and stars all over, riding boots and black jodhpurs (horse riding pants). Apparently from an old East German aristocratic family, he had definitely lost his ways. We thought he had a hole in his head. This coincided with the time I wanted to join an athletic club called "KEMS," that had a good youth handball team-a sport I liked and was good at. By that time, it had become a condition that all kids wanting to join an athletic club must be H.J. members. As all of my buddies, I was then about ready to throw the towel at the H.J. Now the H.J. split up our troop and forced us to join others, which were different, boring, did not offer what we wanted to do, and in which we didn't want to participate. They tried to read some political indoctrination lectures to us, to which we were indifferent. They were lousy and a waste of time. So, I just showed up once in a great while to keep my membership active. Meanwhile I enjoyed playing handball at KEMS.

At that particular time, as I was attending one of those different new H.J. troops, I heard that the larger H.J. organizations were planning a jamboree at the island of Usedom between Stettin and Stralsund at the Baltic Sea. Spending time at the sea sounded good to me; I imagined dunes, the blue, clear ocean, solitude and fun with likeminded fellows. But I soon regretted having volunteered for this disaster. We were squeezed into a tent city which swarmed with little, mean, unforgiving busybodies. Each minute of each day some kind of service or lecture was scheduled-and always lots of kids together doing the same stupid things, with no escape: no town close by for some respite. The tasteless, mass-produced food was absolutely disgusting. We didn't like to be in the dirty tent city, with its smell of open pit latrines and no escape from the sun. We seemed to be always standing for hours around a flag pole with its swastika, listening to some official H.J. leaders in full regalia, who looked like party hacks. One was von der Goltz. We didn't take long to call it quits and withdrew as far as possible-never again this kind of farce! This experience taught me that one cannot give up all individuality to become a member of a mass of warm bodies, particularly when decorated with swastikas. After this additional experience, I left the H.J. movement alone. I had better things to do to prepare for the future.

CONTINUING MY EDUCATIONAL PATH

Around that time, I may have been about 14 years old, I would have normally been thinking about leaving school to enter working life, like my sisters Lisbeth and Ulli. My school (Mittelschule) ended at age 16. It offered many additional instructions, unlike the basic schools. Enjoying languages, I then already had completed two years of English and started with French. Math, chemistry and physics also fascinated me. With the learning experience in full swing, one cannot fathom my surprise when one day father told me about a good job opportunity in a company located close to the Spandau Main train station (closed now). So, crossing the Havel River at the Schulenburg Bridge, we arrived at a tiny outlet for bulk chemicals. They were looking for a kind of go-fer. I could see immediately that there was not enough for me to do, and-more important-I could not learn anything. I still cannot believe that father had the nerve to consider this kind of job. He also may have expected something better, perhaps growing into whole-sale material marketing, but, as I later realized, I am neither made up for, nor happy in sales. Rather, I am good at resolving problems of any kind, but more about that later. After politely bidding good-bye to the owner, father asked me about my thoughts. My unequivocal, quick answer: "No! No way!" It may have been an attempt to not offer me any preferences before the sisters or father would find the burden of education too great. Who knows? Father-and mother-did not communicate their own thoughts, except about such things as getting wood, coals or potatoes from the cellar, etc. After this event I was quite disturbed for some time-I had become aware of the vulnerability of my position in life. I had then hoped that perhaps I could switch from "Mittelschule" to "Oberrealschule" or "Gymnasium," both available in Spandau, which prepare pupils for university entrance. This is what in the US nowadays is called High School, but the curricula were (and still are) much more intense and demanding. Bad performance always meant repetition of a school year, and between 5 and 10 percent had to repeat. This was the case at all schools I attended over the years. For example, it was unheard of that a graduate of those schools could not perfectly compose or write a treatise in German or English about any subject assigned. Although I had top grades at my middle school, which would have qualified me for high school (Oberschule), the subject was never broached by anyone. I don't recall ever pointedly asking my father. It seemed that infamous visit to the chemistry merchant had de facto resolved the subject negatively. This did not make me overly sad or resentful. I think a youngster's mind is very flexible and forgiving. I just concentrated more on the tasks at hand, as school became more intense and demanding.

THE 1936 OLYMPIC GAMES ... AND REASONS FOR MY FIRST REAL SUIT

Germany was now preparing for the 1936 Olympic Games, which was to be a memorable event in Berlin. The area around the old athletic stadium between Charlottenburg and Spandau was completely remodeled and the old stadium demolished. A much larger new one was built, surrounded by huge paved and decorated access avenues. An enormous swim stadium with sport education school and a huge assembly field with an impressive bell tower were constructed, all in grand style. There was a new subway to connect to it, as well as an S-Bahn (electrified elevated train). The bell tower offered a wonderful view of the entire Havel valley with Spandau in the midst. Other support facilities sprang up, especially in Doeberitz West of Spandau, where enormous housing facilities were to accommodate athletes from around the world. These later became air force barracks. Near the bell tower an open air theatre was constructed in the ancient Greek style, which is still going strong today. (Waldbuehne). Because Berlin simply did not have sufficient hotel rooms to house the expected visitors, rooms offered by citizens were registered with a central organization, which inspected and approved them. When guides were needed to show these tourists the way to their lodging, I came into play, as I had just received a bicycle for my 14th birthday and a real, dark suit with long pants. It must have first been used for my confirmation at the Melanchthon Church at the Wilhelm—corner of Adamstrasse, opposite the garrison prison-a more than ugly red brick building surrounded by a 15 foot wall of the same material, which would later become famous-or infamous-for housing those WWII war criminals who escaped hanging. Before that I had worn only short pants in any season, since German boys then wore short pants only. Anyway, around that time my family thought confirmation papers would help my future. The new government was believed to be pro church and pro country. In the past all births, marriages and deaths were registered at the churches. Father and mother never visited them, except for marriages, confirmations and those things. I never heard either parent talk about God, Christ, the Apostles or Luther (we were registered Protestants, which in Germany means

Lutherans). Before I got confirmed in my new black, pin-striped suit, many lessons had to be attended at Melanchthon Church.

Our food was still very simple and invariably made from the most economical ingredients, like potatoes, cabbage, carrots, kohlrabi, herring (pickled, fried or matjes). Sauerkraut was prepared from scratch, green beans used a lot, and mother used them in a great stew with beef bones (Suppenfleisch) or mutton. We ate lots of stews, and everything was nourishing, particularly when potato pancakes were served. Rice was eaten only as a sweet main dish, perhaps accompanied by plum or cherry compote or just sugar and cinnamon.

Our fortunes in the mid 30's had turned for the better, as demonstrated by the improved food. While swastika flags were displayed increasingly by other people in the street on holidays (other flags had completely disappeared), there was none on the Moratz' balcony for quite some time. The Nazi party had become all-dominating. Showing such other flags as black/red/gold, red hammer and sickle (communist), or black/white/red (right traditionalists) would have meant disappearance into a concentration camp. Over the years, mother politely asked father about the possibility of acquiring a flag: everyone had one, and mother was asked curious questions about why it was not possible for us, when everyone else saw fit to do it. Then, one day around 1938 or 39, father arrived home announcing he had a flag, finally! With delightful, slow movements he unpacked a smallish parcel, and an extremely undersized swastika flag emerged, which was immediately displayed on the balcony with relish. No one had that kind of a flag (6x8"). The average, normal size was around 3x5'. In 1935 the Nuernberg laws were adopted and published, which defined who was Jewish and who was not. Marrying Jews was prohibited. Aryans married to Jews were to divorce them, or-I don't remember what punishment was meted out, but it was severe. All Jews then still left in important positions lost them. Many Jewish people had already left Germany; now more followed. I remember an occasion back in the early 30's when Lisbeth, mother and I went to the Gatow swimming meadow (Gatower Badewiese), close to where Margot Voigt lives now. Resting on our blankets, we were looking at the lively scene at the banks of the Havel River, when two gentlemen callers approached Lisbeth, then perhaps 19 or 20, and quite attractive. The three faced each other as they talked at length, while mother was turning her back to them to show she knew nothing and wanted to know nothing of it (just like mother!). These men were definitely Jewish and talked about leaving for America, if I am not mistaken. They did not approach me or mother at all, so, without knowing more, I thought they were a bit clumsy. Funny how these memories return after so much time. I do not know if she ever had a date with them … I didn't even know then what a date was, sorry to say!

Around my confirmation, Lisbeth was getting more and more involved with a certain Werner Ehling, a hunk of a man, blond and blue-eyed. I later learned he was a bricklayer, who was good at his occupation. He seemed very fond of Lisbeth. Funny, whenever I think back, I have memories of her, rather than of Ulli-probably because events tend to be forgotten after 65 years. One day, Werner showed up in suit and tie as if he wanted to go out dancing. One should know that his pattern of speech had a certain lisp, if not to say stutter. Miraculously, father was at home—some understanding must have preceded the meeting, which was far from casual. I was sent out of the room, and then it happened: I think it was a first that Werner got into our apartment, and he asked, stuttering, if he could have Lisbeth as his married wife. They really would like to get married soon, with a church wedding and dinner at the Moratz'. I heard some of it behind the door, but by far not all. This was agreed to, and Lisbeth suddenly had a fiancé. Some months later, the wedding took place at the Melanchthon church. The pair arrived in a black, horse-drawn carriage, as was the custom. I still felt out of place and uncomfortable in my new suit, Werner sported black tails and top hat and Lisbeth a real wedding dress. Usually oblivious to those things, I noticed that she had gained a lot around her midriff, which I quickly forgot amid the other excitement. There were real flower girls and everything. The dinner at Moratz' was sumptuous for our circumstances. Many toasts were exchanged. I believe mother had to stay home to prepare all the goodies. Then the newlyweds took off, rented an apartment in a brand-new development in the North of Spandau, near Neuendorfer Strasse. Soon after the wedding, which was during the year of the Nuernberg laws, in 1935, came the next sensation: a baby girl arrived named Marianne, who looked like her father. Not that I looked much at her; I was quite disinterested in babies and things like that, which would only change very slowly, beginning around 1945/50.

For a good 20 minutes each morning, I walked briskly to school, through Wilhelmstrasse and Kosterstrasse, past Lewin's fur shop. I never met the furrier's son Fred on the road, which I should have … a very quiet person and not one of the brightest, Fred was in my class. It seemed he was to enter the fur business also. In class we treated him as equal. There was no teasing or worse. He appeared to feel comfortable and accepted, although he looked very Jewish, different from the rest of us. However, the learning business seemed to make him ill at ease. He was not alone in this as the learning process intensified, especially in English, French, and the exact sciences. Many fell behind and had to repeat the year.

As mentioned before, after our small scout troop had been integrated into the H.J. around 1936, it disbanded. Bonne, Schwengel and Kasakoff, disappeared from sight. The others got lost in other units or concentrated on such other affairs as school, sports, and-little by little—life after school. My buddies, except Atze Koziol and Koepke (both attended Gymnasium and left the troop earlier, because extra curricular activities began to conflict with academic demands) did not expect to continue school. As for the rest of the group, either the grades did not qualify for continuing toward High School, or the parents subtly let it be known that there would be no more support beyond what had been committed to. I still often met with "Orje" Herwig, who also lived on Zimmerstrasse, Guenter "Tossi" Sossna, and Horst "Osram" Gehrmann. Our interests coincided and we exchanged views. Because the latter two were one year ahead of me, they had to come up with a plan in 1936 what to do for career development. Orje and I had one more year respite, except that Orje entered the honorable bakery business as an apprentice. With Sossna and Gehrman I kicked things around as they made up their minds. We agreed that the future was tech-heavy, and that craftsmen would be in great demand. We also thought that spending three years learning a trade thoroughly would provide a golden basis for further progress. Both took the chance of entering "Heereszeugamt Spandau" (Army Ordinance Factory) in front of me, which offered a good tool making apprentice program. That would qualify them for an army career as weapons specialist/managers (commissioned officer rank).

Seeing so many uniforms over the past years had left the impression that everyone was to be covered with brown, black, blue or gray cloth and shiny buttons. If we had to join the crowd, why not as commissioned officers? This would also fit in with our main goal of a technical position. Otherwise, with a "Mittelschule" education we could not enter an officer's career in the armed forces; those careers were filled with High School graduates, who had been pressed through basic training and then attended the Armed Forces Academies (the Air Force Academy was in Gatow, 8 miles south of Zimmerstrasse). The German forces had no institution equivalent to West Point or Annapolis. Academy training was followed by a commission within at least two years, and later by more training at the war schools. Anyway, my two friends started at the apprentice shop of the ordinance plant on May 1, 1937. I should add here that they could have gotten away by serving for two years as "Praktikant" (intern), a training reserved for people wanting to enter the weapons specialist or an engineering career. The Praktikant did not complete training for a trade, such as toolmaker, and could not work as such later. But to enter an engineering school one had to have worked as

"Praktikant" for at least two years in a related field. (University-level schools required only one year.) So, my two friends had made up their minds, while I floated toward the great experience of the 1936 Berlin Olympic Games. TV did not exist, so I could not watch them (except that they were shown in the movies later). The radio transmitted some reports, but I don't remember listening to a single one. Though the events occurred in walking distance of my home, I am sorry that I did not attend a single one. Rather, through the H.J. organization, I spent some time attending to a camp consisting of several musical bands sent to the games by the Italian fascist youth organization. I suspect they were as fascist as we were Nazis! I was intrigued by those wonderful uniforms and strange instruments, which included several saxophones-then totally unknown in German brass bands. I don't recall quite what I did there, only that I was in the middle of a big, dirty mess as a kind of liaison. This was the problem: One day I wanted to go to the can to relieve myself, but, before telling more, I must describe the construction of those facilities: a wooden shed and a 30' long row of seats slapped together of wooden planks, with holes of adequate size. One was supposed to sit comfortably, and between holes wooden blinds provided privacy. As I entered and saw all planks totally covered with feces, I almost puked and ran out of this horribly smelling mess, thinking I had to do with a bunch of pigs. But the explanation was simpler: German organizers had not inquired about Italian toilet customs, which reach back a few thousand years. Holding onto special handles, one squats down over a hole in the floor, like a scout in the woods. So much for my first culture shock, but the Italian visitors must have been even more disgusted than I was. Whatever I did for them cannot have been much. My main occupation during the Olympics was to serve as a guide for foreigners, using my limited English skills. Usually they came in automobiles. I showed them to their quarters by bicycling quickly ahead of their cars. Earning a pretty penny with my new bicycle was more important to me than wasting my time watching the games. The entire year 1936 was filled with preparation and follow-through of Olympic activities. Otherwise I was very active in handball and things like that; H.J. service was on the back burner.

THE BALL STARTS ROLLING

Well, it was more like an avalanche, in summer 1937 a big propaganda campaign was unleashed by the government's media to prepare the populace for the historic events to unfold. The armed forces crossed the Rhine, settling on the left or Western bank. According to the Versailles treaty of 1918, German troops were not to be stationed on this German soil. Now the German government (read Hitler) broke that treaty. Rearmament had begun four years earlier, the draft instituted, an air force organized, and large Navy vessels had been built-all activities prohibited by that treaty, which the press, government and German historians were calling "the dictate." There was never any serious reaction by the signatories of Versailles. The U.S. had never signed that treaty to protest its content. Woodrow Wilson, U.S. President in 1918 and a college professor, had specifically promised the Germans a fair treatment and treaty, but, unable to influence the other, revenge-seeking allies, he left the spoils to the others and returned to New York City. Many of those treaty demands were now revoked and, as I saw from the reaction of the people around me, the population solidly approved. While even father did not gripe about it, I could tell he was worried that Hitler might single-handedly start another war. He neither easily volunteered opinions, nor did he express his worries daily. But from the movements around the nearby barracks, Seekt Kaserne near the Park and artillery barracks a little south on Wilhelmstrasse, one could deduct tense concerns by the leading military and party circles. History accounts later confirmed that the military had advised Hitler that the armed forces were not prepared to take on the combined forces of France and U.K. Thus the old allies missed one of many opportunities to get rid of Hitler. Had they called his bluff, the German military in all probability would have broken with the brownshirts. Since it had turned into a glaring political success for Hitler, people were relieved that there was no war, and the Rheinland was again unquestionable German territory.

SEARCH FOR A CAREER

In my efforts to seriously prepare for entering the work force, I temporarily became infatuated with becoming an apprentice in the "Deutsche Beamtenversicherung" (German Government Insurance Company). I was asked to submit my application and then waited for a long time. Then one day my carefully composed and painstakingly, neatly handwritten document was returned. I had been rejected because of one comma-mistake, which was prominently circled in red. The comma position was actually debatable, and it was certainly irrelevant! Left mad, I crumpled it into a ball and threw it out. Later I was glad I had not gotten caught in that bureaucratic outfit. Father, on the other hand, was not convinced that I was well suited for life as a metalworker, particularly not toolmaker. My constant immersion in books led him to view me as an impractical bookworm. But in the end he was glad I wanted to learn tool making and viewed it as a good basis for my future, although, to my recollection, it was never really discussed. So, around the end of 1937 I sent my application to follow in the footsteps of Sossna and Gehrmann. Like Sossna, I speculated that I would later volunteer for the army and their weapons specialist career. I was accepted and began working life as an apprentice on May 1, 1938, without the foggiest notion what tool-making was and how to prepare for it. No one in my family had ever succeeded as a skilled craftsman. Werner Ehling was a skilled bricklayer, but that was generally not viewed as a very skilled trade. Anyway, preoccupied with the baby, with whom I couldn't do much, he and Lisbeth were now so remote from me. I seldom saw them and learned later that Werner didn't like his trade much. Wanting to better himself to work in an office, he prepared himself on the side to become a draftsman, someone with a white collar, rather than performing those tiresome physical tasks day in and day out. Once he showed me a complete sport suit he had sewn all by himself, of which he was very proud. Around 1938 or 39 he found a position as a draftsman at Siemens in Siemensstadt/Berlin. Occasionally he showed me some samples of his drafting, and I was very impressed. His accuracy was that of a computer. It almost looked as clean and methodical as modern CAD-generated drawings today. He seemed to have found his destination. Werner's next occupation: soldier, like everyone else. He got drafted into the air force-antiaircraft artillery.

APPRENTICESHIP

My school days were coming to an end-continuing was out of the question because of the tuition payments. The subject never came up and I could not imagine raising any fuss. I had not been brought up to verbalize any independent thoughts and knew that kind of position could quickly kindle father's wrath. I admit that I was also kind of tired of the monotony of instructions which school offered; I felt it could have been more imaginative and thought school was a bore, no matter what; one could see no goal on the horizon. I wanted to get my hands on something real. I was ready to step out into the world and make RM 9.00 per week (RM=Reichsmark, at the time equated $0.25). Most of that income I left with mother. With my bike taking me to work in 12-15 minutes, I needed no transportation. Mother packed a luncheon, and dinner was at home. So there I was, dressed in a gray, long-sleeved cotton working coat I had bought, with some pockets to hold such small things as light tools or calipers. All of us got introduced to the foreman and his substitute, and two or three helpers. I have forgotten the names. Our training facility, separate from production, consisted of a large room with five or six rows of benches and space for about 20 apprentices or interns, another room with a forge and pertinent machines and tools, and a large room with about two dozen machine tools, such as lathes, turret lathes, horizontal and vertical mills, drilling-, grinding- and tapping machines, shapings, etc. etc.

Life started at the bench where we were given a vice, measuring equipment, and two files: that for roughing was 1-1/2 square x 20 inches long, and the other was a flat, bastard file for finishing. Then all guys got a block of steel approx. 2-1/2 inches on each side and were told to reduce to 1 inch each side. All sides were to be parallel and square to each other. What it amounted to was to convert white, soft, unused teen hands into something resembling a metalworker's paws. We soon got blisters, which turned into calluses. To hog down 1-1/2 inches of steel by hand turned out to be a monumental task. The most difficult part was to file it so accurately that the dimensions were kept, the angles maintained (90 degrees), and the flatness filed so that no light could be seen under a precision straight edge. Everyone had to either succeed or start over from scratch. After about one full month of labor, we filed into the foreman's office one after the other to meekly show the results. Those who had completed the arduous task satisfactorily were assigned different-usually easier and more productive-jobs which the production departments sent over. Discipline was tight. Several times during that month the foreman literally jumped apprentices from behind, who displayed idleness or made excessive, loud or gossipy talk, from behind; sometimes he even struck a guy without hesitation.—These were the lessons from the old school. Everyone slowly progressed through the basics of metalworking: layout, center punching, accurate deburring for tool purposes, scraping a flat surface using Prussian blue, drilling a hole to tight tolerances, tapping a hole, and other tasks related to tool making. I learned new things almost daily, interspersed with dry spells. Spending several weeks in a design office with an engineer, I made my first drawings, the contents of which I don't remember. I was quite impressed by the environment of engineers and technicians, who apparently knew what they were doing and were working out solutions on drawings before the shop carried them out. I also saw fellows in army uniform conversing with those engineers, but the guys in civilian clothes always seemed to win their points. The real doers were the engineers, who seemed to solve the problems; the uniformed personnel were merely the administrators. Consequently, the action, technical expertise, education—all those good things were with the engineers. Uniforms made me uncomfortable; I hated to see lower grades strut past higher grades lifting their arm for the mandatory military salute. I found it ridiculous, when a guy greeted a superior NCO each time he walked past and thought there was a loophole in the military code which turned the salute into a farce. There seemed to have been only mechanical obedience to what was demanded, with no respect. I could observe that by the non-verbal expressions indicating it. I started to dislike these shows. However, the NCO's and officers seemed to be really after it, having been taught that this would strengthen discipline. But my own experiences widened daily, and I didn't have to file past anyone to lift my arm to my cap like a robot. After finishing my initial tasks, I got assigned to the forge where a young man could really show what he was made of. I learned how to heat steel without burning it (burning off the carbon). When too hot (like white color), it sparks off little stars and one knows the steel is ruined-scrap. Sometimes the lead man-one of those very old hands-would use me with a 10 lb. hammer to thrash away at a large piece to be formed. He held the piece with tongues and used a two pounder to show me exactly where to hit, and I tried to follow his directives. Then a lively forge sound of ding-dong emanated and the hits became faster and faster until one broke out in profuse sweat. The more hits per time unit, the better the job. One aims to heat steel as few times as possible. Working there three months, I made several test pieces and learned the basics about steel metallurgy. I also did some superficial hardening. While it was a pretty dirty job, everyone had to do it. The first to get in were Heiner Herbold and Horst Gruenwald, and I think I was together with this Gerlach kid. He came daily from Gross Glienicke on a motorbike. Gruenwald arrived in his old three-wheeled small delivery van which he also used to deliver cookies for his father's business. Those were the three guys I was most closely associated with at the ordinance plant. A couple of months at the hardening plant followed. They used such basic processes as hardening in salt baths or surface hardening by carbonizing the surface, followed by rapid-cooling by dipping (water or oil), depending on steel composition and instructions given by the planning department.

As the work started, I began attending a special school for apprentices each Friday, located in Charlottenburg, where I went by streetcar. There we sat on those well-known school benches again, making foul jokes about the program offered, which was tailored more toward the majority who had left school at 14 and thus were two years behind Gruenwald, Herbold, Gerlach and me. Because, due to our advanced educational background we hardly had to lift a finger or think, we considered Fridays a day of rest: we had to work only until 1:00 p.m. on the following day. Generally, the workweek then consisted of 48 hours, after which overtime kicked in (not required of apprentices). One incident stands out from this apprentice school-it must have been in 1938. When school started that day, I observed unusual commotion outside. Gangs of toughs, who normally would have been stuffed in brown (SA) or black (SS) uniforms, roamed the streets; I couldn't understand what they were shouting. Not that the streets were brimming with them-there were some only. Even that was unusual at that time, because crowd activities were generally tightly controlled by police. Crowds one saw would usually be clad in brown uniforms or those of other associated organizations such as NSFK (pilots), NSKK (automobilists), Arbeitsfront (workers' union), police (green), Hitler Youth (HJ), BDM (girl-scout type political organization for girls), etc. etc. Even the horsemen had a Nazi organization ... with the horses not yet wearing uniforms. As I arrived at school, everyone was hotly debating things they had observed. While there was not much to report where I came from, classmates from the central and eastern suburbs told about smashed store windows, broken glass all over the street, and plundering. Our first session that morning was athletics. We knew that the teacher-a tough cookie-was a leader in the SS, which was headed by Himmler, and whose members wore black uniforms with brown shirts. By then Himmler had won Hitler's total trust at the expense of the SA. We had only seen this teacher in civilian clothes so far. Making his entrance somewhat late, and a little out of breath, he announced that he had carried out some "urgent tasks" early that morning. The controlled media reported later: "The people's rage finally struck all Jewish businesses to wipe them out all over Germany." Of course, no one noticed any rage; my schoolmates were not enraged about Jews. It was simply an issue which interested no one. The "civilians" smashing the Jewish shops and department stores were from the SA and SS, since no group could spontaneously band together for such acts, unless instigated by the Nazi organizations. So, everyone was musing on the way home, feeling somewhat taken aback. There was certainly no jubilation by the masses from what I could tell. Did people like me get the idea to help a Jewish shopkeeper? First of all, as I went home, I did not see any demolished shops; there are very few, if any, between Charlottenburg and Spandau. Also, my buddies and I, at about 16-17 years of age, had never been taught about government; had these kinds of lectures been given, they would have focused only on the one-party control for getting things done efficiently and without friction. No one could imagine how the kind of government being perfected by the Nazis in those days would end. On the other hand, the short-term results had been impressive. Besides, challenging the Nazi toughs would have meant immediate disappearance into a concentration camp. Initially these camps were filled with Germans. Willy Brandt, who was to become Germany's chancellor after the war and was then a socialist activist, could only escape this fate by fleeing to Norway. In the aftermath of the so-called "Kristallnacht" (crystal night), Fred Lewin's father must have sold his Klosterstrasse fur shop; many Jews sold everything at bottom prices and left the country. No longer protected by law, Jews were, de facto, no longer considered Germans and had become fair game. I never saw Fred Lewin again after I finished school because we had not been friends.

Another example of the "wonderful" education at that apprentice school was an incident later on, which everyone really considered the pits. One teacher, who quite occasionally would fit into his boring political harangues some sexual hints and observations, told us that any male who masturbated would grow hair between his fingers. The nerve! He naturally wanted to see how many would lower their eyes to check their fingers. This pervert must actually have been counting! We didn't consider it worthwhile to report the guy. As a party member, nothing would have happened to him anyway.

AUSTRIA TAKEOVER

The year '38 offered some more excitement, as the Austrian "problem" was brought to a crescendo. The army marched in and the country was taken over without elections. While the mobs ruled the streets, the Austrian Nazis prepared for the "Fuehrer's" triumphant march into his native country. Austrian by birth, he had acquired his German citizenship by volunteering for the German Army in World War I. His return triggered a flower war similar to the time when the German Army had reoccupied the Rhineland in 1937. But around me people were quite indifferent. Naturally, everything was exciting, with seemingly no danger of war breaking out. So, people shrugged their shoulders and viewed the "enthusiastic Austrian crowds" they saw in the movie newsreels with amazement. But father never watched movies and mother seldom did. As for me, I would spend 50 Pfennigs perhaps every other week on a Tom Mix film about the wide-open ranges. Hence, nothing actually changed around us common folks, while naturally some of the big shots kept improving their positions. So, the last peaceful year came to a close. Not knowing what was ahead, I was consumed by my work. I worked for some time in the coating and conversion plant, which offered such exciting things as coating and conversion, applied phosphate coats and providing black oxidizing to weapons parts. Looking at a weapon like a pistol, one sees the nice, uniform black finish. This is done in a special chemical bath, with several successive rinses. Here I saw for the first time rifle parts and the army regular pistol, the 9 shot Luger. After circulating through different departments for one year, I was now getting ready to enter the machine shop, a very important next step in the tool making career. While I was preparing for all this, more happened on the national level. People were getting used to expecting daring political moves, such as the news about Austria, just about monthly. The dumbbell Pechstein, on the fourth floor of the back court building in Zimmerstrasse, started singing with his kids (equally mentally endowed) blatant Nazi songs such as: "Seht ihr im Osten das Morgenrot, ein Zeichen zur Freiheit, zur Sonne!" (Can you see the red glow of sunrise, a sign of freedom and sun?).—a very notorious Nazi chant of the times. We rolled our eyes and shook our heads in disgust. But what can you do? The poor slob, who finally had a job after years of unemployment and misery, was proudly showing off his party membership-the swastika button-on his coat. He was one of the late bloomers joining the fray (Nazi party or NSDAP). Most people in government jobs gradually were coaxed to fall into line by joining. Not to be a party member meant no promotions, no raises … it was very simple. The wife and kids want more goodies, so what does a guy do for the sake of domestic tranquility? Join the party. This did not mean that many compatriots were enthused about the way things were going and did not doubt the methods used. Father never became enthusiastic-no way; neither was I while I concentrated on systematically furthering my career. The party's long arm could not reach people employed in industry; Nazis could not simply infiltrate commerce or industry, since they lacked the necessary know-how. It was a much slower process, and no noticeable inroads were made up to the end of the "thousand year Reich." Schools and universities were dealt with same as the government: join or else-no rewards. This system was used later in Eastern Germany until the Berlin wall came down. Millions were asked or pressured to join the "STASI" as informers. Refusal meant no promotion, no chance to get into professional positions, and perhaps loss of job-entire families were excluded from higher education, resulting in perpetual misery and isolation. For working people in 1938/39 there was generally no pressure to join the party, but workers had to join the "Arbeitsfront" (labor union), the successor union to all former free labor organizations which had existed before the Nazis' total control of the country. Union leaders were often also members of left-leaning parties and were sent to concentration camps early on. Nazi cohorts got the fat union jobs, displaying uniforms especially created for those stooges. Such other aspects as benefits and salaries were dealt with by government decree. This was the end of the free labor movement as we know it: no one was asked, membership was mandatory, and fees were deducted automatically. Those were then used to lavishly support the Nazi leaders and to create vacation travel opportunities by promoting the "Kraft durch Freude" (strength through joy) program throughout Germany. It offered vacations in many places, and large cruise ships carried German workers to foreign shores-all this under the swastika emblem, while many foreign countries, including the USA, were still suffering from the effects of the great depression. The old toolmakers, whose sidekick I had become later to learn their trade, were not fond of the new union situation. They would have preferred their freedom of choice-but "the train had left and inexorably picked up steam."

CZECHOSLOVAKIA ANNEXATION—SEARCH FOR A CAREER PATH

Meanwhile, the media more and more frantically reported excesses of the police and government toward the German population (as many as 3-4 million) in Czechoslovakia, with concentration along the borders. Though there never had been complaints before, now a Nazi Party was formed in that country, which needed a leader: Mr. Henlein. One thing led to another, resulting in a crisis. Horror stories about Germans fleeing Czechoslovakia were published and it was said that Big Brother Germany could not remain idle while fellow countrymen were mistreated. To solve the problem, European leaders convened-I believe in Munich-under definite threat of war. Unfortunately the U.K. and France still needed time for rearmament. The outcome was that all of the Czechoslovakian country occupied by German majorities would join the German "Reich." The army marching into those areas was greeted enthusiastically; flower wars were becoming routine. At home, we wondered how it would end, but could breathe easier when learning of the Western powers' appeasement. During that time I switched to the machine shop and got so involved in mastering all of those difficult processes that the "Sudetenfrage" (annexation of a little part of Czechoslovakia) made little impression. Some of the tasks on which I was concentrating very hard were quite dangerous. One day, for example, I was filing down the size of a round piece using a mechanical lathe at high speed, the spinning piece with the machine headstock to my left. As I was holding the file with my right hand at the wooden handle and gripping the tip with my left hand, suddenly a tremendous force started to pull my arm away. Fortunately my long-sleeved coat was kind of old and the sleeve was ripped off with a bang-not my arm. I stopped the machine, face white like a sheet, sweat rolling from my eyebrows. I had been incredibly lucky. Even now, after so many years, I shudder at the thought of what could have happened so easily. So, never wear long sleeves when working with revolving equipment.

At age 17 I had developed serious doubts about volunteering for the army for a weapons specialist career, rationalizing that my future should be a thinking man's job. I enjoyed working out things; any education to further this would be a giant step in the right direction. I think Gehrman, Gruenwald, Herbold and Gerlach had similar opinions. We kind of revolted against being pressed forever into a uniform, even if gray and not brown. What to do about it? Engineering education would mean serious money, which father did not have hidden around. Visibly relieved that I had changed my mind about army life, he agreed completely with my plans and promised I could live and eat at home during those years. Since he had no money for tuition and books, I had to think about earning it. I could, for example work for two or three years as a journeyman toolmaker. I could make good money, but it would mean interrupting the learning process and probably more problems at college than necessary. Or I could take evening courses and get a degree the hard way-nothing but blood and sweat for at least eight years. One very intelligent, married young man (Mr. Rauschenbach) in the large gauge department was the only one in the entire outfit who went through it. He said it was very difficult and the program not as good as day classes. Then I found out I could make some money delivering newspapers early in the mornings to the doors of customers. I applied, and, since lots of jobs now went begging, was hired on the spot. Let's face it: who wants to get up at 2:30 a.m. summer and winter, seven days per week, rain or shine, to slip those papers directly through door slot after door slot? It meant unlocking each main entrance door and running up to the fourth or fifth floor 2-3 steps at a time after picking up the load downtown. I had to bike to the assigned delivery zone in the eastern part of Spandau along Ruhlebener Strasse. The apartment blocks are still there, unchanged in all those years. Because that also started in early 1939, I had little involvement or interest in the entire patriotic hullabaloo. I just could get up at 2:30 a.m., run after the papers and bike to Ruhlebener Strasse. When finished, I pedaled to Neuendorfer (my regular job) and returned home about 4:30 p.m., where I wolfed down the meal, read the paper, and went to bed. Extra activities were impossible, and I was permanently excused from H.J. service. This schedule was only surmountable with my goal in mind. That was illustrated each morning, when, gasping to the fourth floor, I reached a polished door nameplate fastened in the German tradition, which read: "Dr. Ing. E. Ruska." He was always very sympathetic to my agenda; of all customers he would give me the largest monthly tip. I learned many years later that he was the developer and inventor of the electron microscope and received a Nobel Prize for it in the eighties. Then I did not know what he did, but that brass plate was very important to me and my endurance-he was my shining example and didn't even know it. What papers did I deliver so diligently? The "Voelkischer Beobachter," owned by no other than Mr. Hitler-which had become an official organ of the government and was the most widely read paper in Germany. No other paper, like the "Morgenpost" or "Lokalanzeiger" wrote anything different. They were totally controlled and their editorial staff had come to consist of party sympathizers (at least) or members. Besides the "V.B.," I also had the "Schwarze Korps" (organ of the SS) and "Angriff" (party organ)-both read by almost no one. I sometimes glanced at the Schwarze Korps, disgusted by its content: one harangue after another about Jews, without any foundation. I wondered who would read this crap. Did I draw any consequences? Hey, I was making money for college, with little time for anything else, unless I would stop sleeping. What could I have done against the contents of the Schwarze Korps, if I had wanted to? Nothing … like Don Quixote fighting the windmills on horse Rosinante. But those thoughts did not surface … just disgust. Frankly, I didn't understand it and considered it more of a pretty bad joke. I didn't spend much time on it or on any deep thoughts about the consequences of those papers. Germany had no history of educating people in the affairs and consequences of government behavior. In my daily life I did not see that these dirty tabloids would make the least difference; reaction around me was indifferent, and I wondered why anyone with any taste would ever order and read this. As I made real money now, I realized that the law required me to deposit part of my gross earnings in a savings account to which I did not have access. This law, which covered all wage earners and forced them to save without the right to withdraw, withheld billions from circulation and consumption. If people would have used the vast amount of money, inflation would have followed. These sums were now invested in the exploding armament industries, armaments, military expenses and infrastructure such as the Autobahn. As a particular propaganda instrument, this enormous construction project was used to expound the superiority of the German government as compared to those of such Western democratic countries as France, U.K. or USA. Since only the wealthy could afford automobiles, people might have wondered how those marvelous superhighways would be filled. Simple: another huge people's propaganda wave was created to launch the Volkswagen which was designed and tested in 1937. The designer, Dr. Porsche, had revolutionary ideas for his time to build an inexpensive, but sturdy car. The goal was to make a car available and affordable for every German. It is revealing that the advertising campaign left no room for the possibility of also selling this new vehicle to foreign nationals or countries. Germany was by now totally focused on itself. Now, how to produce millions of cars without a production facility? The Nazis never ran out of ideas for their purpose, so here we go: The new "Arbeitsfront" (workers' union) set up another savings system in conjunction with the purchase of a VW. Once purchased by a lucky individual, the buyer only had to pay a modest monthly sum in exchange for a promise to receive a car after all installments had been paid. Even serial numbers were assigned in advance. The money went to the Wolfsburg factory. Actually, the city of Wolfsburg did not yet exist, but was erected overnight along with its huge, impressive assembly buildings. Thus, billions more were bilked from the trusting Germans. The Nazi organizers were more ruthless than the worst robber barons on Wall Street-Rockefeller was a novice compared to them! But by now everyone was impressed and enthusiastic about Hitler's effort on behalf of the long-forgotten working stiff who could never even dream before of having a car to take mother and the kids for a spin in the country. In reality these savers would never see any nuts from their cars! Since it was still too much money for our budget, father never bothered with it. We could not yet even afford a radio in 1938 and felt the VW was more for the middle class and up.

The promising news about economic initiatives almost overshadowed the new troubles with Czechoslovakia. This time there was nothing to be liberated. The troubles were cooked up in Berlin, and many people were again afraid of war. I worked day and night and could read about it in the Voelkischer Beobachter. We didn't get a daily paper, but sometimes father brought one home that had been left in the streetcar. Now, this may not fit well with the notion that newspaper was used for toilet purposes, but that's how it was. Right now it appears to be a mystery where the supply of newspapers came from for those needs. Some may have been leftovers from my route. Should I also narrate how strenuous it was sometimes in winter or during rainstorms to negotiate the huge stacks of papers on Sundays from the downtown Breite Strasse distribution center to Ruhlebener Strasse? The stack, between three and four feet high, was balanced precariously on my rear luggage rack, sort of swaying with the wind. Unable to pedal, I pushed my bike hard all the way. One day mother asked about my progress. My parents were still doubtful that I would be able to go through with my plans. But now she wanted to see for herself if she could do the same, in order to buy a new, modern radio. It looked as though we could never get one from what father earned-perhaps only after Ulli and I left for good. So, she did very well in helping me climb the stairs, and then decided to take one route by herself. She also had a bicycle available by then. It may have been purchased for the paper route's sake; she really had no other needs for more mobility on the street. I taught her to ride it. Initially it was an almost insurmountable task to get her on top of the saddle, shift her weight, and quickly position her in the center of the system mass, let alone to get her to pedal through all the commotion! It seemed to take forever, but it finally clicked, but I wasn't too sure mother would make it downtown and from there to the other end of Ruhlebener Strasse. But luckily there was no traffic at 3:00 a.m., except for an occasional bicyclist. Mother would return home around 7 a.m. while I went to work.

LOSSES AND DISAPPEARANCES

Meanwhile, the lively weekly open air Spandau market suffered a great loss. Samuel Intrator, the best, and perhaps only, cheese vendor was gone. We would have never thought of describing this couple as Jewish, only as the best place to buy cheese. They were there summer and winter, always slicing you a little sample of what you wanted. Even after they were gone, we did not speak of them as Jews. These kinds of thoughts neither surfaced nor did we link them to the increasing media blitz about the races. Perhaps we were naïve or not very deep thinkers. I admit that no prolonged rationalization about the Jewish people's plight was discussed. On one hand, there was no information as to who lost his job, who sold his business or property, or who left the country. It did happen, but my direct observation only involved Fred Lewin and the Intrators. Our family had simply no other connections to Jewish people, and it therefore was not something we knew or thought about.

At work, I progressed through several machine experiences, e.g. some time working on shapings and on large turning machines. Here I was first exposed to a new hard cutting metal from Krupp called WIDIA (Widiamant). They had developed it and slowly introduced it to industry. It was a piece of tungsten carbide soldered onto a steel shank, which served only as a carrier for the tungsten carbide. I practiced with it on the end of a 12" alloy steel bar. The end was irregular as it came from the forge and therefore almost impossible to cut by regular high-speed steel bit. The forces generated were enormous, the chips red hot, and the huge machine sounded as though it was being demolished. It was too much for it. That was very impressive. Soon much more sturdy machines would be developed to accommodate the vastly increased cutting forces of WIDIA. Later I worked on a horizontal mill and experimented with new carbide-tipped mills. The versatility of these machines was also astounding. In 20 minutes I learned to mount a vertical head. Some time later I was cutting large threads, worm gears, even special form mills for one of a kind services in the production departments. The theory of calculating the different drive gears, etc., was transmitted through that Charlottenburg apprentice school, but much of it I learned quickly on the job. I quickly realized that, to be a good journeyman, technician or draftsman was the future in engineering and industry, and a solid learning experience like mine was an enormous value and advantage. Consequently, I had done the right thing under the circumstances. Of course I could have complained about not being able to finish high school and enter university, but complaining was never my style. If the possibility had existed, I would have asked for it-but there wasn't any.

Fairly soon mother showed us her new family acquisition: a brand-new SABA radio with polished wood veneer box, large scale for station selection, and even short wave bands. It was handy for listening now to the political games being played with the rest of Czechoslovakia. I have forgotten all of the pretexts used to knock that poor country into submission to Hitler's demands. Finally, the German army occupied the remainder of the country, without any resistance. No flowers greeted the soldiers this time, only angry faces. It happened so fast and methodically that no one around me had a comment. As usual, adverse remarks or opinions were not published, and the Western allies seemed to have gotten surprised again. They sort of sheepishly agreed in Munich, and Hitler promised that this was his last territorial demand. England and France, though, did not lose any time to conclude a defense treaty with Poland-potentially the next target. Thus the final stage of the relatively quiet period reaching from Hitler's ascent to power until the annexation of the rest of Czechoslovakia came to an end. Periodically, exciting events were taking place, yes, indeed-but they did not really reach into the fabric of the families. This time was characterized by increased opportunities as well as better and full employment for the population at large, as I knew it. There was a great deal of skepticism and exhilaration, of which I could neither make a statistical study, nor did I know yet what they were. I only describe my own observation and the impact of actions as they affected me. I can't help saying there was plenty of careful skepticism, but there was absolutely no mechanism left for venting it. All organizations were controlled and belonged to the NSDAP (Nationalsozialistische Deutsche Arbeiterpartei=Nazis). Other organizations were allowed only by special permits granted by the government. Although some, such as glee-, sport-, bowling clubs, etc. were not directly part of the Nazi organization, they made sure there was no adverse politicking. If such things would occur, then one could never be sure there was not someone reporting to the security police (GESTAPO), with dire consequences. At that time one could see the most glorious and powerful movie strips covering the movements of the mighty German army racing through Czechoslovakia. Little was seen of the air force, which seemingly did not need to be deployed. Also, Hitler was shown racing through the lovely countryside in his large, specially built Mercedes-Benz command car, with a mercurial warlord aura displayed for the world to see and fear. I must have seen a movie then, preceded by the usual program showing a 10 to 15 minutes newsreel, as also customary in the US and elsewhere. I could not see movies very often. Neither I nor anyone else I knew understood very well from all the media hullabaloo why Germany had to, or wanted to, take in or occupy Czechoslovakia. There was no historical link or adhesion between it and Germany. When Bismark founded Germany in 1871, and earlier, when Prussia defeated Austro-Hungary in 1866, he opted for a "small Germany" excluding the Austro-Hungarian Empire with its wild mix of nationalities. So, from a historical point of view it made no sense. I realized that, and that's where I largely let the matter rest. But without my knowing it, an epoch was ending.

NUERNBERG PARTY RALLY 1939

Around that time the H.J. leadership invited me-even though I was hardly in attendance because of my oppressive work schedule-to participate in the annual party ritual. The H.J. organization had to carry the flags of the Berlin-Brandenburg units to the gathering in Nuernberg. I cannot explain why that city was chosen, where a huge area was set aside outside Nuernberg, with huge displays of flags and party emblems, designed by Hitler's preferred architect, Albert Speer. These grandiose events (Reichsparteitage) lasted about a week and were to eclipse everything ever done in this genre-even by the ancient Romans. The important party heads spoke, with parades of army, navy, air force, SA, SS, Hitler youth male and female, working service (Arbeitsdienst), etc. etc. In 1938 they actually showed tank battles on the field, and jumping of air force paratroopers. Whole battle scenes were enacted before large crowds-mostly party hacks. The only thing missing on the field was a dead corpse. I wonder if the crowds had any thoughts about it. But this is an old phenomenon: everyone thinks the other guy will be hit! Gehrman and Sossna had also been invited. They may have dropped my name because Gehrmann's dad was a fully employed party bureaucrat, about which Gehrmann never talked-he must have disliked it. If he had followed in his father's footsteps, he might have evaded the draft, but he didn't. Just like Gehrmann did not mention his father, talking about parents or family was kind of taboo for us. They were almost non-existent. Anyway, I thought a respite from my work would do me good and this flag-carrying stint would be my last H. J. engagement. After that, young men were normally transferred to more grown-up party organizations. Knowing that at work they would have to give me time off with pay, and the "Voelkischer Beobachter" couldn't block party activity either, I joined. The party congress was planned for the last week of August or first week of September. H.J. units from the different regions started marching at different times, depending on their distance from Nuernberg, in order to all arrive on the same specific date. The Franconians had one day to march, and the East Prussians three or four weeks. So, our little troop left with 20 to 30 flags flying. They were pretty big and a pain in the a … to carry such distances each day. Sure, there was a spare guy and we switched occasionally. The mileage from Berlin is about 250 miles or 400 km on today's Autobahn. In 1939, marching along the highways was somewhat more … maybe 450 km. This means about 32 km per day (20 miles), with those blasted banners. On the first day we could not walk that much-we had to adjust to the march. We developed blisters, the muscles ached and shoulders crunched under the swastikas' weight. My visions of walking animatedly through the beautiful German forests and meadows, crossing rivers, and seeing new sights and towns had been too romantic—now reality set in. The first night I spent in a room with an architect family in some town South of Berlin-perhaps it was Luckenwalde. An elegant house, upper mobility people, nice crystal, fancy food, and nonchalant talk of the war to come. I could hardly follow because I was falling asleep on my chair. And the next morning I was to go on! More kilometers: later we occasionally did 40 km. This experience must have profoundly influenced me not to become part of the German infantry later on! As the days went by, we sometimes got invited to a village or town dance after dinner. Most guys grabbed the available girls and danced to those old-fashioned polkas or waltzes. Modern English or American-sounding selections were not offered. I usually hung around bored and tired, not knowing how to dance, hold a girl, or entertain one. That notion was so strange to me. Feeling out of place, I always wished the affair would be over sooner than later. They should have given us dancing lessons before sending us to Nuernberg, I thought-but then, the H.J. was not really a social club. We brought the flags to the party congress in the allotted time; a day or so before our scheduled arrival we were unceremoniously packed into a train and in Nuernberg a big tent city in the festival area awaited us. We had hardly had time to unpack, when all elders, usually commissioned H.J. leaders, bade a quick "good-bye." They had to join their reserve army units overnight.

WORLD WAR II BREAKOUT

War had been declared on Poland. As a result, England and France declared war on Germany. Everyone had to go home immediately, and the party congress was cancelled. I was somewhat relieved that I didn't have to stay in that terrible tent city. But the idea of war made me feel very uncomfortable. Returning to Berlin by train, I saw vast amounts of war material, cannons, howitzers, tanks, soldiers, etc., etc.-the entire system overloaded with army units and support material. A tremendous organization seemed to shift all those things around. Some went east, and from the East came others to go west toward the French border. No one had ever seen this kind of impressive action. Disembarking at one of the large Berlin train stations, we heard the air warning siren's sound. No one knew what to do. Bomb shelters were not yet available and, had they been there, I would have rather opted to have a good look at whatever action would occur. Luckily, there was none, and I arrived home safely. I took off my H.J. uniform, never to wear it again. In the next days I could study what happened to make the German government declare war on Poland. Negotiations had been in progress for a German-controlled railway link to East Prussia through the Western part of Poland, which was wedged between Pommerania and East Prussia. Before 1918 all this territory had been German and most of the population as well. The 1918 Versailles treaty ceded all of this land to Poland, without elections to determine the people's preference. Now Hitler tried to force this railway link to East Prussia. Based on their defense treaty with France and England, the Poles resisted. Suddenly, the media reported riots in the border areas, and one morning, German troops dressed in Polish uniforms crossed the border and attacked a radio station near Gleiwitz, Silesia. They further reported that the provocation was quickly answered by German troops invading Poland: war had broken out. A few hours later, Germany was again at war with England and France. The outcome is known: The poor Poles were so badly mauled, it was pathetic. I saw pictures of Polish cavalry units attacking German Panzer units with drawn sabers like in the Napoleonic wars. England and France could do nothing to prevent Poland's occupation, but neither did these two countries call it quits. The war continued. As the German armies marched toward train stations to be shipped to the East or West this time, neither the populace nor the soldiers displayed any enthusiasm in the streets. No flags were shown, no flowers were thrown. In 1939, there was somber anxiety instead of the proud show of commitment demonstrated in 1914, when the whole nation had exploded with patriotism, ready to follow their emperor. Now they left like sad sacks or puppets. People and material were moved according to a plan, and everyone followed automatically, without noticeable emotions. At work I heard many voices doubting the wisdom of all this.

Will the Allies retaliate?

By now everyone awaited the allies' counteroffensive, which did not come. All winter the armies confronted each other-no action. Most German units were moved from Poland to the Rhine. This war had only been made possible through a treaty Germany had signed with the USSR in late August 1939-both promising not to attack each other. The two countries exchanged an enormous amount of goodies, foodstuff (wheat, corn, rye, etc. for Germany, and machinery for the USSR). The latter was allowed to annex Lithuania, Latvia, Estonia and all of Poland east of the Vistula River, a good deal for both parties. The winter 39/40 was full of speculation. People became very anxious and could not figure out how all of this could ever end in their favor. I had my hands full at work. In early '40, my last year of apprenticeship, I was transferred to a production facility.

My first real work assignment was in the department producing all special gauges to control the working gauges in the different factories-private corporations or government armories-throughout Germany. These gauges were for quality control of any size weapon used by the armed forces and, at the same time, interchangeability of all parts. Today computer controlled Q.C. machines make this task much easier. Three-dimensional curvatures used on gun breeches required devices, which were extremely difficult to build. One design office worked on the drawings and one office prepared the work and developed work sheets, including estimated times, for carrying it out. The piecework was based on these times. If, for example, 100 hours were estimated for the job and the journeyman needed only 60, he still got 100 hours credit against his payments. These credit vouchers were used like cash. Quite regularly, if a man got too much credit, he started "working" very leisurely or stopped altogether, just pretending. If he got stuck with a very tightly calculated, difficult job, he could use time from other jobs to receive his customary (very good) salary plus incentive pay. They all took care not to turn in too many hours, never in excess of 140%, lest the calculations might be squeezed. The piecework calculators were old hands at the game, with more experience in this than the journeyman on the floor. I got assigned to Brauer, an old hand in his mid-fifties, kind of overweight, with a pronounced stomach, and very good-natured. He could use me as he saw fit. What I produced for him was his gain. I noticed that sometimes he hardly worked for weeks—mostly, of course, due to his enormous skill and knowledge. He worked together much with a guy named Rautenberg, who was attending evening courses for his engineering degree. Although he was an extremely able professional, it almost killed him, which confirmed that I should attend daytime engineering college. So, there I was as a sidekick to Brauer, who loved chewing tobacco. In back of us was Heiner Herbold's father, a tall, good-looking, blue-eyed chap who looked more like a banker than a toolmaker. Brauer showed me lots of tricks. One day he picked a bastard file (about 10" long) and started working on a piece of steel. After a while he measured the straightness of the worked piece with a super accurate, lapped straight edge and showed me it was dark. This meant he could work with a file as accurately as a grinding machine. Now I was to try. I did my best for a long time, but it never worked! As a result, my respect for this man, who often acted as a consultant for other journeymen, who had difficulties with their assignments, grew immensely. To produce a certain piece, they often first had to conceive a complex setup on one of the high precision machines, or they had to figure and build an auxiliary fixture or gauge. He freely used his own time to support his younger colleagues—he always had more than enough time in his pocket. Brauer lived on Ruhlebener Strasse and was not a "Voelkischer Beobachter" subscriber. From what I could gather, he was very skeptical about what was happening-particularly the war bugged him—same as Herbold. Although they did not openly discuss things with their apprentice, I drew conclusions from occasional remarks. They were as much prisoners of the regime as father and millions of others. Unfortunately, there are no statistics about average people's sentiments at the time. Nowadays, proof of the Germans' agreement is in the form of movie strips from party congresses or Hitler's speeches in the Berlin Sport Palace. This type of proof is somewhat popular still today. Often, when a U.S. President, for example, speaks (in front of selected audiences), only enthusiastic applause can be noted. Anyway, Brauer put me to work on something he needed quite badly. He wanted a layout and checking flat plate, made from gray iron, ground and lapped within about 0.00005 inches. This means optical flatness criteria, measured by a lapped straight cylinder. This device was the best straightness measure that existed at the time. It was hardened, and, when placed on my plate in any direction, no light should penetrate between plate and cylinder. Now, this is easier said then done! I started grinding on a horizontal grinder, the best, very expensive high quality machine available. When measured, there was a huge gap-even a feeler gauge could be squeezed through at the extremes of the geometry. Grinding was followed by scraping by hand and then lapping one plate against another. It took about one month of lapping until this torturous thing was complete—the best, lapped, flat plate in the department. Nowadays you can purchase granite plates to the most extreme requirements. This exercise taught me the price you have to pay for accuracy. Afterwards, Brauer entrusted me with entire gadgets to build on my own of ever increasing complexity and accuracy. We established a good relationship, and I also told him what my goals were, and that I looked at Rautenberg as what today might be called my role model. He encouraged me to no end. I had a good time in that department (Lehrenbau), learning many things and feeling I was on my way to something I might like later on. I always had an eye on the future and liked to prepare for it. I was getting up there in age-18 or 19, and had to start thinking about journeyman's exam and military service.

Before that phase began, I had one more encounter with the party organization. Not having attended H.J. activities since the ill-fated Nuernberg party congress, I was asked one day to join one of the adult N.S. organizations. I only remember attending a N.S.K.K. (Nationalsozialistisches Kraftfahrer Korps or N.S. Automotive Corps). Consider the irony: an organization of auto drivers in brown uniforms with special NSKK emblems, of whom none owned a car. I thought they might teach me to drive one or perhaps a motorbike. Car owners didn't join; their free time was spent enjoying the luxury of having one. So, there we were one Sunday morning enduring the usual lengthy roll call in front of the Olympic Stadium. In front of about 150 NSKK prospects, three motorbikes of the DKW production appeared-about 100 cc jobs, 2 cycle engines, very light. After a show and tell, we were offered a spin. I waited for at least an hour for my turn, then up on the thing, coupling out, first gear in, slowly activate coupling, and, increasingly turning on the gas, I took off. This was so easy! I only needed a bike like that. Here is the rub: I couldn't get one! Back home, I did not think highly of the NSKK and never attended again. I couldn't see how they would fit into my life and schedule. That was the last I saw of a Nazi organization and vice versa. In the last few years, I had hardly ever used the uniform, but now: never again: never! Therefore I was never transferred from the H.J. into the party. Apparently not a great believer, I was not a big loss to them. But they would take anyone who could pronounce "Heil Hitler" and lift the arm for the Nazi salute, which was called "German Greeting" (deutscher Gruss). Something comes to mind that I thought was long forgotten: in my last years in the H.J. we sometimes had to line up to go on the street in wintertime to swing a collection can for the "winter assist program" (Winterhilfswerk). I think they caught me for this once or twice. What the party would do with all the money collected was never explained. All party organizations participated in this all-out effort. With a red painted can I had to walk the corner of Pichelsdorfer and Wilhelmstrasse and swing it in front of the pedestrians' noses. Very few softened to contribute; most were annoyed, and I was furious, because I hated bothering people for something

I could not explain. But I had to return the can, which couldn't be empty, and deposit it in front of one of the leaders. So, after a short while I went home, got some of my precious savings, exchanged it for pennies, filled the can and returned it. What they did with the cash is a mystery; I never saw a program for distribution and there was practically no unemployment—and unemployment compensation and social services were Europe's best, perhaps the world's best. I suspect it went into party coffers for beer and champagne. In the winter of 39\40 not much was happening on the Western front, except that air warfare against England steadily increased. Germany didn't suffer much, and occasionally an English bomber appeared at night over one of the German cities, doing little damage. German units of the air force, likewise, didn't do much harm to British cities, except to the defense industry, which became critical for the British war effort in 1940. It was initially more of a cat and mouse game. The French did not seem to possess any air force at all. That winter's war effort was confined to defensive lines-an infantry warfare like that of WWI, except that there was little effort. Life at home continued unchanged and peacefully. Due to the Soviet food deliveries the rations were sufficient and no one went hungry. Little luxuries like bananas, pineapple and other tropical fruits slowly disappeared. Entertainment industries worked full blast with theatre, opera, operetta and other recreations galore. Music ensembles propagated modern German dance music and people liked to dance. Most anticipated heavy fighting to commence in spring and no one dared a wager on the outcome. While not be merry while one could? I did not worry about it much, with my newspaper route and my last year as apprentice. I saw the war as far away and not touching my routine except that all houses were blacked out as well as streetcars, trucks and cars. Even my bike lamp had to carry some special equipment for cutting the light cone to a tiny slot. Streets were no longer lit-all was dark, especially since apartment windows were darkened by black shades. The general mood was foreboding. Something was up and coming. But these feelings were somewhat subdued, while I concentrated on my daily, tough tasks, like pushing a bike with a stack of newspapers 3 feet high, often through snow, biting cold or rain.

Early 1940 marked Germany's invasion of Norway and Denmark under the pretext that British troops had assembled conspicuously in England to establish bases in Norway. It may have been true. But whether I believed the news stories was pointless then. Soon the real fury of war was unleashed in the West. This time Germany didn't have to defend its Eastern borders against Russia due to the non-aggression treaties signed in August 1939, which were advertised as a particular strike of genius by our "leader" Hitler. Indeed many marveled at this turn of events and all was done to let them hope that this time-other than in WWI—the decks were stacked in Germany's favor. But from my observations, the country was not really preparing for a prolonged, difficult war. Many people were not employed yet, particularly women generally stayed home taking care of domestic tasks as if nothing was happening. Entertainment was in full swing. People worked regular eight hour days, weekends were still used for recreation, and holidays and vacations were taken as usual. The authorities treated the population very well. The mighty assault through the allies' defenses impressed the average people, who hoped that, once the great victories were accomplished, the war could end quickly. The defeat of France/UK was so complete that the German leadership appeared more surprised than the enemy. It presented the perfect opportunity to take the entire British armies prisoners at Dunkirk, but-as later learned-Hitler himself intervened to stop the Panzers' advance, allowing them time to escape. Arriving at the Channel ports without further operational plans, the Germans wondered what to do. None of the leaders appeared to have had enough faith in the enemy's defeat to justify development of plans to leap over the Channel into England-what a way to run a war! Because Germany had never had a good understanding of global or maritime war, tactical plans and logistics for crossing a great body of water were utterly strange subjects. No special crafts existed to carry troops to enemy shores. The Navy, too small to take on the mighty U.K., could not protect a crossing, neither could the air force. Therefore, the German armies did the next best thing: enjoying French champagne, wine, and any other luxuries found. I heard that some river barges were assembled at Dutch ports, but-unfit for the rough Channel waters—they could accomplish nothing. As a result, the state of war with England was unchanged, with no end in sight for the time being. Germany's air force commander Hermann Goering battled the growing British air force with no success. The papers did not report the mounting losses, but the fact that the air force war over England continued proved the enemy's resistance and ability to retaliate.

Raids now began on German cities, with ever-increasing bombings at night, against hopelessly inadequate defenses. It was obvious that the war would last longer than projected. Italy joined Germany, and most people I knew only laughed about it. Joining with Italians-considered unreliable and better at things like wine, women, songs and food than at making war—was a bad omen. Anyway, they annexed a part of France for their effort. This was part of a deal cooked up between our "Fuehrer" and the ridiculous figure "Il Duce." At one of those periodic party rallies on the vast lawn between the Olympic Stadium and the clock tower overlooking Spandau and the Havel valley, I heard the Duce give a speech in German after Hitler had finished one of his bombastic diatribes. Among the 50,000 to 60,000 people in party uniforms, I and those around me thought it was very funny. The Italian connection must have originated in the late 30's, and now around the early 40's Il Duce set out to complete his "Imperium Romanum." He took off from Tripolitania (today's Lybia) to take over Egypt and was badly mauled and devastated in the process. Germany had to rescue the proud Italian forces from total annihilation, which led to the concept of the "Africa Corps." There was no strategic principle. The Italians were to take care of that theatre of war and push the weak British contingent into the Red Sea, but it didn't work. Further developments of the war in North Africa are well known. Germany had to quickly equip a special army for mobile desert warfare—very valuable and modern mechanized divisions fresh from their success in France. Miraculously, they could ferry over the Mediterranean Sea-which had not been possible at the Channel. So, at least there was some use for all this mobility and firepower. Valuable air force units were also transferred, distracting from the real war over England. People whispered about Cairo to be taken, and that was not far from the vast Saudi and Iraq oil fields, wasn't it? They thought: "My-are we going to take over the world? What is this leading to?" No one had any idea about the real power centers, e.g. little was known about the U.S. It turned out later that our anointed leadership, and particularly the "Fuehrer" himself, did not know anything either. The U.S. was believed to be in terrible shape economically, with the depression yet unsolved after ten years. Because Germany had overcome the deflation by deficit spending, the U.S. was viewed as a basket case, and its enormous industrial capacity, which allowed most people to have automobiles, whereas in Germany almost no one had one, was overlooked. And that powerful country started to supply Britain with everything she needed on a "Land/Lease" basis, with gradually noticeable results. Britain even received entire warships, while Germany lost ten destroyers alone during the Norway invasion. These were bottled up in a Narvik Fjord and then slaughtered by big British battleships. A terrible tactical error. Except for the U-boats (submarines) the German Navy was never heard of again.

In 1940 I was keenly observing it all. People started following the German troops' positions all over Europe. In the East, Germany now began at Warsaw on the Vistula (Weichsel) river; the Soviets had taken over East of there; in accordance with the August 1939 treaties, the UDSSR had occupied Lithuania, Latvia and Estonia. There was a huge campaign to repatriate all German peoples from those countries; many of them came, opting for a life without communism. Previously, the Nazi propaganda had invited all German expatriates to partake in the promising opportunities offered by the "fatherland." Many of these unfortunates took the bait. I met some of them later after they had returned to Brazil. Now German influence reached to Northern Norway, the Spanish border, and the Atlantic. Its U-boats operated directly from Atlantic ports, and now the German troops were also in North Africa. Looking at the world maps, the common man was impressed, and so were the people busying themselves with trying to lead. But what next—how would the war be settled? I believe I had an inkling of the problems, but started in the fall of 1940 to prepare for the life ahead. To many Germans I knew things were confusing; they didn't even try to rationalize what was ahead and withdrew into their shells, hoping for the best, with daily tasks their main preoccupation. I would be drafted into one or the other branch of the armed services soon, as had Sossna and Gehrmann earlier. Sossna had picked up his weapons specialist career in 1940 and Gehrmann just dropped out of my sight. He was drafted into the dreaded infantry.

Once I met "Bonne" Bornschein-a private first class in the artillery-after many years. Dressed to kill in a smashing army uniform especially tailor-made from fine officer type wool cloth, he wore long pants, spit and polish shoes (to be pulled on! No strings), and sported nicely made shiny silver spur (the type without a real spur for evening occasions indicating that you belong to a mounted regiment-definitely not infantry), huge saber dragging at his side. I wondered why, because he was to shoot with a big cannon or howitzer. Looking like an operetta hero, he was a sad sight, which made me wonder why I had attended his scout troop for so long. After this last time I saw him, he must have disappeared on the vast Russian plains. Werner Ehling was drafted and joined the FLAK (air force anti-aircraft artillery). I visited him later, when he was temporarily stationed in Lankwitz, south of Berlin, to train recruits.

I have not mentioned Ulli for some time. I don't even recall when or how she moved away from home. But, still a civilian, I visited her in Frankfurt on the Oder River around 1940 in her apartment on the east bank of the Oder. I think she had a small child. Her husband, Oskar Jahn, was a corporal in the air force with a 12-year commitment. He came from the Baden area. Since there was no great wedding celebration at home, I don't know how they met, when they married, and why she was suddenly in Frankfurt. I regret my lack of recollections, especially about her involvement with Oskar. Young married couples could then obtain easy credit to get established, since the regime greatly encouraged families and childbirth, under the slogan: For a sound future, we need sound families with children. Mothers of four and more got medals (Mutterkreuz), which some proudly kept, but few displayed.

With Sossna and Gehrmann gone, Gruenwald, Herbold and Gerlach-excited about the fashionable air force—considered volunteering for flight training. One consideration must have been that these young officers in their evening dress looked smashing. Attending a Wintergarten show in Friedrichstrasse, I saw them leave the subway: irresistible, like trained models, shining lights, heroes, or something. Rich, white silk shawls bulged out of their light blue topcoats. Their deep tans came from flight training in Elstal west of Doeberitz, where the J.G. 1 (Richthofen) was stationed (Jagdgeschwader—fighter squadron). Everyone guessed that these guys were the same who helped another dictator to power in 1938 in Spain. Along with all the other excitement, the "Legion Condor" returned from Spain that year after the republican forces-said to be Bolsheviks—were defeated. A huge parade commemorated the victory. I saw the soldiers-the paratroopers of the airborne regiment the most impressive—passing for four hours near Berlin's Tiergarten station. So, my three guys were kicking flight training around. I was no longer that close to them, because they had gotten jobs in the fixture production plant. Later I heard they had volunteered for pilot training and had to wait for quite some time for acceptance. They wanted to use the time in the service to learn something worthwhile and provide another basis for future development. While I prepared for the journeyman's exam, I mulled it around in my head. Those who did not volunteer for a specific service were likely to wind up in the infantry. Since I no longer considered the weapons specialist career an option, I did not want to stay in the forces longer than necessary. There was not really anything else. Not being the daring type, paratrooper was not my cup of tea, and, knowing nothing about the sea, navy was also out. But air force pilot didn't look too bad. I finally submitted my application around March 1941, much later than the other guys.

For the journeyman's exam I had to design, draft and produce a substantial piece of equipment on my own, to be turned into the committee for approval around March 1941. I selected a precision drill jig for drilling holes absolutely on center of such round cylindrical pieces as shafts of sizes between 1/2 and 4 inches. The department where I had worked for the last year needed such a device. After approval, I worked on it uninterrupted for one month, as did the other finalists. Upon completion, I took it home, because-lacking any perception of industry and what was needed to make products under modern conditions—father could not quite figure out what I was doing all this time. Marveling at my product, he finally seemed to understand that I was succeeding in making something of myself. He would not have thought I was handy enough to make such a masterpiece from scratch. It is the kind of surprise many fathers get when finally the "kids" do something that puts them on the right road. Shortly before the fixture was submitted to the committee, three experienced master journeymen gave the oral examination on April 1. It was easy, since they had long forgotten most of the theories and dwelled mostly on the practical.

My time as a new journeyman with a good salary lasted but one month, since my conscription papers arrived through the mail a few days later. I was to report on May 1, 10:00 a.m., at the barracks of the air force communication regiment in Kladow-Hottengrund, close to Spandau, reachable by bus from Pichelsdorfer Strasse in 30 minutes. The fact that my application for pilot training had not been processed in time didn't depress me-at least it was not the army, where all the fighting occurred, which I loathed. With my keen sense of survival, I realized I had pulled the grand prize, meaning training as a radio or telephone operator or similar chores away from powder and blood. While I would not completely escape from the injustices and humiliation of a soldier's life, this was something one didn't have to anticipate with trepidation. My parents were also relieved, because it had become obvious that the German air force must have had terrible losses, while England's stepped-up bomber campaigns over German soil were becoming more and more successful.

LIFE AS A RECRUIT—KLADOW-HOTTENGRUND

On May 1 I arrived in Glienicke, West of Kladow, at the Hottengrund barracks. Used by the British after the war, they are now senior citizens housing. We were rounded up, assigned eight to a room, and sent to the stockroom for our gear. There the ubiquitous steel helmet, a blue uniform of very rough wool, German-style pull-up boots, a working outfit of white cotton, leather belt and all the rest were thrown at me. Since nothing fit right, we started trading to look halfway decent. Then they threw us out of the barracks into the courtyard in our whites and the cap, and let us stand at subzero, while it snowed profusely for hours. We hung around in that cold, freezing to all colors of the rainbow. It was really obstinate, with no one to complain to. This crazy first of May marked the beginning of my military training. They wanted to toughen you up, you know. But toughen me up? Since I was in superb condition because of my daily running endless times to the fifth floor and down, this was child's play. They started teaching us the military salute for days on end, which no one had used before. When greeting a superior anywhere, we had to change our leisurely steps into a military rhythm, assume a military posture of deference and lift our right arm fast and precisely to the cap, while moving our head so as to look the superior directly into his lovely, caring face. Passing him, we had to move the head always such that we were focusing on him. When passed, the head had to be immediately and quickly moved into the direction of the walk, the hand remaining at the cap, and only then the hand must be brought down in an abrupt movement (zackig!). Meanwhile the left hand must not be idle. It and the entire arm had to be held straight and stiff at the left side of the body, fingers all straight pointing toward the ground, thumb straightened at the side of the indicator, and the hands must never be placed in the pockets. I mean, did the reader get all this? Making us understand this nonsense was quite a task. Not quite willing to listen, we learned passive resistance very quickly. When we didn't wear a cap, for instance, upon entering an office or storeroom, we had to lift the hand to the "German" salute, i.e. the Nazi greeting. There were another few days of harassment to drum all that into us knuckleheads. In time, we all got numb and hungry. The miserable food was prepared without care or knowledge. Mornings and evenings the traditional heavy army bread with jam (a.m.) or a piece of sausage (p.m.). Coffee was an ill-tasting barley brew totally without coffee-like flavor. Coffee was no longer essential and didn't make it through the blockade anyway. For the first few months we were confined to the barracks; no city passes at all, and day after day the endless infantry drills. How to pick up a rifle, hold it at rest at your feet, shoulder it, march with it … individually, in groups and platoon. Days were spent to train presentation of the rifle, for example during a parade. When an officer passed through the gate, the guard had to present the rifle. Endless repetitions were needed to bring each detail movement to perfect execution. For example, when the entire platoon shouldered a rifle or presented arms, only one sound in unison must be heard. If not, they chased us through the landscape endlessly or let us do various strenuous exercises with the rifle, the preferred one being to hold the rifle with stretched arms horizontally, go into deep knee bend, and then let us jump from knee bend to knee bend till hell froze over. The can (incarceration) was the punishment for dropping a rifle-bread and water for three days. We also had to learn to sing in marching formation. When the sergeant ordered "ein Lied" (a song), he expected it right away, or the chase began. Not knowing soldiers had to sing, we were unprepared initially, so it was quite a disaster. Singing lessons or a glee club were not offered. Since we had to, or else, soon everyone could belt out the required four to six songs to make the premises shatter-not pretty, but loud-so loud that, after a while, out of passive resistance and to save energy, I only opened my mouth without sounds. But it would happen that, when the first man in the formation shouted his "one" "two" "three" to start us, all of us only opened the mouth silently. Then we had to suffer again. They even taught us how to dismantle rifles and pistols, and how to shoot. I never amounted to much. I was not a marksman. It probably did not interest me enough. After three months we got a day's leave. Since we had to wear the uniform at all times, I could only go home and get some decent food. Stuck in the barracks, we sometimes heard American jazz music, since one guy had a phonograph, playing the "Tiger Rag" and similar attractions to no end.

TIME AS A RADIO OPERATOR

One day we were divided into different groups: radio operator and telephone installations, and got real instructions. I was in the first group. The routine of the Morse alphabet followed for days on end. In a few weeks I brought my speed to 90 (letters per minute). Real pros had to do 120 or more. I can still tap it today after 58 years.

While I was wasting away in Hottengrund, the war came slowly alive again. In the summer Italy invaded Albania to occupy it. I can recall no specific reason, except it was time for the "Imperium Romanum" to expand. For good measure they also tried to take in Greece, but that did not work very well again. The bersaglieri, who always looked so fierce on parade, got bogged down in the mountains between Albania and Greece. The real thing was simply not their bag. Hitler's request to Yugoslavia for free passage to assist Italy in Albania was denied, and the German armies again invaded, taking Belgrade and the whole of Greece in no time. The British tried to assist, but had to evacuate. We tried to follow all that, but were usually too busy to make sense of it. Then the air force invaded the isle of Crete by dropping parachute units, resulting in awful losses, which the tabloids did not report. That was the last parachute drop of the German side. I later learned that Orje Herwig dropped there and received the Iron Cross first class for some heroics. In Hottengrund, rumors now circulated about transfers. Supposedly there were new electronic devices built in Koethen (Saxony). Some or all of us would get trained to use them in North Africa. We were also to get tropical uniforms, etc. One day we got marching orders to Dresden, where barracks near the Heller awaited us. No one there seemed to know what to do with us, so the recruit training started again on terrible terrain-all loose sand like a desert, and wavy. For days we raced up and down those sand dunes, sometimes with gas masks-terrible and depressing. On weekends we could see the town, where I even saw one operetta "The merry Widow." Then Monday mornings the same lousy routine started over. We had to sing while running under gas masks. At least we got so used to the useless routine that passive resistance improved daily. When the bull (the leading sergeant) called for running, we trotted at a very restricted pace which we knew we could hold for hours. When he yelled with threatening under tones "faster," we moved the legs a bit faster, not increasing ground speed, only to soon fall into the old trot. Finally, the exasperated bull ran ahead to show us the speed he wanted. We followed cautiously until he stepped aside, and then fell into the same old trot. That continued until the s.o.b. got tired of it, wanting to have a good time in town, while we had to stay in the barracks, only to get out on weekends.

The rumors about North Africa intensified. One day several radio transmitter special trucks appeared. We started training how to operate the equipment, transmit coded messages and things like that, all specialized to report aircraft movements and whereabouts. At that time, Soviet foreign minister Molotov (translation: "the hammer"), a very tough cookie, paid a state visit to Berlin. Among the specific demands of the Soviets he brought along were: a free hand to arrange control over access to the Baltic Sea, i.e., control of Denmark and Sweden, the German o.k. for control of the straits of the Dardanelles for accessing the Mediterranean, and the German consent for access to the Persian Gulf, i.e. control of all Arabian oil. At least this is what later publications disclosed; these facts were not widely published then. What I observed in 1941 was Molotov's unceremonious departure. No one knew what to make of it, but it did not bode well. Sure enough, some time later the huge German war machine entered Soviet space by crossing the Vistula River—quite late in the year to start this kind of thing. The war in Yugoslavia and Greece had delayed the Russian campaign by at least a month. Because Hungary, Romania and Bulgaria now had friendship treaties with us, Germany controlled almost all of Europe except Sweden, Switzerland, Spain and Portugal. Its eastern front reached from Northern Norway to the Black Sea-an enormous expansion for a battlefield. The largest, bloodiest war of the human race had begun, and I knew it was already lost: Germany could no longer maintain its superiority, since the U.S. supported the U.K. and the UDSSR (Russia). One look at the map sufficed to realize the colossal people and material power assembled against Germany. Its treaty with Japan would hardly help. Few people foresaw that the U.S. would be drawn into this conflict. I discussed this with my two new friends in the outfit: Helmut Neumann and Hajo Lokat; Helmut was from Thuringia with relatives in Cologne, Hajo from Babelsberg near Potsdam. Hajo was a physics student, who no longer could postpone the draft, and Helmut had just finished high school at a boarding school in Strausberg between Berlin and the Oder River. We rationalized that the condition to complete Germany's doom was again fulfilled: A war on the East and West side, and one to be waged in Africa (since the Italians had lost their composure vis-à-vis the rough British). We did not know what prompted Hitler to invade Russia so recklessly. It turned out later that Russia—realizing Germany's inability to defeat Britain with all the help Britain had from the U.S.—found it opportune to extract concessions from the "axis powers" which would be designed to enhance the Soviet strategic positions. If not met, they had better join the Allies. As usual, Germany was diplomatically check mated. Now would have been the time to end the war, because Germany could not expect a favorable outcome with all the material, supplies and people power stacked up against it. At that time, though, we simply thought everything was lost. The three of us were kind of desperate. Whatever we did was done with reservations, with the waste of our skills and intelligence the dominating factor. What was this all about? Day in, day out these basic nonsensical drills were meted out only to raw recruits in their first month or two. Obviously there was no plan for us to do anything significant. A young man wants to prove himself, hone skills, etc.… nothing of the kind. Our preparation looked and felt as though we were getting ready for infantry warfare in the Russian plains, but, on the other hand, there were those rumors about North Africa … Some of us were to be trained on new, special and extremely secret equipment in Koethen in Sachsen-Anhalt. Then one day we received new, lightweight cotton uniforms and nice short-sleeved shirts with collars. Africa—what were we to do there? No one had the faintest idea. After about two months we were put on French Renault trucks, which hit the Autobahn together with our special mobile radio trucks—not south, but North. Arriving at a location East of the city of Stettin at the Oder estuary, we were put in some primitive accommodations-to wait again. Sometimes the numb waiting was filled with the ubiquitous drills, which some of the noncom's seemed to love. Since they had signed for 12 years, there was a vast chasm between them and us. Most of us had started university education or had high school. I was an exception with "only" Mittelschule, but with very good practical experience and good quality schools. The noncom's had basic school (Grundschule), which finished at 14, and-more significant-they were primitive, sadistic minds, if you can call what they had "minds." They were happy as long as they could play the superiors.

I had heard that Oskar Jahn was stationed in Stettin on an ocean liner, which served as military accommodation for flying personnel or those being prepared for flight training. Basic training and probably some preparatory lectures on aviation, meteorology, etc., were given. I visited Oskar there, who was a corporal, having signed up for 12 years (12 ender). I knew I would have to deal with him carefully. My experience with those types had shown them to be unpredictable and primitive. He showed me the ship and we had a beer in the noncom bar. After an hour or two, I walked away unimpressed—not really having gotten to know him. He later served as an administrator at German airfields in Italy and rose to the rank of staff sergeant (Stabsfeldwebel). The Jahn family relocated to Lahr/Baden, the home of Oskar's family. He must have seen the disaster brewing just in time and could thus save his family of five from the worst.

STATIONED IN ROMANIA

In the fall of 1941 two or three-dozen others and I received orders to report to a factory in Koethen, where we went with all our gear, guns and everything. There, a train loaded with ominous-looking equipment awaited us, which I could not identify. There were some large cabins with all kinds of boxes stacked up one on top of the other. They were fabricated from aluminum, and lots of cables went from one to the other. Obviously, this apparatus had something to do with radio transmission. Packed in huge boxes was a parabolic mirror also made from aluminum members—something like 40 feet across! There was also a huge pedestal for the mounting of mirror and cabin. The entire contraption was movable around a vertical axis in a horizontal plane. It looked like the mirror could be moved in an azimuth, i.e. the face of it, from a vertical position to horizontal. We did not worry much about its nature and hunkered down in the cabins as best we could without beds, kitchen, etc. We were to guard this highly secret equipment until Bucuresti (Bucharest), the Romanian capital. No one could come aboard and inspect what we guarded. We received ammo to be able to make a difference. But we were not told how far we could go in case of a confrontation. The usual thing: We were left dangling in the wind … to use our own discretion. We only heard later that we had "Wuerzburg" and "Freya" type radar equipment on board. The train took off toward Dresden and south along the Elbe River to Prague, Bratislava and then Budapest. When the train stopped at a switching yard there, we had time for a short look at the town, which was fairly rich. Shops were full of delicious food: salami sausages and hams-not seen for some time in Germany-were hanging by the tons. Unfortunately we could buy nothing. Helmut and I came to talk to some pretty German-speaking girls who took us to a restaurant, where we ate legitimate Hungarian goulash. We would have liked to remain in that friendly town, but our shift was to start soon, and we had to leave-sadly. We went on to Scolnok, Temesvar and those little German towns in Siebenbuergen, a country settled by the Austrian crown with Swabian people. Everything looked like Germany. Schluesselburg, Kronstadt (Brasov)—super clean towns, organized like in Germany, architecture typical as well. Few Hungarians or Romanians could be seen. Siebenbuergen was attached to Hungary, as this country became Germany's axis partner. It was given to Romania after WWI, I do not know the reason; now it was Hungarian again, demonstrated by the railway employees with those well tailored bluish Honved uniforms with their classic chic K.u.K. caps. (Honved means Hungarian army and K.U.K. stands for "Kaiserlich und Koeniglich"—the Austro Hungarian Danube monarchy.) They saluted us solemnly and super elegantly as we passed their beautiful country. In the far south toward Kronstadt loomed the very high, forested Carpathian Mountains. More engines were added for climbing the pass ahead. On the other side: Ploesti with its large oil fields and refineries. Romania was now also an axis partner, apparently with little choice. The Carpathians were devoid of people. The war might not have been possible without those badly smelling oilfields, where pumps stood as close together as a dense forest. We finally stopped at a switchyard in Bucharest. The next day another train arrived with the rest of my outfit and their mobile radio transmitter stations. We mounted the trucks and took off to the East through the dusty roads well north of, but parallel to, the Danube River, which became visible when Tulcea was reached where the platoon headquarter was installed. The company staff remained in Bucharest.

Our troop of about 20 guys left for the East until arriving at a forlorn place called Babadag, where all houses were of dirt. The town had several Minarets, showing the population to be partly Turkish. Not long ago this country had been Turkish-controlled. Romania was created after Turkey lost the Balkan War (perhaps in the early 20th Century). When it rained, the streets (dirt roads) turned into something like soap. The town we came from (Tulcea) had at least some cobblestone streets ending at the Danube. The banks were fit for bark and steamship mooring. But in Babadag there were only a few open-air bars serving mainly soda, zuica (slivovitz or plum brandy) and coffee, which was prepared in the Turkish tradition. A copper mocha cup on a long handle filled half with ground coffee and sugar and half with water was held over charcoal fire until boiled, then poured into a demitasse—everyone drank coffee that way. Men sat motionless all day around the bars or coffee shops. Women could not be seen. All huts or houses had no windows facing the street; we never saw what happened inside. Little work seemed to occur, at least by the men. Plunked in the midst of this—what should we do? We were assigned to the largest house in town, which was empty and had about four or five rooms. In each we installed four to six bunk beds. There was plenty of space for beds, but not much else. There was a kitchen with a primitive wood-fired stove. What we did then was to organize daily life. We got rations from headquarters plus Romanian currency to supplement our rations on the market. The currency was "leis." Our salary was also partially paid in "leis." Soon we were in the courtyard sawing and splitting wood for the kitchen or assisting the assigned cook, Ferdi Richter from Cologne. We slaughtered pigs by shooting them point blank in the head with one bullet of the rifle. Then we helped with rough cleaning of skin and guts, whereupon Ferdi took over to use it up in the kitchen. Finally we got some halfway decent meals after many months in the military surviving on tiny rations and tasteless, carelessly prepared food. This was no French cuisine, but when eating a bean soup or veggie stew one also found very adequate protein content. We seemed to be mostly concerned with the new environment and our own supplies, supplemented by an enormous, constant stream of red wine. With all of this, our job became a secondary item. Near the village we placed an observation station at the highest hill, which three of us always occupied. A phone was linked to headquarters in Tulcea, and we watched the air traffic around the clock with huge binoculars and our ears. We were to report types of aircraft, height and direction as far as possible. By night there were only noises. It was an air-warning network. Each time, going up to the hill, we took rifles, steel helmet, bayonets, and gasmask—ridiculous. Once in a while some noncom—especially at night—checked if we were awake and doing our job. Aircrafts almost never came along—no friend or foe to report. It dawned on us that someone must be concerned about the Ploesti oil fields, speculating that Soviet bombers could penetrate there, though the front line meanwhile had receded toward deep in Ukraine and German troops were spoiled to invade the Caucasus area. The Black Sea threatened to become a German domain. Crimea with Sebastopol was in German hands. And now the winter 1941/42 arrived. Life became very monotonous—no change of pace or entertainment, except hanging around the huge barrel of wine (perhaps 200 liters), singing and drinking the dark red/bluish wine which was almost like ink and tinted our mouths. When we couldn't stand life in our quarters any longer, we visited a cafe and drank zuica out of water glasses until happily wavering home and falling into bed. Since the house had no toilet facilities, finding the stairs in the middle of the night and going down across the courtyard to the John became almost impossible as winter progressed. It was Siberia-like, we thought, with cold winds blowing fiercely from East, going right through our inadequate clothing. A steel helmet is good for bullets, but doesn't help against a bone-shattering East wind in January in those parts. We saw the natives wearing sheep vests and hats, and they sold us whatever we needed. But the German soldiers who penetrated up to Moscow and

Leningrad were less lucky, facing an unusually harsh winter with the same flimsy clothing we had. Another advantage was that we could spend most of our time in the woodstove-heated building, listening into the deep frozen nights out on the hill. We wore special hooded, floor-length guards' coats of thick wool. To prevent aircraft noises from remaining undetected it was better not to use the hoods. Since they were so comfy, we made it a distinct game of risk to wear or not—without them one could also better pinpoint a noncom's approach. But the poor infantry in Moscow or Leningrad were mostly outside and treated like frozen meat. The local Russian population had their traditional winter gear: fur caps, feather-lined coats and pants, and special felt boots—superior to anything under those conditions. Obviously, the German leadership had never prepared for those winters: more soldiers were injured by the temperature than by enemy action. The winter turned out the biggest enemy of the German forces, while the Soviet forces were prepared as a matter of routine. Other effects of the cold were difficulties with the German troops' mechanized equipment. To start engines in the morning, fires were set below them to preheat them, gearboxes, etc., before attempting to start. Everything ground to a halt on the German side, while the Soviet winter counter offenses with special winter troops caused heavy losses. No one had anticipated that winter warfare could be waged at the kind of scale for which the Soviets were prepared. For urgently needed protection of its soldiers in the East, the German government and party organization belatedly started a gigantic winter clothing drive. Everything was taken: socks, gloves, blankets, wool and fur coats, hats, etc. This confirmed the German leadership's naiveté and more and more Germans were now becoming anxious about the course of the war, recalling another "invincible" war hero, who had earlier been subdued by enemy winter in front of Moscow (Napoleon). Unable to judge the effect of the clothing drive upon the war's progress at the time, I suspect the result was less than negligible. Little by little the fighting German troops got winter gear similar to the Soviets' until a German soldier in winter was distinguishable from a Russian only by his hat: red star vs. eagle and swastika.

Much of our domestic work during that and the following winter was performed by Ukranian nationals, so-called "Hiwis" (Hilfswillige or service helpers), who volunteered for this service in the German units. We had at least two fellows; others of our units employed them also. Very tight-lipped, they spoke a little German. Trying to strike any kind of conversation to find out where they came from or why they joined the German cause was futile. However, a large number of people had welcomed the German troops invading the East in 1941, with many men volunteering to join the German troops. Organized in military units, they received German uniforms and weapons and fought at the front. Those who did services for us (e.g. Hiwis) also had German uniforms. As the war progressed and German administration was introduced in the occupied areas, the conquered people noticed that they were not treated any better compared to Soviets. Their initial enthusiasm dissipated quickly, and soon they joined the partisan movement. This was another fundamental mistake by the Nazi leadership. Many of those simpletons in high places may have even thought the Slavic peoples, recognizing Germany's "benevolent superiority," would submit to the victor's desires and policies. This was only one of many fatal errors! But, as it sometimes is with mistakes, the consequences have a very delayed effect. Trying to level with the Hiwis was no use; in 42 or early 43 they just disappeared. We had neither understood them nor had they opened up to us, and we suspected some of them might have been spies.

Some of these observations were then made by me and my friends, and the general despair about the war's progress, or rather non-progress, certainly depressed most soldiers. We exchanged absolutely no views with the superiors. In Babadag there were only a corporal and a sergeant. The nearest officer was in Tulcea, three hours away by car, which amounted to many more hours in winter, and we did not possess cars. One must consider also that we received no lectures on the war effort and how we related to it. Stuck on a spot of a map, we were just there, reporting to two guys who just about ignored us, except that food, drink and beds were provided—an eerie state of affairs. For the most part, though, everyone was fairly content with his fate, considering what millions of others endured farther East.

Meanwhile, the extent of personnel losses necessitated mobilization of the allies, like Romania and Hungary, and the dispatch of large numbers of troops to the East. Equipped with German arms, they lacked heavy weapons and mobile equipment such as troop carriers, trucks and cars. The only transport equipment was the horse-drawn carriage or wagon which most Soviet troops used also. Spain also sent a division of volunteers to the eastern front in appreciation of the help received from Germany in 1936–38. They didn't last long. After a few months they were not heard from again. Why would they want to freeze to death on the plains of Eurasia? The vigorous resistance of these smart people to German pressures to repay their debt and join the axis was another big letdown for the Nazi leadership, which could not fulfill its aim to control the straits of Gibraltar. That would have helped in North Africa. In that fateful winter the Japanese Imperial Navy attacked Pearl Harbor without notification of, or coordination with Germany. We heard that, on top of all this, Hitler had single-handedly decided to declare war on the U.S. without a contractual agreement with Japan to that effect. We were devastated. Now we were sure how the war would end and became deeply depressed. While Germany could not even adequately clothe its fighting men, another vast continent with a sea of men and material power joined the war. The change of the constellation could not be immediately noticed, but we could well project future developments. It was significant that the combined Anglo-American navies would sweep anything German from the seas. For the present a fierce submarine war was raging, but none of us then expected that the U-boats could interrupt supplies across the Atlantic. We did not know how bad the situation would soon become, because the German media did not report U-boat losses. Stationed in Tulcea later, I sometimes listened to the BBC while attending to our radio transmitter, which also had a receiver—but I had to be very careful with this. Now we had another World War, larger than the first, which would be decided by endurance, stamina, and ... supplies, supplies, supplies.

In Babadag, we kept on killing an occasional pig, and often chicken, which always made a good soup, stew, or both. Paprika and Garlic were freely available. During an outing to Tulcea or once in a great while to Bucharest, one could even purchase quality items like Swiss wristwatches. Those items had disappeared from shops at home long ago. Leaving Babadag on furloughs required going to Tulcea and Bucharest first, staying overnight near the main train station. The rest of the afternoon was spent getting a haircut and shopping for goodies to take home. I always took a canister (1-1/2 gal.) of Sunflower oil with me, also bacon, things one only could get on ration card back home, and rations were inadequate. Bucharest was good for buying additional salami, etc.; the Romanian shops were still normally loaded since the country's agricultural supplies were still ample. Switzerland needed the excellent wines, meats, wool, etc., in exchange for its watches. I bought a nice Swiss wristwatch, which lasted to the war's end when I exchanged it in a U.S. army prisoner camp for a few cigarettes from a G.I. guard. Some lousy buddies with terrible withdrawal symptoms later smoked those. Swiss goods were in high demand. Their technical quality was high, and things like Oerlikon anti-aircraft cannons found takers on all sides of the war. The Swiss and the Swedes were truly neutral, selling to anybody with money or equivalent. Returning to Babadag, I had to retrace the entire route by which I had come. In Scolnok, Hungary, another lengthy stop provided an opportunity to spend the last money on salami, cheese and wine. Hungarian Salami was also excellent, and I ended up loaded with provisions. Upon returning, I was glad to have escaped the monotonous loneliness of that Romanian desert for a while.

One could see at home the effects the war started to create. Here and there, destroyed, bombed out buildings stood out; shops no longer offered goods as they had one year earlier. Shoes were rationed, and one could expect all other goods, such as shirts, suits, coats and other clothes, to be rationed soon, since the country was now essentially cut off from most raw material supplies. There was no cotton and very little wool. I had purchased a woolen sweater with tight fitting turtleneck in Babadag, especially knitted for me by a nice girl. People needed the work and income, and most buddies did the same. These things had become priceless in Germany, where the entire economy was being turned around to benefit those with access to the shrinking flow of goods. Average people wore only old clothes: clean, but worn at the edges. Soap was also rationed, i.e. people did not have enough, and so I brought some along also. When Ferdie the cook had a pig or two spoiled due to lack of refrigeration, he found some caustic soda, threw them in, and made some wonderful laundry soap. For my parents' personal use I brought some real good bars from Bucharest. By the way, the Babadag populace did our washing, with women coming by periodically for pickup and delivery. Our currency seemed worth much more than their "leis." It beats me why, since Germany no longer had much to offer. Everything was being turned into weapons and ammo. One item in great demand, artificial sweetener, was impossible to find in Germany for those without business connections. One of us, Borchert, who owned a high-class hat shop at the "Unter den Linden" corner of Berlin's Friedrichstrasse, which was said to supply Hitler and his brass with fine "Borsalino" heat wear, always returned from furlough with loads of sweeteners. He then disappeared into town and made his deals. Nobody ever knew what he dealt in, but he always had an abundance of the finest supplies.

FURLOUGH IN BERLIN

Back home I didn't do much. My friends were gone without exception. Girlfriends I didn't have. When I was in Hottengrund for boot camp, lots of buddies were picked up at the gate by their girlfriends or fiancées. Almost no one was married. The only person other than my parents was Lisbeth, or I could watch movies. When I visited Lisbeth one day, I got introduced to Mrs. Dumlich, an attractive person who lived in Charlottenburg and was married to a handsome, dashing young man in SS uniform. She showed the photos and said he had joined a special SS unit (Totenkopfverband) on assignment in the occupied areas of the Soviet Union. She had no idea what he was doing. Those at home usually had little information on the whereabouts of their relatives. They couldn't give details about their units and locations or describe their assignments. The mail was censored. The Dumlich woman had a thick accent from Dresden. I heard from Lisbeth much later that he was killed in action. Daily the papers were filled with the typical soldiers' obituaries. All ads displayed the "Iron Cross." Sometimes dozens of those appeared. Soldiers wearing Iron Cross decorations were growing in numbers. I hated going to the Zoo area near the Kurfuerstendamm in my ill-fitting, miserly uniform, to be surrounded by all kinds of live heroes, strutting around in tailored, smart uniforms and decorations galore. Passing one, I had to lift my arm to a standard military salute each time—perfect, obnoxious nonsense! And some of them really wanted you to salute, especially when accompanied by girls, in order to look sharp. Sometimes I saw something like a colonel or so with monocle squeezed in one eye! Those outings were a study of human follies. All these walking heroes could almost make you think that Germany was well taken care of—nothing was wrong—although close scrutiny indicated otherwise. In early 1942 the entire propaganda was pounding home the fact that Germany controlled almost all of Europe; the rest would follow as soon as the snow would melt. Everything appeared optimistic on the surface. Lack of contact prevented me from judging the people's mood, but my opinion did not reflect the propaganda at all. Unable to wear civilian clothes during furlough, I was somewhat uncomfortable. I didn't want to detract any heroic deeds the medal wearers may have accomplished, but I did not give them the military salute because of their medals—rather, because I feared retribution. While not always 100% conscious that the war would have a terrible ending, in times of reflection with like, reasonable companions, I had serious doubts. Not that doom and gloom poured out of all my pores; there were moments of conversation with others, movies, and then: one day I decided to see an opera. And it had to be the best: The Staatsoper Unter den Linden. There was also the Deutsche Opera in Charlottenburg, and there were light opera theaters like the Metropol on Friedrichstrasse North of the train station.

This brings me to the entertainment offerings in Berlin, which were simply superb, with many repertory theaters like the Schiller Theater in Charlottenburg, the "Deutsche Theater" am Gendarmenmarkt; there were variety shows like the Wintergarten on Friedrichstrasse. Soldiers on furlough got preferred seating in all of these establishments. The regime wanted to keep the appearance of normalcy, with its main vehicle being the entertainment industry. There were many more popular offerings to please the masses. One of the propaganda efforts was the radio "Wunschkonzert" (call in concert), which blared march music, soldiers' songs, and regional country songs everywhere. The speaker would announce a call from Sgt. Meyer, Narvic/Norway, for instance, which wished this or that to a Private so and so in front of Moscow, through that and that song. The idea was to demonstrate the omnipotence of German might. On the other hand, it meant a little to a poor, forlorn guy at a boring, lost and dangerous place. It didn't mean much to me, since I hated marching songs. So, what about opera? Benjamino Gigli quite often sang there, who was second only to Caruso—perhaps only because he had steadfastly avoided an appearance at the Met in New York over the years. One early morning I went to stand in line at the Deutsche Opera. Because the line for "Landser" (G.I. Joes) was short, while the regular line circled the building, I quickly walked away with a ticket for what I believe was "Rigoletto" which the Berliners had dubbed "Riegel-Otto." It was a memorable experience: the formidable decorations, regular folks with tux, evening gowns, and I with my ill-fitting garb from Hottengrund. I could neither change it nor did I try very hard—rather, I was a bit coquettish about it. The regular belt I always had to wear sat much too high directly under my chest, because of the badly placed belt hooks. I looked like my belt was squeezing me. Fortunately, it was still cold and I could wear my great coat outside, which covered all. But once I took it off, everyone could see that I was neither a great hero nor someone important—rather, a "Buschkote" (nincompoop) investigating if opera was for him. Luckily, the mass of humanity getting to their seats was so dense that greeting superiors with the military salute was impossible. Glancing around, I soon found out what to do or rather not to do. Being able to rub elbows with a major here and a colonel there, and even generals, made me feel important. Because I saw few soldiers or noncoms, I suspected that the officers had made the soldiers stand in line for the tickets. When the lights went out, all the impressions of my environment left me. I took in what was offered and was totally delighted. It was so good that from there on I became a fan of opera and classical music. To my knowledge I was the first Moratz/Boehlke who ever visited the opera. And this one was one of the best in the world! During intermission I did not leave my seat due to the congestion in the corridors, and I did not have to offer my consort a glass of champagne. But that would have really been in style, right? This experience must have awakened my awareness of good things. Not that I went out to round up a consort … which would not have been difficult at all, since few young, able men were around. Most were in uniform, many on crutches, or similar. Walking toward Friedrichstrasse station, I was still humming the tunes and soon squeezed into the overloaded S-Bahn (elevated electrical train), which ran every two minutes. It was quite a night!

Returning to Bucharest, the opera was still on my mind. Seeing my parents so relieved that I was still alive in a safe place for the time being, and having left many useful things with them for their badly needed calorie intake, made me feel really good. Calorie supply had become scarce and would diminish even more in the future. I had not heard from any friends during my visit. I had not really been close enough to anyone to consider a correspondence … the idea had not even come up—perhaps a sign of lacking maturity. We had the notion that we might see or hear from each other; it would just be a matter of a short time. We just met, did our things of the moment, and parted cheerfully. No one was convinced that friendships, acquaintances or camaraderie were to be something of permanence. This may explain why I neither visited the parents of my former buddies, nor did they visit my parents, although it sounds strange. Of my contemporaries of the crop of 1921—a devastated lot—I met none ever again.

I returned to the early-commencing Romanian spring of 1942 without any artificial sweetener, to my regret. There were then no good deals to be made, and I had to subsist like everyone else on the meager soldiers' pay, which was good for Romanian cigarettes, zuica, and little else. The rest was set aside for the next furlough, which was always in the nebulous future. But, in case it would suddenly come up, it would be a real letdown not to be able to take lots of needed supplies home. The old Babadag routine set in. Before the snow melted, Helmut and I went out one cold afternoon to try to shoot a rabbit. Encountering some, we blasted away at them with our rifles without success. Disappointedly stumbling home over the frozen cornfields, I saw a mole or mouse sticking its head out of a burrow and quickly, thoughtlessly, swung the rifle butt at it, which landed flat on the ground without hitting anything, but I heard the sound of cracking wood. I was shocked to see that the butt had broken off from the rest of the rifle stock: disaster! Willful destruction of government property carried a minimum of ten days behind bars at bread and water. One must consider that we were trained to believe that the rifle is "any soldier's bride;" he must protect and maintain it very carefully. The serial number was registered in each soldier's pay book. I was caught with no escape! The only question was whether to report the incident immediately or hang on and hope for a miracle. I decided to wait and, if the truth would emerge late enough, go to the slammer in the summer when it would be more comfortable. Each time there was a reveille (Appell) or other service requiring a rifle, I borrowed one from a buddy, while my own was securely hidden. After several weeks I awoke one dark night from a big commotion: fire! Everyone was running around and grabbing supplies: valuables, rifles, uniforms, blankets, etc., throwing all out of the windows into the snow, especially from our second floor windows, since we could not carry anything down so fast. Later, assembling our belongings out of the mess in the snow, I feigned surprise: my rifle had not survived the throw from the window. The miracle had happened! I reported to the sergeant who made another report to the weapons sergeant in Bucharest. Coming later to inspect the character of the break, he mumbled something about an old break, but let me get away with it. Any halfway seasoned expert could have seen that the wood on the break surfaces was weathered and at least several weeks old. There was a good guy for a change.

The burned-out building brings back memories of some wild parties we had with the officers of an adjacent Romanian infantry battalion. Sometimes, looking into their courtyard, I observed some very strange scenes. Watching the comings and goings, I noticed that often soldiers, strapped to a post with exposed back, were severely flogged with a leather whip. The officers ran around with a short stick, which they also used profusely. An enormous cultural and social gap seemed to exist between officers and soldiers, with officers apparently much more educated and dressed in sharp, meticulously tailored, olive green uniforms, with jodhpurs, elegant, shining riding boots, and enormous hats resembling those of Russian generals. The most peculiar thing was that all officers liked to splash themselves with cheap perfume, which was reminiscent of a cathouse, literally walking around in a cloud of mist. They all spoke French fluently. The average poor soldier was illiterate, shabbily dressed and always seemed bewildered. Obviously drafted, they couldn't figure out why they had to suffer through this; they had no interest. Passing us on the street, they saluted us as if we were their officers. From what I could tell, those forces were ill trained, ill equipped, had no spirit as a fighting force, and lacked cohesion—a sorry lot.

Occasionally, those officers showed up for a party with us. Though we were not officers, they treated us as their equals, perhaps because we were educated and some of us spoke a little French, their favorite language. I even still could cough up a few phrases, although I had not practiced since learning French four years earlier. There was a fairly large room with several tables on the second floor, normally used for taking meals. They brought some wine, zuica and food, which sometimes included their "icre," a mix of sour cream and fresh caviar—then available in abundance in the Danube estuary, where fishermen regularly landed sturgeons. Since one no longer hears of Rumanian caviar, it must be gone now. With plenty of this delicious mix offered, we poor guys, who had never seen caviar before, were eating the stuff by the pound, which greatly raised spirits and sense of well-being, especially since we washed it down with lots of wine followed by zuica. The conversation blossomed, but all got almost drowned out by a gypsy band, brought along by the officers: marimba, bass, cello—mostly violins. One really accomplished gypsy artist stood out from all the others. They offered the typical tunes heard throughout the Balkans, starting in Hungary. But the more melancholy Rumanian gypsy tunes reflected the vast spaces of the endless Danube plains. As the evening progressed, the music seemed to get more and more melancholic until the officers started embracing the principal violinist and kissing him in an unusual, violent manner in what seemed to be some kind of ritual. He did not seem that amused, but played along to keep them in a good mood. I think the musicians had to do this, because they were totally dependent and could not dare to have or express their own opinions. These wild parties usually ended in everyone's losing his senses and conking out. The next morning's hangover was enormous. Helmut and I would take a long walk to work it off. There was little or no drill at the Babadag station. The noncom's tried to live alongside us, and all were mostly concerned with passing the day, working for provisions, or do the ridiculous air traffic observation service up on the hill, out of town.

MOVE TO TULCEA/USING MY RADIO OPERATOR SKILLS

In 1942 my gang was transferred to Tulcea, the larger town upstream on the Danube. There was more traffic to be observed in town. Our radio transmitter truck was taken from us; somebody had finally noticed that, for what we were doing—if anything—we didn't need an expensive, idle, special truck, which would be more useful for a forward airfield in mobile warfare. The transmitter and encoder were removed and installed in a room at the second floor of the house that served our platoon. In Tulcea, the reports of three to four surrounding observation posts were encoded and transmitted via short wave and Morse code to headquarters in Bucharest, where a small contingent of fighter planes (Me109) was stationed. Here I could finally use my radio operator skills and listen to the BBC at night when no one was around. Ferdi came with us from Babadag. We now had a platoon leader, Lt. Wagrandl, from Vienna, who had been transferred to the German air force after the Austrian takeover. About 35 years old, he lived in a separate house, since a German officer could not live with soldiers. He actually had a family life of his own, living with his girlfriend, Miss Morosov, whom he seemed to cherish. Therefore we rarely saw him. When he did turn up, he immediately created asinine trouble, like ordering inspection or military drill, which included marching through town, singing German marching songs, which we hated. They sounded terrible, since our military singing skills had markedly suffered during the past year due to non-use and our infatuation with the gypsies' entertainment. This boor Wagrandl always turned up in a sour mood when he seemed to be in trouble with his girlfriend, squirming because of his domestic travail. We found it entertaining and took the little discomfort he meted out with relish, knowing that he was in an emotional vacuum.

The service in Tulcea was scheduled carefully so that everyone had some free time. There were radio service, kitchen support, a little drill just to go through the motions, and the rest was leisure. Those who had found girl friends split the minute they were free and returned late at night. Why not? The platoon leader did it too! Others hung around town, talked with the local girls, searched the market for bargains or mingled with the local Turks in their coffee shops, where coffee was always delicious. We assumed it might come from Turkey, which was not very far. Commercial connections must have also existed to Arabia, where a good coffee came from, although I had read in Karl May volumes that Arabs prefer drinking tea. Small, very sweet, bite size cakes were also offered, which I did not like very much. One of us, Bussman, did not talk or associate much with any of us. The rumor was that he came from Torgau (tough military prison) and had been convicted of gay activities, which carried a lengthy prison term. We sometimes saw him hanging around with young Romanian men, whose language he had learned very quickly. No one bothered or teased him—he was left alone. Many had strange peculiarities. One older, leathery-looking guy smoked like a chimney and looked twice his age. Our cook Ferdi, who had free access to the 500 liter wine barrel, was always drunk. I slept opposite his bunk in the upper, he in the lower bed. Waking up mornings, I sometimes saw his arm moving first, searching for something until he found a filled wine bottle under his bunk, which he picked up, uncorked and put to his mouth, eyes still closed. When it was empty, he finally bothered to get up, ready to face the world. Without his first bottle, he had no incentive for action. He had recently learned that his large bookstore in Cologne was bombed out and all is belongings were lost. A beggar now, whatever he owned he had with him. Can one blame him? No, especially since he lost his wife in the same raid. Always drunk, his face was never anything than red, but he never swayed in the wind: the last stage of alcoholism. Another guy from Posen, now Poland, continuously got enormous food parcels with German delicacies, but no one ever got a taste of it. He was obsessed with school girls and had found one 12-14 years old, don't ask how, whom he could visit at home without anyone else around. One of the few with a camera, he liked to take the girl's picture in the nude. Naturally, not all of us had such way-out habits; most just struggled along to see what the next day might bring.

In 1942 the German side had cranked up the war to maximum intensity, while the allies were slowly converting all industries for war material production. German armies broke through Ukraine, into the Caucasus area, and headed toward the rich oilfields in Georgia and Azerbaijan. This slowed the advance toward the Volga River, which controls central Russia. The Soviets had time to disassemble all vital industries and destroy the rest. While the victorious German Panzer armies moved further east and south, I and some others sometimes made a foray across the Danube into Bessarabia toward Odessa deep into occupied Soviet territory to look for good wine—even cheaper there than in Romania. We usually had to stay overnight among the native population, which was friendly and poor; the reed-covered houses, made of mud, with few windows, had dirt floors and big wood ovens for the harsh winters. Food was simple, usually some cabbage soup. Sleep was impossible since all huts were teeming with pests, mostly fleas, but also bed bugs and lice. It felt like whole armies were poised against each one of us. The natives did not seem bothered. The wine was always hastily bought, and off we went with another 500 liter of the precious stuff. Where we got the wine must have been close to where Dr. Konstantin Frank, the deceased Hammondsport winemaker, headed a winery in those days. He mentioned coming from Odessa when we met him later in the Finger Lakes. The road back was dusty, as usual, and cumbersome, and led to another perilous crossing of the Danube on a decrepit ferry, which started about three miles upstream to get us into Tulcea. The strong currents necessitated this advance to make it across and end up in the town.

The summer of '42 was long and almost without remarkable events, until late that year word spread that something was afoot. Also, on duty at the transmitter end one evening, I could overhear a phone conversation between our fearless leader Lt. Wagrandl and captain Storm, the company commander, who had apparently just informed Wagrandl of the preparations for his transfer to the Eastern front. Losing all blood from his face, Wagrandl turned white as a sheet and gasped for air. This was the only phone available, and he couldn't delegate me out, since I had to listen into the airwaves to pick up occasional communications. Meanwhile he was panting, chest heaving, grasping for the right words to convince Storm to leave him at his beloved Tulcea with his fiancée and easy life, protected from the vagaries of the changing times and war. "Why me, my dear captain?" he wailed in his Viennese slang, which must have sounded like an insult to a North German professional officer (Storm). "There are so many other, much younger candidates. I always accommodated you! Did I do anything wrong?" and "It can't be true that I'm thus betrayed," and, "Please, please, dearest Mr. Storm, please leave me here. You'll never be sorry—I guarantee it from the bottom of my heart." I never had thought it possible that an officer could lower himself so much. He just about crawled into Storm's behind. Surprisingly, he remained in Tulcea and even made first Lieutenant some weeks later. Still a private, I had no other ambitions.

So, there came the rumors, then news. Finally, a construction program was underway to install all those "Wuerzburg" machines (radar in modern language) in remote corners of Romania, for us to operate and maintain. Over the months, those of us with electrical/electronic experience, and any all around electrical technicians were sent to Koethen, where the equipment originated. Unsure what it was all about, we guessed it had to do with the oil in Ploesti north of Bucharest at the foot of the Carpathian mountain range. We were kind of aware that the North African campaign was turning against Germany and that soon the German armies deployed there would take a nice trip to visit the U.S. We had no idea that vast airfields were being built at a feverish pace, to base enormous bomber armadas. Ploesti was assumed to be the primary target. But these consequences were not paramount in our minds. With little or no instructions as to our destination and purpose, we were too set in our boring ways. We were also not told what other things going on in Romania might impact our tactical situation. Large contingents of antiaircraft artillery were installed in and around Ploesti, and the fighter force was beefed up. We were just lost country bumpkins preoccupied with our daily chores, nonsensical reports and speculations about the next furlough, the latter theme overriding all others.

One day in late '42 or early '43, a truck came to load me and some other (mostly younger) fellows with our gear. After going through the Romanian plains (Walachei) and crossing the Danube, we arrived at a sorry-looking place in the midst of nowhere. Not a hut or village in sight up to the horizon, except for two wooden barracks. About 300 yards from there we could see the outline of an assembled "Wuerzburg" type radar, with some technicians monkeying around the electronic housing, which was almost the size of a living room. I knew that more regimentation, work, less sleep and increased boredom were ahead. Imagine, not even a town around—only a few shrubs, but no trees. The entire area was planted with poorly maintained grapevines.

After moving into the empty barracks, we were assigned to working details. Many things needed doing: split wood, get massive amounts of water, dig latrines, help in the kitchen and, most of all, guard service around the clock. After dinner, guard service began through the night. With more superiors, including officers, running around trying to prove their importance, all had changed. Living in a separate house and not mingling at all, these officers always wore gloves when making an appearance, which was only when they wanted to put more work on the rest of us or rant and rave about our sloppy dress and lack of discipline. The military salute—demanded to install that ever-important discipline-became of paramount importance again. Military basic drills were reintroduced, just to show who was the superior and could mete out punishment for our innumerous transgressions, which were found daily with ease. Consequently, we became very stoical, assuming passive resistance. Everything slowed down and was done sloppily. When volunteers were sought by barking: "Three volunteers!" some hands were expected to show, though it was never explained what the volunteering was for! No hands showing meant immediate reprisals with vengeance. Drill for hours on end, then work, then night guard duty—ridiculous! The site was so remote, we never saw anyone. The vineyards must have been abandoned a long time ago; they hadn't been pruned for years. During night duty I was sometimes so terribly sleepy, hanging around with my rifle over the shoulder, that I lost equilibrium when pausing from my trot, swaying over to almost collapse until my senses caught the fall and made me move my foot to counteract the impending fall. Sometimes this game repeated itself every other minute or so, until, after my two hours, the next guy came stumbling out of the bunker to repeat everything. With inspections looming at any moment, we could never be sure of anything. A soldier found sleeping on guard would have been tried before a military court, and the soldier was always "guilty as charged." He would face two years of military prison, i.e. punishment battalion in the East and almost certain death. Although aware of this, I once found myself flat on the ground staring at the stars without knowing what it was. Suddenly realizing that I had fallen over, I jumped up as though bitten by a tarantula. Luckily, no one found me. I did not know how long I had slept.

One of our first jobs was digging up a defense system around the Wuerzburg, consisting of ditches, machine gun emplacement, hand grenades, etc. Continuing week after week, this never let up, with more barracks, dining hall, officers' house, garden arrangements, equipment stalls … you name it. The fertile imagination of the superiors, who never worked, was endless.

In midwinter 42/43, the horrible debacle of Stalingrad came to an ugly conclusion, confirming my worst fears. Often discussing the situation, Helmut, Hajo Lokat and I agreed that the war had been lost already a long time ago. We also talked of bypassing the terrible end by seeking refuge in neutral Turkey. We would only have to go south to the Danube and cross Bulgaria to reach the Turkish frontier, perhaps a three or four days' march. We kicked this idea around a lot without knowing the country to be crossed: no maps, language, sympathies of the population, their police and army, guard density at the border with Turkey unknown etc. Such factors would make this plan very risky. Getting caught meant certain death for desertion in time of war. We also considered it dishonorable to leave country and parents in wartime, while Germany faced its worst time in centuries. Based on our limited information, we were unable to conclude that Germany had committed crimes when the war began. Even if we had thought so, I doubt we would have faced the huge risks involved in crossing Bulgaria on our own. We began to realize what our presence in the middle of nowhere was for. We could look into the electronic display and pinpoint targets in the air as far as 40 miles away, much farther than one could see with the best binoculars. The height above ground could also be determined accurately, which allowed sending aircraft aloft in pursuit and directing them to their targets. For the anti aircraft artillery it meant early warning and accurate height information. Our radar was the farthest to the East of Bucharest of several Wuerzburg stations throughout Romania. We did not have to expect making contact with allied bombers coming from North Africa, but were more concerned with flight traffic from the East, the Soviet Union. The front was now pushed back west considerably, and the Caucasus units withdrew helter-skelter. The German power was dangerously overextended. The 1943 summer and fall saw gradual withdrawal of German forces toward the West, usually involving considerable losses of men and material. Hence, lately we had seen increased large aircraft traffic from the East, presumably support supplied to the Yugoslavian partisans. Our tasks were getting more complex. We were building another large structure to house a command center for night interceptors. This traffic from the East always occurred at night, making simple Me-109 fighters useless. The target had to be located by "Wuerzburg," the location was projected and by means of comparing it with that of the target on the command table, the lead officer gave the night fighter/interceptor exact direction toward the target until having it on his own radar screen. Then the target was usually doomed. The night fighters were Me-210's, equipped with on-board radar and cannons. What an elaborate effort it was just to interdict a few lousy Soviet aircraft, which happened about every other week. Once the enemy found out, he surely would take a more Southern route. Anyway, the measuring data from the "Wuerzburg" were phoned every 30 seconds to the command table, where female air force helpers revised the location according to the data received.

These young women had been sent into this forlorn corner of the world after being drafted into the services. They were taken only if they were not employed in the defense industry. Some were glad to escape the bombed cities; others were sad to be suddenly exposed to the risks of a soldier's life, and all felt quite uncomfortable. They were now selected to maintain the officers' quarters, and soon I could observe some of them joining the officers at night for lively parties. As I sometimes stomped around the officers' quarters on night duty, I heard commotion, laughter, shrieks, clinking glasses, etc.—signs that those inside enjoyed themselves to no end. The windows' solid shutters were locked from within, which was officially necessary to prevent light from being projected out, since everything had to be pitch dark. Therefore I could see nothing, but it was clear that the officers were inviting the more attractive women into their quarters to commiserate and have extensive old-fashioned fun.

This kind of "commingling" going on at the highest level was freely copied throughout the place, with the difference that the simple guys couldn't take women to their rooms. We met and talked in the mess hall, had our beer—or mostly wine—together, etc. Many of the men started relationships that increasingly resembled marriages, although those were never celebrated. Among those who did not get involved were some married men and those who were young and uninitiated, including myself. Helmut got involved with a very nice woman from Thuringia, perhaps because he was from there and one thing led to another, etc. etc. She was devastated about being in the service, especially in this godforsaken place that did not bode well for the future. For example, what would happen, should the eastern front move closer to Odessa and Romania? The front inexorably moved west week by week. One could almost devise a timetable forecasting the Soviet armies' invasion of the Balkans, including Romania. We didn't really speculate very much about this development, since the daily chores as well as other anxieties overshadowed everything. But the women—usually more sensitive than men—must have speculated about it. Helmut told me that his girl, who was definitely no floozy, repeatedly begged to have a baby with him. It became some kind of an obsession, which he discussed with Hajo and me several times. Pregnancy was the only way for these poor girls to go home and leave the service for good! Helmut was close to caving in, but decided against it in the end. He couldn't decide if she would be the one he would marry. Things would change so much between then and the war's end that no one could know who would be left alive and under what conditions. He had also no profession and had never worked. How would he feed a wife and baby? You had to be on solid footing to father a child. This must have gone on between many or most other "couples," except, of course, the officers. Incidentally, Wagrandl, my glorious leader in Tulcea, who was promoted to first lieutenant (Oberleutnant), did not transfer with us. I wonder if he really remained in Tulcea. I briefly befriended a fairly young girl from Silesia, but broke it off. The public display, gossip, and the prospect that soon men and women would change hands were simply not my cup of tea. I settled for talking to one or the other and sometimes drinking with them, the only form of entertainment we had. One evening we were sitting in the mess hall with lots of red-bluish wine, when I happened to talk to a very sturdy woman with a Bavarian accent. She was one of those beer-carrying waitresses in the Munich beer halls, e.g. the Hofbraeuhaus, who carry ten large full beer glasses of about a quart each simultaneously. Can you imagine the weight? Since beer production was reduced to almost zero due to food shortages, the employees had been drafted into the air force. We were chatting and drinking, until she proposed she could drink double the amount of wine I could. Both of us would drink until I would drop from my chair, and she would then carry me to my bunk. Never having known a Munich beer hall waitress, I made the wager—only to find myself neatly tucked into my bunk the next morning, not remembering how I got there.

It's amazing how we could exist in this desolation until some guys got together and offered to run some classes for those interested. As mentioned, some soldiers had several semesters of advanced study in physics. The classes we started in mathematics, mainly calculus, were quite interesting, especially because I would have to go through all this later on anyhow. We kept this up for a few months until in early 1944 Hajo left for an officers' course in France. I believe he and Helmut also went to a noncom course in fall of '43, soon to advance to corporals. Meanwhile, I had "advanced" to private first and second class (Gefreiter and Obergefreiter), which meant nothing, just a few more pennies' pay.

A SECOND FURLOUGH IN BERLIN

In the fall of '43—or perhaps winter 43/44—another furlough came up, initiating the usual preparations: arrange a canister of sunflower oil, etc., adding sausages, wines and chocolate in Budapest. Just before I left, Helmut asked me to look up his uncle in Berlin, a school principal who lived near Nollendorfplatz. He also talked in the best terms about a female friend from his school period in Strausberg. If I liked, I should look her up and report to her about our times together. She might be interested in his fate, since they had had no regular correspondence. She lived in Oranienburg, North of Berlin, in Kremmener Strasse, the same street as my Uncle Fritz. Promising both, I left in good spirits at the prospect of again escaping the drudgery of my soldier's life. Salami and chocolate had become hard to find and much more expensive. The city was less friendly. Something was no longer right. Also in Hungary the usual ample supply of smoked ham and salami was much reduced—a sign of the times. The war was going badly, and the consequences showed more and more. Especially the situation in Berlin had become very depressing, with large areas of bombed-out apartment blocks. Although this damage was still less than in smaller, heavily hit cities such as Cologne, Schweinfurt, Frankfurt, Hamburg, etc., it was quite extensive. Clearly, the Allies had gotten the better in the air war and were improving their advantage daily—the result of the accelerating U.S. war industry and machinery. I had realized early on that Germany could not wage a war of attrition. Unable to change the course of events, I opted to make the best of my days at home. Father and mother were delighted about all the goodies and used the oil for wonderful potato pancakes—the smell of the brownish crisp frying pancakes must have tantalized the neighbors to no end. The supply of meats and fat was no longer sufficient at home. Those without relatives or connections in the countryside, i.e. most Berliners, had to live off their inadequate rations and were losing weight; fat people were no longer seen. The air raid sirens, which went off almost nightly and sometimes more than once, told me to grab my gas mask and steel helmet and run to the basement, which had an air raid shelter, reinforced with timber, plus a secure door. Several people, mostly the available and able men, stood guard around and in the four-story house. At each level and on top, containers with sand and shovels had been placed. These could be used to quickly smother any incendiary bombs that hit the premises. If not covered, they would immediately set off a large fire and destroy the house. Water was no use and only made things worse. Each apartment building had an air raid warden to take care of all those details. Once an explosive bomb would hit, it was very unhealthy to be stationed somewhere around, or on top of the house. But if the bomb would bury the air raid shelter, the outcome would also be mighty unfavorable. A certain amount of luck was needed, and mother had always told me I was a very, very lucky boy. One night during an air raid, the bombers dumped some of their goodies over Spandau, which, amazingly, did not happen very often; Spandau escaped with relatively little damage. Who knows—perhaps the British had already selected it to house their soldiers in 1945. Normally, my place was in the street, to observe falling incendiary bombs. They looked like sticks of about 2" in diameter by 1-1/2 feet in length. As the engine noises approached us one night, soon enough some incendiaries landed and burned fiercely in our street. I jumped at them eagerly with my sand pail and poured it over them, never aware if I had an incendiary with explosive delay charge (a deadly thing). The bright light of the potassium compound could show the bomber crews exactly their location—undesirable from our standpoint. Thus occupied, I heard the whistling of incoming larger bombs and was suddenly lifted off my feet and thrown head first from the middle of the street against the building wall, a distance of 15-20 yards. Crashing my steel helmet first, I fell on the ground like a sack of potatoes while an enormous explosion rang in my ears. Pulling myself up, I saw fire and crumbling walls down the street toward Zimmer- and Jaegerstrasse. Getting up and running over to see if I could help, I saw that I was not needed. A big bomb had totally collapsed one large apartment building and partially demolished several surrounding ones. Orje Herwig, on furlough from his parachute division, was in the street. He was one of the fellows they dropped on Crete with horrendous losses, and had survived with a wound. That was in the summer of 1940. His parents' apartment and all belongings were lost. He was to return the next day. Those losses in '40 were so dramatic that German troops never attempted airborne operations again. Tactical conditions favoring their use were no longer existent. So, I had to be back home to get a whiff of real war conditions. In our quiet spot in Romania there hadn't been a single sign of it. Not that I longed for it: sometimes I saw on the railroad trainloads of wounded soldiers returning home. Those were the lucky ones who might make it. No statistics were published about losses in the field—one could only tell their extent by the number of obituaries (flagged with the Iron Cross) and soldiers with bandages and/or crutches. People started to whisper that one should enjoy the war; peace would be terrible. One day during furlough I did visit Helmut's uncle and also contacted his friend Ellen Mosebach in Oranienburg. I went there on the electric train via Gesundbrunnen and also briefly visited the Boehlkes on Kremmener Strasse before crossing the bridge to the last house on the street on the left, a one-family dwelling. A good-looking, blond, blue-eyed young woman opened the door—obviously well brought up and protected by the parents. I was happy to have afternoon coffee and cake with her and her mother. The father was in the East, a captain with the police. Political themes were not touched. The two women seemed to have neither the stomach nor an interest to waste time with it. I must have spent two hours before bidding good-bye and returning to the train station for the long trip back to Spandau, which took about 1-1/2 hours. Ellen came along, taking my arm, and I felt quite happy. We discussed going to the opera, and she agreed to meet me in downtown Berlin. The next day I went there to get tickets. I don't remember how I let her know I had some. We may have met a few days later at or near the Zoo station. A few days thereafter we met again at Friedrichstrasse station and left for the nearby opera house. Since it was already fairly cool or cold, I wore my great coat, which covered up my miserable, ill-fitting, disgusting tunic. We attended the "Magic Flute' by Mozart, conducted by Herbert von Karajan, then a young, fledgling conductor. The memorable Erna Berger had Tamina's part. It was an unforgettable evening, and both Ellen and I were very enthusiastic and emotionally involved. One has to know that the absolutely non-musical Helmut could not hit one correct note or bar when singing. She liked my enthusiasm for music and art. Having completed her high school degree (Abitur), Ellen's school education was better than mine. She may have attended university at that time, but I think we never touched that point, or I have forgotten. Being with her on that special evening was a marvelous experience. You know what young people discuss ... I talked about my aspirations and my past, which must have sat well with her. I may have also mentioned my lack of ambitions in the military. Accompanying her home in the middle of the night to Oranienburg, I couldn't even invite her for a refreshment or food in a restaurant. Hardly anything was offered: no beer, wine—nothing. Still, she was visibly happy, and so was I. As it was in those times: no kisses or things like that.

TRANSFER TO FLIGHT TRAINING

A few days later I had to return to Romania to face the usual boredom and chicanery. I told Helmut about my experiences and soon started receiving letters from Oranienburg, as well as Spandau. I had regularly corresponded with my parents; they always knew where I was and what I did or felt (sort of). On the last visit I had told them about my plans to volunteer again for flight training, as somehow I had gotten wind of that possibility. I thought it would benefit my technical development to enter this promising field. What I overlooked were the risks. I should be partially excused, because real losses of the air force were not published and the enormous daytime bomber attacks by U.S. forces, protected by long-range fighters, had not occurred yet. Germany had nothing equivalent to defend itself against these forces. These fighters were far superior to what our air force could throw against them. Therefore, flying a mission in early '44 against a bomber group was just about suicide. But, I volunteered and soon was invited for an ability test and medical examination in Bucharest. One test I remember went as follows: they put an airtight mask over my head, which they connected to oxygen and nitrogen supply. First, the air supply was normal, like ocean level, and then oxygen was gradually reduced to simulate increasingly higher altitude.

Meanwhile I had to repeatedly write down a simple sentence. As I was cheerfully following the simple task, I felt someone abruptly pulling the mask from my head. Looking at the sheet with the repeated simple sentence, I realized that the last line consisted of undecipherable, confused scribbles. I must have lost conscience without noticing it. This happens when going up too high in an airplane without artificial oxygen supply. It is very dangerous. Each individual has a different threshold, and the test was designed to determine mine. Thinking that the day had gone very well, I returned to my unit in good spirits to await further developments.

Not much newsworthy happened in the radar outfit. Once in a while we picked up Soviet targets and directed night interceptors toward them. All this became routine without excitement. Because the large and dangerous bombing raids in Ploesti far exceeded our range, we were never involved. One day in spring of 1944 I learned of my acceptance for pilot training. I was to report on a certain date at pilot school A-4 (Flugzeugfuehrerschule) at Neudorf near Oppeln in Silesia, southeast of Berlin. This must have been at the beginning or in the middle of March, 1944. Before showing up there, I could spend one week of special furlough in Berlin. So, I again rounded up as much oil as I could, but salami, chocolate, perfume and other luxury things could no longer be found in Bucharest. The city appeared to be in a panic; normal life had stopped. The Soviets were coming fairly close. I think they were retaking the Crimea. From there it was not far to Odessa, Bessarabia, and the Danube. I was glad I could return home, feeling sorry for all those who remained behind, particularly the women. Years later I heard that this radar station was not warned in advance about the Soviet invasion, the leadership always wanted to hold the fort until the last man, and no one would admit to a timely withdrawal for fear of being court-martialed as a traitor. All men and women were killed or taken prisoners. Most never returned from Siberia. To be taken prisoner was practically a death sentence, especially for females. To quote mother again: "Sohni" was always the luckiest boy in the world! Without that, and a nose for things, you were a loser in those times. Rudolf Bernsee of Erlangen told me years later of his experience in Ploesti, where, as Engineering Manager for Siemens Construction Co., he was in charge of maintenance and repair of the enormous oil facilities. Despite many connections to the military upper echelon, he was not forewarned of the rampaging, fast-approaching Soviets. By coincidence, one day he tried to get the latest information from a military liaison colonel. Finding the offices empty, with some people burning things, others leaving hastily on various vehicles, he was asked what he was still doing there; he should get out as fast as he could. He did and lived to tell the tale.

So, I had another furlough on my hands in Berlin. I must have spent much of it with Ellen, either in Oranienburg, or meeting her around Zoo and Kurfuerstendamm. The time passed quickly. We got quite comfortable with each other and liked the togetherness. I told her that Helmut had also left Romania and attended an officers' course somewhere. I did not see him again until much after the war. He had discussed with me at length what to do with his life. His family was mostly in the teaching profession, but there was an uncle in Wuppertal, who owned a good bookstore. Helmut wavered between following teaching or book sales. I thought teaching could be stale and advised him to do something more dynamic. Book sales were always big business in Germany, since public libraries were less lavishly equipped than those in the U.S., and people on average spent much more on books than the average American. He decided on this when the dust had settled. His uncle provided an apprenticeship in Southwest Germany, and then he joined his uncle in Wuppertal. To end his story: He later married a very beautiful woman (Flick) and had two daughters. Thereafter he became quite ill with schizophrenia, sometimes becoming so manic that he was placed in an institution, where he committed suicide. No medication existed to help him at that time. Today, this illness has a good chance of being stabilized without too many problems. It was a tragic case. His wife married him although Helmut had told her of his father's death from the disease. A very cultured man for his age, he taught me a lot. Sadly, the winds of war blew us in different directions. While institutionalized, he even tracked me down in Brazil, to be able to correspond with me. He must not have found another or better friendship than we had, and/ or perhaps everyone had given up on him, which unfortunately happens so often. Anna and I later visited his wife on the island of Sylt, where she had remarried and appeared happy. Her husband was a painter of North Sea scenes, popular with the tourist crowds, and he seemed to make a living of it. When seeing Ellen, I always thought of Helmut. I did not know how close they had been, and it was unimportant to me. Rather than dwelling much on him, she concentrated on the present and future. I do not remember what Ellen wanted to do with her life—no wonder—those demanding and confusing times made planning ahead difficult and futile. My immediate direction was clear: pilot school. We parted with hope for the future: that things would work out somehow. We never much discussed Germany's horrible problems. I did not ask about her father's occupation in the East, and she volunteered nothing, perhaps unaware of the assignment's details. It is common knowledge that those officials revealed nothing. Having been the chief of police in Oranienburg, he was a party member, but I never questioned her about this, either. While in Oranienburg, I always looked up Uncle Fritz, who had worked his way up to department boss in a nearby factory (Auer). The place made gas masks, which every soldier and many civilians had to have. They were packed in a metal container, 4" in diameter and 8-10" long, and carried on the back by an adjustable strap over the shoulder. His job entailed deferment from military service. When the Soviets approached at war's end, Oranienburg was bombed once more, wounding him badly, and he was treated in the local hospital. As the Soviet army took it over, he must have been thrown out. His wife or relatives told us that he was never seen again. He simply vanished.

NEUDORF—PILOT TRAINING

My trip to Neudorf was uneventful and fairly short. Reporting in military fashion, I was assigned to my unit. One of the first actions was exchanging my hated jacket, etc. for a brand-new flight personnel tunic with the appropriate insignia, nice shoes and light flight overalls, which were opened by a large zipper. We dubbed the latter "Knochensack" (bone bag): it would keep the bones together in case we didn't make it; we could be carried away without even opening the zipper. I returned fairly satisfied to my room, shared with three buddies who came from all over: one from the eastern front, another from Italy … all from some air force units, with their bluish uniforms. All now changed their different colored collar squares to the prominent yellow collar of the flying units. Brown (my former color) was communications (Luftnachrichtenverbaende), red antiaircraft (Flak) artillery, and pink belonged to engineering units such as maintenance. Werner Ehling, who served for a long time on an antiaircraft artillery unit in the East, sported red. His unit was mainly used to fight Soviet tanks. He was on an 88 mm piece, the most effective artillery weapon in the German inventory. Very flexible, with a superior muzzle speed and therefore armor penetration, it was used against air and ground targets. On the latter, direct aim and hit were used, same as tank- or anti-tank guns. When I started in Neudorf, Werner had become a corporal and was stationed in Lankwitz South of Berlin, in a recruiting and training unit for anti aircraft personnel. He must have been drilling new recruits, although I didn't see him at it when visiting him briefly before leaving for Neudorf. After showing me his quarters and the facility, we left for a café. It beats me what we did there, without beer, coffee, etc., but the room was full of soldiers with their girlfriends; there was really nothing else worth doing. Close by sat a soldier with a nice looking girl. When listening more closely to their talk, I heard them speaking French. Werner started acting up, mumbling to me that the guy was out of line speaking in a foreign language (he had never learned any languages). In his opinion, a German soldier must use German to communicate, especially in public. I told him it made no difference to me, as I had never been advised during my soldiering years that I must not use anything other than German. But, in a sudden and eager, official posture, Werner started to dress down the guy, who was clearly not impressed. He answered in a submissive, official voice: "Yes, Sir," and "Yes, Sir," while his non-verbal expression meant: "You poor s.o.b., don't you know it won't affect me in the least?" I found the scene utterly distasteful, but it may have been typical of Werner, who knows? Arriving home, I considered the trip to Lankwitz a total waste of time. Werner appeared oblivious as to where the whole mess was heading. He may have only wanted to show off in the café—that kind of thing had never been to my taste, then or later. The French soldier could have been from the Alsace, preferring French. Those people had been drafted into the German forces when Alsace had been declared German territory after the victory in France. Most of its inhabitants are bilingual. The girl may have been a French contract worker. Germany was brimming with foreigners, since German men were wasted at a quickly accelerating pace; logistic supplies were fast diminishing, and to equalize the shortages, men with light weapons were sent against enemies superior in numbers and equipment, with catastrophic results. Meanwhile, the leading hierarchy, who no longer ventured outside their safe concrete bunkers since the Stalingrad disaster in early '43, had literally abandoned Germany. Of all this I had an inkling, but no concrete information or data. Everything was nebulous and frightening.

With yellow collar and coveted insignia of flying personnel, I was now ready for action in Neudorf. In this beautiful spring, we were first delegated to another camp about two hours away toward the Sudeten, the mountain range dividing Silesia from Bohemia (Czech Republic today). Just being in the camp amid gentle, rolling hills with meadows and forests was sheer delight, and I would have liked to stay there for the rest of the war, doing absolutely nothing. But soon instructions started about flight dynamics to prepare us for lifting off the ground by ourselves. Flight dynamics is a fancy word for examining the forces that occur when flow is established on a wing. That was easy for me to understand; it simply states not to move too slowly, or you risk falling down. It contradicted mother telling me when I left Spandau, not to fly too high and too fast. Naturally, the higher you go, the safer you will be! Later I saw many a pilot flying too slowly in new aircraft and falling down without jumping. We were then instructed also how to use a parachute, but there was no training in actual jumping. I'm glad, since I'm not sure if I would have mustered the courage to jump from a plane. The consequence would have been transfer to a fighting unit in the East. Those who didn't qualify on any of the following tests had to face that transfer, and many didn't make it for one reason or another. Soon, one morning, we found ourselves on the meadow for flight training on gliders. First there was this primeval glider contraption sitting on the meadow, ogling at us with contempt, it seemed. In principle, it was a piece of 2x6' timber, with stick and pedals. Stick for ailerons and pedals for the tail rudder. The darn thing had no brakes but had a little flat wooden seat, which was too big, so that we were always kept uncomfortable. There was a strap to tie the pilot to an upright, connecting to the wings. They had the ailerons, one left and one right, which connected to the stick. When making a left turn, for example, the left aileron would lift and the right would drop, thus rolling the entire craft on its long axis to the left. To initiate a curve, one also had to step gently on the left pedal, very gently. These things were sensitive. When you wanted the kite to descend, the stick had to be pushed forward. All was very simple and straightforward. About four to five gliders were lined up in a row on top of a slight elevation. A rubber rope was fastened to each plane, and six guys picked it up to be stretched to its limit; another two guys were holding the glider. Then, at a command, the fellows at the glider let go and the rope crew ran quickly down the slope. In this manner the glider took off to an altitude of about 30 to 50 feet. When arrived at apogee, the pilot had to release the rope by activating a pull string provided with a ring. All of us were a little tense until we got the hang of it. This way, we learned to keep an aircraft level and flying until the natural glide angle would set it down unto the meadow. Then the whole thing had to be dragged back on top—a healthy workout! After one to two weeks, it became a bore, and we were now in the middle of April. We had already seen what the next step would have to be. A winch was installed at the end of a grassy field. It was connected to a motor. The gliders were lined up in a distance of 100 to 200 yards on the other end. When a glider was to be started, the cable of the winch was dragged by a motorbike to the gliders and hooked up. Then, at a command, the winch was engaged and quickly pulled the glider. The pilot had to pull the stick all the way to his chest, which let the glider gain altitude at a fantastic clip. Meanwhile, the pilot had to look at the winch and a flagman posted close to it. At the apogee the pilot had to release the cable again by dipping the stick forward. Then the nose would dip, too, giving slack to the cable to release it quickly. This was done when the winch stopped and the flagman simultaneously waved his flag. If one would not release the cable, the glider would descend very fast on a course dictated by cable length, and hit ground, nose first. It would be 100% fatal. While the glider was heisted aloft, the motor-bike drove back to the winch to pick up the cable for the next launch. This was our next fun thing to try: to sit on this completely open 2x6 during a catapult-like launch to about 100 yards of altitude. When my first term came, I didn't feel very well. I was instructed to get up to 100 yards, make a left turn four times, and descend. The glider, once it was up, constantly lost altitude, determined by its characteristics. After the last turn I was only 30 feet high and had to ascertain a good landing. The ascent was a wild experience. This kite really got going. It was hanging in space at an about 45-degree angle. I tried to make out winch and flag-man. If I released the cable too soon, it would not snap out of its seat unless I also lowered the nose first. That would be a sign that I had my pants full. Missing the flagman's wave would be noxious to my health. Therefore I looked, with anxiety building up, to the fast dwindling flagman. It seemed to me that I was already 300 meters up, when he finally caved in. He must have heard my prayers (if there was time for that). I didn't even wait a split second to eagerly follow instructions. I thought I was too high up—which is what mother had warned me about. Now I had to lean into a left-hand turn, a trick I had never tried before. It went fairly smoothly. Meanwhile I had to maintain good speed or the crude glider would spin out of control. All went well—another left turn, a long straight ahead, and now there was time for me to take in the scenery. Below was the camp, beyond the meadows and trees was the village, and I thought: "Hermann, you like this. You got the hang of it all. It's a cinch. Man, this beats infantry duty in the East." Jubilation started to trickle through my senses. In the back of my mind I had believed that this might not have been for me. Maybe I learned a great thing: "You must keep trying; you've got to try to win; without it you are nothing!" This entire flying thing was an enormous challenge—something I had selected over being bored to death. It was technical, and, what one would call today an "in-thing." I was on the right track. That much I was sure of.

The landing maneuver was a little trickier. The glider had to be brought to the required low speed by waiting your time, pulling the stick a little and then letting it go on and off, as the end of the field approached too quickly. As mentioned, there were no brakes. Finally, at minimum speed, the glide rail touched ground until grabbing it snugly and elegantly, then the kite decelerated until the right wing tipped toward ground to touch it. The fun was over. What started as enor-mous anxiety ended as pure fun. I loosened the seatbelt and got off nonchalantly. I had done it. Flying relates to all kind of emotions and how to overcome them.

Now the opportunities for flying came much faster due to the mechanized winch service. While we were hanging around the field for usually half the day—weather permitting—I went on a glider perhaps twice to make a turn around the field—about 3-4 minutes each time. The other half of the day was spent with all kinds of instructions: maps, airport approach, compass, orientation, aircraft instruments, weather service, aircraft type recognition of friend and foe, etc. etc. After about two weeks it was time to move on to the real gliders with enclosed cockpits, spoilers and soaring capability. The pilot was sitting comfortably in an enclosed space. They had one and two seaters. The "Grunau Baby" (one seater) and the "Kranich" (two seater). I could show Bill both models when we visited the "Rhoen" glider center in Germany near Schweinfurt in 1986 or 87.

First we did what we had practiced before: hook up to the winch, rise to 100 meters, make four left turns and a pinpoint landing at a large white cross which marked the ideal landing spot. With the first training, we were not required to hit the cross, because the initially used hang gliders had no brakes, i.e. a spoiler in the wings to slow down—or not—depending on one's gliding situation. Now we were told to use the brakes and later also to slip the plane, a maneuver that got it partially out of control—used only temporarily and just when needed to pinpoint the cross. Things were much more relaxed in the "Baby." I didn't feel any more like sitting in the middle of nowhere without anything to hang onto. Also, the turn around field was much longer in time, because the gliding angle was much improved. As we merrily went through our daily flight instructions, I looked up as a buddy was pulled up with the winch. Suddenly, the returning motorbike stopped. The driver got off and started working like mad on his bike. Soon I saw the "Baby" hanging over the bike. The flagman waved his flag and yelled like crazy. The "Baby" was about 50 meters up and no longer gained altitude. With the wire taut and seemingly stuck in the bike, there was only one maneuver to be done: lower the glider's nose and unlatch the wire. The pilot-buddy didn't do it and went straight into the ground at tremendous speed—nose first, with an enormous crashing sound of splintered wood. Only a heap of broken wood was left. Everyone ran to the glider, but we could do nothing more. The buddy was dead instantly. He must have realized that he was not high enough yet by a far shot and therefore didn't bother to look at the flagman yet. That was his undoing, because he could have noticed that the tow wire got entangled with the motorbike and therefore his apogee was 50 meters short. We all knew he had been out the night before to some neighborhood village festivities into the wee hours, climbing the fence on his way back. The security was very relaxed in this place. I think his senses were still somewhat fogged up. The flying business is unforgiving. Any mistake you make can do you in, and each also increases your risk exposure too much to escape unscathed. Going up on a tow wire, I always had the flagman in my focus, no matter how high up I was, until I could hear the audible snap of the wire being released. For the rest of the day training was cancelled, and we went to quarters in a somber mood. The next day, everything started anew. With the glider remnants removed, things looked brighter. Flying in the "Baby" was an exhilarating experience. Controls were super-easy to handle, needing almost no pressure; I could fly this thing with thumb and pointer touching the stick. The slightest finger move made the kite react and do immediately what was needed. After about 15 turns around the field, I was ready for the next step in the development. Now it got exciting. We were introduced to the two-seater "Kranich." All aforementioned experiences took relatively long because of the insufficient amount of gliders and equipment. Sometimes it took many hours before each turn came up. What they did with us now was simple: Sgt. Kipper loaded me into a Kranich, which was hooked up to a tow plane, a Fokke-Wulf 44 biplane. This was a two seater, with open cockpits and double wings. It looked like one of the fighter planes of WWI. As the tow plane slowly got to move first, the tow cable was tightened, and the excitement started. The Fokke-Wulf accelerated slowly and then lifted off gently. The trick was now for us to keep the horizon line right between the wings, exactly in the middle. I was certainly not used to the extreme speed the FW provided to the Kranich. The glider was designed to an absolute speed of 50-60 km/h, and here we were being pulled along at over 100, resulting in extreme sensitivity of the control system. The slightest pressure on the stick made the glider jump abruptly, up or down. If I got so high that I actually could look down on the tow plane, I had to gently nudge it down by pressing the stick forward little by little. Pressing was not indicated. Only an ever so slight whiff of a tendency was needed—almost a thought was sufficient. If it were too abrupt, my glider speed would increase as I lost height, and the cable would slack. Then, when leveling with the tow plane, my speed would decelerate and the cable would suddenly tighten up with a terrible bang, which would shake up the inexperienced pilot-trainee, and Sgt. Kipper would chew me out. Well, there was a weak cable piece woven into the tow cable. It was designed to break when the cable impact became too large during slack pickup. It happened to many beginning glider pilots that the cable snapped, the tow plane made a steep turn, dropped the cable and landed. So, the desire and pride of all of us was not to snap a cable—which was more easily said than done! On that particular day, Kipper showed me the ropes with regard to properly remaining behind the tow plane, horizon between wings and cable always tight. I got the hang of it pretty fast. I mean there were initially some minor episodes of cable slackness, but I sort of got out of it without losing my nerve or sweating profusely. As we got up to about

2000 meters, the tow pilot waved his hand, signaling me to lower my plane (slack the cable) and unlatch the glider from the tow plane. That done, we were free. The tow returned with a steep banking curve, and the motor noise disappeared. Also, the loud hissing noise of the airflow over the wings diminished rapidly until hardly any noise was heard. We were soaring elegantly over the beautiful Silesian countryside, but there was no time for romantic musings. Kipper told me what to do: 90 degree left turn, 180 degree right turn, etc., until all of a sudden I noticed a bump on my behind and saw the accelerometer indicating a climb. The altimeter showed that I gained height. What happened? Kipper had maneuvered me underneath a sizeable cumulus cloud. There are usually updrafts under those. In an extreme case, for example under a thunderstorm line, one could climb several thousand meters. This is the method long distance gliders use to gain their altitudes. They fly from cloud to cloud until they run out of them. Kipper now had some fun also. He was an old glider ace, hanging out and waiting in Neudorf for war's end, like the rest of us. We managed to stay up some 20 to 25 minutes until having to descend to give the next aspirant his chance. That day many cables were broken. I was lucky and perhaps a little better skilled than some others.

The atmosphere was now more professional. We had instruments to observe speed, altitude, and accelerations in all directions, and we strapped on a parachute—just in case. We were taught how to operate it, but we never actually jumped. They must have trusted us to get out when necessary. No one had to do it while in training. This fairly cumbersome chute was a very large package of about 15-20 lbs. It hung on our behind as we entered the plane, or sometimes the package was in the plane or glider, and we sat down on it and had to adjust all the straps so they would tighten around our bodies—everything just in case! If the straps were loose when jumping, you could be badly hurt. But usually we were hanging around the starting point strapped in the chute, bone bag on, flight cap and goggles pulled over the head, waiting for the next turn to get into a glider. Much time would be wasted at this point, but, young and dashing as we were, it hardly crossed our minds. I got so eager about this flying thing that I could hardly wait for my next turn. If something had gone wrong, the punishment could be one turn around the field, chute strapped on—a big pain, because the chute was hanging and dangling below you with its heavy pounds—and then running? The worst was that we couldn't sabotage it by slowing down deliberately, since all of us wanted to stay in flight training. We had to grin, bear it, and put on a good show. But this only happened seldom; the general climate was civilized, different from that of the radar station. The instructors were educated fellow travelers whose gratification didn't depend upon making us miserable and obedient. They had to teach us a subject, and I always welcomed a learning experience. Again, I was fortunate to be at the right spot at the right time. We were introduced to the new features of the Kranich and the Grunau Baby gliders one by one. There was instrumentation, and both were equipped with spoilers—a kind of brake. I could also move a wing upward while turning the fuselage around its vertical axis, so as to provide added resistance to the airflow. This maneuver reduced the speed, making the glider (or any other plane) lose altitude very fast—like an elevator. Although the maneuver looked quite hairy and challenging, it was easily executed once learned. I got the first taste—the slip—when going up with Kipper in a Kranich one day. On return, he wanted to show me how to place the glider exactly on the landing cross. As we approached relatively high above ground, he took the stick and told me just to feel along with him. Sitting behind me, as usual, he latched violently into the left rudder and moved the stick all the way to the left, too, which made the plane kind of lose control. It moved 60-80 degrees to the right and dropped the left wing down 45 to 60. It felt like dropping out of it, while the whole thing went down like a rock. Continuing that way would mean a crash. Then, at a selected moment, he latched into the right rudder, moving the stick to the right also. This made the kite straighten out to normal and—as if nothing had happened—it elegantly floated down to land exactly on top of the cross. The experience was truly hair-raising. It felt like crashing and then—at the command of Kipper's fingertips—everything got straightened out. This maneuver was the only possible way to land a plane on the spot, in case there were no landing brakes, flaps, or other help. Not all older planes were thus equipped; for example, the tow plane FW-44 didn't have it. Therefore I later thought it was real fun to fly. The landing cross was very important to the pilot as a suggested touchdown spot. If one touched it on descending, a safe landing was assured. Touching down much beyond would mean danger—one could run out of prepared strip and crash into a tree, hollow, or rough acreage. Besides the obviously serious consequences, wrecking government property was not recommendable. One of the next days I again went up with Kipper, this time to 3000 meter on a marvelous spring day, with clear view to the horizon. It felt like leaving all the ugly problems behind, and around us were silence and peace. Suddenly he placed the glider downward, nose first, and the wings started to spin around the landing cross, faster and faster. The ground seemed to spin around the plane. Then he straightened it and pulled up the stick to the belly. The plane went into a steep climb until we were hanging in our straps—upside down! Then down at full speed and again a wonderful loop. Kipper must have really known what he was doing! Another loop until we were inverted, and then he rolled us into normal position. Meanwhile we lost 2000 meters and it was time to get down. Now I realized why he had carefully checked my belts and tightened them before we took off. A little dizzy at the end, I was very impressed. This was the real thing! My knees were a bit shaky, but I didn't throw up. Thereafter I got clearance for getting towed up alone. Many starts, mainly with the Grunau Baby, followed until it all became a routine.

At the beginning of May we transferred back to Neudorf, to be trained on real aircraft with propeller and engines. In parallel, theoretical instructions were given on various subjects. Basic drills were long forgotten. In the morning of May 17 we marched out to flight training in the usual bone bag, caps and goggles. The instructors jumped into four or five single wing training planes, Bu 181, and drove them to the starting point. The Buecker, Bu 181 at the time, was the standard and most widely used trainer in the air force. We had many others, though, which I will explain later. The Bu 181 had a six cylinder fuel injected engine and a starting mechanism (with battery on board). The single wing was connected low to the fuselage. One had to jump on the wing to enter the two-seater cockpit. Both seats had full controls, so that the instructor could observe and control the trainee. The seats were next to each other, making conversation during flight fairly easy. The cockpit was enclosed with Plexiglas. The wheels could not be retracted. The plane was very light, and the third, small landing wheel was at the tail, not like modern jets, where the third landing wheel is at the front right below the cockpit. First we were taught how to start the engine. After hearing lengthy lectures about engine function, here was the real thing! Since none of us had driven a motorcar before, everything was very unusual, and our senses were honed to the utmost. So, while the pilot was inside the cockpit, another guy had to turn over the prop about twice 360 degrees. To do this, the pilot had to turn the ignition switch to the "off" position, then yell to the guy at the propeller "ignition off," do his thing and step aside. The switch was turned on and the engine started. To prevent the plane from quickly moving away, start blocks had been placed in front of the wheels. As I went through all this that morning with Corporal Kitzhoefer, he waved to the attendant to remove the blocks, grabbed the gas lever—positioned to his right, mine to my left—and slowly we gained speed to roll to the starting position. There we paused and pushed the gas to full throttle to see if the required rpm were reached. Everything was o.k. He explained that, while gaining speed on the runway to the required minimum lift-off speed, I must push the right pedal very gently to keep the plane on my runway. A straight line of movement was not guaranteed, because the propeller turned left, throwing the air stream from left to right against the rudder in the back, which made the plane behave a bit irrationally, always turning to the left. I soon noticed this irritating behavior, but managed to control it by holding my right foot against the pedal and adjusting the foot pressure diligently to maintain straight-line movement. I remembered buddies aborting the takeoff by braking out to the left. Then the tail lifted up—a sign of increasing speed—and soon Kitzhoefer signaled me to gently pull on the stick. The plane obeyed my suggestion and lifted off. The sound of the rumbling wheels faded, and only engine noise was audible. I got up to roughly 200 meters, then a left turn and straight back to the starting point. This was quite different from glider flying. The engine noise was deafening, and I no longer depended on the glider's ability to remain in the air without updrafts. My new limits were my gas tank and orders given. For the next few days the goal was to get me safely up in the air and down—the landing being the harder part. A good deal of judgment had to be applied when descending toward the cross for landing. The altimeter gave the height and your eyesight the distance to the cross. Now you had to reduce the gas to zero, so that the plane would gradually float against the cross. The aim was to balance everything such that you set down the plane exactly at the cross without cranking up the engine again or arriving too high so as to set down in the middle of the air field. Before starting the descent, I had to lower the flaps to increase resistance. When I came in short, I could pull in the flaps or push in for gas to gain speed. When I came close to the ground, it was most important to exactly guess distance to ground, which was difficult for many guys. Everything looked different when close to ground, compared to an altitude of 200 meters, much more difficult when coming down from higher altitudes. What had to be learned now was to slow the plane before setting it on its wheels, i.e., I had to pull slightly on the stick such that the plane was now flying parallel to the ground, slowly reducing speed until the correct touchdown speed was reached. Then, by pushing the stick gently, the wheels finally and easily touched ground and the plane rolled. This time, no correction with pedals was needed. As speed diminished, the third wheel in the back finally touched, enabling me to guide the plane with the pedals. They were connected to the wheel in the back. This all sounds so easy, but took an enormous sense of judgment and concentration, especially for novices. If the plane would hit the ground too hard (too much speed), it would jump right back up, high into the air. Then the pilot had to push the stick to get it closer to ground. Because usually corrections were too hard due to excitement and fear, the darn thing hit hard again and again. A landing could look more like an old Billy goat jumping up and down. Some of those pathetic shows made me feel sorry for those guys. Sometimes a run around the airfield with parachute was ordered as a "cure." On my first start on May 17, 1944, I was shown all of this. While having a healthy respect for the subject, I thought I could handle it. I had two flights that day. Next day it was just a turn around the airfield with Sgt. Renner to train starting and landing. So it went for six more days, with four tries each. Soon they gave me control of the plane, and I did the turn while the instructor relaxed in his seat. At times it got scary. On a hot day, flying over a forest, the machine suddenly started to get a kick under the right or left wing, which required instantaneous corrections. The Bu 181 was very susceptible to the slightest vertical drafts and needed constant attention. On the 27th of May they let me start alone after the boss (Renner) had given the final o.k. The first solo start is a big milestone: now one got the hang of the basics. I accomplished this at the 21st start—not bad! Now I got qualified for better things.

For the next few days, turns around the airfield continued until, on June 2, we were introduced to a strange kite, which looked more like a toy than anything else. It was a one-seater and yes, it even had an engine. It sounded more like a sewing machine or a modern-day lawnmower. First things first now! How to get this thing going? The absence of a start switch meant someone had to grab the "Quirl" (German slang for prop) and pump it a few times first. With ignition on, one had to then forcefully jolt the prop to give it good momentum, hoping the darn thing would pick. When it happened unexpectedly, one had to be sure the hands or other body parts were not in the perimeter of the revolving prop. Miraculously, no one got hurt doing it, although it looked daring. This was an Italian plane; captured when the Italian army had surrendered to the allies a few weeks earlier, and now we were stuck with it. I got a few good words from Kipper, and off it went into the blue yonder. Starting was a piece of cake, but landing was the opposite. The darn thing just wouldn't set down, although my speed was well reduced. So, I fussed around seeing the forest at the end of the field approaching until it finally decided to quit, settled down, and stopped. The starting point was about one mile away. Not only did it stop, the engine quit, too. There I was—got out of my belts, jumped down from the wing and scratched my head. I tried to lift the tail, since it was very light—almost weightless. I picked it up and started pulling the kite on my back toward the start. Some buddies soon arrived and helped push. It was the joke of the month of June '44.

Some days later another plane was tried: a Klemm KL35, a well-known light sport job of the mid-thirties. It had two open cockpits and was easy to handle, except, again, for the landing: it took forever to nurture the plane to set down. Many guys gave a sorry spectacle. They hit the ground, the plane bounced back high into the air, and, knowing he was in for it, the pilot tried again and again, with the kite jumping back up. Each time it looked as before: a bucking horse running down the airstrip. One of us hit so hard he planted the nose into the ground. Obviously, the KL 35 was not very well liked.

During all of this we were protected from any information about the war in our fairly isolated outpost with almost no newspapers, and few had a radio. One Sunday morning, a buddy and I walked through the beautiful, sunny country-side. Resting on a hillock, we overlooked a large valley. In the far distance we noticed a huge gasoline manufacturing plant—one of those producing gas from coal. Suddenly, high up, we heard the alarming sound of engines: a huge stream of allied bombers. Their target was this plant. Not one single German plane was in the air, and there was no anti aircraft fire. We saw the bombs drop and pulver-ize the entire installation, with no resistance by the German side. This sad and significant spectacle showed that the war would end soon. There was no doubt, not even for the most stubborn "believers." What on earth were we training for here in Neudorf, with no more fighters available? Not that I longed to "defend the fatherland."—Stories were going around that fighters had to ram bombers in mid air to make a kill. The number of German fighters and light weaponry no longer sufficed to attack bomber groups with at least some success. These stories made me realize that my situation was scary. I had not expected to be slaughtered without any chance of survival. I thought that infantry soldiers in the Russian campaigns had better chances. No wonder that doom beset us once in a while. We knew by now the fate of Germany was sealed, but the overriding concern became individual survival, except that I could do little to get into a safe harbor. I depended on bureaucratic decisions by people I would never meet or know of.

In the next days flight traffic continued. Another trainer type got me excited: the Buecker Bu 131—an old-fashioned looking double wing job, but with very modern design and lines. This sporty little two seater was a delight to get off and on the ground. The few rounds I could do were exhilarating. Later something better came up: Kipper got me into a Bu 181 and explained to me that I was to train for emergency landing. In case I was to run out of fuel or the engine would stop, quick decisions were needed to get the kite and me to the ground, prefera-bly hitting the next airfield. It would mean pulling the signal pistol, opening the window and firing the shot in direction of the field. The charge was made up of several bright red stars, notifying people on the ground that I had to land, no matter what and that they had to clear the landing strip immediately. If there was no airfield around—then what? Kipper explained that I had to quickly find a plane field with as few obstructions as possible and get down for a rough landing. My life would be on the line, and all depended on my wits and—luck! Should the aircraft be on fire or a wing fall off, there would be one action only: bail out! However, the goal of the exercise was to rescue both aircraft and pilot by swiftly locating a suitable touchdown surface—preferably a cultivated field, meadow or large highway. Such obstacles as smokestacks, high voltage lines, etc. had to be observed and avoided. The latter were especially dangerous and difficult to detect. So, we went up to 2000 meters and somewhat away from the airfield. Then Kipper pulled the gas lever to the zero position and gave me the signal to land. Below were lots of forests, a little river, meadows along the river and cultivated fields. The meadows seemed too wet and short, always ending in shrubs. One field didn't have large trees or shrubs, and—not knowing anything better—I made the turn to direct the aircraft toward the wind when landing. I could tell where the wind came from by observing the red-white wind direction sack at the airfield, and I had correlated my position with the airfield. A smokestack in the distance spewing a trail of smoke confirmed the direction. Landing against the wind greatly reduced the speed over ground. Let's say, if your minimum touch down speed were 60 km/h and the wind 20, the speed would be reduced to 40. The aircraft carriers also help by steaming at 30 knots against the wind. That trick can be the difference between getting down unhurt or drilling the craft nose first into the ground. In my first attempt of emergency landing, I soared toward a freshly mowed field, covered with shorn clover—almost ideal for a landing. As I was ready to set down at about one or two meters altitude, Kipper pushed the gas and the engine started again, increasing speed and altitude immediately. He signaled that everything was fine, and we returned to the airfield, unable to complete the emergency landing, because that would have been dangerous. From 2 meters up, the chance for completing the landing could be judged. More training followed to improve our pinpoint landing skills, i.e. getting up at a good altitude, cutting off gas and then soaring exactly to the cross without the engine's help. After another six to ten times, the landing thing was no longer a major problem. Descending from greater altitude to exact landing remained a challenge, and we had to collect all our skills to prevent disaster. I even saw terrible landings by experienced pilots. Once, an Me-109 tried to land in Neudorf, coming from the East. Touching down too late, the pilot didn't have enough runway and crashed into the forest beyond, shearing off both wings between two pine trees. He scrambled out cheerfully, unhurt. It always pays to use your belts!

By mid-June they rolled out a completely different aircraft—the FW-58 from Fokke Wulf, a two engine, larger job, to train for things like flying transport planes or bombers. It had lots more instrumentation because of the two engines. All indicators, oil pressure gauges, etc. were duplicated. A control column, as used by modern, large passenger aircraft, replaced the stick. The cloth-covered fuselage was very simple. It held six people. Taking off was easier now, with two engines and props! Since revolutions were opposed, you did not need to correct your direction as required by a single prop job. I saw a FW-190 fighter taking off with loud noise and suddenly turning to the left, heading straight for the hangars, crashing miserably. The pilot had to be peeled out of his cockpit. The necessary correction during takeoff in a single prop craft was always tricky, and it was a different experience in each plane. In this FW-58 it was a piece of cake. Also, the taxiing on the tarmac was simplified through use of the engines to change directions quickly. To move left, one accelerated the right engine slightly, and so on. Once in the air, it did feel somewhat sluggish. The smaller aircraft reacted to each little updraft quite wildly, requiring constant manipulation of the controls to maintain balance. Sometimes both wings—and sometimes only one—kicked up or down. There was never a quiet second! It was like riding in one of those small propjets from Philadelphia to Ithaca in bad weather and landing in a storm. The relaxing FW-58 was truly boring. I was now sure that I could take off in the cockpit of a JU-52 transport or a Heinkel He-111. Those craft offer little challenge. Where it gets interesting is when there is instrument flight and navigation, i.e. flying without the benefit of the horizon, flying in clouds, fog, or at night.

On June 20 Renner, who had made lieutenant, took me to a plane in his new uniform, and we got up, with three other planes following, to try formation flying—naturally without touching each other! One was the leader; the others followed fairly close in staggered order, like geese have done it forever. The distance between planes was about 15 feet. This sounds like an easy task … and it was a quiet day. However, with choppy weather the wings bumped up and down, and the entire craft would jump without notice. We used the Bu-181 single prop; with the result that everyone started sweating profusely. When Renner occasionally signaled to make a left or right curve, the others had to adjust their flight pattern to maintain their spot in the formation. For example, on a right turn, the pilot to the left had to accelerate and slightly gain altitude; to the right it meant the opposite—tricky indeed! But we were now so well adjusted that nothing happened. Much later, on a quiet day with not much bumpy weather, I flew one plane alone with Corporal Kitzhoefer flying another. He slowly moved his wingtip closer and closer to mine, until his was located about one or two feet above mine—very, very close! Then he manipulated his controls such that—slowly but surely—his wingtip circled exactly around mine. Naturally, he bet that I wouldn't budge and we wouldn't meet a sudden up- or down draft. This went on for quite a while. Convinced that only the most careful pilots could survive, I didn't like it one bit, but I got through it o.k. I could do nothing against an instructor! It was hardly worth thinking about. I had heard of all kinds of stints; some guys flew underneath bridges or transmission lines, and one buddy boasted of having thrown his dirty laundry in a girl's back yard from a plane for cleaning. When we took off for lengthy solo flights to distant locations, anyone caught with those kinds of extracurricular activities would be terminated after some time in the slammer. One guy, returning from a long-distance flight, couldn't explain why color and consistency of strange dirt on his wheels differed from our region. That was the last of him. He later told of landing in a field to meet a girlfriend, just to show off. How foolish people can get!

Getting out of the plane upon landing that day, we found no one around. The planes were taxied to the hangers, and soon we were told that the base commander would address the entire personnel stationed there. He informed us that an attempt at the "Fuehrer's" life had been made, that he was alive, and that the culprits had been or were to be dealt with. The usual nonsense followed about winning the war, secret weapons, etc. etc. It was very depressing to hear. At the time one couldn't discuss these issues with anyone. If I would say to another guy that the war was inevitably lost, and he would snitch on me, I would be indicted for "undermining the country's defense," always resulting in a hanging. Since we came from all over, I had no close friends and could trust no one. It takes a long time until you know what your buddies are made of, and Helmut or Hajo were not around. I sensed that war's end had again come another giant step closer. If the generals had made that desperate attempt, it must already be five minutes after 12. As a rule, German generals had never been good patriots, most having confused their personal honor with patriotism. They were unaware or ignored the fact that the regime had cooked the books, and it all happened under their eyes and watch. They were primarily responsible for the mess Germany was in now. This shabby, bungled attempt to right things almost looked as though they wanted to forfeit success, to be able to claim later that they had tried. Some historians would bring up this point in the future. To us, the most visible result was that, instead of the military salute, from June 21 on only the "German" (Nazi) salute was allowed in all armed services. In his fury, Hitler wanted to humiliate anyone who no longer believed in him, his party, or his actions. Perhaps he sensed that there were, and always had been, many people out there who doubted him. Formerly we had to use the military salute outdoors (with cap on) and the "German" salute indoors (cap off). Only the SS troops, as well as all Nazi organizations, used the German salute throughout. At this point it felt kind of silly, and initially some of those around me made fun of it, until it soon became another routine. There were other things to worry about, especially: when would the Soviets arrive in Silesia? They were already close to Romania and would flood that country soon (in August). I worried about my buddies there. But in this kind of terrible conflagration you had to take care of the biggest priorities first: yourself! As far as possible under the circumstances, I sometimes considered getting into an aircraft and head north toward Sweden—but this was only a dream I went to bed with. For practical purposes it was not worth a thought; there was not enough gas in the tank!

Until the end of June, more formation flying followed when we again got into the Fw-58 (bi-motor). This time, up in the cockpit, I was instructed about how to control via instruments only. Since one does not see horizon or ground, only compass, attitude instrument, accelerometer, and altimeter could be used to observe the craft's status. Control was as usual. Compass gives the flight direction; the complete horizon is divided into 360 degrees, zero North, 180 South, etc.: magnetic compass indicator toward magnetic North, which is much different from geographic North. Therefore, this instrument needs a correction, depending on global location. There are tables for navigators showing correction as a function of geographic longitude. Somewhere in the U.S. the correction is zero. For us in Neudorf it was always a certain constant, which was easy. The attitude instrument preceded the present artificial horizon, an electronic device coupled with a gyroscope, which conveniently shows a craft's altitude: banking right or left, rising or descending. More convenient is a display of an aircraft's cross-section against an artificial horizon. We had no such thing. Our instrument had an indicator (Pinsel) and a ball (Kugel), placed in a curved glass tube. When making a turn to left, one had to see the indicator swinging to the left while keeping the ball on center. Being very sensitive to G-forces, the ball was capricious, difficult for less experienced pilots. On a left turn, the ball's flying to the right meant a turn was in progress without banking the craft. That meant one could feel G-forces pulling to the right—not good. Its rolling to the left with the indicator meant that the plane was banked too much, and the craft might lose control and spin to the ground. The fight with indicator and ball was always tense. I saw many a young pilot falling helplessly out of the clouds. This was always done at sufficient altitude, so that a plane could be recovered in time, and was always combined with loud whining of the engine, an impressive display. The trainee would be placed behind a black curtain, while the instructor enjoyed the view and didn't like it very much when the kite started to spin out of control. It upset their digestive tract, and the poorly performing trainee was always somehow retaliated against. In the FW-58 it was still very easy: we just flew straight to get the idea. The torture started later in the little, sensitive Bu-181, where indicator and ball simply went wild. Sometimes the poor novice got so disoriented that he no longer realized what was up, down, left or right. Some found having to fly without the horizon's assist to be a nightmare. At the end of June I got introduced to another plane of the inventory: a FW-44, which was a bi-plane (Doppeldecker) and a two seater. With cockpits arranged in line, it was the original trainer for the air force. It had an air-cooled star engine. In the olden days, the stick could be unscrewed, and the instructor loved to throw it out to tell the trainee he was on his own. Another one was hidden in his cockpit, just in case the trainee would get a nervous breakdown. But, being beyond this phase, this kid stuff couldn't scare us any more. The FW-44's engine had to be primed and started like the Italian kite. The prop had to be swung well and hard enough until the engine kicked in, coughing and stuttering. Flying this one, which was more stable than the Bu-181, was a pleasure. Its funny, old-fashioned gas gauge was a float indicator, sitting between first cockpit and engine. Since it had no landing assist, to get down smack on the cross required lots of slipping and/or use of the engine. All in all I felt comfortable and, taking off in that kite, must have looked like one of those old-fashioned men in their flying machines. I later regularly used this plane for cross-country flight assignments. (Remember, this plane was used also as tow plane at glider school!)

In early July, the real thing came up: acrobatic flying! It began with one of those initial show-and-tell takeoffs. Kipper got up with me, and I had to do all the honors. Three air spaces around the airfield were reserved for this purpose. I climbed up to 2000 meters, and then Kipper took the stick of the Bu-181, which was a reliable plane, but not really ideal for acrobatics. Now he just wanted me to get an idea what the different figures to be learned felt like. First he did an "Immelmann" turn, named after the pilot ace of World War I. After dipping the plane for maximum speed, he jerked the stick back. As a result, we climbed up with maximum gas throttle, at a very sharp angle—engine whining. The plane finally hung below the prop and quickly lost speed. The engine noise gradually decreased and the plane started to vibrate, with almost no speed left. At that moment Kipper stepped on the left pedal, which made the plane turn left about 180 degrees, and down we went wildly at tremendous speed and increasing engine roar. When we had enough speed, he let me do the next turn, etc. etc. I did that a few times until it became a piece of cake! But it looked and sounded impressive. The loop he showed me next was hairier. One has to start as though making a turn, i.e. pick up lots of speed by diving, then yank the stick back, so that the plane shoots up, but now, as there is still some speed left and the stick close to the chest, the plane goes upside down. As the apogee is reached, with the pilot hanging upside down in his belts, the stick must be thrown briefly forward to momentarily stabilize in this position and then back again to make it slide down and fully complete a loop. Diving from the apogee, the throttle must be reduced as the ground quickly approaches. If the stick stays in the forward position at the apogee, the aircraft continues flying in the upside down position. After showing it, Kipper let me do the next loop, made a few corrections, and—another piece of cake! What looks so impressive from below is just a sequence of well-learned little moves. I admit that, before going up, all of us were nervous, adrenalin pumping considerably. But calm and composure returned quickly as the show went on. The roll—probably aviation's most intricate figure—followed. It can best be imagined by sitting on the ground, stretching out, face down, and then rolling the body about 360 degrees back to the original position. This is the figure he showed me, except that the plane moves forward while doing it and remains on course; it does not move sideways. Kipper did this very quickly. There are a fast roll and a slow, controlled roll. One can even imagine doing a 90 degree roll and then flying straight, which is very strenuous and challenging for the pilot, who hangs in mid air and has to switch the importance of the control surfaces (the tail rudder now becomes the altitude adjustment); in other words, stick and pedals reverse and interchange their usage. First Kipper did a fast roll, jerking the stick to the right for a right roll. The plane quickly dropped the right wing and flipped around. Just before completion, he moved the stick to the left, whereupon this kite stopped the wild roll and remained straight as if nothing had happened. To see sky and ground turn around you was a half-threatening and half-exhilarating experience, with lots of G's at work. Because it was hard on the system, I began to realize why the instructors preferred to quickly introduce us to all this and remain on the ground—to critique us after we landed. (It had never been right!) Enduring all our terrible mistakes was just too much. It was bloody murder up there. Every other minute a fellow fell from the sky, out of control. Some needed considerable time to mount a halfway acceptable show. All following acrobatic assignments were solo affairs. The instructor just gave the exact assignments, like three fast rolls left, five right, etc. etc. On my first day of acrobatics Kipper also showed me the slow roll, which differed from the fast one; he used an intricate pattern of pedal and stick moves. He could stop it in any position during its 360 degrees course and start again. I realized that it would take a lot of practice to equal his expertise, the key being handling and coordinating stick and pedal actions so precisely that the long axis of the aircraft would not describe a circle. Later we would always be reviewed, endlessly. A novice simply could not do it perfectly. Very exhausted after a dozen or so of those slow rolls one always more than welcomed the descent.

Some days later I was to take off with Kipper for my first cross country flight, in a FW-44, a biplane as described before, and go to Bohemia across the mountains which separated it from Silesia. First I had to get a formal, written weather report for the area between Neudorf and our destination from the meteorologists. In bad weather, e.g. heavy thunderstorm fronts, they wouldn't let us go. In case of local weathers developing, we would have to fly around them or head for home, if enough gas was left. If not, we would have to choose an airfield close to the position. We simply didn't have sufficient training yet (instrument flight) to venture into a large bank of clouds. Then a map, a signal pistol, and a sidearm, usually a Walter PK7, were obtained. The pistols came with ammo. The neat little 7.35 mm Walter was the weapon for officers in the German services. The 9mm Luger, also known as "Pistole 08" (German official model) was for real war. In my extensive training on pistols, one of the most important aspects was the maintenance of each model; same with rifles, submachines and machine guns. Much time was spent disassembling and reassembling each, sometimes blindfolded. If a speck was found in the bore of a gun during the frequent inspections, penalties usually followed.

There we were: the flight controllers registered our departure and port of destination. With map and pistol, I climbed into the first cockpit, buckled up. Earlier I had studied the weather report and determined my compass reading to Beneschau (Benesov) in Bohemia, south of Prague—about two flight hours away. Altitude of the hills to be crossed was roughly 4000 feet. Compass reading was determined by destination, wind speed, and direction. It sometimes felt funny when observing the plane being shoved sideways by the wind. Soon after Kipper signaled to taxi away, I lifted off into the blue yonder—a fantastic feeling! But Kipper had cautioned me not to get too excited about this wonderful little excursion. In the distance the outline of the "Eulengebirge" soon appeared, ahead were the Neisse River and town of Neisse with its airport, which had a fighter squadron training school—perhaps the next station in my aviation development, I mused. My pencil mark went right through Neisse. While pursuing the destination, I had to compare the map and look for landmarks to confirm my course. One could never fully trust the wind. Once above the hills, I looked for the Elbe River, supposedly a few miles north to the right of my course. After one hour in the air, there it was—the same Elbe that passes north toward Dresden and then Hamburg. It comes from the west slope of the "Riesengebirge" and is the main drainage of the Bohemiam plateau. Everything went as planned, and there was not a second when I didn't know where I was. With one eye I always looked at the nearest airport or landing strip marked on the map. Noted in red, they could not be overlooked. The altitude was also noted, in case of an emergency landing. Then the altimeter had to be adjusted, so that one had the exact altitude over ground. The map showed altitude over sea level. Soon I landed in Beneschau, where Kipper and I had a good meal in the NCO mess. Since this was Bohemia, the food was out of this world, compared to the miserable stuff in Neudorf. Much of the Viennese cuisine originated in Bohemia (Boehmen), and Moravia (Maehren). The cooks seemed able to get good and ample supplies in the neighborhood. Judging from the taste, they were local people. Earlier, coming from Romania to go home on furlough, I once had taken a train, which stopped in Prague for an hour or two. At that time, the amount of good, tasty food available also resembled peacetime. In German cities, nothing could be had during those times—no chocolate, no fruits, etc. I wondered why always the dumb Germans got the short end of the stick. Although our meal in Beneschau really called for a little snooze, we couldn't afford to return at night; it was getting late, and the road home was long. I think the return flight led me further north to return to Neudorf coming from the north, from the Schweidnitz area. Kipper was visibly pleased with me. I had never gotten disoriented or lost my way. I always knew I had a sixth sense for orientation, my memory never failed me, and I was very methodical and cautious. At the end of this trip Kipper told me that I would make future cross-country trips alone—a pat on my back! Few guys performed as well during their first cross-country flight. It was a memorable experience.

A couple of days later I did my first solo cross-country flight, which took about three hours without an interim landing, on another one of those beautiful summer days so inviting to enjoy life. Dawdling leisurely above the landscape, I was no longer 100% sure that I was on track. I looked for a railroad, always a safe pointer for us with others being large highways, canals, rivers and cities. I preferred remaining between major landmarks, in this case between Riesengebirge and that railroad. But I wanted to know for sure at which town along the tracks I was. Easy! Seeing a train station ahead, I lowered my cruising altitude and got close enough to read the name of that smallish town. Meanwhile I waved in a friendly manner to those waiting for their train, and they waved back. I only regretted that we hadn't been issued colorful shawls that could flutter behind us. I did have the pilot's cap, goggles, so why not? It might have positively enlightened the scene. I felt fashionable and relaxed, especially since I now had a better idea of where I was along the railroad. From Kempen I turned back toward Grottkau and then home. Except for looking up my location on the train station, the flight was uneventful, but, when landing in Neudorf (between Oppeln and Neisse in Upper Silesia) I had trouble judging my height above ground for a smooth landing. I just couldn't get my bearing, coming from about 2000 meters altitude. Since the altimeter was not sufficiently accurate to tell me whether I was 2 or 12 meters up, I set the FW-44 down quite hard, making it jump up again. Being very tired after this long flight didn't help my judgment. I pushed the stick slightly forward, gave a little gas, and the problem was over. Without doing this, the craft would lose speed and set down hard again and again, until sometimes the wheels would get knocked off. As I write this, a terrible event resurfaces in my mind. I can no longer pinpoint location or date. It was another F-44 biplane in which I took off for an airfield round. As I came down for the landing, they shot a few red star signals in front of my nose. Not knowing what was meant, I pushed the gas and aborted my landing. Their signals had totally surprised me. Perhaps another plane was doing an emergency landing? But I saw nothing coming down. Meanwhile, aircraft traffic had ceased, and a bunch of instructors were watching me intently, reloading their signal pistols. I tried to land again, and the red stars re-appeared. I looked at the instructors, who were making baffling, funny signs toward their feet. I took off again and made another approach, only to see red stars again. But this time there was a guy standing there, holding up one aircraft wheel, and everyone pointed at it. It dawned on me that I must have lost a wheel during, or shortly after takeoff. I pushed more gas and wiggled my wings left and right to indicate I had understood. On return to the landing zone I saw the fire engine and an ambulance pulling up. Was it that bad? I had never seen anyone making a one-wheeled landing—it almost never happens. Modern aircraft, and all fighters and bombers at the time, would retract their wheels into the fuselage and/or wings to reduce flow resistance. If a pilot could not crank down and lock the wheels due to wheel systems trouble, he had to do a belly landing. All those aircraft were tested for it. That was not very safe, but preferable to staying in the air forever. It usually worked out all right. No one had ever told me about a single wheel landing. I could not retract my wheels at all. There were two ways of getting down: a one wheel landing, or to jump out in the parachute. Those below had only pointed out my problem; perhaps not knowing either what would be better. In aviation there will always be situations that leave the pilot to confront the unknown or unplanned, requiring a unique decision to solve the problem. I thought jumping was not the solution. It would destroy the aircraft … and then there was a chance to get the kite down intact … but how, halfway safely? Well, the usual travel speed was about 120 km/h or 75 m/h—not too good when sitting in a cockpit surrounded by thin aluminum tubes and fabric. The usual touchdown speed was 40 or 45 mph. The trick would be to get close to the ground with minimum speed, then gently touch with the one wheel and let it roll, thus gradually reducing speed. Then the stick must be used to diligently keep the craft horizontal as long as possible, until the reduced air speed would make control no longer possible. Then the right wing would fall to the ground (the right wheel was gone.) As it would touch ground, one would have to close the eyes and hope for the best. The trick would be to hold the craft in the air until the controls would get mushy and almost not react ("aushungern"), and set down during that last moment. That's what I did. It was well executed, though never learned. As the wings touched, the entire aircraft spun around wildly in a big cloud of dirt. It was a terrible ruckus, but nothing broke, including the pilot. They lifted me out of my cockpit. It was quite a celebration!

Later we had some days of formation flight training and acrobatics. Formation flight soon became routine, but in acrobatics things could always go wrong, and they did. The roll was everyone's enigma. The fast roll was a cinch, but it took a while to overcome a terrible feeling when making a left roll. While the right one soon was no problem, the left roll took a lot of courage. Sitting in a flimsy cockpit, you suddenly fall into nothing. On the right roll, I could see the adjacent cockpit as though it was something solid. But you have to do it to know the left roll's terror. It must be similar to parachute jumping. After getting the hang of it, this feeling lessened somewhat, but it never really left me. I always had to overcome a resistance to initiate a left roll, and the slow roll, which took an awful lot of practice and was something that separated the men from the boys. Since coordination of the pedal and stick moves was so difficult, many a pilot simply lost control and fell out of the sky with engine whining threateningly, until they pulled back the gas. Luckily, I never fell down, but some of the rolls initially looked awful—long axes describing huge circles. This got you into enormous G-forces and didn't feel too good. While waiting at the starting, everyone was making dry runs of the control moves over and over, to get prepared for the upcoming ordeal. By mid-July, I could state with some confidence that acrobatics, at least the required figures, had become a welcome routine. It beat sloshing around as infantry (Landser). We did not yet have to make slow rolls while flying a large circle or doing rolls while ascending on a turn. Some instructors occasionally went up along to show us their skills and superiority, but I think it was more the former. These high performance acrobatics were just skills, not a daredevil show, which they would have been if performed close to ground, and that was simply not tolerated!

On one of the first August days I picked another FW-44 biplane for a cross country sojourn to Lodz (Poland), then called Litzmannstadt, probably named after Mr. Litzmann, who was a WWI general. During those war years 1939–44 many Germans migrating from the Baltic States were settled in the vast plains of Eastern Europe. I think the Nazi regime's "grand" design was to settle more Germans farther and farther east to "germanize" those conquered lands. Ironically, many Germans had, and still have, Polish, Czech, Russian, Latvian, etc. names, since Germany was always a mixture of tribes and nationalities. In school, for instance, in addition to German names, Polish, Jewish, Dutch, French, Russian and other names were also represented. In my youth group there was Mahmud Kasakoff, who behaved just like the rest of us. One buddy looked like a light-skinned black man and was nicknamed "Neja," the Berlin dialect pronunciation for "Neger" (German for negro). Kasakoff never talked about his racial or ethnic background. For that matter, we didn't even know if he had live parents and never asked if he was Cossack or whatever—other tribes also have names ending in "off." Anyway, I was off to Lodz—a considerable distance from my Oppeln region in Upper Silesia. It was 2-1/2 hours to that airport. Vienna would have been closer. So, I got my usual things straightened out: pistol, map, signal pistol, and weather report. The pistol was for self-defense in case of an emergency landing in the countryside—only a very distant possibility. The flight was fairly uneventful. Orientation was easy. About 50 km away from my destination, I happened to look at the gas gauge and realized I might not have enough to make it. The gauge was a simple float. When it hit bottom, I didn't know how much was left in the tank. There was still some little indication. Had I been in an automobile, I would have stopped at the next gas station. But this was not a car. And I was up in the air wondering why they put so little gas in my tank. With another 40 km to go, that kind of thinking didn't help. The map showed no airport or airfield between my location and Lodz. When there were only 30 km left, the float hit bottom: no more gas. Now I had to gamble. I had the idea to drop the plane quickly. If there were gas left, the drop would create waves in the tank, lifting the float temporarily. And the float came up. No one had ever taught me this little wisdom of hydrodynamics, but dire need makes one invent things quickly. So, I had a tiny bit left, and the engine continued to roar calmly. How long would these few drops last? Wouldn't it be better to look for a safe place to set the kite down? I started scouting for a landing spot while checking if the gas tank float still came up when dipping the plane. It was another 20 km to Lodz. In the distance I started to see some smokestacks. Because the airport was at the West side of town, I didn't have to look very long to find it. Another 10 km—and then the float quit. Gas level hit rock bottom. Although the tank was dry for all practical purposes, I still heard my engine. Then, in the distance, I saw the airport with its hangars. I got the signal pistol out and cocked it, with one hand on the stick and the pistol in the left. I had already reduced speed and altitude. When I saw planes on the start ready to take off, I shot my red stars to indicate my need for an emergency landing. They quickly moved aside, and I set down the plane, cold sweat running from my brow. I was soaked. As I rolled out and reduced speed to arrive at taxi pace, the engine stopped—in the middle of the runway. I got out of my belts and stepped off the plane to enjoy the fresh air and my salvation. From there a truck towed me to the hangar to fill the gas tank. I had made a successful decision after all. I could have decided on an emergency landing somewhere on a field, but lacked assurance that this would end well. What kind of trouble would I have faced after damaging an aircraft? So, from the beginning, I was highly suspicious of this and rather engaged in an educated gamble. But, no matter how I viewed it in retrospect, I had been an extremely lucky boy. With slightly shaking knees, I reported to the officer in charge, who invited me for some snack or supper. I still had to continue to Ohlau, located between Breslau and Brieg on the Oder River. I arrived there after 9:00 p.m., still in daylight because of midsummer. Germany is much further north than New York. Returning, there were no problems and gas was plenty. Next morning I returned to Neudorf and reported my close call. I don't remember why I ran short of gas. Although the wind may have shifted from westerly to easterly, adding flight time, I think the gas should have never been so tight. With the assignments I got from Kipper there was always a full tank. Considering the prevailing wind forecast, I had plenty, but apparently too little for changing weather conditions. Since Kipper was more involved than I, no blame was heaped on me. Rather, I came out smelling like a rose.

The rest of July passed quickly with formation flying, acrobatics and other cross country assignments. I now marvel about our almost total disconnection from the history-making events taking place throughout Europe, especially in France. The allies had landed and broke out from their bridgeheads in the Normandy to start their inexorable advance through France. Germany could no longer resist effectively; the air force, for instance, had become just about extinct. The same could be said about the Navy—if Germany ever had a Navy to speak of in WWII. We received only sparse information and rarely discussed or thought about how this war would or could be waged further. Since we were confined to our pilot training, somebody must have thought that there would be planes, ammo and gas for us, once we were finished. The next step after the "A" pilot certificate, the "B" certification, required attendance of a B-pilot school with more sophisticated trainer planes, where training focused on instrument flight, night takeoff and landing, more formation flight, and acrobatics. Assuming a contin-ued brisk pace, we would be ready for B-school in November. Not that we were counting the days to be transferred—no! We lived one day at a time, complaining about bad food, not enough alcoholic beverages or none at all, and never any luck connecting with girls outside. Civilian life was so far removed from us that it almost didn't seem to exist. Even though I was stationed only about five hours by train away from Berlin, I never received more furlough. I believe each soldier was entitled to one per year, except in such special circumstances as being wounded in action or things like that.

Life in Neudorf was about the safest in Germany. All large cities were now potentially bombed daily. When bombers appeared on the radar screen, no one knew where they were headed. Therefore the population had to move to the air raid shelters nightly. In the morning they would get up as usual to head for work or school. Often public transportation was interrupted due to damages. There was nothing but problems day in, day out, while in Neudorf we enjoyed a bucolic peace. Nothing disturbed us, except the implied threats of transfer to the front in case of poor performance. In this way July ended with lots of daily acrobatic training.

I now flew mostly alone, except when Kipper wanted to show me another fine point. As mentioned, the instructors couldn't physically endure the punishing acrobatic figures all day long with someone else at the stick. Even if done alone, it would have been too much. At the beginning of August, I was to fly cross country again—to Bohemia: first to the town of Pardubitz (Pardubice) on the Elbe River, and from there north toward Bautzen in Saxonia, east of Dresden. So I had to go southwest first and then more or less north. After the preliminaries, I was soon happily moving along over pretty Bohemia, looking for Pardubitz and the Elbe—a distinct location, since there the river changed from an east-west direc-tion toward north. I found the town easily, but was very uncomfortable to read a map on my knees without a holder. Also, one hand was always on the stick for the constant corrections needed. When the flight lasted over one hour, it became heavy in the hand. This happened because gas was used up to the point that trim-ming of the plane got out of kilter. The tail end became lighter (gas tank in the rear fuselage), increasing the feeling of weight in the stick. Without compensat-ing, the aircraft would head down. Modern airplanes have trimming surfaces that can be adjusted from within, but ours didn't. Anyway, I was heading toward Zit-tau. In that area steep hills of about 3000 feet altitude separate Bohemia from

Saxonia. Coming close and seeing some figures on top of the mountain, I decided to get down to have a look. Soon I found myself at the height of the mountain on the south side and saw about 20 girl hikers waving at me. I waved back, cruising by a few times to have fun. Too bad I couldn't get off. So, I had to gain some altitude to hop over the mountain rim. As I had reached just about enough height, a terrible ruckus started. The entire plane shook so badly, that I couldn't read any instrument, and—worse—could no longer increase altitude. I just about made it over the rim and then looked at my map for the next airfield. In those mountains, emergency landings or bailing out meant suicide. There was insufficient height for that. I immediately found a landing spot down the mountain valley. Luckily, I had studied my emergency landing fields before, as always, and just about knew where this one was. Meanwhile, things got worse. I began to lose altitude and the engine coughed badly. Gliding down the valley, I found a tiny landing strip close to a small mountain hamlet. I dropped the kite badly, but I didn't care if anyone looked. I had made it just in time. There were even mechanics at the hangar. They put in new plugs, which they happened to have around, and started the engine again. Everything was o.k. Then I tried full throttle speed: also fine. Meanwhile, I had recaptured my composure, thanked the guys, got in and lifted off toward Bautzen, an industrial city to the north, perhaps half an hour away. On that last part of my 2-1/2 hour flight, I mused a lot about why I had to get down so close to those mountains. Of course, there were the girls, and I had to show off. Aviation is unforgiving. If I would have maintained safe altitude, I could have easily glided down to any spot in the low lands for a classic emergency landing, if needed. But so close to the mountains there was no way out. It was my good luck that made me survive—not my skill. This tiny landing field in the midst of nowhere saved me from an inglorious end. I spoke up aloud in my cockpit: Only cautious pilots live long! Never again this foolishness. Last not least, aircraft are not failsafe, particularly not those small jobs we were handling, and who knew at the time if all those mechanics were sufficiently thorough? Why did three plugs out of eight suddenly stop working? Something was wrong with the maintenance. I didn't stay in Bautzen long; the return home took another 2-1/2 hours. This was the longest flight I ever made. I now felt quite comfortable doing it. If someone would tell me now to go to Vienna or Munich or any other European city, I was sure I'd find my way and then some—provided I didn't make any foolish mistakes. But this experience in the mountains was quite a lesson—for life! Never show off ... be conservative ... be modest!

After this last flight, our entire school got transferred to another place in Beneschau for about two months. Flight training stopped entirely. Presumably gas was becoming scarce. Something had to give, but high command, for political reasons, could not yet admit that the war was quickly becoming a desperate affair, to be lost soon. Under those circumstances the Nazi politicians would send everyone, except themselves, to the eastern front to stave off the Soviet "hordes." Hence they must have intended for us to soon mount those Fokke Wulf fighters and dive into the allied bomber and fighter formations, suicide-style. Luckily, high command could not rationalize correctly—or perhaps some of the fellows had some benevolent reasoning, which, however, was unlikely, since that was not a typical train of thought in those days. They wanted to prove to the "Fuehrer" their ability to transform as many healthy soldiers into dead heroes as they could—the normal order of the day. In his contorted mind, Hitler had become convinced that the German people and soldiers were not tough, or readily enthusiastic enough to deserve offering their lives on his behalf. Hence they were therefore unworthy of him.

I found myself in some barracks performing occasional guard duties for about two months. It was too far for a visit home, which would have required travel documents. Those were simply not issued. Being caught on the railway without documents would have meant immediate court marshal and possibly death. I remember only one episode from that time. After another one of those endless bomber raids, five American soldiers were brought in as prisoners. They had jumped from a bomber. Lacking anything like a prison, they were put into a small barrack hut with only one door and one window, sufficient bunk beds, one table under the window, and one chair. Someone was to be selected to watch over these American prisoners of war—supposedly very reliable, experienced soldiers and not greenhorns. Since our camp consisted of recent draftees and young pilot trainees without soldier experience, several buddies and I were chosen. We had no combat experience either, but the advantage of having been subjected for many years to the stupid, repeat drill sessions, which make one entirely indisposed to reception of unusual mind stimuli. So, I found myself sitting on that chair, two 9 mm pistols 08 (Luger) in front of me, safety pulled, guns cocked. I had brought one pistol with me; the other was already on the table. Knowing mine contained a fresh clip of bullets I checked the other, which was also loaded. Then I looked over the situation like a suspicious pilot would. The guys were snoring in their bunk beds like logs. They had taken everything off, except their long johns. Bomber jackets and pants of first-rate quality were at the foot of the bed. I wished I could have one of those jackets. But, had they been awake, I certainly would not have asked for it. One and a half years later, a Soviet soldier took my bike without asking. His strong persuasion was the submachine gun slung over his shoulder. Taking a jacket didn't even occur to me; stealing from a P.O.W. would have been a terrible offense. Anyway, there they were, all strong, blond young guys, built like trees. They were happy to have gotten out of it alive. I could tell by the snore. Then I thought that if they really wanted to escape and do me in, they could have done so easily. One simply does not place a guard in the same room with his prisoners. If they would have pounced on top of me in unison, I could have shot only one, at the most. So, I sat there nervously during the whole time. This whole thing was organized by a complete idiot, of which there are plenty in the military.

On the next day we went to inspect the downed bomber's remains. We were amazed at its rich equipment; everything was from the best material. All hydraulic tubing was copper. All instruments were made with good copper alloys. The best was used and lavished on the design. German aircraft were all made from substitutes. Copper was not available since long ago. Also, the multitude of gun emplacements in all directions was amazing, demonstrating how difficult an attack might be when these bombers kept close together in formation. That's all I remember of these two months.

In mid-November, the training started again in another pilot school in Beneschau for one whole day. Meanwhile various instructors evaluated our prowess. I had about half a dozen starts. In the evening we were told to get our belongings together. We were to be transferred again. Wild stories began circulating: "This is it! This is the end. Transfer to the infantry, finally! Transfer to a special rocket plane school!" Another one: "transfer to a fighter school!" Anything could happen, anytime. Although we were far from qualified to begin fighter training, some bureaucrat could have promoted this kind of nonsense.

The next morning, divided into three groups, with one leader each and travel documents, we left toward Dresden and then west until arriving in a Hessian town south of Kassel, named Fritzlar. As usual, we soon got packed into a makeshift barrack constructed from wood. There were only bunks, and everything was dirty. We were so tired that we only wanted to sleep. It was cold. The room had only a small round stove, which only radiated heat when red hot. Guys close to it almost got fried; those further away froze miserably. Guards had to be appointed to keep it in red-hot heat. Miraculously, someone had provided for the coal. Next morning at parade time, as we shivered in the wind, we were assigned to working details and walked to a quarry some two miles away. There we received 10 pound hammers and were told to use our undernourished bodies to split those large rocks apart. Our "breakfast" consisted of some coarse bread and very little jelly, washed down with thin barley coffee. As we marched out, we were already hungry again because of the insufficient calories administered to tone down the appetite. What we would have needed was a pound of ham and eggs, but we could not imagine when in the future this kind of luck would shine on us again. We were just cold, hungry and miserable standing there, poorly clothed for an outdoor job with a 10 pounder, which few could easily lift. No one showed any zeal for hitting the rocks. The small, knocked down pieces were shoved to a landing strip being built for the new jet fighters. A very long surface needed to be perfectly leveled, which no other airport possessed. There we were, some hitting the rocks, others loading them on some primitive, small steel rail cars, which could be dipped for ease of unloading. Others pushed the cars to where the rocks were needed, about a mile away. So it went all day long, ad nauseam. The only thing on our minds was lunch in the warm barracks, a hot meal—the only positive remark one could make about the food. Luncheon in Germany always means the big meal of the day. And then back into the cold, hopeless drizzle or snow flurries. The enormous effort of hitting the rocks all day long met with very disappointing results. One day, an old man showed up with a chewed up pipe in the corner of his mouth. He wanted to show us how to do this comfortably. He picked up a hammer and walked around a huge block of a rock, almost as tall as we were. It took a while until he settled on a spot he wanted to hit; he lifted the hammer about one foot high and let it drop. To our astonishment and consternation, the rock broke apart in the middle—effortlessly! The next followed the same routine. At that pace this old fellow did more than 20 or 30 of us. He wanted to show us exactly where to hit, utilizing split lines in the crystalline structure of the rock, which we did not find, hence we could never do what he did with amusement. With our diminished energies, we thrashed wildly at those things with miniscule results. Luckily, I didn't have to do this for long. Some people were needed to repair those railcars in a shop in downtown Fritzlar. There at least I worked in a warm room, doing mainly welding with oxy-acetylene torches. It was new to me, but I had claimed to be proficient in this (a good training for my later job claims in the U.S.). Once I was in that warm place, they would never get me out of it again. Soon I had mastered some primitive welding skills, and I was familiar with all the other metalworking tasks. Two more buddies hung out with me in this welding shop. One day I observed one guy trying to light a torch when something went wrong. Opening the gas valves directly provided at the torch, one for acetylene and another for oxygen lights an oxy-acetylene torch. I didn't see what he did, but saw a flame crawling slowly and steadily from the torch toward the storage bottle—a bomb-like high pressure container, which can act like a bomb when fire strikes. As I saw the fire, everyone jumped screaming to the exit, while the owner and I jumped to the gas bottle to close the main valve. Just a matter of timing! He got the valve handle before me. We were both kind of pale in our faces. These bleak November/December days with cold, wet, snowy weather, along with our ever- diminishing poor-quality food supply, were depressing. Most people in small towns like Fritzlar had some extra food, either from relatives in the country or from their own garden plots, but the poor soldiers depended entirely on their rations. I suspect many people in the supply chain (who appeared well fed), chiseled away at the poor rations. Farmers, bakers, butchers, military purchasing agents or supply NCO's looked almost as well nourished as American GI's. I guess we must have spent that Christmas season warming our hands over the stove while listening to the bad reports. All fronts were rapidly closing upon Germany proper. It was just a matter of time before the first foreign units would step on German soil. Actually, they were already in East Prussia, and I believe some U.S. units in the Huertgen Forest near Aachen. The assignment in Fritzlar lasted until January, when we returned to Beneschau.

Four or five days later I picked a Bue 181 with a staff sergeant Zink, an instructor, and returned to Neudorf. The black and white landscape below looked depressing, almost lifeless. Upon arrival we were to pack our things to prepare for some immediate action. The eastern front had come so close that on a clear night one could hear rumbling of artillery fire. There was talk about going up in those kites at night to throw grenades at the Soviets. We considered this senseless suicide. According to other rumors, we were to transport the wounded. With our tiny planes—without gas being available for fighter planes? Many people became quite nervous, not knowing what would happen next. The most plausible idea was service in the front lines, to be thrown into the great German meat grinder. But little Hermann got another reprieve: Sgt. Zink picked me to transfer the Bue 181 to Warnemuende north of Rostock at the Baltic Sea … a welcome distance from the rumbling. Seemingly, Zink also had a great interest in leaving Upper Silesia, which was becoming a real hot spot. We were told to look out for Soviet or US fighters on the way. Without German fighters to oppose them, they were hunting freely throughout German territory, hungry for action; I would have been an easy feather in their hat. What would we do if attacked: dive deep over ground and play cat and mouse around hills, forests, etc.? Boarding the Bue 181 together with Zink, I realized that the end was coming and the allies were positioning themselves at the border for the occupation of Germany. Our forces had no more countermeasures available—it was too late. We were to endure what others had planned. I did not understand why our "government" never attempted to settle this war and save millions of lives. But, the sad truth was that we had no government—only the "Fuehrer," a crazy gambler who awaited some last-minute chance to split the allies. On this dark, foreboding January day, we flew to Liegnitz, to move onto Guben south of Berlin the next day. The following morning we continued to Prenzlau northwest of Berlin, and then Neubrandenburg. Before taking off each time, we heard the latest reports about roaming enemy fighters. We did not see any. Flying very low, we took cover over forests wherever possible. On the last day we flew via Guestrow in Mecklenburg to Warnemuende on the Baltic Sea some 67 miles east of Luebeck, not far from Hamburg. Heading toward Rostock to get to Warnemuende, we crossed over the Heinkel aircraft factory, once an enormous installation. Now we saw only bombed-out, flattened buildings. There was apparently still some life left down there, though: As we landed in Warnemuende, we found many other small aircraft lined up. This appeared the last station for many planes once belonging to many pilot schools in the east of Germany. I was sure flight training was over. Now, what was in store for us leftovers? This airport had also housed a pilot school. The buildings were very solid and well kept, everything done in red brick, as is customary in Northern Germany. In Neudorf (apparently initiated during WWII to satisfy the ever-growing need for pilots) there had been only primitive wooden barracks. The increasing enemy air armadas required a German reaction, although that feeble response could never match the allies' grand design. Also, the fast-paced attrition on the German side required more pilots. In the end I was part of the stream of pilots in the pipeline, who could no longer expect an aircraft ready to fly when emerging from the pipe. Enemy planes hovered all over the landscape to find targets. When not finding any, they emptied their bullets at everything crawling below, shooting at any cars that were left, buses, farmers in the field, cows, anything. We went to our quarters, and then to the mess hall. The meal was very disappointing, "take it or leave it"—only boiled potatoes with an undeterminable sauce. I had gone in hungry and left the same way. We had received some colored pieces of paper in the office with printed letters, such as "M" (main meal) and "R" for other bread rations. Losing those pieces would mean losing the food, period. I noticed that this paper could be bought in any stationery shop. The crude letters were made by a rubber stamp. Wondering how I could make a stamp for myself, I found a new potato somewhere and carved it until I produced an "M" exactly like that on the ration slip. With the right paper and inkpad, I was ready to go. The perfect result enabled me to get second portions from then on; my deceit went unnoticed. Since I gave my roommates some extras that evening, we got second portions the next day, which filled us up better. One must know that seconds were not offered. Otherwise, in Romania, I could eat as much as I wanted, but not in Germany. The fun lasted for only a week, after which I saw an extra bull at the chow line examining those stamps very carefully. I had to drop my risky scheme. During that time we were sent to the Heinkel aircraft works, to man several anti-aircraft machine guns—a useless endeavor, since the installation was already demolished. If they were to bomb, it would be a high-level job—no use for a machine gun. With our guns we were very close to the starting point of the landing strip, which was all lawn—no asphalt or concrete, where a sizeable number of very small jet fighters were always positioned. Daily, experienced air force pilots were trained to take off and land with those weird-looking things. Their fuselage was made entirely from wood, and the cockpit was so small that the pilot had to squeeze into it. In front of him were two 20 mm cannons—the only weapons on board. The wings were on top of the fuselage. Above them the gas turbine was mounted, which supplied the thrust to the contraption. Called the "Volksjaeger" (people's fighter), it didn't make a very reliable impression, looking more like a glider than anything else and about the same size. They took off and landed day in, day out with those things. The takeoff noise at full throttle was ear deafening. People were crashing daily, usually on takeoff and when making the first left turn. They regularly fell down like stones, as though the plane didn't have any wings. They lost control without having reached sufficient altitude to bail out. I also suspected that the cockpit was too tiny for a quick exit. They fell so swiftly that there was literally no time to remove the belt and wiggle out of the seat. Something was wrong with the plane's design, which had not been completely tested, but pushed by the leadership to simply get something into the air. Many good pilots were wasted. I must say some of the plane's parameters were very impressive. When buzzing the airfield and pulling up, it shot up easily at an impossible 80 to 90 degree angle and kept going at enormous speed until disappearing as a small speck into the blue yonder. One day the test pilot made a belly landing, simulating loss of wheels. I didn't think landing a wooden box at about 250 mph could succeed, but he did it! I wouldn't have wanted to have to duplicate that feat. While some of the plane's characteristics were fabulous, others were questionable. Naturally, it was too late to change the course of events. By now the allied fighters hovering around those long, paved landing strips were waiting for jet fighters to take off or land. They were then easy prey. Under those conditions the jet pilot didn't have a prayer. This also happened to the famous ace Adolf Galland, leader of all fighter forces, who was lucky to save his life. He got blamed for the demise of the air force's fighter squadrons, which got wiped out by overwhelming enemy bombers and fighters after he had pleaded in vain for building more fighters. Hitler wanted more bombers to still his thirst for vengeance against the British. Galland got demoted from leading all fighter forces to a lowly pilot. But—as we know, Germany was too small a country to take on a prolonged war. Hitler's game was long over; the populace had to pay the price. I saw this one day when we were sent to a small port, normally used only for pleasure craft or fishing boats. There one of the last ships making it through the storm-tossed Baltic to safe ports like Warnemuende was discharging a cargo of human misery. The large liner was filled with refugees from East Prussia. Most of them had been forced to stay at their places to the last minute without warning that the fronts were collapsing and the army was being smashed. Party hacks passed on only what Hitler wanted: "Hold out! Germany has an array of 'miracle' weapons that will totally destroy the enemy." Instead, Soviet forces, overcame them with untold thousands taken to Siberia, killed senselessly—or worse! Here I saw the remnants: those who had miraculously escaped imprisonment and such adverse conditions as weather, lack of food and shelter, days and weeks of exposure—until finally making it on board. Many had to leave loved ones behind to a terrible fate at the hands of a vengeful enemy, whose stated policy was cruelty and whose aim was to clear the land of German people, to make it look like Siberia. That they accomplished. We had to carry most of those people from the ship—many wounded, with frost damages, clothes tattered, all emaciated. Most could hardly walk straight. Meanwhile I noted some party hacks in neatly pressed bright yellow/brown uniforms, surrounded by delicate French soap aroma. One looked more like a pig than a human being. They tried to direct the traffic, but no one seemed to listen. I glanced back and forth between the victims and the "leaders." Here was the staunch party faithful, who, by joining the party's inner circle, reaped the benefits of its ascent. They got the good jobs in government, so that more and more extreme party programs could be installed. Lacking original thinking, ethics or morals, they obeyed the "Fuehrer" blindly, and now I saw these criminals, who had fattened themselves at the expense of the silent, inactive majority, who always pays for the reckless opportunists. I think at that point I resolved to neither attend political rallies nor join any party in the future. While the party hacks may have felt out of place that day, it is possible that they had prepared their exits some time ago by arranging other identities, foreign currencies, etc. Those impressions affected me deeply. Doomsday was sure to begin.

END OF WAR AT HERMANN GOERING GUARD DIVISION

We soon noticed changes coming. We were all picked for something. But where would they direct us? The bet was the eastern front, where an acute need for warm bodies existed, to be expended at a horrific pace. Also, by transferring many units from the west to the east, the leadership tried to stem the red tide and rather let the Anglo-Americans advance into Germany. Finally we received our orders: travel to Reinickendorf, a northwest Berlin suburb, base for the "Hermann Goering" guard regiment. Like Hitler, Hermann Goering early in the regime had initiated a guard, which grew into a corps during the war, similar to what happened with Hitler's "SS-Leibstandarte." The Goering unit had grown from a parachute unit to a fully motorized division with parachute capability. My fate now apparently was to be part of Goering's guard unit's last rites. I received all regalia: parachutist's outfit, a very practical combination of an overlong jacket, which reached to just above the knee and had handy pockets all over, and pants. One could place more than half a dozen wine bottles into the camouflage-colored jacket's pockets without any strain. The parachutist's helmet was different from the regular army issue. I hated to put it on. I got permission to go home, but had to return the same night. It was just an hour by subway. Traffic was still functioning, but on the surface there was little left. The subways were also used as bomb raid shelters. The people looked terribly tattered and worn out. Many wounded soldiers testified to the increased losses the forces were taking now. On my way home, my documents were checked at least three times. Every soldier on the street had to carry a permit for leaving his unit. Without it, one was immediately suspect of desertion, which carried automatic hanging, then sometimes on the spot, without trial. The military police were widely hated. Because they wore an oval, chrome-covered brass shield, fastened by a chain around the neck, they were secretly called "chain dogs" (Kettenhunde). They were to maintain discipline in an otherwise disintegrating army. Berlin was swarming with them. My visit with the parents was to be the last before war's end. We discussed my staying on and hiding, but one cannot do this in Germany, ever! Some people had seen my arrival; had I remained at home, they would surely have denounced me to the authorities. Why should I have a privilege they can't have? I would have hidden 'til war's end if I could have, for sure. But then, no one knew when the end would come. There were rumors about negotiations with the western allies to reach a separate peace treaty. If true, the war could drag on another year or two! I definitely had to return to Reinickendorf. On the next day, Ellen Mosebach came from Oranienburg. She was frightened about her future. What if the Soviets invaded across the Oder River, encircling Berlin? Should she remain there with her mother or move west, where they had relatives in Frisia close to Emden at the North Sea? She must not have had communications with her Dad recently and had to make decisions on her own. Perhaps her mother was out of her wits, incapable of initiating any action. Some people also believed things would resolve themselves, but they couldn't figure out how! Usually, the majority would be caught in the events as they unfolded ... millions of passive victims. I advised Ellen to prepare for evacuation, take the most valuable things, but mainly the necessities, and hunt for shelter further west. I am still glad to have said that. Women were known to be terribly abused by the invading Soviet troops. Most suffered horrible traumas, or worse. With the father a police officer and party member, the family would have been thrown out of their house. I think they never saw him again. I could leave the compound briefly to be with Ellen. We could only go to a small park nearby, where other couples were already trying to be with each other before the inexorable move to the frontline would take place. We looked for something like a café, but in vain. Ellen became very emotional, and I noticed she must have been fond of me. But the encounter's circumstances did not support anything like a romantic tête-à-tête. She was also quite shook up by the decisions she would have to make when returning to Oranienburg. On the other hand, I must admit that I was also concerned with my own immediate fate. As usual, we were told nothing until a command came, and off we went. Ellen and I had a tough time parting from each other, not knowing if and how each of us would survive the last convulsions of the "Third Reich." I felt very sad and helpless and would have rather liked to help Ellen and to see that she was comfortable. That was the last I ever saw of her, but I know she survived. After the war in late November 1945, she surfaced around Leer near Emden in Northwestern Germany. I returned to the barracks, which were beautiful, solid brick buildings, for one more day in Berlin.

Early the next morning we were driven to the "Anhalter" railway station in downtown Berlin. All we had was what a front soldier needs—mainly weapons, ammo and bare necessities. All other things I had carried were now with my parents. The mess tins were filled with rations and cigarettes; they even handed out some chocolate. These kind of delicacies were reserved for flying personnel and submariners only. They must have hoarded this for Hermann Goering, same as he hoarded and stole so many other things throughout Europe. In these days one no longer heard of him. Hitler never forgave him his inability to win the air war over Germany. They must have dealt with each other more like spoiled brats than responsible statesmen carrying the fate of their country on their shoulders. One never heard of industrial capacities or production rates in publications. Their problem was just that. There was an alliance of the largest industrial powers focused on Germany's destruction. Their very efficient production outclassed Germany's by a ratio of at least 3:1. The U.S. alone had large automotive facilities set up to produce millions of vehicles per year, dwarfing Germany's industry. They possessed very refined industrial engineering techniques—then mostly ignored in Germany. Those January days were cold, snowy, dark and hopeless. We went to Anhalter station to trains headed south. It seemed we were to leave Berlin. Initiatives were underway to make a last stand in and around that city—as if there was anything to defend at all! The inner city was already a mountain of rubble, and the other parts didn't look much better. I wondered where all those people slept and cooked their meager meals. Most children had long gone to the countryside. (I knew Marianne stayed with aunt Ulli in the Black Forest in the town of Lahr.) The adults had to man the factories, located mainly in the large cities. The facilities also had to be constantly repaired because of bomb damage. Ulli had left Frankfurt/Oder, which is east of Berlin, at least one year before after a heavy bombing raid. She had two or three children. Her in-laws set her up near their place. Lahr was small and never got bombed. Ulli was lucky she didn't have to undergo Soviet occupation and related hazards. Slowly we pulled out of the switchyard, where we boarded and inched south. There was an enormous amount of repair being done to the yard and the railroad tracks to the south. These facilities were main targets for bombers. Not functioning, that freight could not reach the points were it was needed; it was as simple as that. After a few hours, we came to Koenigswusterhausen, normally a trip of about half an hour. Next were Luebben and Cottbus, then Sorau, Sagan and Sprottau. Crossing the Neisse River, we now headed toward Sprottau and the Oder River. It was evening by now, and I felt like getting ready for a nice meal. Naturally, there was none. We headed east perhaps another 20 miles, until being ordered to get off the train and assemble. One could hear noises in the air like sewing machines; persistent like hornets or wasps, they never died down. We quickly moved away from the tracks. Soviet planes appeared to be in the air to find targets on the tracks. They were very primitive larger bi-planes, very slow, but well provided with armor plates from below, and impossible to shoot down by rifle or machine gun fire. The Soviets used tens of thousands of those by night, only to find targets of convenience—which they always found. Suddenly there were explosions behind us near the tracks, followed by a hit at the engine. Just like that, a valuable locomotive was gone and the tracks blocked. We were lucky to have moved off quickly.

Continuing to the next village, we heard sporadic artillery fire from the east near the Oder River. An uncomfortable, cold barn served for overnight stay. We moved closer together to get some heat from the next body, but it didn't help much. Because of the cold and anxiety about the next day there was little sleep that night. The rumbling from the east and engine noise above didn't help. Once in a while there were explosions and antiaircraft fire. So, we were close to the action.

Next morning we marched along the highway in loose formation. All kinds of vehicles were transporting supplies. Other military units moved in the same direction. From the east came transports with wounded. At times we could see prisoners of war being marched west. We were always on the lookout for "jabos" (Jagdbomber or enemy ground support fighters). They were dangerous, because the highway was so exposed. I always made up my mind what to do immediately when we saw them approaching. Since the landscape always changed between fields, meadows, brooks, forests, hills, valleys and villages, buildings, bridges, etc., I got prepared each minute for a different, explosive dash. Once at the end of a forest and marching into the open, we saw several Jabos approaching from the east, ready to strike. We split into the underbrush and took cover. They didn't hit us, but we heard gunfire and explosions behind us. So it went for a while. After an hour, several burning trucks were on the road. Soldiers, dead, and half-dead, were being carried away. Then we turned into a small, unpaved road and, after a while, reached a hamlet in the woods. Here we got introduced to the battalion commander. He wore the same garb we did. We were the reserves to fill out his losses. Pretty soon a sergeant picked me and a handful of others to lead us to join the company deployed further toward the Oder River—and the front.

The situation was desperate. The Soviets had rushed up to the river. They literally had smashed everything ahead of them. German units posted there finally were so weak, small in numbers and lacking armor and artillery that they could no longer muster a halfway organized resistance. Now the Oder separated the two foes. The job of the Soviets was to ferry troops over the river to create a bridgehead, i.e. anchor their troops on the opposite side, which was to be gradually enlarged by pushing relentlessly, so that entire armies could be stationed. They then would be used to break out with their armored units to strike deep into German heartland. In this bridgehead they would build several pontoon bridges to transfer vast amounts of material to the other side of the river. Those bridges were defended by an impressive amount of antiaircraft guns of all calipers. Not that this was so important now—there was hardly any German fighter in the air to interdict bridge traffic. We were located somewhat north of Glogau. The enemy was already forcing a bridgehead further north in Frankfurt/Oder to prepare for the final assault. It would take several weeks before they would complete these preparations.

In our section, things were relatively quiet, although artillery shelling, grenade launches, grenade and rocket fire, etc. could occur at any time. We were working constantly on defensive reinforcements: more ditches, bunkers, machine gun emplacements, etc. Work never stopped. And there was guard duty in addition. We had to be very careful when moving around. The enemy had lots of sharp-shooters watching us, which was a real pest. If we got to a spot where the guys across the river could see us, it meant getting shot. We had several such casualties, but the worst danger was the large caliper weapons. One was always exposed. Our company slowly but surely lost about 30% in one month. Most were wounded, but some dead. It became daily life. I had to learn quickly from the old hands how to react to the different noises. There was the "Silesian," (he spoke with a Silesian "tongue", bordering on the Polish), who was not called by any other name. The Knights' Cross to the Iron Cross was hidden around his neck. He had gone through the entire Russian campaign into Russia and back, and it showed. The prototype of the German "Landser," he had seen it all and survived against all odds. He had confirmed kills of twelve T-34 tanks, done with a shoulder-fired rocket. At the time this was an act of unbelievable courage. One had to let the tank come as close as possible—for a sure success within 40 to 60 feet. Since the aiming devices were very crude, all depended on a good, effective hit at the first try. When a spot was hit without a total kill, then our poor guy was a dead duck—same in case of a miss. The rocket launch would be seen immediately, which meant all fire of the opponents would be directed toward the hapless launcher. What a gamble! These weapons were used against tanks, since heavy anti-tank cannons became more and more scarce. I didn't see any within some distance. This made sense, because regular Soviet tanks couldn't swim through the fast-flowing river, which was fed by the beginning spring melt. As far as I knew, Soviets also did not then have armored amphibian vehicles.

So, I had to quickly take some practical courses from the Silesian and to a lesser degree from Arthur (Atze) Assmann. There were discharges of Howitzers far away. That meant: watch out—perhaps a load is coming in soon (5-10 seconds). Then we actually heard the noise of incoming shells. If it was high up, one didn't have to take cover lying down (if in the open). Those made a swishing sound—they were gone. If they came toward you, the sound was more threatening. That meant: take cover. If the hit was close, one best jumped into the crater forthwith. If a Howitzer fired again with the same setting, it never hit the same crater. Then there were the tank cannons, of which the Soviets had a tremendous arsenal. They used them almost at will and to hunt single soldiers. They had no parabolic trajectory and were nasty. Therefore, one heard only "ratsch"—"boom" in close succession, with almost no time to take cover. It was especially dangerous if in the open and no trench or suitable cover could be had. We called them "ratsch—booms." Then there were the grenade launchers. When they were fired, there was only a "plop." Luckily, they traveled on a steep trajectory, allowing time to observe the incoming load. They made a higher sound. While one was usually safe in a trench, to be in the open meant disaster. Among different ammunitions were some which dug into the ground, making craters. Others exploded close to the ground, making cover useless. And there were rockets, launched in a distance with tremendous hullabaloo, and one could observe the trajectory. Not used much in our section, their purpose was to strike a massive blow to an entire limited area, wiping out everything alive. Whenever some of these loads were thrown our way, I simply imitated what the Silesian or Atze did—they usually explained later what it was. This is how I became an experienced soldier, learning how to keep my skin un-punctured. We were not located at a point or section where major actions were going on or planned. Apparently the Soviets had to straighten out their supply lines after their earlier, huge advances. They must now look for suitable places for creating bridgeheads. Definitely, no advances were planned in our section by our side. Since there were few heavy weapons and no mobile forces, including armored units, our goal was to keep the Soviets from penetrating across the river. It became difficult one night, when suddenly they let loose with everything on our section concentrating mainly on the trench closest to the river. We quickly retreated into the second and third to await the end of the carnival or a signal from a few fellows left to observe the scene. They fired the usual flares, flooding the width of the river with bright magnesium light. After some twenty minutes it stopped, and we rushed forward. We realized it was a gamble. Perhaps the enemy just waited to send more fire. In our case, they came with about twenty boats. Our artillery wiped out half of them before they came close, and the others got grenade, machine gun, and shoulder-fired rockets fire until they had enough and returned. I wondered what they wanted—they may have been probing if there was defense on our side. They had to determine the easiest point for crossing the river. We didn't think it was in our section; there were no extensive road systems on the opposite side. To mount a forced river crossing and build up a bridgehead, good transport facilities, including railway links, would have been needed.

Totally exhausted, we were pulled out again and had to march back to where we came from. Another army unit took over our section. Marching back to our village, we got attacked constantly by fighters. Although things went more easily, since much of our ammo was spent and I lost about 30 pounds, it was obvious what was about to happen. The Russians would enlarge their bridgehead over the next two weeks, until they had a few armored armies positioned and fully supplied, to spearhead an advance into central Germany. The question was whether Americans or Russians would move the fastest. Again, the overriding concern was for us to avoid being taken prisoners. When the Russians would break out of the bridgehead, they would roll ahead, outflanking us to their north. The danger was that their units directed north to protect their flanks would interfere with our path of retreat. It remained to be seen who would be faster, unless some stupid gave the order to defend to the last man. But I trusted that our officers were more enlightened than that. They had to protect their own skin. My platoon leader and company commander, both from the reserve, not professional soldiers, were from around Frankfurt and married—a teacher and an architect. So, after another two hard weeks of digging, guard duty and ducking ordinances, we awoke with the horizon to the south being ablaze. We knew that meant that the Soviets had broken out of the bridgehead. Meanwhile, it was the end of March and the air was milder. What would we do now? Sure enough, we had to pick up everything and start marching in the middle of the night, hoping no one would cut us off from our designated direction. One could hear by the moving battle noise and lights that everything on the German side got smashed. We hoped some units still found the time and means to retreat in order. Marching as fast as we could, we were always being harassed by fighters. Sometimes we heard light fire from the south, but never had to develop battle formation. Scouts were out to the south protecting our route; we were not bothered from the rear. They first had to gain this side of the Oder River before pursuing us. After about 12 hours of moving at a fast pace, we came to a smaller river. The bridges were still standing. Crews were ready to blow them up. It would give us some respite from the pursuers. We marched into the night. There seemed to be no attempt to establish resistance at that small river (Bober). We were in the Sagan/Sorau area and moving toward the Neisse River. This is a different Neisse river than that in Upper Silesia, where the Neudorf pilot school was located. After the war it was to become the border between Poland and Germany, separating all of Silesia from Germany. After marching another two or three hours, we reached a village where we stayed overnight. At last some hay, good food and a few hours sleep. The villagers shared whatever they had left; we should have it, not the Russians. We assembled before daybreak for milk and bread and continued toward the Neisse River, which we crossed in the early afternoon, moving slightly north where a section was assigned to us. The new resistance line seemed to be the Neisse River, the last obstacle before central Germany—and Europe—was fully open for the final Soviet advance.

The next North/South river was the mighty Elbe. But when the Soviets would reach that river, the war would be long finished. Then it would only be a mopping up operation. There we were at the last line of resistance, but there was not much of a line. We were a much-reduced force. The daily attrition had left only half. Some young guys were added now, but this was far from our original number. A company had 120 to 150 men, and each platoon about one third of that. We were now about 30, including the additions. Luckily, the "Silesian" and Atze were still with me. I no longer need to look at them to find out what to do: it had become routine. Now more troops trickled in daily, as we dug in fast along the fast-flowing and deep river, which was roughly 400 to 450 feet wide at our section. Both banks were covered with willows and shrubs—not too good. First, we cut down everything on the east bank, which was difficult, since chainsaws were not yet available. A few tools, which came from the adjacent villages, were still insufficient. We had to work through the night in shifts; some villagers helped us dig trenches, but there was not enough time to accomplish much. Lack of barbed wire, mines, construction timber and material also precluded a thorough job. Soon the Russians arrived and settled on the other side. Some tried to go into the river to scout out our side, but had to retreat from our fire. Since they didn't try to cross the river immediately in our section, the front stabilized again along the river. We could expect the same kind of warfare we had gone through at the Oder River. The Soviets would pull up all their heavy equipment and engineering units and then select a suitable crossing point at their leisure. Until that time it was trench digging, barbed wire stringing, mine planting and evading the never-ending fire from ground and air. It was desperate just to sit, work and wait for the inevitable. Too weak and lacking heavy weapons, we could not think of making forays into enemy territory. Daily casualties were unavoidable. Harassment fire continued day and night. They didn't seem to count their ammo. One of our more dangerous tasks was to recover casualties, dead or wounded, and carry them to the rear. That was usually combined with carrying chow or ammo to the front line. When I walked back, it was first trench, then a wooded area that provided some cover from being seen. Some light artillery pieces were hidden here. Coming out into the open after about one mile, one could see civilians working on a secondary resistance line—unenthusiastically, since they knew that, once the

Soviets crossed the last river, no trench of theirs could stop them. Usually, around there we found a truck or horse-drawn carriage to pick up our loads. The nearby battalion command post harbored chow and whatever else needed carrying forward—sometimes bottles of wine or cigars for the company chief. Mail deliveries were a thing of the past. There was communication equipment, and I heard that the Americans were crossing the Rhine. Apparently there was still phone communication with the regiment, etc. All kinds of wires were visible. While there was still a semblance of military organization, the question was for how long? I figured that, after the Russians would cross our river, we would be dispersed by events beyond our control.

After about two weeks we were pulled out to return as reserve unit. Some reserve was always available in defensive positions to throw manpower at any penetrations that could occur. Also, we could sleep for a change and wash our clothes. I think our smell in those days must have been horrifying. We didn't notice it any longer. The "Silesian" never washed or changed socks, but wore them until they fell off his feet. The feet we couldn't see—a mess of smelly crud. When the socks fell off in tatters, he pulled out another pair and put them on his feet, which lasted another month or so. Meanwhile, he arranged for another pair—those were the essentials for him. One thing he was afraid of was to be caught by the Russians. His decorations, and list of what they were for, were in his pay book. He told of having been a POW once for a while and of escaping again—two attributes to which the Soviets would not take kindly. Everyone was terrified of being taken prisoner—it would be far better to get hit. I thought I would do everything in my power to resist being taken, but, rather than musing about this, I decided to leave it in limbo, to be decided when the time would come. At the battalion, seeing some SS officers talking with our guys, I concluded we were neighbors to some SS outfits. They usually had better supplies and first choice of equipment. Perhaps we also got something from the same line.

One night, as we were fast asleep, general quarters was called to be ready in five minutes, and off it was to the front, which was about two miles ahead. There was nasty shelling from across the river. We were told "Ivan" had made it across with some force and had to be thrown back. "Ivan" was the common designation for anything Soviet. We joined with our troops at the defense line. All of us had hand grenades and the usual, including flares, bazookas, etc. We heard our artillery opening up and off we went toward the break-in. There was enemy artillery fire, poorly aimed. They may not have known the situation. Soon there were enemy flares. You fall to the ground, make yourself small and glide forward. Then you see muzzle fire and you hit it quickly with a few rounds. Then you roll like a ball to the left or right to protect yourself from incoming gunfire. Then you get close and throw grenades, one, two or more, like everyone else, and suddenly a whistle blows and you get up firing like a madman. Apparently there weren't too many left: whoever wasn't dead or hurt had made it into the river. As dawn approached—a foggy morning—we saw the situation. They had made it across with some boats—perhaps 50 to 60 Ivans. There were about 30 dead and a number of wounded. We had lost maybe—well, I don't recall those details, but it was costly. To me each one was too high a price to pay. We left again toward the rear amidst increased artillery fire. At last we had shown there was someone. This showed they were starting to cross the river.

It was mid-April by now, and I found myself near the small town of Bad Muskau. The final assault could start any minute. In the village and in the countryside, early flowers were appearing—a sign of hope, but I admit that they had little impact, with our preoccupations regarding our fates. Early one day we heard heavy fire from the south, always a sure sign of major action. With all the associated air traffic around, we knew what was up. Since we were in the reserve, we saw the SS units gathering as they emerged from their camouflaged positions. It was a large, impressive-looking armored unit—perhaps one of the last that was fully equipped and trained. Passing us in a hurry, they were to stop the bridgehead, but accomplished nothing. As they proceeded on the road, the Soviet fighter-bombers arrived wave after wave. We saw some fighters coming down, but also many hits and explosions. I guess they never arrived there as a useful fighting unit. We could hear that "Ivan" made progress. Within three days the bridgehead almost got increased up to where we were. So, what were we waiting for? They would break out in huge numbers and would stop only when they decided, to get their logistics straightened out. We couldn't stop them. The bridgehead died down for a few days—the quiet before the storm. One day, the noise started again, and we could hear the progress toward west. Discussing that in bewilderment, we received orders to get ready, and we moved quickly toward west. We could be cut off easily if we didn't retreat. We packed the essentials—food, ammo and grenades—and walked as fast as we could, regardless of our units behind us at the front line. I neither knew where to, nor did I have a map. Now we had to be careful. Scouts were marching ahead and on the sides. When there was a forest, we stayed close to take cover against fighters that bothered us constantly. We were lucky not to have trucks, which would have required paved road. Those were dangerous to use. We checked each village carefully before approaching—there was nothing we could be sure of anymore. Then, in the afternoon it happened. We got fire from a village ahead of us. A light unit of the Russians was first. If we didn't throw them out, we would be cut off from the west—disaster! I could see now that our commanders were as eager as we were to head west. Communications with other units must have ceased by now—the company was on its own. After resting a while, we got our orders. My platoon was to walk through the woods around the hamlet and attack from the west. The others came from north and east. A gap was left open for Ivan to retreat, so he would not get desperate. We didn't want to get bogged down. As we developed our advance in the usual way—walking in widely drawn out and staggered lines—we were soon caught in infantry fire and also heard fire from where the other platoons attacked. Then our machine gun opened up and rockets were launched. Meanwhile, I was as close as 150 feet to the first building and could make out some targets. Those now kept retreating toward the rear. It seemed to be too much, and they didn't receive reinforcements—our lucky day. After another hour resistance ceased. We saw Ivan retreating hastily toward south—mission accomplished with only minor casualties. But at this point nobody cared. We couldn't report to anyone, and there were no replacements. Afterward we quickly moved further west. More Ivans were expected soon, probably with armor, etc. Meanwhile, our survival seemed to depend mainly upon swift movements through the woods and good observation and prediction of Soviet moves. For the night we had some hay and straw; early in the morning we continued our march. Not much was visible or audible from the main battle, at least not to me. Oblivious to our destination, I just followed orders. Luckily, so far I thought they were reasonable. The move toward west was the only fair thing to do. We couldn't move north, having heard Ivan was surrounding Berlin and was about to close access from the west. I thought of poor Ellen and her parents, but not long. I was much too busy. To move south made even less sense. There, an entire population of Czech people was waiting to take their anger out on anything German. My dream was to make it to the American line and then get demobilized. I was oblivious to any Allied agreements stipulating that U.S. or British troops had to return all German soldiers, who arrived from the Soviet zone of operations in the east, to the Soviets. But many days of hair-raising experiences still awaited me before coming close to that possibility. A few days later we came close to a road trap set by SS field police. After they negotiated with our officers, we were included in some task force. At the time, most local commanding generals had lost contact with their divisions, regiments etc., of which, in most cases, there was little left. Short of going home and forgetting the war, they got busy collecting free-floating units and stragglers, wanting to protect their turf to the last minute by organizing fighting units. Soldiers found without valid papers, i.e. pay book and marching orders, were hung on the spot on the nearest tree, utility pole, or whatever, without court- or similar procedures. There was no time for those minor bureaucratic details. We tried to make sure not to lose contact with our gang (Haufen in German), suspecting it would mean the end. We now had arrived at the Spree River, which flows toward and through Berlin. It originates not far from where we were, in the mountains to the south, which separate Bohemia from Germany.

Our nameless new outfit got organized quickly and was ordered to defend the Spree River line. Apparently some Nazi chieftain had the last ditch glorious idea of having a line on the map defended. We weren't happy about it and, from what I could figure; our officers didn't like it either. No positions were prepared, and Ivan was close—a joke, but a potentially bloody one for us. All we could do was wait for chaos to strike, when Ivan would start plastering our "defensive line." The first to run were always the party hacks, generals, and field police, who were much more concerned about their health than we could ever be. Once Ivan had broken through with his armored penetration units, they would mostly look for command posts. Those types knew that very well. The disaster followed soon. Suddenly tanks appeared on the horizon, visibly overcoming us. There was no resistance. We fired a few shots to keep Russian infantry away from us, but there were so many, and there was so much rolling equipment that it was pathetic. Our officers decided to retreat. We marched all day without a stop. Passing through a large airport with an aircraft factory, we saw hundreds of abandoned brand new jet engines. Good bounty for the Soviets! I wondered what was being done about all those complex records needed for building those new engines and aircraft.

Our group by now had turned into a real "gang," with the overnight disappearance of two guys, who were from the area. One of them had told me that his father was an old communist party member, implying that he would join his father in welcoming the Soviets and build a new "socialist" Germany from scratch! Things were sure changing fast! We never saw those two again. All day long we had to avoid probing Ivan forces. At times there were exchanges of fire and sometimes light armor chased us. All we could do was to fade quickly into brush and woods. Fortunately the area had plenty of forests and small hamlets. A day or two later we again ran up against a field police trap—the usual thing. Still hell-bent to save the country, they were putting up a defense to prevent the Soviets from reaching the Elbe River. By now we were near the Kamenz-Grossenhein area north of Dresden. We sensed that these characters had neither seen a front line nor had an inkling of what is needed to wage a war. Eager to do something, they chose the easiest: catch the stupids and make them confront Ivan until they could withdraw safely with a truckload of goodies and civilian clothes plus new identifications, to safer places out west. Quite a few soldiers were gathered this way. They combed the whole area. They had no heavy equipment, just rifles, etc. If we really attacked, we would become mincemeat before even coming close to Ivan's lines. Well, this is what really happened. My last advance toward Russian lines was around April 25. From the beginning, we didn't have a prayer. There were all kinds of artillery, rockets, grenade launches, anti-tank guns, fighter-bombers, etc. I mean, as soon as we developed our units and came within half a mile, it began hitting us relentlessly. Casualties mounted, and there were no provisions to take care of wounded. When withdrawal was finally signaled, we gladly jumped from cover to cover back to where we had come from, only that some didn't make it. Now Ivan advanced, and we had our hands full. It started to rain and Ivan fell behind. We shook them loose, but they kept coming without stopping. I was delegated to the rear guard—the fellow who watched the back against nasty surprises. While the main troop marched fast to make distance, the rear guard watched what was coming from behind, what kind of units, motorized, armored, and would they pursue with vigor or not? You sometimes got into firefights to stop them; then we disengaged. I was with Atze; the "Silesian" had vanished from sight. I don't remember what happened to him. We observed the Ivans as they had taken cover, and then we withdrew through the woods, walking gingerly to avoid breaking twigs—their noise alone can give you away. Then we quickly crossed some acreage—always a big danger. First, we watched if there were any movements—nothing. Walking in the middle of the opening, we heard an anti tank gun opening up. I don't know where these guys had come from. We hit the dirt—grenade about 80 feet from us. Up we jumped as though bitten by tarantulas. We couldn't believe it: they hunted us with an anti tank gun—not too easy, since Atze and I were running, jumping and ducking for our lives. There were still some 250 yards to the cover of a piece of forest. We made it, but gasping for air, covered with dirt and sweat. That was terrible, and we quickly proceeded for a hamlet with a large estate—apparently a winery. We lost touch with our outfit. In the winery there were thousands of bottles of wine: welcome bounty for Ivan. We each stuck four or six bottles into the various pockets of our parachute outfit. We looked funny loaded with ammo, grenades, guns and wine bottles. No time to drink: we had to stay alert. Attempting to make contact with our people again, we continued to the next hamlet, where we could not evade two big Mercedes staff automobiles on the commons (Dorfanger). An SS general with all his impressive regalia signaled us to approach him. As is the military custom, we reported who we were, what outfit, and that we were on rear guard duty trying to catch up with our people, that we had contact with Soviet antitank forces and that Ivan, generally, was losing no time in following us. Red-faced, the guy implied we were deserters and looked like such, forcing us to drop all our precious bottles. Accompanied by six to ten tough-looking SS guys who were armed to their teeth with guns cocked, this idiot had such a tantrum that I feared for my neck. We didn't have chance. This war hero then showed us the way to the front (where we came from). Red in his face, he yelled as though talking to a whole regiment, that we must proceed there to hold off the enemy. If he would ever see us again, we would be hanged! Perhaps he had had too much of the white wine he made us drop. Losing that wine was a pity. The trouble was Atze and I were much more impressed by Ivan than that crazy SS general, who seemed to have lost his followers by having all of them butchered by Ivan. What to do? We didn't want to return toward Ivan. From afar, we watched him ranting and raving with other stragglers also; surrounded by the few fellows we had seen. There was no chain of field police. Making a large walk around the hamlet through the woods might keep us from getting caught. That's what we did—but very carefully, and looked out as if looking for Ivan. Guns were cocked. If anyone wanted to stop us again, we knew what to do! In those times, one had to defend even against one's own. About an hour later we made contact with our outfit. We now became an entity in search of our destiny, left alone by our people and Ivan. For some reason, we swung more south and aimed at Dresden, arriving there around the beginning of May. Before that, I must relate a speech by some colonel at the last advance, who tried to tell us why we were still fighting. He explained point blank that the German government had concluded a separate peace treaty with the western allies and Germany would from now on fight together with them to drive Ivan back to Siberia. Were this true, we would have had to find the western allies. I mean, we were all so confused at the time that only one motto mattered: get some food and protect your skin and your buddies! And then we entered Dresden! Having heard earlier that the "Fuehrer" had fallen (KIA) at the head of his troops in Berlin and that Admiral Doenitz was now head of state didn't impress us as much as wandering through miles of rubble—not a soul to be seen. The population had disappeared. In 1941, I had been stationed in Dresden for three months, but now I recognized nothing—a tragedy. All that was left was to walk through this rubble as fast as possible. We had never heard about this massive bomber attack before. Because the Nazi propaganda machine always de-emphasized the damages, we had no inkling of that catastrophe. Since we knew by then that Germany was finished, it didn't add to our concerns in general terms. We didn't see any people, so we were not musing about them in detail.

We just took step after step in a direction, hoping we would be all right. The steps were leading away from Ivan for now.

We no longer moved with guards, since Russians were no longer in sight. About 20 buddies were left, headed by an officer. We still had some kind of legitimacy, which let us withdraw supplies whenever we came across military supply depots. South of Dresden we moved toward Freital and Dippoldiswalde. I'll never forget those names. We came upon some released prisoners dressed in striped prison clothes, who were even more emaciated and apathetic than we were. There was no time to talk to them. It is just a flash in my memory. Then we moved slowly into the extensive wooded area bordering on Bohemia to the south of Dippoldiswalde. Our leader must have had this planned long ago: disappear into the woods of the mountains and move west to resurface somewhere in Franconia or Hesse—where he was from! I didn't mind. I think the last supply depot we found was in Dippoldiswalde—around May 5 or 6.

As we made it into the woods, we now finally saw Ivan swarming all over. All paved and unpaved roads were now unsafe. One day we watched from a top of a hillock as a Russian motorized company moved in on a hamlet down below, using motorbikes with sidecars, three soldiers to a bike. They crossed open fields, dismounted and moved slowly toward the first houses. As they did that, one or two of our gang started firing at Ivan—who was about 150 soldiers strong, against our 20 or so. They had lots of equipment and machine guns and ammo on their bikes. We quickly jumped these two stupids and stopped the nonsense. We no longer cared about fighting—only about a way west. Since we knew now there was no longer a chance to march on roads, we started walking only at night through open terrain, guided only by the compass. It certainly didn't make us much mileage per night. During the third night or so we saw wild shooting around us in all directions: lots of tracer ammo, rifles, machine guns, artillery, everything. It appeared more like fireworks than battle action. We thought then that peace had broken out for Ivan—not for us. We had no idea about our status. It could only be an armistice with unconditional surrender, meaning, for example, the allied forces could do with us whatever they wished. It must have been May 9, the day Admiral Friedeburg signed the instruments of unconditional surrender. We discussed it briefly, decided what the shooting was about, and realized we were completely surrounded. For the last two days we had no longer noticed German soldiers, groups or units. It looked like we had made some unique moves, which under the circumstances would be essential for keeping out of trouble. So we stumbled along through the woods …

PRISONER OF WAR

As morning's dawn slowly crept up around us, we found ourselves in a dense 20-30 year old fir forest. Those are planted in neat rows in Germany. The ground was covered with dry twigs. The trunks were not totally cleared of branches. So we had to fight stems, branches above in the darkness, and twigs below. We tried to be as quiet as possible so as not to alert any guards who might be near. Dawn slowly turned into a foggy morning, which takes a while. If the reader has stumbled through a foggy night and seen the daylight rise, he knows how endlessly slow that can be. As the light increased through the fog one could increasingly discern more tree contours, buddies, first close, then further apart. That morning, as the light increased, we realized to our horror that we were close to a tent or two. Then we saw more and more—a sea of tents, neatly erected: a Russian bivouac! No time to count those hundreds of tents. I could make out snoring sounds emanating from the tents. What was going on? We had landed in the middle of a Russian encampment, but how? In the German army there were always guards, day and night, peace or war, Sundays and Holidays. At least one should see some Ivans coming out to relieve themselves! But even that didn't happen. So we quickly went on our knees and crawled for about 100 yards until the forest provided us cover again. Anyone seeing us would have been the end. Opening up on them was impossible: there were at least a thousand soldiers against our 20 lost souls. And our goal was walking west—not to shoot—as long as we could help it. That was one of the luckiest days of my life—like being newly born. As the day progressed we put some distance between the bivouac and our group until we stopped at noon to rest and refresh. There was a spring in the area. The water tasted delicious. Food was just bread, and there was hardly any left. We now had pow-wows daily with the boss, who included us in decision-making. We had noticed increased traffic on the roads and once in a while patrols also. We decided to add one more night of strenuous walking to our pilgrimage. Next morning we wound up on a wooded bluff, overlooking a road in the valley. First there were some hours of sleep without our shoes on—a welcome relaxation—followed by bread and spring water. Our rations were just about used up; I had one end of a bread and half a tin of lard left—good for energy, but no good without something else. Our gas mask cans were depleted long ago. Clearly, something had to happen. It was too dangerous to venture near a house or hamlet, which were swarming with Ivans, who were looting all over (and worse) by now. We had never seen looting before, which was apparently condoned by their commanders. As we scratched our heads about what to do, a German soldier came walking along below, heading west—our direction. He just had his military issue bread bag with canteen slung around his leather belt and sported a white armband around his left arm. He walked briskly ahead and made about four times as much mileage as we could at night, while expending far less energy. That's important when supplies run out, although one could survive for 10 to 20 more days without food as long as water was around. Anyway—that looked strange, and we wondered how long that poor slob would remain free. He had no weapons; even his bayonet was gone. A German soldier without a bayonet? Unheard of! We almost had to wear it in bed as well as this useless steel helmet—a heavy burden at best. We decided a long time ago: what use is a steel helmet when you get it in the belly? It kept us from being quick and on the ball. So, when we discarded the helmets, the officers did too. Now, there came another soldier with the same white decoration, followed by three or four more guys. All were walking happily toward west. When one of us went down to scout about this phenomenon, he reported that Ivan let everyone walk wherever he wished and did not take prisoners. With more and more soldiers parading past us, we decided together that we would also drop our ammo, weapons, guns, bayonets, etc., and split up. War was over—everyone was on his own. Were we to parade as a unit past the Ivans, they might not take it kindly. And then—war was over. No command structure was left, no government—nothing. From now on we would fend for ourselves, begging for a little food here and there. We grabbed our weapons, disassembled, then threw the parts away, and smashed and broke what was left. While doing this, everyone started crying. I had never seen this before and would never see it again: grown, hardened men, crying like little boys. It was an expression of desolation. What would happen? All those years of serving, so many people dead or maimed! What had it all been for? What was life's meaning? A moment of utter despair! Slowly we split up. I joined Atze Assmann from Westphalia. Groups were of two only. Two can make quick decisions—not three. With two, one would watch the other's back … two is a perfect team. Atze and I fastened the white bandanas and hit the road. He was looking to quickly return to Dortmund, known to have been taken by the U.S. army. I knew Ivan reigned in Berlin. I simply didn't trust Ivan one iota. I couldn't believe I would reach Berlin that way. I was so sure of winding up in Siberia, I didn't give much thought to heading north. To me the only course of action was to reach the first G.I. Joe on a straight line, if possible. Well, still talking about it, we reached a little hamlet where Ivans were lining the road. I had hidden my wristwatch in a pocket. No one searched us. We had removed rank insignia. They were looking for anything valuable. One German guy ahead of us gave up his golden wedding band.

Another guy had to take off his shoes. Our shoes were completely worn, so they weren't interested. But all Ivans had their weapons at the ready. No fooling with them. We met one mounted on a horse leading another one, in both hands a heavy pistol, whipping them nonchalantly toward us. Then we came to a meadow along the road, where we saw two German soldiers, stretched out—dead. Shot a short time ago. We walked briskly past this eerie scene to put it behind us. Then once in a while there came heavy horse drawn farmers' wagons, loaded to the hilt with apparently everything they could lay their hands on. Cows fastened to the rear. Those were Russians, or Ukrainians, who had worked as laborers on German farms, leading much better lives than many German soldiers. Now they plundered their hosts. We passed hamlets where people were simply terrified. Whenever they saw Ivan approaching, they fled to hideouts in the thick forest. Some never came out. Killing and raping were widespread. It was like the last judgment had descended. Those poor people always gave us a boiled potato or a little piece of bread, not knowing if they would survive the next day, either. The area we were passing was one of the poorest in Germany, with mostly forests. Crops were rare due to the poor soil. Hence most people in that poor, but beautiful area made some money crafting toys. It was the toy center of Germany (Erzgebirge or mineral mountains). Most minerals, like silver, were long exhausted. There was only one mineral left to be exploited: uranium ore. At the time it was produced at a very limited scale. Indications of uranium were the radioactive spas across the border in Bohemia in the town of Karlsbad. Descending into the next small town, Atze and I noticed a commotion in the town center. There were Ivans coming out of a factory, which happened to be a distillery for hard liquor. They were loaded with bottles, and, to demonstrate what communism was all about, they handed the full bottles to anyone in need. Frankly, everyone and his brother were in need then. So, in accordance with Marxist doctrine, I received my bottle, and so did Atze. We looked at each other and got our feet in highest gear possible. Get out of town! Drunken Ivans were simply a curse. In that state they would be capable of the worst. And no one would pop up to restrain his or her callous excesses. We made another five to ten miles that afternoon before staying overnight in one of those small hamlets. We were approaching higher and steeper mountains. There were only forested hills, with the road running in a valley between them. That night we had a meal of fried potatoes (Bratkartoffeln) made with my lard. We were lucky to exchange our dear brandy for a loaf of bread; on top of it came a good night's sleep. Things were improving. The people also had not seen a great number of Ivans yet, but had heard about the excesses and were terribly afraid. It looked to them that the Soviets would be their occupation force, a dreaded fate. No one knew where the U.S. forces were.

Next morning we were refreshed, though realizing it was still a good distance to the first G.I. It puzzled us tremendously that the Ivans didn't take any prisoners. They all seemed to be in a mode of celebrating their victory and neglecting everything else. We thought caution was indicated, but did not know how much. We could not address that at the moment. We now followed the increasingly winding mountain road in a westerly direction and had walked about three hours. The paved road was lined with 10-12 year old fir cultures, densely planted. Many must have been used to decorate German apartments at Christmas. Only during the long war years there was no harvesting. The rolling stock (railway) had to be used for more important cargoes—less income for the economy around us. As we mused about this and the chance of mushroom picking, we made it around another of these tight bends in the road and suddenly froze: We were right in front of a very long column of what appeared to be German soldiers. But within a split second we realized they were not soldiers. Wearing tattered rags and totally emaciated, they were so weak that they could hardly put one foot in front of the other. They seemed to have been projected from a Siberian prison camp directly onto this road. They must have been POW's for days on end with no food or other basic comforts. In front, two Ivans with their dreaded machine pistols waved us a friendly "Dawai," which means, "Come on join the party!" We could tell where they—or better now: we—were going! Straight to Siberia. Many would never make it there. We were now the first line in the column and the two Ivans fell slightly behind. There were many others further behind, but we had no time to count. As we slowly crept into the bend, at a command the Ivans yelled which sounded like "Pause" (break), all German soldiers went down to the asphalt as if hit by rocks. They were completely exhausted and at the end of their ropes. They must have been through something awful, with a much, much worse future. That, of course, created their enormous despair. Glancing at them, we exchanged no words. This all happened within seconds filled with adrenaline pumping my system to an absolutely perfect, instantaneous response pattern. Atze and I exchanged a look—without speaking. Then we both did the same: We stumbled forward using the prisoner's gait and trot, one leg after the other. In my mind I saw the dead German soldiers along the road we had passed, and the Ivan's starting to aim at us. But hopefully they would yell to stop ("stoi") before shooting. Yes or no? Meanwhile, another step, another, and then another, five or ten quick ones, like a panther, and then the look back: We were around the bend, no Ivan or POW in sight. Then, an enormous jump into the thick fir woods and running up the hill as fast as our lungs and legs could carry us. No look behind, just a sprint to freedom. Finally, way up the hill, we fell down to get some air and pressed our ears to the ground, listening if anyone might follow: no sound. Also, from the road no sound of alarm: we had done it! They hadn't noticed our escape. What jubilation! What a good feeling! What luck we had had! It is rare to be that lucky. Everything had come together. The pause for the POW's, the Ivans falling a little behind, and our instinct to try the impossible or improbable, a simple, old fashioned dare and gamble for our lives: Siberia or freedom! Wasn't that worth the ultimate gamble? We both sure felt it was—after it succeeded! Now rested, we climbed the crest of the hill to continue our quest for freedom. No longer did we walk on any road. Before crossing one, we carefully crawled close and watched for movement. Then we jumped quickly across. Orientation was by sun or moss on the trees, the latter grows on the northwest side. No longer trusting villages, we took pains to avoid them for fear of encountering Ivans hunting for us. That, of course, made us very hungry. The next day our bread was finished, and I had only a smidgen of lard left. Walking cross-country, we finally reached a larger town. Looking down from a hill, we saw almost no life. It was noon, but only some civilians—with red armbands and equipped with rifles—were patrolling the streets. We didn't trust this setup at all. There had to be Ivans where red armbands appeared. These guys looked like Spartacus followers of the early twenties. When a boy came by with a goat, we asked him about any Russian forces. No, they had not seen any, but were waiting for them to arrive. He told us about a soup kitchen in the central square, and that we were in Annaberg, about 18 miles from Aue. Even without a map, I could roughly visualize that we were on the right track. From Aue to Plauen (Voigtland): another 30-40 miles. In the town square we found out from the types with the red arm bands and rifles that they were from the "progressive socialist league," organized ad hoc to maintain order until arrival of the "liberators." They meant Ivan! They showed us the way after telling us that Russians were not in town yet, but would come soon. They didn't know what "soon" meant. Therefore, all we wanted was to fetch our barley soup with some potatoes in it and leave town. A more affluent farmer reluctantly agreed to let us spend the night, feeding us some peeled potatoes. We couldn't see what the farmer's family had, but it smelled like something other than potatoes only. Well, by then we knew the ways of the world, and that we had become mere beggars—a nuisance. "We" meant all displaced soldiers looking for a safe haven. Next day we made it to Aue, an industry town, with nothing to eat and no soup kitchen. At the train station there was a train with a locomotive under steam, with only open wagons hooked up. The train was said to leave for Plauen—the first train since everything had broken down. A couple of hours later we started moving. Meanwhile, all railroad cars were jammed with civilians and soldiers. It was exhilarating to ride comfortably and quickly away from the nightmare called "Ivan." Lots of people did not know yet what to expect from him. All hoped that U.S. forces would take over that part of Germany. How disappointed they would be soon! The train ended in Plauen, where we got out, heading west into the countryside, because there was nothing a beggar could gain in the towns. There were usually some potatoes at the farms. The more we got away from Plauen toward the west, the less people believed that the Soviets would eventually take over, but they had not seen any U.S. forces, either. Another guy had joined us, to which we agreed, since the danger of being caught by Ivan had subsided to zero. He was from one of those fighting SS divisions, which were completely wiped out at the end. Only few could escape with their lives. He, too, had removed all insignia; that way one could not tell army from SS. We were identifiable as air force through our uniforms under the parachute overalls and, of course, the pay book with picture. He was worried about being identified by the U.S. authorities later on, but we didn't see any yet. For him it was best to pass as an army soldier. What would give him away was the blood group tattoo under his left arm—a practice only the SS had. This was done to help a wounded soldier more quickly. We knew that, toward the end, many young men got drafted into the SS. Our new buddy claimed to have been a draftee. Actually, at that moment we couldn't have cared less about his past. We looked at every soldier to be in the same spot—left on the road as beggar, fighting to survive and return home to begin a new life. We proposed cutting his tattoo with small scissors, which Atze had as precious possession. I had saved a pocketknife and my wristwatch, purchased in Bucharest, Romania. Atze cut and removed the darn tattoo, accompanied by a lot of moaning. Usually all these fellows would be caught later in the U.S. POW camps, because the scar could be found: tattoo or scar would be the clue. The SS men were then separated and kept in extra tough camps for quite some time. They were also investigated to see if they had participated in any atrocities.

A few hours from Plauen we then came upon some trenches dug in the middle of a field. A trench in that location made no tactical sense. Strangely, all trenches were loaded with empty cans. Picking one up, I saw they were from the U.S. No one was near—they appeared to have gone home. They had finished the war. Before that, they had tried to get rid of the surplus food. Looking around further, I saw a paved road in the distance and—there was a figure in an olive-brown uniform leaning against a tree with a peashooter dangling in his hand. No one else was near for a mile or two. So I made it over there to find out what the deal was. When I came close, I didn't know I should say "Hi." So, I said "Good afternoon." My several years of English came in handy now. I found out that West of this point was U.S. occupied Germany, and he could not let me pass through. I didn't understand: it seemed so stupid to me. Here was one G.I. on that road and no one else, as far as I could see. That we were not to pass to the U.S. side seemed absolutely ridiculous. There was some kind of a catch. So I asked the GI what would happen if I would go 100 yards into the fields and then walk west cross-country. He chewed intensely on his gum, took a deep draw on his cigarette, responding: "I guess nothing much—there's no guard over there as far as I can see. But you can't go here on this road toward the west." I gave up asking for a reason if there was any. The poor guy must not have known himself. So we trotted off musing about these strange Americans who didn't seem to know what they were doing. This impression stayed with me for years until I learned that, according to the Yalta treaty, all German soldiers returning from the east were to be delivered to the "care" of the Soviets. Since U.S. commanders were instructed accordingly, the U.S. army commander in the area I chose to cross over had issued orders not to let German soldiers cross to the west, and he positioned one G.I. on each major road. There were miles between roads. Obeying orders, he made sure all of us could comfortably escape west. I guess we found ourselves in an area commanded by General Patton known to hate anything communist. This was my luck and Ivan's loss. Remember: mother was always convinced I was a lucky boy.

We found ourselves happily walking west again. We had made it. Since the U.S.-Army was not chasing soldiers, we made good mileage. Farmers would give us soup and a piece of bread—sometimes milk. Atze started talking about taking a more northwesterly direction, which would lead him to Westphalia, his home. During our daily hikes we came through a hamlet where people told us that "Amis" (German nickname for general infantry soldiers) were cruising around on a jeep, looking for something. We evaded anything in uniform equipped with deadly weapons. Since we knew little about the Americans' intentions, we took careful position, retreating into a dense piece of shrubbery. While we were waiting for the thing to blow over, the soldiers passed slowly in front of us about 5 feet away, in their jeep. We hadn't heard such a quiet engine when in low gear. It was unlike our VW personnel automobile, which made an awful noise at any speed. They stared at us and we at them. We thought for a moment they would take us in, but they didn't. We had never heard before that the U.S. army corralled German ex-soldiers. As a matter of fact, it was a mystery that Russian troops would not take us prisoners shortly after armistice on May 9. To the contrary, they told us to go home. This obvious misunderstanding was corrected several days later when I was taken prisoner briefly. Where I was at that time may have been a unique place, where a Soviet commander issued orders to let us go home. From any other location I only heard that everyone, uniformed or not, was taken on the trek to Siberia, leading to eventual misery, death, or both. Now the soldiers looked at us so curiously, we felt they had some thoughts that may not have been very favorable to us. So, we decided to evade any jeeps from now on as far as possible. At that time, soldiers never walked, but only moved in jeeps. They were hanging in their seats, legs draped over the sides, smoking cigarettes, chewing gum, and looking bored stiff and superior. After all, they were victors! Next day, an increase of jeep traffic signaled something significant. As we took cover, a jeep passed by, carrying a German soldier. It looked like they were hunting us now. Coming through a hamlet, we took cover and observed a Polish farm hand pointing toward our hiding place. They came close with their jeep and waved us to step up to them. They didn't bother to have their weapons at the ready or to search us for weapons. They offered us cigarettes and we had a smoke. I had not had one for weeks. As usual, I did not particularly enjoy it. We talked a little about where I came from, etc. They wanted to know what I thought about the present situation. I expressed the opinion that in the near future we would join and be allies. They were very interested, but didn't offer their opinions. Then they asked me to sit in front on the hood of the jeep. I could only hang onto a vertical T-shaped bar placed there to protect against enemy wire strung across the highway. They drove me to some large estate, where the jeep ascended over about 50 steps leading onto the top of the hillock. There they dumped me in front of an officer, who recorded my data on a form. Now I was POW of the US Army for a change, which I remained for about nine weeks. This must have occurred around May 15. We then drove on a 3-axle truck to Naumburg on the Saale River north of where I had been apprehended. There I was placed in the middle of an open field, which was subdivided into about 50x50 feet squares by barbed wire fences. Between the fences a few soldiers were patrolling, and armored scout cars were stationed on each corner of the compound, to guard against escapes. A primitive latrine some distance from my square consisted of a singletree trunk with bark still on it. There was lots of chlorine in the ditch. When we had to go, the guard had to be signaled for his permission. Otherwise, there was no shelter—no beds, blankets, roof, nothing. Because May is usually mild, I didn't freeze too badly. Our keepers were very concerned with our entertainment. They must have invented the hunts we conducted daily for hours on end. In my quadrant there were about 100 soldiers. All engaged endlessly in the hunt—for lice! I had never had them before, but in close quarters with others, they seemed to spread overnight to everyone. I could not get rid of them as long as I languished in this quadrant, of which there were perhaps 50 or 100 others, so many that I could not count them. Aside from the daily hunt, food distribution was the only other excitement. One, on the second day, was a German army ration of pressed coffee rounds consisting of 70% roasted barley and the rest was very roughly ground coffee. Each pressing was about 1.5-inch diameter by 0.5 inch high. I got three of those and thought this was a joke, or that soon more food was coming. Nothing of the sort! That was it. Next day, each got only half a can of green beans. Once a week there was a German one-pound can of beef for five people. Apparently, we were in the middle of a German army supply depot, and they slowly dumped on us whatever they found. Since it was very little, everyone soon became half-crazed from hunger. It seemed they wanted to do us in. One day one of us—beside himself from hunger—tried to run and was shot dead. They really meant it. The war was long over, but we were kept interned, which was against the Geneva Convention. Did we have no rights because of the unconditional surrender? Who knows? But, of course, everyone was then mad and furious—but helpless. Also there was no explanation as to why we were there and how long our deprivation was to last! Nothing—it seemed we were written off from human inventory. When it rained—often—we stood in the mud into the night as long as we could endure this kind of water torture. I was told later that prisoners in Siberia at least had fabricated huts. Also, any military prisoner in Germany had a shelter from the weather. We were an exception. When it was dry, we slept on the bare ground, huddling together against the chill of the night with hardly enough ground space for all. When it rained, we slowly plunged into the mud when sleep took over while we were standing. After a while we looked and felt more like pigs than human beings. And the hunger slowly cut the guts apart. The worst with this hunger business is not to know what is ahead. Was I going to end this way? Had we known that, we could have tried a breakout, at least killing some of our captors. But even that information was withheld. There were different rumors going around daily. One day it was that we were to join the Western allies to fight Ivan (hadn't we heard that one before?). Next day it was that we were to be transferred to the French to be used in African mines. That raised sheer panic—to be worked to a slow death. We were getting a taste of it right then and there. Or: we were to be given to the Soviets to be used as labor. Little did we know this was actually the policy established in Yalta. And so it went, day after day. Then, one day, one man of each quadrant was selected to go into the supply depot, where huge amounts of sacks were stored, full of barley. I could fill all my pockets and cap with it and returned. But how to eat this stuff? I mean horses like to feed on it as a kind of power meal—lots of calories. But human teeth and stomach just don't know what to do with it. Some thousand years ago, our forefathers invented cooking and baking! We had all that barley and didn't know what to do. One guy found a large one-inch bolt used on railroad ties. There was a railroad trunk line leading through our quadrant—the feeder for the depot. The ties were wooden. One buddy took the large bolt and an old can, filled barley into the can, and started hitting it with the bolt head. Soon there was something down in the can looking like very coarse flour. We tried that, but couldn't get it down. Then we mixed it with water and still couldn't swallow it. Then another guy and I started fashioning a small tin oven from one of these ubiquitous cans. There was a little grill on top and draft holes on the bottom. Firewood we carved from the railroad ties. Some guys had matches or cigarette lighters. Soon a little cookie was baking on the grill, and it tasted marvelous—the first "bread" after a long, long time. Now we made cookies all the time—which didn't provide many calories, but we had a purpose and a tiny reward! On days we got the coffee as a ration, some guys tried to eat it. There was a little sugar in it. Some guys tried to smoke it with their pipes. Some almost had heart attacks while eating it. On days like that, we were all disgusted. I no longer could see Atze Assmann. He was in another quadrant and I lost track of him. I had so much hoped to be taken by U.S. troops, and now I experienced total neglect and what seemed like a descent toward total oblivion. I simply couldn't believe they wanted to finish me off after I had made it through that war. From what I understood of the U.S., that would not be the American way. I then really didn't know anything about America, but more than my ex-"Fuehrer" Adolf Hitler and his general staff. My hopes were dwindling in the mud because of severe hunger pains and emaciation. If they wanted to retaliate because of the concentration camps—sorry, I was the wrong guy. How can one retaliate against someone who had never seen or heard of these atrocities? But then, since I didn't know, they still could! To me that treatment by the U.S. troops was an atrocity in itself. That's the way I saw it, fair and square. Some people got dysentery and other diseases, and there was no treatment. Then, after weeks, some were finally carried out, half-dead. I don't know where they were taken. It should be understood that no communication existed between POW's and the U.S. Army. They were totally anonymous to us.

One of those dreary and hopeless days I caved in. Some guys had bothered me for some time about my beautiful Swiss wristwatch, my only and most precious possession. They had observed some of the soldiers on duty make the prisoners exchange their precious things for commodities such as cigarettes, sugar, chocolate, etc. Some of these guys were starving for a smoke. So I traded my watch for eight or so packs. At least the soldiers didn't strip us of everything, like Ivan did. They did it the smart way. As a result, my fellow prisoners were constantly all over me begging for cigarettes. In no time they were gone. I felt stupid about it, since I certainly did not need a single cigarette. Looking back, I consider it a silly mistake. You only please an addict if you can offer him something. When the cigarettes were gone, no one bothered with me any more. This was a big lesson for life.

Slowly our condition deteriorated; mostly we became physically weaker and sicker. But, in mid-June something started to move. A few days later it was my quadrant's turn. We were led into what looked like horse stalls, probably former barracks for horse-drawn artillery (some artillery was moved into battle in 1939 in this fashion). There were long lines before some tables, behind which GI's asked questions about identity, last unit, etc. Some people were checked for tattoos under their arms. Those with tattoos (SS members) were separated and never seen again. I went up to the second floor, happy to be under a roof again. There was nothing in that large room, which measured about 50 by 150 feet and had formerly been used to store horse fodder. A grandiose night was ahead—under a roof. Then we got called down to a soup kitchen, where hot noodle soup with plenty of corned beef in it, and—wondrously—a piece of bread, each about ¼ lb. awaited each of us. The hot soup awakened our spirits and was immensely nourishing. Most fellows couldn't wait to wolf down their bread, but I thought I had eaten enough and left mine for the next morning. I was right. Since no breakfast was served, I sat down with some water and started to savor the precious bread. It tasted much better than any fancy cake I had ever eaten or seen—a delight for a king. From then on, life started to normalize. There was always hot soup and bread—mornings and evenings. But I cannot remember things like roast beef, sausage, cheese, peanut butter, butter or jam. It must have just been the plain bread. At the time it didn't matter. All we wanted was a chance to survive, and it looked like they were preparing us for it. That phase lasted another three weeks to the month of June. The floor on which we slept became increasingly hard and the anxieties took over again. Not knowing one's future can really destroy the mind. And it was boring in the absence of "entertainment," since they had sprayed us with lice killing chemicals, which were totally effective. All we had left to do now was wonder about the future. It is interesting that we never discussed the past. But, who wants to rehash all the horrors we, or at least most of us, had experienced? It would be unproductive and without purpose. I kept wondering why we had not been transferred earlier into the horse stalls, which had plenty of room for all. I'll never know the answer. I can dream for the rest of my life about the total misery in the mud of the POW camp of Naumburg. In the horse stalls, food was also quite restricted but it maintained our emaciated state. No one gained an ounce. This means that, before falling asleep there were always the hallucinations about Linzer or Black Forest cherry "torte" or fine cheese, sausage or Westphalian ham with Pumpernickel. I had not had much or any in peacetime, but that is what sticks in a German mind when thinking of gourmet food. What that means is that in the evenings we were still hungry. Since Germans did not organize any kind of military order in the camp, there was no military discipline. It was unnecessary and had no purpose. We started to realize that, whenever we would be free, there would be no government or military order. The German forces no longer existed. It seemed strange that no German die-hard NCO was trying to institute military order!

Things were now really changing for the better. One day, as we were talking about the latest gossip, a huge number of those standard U.S. army trucks lined up and soon the first of our group were loaded and driven off. It didn't take long until I got stashed on one of them, together with 59 others. The trucks were open, with wooden lattice all around, and their rear doors were latched. Even though we were thin as toothpicks, they sometimes had to encourage us with rifle butts until the door latched for good. Then we were driven off through the winding roads of typical German provincial towns. At each corner, the latticework groaned and creaked dramatically. But, packed tightly like sardines, we could not fall out. The truck's structure had to take all our weight. The drivers were all black. They didn't care that we worried about the soundness of the superstructure, its bending, weaving and creaking. They just drove like crazy toward south with us like an elastic pack swaying with each curve. And each time the planks of the superstructure were moaning ominously, so were we, because we couldn't move one iota. We could hardly shift weight from one leg to the other. Moving along, hunger and thirst overtook us. For lack of time we had not been able to take anything but our miniscule belongings. There hadn't even been time to empty the bladder or ask questions of the GI's or anyone else. The general direction was south. In that way we would have to intersect the Autobahn Berlin-Nuernberg-Munich. The highways we passed were stacked left and right with artillery shell cases—dumped by the millions, it seemed, without future use. The strangest part was that there was no one posted to watch all this. No one seemed to care about the tremendous inventory. We had never seen this kind of spectacle before. Apparently, those Americans worked with different rules. They knew no one could remove shells, because the German population had no trucks. If anyone did remove some, there were no artillery pieces to shoot them with. If anyone blew up a few stacks of shells, they would be glad, because they would not have to transport them back to the U.S. Therefore, posting a guard would have been a waste of time. Their time would be better spent with baseball or girls. I marveled at the endless line of trucks in our column. As far as I could see, their trucks with our POW's—all brand-new and of the same make—were the only type of trucks that would be seen on the road. They all had three axles and were equipped with multiple three-axis transmission drives. The amount of jeeps and other automobiles was also overwhelming. For each purpose there seemed to be one type of car exclusively. Compare that with the German rolling stock for the past few years. First of all, our trucks were equipped to drive with gas, generated by an on board gas generator fired by wood, reducing the engine power by 30-40%. Of our many different trucks none had 4-wheel drive. Then, the outfits I served with at war's end had hardly any automobiles left. I could see now how we had to lose this war. What I had been already sure of in 1941 was demonstrated here on the roads of the "Voigtland," as we rolled along south. That drive was a field trip into history for all to see who had open eyes and a brain behind them. Soon our discomfort became so great that they stopped to let us relieve ourselves. The black soldiers got some ration packs, but only after we had climbed back onto the truck. They started their second breakfast—biscuits and cans of corned beef or Spam, and they didn't look very happy eating it. Meanwhile we watched them with mouths watering. There was not one crumb for us, or water or cigarettes—nothing. There was also no chance to talk to the drivers who behaved peculiarly. I could hardly understand their strange language, which didn't quite sound like English to me. They played totally dumb. They may not have known much of anything or may have had orders not to talk to us. Soon we reached the Autobahn and continued on a southerly course, which would carry us into Bavaria, and who knows where? I regretted being moved farther away from Berlin into an unpredictable future. I had hoped to be released in Naumburg to return home, and that Berlin's situation would be stabilized. To what extent and by whom I could not imagine—it was just a dream. I was sick of wandering around as a beggar or POW. I wanted to get my life started again. Now we passed Hof in Bavaria—a beautiful scenery, except that my receptors were not at all calibrated to nature's bounties. An hour later we reached Bayreuth, then Nuernberg, where the entire mass of trucks got off the Autobahn. In the afternoon we saw the next city, Ansbach. The bets were on now. Most guys believed we were going to work in

France under harsh conditions in mines, or perform other duties to rebuild the French economy. It now looked like the next destination was Stuttgart. But where would we stay overnight? We still had not ingested anything all day—not even water. About one hour after Ansbach, the trucks stopped. We climbed off to stretch and do our thing. Hanging around, we heard no one telling us to climb back up—not one word. I couldn't check the time—I had sold my watch. But it must have been 20 to 30 minutes. Then everyone got nervous. "What is this? What does the 'Ami' have up his sleeve?" One white GI was leaning against a tree in the distance—carbine slung over the shoulder, and dozens of Germans around him. He was totally unconcerned that they might do something to him. In his case, I would have been more careful. Also, I believe the black GI's were unarmed. I was getting curious what that meant. If the US army had counted on us to remain their POW's they would have taken more precautions, like they did in the POW camp with its barbed wire quadrants. Since the long legged, smoking GI looked very relaxed, I asked him something like: "Are we going to continue?" He took another draw and looked at me, replying … "nope." That was quite some news! I couldn't believe it. What did this mean? What was there other than continuing the ride? Then I asked him another, trickier question: "What's going to happen now?" His very intelligent answer was: "I don't know." This had become sinister now. I was sure someone had to give some orders as to what to do with this melee of German POW's. In the German forces orders were always issued and available. But here, we were no longer German forces. If the guy didn't know what would happen next, perhaps I could make an acceptable suggestion. I asked him, if I were to walk across that field into the hamlet at the forest's edge about half a mile away: would that be OK with him? He straightened out and acted as if he had heard the first reasonable thing that day. I noticed that, according to a lot of décor on his sleeve, he must have been a sergeant or more. He said: "no problem," leaving me flabbergasted. What if the guy were to shoot if I were 20 feet away? Nothing worse than to get killed this late in the game! But then, they were not equipped to have us all murdered. Of the thousands on the road they could get only a tiny portion. But I didn't even want to be the only one killed that day. So I wanted to make sure: "If I go way yonder, you won't shoot, for sure?" He assured me: "No way, absolutely not." So I started stepping into the field with direction to the hamlet, turned around again, and wanted to make sure: "You sure? You won't shoot?" He was quick this time to yell at me: "Hell, no, I won't shoot. Go ahead—beat it!" I concluded the fellow didn't mean any harm. He may have had the order to get rid of us. I walked slowly across the field and looked back several times. No shooting—and then I saw some more guys slowly following me. I came to a cherry tree on a road full with ripe and yellowish red, large, delicious and inviting fruits. Though terribly hungry, I decided to forego them. Had I started, I could have never stopped. The end would have been dysentery of the worst sort. First thing in the hamlet was a bakery. I went in and asked for bread. They did not hesitate in handing me a piece and pointed out a large Swabian style farmhouse, where I could get a decent meal or two. The family was just getting ready for supper. They were extremely friendly and asked about my situation. Several of their clan were also still missing somewhere. They hoped someone would nourish and take care of them, as they would do to me now. Then there was everything on that table: beef, sausage, "Spaetzle," (Swabian noodles), veggies, rich gravy, everything. I had not eaten for so long! I just couldn't help it. I stuffed myself and then went to the barn to sleep in the straw. I was terribly sick to my stomach for three days before I could get up again. My system couldn't take food any more. It had to be slowly acquainted with normal food and quantities again. My nightmare in the forces and as POW had now terminated. I was a free man and could go where I wanted. But where would I go?

My trek on a GI truck across Germany ended around Crailsheim, 35 miles Northeast of Stuttgart. The events that saw me transported from the Naumburg POW camp to that town left me dumbfounded. Why would the U.S. take me prisoner, when they let everyone walk around freely initially? Many soldiers must have then made it home safely. For me there were those punishing experiences bordering on a death camp before I was trucked across Germany, just to be dumped on a remote highway. About ten years later I learned of an agreement between the Western allies and the Soviet Union at the Yalta Conference to deliver all POW's the US had taken in the Soviet zone back to the Soviets. Also, those streaming West coming from the Soviet zone of occupation were to be delivered to the Soviets. When I was evacuated from the Naumburg POW camp, the Soviet troops finally moved west to occupy all areas of the Soviet zone that had been initially overrun and taken by U.S. troops. The U.S. army then withdrew to what later became the Iron Curtain. Poor Naumburg became Soviet occupied for the next 45 years or so. The local U.S. army commander took it upon himself at that time—I am sure against orders from Washington—to liberate and rescue us poor souls. This smacks like another General Patton caper. Bless his soul. I'm forever grateful to whoever made the decision to push us onto those trucks helter-skelter. It must have been an overnight shoot from the hip decision. For that reason I wound up on the roads of Swabia without duly authorized release from POW camp. No one ever asked for it anyway.

THE ROAD HOME TO BERLIN

I was knocked out from exhaustion and dysentery for at least three days in that farmer's barn, not able to eat or do anything before I recovered and could face reality again. The farmer offered all kind of help, but all I needed was rest and quiet. Then the appetite returned and, with something to eat that I could hold down, my strength returned. Since I learned from those country folks that Ivan occupied Berlin, I decided not to go home. But the farmers were not sure. They had heard only rumors. There was no radio service or newspaper. They couldn't listen to the U.S. army radio for lack of English. Whenever I tried to listen, there were no news, or only some silly sports games in the U.S. or the war in the Far East were being reported. There was another, older guy in the barn with me—maybe end 30s or 40 with four kids, who was from Rostock. I decided to make it closer to the border of the Soviet zone of influence to obtain more up to date information about the fate of Berlin and the Berliners. One day the Rostock man (for lack of his name) and I grabbed the walking sticks, heading northeast back the way I had arrived by truck. The Rostock man originated from a different convoy and came from Italy somehow. He wanted to make it home, but seemed reluctant to do so, perhaps dreading responsibility for his brood in times when everyone was wanting. And there might be the Soviet occupation on top of it. Without sufficient goods even in Russia—how could they care for their German victims, too? Both of us fortunately did not know at the time where the demarcation line was to be found. Perhaps Rostock was British? After finding the highway I had traveled before, we made some good mileage. A piece of bread was given to us. At noon we found a farm where we were invited for a meal. The people spoke the Swabian dialect when talking with each other, which was like a foreign language to us. They did try to speak good German so that we could understand them. When one of those U.S. trucks passed us, the Rostock man always looked out for cigarette butts; he was crazy about them. Whenever a G.I. threw out half a cigarette, he picked it up and continued smoking it. I preferred not to smoke at all. Since I was not used to having cigarettes, it made no difference to me. We passed the next day in the same fashion. We were accustomed to knock on doors, hat in hand, and ask for a handout. As long as we were in an area where Swabian was spoken, we were always welcomed with open arms. But after a few days, the dialect changed to something we made out to be Franconian with a little Bavarian mixed in. Most of the doors at which we now knocked remained closed, but we had the strange feeling of being watched. One or two doors opened, but they offered nothing. There we were on a hot day, tired and hungry from walking and nothing to eat. Finally, a girl suggested knocking on the pastor's door. It was a protestant community—in those parts villages were either catholic or protestant, not mixed. We tried—nothing doing—then tried again a few times. Then we heard noises of silverware, pots and plates being moved. After a while the door opened and we were let in. The people looked a bit sheepish and wanted to know who sent us to the pastor—of all places! They were miffed, but finally agreed to serve us soup. There was not much in it. We left almost as hungry as we came. This pattern continued as we made our way slowly across southern Franconia past Rothenburg, Markelbach and Herzogenaurach. We never touched the larger towns, since we felt we couldn't fetch any grub there. It was more profitable to stick to the small hamlets. We thought the farmers always could spare a bit of their food. But, from day to day it took more time obtaining some. It looked like the day would come when we weren't offered any. We met some walkers also, coming from the Northeast from the Soviet zone. They cautioned that Ivan was in Berlin and also Rostock. As we discussed the situation, I wanted to hang around until there was more news about the Berlin situation. I had to know that there would be food and safety from becoming a POW again. Also some news about administrative policies was needed. The Rostock man simply didn't have the guts to see his family, which I couldn't understand. My parents were relatively self-sufficient. Dad was 57 years old and had a job. The first thing they would do is to produce energy and get the trains and streetcars going. He was also very adaptable and good at taking care of things.

On our way we saw many crops being harvested. It was time for winter wheat, rye, barley and oats. Going around Erlangen, we found a little hamlet south of Forchheim, where we came upon a 35-40 year-old woman who headed a farm with her grandpa. She needed two misfits like us and offered bed and food. In return, we had to help with the harvest or whatever else there was. As a come-on she served us each a great glass of home-brewed beer. She had a tunnel dug into the side of a hill behind her farmhouse for storing the barrels. The temperature in the tunnel kept constant through the year at an ideal 48 degrees F. We marveled at the thought of expecting beer each day with our meals. There was a tight door at the end, which she locked with one of the keys from her huge key ring. She always had the keys on her. I guess she slept with them also. The entire farm, i.e. all buildings, were located in the hamlet—the large house, the building for the horses and cattle, a utility shed and a barn, all neatly draped around the huge dung heap. Its aroma penetrated right into the adjacent kitchen. On the first day we headed out of the hamlet into the fields. There was wheat to be cut, using a scythe. We both had never done it. So we picked a scythe and grabbed a sharpening stone to dress up the edge. I looked to people in the nearby field and observed what they did. As a toolmaker I should be able to do it better than these guys. I checked the sharpness: it was tolerable; though I wasn't sure I had improved it. Then we started cutting. The darn wheat had very tough stems. It wasn't easy to cut. Matter of fact, it soon went over the arm muscle, and then the hip started hurting. And we had to do it all day long. Not 8 but 12 hours. The woman came out at noon with lunch. It was usually potato dumplings with some sauce on top. I never saw any meat. I hope my memory doesn't play a trick on me and there actually was meat once in a while, because the chimney was full of smoked goods. We knew it when she sometimes sneaked upstairs and could later be seen in the kitchen, gorging and chewing. She didn't have chewing gum! But this wheat mowing was tough! My emaciated and untrained body really revolted against such mistreatment. The nights were about as painful. I had tremendous muscle pains and there was no aspirin or the likes. This continued for some days, with a few girls picking up the wheat and bundling it. One day in mid-August, as we were working alone, it got very hot. We walked over to a nearby brook, took it all off and dived into the inviting clear, cool water—then, with a tremendous yell, I tried to jump out. My lungs had frozen or shrunk. The water felt like 40 degrees F. It was just too much. What a surprise that was. From then on the brook was off limits. We had to continue with the primitive well and hand pump in the farm courtyard. Since the food was monotonous and not very nourishing, my Rostock man set out to arrange for supplementary rations. When the owner woman was not around and grandpa was not looking, he would look for chicken nests in the barn. He always found some eggs, which we had to drink raw. Sometimes he exchanged them with some displaced people from the east for some other goodies. They didn't ask any questions. They knew well what life was all about when you were completely disenfranchised. Not that there was no food. The woman and her father-in-law always ate all those smoked pork goodies separately. They never showed us what kind of food they prepared for themselves, but sometimes we saw the women climb into the attic with her big bundle of keys. There the chimney extended from the kitchen through the roof. Made completely from masonry, it had been carefully crafted ages ago. There was a huge wrought iron steel door, held by large hinges, which had a closure with an impressive lock. Inside there must have hung countless homemade sausages, bacon, smoked meat, ham, etc., because farmers had their extra supply of hogs and geese. Fall was traditionally the time for slaughter and preparation of the meat. For preservation a vast portion was destined for the smoker—which, in case of a Franconian farm household, was located high up in the house chimney.

Sometimes the local Catholic priest came for a visit. We could always tell by the activities in the kitchen when high visitors were expected—and he was the only one. On such days we were fed quickly and ordered out of the dining room, whereupon the very well fed representative of the Pope rumbled up the stairs to take his seat, expecting the best. He never spoke with us displaced non-believers. For him, we did not exist. The feast he was served was always first class, including plenty of beer or wine. As for us, we hadn't seen beer again after our first day. The black frock also always left with a neat package of treats.

One day we had to go some distance out of the village, to another field, to cut rye. The woman came with us to bundle and stack up everything for drying. It was a hot summer day and suddenly, as we turned around toward her, we saw her spread her legs under her long skirt and, as she sheepishly grinned at us, we heard and saw a waterfall descending from underneath her skirt towards the ground. It looked like a cow urinating. We didn't get as far as speculating what her under-garments were like. It was too unappetizing for us. Neither did we ever find out if that was a common procedure in those parts. Anyway, we surely did not return her grin (or was it a come-on?—I'll never know). We quickly returned to the mowing task.

By mid-August all the rye, barley and wheat was finished and the oxen and wagons were taken out to transport the harvest into the village for further pro-cessing. There were no modern combines. Separation of the wheat, etc. from the straw was handled by a village-owned machine, which was dragged from farm to farm. Left over were then sacks of wheat, rye and barley, and bales of straw. The straw then had to be transferred high up into the barn. Since it was slightly driz-zling that day, the bales were wet and therefore heavy. They had to be picked up with a fork and lifted high up overhead into the barn opening, where another guy was waiting to push them further into the barn. As I lifted the bale, my knees were buckling and my hands with the bale swaying wildly. I was almost breaking down under the load, not having eaten any substantive food in the past weeks and not being used to lifting that kind of weight. Suddenly, one of the village maidens grabbed my fork and showed me how to do the job effortlessly—seem-ingly without exertion. She continued, and she loved it. I was no match for her. And she did not look the least overpowering—just a normal-looking girl, 22 or 23 years old. If I had ever thought of going into agriculture—this event ended such ideas once and for all, as this work made me feel very uncomfortable.

The next task was to spread the manure over the fields—apparently an annual requirement to prepare the fields for the new crop. Also, there was so much piled up on the dung heap that something had to happen. When we cleaned out the cowshed, there was no space left for depositing the manure. It had to be loaded onto a wagon and dragged by oxen to the fields, to be unloaded again in small heaps spread out in a geometrical pattern all over them. Again, what sounds so easy turned out to be a very heavy, stressful and excruciating task, because the manure was very old, having almost turned into concrete. After prying it loose from the heap, we had to pick it up by fork and spread it evenly over the entire field by shaking it rhythmically and violently. Since the manure was so heavy, our arm muscles received a violent, painful impact each time. This work lasted all day and continued into the night. My arms got so sore that the nerves played an ugly trick on me by continuing through the night, with no aspirin or Tylenol available. On the next day the torture continued, and so on. I could never become used to it. Eventually the dung heap was used up and better days lay ahead.

By now we were hearing rumors that the USA, Britain and France had moved into Berlin—each nationality, plus the Soviets, occupying one sector of the city. That could not be immediately confirmed, because radio or newspapers did not yet exist. I heard also that there were sometimes trains going somewhere—just freight trains, but people just piled on them to go home or somewhere, where they thought things might be better.

It was mid-September. If I wanted to travel in the open air, I had to do it before winter would set in. As more and more refugees from the East came wandering past, I had to believe the news they brought with them. Berlin had all of the Allies, but Eastern Germany (the Soviet Zone) was a hellhole of the first magnitude. The Soviets dismantled anything valuable. Whole factories, railway installations, personal property, agricultural assets, people, soldiers—everything got shipped to Russia—whatever they could think of or could get their hands on. In the process, many women, young, old, even children … got maimed and raped. Everyone I met told more horror stories. Discussing this with the buddy from Rostock, he could not make up his mind to return home. By now, we knew Rostock belonged to the Soviet Zone. But I decided to give it a try—I had to find out how my parents were. I had no idea if Spandau was damaged by the battles or not. They might be sick, lonely … in need of my help. And I was sure they wondered about my own fate. Also, there must be life to be picked up somehow! I told the farmer woman I would leave for home the next morning. She gave me some bread and a little piece of sausage, good for two days at the most, and 50 marks, which then was worth nothing. I started arguing with her and told her my journey home would last one week at least, and the bread would last only a day or two. How about some plum brandy? I knew all those farmers made it and had plenty. Reluctantly, she gave me one third of a bottle of the stuff, which filled one third of my canteen. This way I started walking toward Forchheim, a small town north of Erlangen/Nuernberg. I cannot recall the name of the hamlet where I had stayed for those weeks. I would have liked to go there again, but trying to revisit the past usually ends in disappointment.

As I approached Forchheim itself, I came across some park-like green meadows surrounding a pond, where some ducks were swimming. There I saw some GI's (Amis for the Germans), endlessly throwing a fairly large ball at each other. Watching them while I was sitting down, I noticed that they were constantly chewing something in their mouths. I soon realized it must be chewing gum, which I had never seen before. In my former contacts with this human species, I had never paid attention to this phenomenon, as there had always been stress and my mind on how to survive. Now I could watch them up close. They were somewhat overfed, happy guys who seemed completely relaxed and carefree and didn't even have guns close by. Their attention focused only on their game, they did not notice me. After a while it occurred to me that I might try to exchange my plum brandy for something more worthwhile—perhaps cigarettes? I had heard rumors that the U.S. armed services did not issue liquor to the troops. They had to try fetching it from the population. The landscape was then entirely dry. Besides nothing to eat, there were no liquor stores, and breweries were not operating; that would have to wait a few more years. The first order was to feed the population, to keep the people barely alive. I guess supplies of wine were also entirely used up, due to the enormous demand during WWII. The fighting men and everyone else had to be kept in a happy mood. The Soviets even issued extra-large vodka rations before large offensives, so that soldiers often went into combat in a drunken state. Thinking this over, I tried to muster my English, got up, straightened out and approached the first G.I., who watched me suspiciously, perhaps thinking I wanted to bum a cigarette, chewing gum, or food. But as I offered him plum brandy for sale, his face lit up and he wanted to see it. I took my canteen from my "Brotbeutel" (bread bag) and unscrewed the closure, holding the spout under his nose. I need to explain that the bread bag was standard issue, together with the canteen (Feldflasche) for all German soldiers. It was enclosed in a gray layer of felt, probably to camouflage the bright aluminum, and it was fastened on the bag with a snap-hook. The bag, about 14x10x2" in size, had loops to secure it to the main leather belt. It was made from heavy canvas. This combination of bag and canteen was always carried in the back and filled with the soldier's essentials, like iron ration, knife and fork, spare socks and whatever each individual decided on. The standard issue mess container could also be fastened to the bag, but I will not go into this now. Anyway—this G.I. got quite excited and asked what I wanted. I responded: "cigarettes," then the only currency of value in Germany. He took the flask and said to wait a moment. He would be back with the empty flask and cigarettes. I didn't tell or demand to know how many cigarettes, or how to proceed with the transaction. I should have insisted on keeping the booze and wait for his return. But everything evolved so fast, and his approach was so natural that all of a sudden I saw him running through the meadow with flask in hand. He seemed happy, but I began having second thoughts. If he were never to come back, there was nothing I could do—nothing! I stood there dumbfounded, writing off the only asset in my possession, when I saw him miraculously reappear in the doorway he had entered a while ago. He returned with a whole carton of "Lucky Strikes," the best-known currency at the time. Much relieved and happy at having encountered an honest man, I thanked him profusely in my fairly broken English and bade him good-bye and Godspeed. Around the corner I opened the carton and distributed the packs into all of my pockets. Carrying a carton of cigarettes at that time was as dangerous as possessing gold.

Next, finding a train station didn't take very long. One could always find a great number of people hanging around train stations—mostly folks coming from the East: East Germany or Czechoslovakia—displaced soldiers of all services, army, air force, Navy, SS and/or civilians. Everyone had stories to tell. People from the East had lost everything they ever owned and then some. Of course I could not listen to all of the stories. But, looking into the faces, one could imagine the trouble, misfortune and harm they had experienced, and it had not ended yet by any means. While the soldiers usually wanted to go to their parents, wives or siblings, the displaced people from the East had nowhere to go. Governmental organization was not noticeable at the time. Also, the U.S. occupying powers were woefully behind in resolving all of the problems. This would take years. There was nothing to be had at the train station: no warm room, no water, no food, no government representative, local or provincial. All of these people at the train station were on their own and anxiously held on to their meager possessions. A desolate scene. Rumors were circulating among the masses as to what was happening in the East, when a train would go, and in what direction. No stationmaster was in sight. When night fell, the people bedded down wherever they found space. Bedding down, naturally, was a luxury, as there was no bed. Not even owning a blanket, I curled up, using my bread bag as a pillow, and fell asleep. Because it was September, temperatures were still just about tolerable. Next morning I woke up to the rumor that a train would soon pass through, heading north. Indeed, a freight train pulled into the switchyard and stopped—the general direction was north. There was no time to lose. Most cars were of the open kind, used for bulk products like coal, gravel, etc. There were no passenger trains yet, so I climbed onto the open car and waited for the next excitement. There was no railroad or other police, either German or U.S. No one tried to regulate or interdict. People just climbed on and waited for what would happen next. Luckily, the train pulled out of Forchheim within the next 60 minutes, and I was on my way, figuring that my best approach to Berlin would be to reach Northern Germany. The best base might be Hamburg, and the cities and villages of Schleswig-Holstein, such as Ratzeburg and Luebeck. I had a vague notion that the demarcation line must be in the area east of Ratzeburg and west of Schwerin. I had no map, but I had always had an excellent ability to orient myself. I just about had the important details of German geography in my head. This came in very handy now. Soon the train chugged into Bamberg, where it again stopped at the switchyard. People got on and off. Then, luckily, it continued west toward Schweinfurt. I remembered that in this fashion I could probably reach Wuerzburg, where there was a main railway line intersection. This was a north/south spur connecting the north to southern Germany. Pretty soon I passed through a town situated on the Main River. The train slowed for some reason, and so I could observe the utter destruction meted out here in all details. From the railroad car I could overlook the entire town. Not a single building was standing. Factories, recognizable by some twisted girders, apartment dwellings or single-family homes—there was no brick left on top of another. There was only rubble, as far as I could see. Even streets were no longer discernible. I think there was a church standing in the far distance, and I saw a smoke stack with two large letters, "F&S." I later learned from my son during his stay in Schweinfurt that the natives interpret those to mean "feeding and boozing" (German: Fressen und Saufen). That's all that was left of Fichtel und Sachs, a large manufacturer of mechanical parts, bicycle, motorcycle parts and small engines. I soon realized that this had once been the great traditional Franconian (Fraenkisch) town of Schweinfurt, totally destroyed due to two large bearing companies, SKF and Fischer A.G. Old Fischer had invented the centerless grinding process, which initiated vast industries throughout the world. The train didn't even stop in that forlorn town, where no signs of life could be seen. What a difference I found when visiting my son Chris (William Christopher, earlier referred to as Bill) there in the 80's. Everything had been rebuilt in the original medieval style!

Next was Wuerzburg, also a picture of utter destruction, but there were still ruins and dwellings standing. I could observe people moving about, and there was some life around the train station. Ending up in the switchyard, as usual, I learned that I had to find another freight train, in order to head north. That meant an overnight stay in the open air. There was little train movement. Next morning I realized a train was being assembled and a locomotive placed in front. I found out it was going to Bremen. Like many others, I simply boarded, although I would have preferred Hamburg. I was getting anxious. My provisions were running very low. I had possessed only some bread and sausage, and now there were just a couple of slices and perhaps 100 grams of sausage left—that would not last long for an already emaciated 23 year old! It would last me another day if I stretched it and calmed my rebelling stomach with cigarettes.

The train started moving reluctantly. It seemed to wait endlessly in each little town it stopped at, and then moved slowly on. By evening, I reached Kassel. Jumping off quickly and walking briskly toward town, I hunted for a bakery shop, and, with locals' direction, found one close by. Having repeatedly been hard hit, Kassel was also in ruins. The baker happily exchanged half a loaf of bread for two packs of cigarettes—enough for supper. I hurried back, finding the train still parked in the switchyard, and climbed on to start supper. Two buddy ex-soldiers got a slice, too, and all was gone in no time. I passed the night on the train. There was lots of smoking. The buddies got their share—the thing to do in those times. The train finally rolled into the Bremen switchyard the next afternoon, having passed through Hannover. There I was, without food; cigarettes were gone, and I was hungry, very hungry. In the next business district, I tried my luck at two bakeries and a butcher shop. Butchers carry all those irresistible German sausage delicacies, smoked hams, etc. etc. They did not offer much then, but to the disadvantaged, displaced beggar that I was any smoked morsel seemed worth its weight in gold. But without something in exchange, not a single crumb would have been given to me—nothing at all. This was a city, and all foodstuffs were accounted for. Food was available only with ration cards. Perhaps somewhere there was a local government office, which handed out food ration cards to the myriad of transients. But that idea did not occur to me then. So, after strolling back to the switchyard in a desperate, hungry mood, I sat down at its edge, observing the traffic. Suddenly I realized that all of those trains seemed to contain supplies for the U.S. forces in Southern Germany, because each had a caboose at the end, which was guarded by an infantry soldier. The cars were of the enclosed kind, with roofs and sliding doors, and there seemed to be no locks on the sliding doors. But I was not sure of this. Watching the comings and goings, I realized that there was no real schedule for the G.I. guards. Eating, drinking, smoking and chewing gum, they didn't seem to take their duties very seriously. They never came out of their caboose and seemed bored to death. I knew that feeling from my own experiences. They also didn't feel threatened by anything or anyone.

This relaxed bunch was oblivious to being observed or staked. I concluded that an attempt to open the sliding doors could succeed. But being caught by the guards would result in a military court and long prison. Running away when discovered would mean getting shot. And who knows what kind of a marksman I might come across? And then, I got hungrier by the minute. The only thing to do was trying it at night. I knew that the hours between 2 and 5 a.m. cause any good man to lower his guard and relax. In those lonely nocturnal hours night hallucinations take over, and the senses are almost shut off, even though one isn't yet fully asleep. So, way after midnight I slowly approached the freight train far away from the caboose. Only one train was left which was apparently loaded with goodies. The others were empty, waiting to be pushed into the port of Bremen to get loaded. Crawling underneath, I carefully paused often and listened for steps or other events. The noise in the guards' caboose had subsided now; it was very quiet. Finally I was at the train—alone. Some others at the edge of the yard didn't dare come along. Who wants to get shot so miserably after having survived history's largest and ugliest war? Better go hungry some more. So there I was, straightened up at the first sliding door. I unlatched the door, which was unlocked. I pushed the door slightly open, perhaps a foot, which made a loud noise. I fell to the ground and listened, rolling underneath the car. No opening of the caboose, no approaching steps. I got up and reached inside. I felt bags filled with something flour-like. It was not sugar or beans, or coffee beans. The bags were too large and heavy to carry them into the yard. Bad luck. Perhaps the entire train was loaded with flour bags? That would be something! Off to the next door, same procedure, same result. My spirits started sagging. If my daring was to be rewarded, I must keep trying. Next door, I stretched out my arm, and this time I felt cartons. The entire car was full—top to bottom. I could feel cans inside, but it was so dark that I could not decipher the print on the cartons. The entire yard was pitch-dark (which is what made my operation possible). What to do? Carrying a carton was doable, but I could be carrying something which would later turn out to be worthless and of little or no nourishment. What we needed at the time was the more calories, the better. Pure lard would have been highly valued! Not fooling around much, I swung a carton onto my shoulder, closed the door gingerly, and briskly crossed the yard, on my belly underneath the cars, up again, and so on. Soon I had reached the yard's edge where the fellows waited. We went into a shed. Somebody had a lighter: "What did you fetch?" The opened box revealed—I couldn't believe my luck—California peach halves in heavy syrup. Quickly each of us opened a can, and we enjoyed the heavenly nectar. We had not had such a delicacy for at least ten years and didn't even remember ever having enjoyed this kind of canned fruit! Some guy offered me a canvas bag for some of the cans, and I walked happily into the dawn. Now I needed substantial food with calories most of all: bread, butter, meat or sausage. The next morning when the stores opened, I again politely asked for a little piece of bread. The bakery shop people tried to shove me off, but I waved a can of peaches in front of them, and in no time I had a nice, fresh, large loaf of bread, hot from the oven, in my hands. The same happened at the butcher, where I got a nice piece of salami. I felt better now. It was a nice day, and I sat down on a park bench with my breakfast. Having the belly full felt good. My spirits improved in direct relation to my calorie intake. I went into the yard with my satchel over my shoulder, sure that the provisions would help me get to Berlin. Soon a freight train left for Hamburg, which didn't take too much time. I thought there I could exchange some more peaches for bread and for smoked herring—another delicacy I had not enjoyed for at least six years.

Then I left toward Ratzeburg. I had heard that the demarcation line (East-West Germany) passed somewhere east of there. Schwerin in Mecklenburg was already Soviet-occupied zone, while Ratzeburg in Holstein was under British occupation. Nothing could keep me in Hamburg, of which there was almost nothing left—mostly rubble, where primarily women, young and old, were recovering bricks and other useful material to be used for reconstruction later. I could already see many orderly piles of bricks along the streets. I heard that people of any age had to do this work to receive the meager ration cards, except those with other occupations or jobs. Arriving in Ratzeburg, I asked how to get to the border and got strange looks: "What on earth do you want to do over there—in hell?" Thousands had fled to the British zone. Unable to make anything out of this, I soon found the narrow highway east toward Schwerin and the border. I had no idea about the details of this demarcation line. Were there guards—British guards on one side, Russians on the other? Was there a fence, perhaps barbed wire—were there even mines? Approaching the village with those thoughts, I passed an endless stream of refugees coming from the east, some with hand-drawn carts loaded with bedding, blankets and some utensils, others with baby carriages or simply carrying things on their shoulders. They looked hungry, exhausted, dispirited and homeless. Sometimes entire families dragged their feet along, not knowing where to go, only that it must be toward the West, which is what I had thought shortly after armistice. The result of their first hand experience with the Soviets was flight. I found it strange that the Soviets were letting them go. I was able to talk with one of the refuges, dressed like an ill-clad farmhand, who was about my age. His clothing was dirty, smelly and ready to be discarded. He looked like one of those Russian "guest" workers found on German farms. He told me about the east: People disappeared; thousands of women were raped; there was no law and order. Individual Russians looked through everything, simply taking what they liked. Things were totally out of control. Germany seemed to be plundered for good, with no end. Soviet-organized troops were dismantling all factories. German workers were forced to dismantle and load everything, including entire railroad lines, lock, stock and barrel, for shipment to Mother Russia. Anything that could be removed was taken. Small tools, such as hammers, screwdrivers, chisels, etc., etc., were packed. It seemed that only forests, empty building shells and pastures would remain in Germany. The young refugee looked at my nice parachutist's outfit and said that a crack soldier was a loathsome sight over there. He said that looking like a farmhand in his dirty outfit would get me through the Russian zone. After exchanging clothes, I looked much different.

In the next village there was supposed to be the border. Someone showed me the demarcation line. The word was that the Russians for mysterious reasons didn't let anyone pass over to the east. What to do next? It was evening and the sun was setting behind me. Running into a British soldier, I asked about the chances to go east. He took me to a bluff overlooking a meadow and small patches of forest in the background. He said if I would start at 2 or 3 a.m. and pass between two areas of forest way yonder, I would make it through. He said Russian guards were posted there and pointed out the exact location. I should walk carefully right between two posts; the Russians were usually fast asleep at night. I felt he was o.k. and wanted to help me. Wishing me luck, he left me to contemplate my nocturnal moves. Soon it was dark and I curled up for a nap. Since my watch was in the Naumburg prison camp with a G.I., I could not check the time. The village had turned quiet, and the dew began rising, which would make me less visible. As I was trotting through fields and meadows, the loose soil muffled my footsteps. After an hour or so I noted the patches of forest to my left and right, where the Russian guards were supposed to be. I expected the fateful: "Stoi," Russian for "stop," at any moment, but all remained quiet. Reaching a path and then a small, unpaved road, I then saw the beginning of dawn and heard bells ringing here and there. I soon saw a herd of cows. A farmhand was milking them. What an opportunity! I bade good morning and asked for some milk, which was given freely, without hesitation. I also found out about the way to Schwerin, and that there were real passenger trains daily to Berlin! Soon I was on my way to Schwerin, a good 4-5 hours away. The only vehicles on the road were those of the victors, so I had to walk. After about another hour, approaching a hamlet, I was negotiating a bend in the road when I found myself in the middle of a Soviet infantry outfit resting along the roadside. Fierce-looking characters, most from some Asian tribe out of Siberia, they looked ready to commit any atrocity at a drop of a hat—just for fun. Hoping not to show my panic, I steadfastly walked through the bunch. They looked me over top to bottom, appearing to hope for valuables. But I looked so desperately dilapidated that, thinking I was a farmhand, they realized there was nothing to be had and didn't stop me. I had received good advice! I will never know if my camouflage protected me, but am convinced it helped me a great deal. And then—as mother said—I am a lucky boy! Having arrived in Schwerin, I looked up the train station. Indeed, a train was leaving within the hour for Berlin.

RETURN TO BERLIN

Arriving at the Berlin-Spandau (West) station in the late afternoon, I walked briskly down Klosterstrasse toward Wilhelmstadt. Spandau was in relatively good shape, never having suffered a massive bombing raid. Some bombs had fallen here and there, like the one in Zimmerstrasse while I was on furlough in 1943. This had left Zimmerstrasse partially wasted, but luckily not at the end where we lived. Although I saw marks of infantry weapons everywhere, the apartment was still inhabitable. My expectations and anxiety grew with each step I came closer to home. There was Pichelsdorfer, but I selected Wilhelmstrasse. Soon there was Metzerstrasse, which looked like five years earlier, only that people wore shoddy, colorless clothes and had thin, pale faces. To the right, beyond the park, I saw the barracks, which had been built in 1935 or '36 to replace a wonderful sports complex, where soccer, handball and field hockey competitions had been held each weekend. In those times, many amateur sports clubs had existed for the common folks. Lots of people participated, with leagues for old gents, juniors and kids. Now I could see British soldiers in the distance. And now … a gasp! I rounded the corner into Zimmerstrasse, and—everything was in sound condition. There had been no more destruction. The 4-story apartment house, where we lived on the second floor, was standing solid. What a relief! I ran upstairs and rang the bell, heard movement and shuffle inside, and the door opened: "Der Junge" (the boy)! Mother's cry echoed through the building. Father came, tears were flowing, and all of us were mighty happy for the moment. Mother brought out something to eat. The pot roast tasted wonderful. I couldn't understand where this meat came from, but didn't ask any questions—yet. The apartment was as I had left it, with all furniture, draperies and carpets in place. Russians, who repeatedly searched all houses, were looking for valuables, which we did not have, or—girls or women. They didn't want regular household utensils or bedding. Many people lost cameras, watches, and jewelry. Father still had his pocket watch, though, which looked like, but never got close to being gold. The Russians would have liked to get their hands on bicycles, which father had hidden in the basement. Such things were not available to them in their "workers' paradise;" when they saw one, they took it. Russians also routinely searched any existing backyards, especially in the suburbs, probing around for hidden valuables with long steel poles. Our apartment house had a concrete paved courtyard.

Dad told me about his last days of war, while I was fighting in the Lausitz and Saxonia areas. They had wanted to draft him into the Volkssturm outfit, which consisted of very old, ill-equipped, ill-trained and unwilling boys and men, to be used as cannon fodder for the Nazi leaders' benefit. Dad, then 57 years old, had arthritis, angina pectoris, and probably high blood pressure, although, knowing him, he probably never had that checked. He attended a few meetings at which some of those "hot leaders" wanted to drum up enthusiasm for the fatherland's defense against the onrushing Soviet hordes. Terrible reports of killings, mutilations, rape and savagery were told, already known through rumors and refugees' accounts. No weapons or training were offered to the poor audience. So, father missed more and more meetings, and gradually things got so confused and disorganized that the organization fell apart, especially since the "leaders" started to disappear, i.e. they escaped to the West before Berlin's total encirclement. That was when battle noises came from all four directions: north, south, east and west. Until almost the last minute, the electric streetcars were in operation. In the last gasps, soldiers, ammunition, equipment, food, medical supplies and wounded soldiers were transported. Civilians no longer ventured into the streets, where battles were being fought. The Soviets didn't have to use much heavy weapon fire. Germans were fleeing, only trying to save their hides—at least in Spandau. The end had finally arrived. As for myself, I had been convinced already in early 1941 that the war was lost, but I had not imagined that it would come to this devastating, irresponsible end.

In the last hours before Russians gained control, the people from Zimmerstrasse and surrounding streets stormed into the army barracks and laid claim to all valuables they could find. The sergeants in charge of the supplies tried to desperately defend their fiefdom's possessions, but the crowd was too large and just broke everything down. Wholesale plunder started. Officialdom wanted to keep everything, no matter what. If they supplied something, a request had to be signed by an officer, and a receipt, etc., etc. That meant the Soviets would have gotten everything. The people won and carried away all foodstuff, blankets, and anything they could use. It stopped when the first Russians showed up. During these last days, Mom and Dad didn't have any contacts with Lisbeth (and her daughters). Ulli, my other sister, had lived in Frankfurt/Oder with her children, while her husband Oskar Jahn was stationed in Italy with the Air Force. Werner Ehling, Lisbeth's husband, was with a flak unit in the East. Oskar was a Master Sergeant, and I think Werner was a Sergeant. Ulli left Frankfurt/Oder before the Soviets arrived and moved to Lahr/Baden, close to Freiburg, to be with Oskar's family, for better protection. Also, extra food was more easily obtained there than in Berlin. While my family had no connections with farmers, Oskar's family was well placed and never suffered from want during the war. My parents' only additional supplies were those I carried home from Romania. Those helped significantly.

As the battle noise slowly crept into Spandau, father heard that a bunch of Schultheiss brewery horses had been hit by artillery on the Brunsbuetteler Damm toward downtown Spandau, a walk of 10-15 minutes. Knowing what that meant, Dad hurriedly assembled his handcart, gathered knives, saws and an ax, and rushed to Brunsbuetteler Damm. He said that bullets were actually flying, but the image of a good supply of horsemeat must have kept him going. Food was expected to be in even shorter supply, and then—he actually was already hungry. Upon arrival he found the horses badly hurt or already dead. Some people were busy butchering the large Belgian horses used to drawing the huge beer wagons. Well-nourished, they had lots of fat and protein. Between occasional grenade hits nearby, Dad got his tools from the cart, working with all the haste he could muster. He loaded as much on the cart as he could justify under the circumstances and started pulling toward home—one more occasion when this old contraption of a cart proved its worth. It could be loaded full of sand, manure, or potatoes—whatever came along, even horse meat! A Shetland pony or two could have been harnessed to it, but, sadly, it saw only human power. Father arrived home unscathed and began to unload. The watchful neighbors, seeing the skin still on the meat, shrunk away from the barbaric scene, but father knew better. He had survived in WWI on Russian or German horsemeat much tougher and more leathery than the delicious pieces he had now brought home. My parents quickly set up a production line in the kitchen to prepare the meat, cook it, and fill the 40-50 canning jars, which we had gotten from the basement. All was saved for the bad times to come. The saying during the last years of WWII came to mind again: "Enjoy the war—the peace will be a nightmare!" And the nightmare was now developing.

POST WORLD WAR II YEARS IN BERLIN

Father had been initially drafted by the Labor Department to work in factory details for Soviet dismantling gangs, whose task was to dismantle machines, furniture, tools, and lavatories—anything movable, to be shipped to the east. For instance, only a shell of buildings was left of the vast Siemens factories east of Spandau. No chair, nail, screw, table, bench or anything else was left on the inside. In many destroyed buildings an enormous amount of valuable tools, equipment and machinery was buried under the rubble. That rubble, and what remained underneath, was not touched by the Soviets—yet. Only a limited time was left for taking as much as possible with the available workforce. The fate of Germany had been decided earlier near Glienicke, south of Spandau, at "Schloss Charlottenhof," the former residence of the German crown prince. There, sometime in June or July, the Allies, represented by Joseph Stalin, Harry Truman, Winston Churchill/Clement Attlee and Charles DeGaulle decided to divide Germany into four zones of occupation. Berlin was to be occupied by the four powers and also divided into four zones. However, because there was to be a free flow of goods and personnel between the zones, one could still see Russians in the streets when I came to Berlin. Incidents still occurred involving them. They continued routinely trying to rip off people, as though they were the sole occupying power. I observed British military police roughing up a couple of misbehaving Ivans in downtown Spandau. Because the British didn't tolerate any monkey business, Ivan slowly disappeared from the street scene.

Dad later returned to his old job as a BVG street car driver. He had been offered a better position as a checker (control of street car traffic), which he declined. This offer had been made because he always was a known sympathizer of the SPD (Social Democratic Party), although he never had been a party member. He hated to get involved in party political brawls and considered bigwigs corrupted, opportunistic loudmouths. A simple man with simple tastes, he didn't need much to be happy. His best moments may have been when he could do things like walking into the woods with me, making me a flute out of a willow branch in the spring, or collecting mushrooms in the forests in the fall. Another pleasure was picking gooseberries at uncle Hermann's, which were pressed and the juice converted into a wine-like concoction.

While father was working at BVG again, mother had to find something to avoid the dreadful "brick cleaner" (Truemmerfrauen) detail. Everyone had to work in order to receive ration cards, which kept people alive in the cities, especially in Berlin. The rations supplied a minimum calorie supply, perhaps 1200 to

1400 daily—too much to die from and almost too little to live on in those times. Everyone was constantly hungry and wanting to eat. People could only dream of food like cakes and sausages, and whipped cream could only be imagined.

Rations consisted of such basics as potatoes, bread, margarine, lard and very small pieces of meat; the daily quantity of fat was something like 20 grams, or less than one ounce. Fruits could not be had. Veggies were restricted to cabbage, beets (Kohlrueben), and onions. People were mostly busy searching for additional food. So, mother got a job at the British barracks, enabling her to bring little pieces of white bread home daily. The "Tommies" unfortunately didn't like or know the delicious, nourishing German bread. This, and the canned horsemeat, helped us over the terrible winter of 45/46.

In the nice recreational park along Wilhelmstrasse there were some lawn areas, where ballgames had taken place in peacetime. The municipality of Spandau converted these into plots for citizens to plant food. Father fetched a piece just in time. Everyone wanted one. Already in the fall, people were salivating about the juicy tomatoes they would harvest next August. But, first came the input: lots of work to dig up the plot. Then, without fertilizer, nothing would grow, and manure of any kind was not available for 50 miles around. Whoever had some, fertilized his or her plot with it. What to do? Well, I am sorry to report that we did our business into a pail in the bathroom.

The fertilizer was carried to the plot daily. The Moratz' tomatoes the following year were by far the best in the neighborhood! Although we had some extra food, we didn't gain any weight that winter of 45/46. The three of us were terribly emaciated and suffered from constant hallucinations about delicious food. The only people who had enough supplies were bakers, butchers and grocers, who cashed in mightily on the phenomenon of shrinkage (Schwund). If you purchase a quantity in bulk (e.g. flour) and mix it with water, salt, yeast and other ingredients, there will always be an opportunity to chisel 1-2% from the original quantity. Partially some flour is claimed to get lost in the process, water substitutes some of it and, in many cases the bakers let kids collect chestnuts in fall to mix into the bread. Thus, each bread yields a 3-4% gain for the baker. By selling 200 or more per day, a pretty good extra non-ration card controlled food reserve results, which can be exchanged on the black market for anything and everything, from cigarettes, meat and fat to nylon stockings, etc., etc. Hence these types of business people never looked or were hungry. The R-Mark (Reichsmark) as German currency was worth nothing, except that one could purchase food on ration cards at controlled, low prices. Salaries were also low and controlled. Some flour could be bought on the black market for R-Mark, but an entire monthly wage would go for perhaps one pound. In order to afford this, many people started selling such household items as linen, woolen coats, shoes, etc. Anything was for sale on the black market. In the evening, groups gathered on the street corners, where the desired goodies were for sale, starting with cigarettes. There was no end to it. It seems the economy, if there was any, was running solely on the result of street corner deals. Almost everyone was involved. Those involved full-time had access to such valuable resources as cigarettes, sugar, fat or flour, which they could exchange for such pre-war valuables as cameras, watches, jewelry and gold. Those then went to the myriad of occupying power sources. An endless stream of parcels must have been flowing back to the U.S., containing cheaply bought valuables. In those days, I met an old classmate from my last years at school again: Heinz Goedicke—the only one I saw again, except old Kampe from Staacken. Most others must have died in the war. He was my age, but appeared 10 years older, with deep lines in his face and some gray hair. He was working the Black market full-time and thought making a living that way was the only way to fly and that the future lay in being a successful wheeler-dealer. I didn't like him much and thought that, if everyone would think that way, soon there would be nothing left to deal. When cameras, watches, etc. would run out, the black market would end.

This stayed on my mind as I tried to figure out a future for myself. There were no legitimate jobs in industry, since, at war's end, there was no industry. At war's end, Spandau's factories had been producing only armaments or ammunition. BMW made aircraft engines, Rheinmetall tanks and artillery, etc. etc. Those facilities had become empty shells, with their contents gone east. The only jobs available were in the brick cleaning gangs. And I had to find a job to continue to receive those strictly controlled ration cards. On my return home I had gone to the police precinct at the corner of Adamstrasse and Foelderichstrasse, filled out police recording sheets and shown my soldier's pay book as proof of identity. A few weeks later, an official identification card was mailed to me, without which one did not exist for the purpose of ration cards or anything else.

One day I ran into Horst Gehrmann, an old buddy from my youth group years, who had just returned from Russia. With his face reminiscent of a dead man and no flesh on his bones, he looked like Gandhi or worse. He was very weak, but recovering slowly. He had been released by the Soviets because he was near death. It turned out that he was taken prisoner while Soviet soldiers briefly detained me. He then had been roughly south of where I was located in Czecho-slovakia. Marching hundreds of miles east, he wound up in Stalingrad. There he unloaded German goods, which rolled in daily. He saw huge quantities of preci-sion machine tools deposited in the open, exposed to the weather. No one knew, or cared, about what to do with them; enormous values were rotting until useless. Many of the dismantled machines must have never been brought to use. The Soviets would have profited much more if they had left everything in Germany and ordered new capital equipment and installations from German industry, which could have revived both the Soviet and German economies. Because of the senseless way in which it was done, both economies fell behind for many years. Gehrmann also told about the primitive and abhorrent conditions in the USSR. He was carried daily by truck from prison camp to the place where German and Russian prisoners, including women, were working. Almost daily the truck driver would stop, point at a woman to step down, and have sex with her in front of everyone. It was done so routinely that Gehrmann speculated it to be a widely accepted practice. And, once they were prisoners in the USSR, these poor Russians were as badly treated as the Germans. Having barely survived the ordeal, Gehrmann was lucky the Russians didn't dispatch him for good, like millions of others.

I visited him in the tiny room/kitchen he now shared with his mother, who had been booted out of her apartment, because her husband had been an official employee of the Nazi party and worn those gold-braided uniforms that came with the job. He never turned up again and must have been deported to the Soviet Union. Like me, Gehrmann had never joined the party despite his father's being a bigwig. Now he and his mother lived in this small room with a very low ceiling, very damp, near the Havel River in Spandau's old town. Close by were remnants of the city's first wall, built in the 11th or 12th century. In thinking about our future in those desperate times, both of us were more than ready to begin with our engineering education. To us the war seemed to have been only a long interruption of our careers. But we didn't know about colleges and universities. Because the phones did not work and the papers did not write about this topic, we could only go there and knock at the door. I think Gehrmann, one year my senior, had already had one year of engineering study. So, he took the suburban to Putlitzstrasse station and walked to the "Beuth" Engineering College, well known throughout Germany. He later told me that they planned to open for winter semester soon, and that they were searching for qualified applicants. Many young men were still out somewhere in the world—in prison camps or on the road—or sick in hospitals. Many of my age were dead. The class of '21 (year of birth) was totally devastated. Looking around in Spandau, I had found only this character Goedicke, and, about a year later, run into a former classmate, Kampe, who lived in Staacken or Falkensee. I think he then was also attending engineering college. No one else was there, and no one could be asked. Back to the college question, attending college appeared quite possible for me, but would engineering degrees ever be useful again? Stories were floating around that Germany was to be converted into an agricultural state, with no industry left standing. This seemed to be confirmed to me daily. Only ruins were left of Berlin's industrial park, and perhaps some broken machines in the midst of the rubble. Railways were reduced to one-way service only, like in Siberia. In Western Germany, the Allies were also disassembling whole industries, sending the machines all over the world. As an example, for Yugoslavia, France, Poland, Czechoslovakia, a simple request seemed to suffice for getting what they wanted; no German government or authority was left to protest or resist. This scene was not conducive to studying mechanical engineering—apparently a subject without a future. Those I knew also had no good reason to proceed with it. Yet, I was convinced that I would be better off using this slack time in German affairs to get some education than by dealing on the black market or cleaning rubble bricks. Students were also entitled to ration cards, but the question was how to fund such expenses as transportation, paper supplies, books and my food. Working a job while studying was impossible, as the program was too intense. I would need to leave at 6:45 a.m., return at 5:00 or 6:00 p.m. and spend the remaining hours studying, completing assignments, or composing my own backup material. Because specialty books like kinematics, static, turbine design, thermodynamics, stress analysis, etc. were unavailable, I had to produce my own materials from notes taken during the lectures—but now I am getting ahead of myself.

Armed with my school records, air force pay book, identification card and tool-making records, I took off for the "Beuth" College in the North of Berlin near Putlitzstrasse station, which is part of the elevated railway ring around Berlin. The electric trains circling Berlin did not function yet. A steam operated suburban train coming from Nauen stopped in Spandau and went straight on a tangential toward Putlitz station. It stopped in Siemensstadt, where in peace or war, crowds of workers, managers, engineers and office personnel left the train for their workplaces. There were the enormous Siemens-Halske and Siemens-Schuckert plants as well as the Siemens Main Administration and Corporate Offices. Many employees had moved more and more into the lovely countryside west of Spandau, around Staacken, Falkensee, Finkenkrug and Brieseland—names which indicate that they settled there to be closer to nature and to relax at least over the weekends, surrounded by forests, meadows and lakes. And then, during wartime, there was less danger of being wiped out. From Putlitzstrasse station I would walk another 15 minutes to the college, since there were no buses or streetcars, and no one owned a car. So, summer and winter, rain, shine or snowstorm, there was this "refreshing" walk at a time when we tried hard to conserve energy. When leaving home, I never felt fed and satisfied. Arriving at College in a hungry state, I toyed with the idea of sneaking up on my lunch, which invariably consisted of dark bread with a bit of fat. Sausage or cheese was a rarity, along with veggies or fruits, which had disappeared from the market and wouldn't have filled the belly anyway.

To the college personnel, who received me with open arms, I was kind of a rarity; they were looking for qualified people to begin studies, tuition-free. I would supply all other necessities, such as books, paper, slide rule, compass, etc. The awful-looking rooms had no glass in the windows and no one knew when they would be fixed. A bomb had destroyed part of the huge building in the last days of war. The heating didn't work. By the end of September the air temperatures turned so low that we needed a coat. Sitting in those buildings for 6-8 hours a day would not be a piece of cake! I got accepted, matriculated on the same day, and was given a starting date in October for the winter semester for the program of mechanical engineering, which would begin with a lot of repetition, since most students, having been soldiers for four to eight years, were unaccustomed to academic work. There were lectures on math, algebra, geometry, analytical geometry, calculus and many related subjects. In spring applied engineering subjects would be added. The semester promised to be tough; these subjects would separate the men from the boys.

Traveling home took another 1-1/2 hours and involved a long waiting time for the suburban, which did not run very often and therefore was always overloaded with mankind in shabby, worn-out clothes. Most people smoked cigarettes made from homegrown "tobacco," which released a god-awful stink. Later generations, not having been exposed to it, can hardly imagine the horror, as the smell was not typical of a cigarette or a cigar, but rather of burning seaweed, grass, or things like that. With the windows closed in the moving train, thick yellow clouds of this evil-smelling steam always surrounded one. While it nauseated most of us, the smokers enjoyed it, and no force on earth could have convinced them to stop. During those times I neither smoked nor picked up cigarette butts on the street, which many people did. The streets were always clean of butts—a self-cleaning arrangement. Although with up to three hours travel time daily life would be tough, I went home feeling good. There was something to do. I could learn something I liked and had a worthy goal. How to find a job later did not bother me much; I was still young enough not to get too worried by speculations about the future. I felt good for the first time in years—maybe, just maybe, something would come of it.

Father was already home and I told him what I had seen and would like to do. I needed his permission, since I would have to rely on his meager income for several years. He could not spend all of his income, because buying our rations and coal did not require much money. The remainder could not be used, since the black market was too expensive for normal incomes. For example, buying a pound of sugar might have required two months' worth of remnant income. One would do this only when seriously threatened by malnutrition. Everyone was always trying to put off coming to that point. I still had about RM (Reichsmark) 600, saved from 1938 to 1941 while carrying newspapers, to spend for whatever meager academic supplies were available on the market. Realizing that getting a degree in those crazy times was the only rational course of action, father agreed to feed and house me. He was also glad to have me continue living at home to help round up extra supplies. That was more important than holding another miserable job which paid hardly anything. I'll get to what those "extras" were later. My immediate future was now determined, and I could prepare for the adventures and work to come. I reported my success to Gehrmann, who told me he was going to move towards electrical engineering with emphasis on low-voltage technology, which then covered mainly telephone, radio and related applications. In the next days I went to Charlottenburg, the Berlin borough east of Spandau, to hunt for engineering handbooks such as the "Dubbel" or "Huette." They were absolutely essential, but books were not in print yet, since publishers were still either not functioning, bankrupted, bombed out, or without personnel. These books had to be hunted down in used bookstores, of which there were many in those days. The first things people discarded, sold or exchanged were books. Why? Simple—they are not very useful for eating or for warming a room. Books of any kind, including the most valuable antiques, were offered everywhere. The supply was overwhelming and prices normal. After days of searching, I finally located the first volume of "Dubbel" and then the second—quite a stroke of luck—and would use them throughout my working career. I also found two or three volumes of "Huette" out of a total of five. Now I was set to attend college for good. I didn't have to buy clothes or shoes—there were none to be had. What I had left from 1939 to 1941 wasn't much, but, compared to the many others who had lost everything, I was neatly outfitted. People then didn't criticize each other's fashions—a completely un-German trait nowadays. Times have changed greatly since then, when people only worried getting through the next day.

My first day in college began with a big surprise. I met Horst Gruenwald, who had also made it home safely. He last had been a flight instructor in East Prussia and had retreated safely. He had had a fiancée there, whom he had lost, having to follow orders, while the civilian population had been told by the Nazi bosses, who were still fantasizing about winning the war soon or other irresponsible things, to remain until further order. Mainly worried about their own hide, they transferred all their belongings to safe places in Bavaria or thereabouts on trucks, letting the ignorant, innocent country folk pay for the Nazi crimes. Gruenwald's fiancée did not make it; she was lost. Three years later, having been released from a Soviet prison camp, she surfaced in Berlin—a completely destroyed woman, a mere wreck, aged by thirty years in just three. Horst Gruenwald had the good fortune that his father operated a small cookie factory and had miraculously saved his machinery through the troubles and confusion of war's end. He was doing well, making cookies for the Soviet occupation forces, who brought him flour, fat and sugar, plus spices, so he could bake to his heart's content. The Soviets never learned that he was mixing chestnut flour, from chestnuts gathered by neighborhood kids, into the cookies, yielding valuable bags of flour. How well he did was obvious by Horst's being slightly overweight when I met him again after 4 ½ years in October '45. He even looked as if he might have high blood pressure—a look few Berliners were sporting. He had been offered a job as a flight instructor after completing his flight training at the Schoenwalde air base northwest of Spandau. He knew that Heiner Herbold and Gerlach had gotten into fighter pilot training and gotten shot down. These two had worked with me as toolmaker apprentices in the Heereszeugamt Spandau. Both were fairly well to do. Horst would always come in his three-wheeled delivery vehicle. Its steering bar served to throw the long front wheel into the desired direction, instead of a steering wheel. It sounds primitive, but it worked. Gerlach, whose parents operated a restaurant in Glienicke, south of Spandau, drove the long distance by brand-new motorbike—envied by all, including me. But I was used to this feeling and did not fuss about it. Both were dashing individuals. Heiner Herbold, the much more brilliant guy, was also a great athlete, well versed in track and field and gymnastics. It was typical of Herbold and Gerlach to have made it into flight training. At the time these decisions were made, I was working my guts out to earn money for engineering college. Herbold's father, a crack toolmaker, was more than able and willing to support his only son. Gerlach's parents were business people. Later on he wanted to attend the expensive Mittweida engineering school in Thuringia, a private institution with a much easier curriculum. I was also hearing about their occasional kayak outings on the Havel River, and I was led to believe that there often were girls involved during overnight camping trips. Having to listen to those tales had made me somewhat apprehensive and sad. I had sometimes felt left behind. Because I simply could not keep up with them, we had never developed a true bond, although we had worked together closely for three years. Generally, during those years, 1938–1941, I had been pretty much a loner, focusing on my goal of getting out of working for subsistence only.

Gruenwald had his place of work with his father, but decided to get an engineering education to round out his tool making experience. Mainly, he could use an engineering approach to mechanize his dad's cookie operation. He also hinted that, while a flight instructor in East Prussia, he had always supplied the important people with generous amounts of cookies, and therefore had never been transferred to front duties, had received frequent furloughs, and his training flights invariably would end up in Berlin. Now we were to continue in the same class for the next three years.

First, we had to keep the rough October weather out of the classroom. All over Berlin, there was no window glass available for any amount of money. What if we offered butter and eggs, which normal consumers ("Normalverbraucher") didn't have? But Gruenwald didn't offer anything either. We then started hunting for cardboard and, after a week, had enough to close all our classroom windows, but the natural light was gone. This "insulation" helped little against the exceptionally fierce winter of 1945/45. We were sitting there in coats, caps, mittens or gloves, wrapped in blankets. Finally it became difficult to move the fingers when writing—a total disaster. Notes had to be taken, the exercises and homework had to be written, and the course content had to be recorded in the absence of textbooks. For tests we could use whatever material or books we wished to bring, but the problems assigned were so unique that we never found the sources, which the professor seemed to have developed himself. For grading the entire mathematical approach was taken into consideration. Any numerical errors in addition, subtraction or multiplication, etc. were not valued very severely, as long as the fundamental thinking and principal development of the problems were o.k. and would have led to a correct solution without those little lapses. One could argue that, in practice, in industry, errors might lead to big disasters, but checks applied by industry to important work would usually prevent disasters. And then—they still happen. My opinion today is that little mistakes cannot always be prevented. It's inhuman to consider mistakes unacceptable in industry or college, where teaching the basics of the many disciplines is what counts. Here my college did a good job—or better: they tried to do the job under the worst circumstances imaginable. On the other hand, it was easier to teach us grown men, ready to absorb what was thrown at us. There were no females in my class, as they simply could not have fulfilled the prerequisites. At least two years of practical experience or a toolmaker apprenticeship in a relevant industry were required. It could be finished in three to four years. Hence, students had exposure to cold or hot metal-working processes, metallurgy, finishes, drafting and design. We were fairly well equipped to deal with any process, including the planning of manufacture and setting of production rates. Later in my life I once had to guide some senior Annapolis (Navy) midshipmen (engineering students) through the Westinghouse plant in Sunnyvale, California. They got thoroughly confused at a N/C controlled vertical boring mill, telling me that first the tap, of course, is pushed through the work piece and secondly the drill. My benign response was that normally we do it the other way around. They went through that plant in a daze, marveling at the enormous technology needed to build their navy propulsion units.

The first winter (45/46) was very tough. Returning home around 6 p.m., after my meager dinner, I had to digest the lectures of the day, transcribe notes into readable form and do my homework, which rarely ended before 10 p.m. I would often fall asleep at my "desk," a dilapidated dining table in the living room, to the right of the picture window, which opened to the balcony. It was the only heated room. We could not heat the two bedrooms, which were so cold in the winter that exhaled air froze in clouds. We had to sleep under enormous feather beds, which we had fortunately saved over the years. Those rooms were not heated in peacetime either for lack of money, but that winter there were simply no coal or wood to be had. It was an act of desperation to jump into the ice-cold bed. One had to tremble a few minutes before the body heat started to warm everything. Mother always pre-warmed her bed with a hot water bottle. When I worked in the evenings or on weekends, mother would gingerly tiptoe around me while father liked sitting at the tile-oven (Kachelofen) (heated daily with coal and wood), where he could expose his back to the warm ceramic tiles—something he missed while working. On rare occasions he would produce a cigarette, which a "Tommy" (British soldier) had given him when descending from the streetcar. Yes, Tommies were capable of this kind of friendly human gesture. We then would both sit and carefully enjoy this rarity—a hint that perhaps not all was entirely hopeless. Weekends were used to wrap up the week's work and prepare for the next. Saturdays were also filled with classes, but I would come home around 3 p.m. After so many years, with my notes discarded, I cannot describe each course I took. Among the few mementoes left is a little formula book perfected in 1946. Since there were no special engineering textbooks, handbooks etc. printed yet, we students would get together to compile them ourselves. One of these must still be around somewhere. The developments, which mainly overshadowed the postwar years, were the struggles to keep alive and warm, which involved the constant search for additional food, and fuel.

Then, as a young man, I also finally started thinking about girls, but these thoughts did not preoccupy me to a great extent, as I was not really looking to find a mate and settle down. There was no chance for that. My energies barely sufficed for the daily routines. In the evenings, going to bed hungry induced the most fanciful dreams about Black Forest or Sacher Torte with whipped cream, or Westphalian smoked ham, delicious Salami sausage, etc. As far as I can recall now, there were never any dreams of a sexual nature; my meager, minimal existence was not conducive to extravagance. I also didn't know any females. The social scene was dead, without movies or weekend dances taking place yet. The only entertainment was in a few pubs reserved for the occupying forces, where you could see Tommies with their German girlfriends. Observing a British soldier standing at a street corner with a one-pound can of coffee in his hands meant that he was looking for a German girl to have fun with. The can would be payment. After acceptable performance, there might be more. This supply chain provided relief for many German families. With an occasional pound of coffee—as good a currency as cigarettes—one could purchase fat, meat, anything. Without coffee I couldn't have stationed myself at street corners, and I wouldn't have done it with coffee, either.

While many girls were hanging out with Tommies, I think the majority rather went hungry. The desolate social scene kept me from meeting anyone, though there must have been a lot more women than eligible men. My age group was depleted, with most dead and many still in prison camps. Then one weekend a young woman knocked on our door asking to talk to me. She introduced herself as a cousin or aunt of Ellen Mosebach from Oranienburg. She lived just one minute away at Bruederstrasse. She told me about Ellen and her mother, who had abandoned their nice home and fled to Leer/Ostfriesland near the Dutch border, where they stayed with relatives. After a while it came out that she was to ask me if I intended to marry Ellen. It was an embarrassing situation for her and for me, to be confronted in this manner with such a delicate affair. Postal service did not function yet and heavens know how this poor woman got this message. And it didn't occur to my parents to retire into the unheated kitchen. So this woman, parents and pendulum clock were all looking at me for an instant response ... it really should have been done a bit more gently. But, of course, I didn't know what kind of trouble Ellen was in with her relatives and/or her mother, to resort to this approach. Relatives would often become nasty with their displaced "loved ones" when realizing they would forever be in their way and detract from their own bit of comfort. Whatever the case, I stood there, astonished and struck by this unexpected confrontation. My relationship with Ellen went through my mind. Because I had only seen her half a dozen times, a real strong bond had not developed between us on which marriage could be based. During those past ten or eleven months I had never thought about her as someone to go home to. We also had never discussed marriage. Knowing that the postwar years would be unpredictable and cruel, we had left that entirely out of consideration. She was a nice girl a man could be proud of … good background, education, and all that. But … was I ready and in a position to marry? Since I had no income, she would have to live in our tiny apartment together with my parents! That wouldn't go well! And I wanted to finish college before thinking about marriage. By that time, Germany's economy might be improved. Apologizing reluctantly, my message to Ellen was that there could be no marriage now—perhaps later after completing college! I felt guilty and depressed for some time afterwards. Last, but not least, this decision touched not only my life. Perhaps the chaotic times had subdued a good, fledgling relationship. I still feel some guilt while writing this, but that's life. While I can never ask her, I hope Ellen had a good life. This does not mean I regret the events, which happened later and seem to have been tailor-made for me, adding up to establish who I am—for better or worse. I never heard from Ellen again. My parents later didn't give input nor did I ask them to. It was so awkward … if one imagines the four of us standing in the living room, not even sitting down. I should describe our living room: there was my desk, as mentioned before. In the middle of the room was the dining table with four chairs (wood with cane seats). Along the west wall was the credenza with our china, glassware and linen. Opposite the window was the door. The tile oven took up one corner, the treadle sewing machine the other, with the pendulum clock hanging above. There was no room for a sofa or armchair. Next to the sewing machine was the door to the first bedroom, which was so narrow that the beds for mom and dad were lined up against the wall behind one another. I slept in the other bedroom. The kitchen had a coal or wood burning stove, where water was heated for washing dishes and where the cooking took place. Along the wall there was a table for washing the dishes in large pans and for preparing the food; we would usually eat at that table. The bathroom had a regular bathtub, which was seldom used, because we then had to heat the water in the kitchen and the daily washing, tooth brushing etc. took place in a large pan, which was suspended across the bathtub, which was of unpainted aluminum. Tub baths took place only once a week. A very narrow balcony spanned the length of the living room. A narrow hallway, in which a small credenza was kept for gloves, mittens, etc., connected the rooms and there were some hooks for coats, hats, etc. Limited as it was, the apartment was still a vast improvement over the earlier years at Ulmenstrasse. Unlike many German families, we were never directed by the authorities to house refugees. Not that I think there would have been room, but millions of people out there were looking for a place to put their heads down. Perhaps Berlin was too close to the Soviets for most who had been thrown out from the areas east of the Oder River. They wanted safety first and distance from the dreaded Soviets.

The confrontation about Ellen still occupied my mind when a few months later a letter from Helmut Neumann, my best friend from the Romania days, came from Wuppertal-Elberfeld. He had made it through the war and had attended an officers' course, same as Hajo (Hans-Joachim) Locat. He invited me to visit there and asked what became of Hajo, whose parents lived in Babelsberg near Potsdam. So, one weekend I made what turned out to be a very sad visit. Hajo's parents were devastated by the loss of their only child. Hajo had been stationed at an officers' training school in the east of France. When the American troops approached, all these young, inexperienced officer candidates were handed rifles and thrown into some breach to hold off the U.S. juggernaut. Against the full force of their mechanized might with enormous firepower, the poor souls with rifle in hand could do nothing. They and poor Hajo were slaughtered. This is how fate deals with the individual. Hajo and Helmut, the most eligible, because they had high school diplomas, which carried the right to enter a university, had succumbed to the incessant pressure to become officers. Hajo had already been studying physics at Berlin's Humboldt University. I had a strange feeling when both left the unit in Romania to attend officers' school, not thinking much of the war's future or the Nazi regime. We knew the war was lost, but didn't realize the full amount of vengeance that would ultimately be unleashed upon Germany when its war atrocities would be revealed. Until 1948/49 I had considered those horrible concentration camp stories, which were published, enemy propaganda. Hajo's life had ended senselessly. He was better than most I ever knew. I am convinced he could have moved the world a little. I wrote this to Helmut and promised to visit during spring semester break. He was staying with an uncle and seemed to work in his retail bookshop.

Around the same time, I met a tall, blond male law student. He had been invited to a little party with two girls, and he needed to bring a second man, without whom there would be no party for anyone, since suitable men were scarce. I mean, where do you find girls who invite you to a party? The apartments were so tiny and packed with people … who would dream of a party, anyway? So, one evening he and I walked up a street leading from Spandau Markt toward

Moltkestrasse, knocked at the apartment door and met two of the nicest girls one could imagine. One was Lore Gaertner (Eleonore); the other's name I don't remember. I never met her again. They had decided that the terrible time of isolation had to end; people would have to meet and exchange ideas. There was nothing to eat or drink, but there were a small self-contained record player and some jazz records. Pretty soon we were swinging the girls around; obviously this is what they had wanted. Since the parents had left for the evening, we were very comfortable. I still don't understand how I suddenly could grab a girl and dance. I think it was my first opportunity for dancing; I had no such chances during the war, neither had I danced with Ellen. Lore was good at it and very smooth, while the other girl, who must have had good connections to the countryside, and was fairly clumsy and heavy-set, was harder to move. After the dance, which ended around 10:30 p.m., both of us men walked Lore home. She lived at the "Plantage" across the river. The two girls were long-time classmates and friends. The other guy left in central Spandau, heading south, which would have been my way home, but I first wanted to get Lore home safely. I felt comfortable with Lore; she was good to talk to. She was one year younger than I and still remembered a teacher, whose name was Horak. He had been transferred from my boys' middle school, since he could not handle us boys. The girls, in turn, made complete mincemeat out of him. When we said good-bye at her doorstep, Lore was pleased when I asked to see her again. This started our friendship; I saw her only infrequently, because the days remained filled with so much college work. Another reason why I did not meet Lore very often was the walk to her apartment, where she lived with her mother and sister. The mother, from a business family involving hotel properties, was divorced. I didn't know or ask how many assets were left. Father, who had a plumbing business, lived on Bruederstrasse, close to our place. Lore, a merry, sanguine person, looked like father, and sister Christel, a tomboy and very reserved and moody, like mother. I seldom spoke with Christel, who was very strong for a girl and liked physical work. She had learned gardening and worked in a nursery.

Meeting and entertaining a girl was difficult at that time and limited to visits at home. Spandau offered no entertainment, and I could not have afforded it. Of course they had a sofa to sit down on and talk for a while. Occasionally we would go for walks. Perhaps I could have taken Lore into one of those corner pubs, but in 1945–48 they had nothing to offer. The occupation authorities had forbidden the brewing of beer, since barley was needed for nutrition. Wine and liquor could only be bought on the Black market, the latter usually British or U.S. whisky at exorbitant prices, which normal people could not pay. And I always found drinking beer in pubs a brainless and poor use of one's time. I still do. During those years, the vineyards along the Rhine and Mosel rivers in Southwest Germany must have produced plenty of grapes, which were usable only for wine production. But no wine ever appeared on the market. It must have been confiscated by the allied officer corps, similar to times during the war when German officers had commandeered it. Common people never saw a drop. I believe during that time of hardship a thought formed within me that I had to get at the better things in life, somehow. The only mechanism I saw was education. And then there was Lore, with whom I started dreams of the future, what I wanted to do and where I wanted to go. She worked as a secretary at the U.S. military government headquarters in Dahlem, a southwestern, plush suburb of Berlin. She must have often been tempted to acquire a G.I. boyfriend and easily could have found an officer, I think. Her English was good, much better than mine, because of daily practice. Once we were invited to a party in Dahlem, where mostly Whisky was offered. I could hardly drink anything in my emaciated state and would have quickly gotten very drunk. These soldiers, a merry bunch with no worries, had no idea what it was like to be hungry for a long time. I found it difficult to speak with them. Lore easily made conversation. She knew some of the boys, who treated her with attention, almost reverence. I could tell she did not commingle closely with any of them. My hopes to fetch a few cookies or things like that were crushed. There was never a repeat party. Lore also did not display things that other girls who had liaisons with G.I.s openly flaunted, such as cigarettes, coffee, chocolate, cookies, nylon stockings, etc. She apparently considered this unethical. I am sure her mother, with whom I got along very well, and who seemed to like me, had a lot to do with it.

In early 1946 the subway was operating again. I could take the streetcar #78 to Charlottenburg (Theo. Heuss Platz), continue by subway to Friedrichstrasse in Berlin Center, and from there to Gesundbrunnen and beyond, which got me closer to college. Part of the subway route was below the Soviet sector, but this bothered no one; traffic moved freely between the sectors. As in past years, many people from the west worked in the east, and many in the east worked in the U.S., British and French occupied sectors. The city essentially worked as one until political skirmishes developed in 1948/49 between the former allies. There was one elected city government in 1946, one BVG (traffic company) and one power company. On the subway one could see U.S., British, Soviet and French soldiers. They behaved mostly like any civilians, except when one ran into a weirdo. One day, I was riding the subway with two buddies from college when a Soviet soldier started to molest girls and women around us, grabbing their breast and worse things. It was too much for us. Forgetting that he might have a gun in his pocket, we pulled him away physically and pushed him toward the door, threatening to throw him out of the moving train. We could not open the door fast enough to prevent the subway train which was entering a station, from stopping there. Unfortunately it was in the Soviet sector. The train stopped, the door opened, and the soldier pulled on me, demanding that I come with him to the "Kommandantura" (seat of Soviet city government, while he was grabbing something in his pocket. To me that meant he had a loaded gun. Making me walk up the stairs, he walked behind me with his hand on the gun in his pocket. Arriving at the top, I expected he would walk me to the first KGB agent; there were legions of them in Berlin. That would have meant my disappearance to Siberia. Many people then still got snatched and vanished. Those thoughts were crossing my mind when he motioned me to go back down to catch the next train. He then removed his hand from his pocket and walked away—perhaps he had faked the gun. He may have gotten scared and was relieved to get away alive. So was I—a reasonable deal. And we had alleviated the women's plight! Had we knocked him down in the Soviet sector station, other soldiers could have appeared immediately to take us in. Our actions would have been considered rioting, punishable by huge prison terms or death. I have never forgotten this hair-raising incident and my so-called buddies' quick disappearance when the going got rough for them. The big lesson was: "Hermann, essentially you are always on your own!" These events formed my picture of the world around me: my first unconscious moves toward becoming a self-reliant U.S. citizen later, although I then had no idea what lay ahead. Only Germans with relatives in the U.S. were then considered for U.S. visa applications and leaving Germany was not on my mind. I was concentrating on survival, college work and visiting the Gaertners sometimes.

The subway enabled me to reach Dahlem, where Lore worked, on my way from college. I could switch lines on Wittenbergplatz, which took me within 20 minutes to Dahlem. Once I passed an officers' club on the way from the station to her place. That was the time of day when I would always be very hungry, often having finished my meager lunch at the 10 a.m. break, with nothing left for later. Upon arrival in Dahlem, my rebellious bowels were making revolting noises, which happen when one is super-starved. And I was approaching an officers' club. I couldn't see it, but I could smell the intriguing, intense and unmistakable aroma of donuts in the air. Its intensity increased with each step I took. Now I know they were donuts, but I had no idea about them then and only faintly remembered that in peace times, mother would bake "Berliner Pfannkuchen" on New Year's Eve, 3" diameter pastries usually filled with a delicious preserve such as prunes or strawberries. Her fresh ones were tastier than those from the bakery, and they were hot! With this on my mind, stumbling past the entrance, I started hallucinating: a big, fat G.I. would appear to offer me a fill of whatever they had in there. It was plain torture, as described in the Greek "Tantalus" saga. Meeting Lore afterwards was an anti-climax. I did not meet Lore in Dahlem often, perhaps even only once, since it was a strain for me so late in the day and required a long walk home in order to sit down with a poor, not very filling meal. At Lore's or any other friend or family member, food or drink, except for a glass of water, would never be offered, since people didn't have enough and were starving. And the Moratz' still had more than most. Remember the horsemeat? Then there were some potatoes in the basement. But toward spring 1946, everything was gone, and we needed something extra.

I talked with Gehrmann, who had been in dire need for some time, having returned to Berlin looking like Gandhi or worse. His mother was not getting ration cards, since her husband had been a Nazi official, although she herself had never been part of an organization. We decided to travel by steamboat on the Havel river south toward Potsdam. Our knapsacks could hold about 40 pounds of potatoes. We may have had some flint to offer in exchange. Everyone was dealing in them. After a very short time the entire German countryside must have been immersed in flint stones, with the farmers ready to look for better things, such as clothing, shoes, carpets or gold. Arriving at our destination in the late afternoon, we tried to exchange flint for potatoes, but couldn't convince the farmers, who were overrun and bothered by hungry Berliners and welcomed only those who offered needed goodies. We felt desolate, cold and abandoned. The ground was still frozen solid, but we didn't want to return empty-handed. No one had offered us even a handful. They were to lose everything later on when all land would be "socialized." We probed around in the cold and could make out a number of earthen hillocks. Usually farmers would store potatoes underground, cover them with thick layers of straw, followed by another thick layer of soil for protection against freezing. In spring, with the danger of frost gone, the potatoes were dug out and taken to the market. Our boat would leave soon, so there was no time to lose. As trained infantry, we crawled to the heap on our elbows. A light shone brightly, and the heap was not more than 70-80 feet from the next farmhouse—too close for comfort. If discovered, we wouldn't have a prayer, since the farmers' dogs were vicious. The farmers would have had to turn any weapons in to the Soviet military government, but in addition to having dogs, they were strong and well fed. We quickly removed the soil and straw with our bare hands and were starting to feel the precious buds, when we heard a dog bark nearby and—oh horror—the door to the farmhouse opened slightly and a head appeared, staring toward the heap. But, blinded by the light behind him, the observer couldn't see us in the dark. He retreated after a while, and we continued filling our bags, swung them over our shoulders and ran as fast as we could to the boat, which we reached just before departure. We felt good about our valuable scoop. The food was simply needed—by any means. It couldn't be helped. Actually, both of us were proud to return home with 40 lbs. of potatoes. My parents were elated about my gift. Something extra to put our teeth into meant an awful lot in those times, although the most important ingredient missing was fat—in any form. Nutritionists nowadays believe one actually does not need fat. Whenever we touch any, especially processed, food today, it invariably contains too much fat, except if it is specially prepared. In 1946/7, if I remember correctly, the daily ration equaled one tiny brick of butter of the size offered in restaurants. Everything was mostly fiber.

Another potato caper involved our raid of the Seeburg potato fields. A typical village of the province of Brandenburg, Seeburg was in the Soviet zone, about 6-7 kilometers (or less than 5 miles) from where we lived at the southern periphery of Spandau. Farmhouses, barns, cow- and horse-sheds were all bunched together in the village on two streets, which crossed each other. Since the fields surrounded Seeburg, it took some farmers half an hour to arrive at some of their properties. When the harvest approached in the fall, a throng of interested Berliners wanted to partake. However, one needed to avoid getting caught by the Soviet guards, who patrolled the fields at night. Strolling into the fields one day, father and I came across a large potato field and quickly dug out 20 pounds. Retreating fast toward Spandau, we were stopped by a civilian who appeared out of the blue. A village policeman in civilian clothes, he asked us to follow him to the village. Disagreeing with him, we pointed toward a stand of trees where we would rather move. We knew that German officials did not have guns yet. This fellow desisted from taking us two husky men into custody. But we beat an urgent retreat, making sure no one was following by bike or other, faster transportation.

A third potato-related event turned out quite differently. The hungry Berliners had devastated the potato fields and large areas had thus already been prematurely "harvested." Soviet soldiers were rumored to guard the remnants at night. We went in the middle of a nasty, rainy night with our bike and two potato hoes and found a suitable patch. I started working close to the field's edge, where a narrow path divided one field from the next. About 20 feet away, father was digging away with his hoe, which had three short steel prongs and a 1-1/2 foot handle. Sometimes, hitting a stone, he produced a loud, pinging noise. Each time I hit one I stopped, straining my eyes, to make sure no one was coming. I had no idea how far this loud noise would carry through the night! It was pitch black, and, even though I was used to the darkness, I could not make out anything 10 feet away. I just about had dug out enough of the buds when I thought a shadow was approaching. I stopped hoeing immediately, but father kept working with his occasional sharp "ping-ping" noises, loud enough to awaken a sleeping guard. I got very excited and scared to death. I was in full cover among the plants, about 3 feet from the path where the shadow approached steadily. The figure, including the head, appeared protected from the rain by a canvas. We thought it was a soldier on patrol—completely alone. He must have been about 10 feet away when we first saw him, and had to be equipped with one of those nasty submachine guns, which I knew too well. What to do? I could not call father to stop digging—things happened so quickly. Now the shadow was next to me, I heard father's "ping-ping," and I almost died. This guy had to be hearing the noise now, but kept on stumbling forward, one step at a time. Then he slowly dissolved into the night. I crawled over to father on my belly to make him stop. What a relief! This Ivan had acted like a typical night guard—bored to death, hardly awake, not giving a damn! Luck had again been with the daring—more than fate owed us! We hastily placed all potatoes in our canvas bag, the kind used commercially for bulk foods, like sugar, flour, rice, etc., and waited for about 15 minutes, listening for sounds of human movement. Since there was none, we carried the bag of about 50-60 pounds to the bike, threw the bag on it and started pushing it toward the Berlin border. We had gained another respite from extreme hunger, which would have meant being unable to do one's job.

These weeks and months in postwar Berlin were filled essentially with college work, commuting, providing for extra food (mainly potatoes), and seeing Lore, with the latter visits spaced somewhat widely apart. Mostly we concentrated on ventures into the countryside, attempting to swap food for dispensable items we still had at home. There was a pair of black riding boots and pants I had bought in 1939 to wear on my march with the H.J. (Hitler Jugend or Hitler youth) to the fall gathering of the Nazi Party in Nuernberg. While short pants had been the rule and more comfortable for the long daily marches, riding boots and pants had been required for the Nuernberg parades. I had never worn this most uncomfortable outfit, because I had stopped attending H.J. events before or after the '39 Nuernberg rally. I had mostly been convinced by friends—friends like Gehrmann and Sossna—and of course we had received extra vacation with pay. Now, this outfit might be useful in the countryside for shoveling manure or attending the cows. One weekend I took off toward Rathenow (west of Berlin), descended at a forlorn place in the midst of nowhere, and walked another 8 miles away from the railway line into virgin country. Moving toward the village, walking in the dark on a moonless night, I could not identify anything. Then I heard voices of people who were on their way back to Berlin. We soon became acquainted in the dark, and I talked with a girl, whose voice sounded optimistic and straightforward, inspiring confidence. She told me her address and asked me to visit. It is somewhat significant that I didn't think of Lore and didn't feel sufficiently committed to her to decline the invitation. In those days one didn't date a girl when seeing another one regularly. It was different than what seems to be the current practice in America. Anyway, I must have stayed overnight in some barn. On the next day I met a farmer who happily exchanged flour, lard and bacon for my boots, etc. It had been a very successful outing, but now there were no boots, pants or any other items left to trade. Some weeks later I looked up the girl I had met in the dark. She had a small basement apartment in Wilmersdorf. I found a disappointingly plain-looking, stocky person, who did not look at all like her voice had sounded. It turned out that she already had a fiancé and was looking for a good man for her best friend. I was not interested in her; she was a listless person. Making some vague promises, I retreated quickly glad to have extricated myself.

Some time in early 1946, I had another harrowing experience. One day I pedaled south on my bike on Wilhelmstrasse toward Glienicke, which was already Soviet zone, while Wilhelmstrasse ran parallel to the zonal border for a few miles. I think I wanted to cut some new grass for the rabbits we kept on our balcony. We would eat one at Christmastime—a delicious and quite filling meal, reminiscent of pre-war times. The rabbits regularly got potato and cabbage scraps from the kitchen, but peels were scarce and thin, and even the rabbits sometimes needed extra food to get fat. Merrily pedaling along a path in the woods, I ran into a Soviet soldier with a submachine gun. Without enough speed to pass him, I sensed that the s.o.b. had sinister intentions. Putting his hands on the handlebar, he made me get off with the words: "this is my bike," and took off for the Soviet zone a few yards away. He had a gun and under the circumstances I could be sure he would use it. The Soviets got away with anything in their zone. Hence, I had lost my valuable bike, which could not be replaced, because bikes were not made yet. We had bought it in 1936/37, just a run of the mill bike with a single gear, simple tourist saddle and straight handlebar—not the type used on racers in those days. I mourned the bitter loss for a long time.

We heard almost nothing from sister Lisbeth and husband Werner (Ehling). She must have been intensely involved with her new baby girl, Sabine, born in summer of 1945, while I was still away. My parents and most acquaintances considered it an irresponsible undertaking. Germany was in tatters without a future for anyone—what was to become of a new child? It meant only more excruciating, thankless work for the mother. Werner was not used to being at home much. I was also told later that he never visited the countryside to search for extra food, which I could not understand. But in those times I was very distant from him, since he was simply not my cup of tea, and I didn't even bother to figure him out. When I visited once around 1947 or 48 on a Sunday morning, he took me to his corner pub, where beer was served, which I didn't like. There he horsed around with his buddies all morning, leaving the site only to sit down at home with Lisbeth's good Sunday meal. Although this seemed then to be customary in many German families, at our home father would prepare such things as potatoes, would get kindling and coal from the cellar—things like that. A fairly frugal and reasonable man, who tried to contribute whatever he could, he didn't hang around with his buddies, especially not on Sunday mornings.

In mid-46, with such extra provisions as canned horsemeat and potatoes almost depleted, we were desperate for some high calorie supplies (fat, oil, lard, etc.) Around that time I had been looking for the old buddies of the youth group days from around 1935. I only knew about Gehrmann and Sossna. Guenther Sossna was supposed to be a purchasing agent in a newly formed company, have gotten married, and have left Berlin for Bavaria soon thereafter. Perhaps Berlin was too much of a powder keg for his taste, or he had gotten a better position. I confirmed this assumption 50 years later in Munich, meeting him again with his second wife. He had risen to the top of "Deutsche Edelstahlwerke," a crack, top-notch manufacturer of alloy and stainless steels and forgings. I also knew that Georg Herwig, who had lived at Zimmerstrasse and had learned the bakery trade, had become a soldier in the German parachute division, which jumped into the island of Crete in 1946. Severely wounded, he had received the "Iron Cross 1st Class," which was seldom given to a mere soldier. I heard he had survived the war and lived in or near Essen as a policeman. Later I learned that he had made a good career as a criminal investigator. Those were the only ones I heard about of the troop of 20-30 boys. From the old days, only Gehrmann remained accessible to me. There was Gruenwald, too, but he was from my later apprenticeship days. Around 1946, Wholleben, from Thuringia, another fellow from Heereszeugamt Spandau suddenly surfaced. Like Sossna, he had gone into the weapons officer's career, and, also like Sossna, spent the war with a tank division. But he had been lucky to spend all of his time in the west. During the invasion, he was stationed on the isle of Jersey, a British possession close to the French coast. He could not understand why a crack Panzer division could be positioned on an island. They did not fire a shot and were taken prisoners by the British. Spending time in England, he found a good girl to marry and was allowed to stay in England. On a short visit to Berlin he showed off his fantastic new trench coat, good woolen suit and fabulous quality shoes. He made it! Gehrmann and I regarded him with envy. That's what one had to do to get a little out of life. I never saw him again. I doubt that he had a good career in England, unless he immigrated to Canada later. England seems to me not a very egalitarian society, with her own good old boys preferred over foreigners. But then we could not look beyond his scented British cigarettes, which he offered freely. Perhaps through this encounter the first unconscious seed of trying my luck overseas entered my mind. Britain seemed to go full blast, while nothing was happening in Germany yet. From a Berliner's perspective in 1946/7, little could be gained by sticking it out there and/or in Germany. The situation required quick, flexible thinking by each individual. After all, there was only one life to live, and I wanted to employ myself gainfully and live a decent life.

Meanwhile, things around me deteriorated further. During another venture into the country with some more spare household goods and cautious hopes that farmers or farm hands might consider them exchange values, I ended up at a mill to negotiate for flour, which mother could make into the most wonderful things. While the man I had approached had left the small mill storage room where we met to advise his mother or wife of the deal we were about to make, I discovered some very old 10x16" simple canvas bags sitting on a ledge. I suddenly realized I had nothing to fill the flour into if the deal would go through. In a panic I picked two of those, only to be caught putting them in my knapsack. Coming toward me and cursing me, he repeatedly slapped my face. I was too embarrassed to resist. He was much stronger than I and, mostly, I had been caught stealing—not normally a commendable act, although the article's value was almost zero. I had to follow him to a living room, where several men and women were staring at me as if I were a lousy thief, although they handed me my flour in paper bags. I left quickly, feeling terrible on my way to the railway station and struggling with the times and myself. I thought: "what can one do?" After all, I was the one on line to provide something extra. Father's job kept him very busy day or night. Walking along, I angrily cursed the times, which forced decent people to employ any means to survive. These kinds of experiences led me to think more and more of leaving Berlin for good, although in 1946/7 I had no definite plans. I think I once requested and received information on immigration to the U.S. Because a permanent visa for me required a 20-year waiting period, the U.S. was out of my reach. Those with U.S. relatives filled the ranks for years to come. Around 1947 France, which had a recruiting station near the college, was looking for skilled workers. An interviewer I spoke with appeared impressed with my tool-making background, but, when hearing that I was a student, he lost interest. They did not seem to need German engineers, but wanted to tap the vast skilled workers labor market. In 1946/47 Germany was not yet supplied with significant Marshall Plan seed monies, which may have been given first to France and Great Britain. Their economies were on the upswing much before that of Germany. General Marshall, then foreign secretary in the Truman administration, had proposed what was to be called the "Marshall Plan," which stipulated loans of vast amounts to the devastated nations of Europe, including the vanquished. Eastern Europe and the Soviet Union were to be covered, but the Moscow bosses declined participation, because they would have become accountable to the capitalist west. Their policy seemed to be to impoverish all of Europe, so that the poor, desperate working class would join the Bolshevik cause and the hated capitalist system would vanish from the liberated earth. This scheme came close to success, since Italy's and France's communist parties already had achieved dominance. Only the slow infiltration of U.S. Marshall Plan funds gradually improved the well being of those countries' population, so that the worst was postponed again and again. Germany did not have a communist problem in those times, except for the countless East German opportunists, who joined the "socialist party" for a few sausages, eggs and other enticements. I later heard that the husband of my cousin Jutta in Koepenick (Uncle Willi's daughter) had joined the police. He wanted to be somebody who commanded respect and would not have to work so hard on a workbench as a lousy toolmaker any more. Thinking the East German communist regime would last forever, countless millions chose accommodation rather than—actually, there were few impressive alternatives at the time. Such thoroughly washed-out concepts as heroism and freedom were no longer respected, but rather looked at with contempt. Prevailing attitudes seemed to reflect those of Bertolt Brecht: "Erst kommt das Fressen und dann kommt die Moral." ("First and foremost is the feeding of the belly; the morals come later.") Attending the play "Mutter Courage" by Brecht at the "Theater am Schiffbauerdamm" in East Berlin with Gehrmann, we marveled at this phrase, which stayed in our minds for a long time. To us, who were permanently hungry, it described the times perfectly. The East German authorities preferred this kind of play, thinking it reflected the oppression of the masses by the capitalists, but Berliners then rather looked for their oppressors behind Soviet uniforms and their stooges.

This is how it was until the "socialist" regime later collapsed under its own weight.

Attending plays in the many repertory theaters in West or East Berlin was about my only recreation: the Schiller-Theater near Kantstrasse, the Deutsche Opera and Staatsoper in East Berlin, but, with no border and traffic flowing freely, one didn't distinguish yet very much between East and West Berlin. Among the plays I saw were Schiller's "Wilhelm Tell," Goethe's "Tasso," "Die Laune des Verliebten"—all with very inexpensive tickets. We always occupied the "Heuboden" (hayloft) way up in the house, with other students who also had paid around 10 Reichsmark, the price of half a cigarette on the Black market. The actors had a rough time, too; they were paid in worthless currency and had to live on ration cards only. I sat across from Gustav Gruendgens, the most renowned actor Germany had produced in the last 50 years, one late evening in the subway on my way home. There he was, also hungry, but with a large ruby ring on his finger, staring ahead expressionless. Everyone recognized him, but no one started a conversation. That wasn't normally done on the subway; it was not for making acquaintances. That's the way it is still today, although famous actors are no longer seen riding it. I find it remarkable that I cannot remember ever visiting the theater with Lore Gaertner or any other females during that time. My memory is blank about this, but I know that we simply never attended the theater together. Such attendances were rare, as time and money were scarce. Even the miserly ten marks were hard to come by, and I could not ask father for money.

I could make extra money via foraging trips into the West of Germany. I sometimes purchased cheap "Schnapps" (potato brandy) in East Berlin, where it was available at fairly high prices, around 50 marks. A lot of it was made in East Germany, while in the west its prohibition was vigorously enforced. By traveling from Berlin to the west and crossing into West Germany, I could easily sell the booze anywhere and later exchange it for such things as oil or fish oil (mainly cod oil), the latter being the cheapest. For around six bottles of booze I could get 1-2 gallons of cod oil. By selling ½ gallon of cod oil in Berlin I had my investment back, and the rest served to upgrade our fatless diet. Mother used fish oil for the most delicious potato pancakes (Kartoffelpuffer) or fried potatoes. One had to eat the fried food while hot. When cooled, the taste became so fishy that, as hungry as we were, we found it too awful to eat. After preparation, the apartment smelled for days like rotten fish. We didn't know then that cod oil is by far the healthiest fat. The only trouble was crossing the border.

Later in 1946 I set up for my first trip toward Helmstedt (West) and Oebisfelde (East). How the border was guarded was a mystery to me. I had to reconnoiter at the border town to see who guarded, and how. The trip to Oebisfelde took about five hours on a terribly overloaded train. People sat on each other's laps, and there was hardly room to turn around. Boarding in Spandau, one could not get a seat, as the train came from Berlin with people already hanging at the sides of the wagons and in between them. It was so bad that the train looked like a moving throng of people fastened to it with thumbtacks. Outside one could at least expect some air. Inside one almost suffocated from the smell of homemade tobacco, reminiscent of old burning mattresses. Arriving more dead than alive in Oebisfelde, people disgorged from the train and immediately disappeared in all directions to pursue their goals. A buddy and I went to the town center, where a local explained that the border was patrolled by Russian soldiers with automatic submachine guns, together with one East German policeman without weapons. This was the set-up in mid-1946. Then the friendly local showed us the way to a small river located at the borderline. We had to get there unnoticed, find a shallow ford and cross it quickly. There were no mines, observation towers, dogs, fast jeep patrols or barbed wire fences. Those were to come later. After negotiating a few corners and frantically searching for a fordable part, we soon found some strategically placed rocks, which enabled us to quickly cross the river without getting our feet wet. My buddy had already reached the middle of the river when I saw the patrol coming around the bend. I hastily danced through the riverbed, climbed up the bank and hid behind some thick willow bushes. My buddy, who was running west, got stuck at a barbed wire fence, installed ages ago by some farmer to keep the cattle from escaping. As he tried to extricate himself, the patrol had arrived—one Russian and one German. They were about 15-20 yards from my hideout. I could observe the exchange of words and gestures. The German yelled excitedly to the stoic Russian: "Come on, shoot him, shoot him," as my poor buddy struggled with the barbs. When the Russian made no move to satisfy the German policeman's demand, the latter yelled over and over: "What are you waiting for? Shoot him, shoot him!" This happened while both of us had already crossed the border and had reached West German soil. I saw the Russian waive off the German with disgust. Then my valuable fellow citizen had another idea: "But there were two! Where's the other guy?" I was "the other guy." They could have reached me by just walking over the rocks, but I was well hidden under the willows. If he had discovered me, he might have come across for me. There was no way I could have dared to run away with the gun on the other side and the German challenging the stoic (or better: wise) Russian: no way! But the Ivan simply didn't want to shoot at people on the other side—perhaps following orders? The unequal pair trotted on: The Russian, followed by the German, still not satisfied that no one got killed, who looked around occasionally for the missing man. My buddy had now freed himself from the wire, and I got up after the patrol was out of sight. I was terribly shocked, realizing that this German was ready to kill his own people only for walking across the "border" from one part of Germany to the other. Times had really changed. This cop, hired by the Soviets, was ready to do their dirty work for miserly pay—a thought that disturbed me greatly. In the East, the German population was being trained to serve only foreign interests. The country had lost its identity and cohesion. Everyone for himself. We swiftly trotted to the next train station. I never saw this fellow again. I don't recall what I brought back from this trip, probably fish oil. I have no recollection as to how and under what circumstances I returned across the east-west border, but I had learned that it was a dangerous exercise, especially because of the eagerness of the fledgling East German border police. While the Russians were calling the shots, there were still ways and means to cross. They did not appear to take things as seriously as the Germans did. Last not least, the Russians could not survive in their own country without breaking laws, regulations etc. They were experts at this and sympathized with those common folks who tried to strike a deal and better themselves.

On another such occasion, I went through Oebisfelde again, picking another approach to get me across the river with dry feet by negotiating a railway embankment and bridge. It was an out-of-service railway spur. I waited for a long time at the town line, overlooking a meadow with a cowshed and the embankment/bridge … for about one hour. All was quiet, with no movement or Soviet guards to be seen. I couldn't see behind the embankment, which was about 15-20 feet high. I reasoned that, had there been guards, they would have checked up on the other, south side occasionally, where I was lurking at a distance. Since nothing moved, I slowly approached the cow shed, stepped inside, and looked through the many gaps between the planks to make sure all was clear and ready for my final assault on the bridge to cross over to the west side. However, I suddenly then saw a Soviet cap rise slowly over the edge of the embankment and then the pertaining body moved to an upright position. He slung his gun over the shoulder and climbed down the steep angle. I still hoped he was just making a routine round, but, when he stepped onto the meadow, he aimed directly for my cowshed. He must have observed me. He was about 50 yards away, and I had about 50 yards to the small wooded area where I had started out. I looked at his gun, expecting others to be aimed at me, too. I should mention that, before all this happened, I had sneaked to the bridge and stopped underneath. Seeing six to seven soldiers on the other side had forced my hasty retreat to the cowshed, hoping they had not discovered me. They had been involved in a lively discussion and might not have noticed me. Sensing something was wrong when the Russian was slowly approaching, I decided not to risk my life and run for the town. One cannot treat similar situations in the same way. How could I be sure they would not shoot me in the back, just because I had once escaped in May 1945? I had a knapsack with six bottles of the cheap booze, and a valuable piece of red wool fabric with a Scottish pattern, enough for a dress, which had been given to me on consignment by someone in need of some edible fat. My entire assets were invested in the bottles, and I now foresaw their contents running down Russian throats. I saw myself wiped out. Entering the shed with a "good day," the guy asked where I was heading. I said my direction was west. Then he inspected my knapsack. He liked the bottles, and I expected to be taken in with my wares. Instead, he proposed in his broken German: "I talk to sergeant. We need one bottle tonight for a dance. You then can proceed to the west. Wait here! Don't run away! We will shoot you!" After walking back slowly across the embankment, he quickly reappeared: "You give one bottle for us. I will go back. After I disappear, you wait five minutes, then you stop on top of embankment, walk normally to bridge. In middle of bridge, you start run very fast. We will all yell very loud 'stoi, stoi,' (stop). We not shoot. I repeat: not shoot." With that he took his bottle and left me wondering if I could trust these Russians. I sensed a chance to have connected with some decent people, since they could have easily taken all I had. I decided to take the chance. After five minutes I crawled up the embankment, walked to the bridge, and started running, a whole choir of Russian voices behind me: "stoi, stoi!" Despite my utter apprehension and excitement, the gamble turned out all right. On the western side, another border crosser had incredulously observed the scene: "Why didn't they simply fire a warning shot and make you return?" Upon hearing the whole story, he shook his head and left to scout for a safer crossing. I believe the Russians had to do this in case some officer or political superior was observing the scene from afar with binoculars. Their action would give them cover. If they had taken me to the "Kommandantura," they wouldn't have gotten their bottle, for which they had taken a big risk. On the way back with an extremely heavy load of smoked herring and oil, I dreaded negotiating the crossing. Since, as planned, father was expecting me in Helmstedt (west), we were able to carry the delicious load. We trotted toward the border through the night, which was a stretch without a river barrier this time.

While resting a few hundred yards inside West Germany, father ate his first load of smoked herring (Bueckling) with delight. Continuing in the dark, we reached forest, meadows and shrubs. As we carefully negotiated through thick shrubs adjacent to a meadow around midnight, a shadow jumped up in front of me, shouting "stoi." A Russian, who had discovered us, then made us walk ahead of him at gunpoint—a scene reminiscent of World War II. Without the heavy load I could have easily sprinted into the brush, at very high risk, but father could not have done this at all. Arriving in a little wood frame guardhouse, where another Russian was waiting, we were asked what we had. They seemed to have no interest in fish or oil. Our captor noticed father's pocket watch chain and pulled it out. It looked golden—something those red-blooded Bolsheviks were after—the more, the better. No question about right, wrong, or equal distribution of goods preached by old Marx. The old-fashioned robber baron instinct got the better of him: take it from the defenseless under the gun and let the powerful have it. This modern-day pirate had a very entrepreneurial idea to soften his robbery: father could have his own old, dilapidated pocket watch, most likely picked up from some other helpless German, as exchange for the "golden" watch. If we agreed with the "trade," we could leave with our goodies. Father agreed immediately, the exchange proceeded quickly, and we happily went off into the dawn. We arrived at the railroad terminal exhausted, where we feasted again on our fat, smoked herrings. Father fetched one and first bit into the head. With cracking, loud chewing noises, he gorged down the whole 12-inch herring, including head, fins and tail. Those were the times when nothing could be wasted. The fingers were licked clean before attacking the next one. Much later we found that the ugly-looking exchange watch ran on time and was used for many years to father's satisfaction. The older, "golden" watch had never worked right, had been repaired often, and sometimes would quit without good reason. That was one of my most successful trips to the West. After satisfying all liabilities, we still had a huge amount of herring left. After a while, when they started smelling badly, mother quit eating them, but father and I ate many more with this bad smell; the taste was not bad yet. We gambled, but no one became ill.

Other ventures into the surrounding countryside or the West ended in disasters. Once I was heading west on an open railway car, where I met another guy who was going to Hamburg also. In those times freight trains were not yet controlled by the Soviets, neither did the British on the Western side bother to control border traffic. I carried a nice piece of light woolen fabric, suitable for a woman's dress, with me, which represented all of my liquid assets, and which I hoped to exchange for the usual oil and/or herring. Arriving late in Hamburg, I had to wait for a connection to Cuxhaven, where the best deals could be had, because its fishing industry was being resurrected, and one could meet leftover U-boat captains dealing in herrings, etc. In Hamburg I had to wait for the first passenger train to Cuxhaven until the next morning. I became very tired, and there was no alternative to bedding down on the floor of the overloaded waiting room. Luxuries like hotels/motels did not exist, and if they had, I would not have had the money. I propped up my head on the valuable cloth, which was in a knapsack. My travel buddy put his head down right adjacent to me. It was kind of drafty and uncomfortably hard. I dozed off, waking up a few times half-ways during the night. When I woke up in the morning, I looked around with alarm: something was wrong. My buddy was gone, so was the knapsack. My running all over the railway station was useless. Staying there was useless; my assets were lost. With no police, complaining would lead nowhere. On any given day these things were happening by the thousands. I did not even know the guy's name, or where he lived. This was my next big lesson: "No one is to trust!" Actually, I didn't trust. My "buddy" just had taken advantage of the fact that everyone was asleep on the concrete floor. He must have painstakingly pulled my cloth "pillow" out from under my head and replaced it with some old newspapers. I could do nothing but turn around and go home. This terrible blow left me depressed and discouraged about trading across the zonal border. The times of the welcome herrings and oil were over.

During that same winter, the Gaertner family ran out of firewood. There were neither men nor tools or carts in the household for getting wood. The father seemed to have little contact with the family. He was never talked about, although I believe Lore, who resembled him greatly, looked him up occasionally. In the absence of other help, I volunteered tools, cart and myself, for cutting some trees. Lore and her mother did not consider facing considerable danger, police lurking to apprehend them, etc. It seemed that, instead of coping with the problem, they would rather freeze. Let someone else do it. I think both were not disposed toward grabbing a saw or ax, or being seen pushing a lowly cart through the neighborhood. But Christel, who knew all about those things, was enthusiastic about the idea. One cold and snowy evening we went toward the outskirts of the Grunewald. Within an hour we had found some suitable trees at the embankment of the "S-Bahn" (elevated electric train, part of the railway system). Christel, who knew how to handle tools, was eager and helpful. Soon we had loaded the cart for the return home, relieved that no one had caught us during that very uncomfortable night. In the end, the three girls were very happy to have some kindling.

In the middle of the same winter, when temperatures were very low, father and I also went to replenish our dwindling firewood supply. Since guards were posted at major intersections to catch tree pilferers, we had to be careful. By early

1948, the population was freezing, even though most people heated only one room to the lowest level they could cope with. Because most people didn't have anything to heat with, the forests in and around Berlin were subject to ruthless clearing by the population. The pressed bituminous coal briquettes used in ceramic stoves in Eastern Germany, the West, and particularly Berlin, had become very scarce. The East German authorities, by now totally controlled by the Communist party, under the name of "Socialist Unity Party" (SED), manipulated the coal supply to put pressure on the Berliners. Therefore, in the evening, father and I searched for trees to cut down and saw into pieces that could be thrown into our cart. When this was done around 10-11 p.m. we walked the 1-1/2 to two hours home to catch some sleep until 2:00 or 2:30 a.m., when we marched back into the woods with our cart to pick up the cut-to-length timber. We selected the coldest nights of the season, thinking that guards would no longer be around to interfere with our illegal actions. Hardly able to manage the heavy load, we pulled the cart down Wilhelmstrasse with no guard in sight. Back home, we unloaded it and took another nap. In the following weeks the narrow courtyard echoed from sawing and splitting the wood until our basement compartment was full. If used economically, this kind of load could last for one year, and few Berliners were as well supplied with wood as we were, even though trees in parks and along the streets were almost depleted. The beautiful Tiergarten in Berlin Center was totally leveled by the population. What had not been destroyed during the intense fighting and last convulsions of the third "Reich" in that area was completely cleared of trees and shrubs in the following three years. This park, equal in size to New York's Central Park, was then converted into vegetable plots for the population. Originally, stately 200-300 year old oaks and beeches had stood here, and in the late 1700's to 1800's the park had been used mainly for exercises of the officers and horses of the numerous military units. Today it has been revived for delightful walks from the Brandenburg Gate all the way through the Tiergarten to the train station "Zoo," its other, western end. This walk takes close to an hour. A simpler way is by a 15-minute ride on bus number 100 from "Zoo" to the congress hall (Reichstag).

In the winter 1947/48 my various games to fetch extra food supplies usually had disappointing and meager results. Another catastrophic event took place in Stendal, about three hours on the train from Berlin to the west, but within East Germany. I again had some nice cloth, on consignment from Horst Gruenwald, to exchange for a specific amount of smoked bacon. Whatever I would negotiate in excess would be mine. I was lucky to strike a reasonable deal and got enough so that I could keep one pound of bacon for myself. Unable to return on the same day, I had to spend another night at a train station, again trying to catch some sleep while sitting with my head resting on a table. Later that evening there was a commotion, and the police arrived. People who possessed suspicious merchandise were taken to the police station, which was also part of the prison. Lined up with others waiting for the interrogation, I was sure what would happen. Since I had no receipt for the bacon, it would be deemed obtained illegally and belonging to the state. As a way out of losing it, I could think only of one possibility: Eat it! Because it was too much for me to get down before my turn came, I cut each of the people in line a piece with my pocketknife. Soon everyone was chewing with delight, and occasional burps could be heard, until the entire piece was gone. When my turn came for the interrogation, the cop stooges looked excitedly for the bacon, which they remembered, without finding any. They had made a big mistake in not taking it on the spot. Maybe the poor slobs learned their lesson for next time. They found a few pounds of flour on me, which they confiscated with delight, but they were still looking for the rare bacon. I lost everything that night, including Gruenwald's share. Now I would have to explain to him what happened. Since I could have pocketed everything, he could never trust me again. There was no proof otherwise—a most embarrassing situation. I could offer him no substitute. My reasoning was that he had also engaged in a high-risk gamble and lost, but with suspicion written all over him, I still knew that he resented it. Well, it could not be helped. I had exposed myself to this kind of gamble, and I had lost. Afterwards our relationship began to cool, and I never saw him again after graduation. But then, I was to remain only one more year in Berlin before my big adventure overseas. During our last college year, several months after he became engaged to a girl he had met, his first fiancée showed up at his door in a terrible state. She had been picked up by the Soviet military while attempting to flee East Prussia at the last minute, and then spent two years in a Soviet prison camp. They had rounded up everyone but the Nazi officials who had forced the civilians to hold out to the last minute. They were lucky to escape the wrath of their fellow countrymen. Lynching would have been the easiest way for them to go. They went west on trucks with their most valuable possessions. This girl was pushed from one prison camp to the next while suffering the most horrible deprivations: hunger, torture, rape, hard work under excruciating circumstances, including the Siberian winters. She looked like a mentally ill beggar or, rather, a returnee from Soviet camps. It must have been a terrible situation for Gruenwald, who had been her only anchor in the whole world. Her family was still missing and would possibly never return, as millions, including Russians, did not survive the Gulag. Apparently no one in Russia cared about human life. After some agonizing, Gruenwald decided in favor of his new fiancée, but I am sure the first one received help in starting a new life.

In mid-48, the border controls became so tight that I tried more ingenious methods to go to Western Germany. When I arrived at Oebisfelde, it was no longer possible to cross the border during daylight and very difficult at night. Resting at the train station to think through my dilemma, it occurred to me that I might be able to board a freight train and just roll through to the other side. At the time, there was considerable freight traffic on the railway between the West and Berlin, with all supplies, except coal, coming to Berlin from the West. In return, Berlin's slowly awakening industry sent its finished goods back. There was no exchange with East Germany. Only the Soviets—then the supreme power in East Germany—dealt with them while specifying the prices of various goods. Since a central economic bureaucracy controlled their own economy, they also determined all prices—to the detriment of poor East Germany. The population soon noticed the results of this permanent bondage held by the Soviets over East Germany, and millions migrated to the West by any means possible. This migration started early on and never stopped, although it was temporarily made very difficult through erection of the infamous "wall" by the East German government (of stooges). Since Russian guards checked all rolling stock for illegal passengers at the border, one risky possibility was to crawl underneath the wagon and stretch out on top of the axle, which was not rotating, but affixed to the structure. Rather, the wheels were rotating around the axle, but on top of it were all kinds of bars, which were part of the braking system. By keen observation and estimation, I had to figure out how those bars could move during the braking process to assure they would not kill or hurt me. Finally I satisfied myself that the brake system linkages would not move close enough to harm a person stretched out on top of the axle. When I noticed that the train was ready to move, I took my position, and the train moved slowly to the border checkpoint, about one mile ahead. Then it stopped. After noticing nothing for a long time, I heard approaching steps and the opening and closing of the railway car doors. I could tell by the boots and pants that they were Soviet guards. At that time, they would have submachine guns! Now my scheme was to be validated. One sneeze or cough, and my travels would end abruptly. Then the boots were right in front of my nose. I could smell their burning "papirossi," the foul-smelling Russian cigarettes, which had a thick, round paper end tube of the same diameter as the cigarette. The end tube or mouthpiece, as long as the cigarette itself, had to be compressed to form a narrow slot before being placed between the lips and then lit. Russians got only 1-1/2 inch of smoke—the rest was paper mouthpiece.

There was no filter. Lying on the axle, nerves on edge, I could have used one of those bad cigarettes. I was lucky. The boots stepped away and, after opening and closing the doors, began to fade. Now I could relax and wait for the engine's pull, which soon came, and thus I rolled over the border! When the train stopped in the West, I crawled from underneath to gain a more favorable travel position. I do not recall how this adventure continued, because I can now only cover the highlights of my life during those hard post WWII years. It is also intriguing that the aspects of foraging for supplies and the associated difficulties and disappointments rate first and foremost in my mind today. Compared to this, the college work was a daily, never-ending drudgery, of which I have forgotten the details. The rare encounters with Lore also do not seem to rate very high, although I admit that there was a certain joy associated with meeting a girl I was fond of. That relationship never got anywhere, mostly due to the meager circumstances, the lack of energy in light of my other obligations, and the few chances we had to meet. College was first, providing supplies second, and friends and/or girlfriends came next.

In early 1948, I looked up my old wartime friend Helmut Neumann in Wuppertal, where, having survived the war unlike Hajo Lokat, he worked in his uncle's bookstore. He had also wound up in officers' school, but I don't know where. He seemed to be an orphan of sorts, but I never inquired what became of his parents, neither did he offer a glimpse into his family or relations. After graduating from a private prep school in Strausberg east of Berlin, where he had met Ellen Mosebach, he had been preparing to attend the university, when the draft caught up with him. Then we served together for about three years. I think I got close to him and Hajo in Dresden, just before we were sent to Romania. I remember that he had been worried about his future after the war. He seemed to have no means left to attend the university, and one cannot do much with a high school education (Abitur), unless one pursues a college degree. He may have envied me a little, because I had definite plans, while he was wavering between becoming a schoolteacher like his father and joining his uncle's book business. He often requested my opinion, which was that teaching could be boring and repetitive, while, by selling something like books, one could be in command of one's time and possibly also make a pretty penny. He seemed to have decided to go into books. The exact sciences did not appear to be his cup of tea. A stylish and cultured man, he was well versed in literature and the arts. His level of sophistication, which could give the impression of arrogance, almost made him look a bit funny as a soldier. Rather, he could be visualized more easily as an officer. He didn't stand out so much from the others, because all of us were quite well educated, and each was kind of an individual. The Prussian drill over the years had never punctured our individualism. One of the lesser educated, I came from a workers' environment, while most others had passed university entrance exam or had studied for several semesters already. That's why in Romania we had attempted to get physics and math courses going, which flourished for a while, until the NCO's and officers stopped them: this was not something simple soldiers needed! They rather need drill—again and again, until hell freezes over! Meeting Helmut again in Wuppertal after three years, I could tell him about Hajo and Ellen. He reported what he had heard from our radar installation east of Bucharest, Romania, near Tulcea. He commended me for my academic progress and said he planned to go into publishing. He later realized this plan and become a sales representative for a publisher. We had a good two days until I boarded the train for Spandau again. This is the last time I saw Helmut. He later married a very substantial girl from a good Westphalian family (name: Flick), and they had two children. Years later, after I arrived in Brazil, he ended tragically. This saddened me for a long time. He would have been a true friend until the end of my days.

Soon after this trip, Lore and I had a discussion and decided to end our casual encounters indefinitely. I cannot remember how it all came about, but know that there was no argument—we had never had arguments of any kind. The reason may have been that we could only meet infrequently and could not visit more exciting places. I think we simply had run out of things to do. Besides, I was starting my last and most demanding academic year. We separated nonchalantly and peacefully and each went our own way. Today I find it strange that I let this happen, because Lore was a very good-looking, well-mannered, educated and substantial woman. There were not many like her that I knew of in Spandau. But our bonds must not have really been strong enough to think or speculate about engagement or marriage. I admit that I also did not miss her much. It had been a somewhat unemotional friendship—very strange—or was it typical for the times? As mentioned earlier, it seemed that Lore never foraged for supplies. I did not give it much thought, but now I believe it was typical for her approach to life—sanguine and a little on the comfortable side. We had not known each other well enough to forge a base for closer relations. After these encounters ended, I was rather relieved to be able to concentrate fully on my studies and degree.

Meanwhile, on the weekends, I got together occasionally with Gehrmann. We would take the hour-long walk from Spandau's center, where he lived, to the large dance hall below the Stoessensee Bridge. It was a delight to swing the girls around there, accompanied by live music, to the exciting rhythms of the modern big band tunes. Why I had never taken Lore there escapes me. It may have been a new project, developed by the owners to squeeze some money out of the property by selling entrance tickets, soft drinks and coffee, all at nominal prices. Both unattached, Gehrman and I could not extend ourselves very much, so our recreation needed to be carefully measured. Without fat on our bodies, we were extremely lean—but not mean; there was no energy for that! On one of those weekends we met two nice-looking girls from Gatow. I latched on to Hertha Theilig, and later we walked them home. The 1-1/2 hour walk was quite a feat in our state of emaciation. Hertha lived in a small wood frame house in front of the British governor's mansion, on the same street—the kind of place where a man could walk in and hang his hat on the first available nail (not that it made any impression on me!). Her husband had died of meningitis some time earlier. There was no cure available for Germans then (1946/47), as the needed Penicillin was not distributed to German hospitals. Hertha and her husband's mother tried to petition the British governor, their neighbor, to no avail. I suppose it would have set a terrible precedent! I did not know the details, but from a German observer's viewpoint it looked like they did not want to become good Samaritans to the vanquished. In the following months I became more closely associated with Hertha. After meeting her a few times she wanted to travel with me to the West to obtain some shoes. I think it was around the time monetary reforms were instituted in the West and West Berlin. Berlin paper currency received a "B" stamp, but was also legal tender in West Germany. We could exchange a certain amount of old "Reichsmark" into "D-Mark." That event made all old paper money and bank accounts worthless, except for the equivalent of 60 D-Marks per person. Some limited additional supplies quickly reappeared in the stores, but most food could still only be purchased with ration coupons. One of the miracles was the sudden reappearance of leather shoes, bags and other clothes in West German stores, while in Berlin such merchandise was not yet offered. In the West with Hertha, I bought a pair of leather shoes and some sausages, which I also could not have gotten in Berlin. Returning to Berlin, we first had to cross the border, which was then patrolled by East German police. There was no police on the Western side. We had to cross a piece of forest and had a long approach before reaching the critical border area, which required caution to prevent discovery and capture. Instead of barbed wire or walls there were only police points and moving patrols, sometimes with dogs! As we marched along, it became obvious that Hertha was not prepared for this kind of adventure. She became tired, and pretty soon I had to carry her satchel too. I think she would have liked to be carried herself! She hated the whole thing. What a way to get a pair of shoes! My thoughts were interrupted by a shout. East German police had discovered us and ordered us not to run, or they would shoot. Dispiritedly approaching them, we were told to sit down at the roadside. I was too tired to run, neither was there a chance. They said we must accompany them to the next checkpoint. When our captors left for a minute, I quickly switched shoes and the old ones went into my satchel. Then I ate as much of the sausage as I could. Still chewing animatedly, both of us were then taken along by the border guard. My sausages were gone, but, due to the quick switch, I had new shoes on my feet. I do not remember if Hertha lost anything, but she never asked me again to come along—one such trip was enough. She expected to be maintained by a man. Looking back, I know she was aggressively trying to land a new, well-heeled husband. In this respect I was a disappointment. I later learned she had a child, whom I never saw when we were together at her home. This baby, miraculously, never made any noise. I later learned that she invited other men to her home, and one day she said there had been a terrible accident. She had brought water to boil on the stove and all that boiling water had gotten spilled over that poor little baby, who died shortly thereafter. I was not invited to the funeral. This episode struck me as strange and suspicious, and I didn't get over it. Hertha—definitely not my cup of tea—was finished. I had known her for about six months before starting to cool my heels. Learning how strange people can be left a bitter taste—always watch out for their angle, or you can get hurt!

While all this went on, I was working very hard on my last academic year. The few "Reichsmark" I had saved in 1939–41 had been spent or had lost all value due to the monetary reform. The Soviets created their own currency. Because of total disagreement between Western allies and the Soviets, Berlin was cut off from any supplies. The Soviets instituted a blockade, which caused raw materials to pile up in the West and finished goods, made in Berlin, to remain there—creating total economic stagnation. Coal formerly delivered for the West Berlin power plants was also no longer allowed to pass. Therefore, the Western allies decided to airlift the bare minimum supplies to West Berlin. Our rations now were the lowest ever. We had no more potatoes. The airlift could transport only dried potatoes, hardly suitable for cooking a meal. It was a disaster. Not enough to live, and just a little too much to die! Naturally the people of Berlin were very grateful (and still are) for the U.S. government's massive initiative. I was one of those who had often rationalized that the U.S. would withdraw from Berlin if seriously challenged by the Soviets. How could I believe a foreign power would exert itself so enormously to assist 1.5 million Berliners? Most or all large corporations headquartered in Berlin thought likewise, for instance Siemens. Many moved to safer shores: Siemens to Erlangen (Siemens-Schuckert, the heavy industry) and Munich (Siemens-Halske, communications). The lack of fuel, especially coal, caused periodic power shutdowns for conservation purposes. On many evenings I studied by candlelight. The major problem remained the search for additional food to soothe our never-ending hunger. With Dad seldom, and mother never going out for this, the task was mine, and I gladly took it upon me. After all, I was grateful for my parents' support.

IMPRISONED IN EASTERN GERMANY

By now, rumors and news had it that the East German police were increasing reinforcement of their police checkpoints around Berlin. They wanted to choke off the influx of anything carried back into Berlin by those foraging for supplies. One of those days I took a train toward Wustermark and Stendal (about 100 miles west of Spandau). Luckily I had exchanged something for about 25 lbs. of potatoes. In the late afternoon the return train pulled into Wustermark station. Soon a crowd of police surrounded the entire station. I had to leave the train, which was full of shabbily dressed, emaciated people from all walks of life, with all my belongings. Those people, mostly older women and men with their small satchels of potatoes—that's all they were able to afford—were clinging to their bags, satchels, knapsacks, etc., hoping to salvage something. This sorry line slowly moved toward the red brick station. As I entered, about a dozen policemen were busily taking all the containers from the group and throwing them, contents inside, onto a growing pile of mostly potatoes. There had been nothing else to be obtained from the farmers who, I think, had by then also started accepting the new Western currency or D-Mark, because their new East German currency turned out to have no purchasing power. The closer I came to the police, the angrier I became at this sight. In addition, I hated the idea of losing my nice, sturdy knapsack! As I reached the pile, one of the policemen grabbed it. He was about to add it to the pile when I protested: "The potatoes, according to your regulations, are yours! But I want my property—the knapsack!" At that moment, another cop started pulling on me, and still another began pushing me. Enraged even more, I started to pull and swing at them—a clue for several of these characters to let me have it, until I was on the ground, defenseless. They had the knapsack, and I, my face bloody, shouted: **"You just wait—some day it is going to be different again in this country!"** Reacting to my angry yelling, they changed immediately. My minor infraction of resisting the apprehension of my potatoes had turned into what was a major political crime in Eastern Germany: casting doubt upon the righteousness of their regime. A large number of cops surrounded me, took me outside the building and placed me into a truck, where several other cops guarded against my escape. Slowly returning to my senses, I realized that I had committed the worst offense possible against a Bolshevik regime. It was close to inciting a riot. Those people were not to be fooled around with. I could not tell anyone my name and address in this moment of confusion. There was no time, and, although there would have been no recourse for them, I had no one with me who could have notified my parents; there were no communication channels between the two judicial systems or the two police organizations. But, at least my parents would have known my fate. Being apprehended by East German police was about the equivalent of a U.S. citizen being taken by South American police and thrown into jail, but the consequences in East Germany at that time were much more severe; one simply disappeared without a trace. Next of kin would not be notified. I was biding my time on the truck with these thoughts until the cops had moved the entire loot to another truck. Then everyone boarded the vehicles for the ride toward the final destination. The train had left and would enter West Berlin territory within 5-10 minutes—without me. After over an hour I noticed the name Rathenow on the side of the road. It is a city on the upper Havel River, shortly before it flows into the Elbe River. Soon all vehicles stopped in the midst of a cluster of red brick barrack-type buildings, typical for the end of the 19th or beginning of the 20th century army barracks. The many uniforms around me were not from the army, but looked more like police headquarters for the county Havelland. I was led into the basement and pushed into a cell. The door, which had a 3x4" opening, to be opened only from outside to observe the inmate, was locked. I was a prisoner who had not yet been advised of his "crime" or what he was held for. I was totally dependent and without any outside advocate knowing where I was. A lonely light of 25 watts or less, which dangled from the ceiling, did not brighten my situation. No light penetrated from the outside through the window, which had steel rod armor. I could not tell night from day, and, having sold my watch to a G.I. in the Naumburg POW camp for some cigarettes, I could not tell the time. If I expected something to eat, it did not arrive. I started to investigate the cot, which seemed to have been provided for my daily or nightly comfort. Instead of a chair or desk, there was only another cot, which made the cell very cramped. The cots' straw mattresses were about as hard as the cement floor, and there was a dirty blanket. A can in the corner was intended as a toilet. There was no faucet. These depressing circumstances were heightened by a total lack of instructions or communications. After a long while I must have fallen asleep.

I was awakened by someone who brought a cup of hot East German roasted barley coffee, a very thin, tasteless, brownish brew. After a long, long while of nothing (there were absolutely no sounds), the door opened and someone handed me a bowl of very thin, watery soup in which the only nourishing ingredients I discovered were bits of cabbage. It tasted awful. By then I was really starved and had been unable to shave or wash myself. I thought I felt like a Gulag inmate, except that I was lucky to be alone. Companions would only have spread gloom and doom. It was tough enough as it was. Later another "coffee" came with a small piece of bread. It must have been evening again, time for bed. That was my second day of confinement. On the third day, another "coffee" arrived without embellishments. My starvation was now so pronounced that my system was becoming numb and shaky. Some time afterwards there was shuffling outside the door again. I was ordered to follow two guards, who led me upstairs into a roomy office. The two left, and an interrogator in civilian clothes was awaiting me. He probably had to do with the infamous STASI (Staatssicherheit or state security). I could sit down and was asked for my identification papers. He filled out some kind of form, the nature of which I did not know. He did not introduce himself by name or say what kind of police or government branch he represented. I believe this was routine. Making prisoners feel apprehensive and helpless facili-tated the work of the omnipotent STASI, master of order and socialist discipline. They assumed everyone knew their identity. The interrogator soon focused on the nitty-gritty of the session. My long-gone knapsack or potatoes were of no interest. He did not bring up my resisting the police, but wanted to know what I had yelled to them. I realized that confessing what I had said would be equal to endorsing a long prison sentence, which would ruin my future. I had already thought it over in my cell: Do not admit anything you said; claim to have been so excited at that moment that you cannot remember. I explained this to the STASI-man, adding that, if I said anything offensive, I was certainly sorry, but I just did not remember. Now he let me know in a superior manner that he knew exactly what I said, reading it to me as written in the protocol and witnessed by the police. I still could not recognize my utterances, but asked, with so many wit-nesses, why would he need my consent? Under the circumstances that would not really add to the procedure! Dissatisfied, he yelled for the guards, who returned me to the cell. Another hot soup at noon and a small piece of bread in the evening was brought while I was sitting in the dark, unaware of how much time had elapsed. This alone was a very depressing element of life in confinement under the harsh conditions imposed by that "socialist" regime. The others were constant extreme hunger—more severe than what I had experienced during the last few years—insecurity about my fate, the inability to do something about my situation, ignorance about the workings of their bureaucracy and who they actually were, and lack of a companion to confide in and talk things over with.

On the fourth day, before the "coffee" had arrived, the door was opened and another prisoner was pushed through the door. Slumping down on the free cot, he buried his face in his hands. I heard some moans. Dressed in totally worn out clothing, he looked dirty. I wondered what kind of fate or act had landed him in my cell. It turned out he came from the high security prison (Zuchthaus) Brandenburg, a town 30 miles up river toward Berlin. He claimed to have spent two years there, usually in solitary confinement. He hinted that he was a political case. I gradually pulled all this out of him. As we talked, he also told me he had become so desperate that he had attempted suicide. There had been an iron stove in his cell which sat on a 3x3' piece of steel sheet. After many hours of bending one corner of the sheet up and down, he had broken off one corner, sharp enough to resemble a primitive knife, which he used for severely cutting both wrists in succession. Rolling up his shirtsleeves, he showed me the two cuts to prove his suicide attempt. I felt much empathy for the poor fellow. It must have been horrible to spend two years in those prisons. But then he started to ask questions about my origin and reason for being in the cell. He specifically wanted to know what I had told the policemen who had taken me prisoner. I thought he showed too much interest! While I had not asked him anything, he had offered his own story as though wanting to rid himself of it. I suddenly became very alert, realizing that he might be a planted stool pigeon, introduced as another witness for the STASI. I clammed up, telling him I didn't recall—the same story I had told the interrogators. In this way day number four passed by. Still without a shave, bath, shower or anything, I felt very uncomfortable. I slept in all of my clothes; otherwise that wet basement cell would have been too chilly.

On morning number five I found myself again in the interrogator's office. There was no progress. After some time two guards took me to another building, 50-100 yards away, where I landed in a large office with a desk, chair, and another chair for me, to face one of the worst surprises of my life. In came two Soviet officers in their olive uniforms with green caps—the sign of the Soviet security police. I was now in the anteroom to the GULAG; ready to be expedited to the place I had escaped from by a hair's breadth in May 1945. Now it was 1948! My heart almost stopped. My thoughts were racing when the two officers came out with a black and white photo, showing an assembled crowd on a market square. They pointed with great emphasis to a man in the crowd, saying: "Das Du!" (that's you). The little German they spoke sufficed to get their ideas across. That was all they said: "Das Du", repeating this dozens of times, while I kept trying to impress on them: "No, that's not me!" The photo was supposed to be from the city of Rostock, where I had not been since early 1945, still wearing my air force uniform. They tried that on me for between 30 minutes and one hour without progress. Although I found this scene stupid and ridiculous, I was not in the mood for laughing. This was certainly no joke. There had to be something they wanted. Sure enough, when the interrogation did not get anywhere, they produced a fairly large hunting knife, suited to do all kinds of mischief. They said: "Das Dein Messer" (that's your knife). The situation became more stupid by the minute. I vehemently denied ownership of the knife, but they persevered with the same line, shouting at me more and more loudly: "Das Dein Messer." This went on for another ½ hour at least. I never learned why they accused me of owning the knife and where it came from. It certainly had not been on me when I had been apprehended. On the other hand, it was known at the time that people were disappearing for no reason. Was that in store for me? After the knife episode also passed, they seemed to give up. Two Germans took me back to my cell. Day number five had been most confusing, under-scoring my desperate situation. Someone in STASI must have found my case significant enough to have the Soviet KGB, an organization not known to distinguish much between guilt and innocence, interrogate me. They customarily made arbitrary decisions, ignoring destroyed human lives, health, family, profession, and so on. Desperation settled inside me, and I fell asleep from mental exhaustion. I found that my "buddy" had left the cell when I returned. I was alone again.

I identified the next day only by the "coffee's" arrival. Again, it was little more than hot water, but we Berliners had not experienced real coffee for years, anyway. As told earlier, my last one, in form of pressed pellets with barley and a little sugar, had been in the POW camp. After savoring the "coffee" in my cell at least for being hot, I was brought to a different interrogation room. It contained a large desk, combined with a nice upholstered chair in which I saw a different individual, whose demeanor seemed to indicate a person in charge. Clad in a good woolen suit, clean white shirt and tie, he seemed ready to make decisions that day. He offered me a cigarette, lit it for me and had one himself. Then, leaning back in his seat, he said that they had ample evidence of what I had said. They really would not need any agreement from me. His decision was to let me go home, provided I would give him confirmation of my utterances. After signing the document in front of him, I would be free to leave for the train station. My signed agreement, attesting to the correctness of the cops' written input, was needed to comply with protocol. Without my signature he could not release me.

He did not volunteer for how long I would be incarcerated. How would I deal with this surprising turn of events? Was it a clever trap? My confession signed, they could do anything with me. But, regardless of my signature, they could do whatever they pleased. If I signed, I might be able to return to Spandau. In bad need of a bath and a shave, I felt rotten. Observing the interrogator's facial expression, I thought I had a chance of making it home. I signed and received my meager possessions. Running rather than walking to the station, I kept looking back to see if anyone followed me. Soon, in a train to Spandau, sure that I was on a police black list, I swore to myself never to return to East Germany. Arriving in Spandau from Rathenow, I ran home as fast as I could, sprinted up to the second floor and entered the apartment, where mother greeted me excitedly. She cried, because my parents had been totally in the dark as to where I was; I had simply vanished. In the aftermath of this adventure I could not help but think about the decline of German society. It had begun in 1933. Now there was no coherence left. Many East Germans did whatever task was assigned to them by the Soviets to gain any advantage they could—the same as in 1933. At least at that time many dumb Nazis believed the program of their party would help the nation as a whole. Now, what the large police apparatus did was in the Soviets' interest. This apparatus was much larger per capita than the Nazi machine. My weeklong ordeal never left my mind and later contributed significantly to my decision to look for sunnier shores.

Several months later the airlift ended, because the Soviets had stopped the blockade of Berlin. During the blockade in 1948 supplies had been insufficient to feed the Berlin population. Berliners would have starved, had it not been for the enormous help of the USA having sent necessities for survival by US military planes. Now large food supplies began arriving from the west, prices dropped, and the populace's calorie intake increased dramatically. The worst hunger began to fade into memory.

FIRST ENGINEERING JOB

Soon my final academic semester arrived and I had to prepare intensely for the 3-day long final examinations. Matters involving women moved into the background. From my class of 28 (one female), only 20 students were left for the finals, because some had left the college due to poor results, moved into other parts of the country, or due to lack of support or the need to fend for themselves. There was no government money available. Werner Ehling, Lisbeth's husband, who was a very good master mason, had started a building contracting business.

Built like a hunk, he could use all of his muscles well. Since 50% of Berlin was destroyed, there was plenty of work. What was left standing had not been maintained for at least ten years. Lisbeth helped in the business, keeping the books. I heard later that it did not prosper. Werner could not supervise people to ascertain a reasonable amount of work, and his work planning and assignment control were inadequate. For years he plugged along without accumulating reasonable resources for investments, unable to buy machinery or acquire larger jobs, needed for growth and success. I doubt that he ever obtained sizeable bank loans, the main requirement in a successful construction business.

My graduation passed without fanfare, parties or ceremonies because there was nothing to do it with. We lacked money, beer, schnapps or whisky, and food. I also had no girlfriend then. All students said goodbye and stormed out the door to quickly start their lives as mechanical engineers. Landing a job was difficult for most, since industry was not yet on the upswing. Only large corporations like Siemens were hiring a few graduates. That was my only "choice." Siemens was about 30 minutes from home by streetcar. My job was in the Geraetewerk of Siemens Schuckert (heavy electrical equipment), which designed and manufactured electrical equipment, such as switches, breakers, and transformers—anything for distribution of electrical power. I began working in the production-planning department, which translated drawings into instructions for the manufacture of equipment. My job included long sessions with engineers and designers about how to manufacture, and to determine whether presented designs lent themselves to effective execution. I was thrown at a new line of air power breakers, of which numerous parts were made of phenol resin. It had an intense, very uncomfortable odor of uric acid. I had much interaction with the shops making these parts. The material, commercially named "Bakelite," had to be baked under heat plus pressure for quite some time. Siemens had a large operation to make these plastic parts, plates, and sheets. I worked in a department of 50-80 people on the 7th floor. Above, up to the 10th floor, were administrative offices; the top bosses were on the 10th floor. Each level of bosses had different sets of privileges. The top guy had a carpet, window shades, a separate round coffee table surrounded by upholstered armchairs, a wardrobe, an oak bookshelf and an oak office desk with a high-backed leather chair. As the level decreased, the carpets, window shades, coffee tables, etc. gradually decreased. Coffee tables became conference tables to spread out drawings or other documents for review. The offices' furniture indicated to which level an individual belonged. These rules were strictly followed. Most people around me were life-long Siemens employees. The company had an intense educational program, and, if I remember correctly, one could even obtain a college degree through their schooling. An entire suburb of Berlin between Spandau and Charlottenburg south of the current location of the Tegel airport pertained to Siemens and its employees, facilities and living quarters. These, mostly comfortable condominium-style apartment buildings, were closely integrated into the facilities, yet, many employees still had to commute from Spandau, Charlottenburg, and other surrounding suburbs. Many of the facilities had been heavily damaged during the war by bombing and by fighting in the final days. The Soviets started to remove all usable equipment immediately after hostilities ended, rounding up all available manpower for the task. Everything was taken—machine tools, any kind of hand tools like hammers, chisels, cutting tools, electrical equipment—you name it. Colleagues told me that in our "Geraetewerk," there had not been a nail or screw left. All floors had been cleaned out. The electroplating tanks on the 6th floor were left, because they would have had to be destroyed for removal. But all transformers, rectifiers and switching equipment were removed. Only a huge empty, ten-story building was left and a pile of rubble, which represented the assembly and the large tool making facilities. After the removal frenzy abided, the Western allies moved into their sectors in Berlin. Siemens was then located in the British sector—same as Spandau and Charlottenburg. At this point Siemens began to organize again, starting with the removal of the rubble and retrieval of all machinery, equipment and tools underneath it. Digging for gold, they found lots of it. Especially the rubble of the huge Tool Department hid treasures of high precision machines, which are any industry's backbone. They quickly erected a roof and began to thoroughly rework the machinery, much of which was rusted. Reconstitution required many hours, but was successful and the tool shop started again. Other machines and equipment were then slowly added over the next three years. A large boost was received when Marshall Plan money became available which was then invested in such heavy production equipment as punch presses or drawing presses. When I started, there was literally no rubble left. A huge court held raw iron and aluminum castings, many left over from WWII days. Although things were orderly, production was slow. The future boom years of Germany could not be foreseen. I had to dig into the details of the subject at hand and to adjust to my environment. The salary offered me was DM220—take it or leave it—worth $55 per month at the time. Most of it I contributed to the household, which improved our standard of living significantly. There was even something left for clothing and recreation. I did not like spending time at bars or pubs. In summer I greatly enjoyed the Havel beaches. Travel over long distances would have been too expensive; people could only think about their immediate needs. As an established Siemens engineer I could now start to think about my future. My schedule had vastly improved. Home around 5:30 p.m., I had time to look at the "Spandauer Volksblatt," the local socialist daily. It had become possible to attend plays, operas or movies. Horst Gehrmann had become my closest and only buddy. He worked at Siemens-Halske, the communication part of Siemens, in a different part of Siemensstadt, which was occupied only by the Halske organization. He expected big investments and advances in this field and was also intrigued by the associated mathematical and theoretical problems. He and I started wondering about our position in life in light of central European and world developments. The airlift was over, but the enormous, enigmatic Soviet-controlled satellite East Germany surrounded our Berlin. We thought that at any time—particularly when diplomatically advantageous to them—the Soviets could restart trouble and starve out the Berlin economy. It was hard to imagine that the U.S. and the others would protect Berlin under any circumstances in the future.

One day Gehrmann mentioned that he had met Lore Gaertner, who told him that she was not going out with anyone. There were few eligible bachelors left in Spandau who could be considered. I thought about her and my subsequent disastrous involvement with Hertha Theilig. I had liked Lore's easygoing, undemanding style and friendship. And—she was mighty good-looking, tall, blond and blue eyed. I always wondered why none of the GIs she worked with had latched onto her. We never discussed this point, but I noticed some displeasure with the manner in which these people dealt with her. It was correct in the office, but when it came to personal interactions, something was missing. I also never learned whether she would like to live in the U.S. There were many issues we had not discussed as far as I remember—perhaps it was my fault. I could have dropped her a note, but felt we were such good friends that, in the absence of telephones, I knocked on her door one day, asking if I could come in, which made her very happy. Her mother and sister Christel were also quite friendly. They were now living more comfortably. Christel had undergone a four-year apprenticeship in the flower trade and worked in a nursery. From then on, Lore and I saw each other fairly regularly. We could go to dances on weekend. "Boehue" no longer existed, but there was now a nice dance hall under the Pichelsberg Bridge. On rare occasions I would pick her up at her Dahlem office. The officers' club no longer affected me so badly, since I had become better nourished. One day, on the way to meet her, I changed subways at Wittenbergplatz. Standing, hanging on a strap, I observed a scene, which may have happened a year earlier; I just don't remember when. On one of the benches which were lining both windows left and right, sat some emaciated Germans; opposite them a G.I. who weighed at least twice as much. He was happily savoring an American cigarette and, when taking a puff, he exhaled directly into the Germans' faces. It was obvious what those men were thinking: "When will he finish ... I really want the butt! Hopefully he'll leave half or two-thirds of the cigarette" and "How can I beat those other guys to it?" Meanwhile, the G.I. disgustedly watched those greedy eyes, which craved his diminishing cigarette. Finally, with a contemptuous grin, he took the cigarette out of his mouth, indicating the last draw. He placed the hand holding it between his thighs, ready to drop the butt on the floor. Three or four Germans jumped up to grab it, but he dropped it and squashed it with his boot. What a demeaning, repulsive display by both, the Germans and the G.I.! It seemed that all decent human characteristics had vanished from our times. This impression haunted me for a long time. It was amazing what people would do, and how they degraded themselves for a cigarette butt, and what kind of cheap triumph someone who thought he was entitled to a comfortable life got out of it. This was most likely an isolated scene; thousands of other G.I.s would not have dreamt of acting this way. But smoking was a widespread vice during and long after WWII. When there were no more cigarettes, I stopped, and I never missed the smoke. I just dropped any thought of it and that was that. Many others, however, played games to obtain tobacco or make it by growing it in a vegetable plot or flower pot on the balcony. Mother worked for some time at the barracks where British troops were stationed. If I remember correctly, she brought home British cigarette butts besides the leftover white bread the soldiers were served. The butts had to be taken apart carefully to produce a mix. All kinds of small, handy cigarette machines were easily available. In addition, one needed tobacco and pre-cut special cigarette paper, which could be bought for little money. Those ingredients were needed to make another cigarette, which tasted almost like a new one. I believe I tried this a few times, but gave it up. I considered it indecent. My Dad may have tried it a little longer. Many people used their homegrown snuff to roll cigarettes. These were kept in silver or gold cigarette cases, and smokers would light up anywhere. The most damaging use was at the workplace in winter, with all windows closed to keep the little heat there was inside. There was no ventilation, as the heaters were of the water circulation gravity type. The entire crowd was lighting up all day long—not real cigarettes, which would have been bad enough, but those homegrown things, which emitted a suffocating stench. Entering the office, one could not see the other end because of the dense smog. Faking work in various other departments, I tried to stay away from it whenever possible.

I soon began to realize that, at the pace things were developing, I would not get anywhere at Siemens for the rest of my life. Their policy was to keep salaries very low, but to compensate with good pensions. But most people did not live much beyond retirement age. To make a splash at Siemens, one needed an influential sponsor to make things smoother. I felt like I was getting lost in a crowd. It made little difference what I did; I never heard a word of appreciation or interest in my progress. Since other industries were not hiring in 1949, I was stuck, waiting for the yet-unforeseen German economic "miracle." Things were bleak, with no upswing on the horizon. Therefore I rationalized with Gehrmann: what were we doing in Berlin or even Germany? West Germany was as strange as a foreign country to us. The difference was only that the latter would have another language, but that could be learned quickly. After all, I had studied English for four years and French for two. Berlin's industry seemed on the downtrend; large corporations were transferring essential operations to the West. A token presence remained, mainly to use the substantial tax advantage, credit facilities and other amenities offered to companies to remain in Berlin. The city no longer seemed a viable place for forward-looking people. I discussed this also extensively with Lore, since it looked to us that we might become a pair in the future, though we did not discuss this until the end of 1949.

My first choice for immigration was always the U.S., but at the time they required a 20-year waiting period for Germans without relatives or sponsors. They (the INS) wanted to push the risk of producing adequate income for immigrants on private parties, not the federal government. Immigration laws were still quite sensible and realistic, with the taxpayers' interest the foremost consideration. So, I looked around for a country where I might feel comfortable and could apply what I had learned—one with an industrial base, ready to develop at a good pace. Trying Canada, Australia and South Africa, I found no interest. The outside world seemed to be shutting me out. I even made an application at the Yugoslavian Military Mission in Dahlem, where all those countries maintained their military missions—it was the best place to be in Berlin. The Mission was housed in a fancy mansion close to Bilsestrasse, where Anna's aunt Gretl lives. Entering the building, I passed several soldiers with huge, five cornered stars in caps and lapels, and automatic guns. They looked fierce and determined and seemed to still be engaged in partisan warfare in the midst of Berlin. They also did not look very bright. Would they receive me in their country as an equal trying to do some good? They gave me the creeps as they handed me the application papers. Thinking that no one in Yugoslavia would know what to do with me, I did not send in the application. Twenty years later, during my brief stay as a consultant to their largest and most important industries, my earlier suspicions about Yugoslavia were confirmed.

As 1949 continued into summer, I remember going often to dances or swimming at the Havel river, just south of Margot's place on Wendenweg. We also used the "Kladower Badewiese" (beach meadow Kladow), easily reachable by bus. The service still exists today. We had a good time, as living conditions had become less bleak than during the airlift and the immediate postwar years. Father, almost 62, and mother, 53, were reasonably healthy and had no serious problems. Those hungry years may have contributed to raising their life expectancy. Father would occasionally light his favorite "Boenicke" cigar. Made in Bremen of Java tobacco, these cigars were favored by many Germans. I think I had returned to smoking no more than six cigarettes per day, which already made me uncomfortable. Towards evening, the tongue burned; fingers were yellowish and smelled bad.

Martha and Gustav Moratz, circa 1950.

Hermann Moratz, lucky boy, circa 1926.

In class in 1939, author seated center.

The young recruit, 1941.

Recruits in Dresden, 1941, author standing right.

On R & R, Romania, 1942, author standing left.

Flight training, 1944.

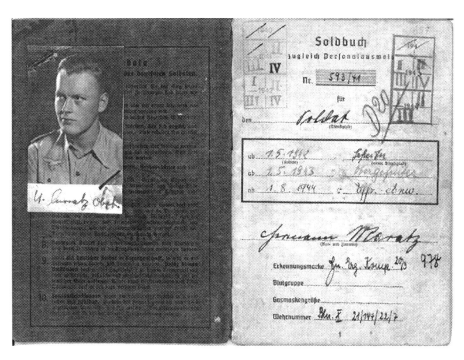

Hermann's paybook, 1944.

German Fokke Wulf 44 bi-plane.

The German Fokke Wulf 56.

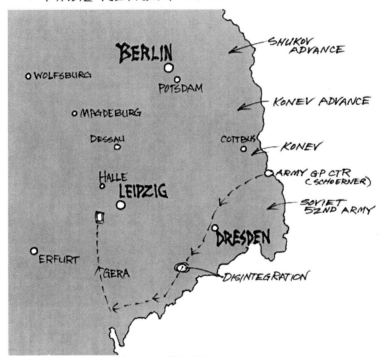

The final retreat. Map Illustration, Ed Robinson, 2007.

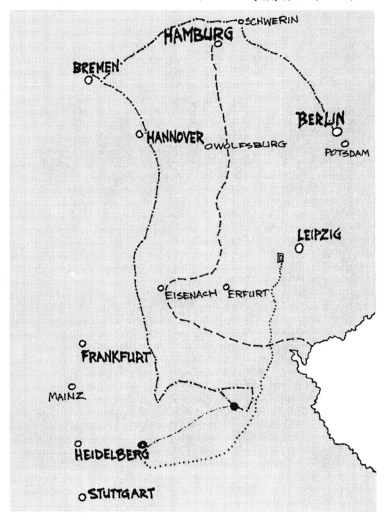

Homeward bound. Map Ilustration, Ed Robinson 2007.

Passport photo, 1949.

Brazil bound, aboard the Duque de Caxias, 1949.

Anna harvesting papaya, 1954.

Anna at work at Mercedes Benz, 1955.

Engaged! Mercedes Benz de Brazil, 1956.

Wedding! March 24, 1956.

Driving a 1937 Mercedes Benz Cabriolet.

On Honeymoon, Ubatuba, 1956.

Aboard the Montevideo Maru, 1957.

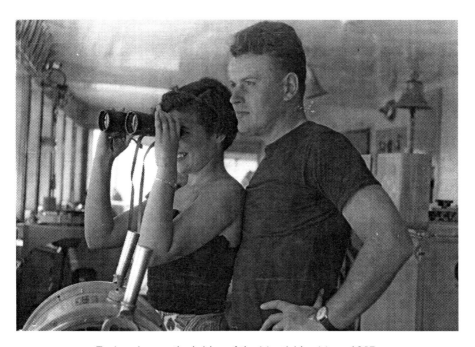
To America, on the bridge of the Montivideo Maru, 1957.

At home with '52 Chevy, Alhambra, CA, 1958.

First trip to Disneyland, California, 1958.

At work at Dun & Bradstreet, 1958.

Anna's mother, Hilde Wagner, comes to visit, 1958.

Martha joins her son in San Gabriel, 1960.

Engineer at work, ITE Circuit Breaker, 1960.

New arrival! Hermann, Chris and Karen, 1963.

The Moratz family, circa 1963.

Karen Annabel and William Christopher, 1965.

On the road to Mississippi, 1969.

A stop in the desert, May 1969.

Oma, Anna and the kids in Berlin, 1969.

To the East, the kids at Berlin border checkpoint.

Karen, Chris and cousin Frank Wagner.

The Moratz Family in Darmstadt, Indiana, 1972.

Father of the bride, Las Vegas, Nevada, 2004.

George, Karen, Anna, Chris, Hermann and George IV in Las Vegas, 2004.

Hermann, William Christopher, Anna and Karen Moratz celebrate the holidays.

Hermann and Anna Moratz, today.

BRAZIL

IMMIGRATION TO BRAZIL

One day during that glorious summer of 1949, according to a newspaper ad Gehrmann showed me, the Brazilian government was looking for German engineers. With free transport from Hamburg to Rio de Janeiro and food it sounded like an adventure! Without any concrete ideas, Gehrman and I speculated extensively about our prospects. We only knew Brazil was huge and had little industry, but thought that agricultural industries like canning, milling, storage, and specialty installations for harvesting coffee, cocoa, sugar cane, tobacco and rubber must exist, and that there must be meat packing plants and breweries. But machine tools, tooling and automotive manufacturing, the backbones of developed countries, would be missing. Perhaps Brazil wanted to participate in the general sell-off of Germany. Even the French and Yugoslavs were fishing in the pool for goodies. While most "victor" nations picked industrial installations for transfer to their shores, the U.S. did not participate in the reparation and dismantling frenzy. They knew that, to install a new factory, it must be the most modern kind! We concluded there was some sense in what the Brazilians tried to do. We got our application from the Brazilian military mission in Dahlem. We also looked for others interested in Brazil immigration without success. We knew the language was Portuguese, but where would we find courses? To be honest, I did not spend much time or emotions on learning Portuguese. I thought that I always could support myself somehow with my tool making and engineering skills. This later turned out to be true, but I also was lucky more often than not. I would have no other mouths to feed, while those leaving for Brazil with wife and kids would have more of a fight on their hands. Some others would indeed run aground, as described later. The discussions with Lore were friendly. If I would be accepted, I suggested I would go alone, because Brazil was so strange to us. Lacking information about living conditions, salary expectations, prices, etc., we should be cautious. One should not expect a well-reared young woman to go to places about which she knows nothing. We agreed she would follow after she could hear about my progress. With that in mind, I completed the forms, including birth certificate, engineering certificate and other required papers. Gehrmann and I left our applications at the Brazilian mission. After a long time, having lost all hope, I received a Brazilian document in October 1949. My application had been accepted—which did not make me too happy. Somehow, deep in my heart I had hoped to be rejected, so that I would not have to stick my neck out; I could continue playing it safe. The letter requested my German identification document (police record card), to which they would attach their travel permit and visa. They told me they had booked me on a Brazilian Navy vessel, "Duque de Caxias," to leave Hamburg in late December, with no word about the type of accommodation. They also required a medical examination certificate and one from the courts and police showing that I had neither been convicted nor was under indictment. While these activities were coming to a peak, I began rationalizing these issues also with Mom and Dad. As far as I recall, they pretty much agreed with me to try life somewhere else after those harrowing years and the total collapse of Germany. A man has only one life and must try his best to use his knowledge and skills in the best way possible. Without negative reactions from them, everything was go. I received my permit and was told to report to the Brazilian Consul in Hamburg around December 14, and to check with the mission about the ship's exact arrival and departure date; these dates would also be published in the major newspapers. As the days passed, I felt more and more like being in an eerie, surrealistic environment. I turned in my resignation at Siemens around December 1. The department manager was astonished: "YOU are the guy who is going to Brazil?" He must have expected someone more like superman, not an average type like me, to leave on such an adventure. According to his few words, he seemed glad someone offered to leave. With layoffs occurring everywhere, things did not look good. Most colleagues encouraged my venture and seemed to wish themselves in my place. But things like sick parents, marriage, kids and property kept most from pursuing my path. Many preferred to stay where they were while others were satisfied with dreaming and lacked the courage and recklessness to pursue their dreams.

Then it was time to say goodbye. I felt better having a buddy along—someone to fall back on in case of sickness or misfortune would make things easier. Since we had similar professions, we could help each other analyze potential jobs, industries or companies and evaluate such other important aspects as job location. Among the few goodbyes to be said was sister Lisbeth, whose husband, Werner, seemed not to care much about it. She was very engaged with her small daughter Sabine. Marianne, a teenager, and her friend Helga marveled about my adventure. With my engineering degree, ready to conquer the world, I was an idol to them—the kind of man teenagers dreamed of. They did not suspect that I was developing more and more doubts about my plan. Cutting off all roots to go into a very uncertain future was a harrowing experience. It did not bother me much that I had no inkling of the language—a gross oversight, as I learned later. But, again, I was to be lucky in getting hired by a company generous enough to provide one-on-one accelerated Portuguese tutoring.

Lore, sanguine character that she was, added no input. She looked forward with confidence to my, and later her future adventures. Was I only one of several irons in her fire? I would not know until much later. For now I was convinced we would later start our life together in Brazil, which consoled me and made me hopeful. When I last visited her at the "Plantage" apartment in Spandau, her mother, Lore and Christel were sitting in the living room with a young man clad in shabby, old civilian clothes. They were very excited about being together. I noticed that my intrusion surprised them, but without telephones I could not have given advance notice. This time I was no longer the center of attention—a change from past years. Taken aback, I wondered if the young man was a competitor. He turned out to be Lore's cousin Heinz Dittmar. Because he lived near our Zimmerstrasse home, I had seen him occasionally from afar during my school years and also at local youth sport competitions. He attended "Oberrealschule," a school leading to pre-university diploma and automatic university acceptance. Lore and I had attended "only" Mittelschule, which terminated at age 16 and did not lead to such acceptance. The schools were separate. One could continue at "Oberrealschule" coming from my school only with outstanding grades, but this was rare and was not encouraged. It was kind of a traditional class arrangement, especially since the Oberrealschule demanded stiff tuition, which was out of reach for average working people. Heinz Dittmar would always compete in 100 m dash events. He and another youngster from the "Gymnasium" were the best in town. The latter was the school where the humanities and old languages like Latin, Greek and Hebrew were taught. Tall, slender, blond, blue-eyed and a first class sprinter, he had always made a great impression on me. They did the 100 m in 11.2 or 11.3 seconds—a real accomplishment for young men of high school age, but not by far comparable to Jesse Owens' 10.3 seconds! I had not seen him in this neighborhood before. Our paths had not crossed, mainly because he was two years older than I, and because I was working around the clock. Like so many other pre-university school graduates in the late 30's, he had chosen one of those dashing careers offered in the rapidly developing armed forces, which indicated that he did not tend towards such subjects as physics, medicine, chemistry, law or engineering. Rather, he had picked a brainless military career, not something interesting like piloting. From officer in the anti-aircraft forces (part of the air force) he moved to captain at war's end. A good-looking man in a well-fitting, impressive air force uniform, (especially tailor-made from special, finely woven wool cloth, while soldiers always wore ill-fitting garbs made from scratchy, low quality fabric), he must have been adored by the female population. On the other hand, I had looked like an imbecile in my first air force uniform. This contrast was by design. The officer had to look the master of his inferiors! I suspected Lore had a crush on her cousin for a long time and will never know why they had not come together earlier. But during my last visit I found the women spellbound by his tales of how he went through the U.S.-Soviet demarcation line in early 1946, wanting to return home four or five months earlier, like I did, but instead he spent the next three years as POW of the Soviets in Siberia. As an officer, he should have known that the Soviets were not signatories of the Red Cross Convention covering behavior of combatants. His dashing officers' uniform had given him away, while I had been fortunate to have the foresight to exchange my parachute outfit for worn out rags when crossing the border. The poor, pale-looking, worn-out cousin had paid a huge price. I could not spend much time studying the scene. Lore and I had agreed that we would meet in Stade near Hamburg, where she had relatives. Her father's family came from that beautiful area of the "Alte Land" (old land), the fruit basket of Hamburg and the North Sea. Bidding Good Bye to the Gaertners, I left with a strange impression of Lore's cousin.

Before leaving Spandau two days later, I had a hard time finding suitable luggage that would outlast the journey to Rio. Usually wooden, luggage was then poorly constructed, heavy and covered with decorative fabric. The heavy contraption I bought even made it to the U.S. after Brazil! While packing and taking care of last minute affairs and paperwork, I met Gehrmann again to coordinate the time and place of our departure from Hamburg. I was shocked to learn then and there that he was not coming along. There had been no word that he had doubted our plans. Later (about 1990 in Munich) he played a similar trick on me. I was thoroughly disgusted with his shiftiness and now regret that I tried to meet him again in Munich. But in the nineties, my recollections of that turn of events were fuzzy. They seem to return only now as I concentrate on them more intensely.

So, there I was, ready to go it alone. Little did I realize that a man is actually alone and must make decisions and face the consequences himself. Soon thereafter I embraced mother and walked to the streetcar station Zimmerstrasse and Pichelsdorfer Strasse with my belongings. Streetcar 75 would take me to Zoo Station for the trip to Hamburg. Father, looking apprehensive and subdued, had never complained about my leaving Germany. I think he wanted me to make my own way, in the best way I could. He was a man of few words, but I could see he was sorry. So was I. Very apprehensive, I thought I was failing my parents. But the dice were cast. I boarded number 75 and watched my disappointed father disappearing slowly. That was the last time I saw him. About 40 years later I heard that he came home crying, afraid of never seeing me again. Unnoticed by any onlookers, it was a very emotional departure.

Arriving at my Hamburg bed and breakfast in the early afternoon, I learned that the "Duque de Caxias" would sail December 14; I needed to board it by noon. The air was frigid and rainy, typical for the North Sea, and I could well use my good, blue, woolen winter coat. But I was going to Rio and did not expect to return soon. There it would be useless, and I looked for someone to take it off my hands. I soon found an interested man, who gave me a down payment and promised to pick it up on the day of my departure. With that problem solved, I slept well. On the next morning I went to the Hamburg main station, where Lore would arrive. We boarded a suburban to Stade, North of the Elbe River, well past all the docks of the harbor, where we walked to her uncle's home. It was December 11. Except for overnight needs, I had left my belongings at the Bed and Breakfast. On the 13th we would have to part again at Hamburg's main station. I don't recall much about our stay in Stade. I did not make much of a splash with the relatives, who had a small printing shop. Skeptical about my adventure, they may have had nationalistic opinions; perhaps they were Nazis? We spent much time eating restaurant meals, having coffee, and walking to see the sites of Stade. Lore was kind of withdrawn, but friendly. Glad and proud that she had gone out of her way to send me off, I savored being with her. On the 13th we embraced in Hamburg, and she left for home. Watching her train disappear in the distance, I felt that the last connection to my past was fading. I could have taken my things and followed her, but it never occurred to me.

When Lore's train had disappeared, I stopped waving, turned around and starting thinking about what to do next. There was not much. The B&B's in Hamburg and Stade had depleted my funds, with just enough left for a meal and a taxi. If the character would come for the coat, I might get another DM40 or 50—my total cash reserves for a trip to Brazil and for starting a new life in a strange land! Now it seems reckless, even silly, to embark on this journey, but times were different. People were hungry for opportunities, of which Germany offered only a few. All had been spent on a reckless war, and Germany was still unable to find its way back to progress. It appeared that the economy would never improve. Only someone knowing those times can understand my behavior. On the other hand, Gehrmann had shown last minute qualms. Perhaps he just could no longer face the risks? On the next morning, the coat-buyer came with the money. Without my coat, I now *had* to leave Germany! Around 11 a.m., a taxi dropped me at the dock. Or was it that I dragged my baggage through the Elbe River tunnel to the dock? I suspect the latter. Before leaving, I had purchased some cigarettes and two bottles of cheap brandy, to drink with my future buddies when sailing across the equator. What romantic nonsense! I made it up the gangway and was on board.

The "Duque de Caxias" was teeming with people, young and old, even children, but no babies. I was shown my berth under deck in the vessel's bow. This was about a 15,000 to 20,000 ton ship built to carry many passengers and considerable cargo. I learned later that it was an old German liner, built before WWI and acquired by the Brazilian government during WWII. For that war, which Brazil later joined, one lonely cannon each was planted on the fore- and afterdeck. A large superstructure contained a multitude of cabins, which were taken by an incredible number of naval officers, up to admirals, captains, etc. Some others had been purchased by Germans with connections to Brazil—former residents wanting to return, or those with Brazilian relatives. Since "Deutsche Mark" (DM) was then not accepted in the international world of finance, all had to pay with hard currency, most likely US$. Ernst and Irmgard Bast (who were to become my friends later in Sao Paulo) belonged to the privileged class with relatives (his parents) in Sao Paulo.

First I needed to find a berth of my own. I descended into the cargo hold. There were two levels prepared. I wound up on the first, closest to the deck. Long lines of cots, each containing a navy blanket, were stacked up in four levels, which required gymnastic efforts to climb into the uppermost one. The rows were so close together that two persons could barely pass each other. There was no heat, but I suspected that this mass of humankind would generate enough of it at night. Up in the bow were primitive facilities, even some showers with a very limited water supply, which, when at sea, turned out to be salt water! My suitcase was pushed under the bunk, which I occupied by advising those loitering around me of my intent. I was on the deck for men only; facilities for women and children were not any better. To keep order, the ship was teeming with military policemen. The pantry and supply store were in the ship's center. Here cigarettes, soap and other rudimentary items could be bought against hard currency, which left me indifferent, since I had practically no money, and my cigarettes would last until arriving in Rio.

Around 3:00 p.m., I watched the pulling in of the gangway and the usual maneuvers for departure. Everyone was on deck. The weather was mild and overcast. It was December 14. Most everyone was quiet and withdrawn as the ship slowly started to move away from the pier. After being pushed and pulled by tugs for about 30 minutes, we reached a ship channel where the proud, but ancient "Duque de Caxias" started to gain speed on her own. It carried the Brazilian flag, which I had never seen before: green, yellow and blue with the motto "Ordem e Progresso" (Order and Progress) inscribed in it. As we approached Hamburg's landmark, the "Michel," (spire of main church), some poor soul started intoning the old German folk song "Muss I denn, muss I denn, zum Staedtele hinaus," ("do I have to leave my little town")—which opened all gates. Men, women and children started crying—a very emotional scene. All were afraid to leave something they knew and loved, and out there in the approaching dusk was an unknown world. Exceptions, like Ernst Bast, were rare. He and Irmchen were enjoying the departure and the prospect of seeing his parents again, in their comfortable cabin. As Hamburg floated by, things caught up with me too. My throat squeezed by emotion, I hastily puffed on my cigarette to overcome the tears, succeeding by a narrow margin. As we passed Cuxhaven, dusk had set in. Noticing that I was hungry, I remembered the Brazilian government's promise of food and quickly found the line. Aluminum plate and fork, spoon and knife in hand, I found the food not bad looking and plentiful. There was rice, which was covered with a generous serving of brownish black beans. They also offered a substance, which looked like sawdust, unlike anything I wanted to try right then. I liked the look of the beans, and also the rice, a rarity in German households, where it was generally cooked with milk and sprinkled with cinnamon and sugar. The rice combined with beans was new to me and filled my belly. I was glad the Brazilians were fulfilling their promises. I was on a ship and was being fed. I began to think I would actually make it to Rio. With that good feeling I squeezed into my bunk, where I needed some contortionist exercises to get into a sleeping position. Slowly the increasing swell moved the ship more and more until I fell asleep at the end of an exhausting, emotional day.

On the next day we moved through the English Channel, stopping in Rotterdam, about which I do not remember much. Soon we were out in the open Atlantic. In the morning we received coffee and white bread with what I now know was Goiabada, made from the Goiaba fruit—a very delicious, sweet and nourishing preserve the Brazilians like and eat endlessly. At noon there was more of the previous day's food: beans, rice and the sawdust meal, which was actually manioc, a root that needs two years to mature. The white meal made from it tastes like sawdust, but, when combined with oil, onions, sweet peppers, garlic and spices, it can assume a pleasant taste. Called "farofa," it is traditionally sprinkled over the beans. I again ignored it, which the dark-skinned cook didn't understand. It was part of what they offered; any Brazilian would have accepted it enthusiastically. This menu would be repeated daily throughout the journey. None of us Germans knew that it was the only meal common Brazilians ate day in and day out. As the same diet continued, some people got quite sick. Although looking at a plate of rice and beans came to be a revolting experience, I always managed to down it and keep myself out of trouble.

As we prepared for another sundown in the midst of the Bay of Biscay, I attended a Brazilian flag-lowering ceremony, where a crowd was gathered which included uniformed Brazilian sailors. Wearing my black, Basque beret, I was enjoying the scene when suddenly someone knocked my beret off my head from behind—a sailor who frowned on seeing my head covered while the flag came down. I became angry, but took no action. He could have let an uninformed bystander, who had never observed this ceremony before, know this in another way. At similar events in the air force we had kept our heads covered. This left a bad taste, and I would no longer be around during this ceremony. I thought the sailor and many others were fairly primitive people whose language I did not understand. There was little opportunity for learning Portuguese on board. Approaching Brazil, I became more and more aware of this deficiency and foresaw serious problems resulting from not being able to talk to a potential employer.

Meanwhile, many people were becoming seasick. I was fighting seasickness, too: the food did not go down any longer, due to its monotony and because of motion sickness pressure and nausea. The ship entered some Portuguese harbor, picked up some uniformed people and quickly left to head south. None of us knew what the next port would be. We wondered if they might take course toward the Brazilian mainland, general direction of the Northeast coast and the city of Natal, but the compass showed us headed for one of the islands on the African coast. After a few days we pulled into the picturesque, Spanish-style settlement of Santa Cruz de Tenerifa. Just before arrival I was astonished to find a piece of meat in my rice/bean combination—a welcome change to the incredible routine. I also tried some farofa, but did not find it worthwhile eating. Compared to the well-prepared farofa I would have in later years, I now know that it definitely tasted like sawdust made from nondescript timber. We were told the ship would remain in Santa Cruz for at least 24 hours to take water and fuel. With time on my hand and my last D-Marks in my pocket, I visited Santa Cruz with some others, which meant climbing up the streets. In this nicely maintained town of white houses with red tile roofs I hoped to buy a bottle of those amply displayed wines. Each street corner had a restaurant where people, mostly men, hung around as if waiting for something. Seeing buildings painted and in good shape, without any destruction, was a wonderful experience compared to Germany with its eternally overcast skies and dirty, gray buildings, which had not seen paint for 10-15 years. Here, the combination of pleasant-looking houses, clear, blue sky and abundant tropical flora made my heart jump, and I began to think that there was something to this Brazilian escape. All people knew we were "alemans." Speaking Spanish, they stared at us intensely. When we asked for a bottle of wine and showed our money, they were not impressed. They had not seen this suspicious-looking paper money before and would not trade with us, even though they seemed to like us. We went from bodega to bodega, until I found one where they acted very sympathetically and, without taking my money, they handed me a bottle and said it was a present. I must have communicated with those folks through my limited English, since lots of them, as seagoing folks, knew some English. I do not recall how, but I managed to spend my last few D-Marks in Santa Cruz and returned to the boat without any cash. If I had saved those few D-Marks in my pocket, it would have made no difference. I was facing the future bankrupt, without the benefit of being able to write a postcard, pay bus fare or purchase cigarettes or food. (One of the first things I learned on board after "yes" and "no" was that cigarette was "cigarro" and cigar "charuto"). It now seems strange that I was not worried about my state of affairs; it never occurred to me that I could be facing disaster! It was as though Tenerifa's blue sky and balmy air assured me that things would go my way.

As the "Duque de Caxias" returned to asthmatically plowing the sea, changes were developing. The nights became so hot that I preferred to stay on deck. With the humidity also increasing dramatically, our clothes stuck to our bodies. It was brutal below. The only relief was provided by the slight draft produced by the ship's moving forward. Since the decks were covered with our humankind, sleeping was a problem. When getting too tired, one fell into a dope until interrupted by noise or movements. The sea was mirror-like. Fish were constantly jumping aboard. Sailing onto the deck, these flying fish, looking like herring, lifted themselves out of the sea by light wings and sometimes landed directly on the passengers' stretched-out bodies. They could sail distances of about 100 yards. We regretted that we could not cook and eat them as a variation to our monotonous meals, which by now had made all of us feel sick. Many passengers suffered from diarrhea. We were kept alive only by the hope of soon reaching the Promised

Land. The days were spent trying to catch a bit of a breeze. Some people bathed in the makeshift canvas pool the marines had erected on the stern deck. Although sea water and very hot, it provided a small, measured relief when one was wet from dunking and exposed to the breeze. My bottle of Madeira from Santa Cruz was long gone. I had not had this kind of heavy and sweet wine before.

After some more days of languishing on the decks, preparations started for the "Aequatortaufe" (equator baptism). The makeshift pool was to serve as "baptism font." The ship's horn announced the arrival at the equator with a terrible ruckus. Accompanied by some assistants, Mr. Neptune himself came aboard in a fancy seaweed camouflage, golden crown and three-pointed lance. Those on board had to go through the dunking, and all were glad when it was over. Now there was only little distance left between the Brazilian soil and us. The Aequator-taufe occurred shortly after Christmas, which no one celebrated much. It was too exhaustively hot, and we had no Christmas tree, presents, or those delicious German cookies to celebrate it with. Had we had the latter, the heat would have melted the chocolate!

A couple of days later I could see islands on the horizon. They turned out to be Fernando de Noronha, uninhabited islands on the direct course to Recife, Pernambuco. After circumnavigating the island group, the ship left for Rio de Janeiro, another 2000 km (1,300 miles) away, around December 26 or 27. I doubt the old "Duque de Caxias" made more than 180 miles per day. Loaded to the brim with hundreds of immigrants and an enormous amount of crew, marines and officers, the ship was ancient, had one screw, oil fired boilers and a very noisy, old-fashioned steam engine. Progress was slow and steady. With no more land to be seen, the only entertainment was watching the dolphins' acrobatics as they raced alongside the ship. New Year's eve was celebrated on the high seas with my last bottle of Aquavit, a terrible "schnapps" left over from Hamburg. The first bottle had been emptied while crossing the equator. I had plenty of help with the bottles, because everyone was in the same condition: bankrupt. We were a merry, lost bunch of negligent, sanguine optimists. Now without money and "schnapps," all that was left for me was reaching Rio to face life. Days dragged out until on January 5 in the morning we could sight an unusual haze in front of us to give way to some bluish clouds, which turned out to be mountain ranges growing out of the sea. After an hour or so I could make out clear white streaks of chalk at the ranges' foot. As the ship approached the beach, the chalk grew into a long chain of high-rise buildings, draped along the beach at the foot of the mountains. It was an impressive, marvelous panorama. Had I possessed a camera, I would have taken many shots. But no one seemed to have one. Later Ernst Bast gave me some photos taken with his camera. According to those in the know, we were approaching the world-famous Copacabana. My blood was running faster through my veins, inspired by the moment, and I was proud at being able to see this exclusive place once in my lifetime. Coming very close to the beach, the ship started moving parallel to it. When it reached the end, where there is a large rock and the boulevard abruptly turns toward Ipanema (I didn't know the name then), the ship turned around and I saw the famous Sugar Loaf ahead of me. Because passengers, crew etc. were now on the portside of the deck, the ship was leaning dangerously towards that side. Therefore, the crew pushed some people in the opposite direction to straighten out the vessel. Soon we negotiated the entrance to the Guanabara Bay past the Sugar Loaf on the left side. Now the entire scenery of Botafogo and the Corcovado with Christ the Redeemer on its top developed before us under blue skies in balmy air. Everything looked beautiful, impressive, new, rich and undamaged. All was painted, and huge palms shaded the avenidas. We discovered trees we had never seen before. I was enraptured. This adventure started to turn out better than I had thought possible. The vessel steamed close to the mooring, where the tugs took over. We were now in what looked like a huge lake, the Guanabara Bay, where Rio's port is located and where an enormous crowd awaited the ship. Most were Brazilians wanting to greet their relatives returning from a long, arduous tour of Europe with its awful weather. But there were also people looking like us—relatives waiting for their homecoming folks, like Ernst's father, whom I would later meet in Sao Paulo. It took an eternity to disgorge all those awaited by relatives. They had to pass through customs immediately. It was dark before the stream of departing people ended. Then nothing more happened. After our usual meager supper, we had ample time to look at the port of Rio. I spent another night on board, where street noise kept me awake all night. There were an enormous amount of automobiles in Rio, which seemed to be honking their horns until past midnight—quite a lively city, compared to quiet Spandau or Hamburg.

On the next morning the ship maneuvered slowly across the bay to what turned out to be Niteroi. From there a launch took us to the "Ilha das Flores (flower island) located just in front of the Niteroi beaches. Through the palms we noticed some low brick buildings resembling somewhat primitive barracks. I dragged my suitcase toward one of them. Men and women entered separate buildings, but families could move into those reserved for them. With only one bed on top of the other, more room between the aisles, a light breeze moving through the rooms, and the roof shaded by trees and palms, I could finally expect a good night's sleep. The lack of peaceful rest for weeks on end had left me pretty much run down. I don't have to repeat the menu; the food offered on the island was the same as on board ship. We still had not gotten used to it.

On the following morning we were examined by customs, got a stamp in our German identification papers and were told that at our final destination we would have to apply for a "Carteira 19," Brazilian identity for legal immigrants. Nothing more happened and we were left to our devices. There was really nothing to do—no library, cinema, games, workout equipment or walking paths. Those with hard currency could leave on daily launches across the bay to Rio at designated hours. Lacking money, I did not go. Little did I know I could have joined the armada of beggars in Rio's streets to earn some money for postage stamps, cigarettes and other necessities. On the island I looked around to make some acquaintances. There was the Westphal family: father, mother and daughter, also from Berlin. He was an electrical engineer in his fifties. Then there were Rubin and wife, Bernsee with wife and little daughter, and others whose names I cannot remember. I did not keep a diary. On the next day I found my swim trunks to discover the bay with another young man. Carefully entering the murky water to swim, I thought it was nice until I panicked when noticing large chunks of human feces floating around my head. I avoided swallowing by keeping my head above the water. That was the last time I tried swimming there. It appeared that raw sewage from the surrounding large cities was simply discharged into the bay. I wondered what the fish thought about this—if there were any left. The evenings were impressive. We could see the millions of lights crawling up on the hills as Rio lit up for another night. The air was full of fireflies, almost as large as birds, making considerable noise. It was all so exotic and exciting to see. In the daytime the air was full of hummingbirds and other unknown birds. I spent much time observing and musing about the new environment.

As I looked back from my position in Rio and thought about my past 10 years in Germany, I already felt detached. This was a new reality. What I had experienced back in the cold north had been a chain of nightmares and deprivation. As I had decided on immigration, it became finally evident and believable that countless millions of people had been cold-bloodedly murdered. I had not believed it until an elected postwar German government had confirmed the reports. I had not been able to bring myself to give credence to those reports by former enemies. Had I known of these goings-on earlier, would I have done something about it? That question may be asked by people who have only known democratic governments in their lifetime. Under the brown dictatorship (we combatants did not call it that because of our ignorance of government affairs), active resistance usually ended in disappearance. But I cannot cite any knowledge of this happening among the people I knew. Today I think the German government waged war not only on foreign countries, but also on the German people. In the final analysis, the vast majority of the population at large also suffered the consequences of the crimes committed. While the Nazi leadership finally had an easy end through suicide, trials or escape, the rest of the population had to pay.

EXPLORING BRAZIL

While I gave some time to these thoughts, exciting developments started to happen in our little community. While some of the immigrants left for their destinations, business people were starting to arrive. About two weeks after our arrival, a serious gentleman came to the island. He introduced himself as Walter Belian, President of the large "Companhia Antarctica Paulista," then the largest South American brewery and soft drink bottler with interests in numerous other enterprises. When hearing the company's name, I really did not understand its and Belian's significance. I didn't have the foggiest idea about Brazilian industry or the country, but I was elated that I could talk with a potential employer who spoke German—so fluently that he must have come from Germany himself. He was looking for six engineers whom he selected from the throng of individuals surrounding him. He said he would return to Sao Paulo and send a personnel manager and an assistant, who also spoke German, to arrange our contracts and transfer us, including family members, to Sao Paulo. He mentioned an initial salary of Cr$600 (Cruzeiros) per month, which people in the know advised was a more than generous salary for local conditions. Together with me, he hired Westphal and Jakob (both electrical engineers), Rubin (mechanical engineer), a fellow with a Ph.D. in mechanical engineering from Borsig/Berlin, and a marine engineer whose name I also do not recall. After Dr. Belian left, the others enthusiastically congratulated the six of us, and we thought that we had hit the jackpot. Three or four days later, the promised personnel manager and Belian's sidekick, Mr. Eichsteadt, arrived. We were given contracts the latter had translated into German. They committed us to the company for three years and stipulated the initial salary and benefits, of which the most important was a health insurance plan, which essentially meant treatment by the company hospital. I later learned that most of the company was held by a foundation, of which Dr. Belian was the administrator for life. Therefore his decisions were just about binding. The hospital was part of the foundation's assets. All employees enjoyed this benefit.

After the personnel man left, Eichsteadt explained how we would get from Rio to Sao Paulo. On the next morning he took us to Rio's Santos Dumont airport at the end of Avenida Rio Branco. Soon we were flying to Sao Paulo with a marvelous view of the coastline from Rio South to Sao Paulo—a very impressive and beautiful part of the world—mostly virgin land with endless uninhabited beaches, islands and mountain ranges. No roads could be seen going anywhere, except the highway connecting Rio and Sao Paulo. Any cleared land or unpaved roads exposed the soil's deep red color. What a difference from Europe where countries were fighting for hundreds of years for each square meter. After this short flight, we landed at Congonhas airport and were driven to a small hotel in downtown Sao Paulo, near the post office in the Rua Brigadeiro Tobias, close to the "Luz" train station. My room had two beds. I shared it with the Ph.D. from Borsig, an imposing man in his fifties. Coming from that company, he was specialized in any aspects of generation, distribution and use of steam. There was plenty of need for this in a large brewery. What I was to do at work was still a mystery, but I would soon find out. Word was that we could live in the hotel for one month—again a most generous arrangement. Eichsteadt had said that he would visit us daily to give us language lessons. After arranging our belongings in the rooms, we started to explore the town. As we strolled past the Post Office, we saw a street sign: "Avenida Anhangabau" (difficult to pronounce). It intersected with Av. Sao Joao, which was then the main drag. I felt uncomfortably hot. My off-white summer jacket, bought in 1938 and hardly worn, was too heavy for that climate. But I noticed that everyone had a jacket. Most were white and made from ultra light linen; others came in very light colors and were made from the so-called "tropical" cloth. My jacket was becoming so unbearably hot that I took it off. Next I noticed that everyone, including men, was running around with an umbrella. Men with umbrellas looked strange. It didn't seem manly to me to walk around with one of those—until it rained. When it opened up, it was like standing underneath a waterfall. Because the wipers did not work fast enough to clear the windshields, cars had to stop. It was like sitting in an automobile immersed in a river. Cars were large American brands, like Chevrolet, Ford, Buick, Oldsmobile, Studebaker, etc. Streets were teeming with them, a scene very different from what one found in Germany. Times must be good, I thought, and they were, because Brazil then had enormous credits in the U.S. having delivered many raw materials during WWII. The enormous resulting unpaid balances, which lasted until the late fifties, were used to buy anything available, and import licenses were easy to get. My first acquisition was an umbrella—without which a "Paulista" was lost in summer. Yes, I had arrived in the Brazilian summer, at the end of January! Eichstaedt had arranged some advance money when we were transferred to Sao Paulo. What a relief! I needed to write home about my arrival and experiences. He had also arranged for some postage stamps, and things slowly began to normalize. My adventure was turning into my discovery about the workings of this new society, which would keep me busy for the next five years. One of the first things I pursued was finding a business that shipped care packages to my parents, who had supported me so faithfully through those rough years. Naturally, this had been a two-way street, with me doing my utmost to contribute, probably more than most compatriots. My parents were a real marvel; we had never had any disagreements. Soon I was happy to find a company which shipped such luxuries as coffee, tea, cocoa, chocolate, cigars, cigarettes, etc.—most were items no one had heard of in the post WWII years, except those with foreign relatives. From then on I would order such packages regularly.

My daily life revolved pretty much around the hotel. There even food was served for all six engineers and their families. Now we could appreciate meals other than rice and beans—chicken, beef and fish, which came mostly from the rivers. For some reason traffic in ocean fish or crustaceans was undeveloped. We could even order veggies and green salads, but rice and beans still seemed to be staples on which each meal was based. I learned that little was going on in the streets during the day—it was just too hot. In the evening things perked up and the population began its activities. Sao Paulo was full of all kinds of small shops. A huge selection of bar-like restaurants served something hot or cold. They had open fronts and one could walk right in, sit down on a bar stool, order a pizza or lasagna together with a cold "chop" (glass of beer), and be served within seconds. Such places were unknown in Germany, but could exist here because of the year-round hot or mild climate. These activities centered around Avenida Sao Joao, Av. Ipiranga, Praca da Republica and their surroundings. Today it pretty much looks the same. Down on Ipiranga there were several tailors, one of whom Eichstaedt recommended to me. I had my first suit made there from very light wool fabric a month later. Since ready-made suits were not available, everyone had them made to order. Mine was reasonably priced compared with my income. Now I looked like a local gentleman. The suit had to be worn with a dress shirt and tie—without the latter, one could not enter any cinema. Around me I saw not only well-dressed people, but also many run-down beggars, who filled the bridges over the "Vale de Anhangabau," along with peddlers, whose wares were laid out in front of their crossed legs. All other streets also swarmed with beggars. When one ventured into certain feeder streets to Praca da Republica at night, girls were accosting passers-by, sometimes even touching their arms when making proposals. It seemed to be a wide-ranging "business." After knowing about those streets, I avoided them. I had not been exposed to this genre before. It was evident that prostitution was customary as well as amply provided and used in Sao Paulo. Later, as I became more familiar with many of Brazil's sociological problems, I would learn why. Not that I knew at the time what "sociological" meant or what to make of it. I had to read up on it much later. For now, I used the time when I was undergoing those experiences to confront whatever problems appeared and to try my best to overcome them.

In the hotel the fellows from the "Duque de Caxias" formed a strong bond. There was Paul Westphal, a chain-smoking Berliner from Siemens or AEG. He was a bit of a loudmouth, but good-hearted. Diplomatically, his wife always straightened out any damage he did in offending others. She watched their only child, her pride and joy, named "Ursula," like a hawk. Ursula was 22-23 years old and didn't have a solid profession applicable to the market place. Instead she was often playing a guitar and singing German folk songs. Next, Jakob came from Saxonia and his wife from East Prussia. He was an electrical engineer who had been in Colombia 1938–1940, installing German radio communication systems for the Colombian airline, which was equipped with the Junkers Ju 52 transport plane. According to his tales, he had made lots of money there and lived like a king, with domestic employees for everything. Dreaming of those glorious times as bachelor in a romantic setting, he wished they would have lasted forever and seemed to expect a similar colonial setting and circumstances in Brazil. Based on his limited spoken Spanish, I doubt that he could write it well. Rather than learning Portuguese faster than the rest of us, he trailed us and never learned it right. The progress of the Ph.D., who was accustomed to organizing his studies, was as good as mine; both of us were the best. Otherwise, the Ph.D. displayed an impenetrable shield of armor. I had trouble relating to him. I don't remember much about the other three, except that I later had occasional contact with Rubin, the first of our group to return to Germany after realizing that one does not get anywhere in Brazil working as an employee.

After a few days of rest we went to work in the suburb "Mooca" at company headquarters, a large brewery and soft drink bottling operation. The installation was huge, even for German proportions. The other five immigrants were introduced to the engineering or maintenance departments. They had their own boilers to generate steam for the brewing procedures, large refrigeration plants to cool the beer storage facilities and a vast network of electrical devices needed to drive everything, from refrigeration compressors to pencil sharpeners. I was attached to Eichstaedt, whose office was near Belian's, for whom he was a kind of a gopher (go-for). Our assignment was to develop a Planning Department. Because the company was constantly embattled in expansions and acquisitions, Belian wanted to apply some method to those endeavors. Eichstaedt had an economics degree from a German university. He had been sponsored by a well-to-do uncle in Rio, who must have paid his voyage and was "gerente" (general mgr.) of the Varig airline in Rio. Eichstaedt liked to give the impression of a man to be reckoned with because of his close association with Belian. Very secretive, he wanted to appear as a man of great influence and considered himself a star in the hierarchy. The actual work in the office was not very demanding. We had an office boy who constantly served us "cafezinho," the strong mocha demitasse the Brazilians adore. Things slowly started to move in the direction of work. Studies were needed for new facilities. There was one plant in Bauru and another in Manaus on the Amazon River. All this required intimate interaction with the Sao Paulo plant, where I picked up the technology by talking to the manager. After six months of having Eichstaedt along, I could do many things by myself. Layouts had to be made of the new facilities, followed by estimates for buildings, equipment, time tables, etc. etc. Later I often had to attend board meetings to report on planning progress and other matters. For the time being Eichstaedt did the reporting, sometimes with me in attendance. From these meetings, of all the board members sitting around a huge conference table, I remember one member very well: a young, tall, blond, blue-eyed fellow, with whom I later went on business trips. He was a von Buelow, from the Danish line of that famous family, who represented the second largest minority stake in the Antarctica. His father had invested in the venture when Mr. Zerrener, a Bavarian, founded the enterprise sometime before WWI. When everyone was seated except Dr. Belian, an attendant entered with a tray of 2 feet diameter, loaded with assorted medications, setting it in front of the empty chair at the head of the table. After a tension-filled five minutes, Belian entered the room, apologized very politely for the delay, and sat down to begin the proceedings. His Portuguese was very well phrased, but his German accent was so heavy that one just about visualized pig's knuckles sprouting from his mouth. By now I knew enough Portuguese to make this distinction. Perhaps this kind of pronunciation was appropriate for a brewery environment, but it contrasted greatly with his super-polite demeanor; his elegant attire was fit for an English peer. Sometimes, when the debates became heated, he grabbed the edge of the table, lifted its top (which was loosely placed) and smashed it repeatedly onto the frame to underscore a point he was making. Not surprisingly, holding an 80% controlling majority, he always got what he wanted.

The company, generous with its products, let employees drink all the beer they could hold on the premises, but it could not be carried home. A cellar master (in charge of beer storage sections) was rumored to consume 20 quarts daily.

Since beer is very nourishing, he weighed around 300 pounds at almost 6 feet. One day I saw a Finnish brew master walking along Av. Presidente Wilson in a very unsteady fashion, as though drunk, on his way home. According to those in the know, this happened when he did not have enough beer. He had a beautiful, tall, slender, blond and blue-eyed wife and two adorable, perfectly raised kids. I always wondered what made him destroy himself. With an enormous income, he had everything, but got stuck on this lousy beer. I never even drank one glass on the premises. I have never been a great friend of beer, but I certainly can tell a good one.

After the month in the hotel was up, the immigrants were advised to look for permanent living quarters. All but the Ph.D. and I found rental houses. The ample supply of these puzzled us, since the average Brazilians did not make as much money as we did. Most of the population had trouble making ends meet. Many families lived close together with the adults staying with parents and grandparents to conserve their small cash income. On the other hand, my fellow immigrants managed to slip into very comfortable, new and well-maintained homes. Next, they had to get their hands on some furniture and household needs. The typical Brazilian solution offered was so handy and tempting that it was irresistible—although the Ph.D. and I cautioned against it. The Antarctica would make loans up to thousands of dollars in today's valuation, at no interest or at reasonable rates. I argued this would make it hard to leave the Antarctica for other opportunities. We had heard about many similar arrangements, which immigrants accepted as a patent solution for their needs—easy on the family, and the wife would be happy. The law in Brazil was that no one could leave employment unless all debts were paid. I later heard of families leaving a small town at midnight to escape their employer's power. As bachelors, the Ph.D. and I were offered a furnished room in a house the Antarctica maintained in the Av. Pres. Wilson in the Mooca suburb for high-level employees. We could get to work without those time-consuming, uncomfortable bus rides.

Stuck in this industrial part of town with nothing to keep me interested or to do in the evenings, I sometimes ventured downtown to see a movie or eat out. At noon I could always eat at the company cafeteria—not very good and fairly bland food, but reasonably priced. I could save most of my income. After the first month, when I acquired more lightweight clothing, shirts and shoes, my bank account was growing rapidly. My parents received parcels, which made them very happy. I reported my fate also to Lore. I could foresee that I could afford the trip for her by late 1950. In addition, we would have enough to start a household and rent an apartment. Meanwhile, I bought the best local newspaper each day: the

"Estado de Sao Paulo," to learn Portuguese. Eichstaedt encouraged me to read the editorial columns aloud and study the unknown words. My command of Portuguese was steadily improving, and I was ahead of the others. On the other hand, opportunities for recreation were scarce, without rivers, beaches or parks nearby. All of Sao Paulo was lacking some greenery, and I started to wonder how the Brazilians spent their free time. Lots of natives were horsing around in the bars, which seemed to be a national institution, with at least one at each street corner. People had their coffee and cachassa (sugar cane brandy) here, and the "amigos" would meet to drink, talk, do some "business," and/or plan mischief. Things like having a picnic or outing in the country or woods were unknown and unpopular. Much later I learned that one could go to the beach in Santos or the most beautiful, sandy beaches of Guaruja, the island northeast of Santos, separated from it by a small channel. At that time one could travel there by car over a very precipitous mountain road, descending about 5000 feet to sea level (Sao Paulo is located on a high plateau) or by train from the "Luz" station. Both ways were not very inviting to the traveler, since they were either very time consuming or perilous and strenuous. And the new immigrants could not afford cars. The material horizon of our bunch centered around living quarters, clothing, food, drink, household items and attempts to establish some savings—an impressive struggle for most. Living here was initially easier than in Berlin, but sooner or later the realities of the new country and its environment began to set in.

Before continuing my tale about our immigrant group, I must report about an incident, which occurred while I still shared a hotel room with the Ph.D. One evening a toothache developed in my left lower molar region, which overnight increased to a crescendo the likes of which I'd never experienced. Unable to sleep, I tossed around moaning and groaning throughout that horrible night. I could not function at work. Eichsteadt made an appointment for me at the company's dental clinic. I tried to lunch at the hotel, but could not eat or think or do anything right, with the pain enveloping my whole body, brain and soul. Before the appointment around 3p.m., I strolled through downtown and Praca da Se into Rua Domingos de Moraes until, hardly realizing it, I ascended the hospital stairs. The dentist said I had a severe infection, and he could not treat me until after the infection had run its course. That would be the safest method of treatment. But he did not have to endure my excruciating pain! It took a long time to convince him to relieve me of my misery and pull the tooth. When he finally consented, another nurse came in. With two nurses and the dentist present, I repeatedly received the usual Novocain. Then he ordered "cafezinho" for everyone. When testing the tooth, it turned out that the painkiller had not taken effect. Just touching it, I went sky-high! When he started pulling, one nurse held me to the chair from behind as he grabbed and pulled, with the pain shooting unbearably through my entire body. And then it happened: the tooth broke off and all four roots remained in the jaw. Using his digging tools, the dentist started digging for the roots. Only the intense pain kept me from passing out. He and I could stand his hellish procedure only for five or ten minutes. Each rest which followed was used to drink a cafezinho. Sweat was covering the dentist, who was by now afraid of breaking the infectious bag under the roots. He did know, of course, which root it was. Had it broken, the infectious material would have entered my blood-stream, resulting in severe complications. Feeling enormous pain and ready to pass out or worse, I couldn't think that far at the time. This enormously painful procedure took about two hours. At the end I was a completely deflated, sorry-looking, moaning piece of humankind. Scared of possible adverse consequences, my tormentor didn't look much better. Finally, with a sigh of relief, he dug out the last root, with the infectious bag of pus still hanging on it, integrally intact. They sent me on my way with some pain pills. Stumbling down the stairs, I could not control the tears. Never since then have I experienced such an enormous, unstoppable flow of tears. I walked for 30 minutes through a very busy part of Sao Paulo, noticing no one, while my veil of tears flowed over my entire face. I only saw shadows passing me, but felt almost everyone eying me curiously. Back in the hotel room, I threw myself on my bed and kept crying—but it was more like letting the tears, which came anyway, flow freely. The Ph.D. tried to talk to me, but I could not be interrupted. Only hours later I could report about my torturous afternoon, after which I slept better and went to work the next day.

Most colleagues from the Antarctica were now settled in a little new "bairro", or suburb, named "Jardim da Saude," which could be reached by bus from downtown Praca da Se to Vila Mariana; from there one needed to change to another bus. Taking a bus was an arduous affair. To reach any point in Sao Paulo, one had to change busses in downtown to the new destination. Going from Jardim da Saude to Mooca took at least 1-1/2 hours. Relying on public transportation was not a good routine. The busses were overloaded, not punctual, unreliable, and the passengers were a varied lot. Many were unkempt, poorly dressed, and some smelled badly. I was lucky to live close to the Antarctica, and I didn't even have to pay for my lodging, even though the Ph.D. and I now had separate rooms. For recreation, I now visited the different immigrant families. The Westphals' house at Jardim da Saude was the liveliest. They always welcomed friends. Soon a group of young people my age met there regularly to talk and mostly play "Skat," the German card game resembling bridge. There was Jose Michaelis, who, a year or two earlier, had joined a brother, who had been a chemical engineer for a large German company before WWII. He ran a company building chemical process installations for the food industry, where Jose was sales manager. The war had surprised him in Brazil, where he elected to stay. Unlike so many Germans in 1938/39, he did not try to return to the "fatherland." Hitler's propaganda machine had tried hard to repatriate as many Germans as possible back into the "Reich." Many—I suspect often those who had not accomplished much—were gullible enough to follow the call. On the other hand, those who had scratched out a decent living were suspicious of the concentrated effort and stayed in Brazil. The older Michaelis had soon started his own company and later hired some of the new immigrants. He married an attractive Brazilian lady and had two children. He drove a large Oldsmobile 99, a classy car for the period, and all of us envied him. Later he brought his mother, who was French, and his brother, over from Germany. The family spoke French fluently. Perhaps, as a wine merchant, Jose's father had much business in France. Serving in the air force as an observer, Jose was stationed only in Northern Norway, to follow the allied shipping convoys. He learned Portuguese very fast—probably from his family members, and his command of French helped him tremendously. He had learned to enjoy card games in Northern Norway, where it must have been the only fun available during the dark, long winters. He had no contact with Norwegians for lack of cooperation on their part. Jansson, whose first name I forgot, also frequented the Westphal home. He was tall, blond and blue-eyed, and we knew little about his past. Also having been in the war, he had come to Brazil through different means of transportation. His constant visits must have had to do with "Uschi," (Ursula). After toying with each other for years, they finally married when I was no longer close to the group. Uschi was invariably seen with a guitar, trying to get us to sing German folk songs without much success. We were more interested in cards, beer and cachassa. Later she became involved with German children's groups who must have been more likely to endure her songs. German folk songs with guitar accompaniment need cool weather, deciduous trees, snow and small village commons. They did not blend well into the Sao Paulo landscape. The last of the group I remember was Mittendorf, who also had not arrived on the "Duque de Caxias." After he had spent the war in Germany, his parents, who had remained in Brazil, had paid his passage. In the late 30's the elder Mittendorf had distributed quality German steel products in Brazil—a piece of cake, because the products were heavily subsidized by the German government. All he had to do was fill out order forms. With everyone lining up for inexpensive German steel, the Mittendorfs must have made a killing. They still lived in a sizable mansion around

fashionable Avenida Paulista. The Westphal's house was always blue from cigarette smoke, and the card games lasted until very late. This, and an occasional
movie, was our only entertainment. Sometimes another enigmatic character
showed up: Ewald, who claimed to have been a seafaring captain on a German
boat. He seemed young for having had that kind of position. He hinted about
having to leave the position, because his very pretty wife had revolted against his
going to sea. Observing her flirtatious character, one could understand his decision. They had a little boy. Ewald now moved about in a Jeep and claimed he
worked on surveying jobs in Santos. He sort of had his own business. But all we
could see was a jeep, a theodolite, and that he was invisible most of the time.
Only Jose also owned a car, a little British MG roadster, which looked very classy
to us ordinary immigrants!

By late 1950 I had accumulated some cash, but do not remember in which
form. A couple of years later I opened an account at the Royal Bank of Canada in
Dollars. In late 1950 I did not yet realize the devastating effect of the Brazilian
inflation, which was about 30% annually. While I still had to buy things such as
clothing for my personal use, I was tenaciously saving money in Brazilian
"Cruzeiros," needed for Lore's passage and to furnish a place to live. The rest of
the "Duque de Caxias" men envied me, because I had no responsibility for wife
and kids. They could guess how much I was saving. We knew each other's salary,
since we received the same amount. This must have been passed on to Ewald,
who, returning from one of his prolonged absences, told us of a big job he had
lined up at the Santos beaches to survey a new development complex. He said
lack of capital prevented him from accepting it. It required purchasing another
theodolite and hiring helpers, which sounded plausible to me. Ewald seemed a
trustworthy, good friend. After a few days I broke down, loaned him about
$1,500 and received a Promissory Note, which, I learned too late, is worthless in
Brazil. Happily, Ewald and his wife thanked me profusely. I didn't tell anyone
about this loan at the time, but a few months later, when causally mentioning it,
I was told that, soon after receiving the money, the couple had bought furniture.
Ewald then confessed and promised to pay. Now I had a promise and a Promis-
sory Note. When I finally received half, inflation had devalued it by about 50%.
The best way to lose a friend is to loan him money. This was the first and last
time I loaned money to anyone. Mostly mad at myself, I chewed on this for some
time. That $1,500 would be worth today at least $7,500 to $10,000. Although in
the post WWII years I had experienced how cruelly humans can treat each other,
I had fallen for the honest looks of a seemingly straight man with a seemingly

plausible plan to invest. In truth he had just been pushed by his demanding wife to cheat on a friend in the cheapest way possible.

Part of the reason I had fallen for the scam was that, before her husband had lamented about needing money, Ewald's Estonian wife had introduced me to the von Tiesenhausen's, particularly Karin. They were somehow related, but Ewald's wife was not a "von Tiesenhausen." Karin later explained that she was a distant Estonian relation. The Tiesenhausen family: father, mother, and three infant daughters, had fled Estonia in the turbulent early 1920's, as the Red Army invaded and took possession of the Baltic states again, while the German "Freiko-rps" (volunteer militia) did not succeed in securing the Baltic states for the Baltic nobility, which was of 100% German stock. That nobility was in control of vast stretches of land, seized hundreds of years before by the "Deutsche Ritterorden," German nobility and their knights, who had penetrated through East Prussia into the Baltic. I had a comrade of the same origin, Heiner von Magnus, whom I had considered a very fine person. The Tiesenhausen's had to flee their vast posses-sions overnight, taking only their valuables. They had come to Brazil through Sweden. The father was described to me as a first-class nobleman with an air of superiority and nonchalance comparable to that of an English Lord or Russian Prince. No wonder the Baltic nobility was amply represented in the government and military circles in the czarist regime. They had assumed the mannerisms of the Russian ruling class over the years. Arriving in Brazil, Papa Tiesenhausen had continued his preferred pastimes: gambling and the horses. He neither knew how to work or do business, nor was he concerned about making money and estab-lishing a new life in a strange society. After a predictable timeframe, money and heirlooms were gone and he conveniently died, leaving the widow with three daughters to bring up. When I met the matron, she was hand painting fine china to make a living. They lived in a "sobrado" (2-story house built snug to the next without front lawn or backyard to speak of) in Vila Mariana. The prettiest daughter, and definitely the most substantial, had married a British manager of a textile company. Karin was secretary to the local, American manager of the Shell Corp. She worked in Portuguese and English and also spoke German and some Russian—four languages which were spoken by her entire family. Her spoken German was stilted, but passable; not surprisingly, the German writing was sub-standard. The third sister seemed to be a forgotten spinster. She and Karin still lived at home.

Before I go on about this development, I should switch back to a sad surprise I had in late 1950 and early 1951. In the Fall I had written to Lore that we could go ahead with our plans and that I had funds to pay for her passage. Before writing this, I had noted that her responses had become rare, fairly non-descriptive and even evasive. I comforted myself that some people just don't like to write (today those people would use the phone!). My letter inviting Lore to join me in Brazil, however, never even got answered. While I anxiously awaited her jubilant confirmation, there was an endless pause. I was getting very lonely by then and longed for a good, close friend to share my life with. I thought I had this friend in Spandau, and that she was also using this time of separation to prepare to join me. But not a word came. Believing my letter had not reached her, I must have written several more times. But I noticed that, as soon as I revealed my readiness to purchase the passage, the response was dead silence. I considered traveling home to see what happened, but this would have depleted my resources and was self-defeating. Such a trip would have required at least three months and might have meant quitting my job. Should I spend so much time and effort to find out that Lore didn't want to leave Germany? And, if my letters didn't arrive, would she not have complained about my silence? Such a trip made no sense. Her silence was sufficient evidence of lack of interest. My anxiety increased during the next several months, until finally a letter arrived from Spandau, from "Gaertner." Opening it feverishly, I found it written by sister Christel, with whom I had cut trees in the winter to heat their apartment. Somewhat withdrawn and perhaps a bit difficult, she had no boyfriend that I knew of. Tomboy-like, she was very strong and almost built like a man. That's all I knew about her. Aware of my letters' contents and that my invitation to Lore had never been answered, Christel wrote about Lore's exploits, noting that Lore was heavily involved with her cousin Dittmar. They were together often, watching bicycle six-day races and similar events—things I would have never considered attending. To sum it up, Lore, involved with another man, was far from coming to Brazil. It was over. Why she could not tell me this herself I shall never understand, but perhaps it was part of her easygoing character. Christel offered to join me in Brazil herself. For a moment I thought Christel had withheld my communications from Lore and wanted to cash in by coming instead. But that was too far-fetched to be plausible, since, in that case, Lore still would have written once in a while. I concluded that Christel may have been fond of me without my noticing it, and that she thought joining me would be a natural thing to do. The trouble was that I had neither thought of her as a prospect nor did we have any emotional connection. Deciding to ignore all this, I wrote to the mother that I knew of the developments, that I had appreciated knowing and visiting her family, and that I now wished them the best for the future. While that ended this episode of my life, I did not get over it for some time, but knew that my dream was over. Thinking about Lore later, I developed some doubts. She may have been too laid back for my taste, and she might not have contributed much to such a marriage. It could have turned into a disaster, and I was later glad it did not happen.

I was now spared from marriage for some time, but kept on looking. The many eligible women in Sao Paulo were mostly of Brazilian/Portuguese stock, intermingled with Italians. During my stay in Sao Paulo I was never invited to a Brazilian home. The colleagues at the Antarctica would not have thought of it, and I sensed from their behavior that they did not like us foreigners. Dr. Belian had implanted us without consulting anyone. I also observed that Brazilians seldom invited complete strangers to their homes. Friends were met at a bar or restaurant, perhaps even at a "cat house." The male "boss" of a household (the "dono") might say he was leaving to do a turn (vou dar uma volta) and would disappear for an unspecified time. The women, I suppose, met women friends in downtown for shopping, or, if German, meet at Café Viennense (Café Vienna) at the Rua Barao de Itapeteninga. That café is still at the same place, with some light Viennese coffee music—a few strings and a piano. The Viennese pastries resemble those served in Vienna. While I had no luck getting connected with Brazilians during the years I worked in Brazil, my German acquaintances would invite me on and off and were usually concerned about finding German women for me who might consider romance.

Getting to know Karin von Tiesenhausen and her family more closely, I found them dwelling on the memories of a glorious past. Mother and the other daughter seemed to consider me as an unqualified intruder, with their own discussions focusing on the family's background and past importance. They mentioned a cousin in the U.S., Count von Tiesenhausen, without realizing I had no respect for the past or their names, but rather expected the daughter to be well bred and educated, which Karin was. Speaking four languages is quite something. When they had guests who spoke Russian only, that was the language used, and they took pride in their Russian connections. I tried to get emotionally close to Karin for quite some time, but something did not click. Very remote, she never lost herself in emotion, and I finally concluded that she was too cool. For a while we would go to the Santos beaches on Sundays, usually invited by a friend. Those times were full of fun, barbeques and games, but Karin, not knowing how to strike a chord with the boys from Germany, never lost her reserve. We found her kind of behavior strange. Her background and experiences differed from ours and did not match well with my crowd, which carried all that WWII baggage. We began to meet less frequently, and after several months we decided not to go out together any more. It was over without my remembering what it had been. But it had dragged on until the end of 1952.

During that time another change was occurring. The Antarctica wanted me to vacate my room in the bachelors' guesthouse. The Ph.D. was already gone, since his family had arrived from Berlin. They remained another year or two before returning post haste to Berlin. There was simply no job in Brazil that matched his qualifications, for lack of companies building steam generating equipment or turbines, heat exchangers, condensers, etc. for the power generating industry. This equipment was imported from the U.S. All I needed was a bedroom, use of a bathroom, and someone to prepare a European luncheon for me on weekends. The Jakob couple had moved into a nice house in Jardim da Saude near the Westphal's. It belonged to Mr. Sturzenegger, a Swiss engineer who had returned to Switzerland for a few years, to be reacquainted with his company's latest developments. He later returned to Brazil. I believe that, associated with Sulzer, he must have been an expert for large refrigeration machinery. The house had three bedrooms, dining and living room, no garage, a sizeable paved backyard (which Brazilians often have instead of a lawn), all surrounded by a masonry wall. Kitchen, living- and dining room were tiled and therefore somewhat cool. The Jakob's wanted someone to share the rent. It was very convenient, because we were able to commute to work with Paul Westphal, the third in the triumvirate. Occasionally, when running late or having to return home quickly, we could take a "lotacao,"—which is a variation of a taxi, which several persons, unknown to each other, could jointly take to a common destination, usually downtown. All travel led to the center of the city. Today much is the same, but some waiting times are alleviated by a good subway system. It was around the middle of 1951 when I moved into the Jakobs' home. I believe he was from Dresden, which you could tell by his Saxonian accent. His wife came from East Prussia. Between 5 and 10 years my seniors, they must have married soon after WWII. As mentioned, he had built a radio communication system for a new Colombian airline, spending several years there. An electrical engineer, specialized in high frequency (radio) communication, he had worked for the Berlin Lorenz Co. before leaving for Brazil. In the time after WWII the Soviet authorities had been hunting down any specialists they could find for building up their own industry, but a friend in the local communist party had warned Jakob one day that he was on the list to be transported to Russia. That night he packed up his movable goods and fled to Berlin. The borders were not yet controlled. In the Antarctica's electrical department he did installations for all kinds of machinery. Having to size electrical cables, fuses, interrupters, electrical motors, etc., was not a job, which required his expertise, but there was little else for him to do. He also had a three-year contract and realized that initially the rest of us were paid more than the average salary for our job category. Unhappy with his duties and his lot, he admired the work Ernst Bast had initiated on his own in the workshop of his father, a printing specialist who lived in Brooklyn Paulista, where he was in printing types and machines. As a first class craftsman, after his apprenticeship the father had qualified as a foreman, which can be accomplished in Germany only after years of work and dedication and a stiff examination. Now in 1951 Ernstchen, as Irmgard called him, set out to build a TV transmitter from scratch, when no such equipment existed in Brazil, Germany, or anywhere in Europe. He made the drawings and electrical diagrams and built all of the parts in his father's shop. Ernst had gotten his education and experience starting in the twenties at the German overseas short-wave radio transmitters in Zossen, south of Berlin, where he had met Irmchen, who worked at the army "Abwehr" (army counter intelligence). Jakob would have loved to participate in this kind of work, but Ernst did not like strangers snooping around. On the other hand, he often discussed detailed electronic problems with Jakob. I think Ernst planned to build and install the first TV transmitter in Brazil and on the strength of this to obtain orders for other regions. Much later he actually succeeded in installing his transmitter on top of the "Banco do Estado de Sao Paulo" building in the heart of Sao Paulo. Since I never owned a TV in Brazil, I don't know how it worked. He failed to receive follow-up orders, which were scooped up by the U.S. competition. He then became technical manager of the station, where he remained until his eyesight gave out in the eighties. An avid skat player, Jakob also often showed up at the Westphal's.

Meanwhile, Eichsteadt's Portuguese lectures had ended. By early 1951 I could make myself understood quite well. I could form sentences, knew many irregular verbs and used grammar adequately in writing. I was now often sent to other subsidiaries, sometimes accompanied by Eichstaedt. There were installations in Bauru, Ribeirao Preto in Sao Paulo State, or Ponta Grossa in Parana state. We once stayed in Ribeirao Preto for some time for studies at the beer filling lines. The lines of workers each morning at the brewery entrance always puzzled me. They waited for a hiring official to count the number of heads needed for the day. The rest of the line then shoved off. I was able to talk with one of these men about the workers on the filling line, who did such manual work as placing labels on the glass bottles, inspecting cleanliness of the washed bottles, or placing bottles in crates. Invariably small and lean, they usually had straight black hair and a brownish complexion. A mixture of Portuguese, Indians and a touch of Negro, they wore white cotton pants, slightly off-white shirts, worn out sandals and straw hats. Their clothes were old and washed out. They mostly originated in the Northeast, where the birth rates are enormous and the droughts everlasting. As a last measure of survival, they had come to the big cities where work was available to survive. The men would come alone, and the family would follow later. After a fellow tried his luck in the line, he would hit the jackpot one day and find himself in a brewery, instructed to place a label or two on the bottles that passed by on a conveyor. He would do that eight hours a day, getting paid when leaving. Having observed this typical worker for three days, I did not see him on the fourth. A few days later, he popped up again, happy as a clam. I asked: "Where have you been?" "Oh, I was home," was the answer. I inquired if he had been sick … what had kept him from working? He laughed, astonished at my concern: "Why should I work? I had money! I bought a bag of rice, and beans and farofa, and also some cachassa (sugar cane brandy). Then I went home, where we all had a good time, plenty of food and fun with everybody. When the food was gone, I went back into the line, and here I am again." So, the cycle started again, ad infinitum. Lacking any kind of education, this type of worker could not read and write. Most did not know the day or month they were in. They could only sign documents by placing three crosses on a line. Their home was the "favela" (slum) without electricity, running water, gas, paved roads or schools. When it rained, the soil, which was clay of deep red color, turned into the kind of mud it takes half an hour to remove from one's shoes. I arrived in the dry season. The car, which took me to Ribeirao Preto, made clouds of very fine red dust. Opening my suitcase, I found my belongings covered with it, in need of thorough cleaning. That was easy, because Brazil is teeming with women who clean for very little money. They also live in favela huts, built of such materials as corrugated sheet metal; plywood scraps or whatever can be found. It is dangerous for outsiders to visit the favelas, which now are controlled by criminal gangs, often in cahoots with police and politicians. A favela is a world of its own—the only place where poor people can afford to live, bare of many basic needs. The concept of social services was then entirely unknown. I was not sure if these people were aware of the misery they suffered. Unable to read, they depended on word of mouth, rumors, or radio transmissions. I never understood in which way the media influenced them. Generally, they appeared happy, probably because they had escaped the dire conditions of the Brazilian Northeast, where people were perishing because they lacked even the minimum needed in food and medical care. Here they could at least get out and work for what they needed. Beyond those basics and a little "entertainment," they were incapable of making plans for improving their future. I started to realize how fortunate I had been in Germany. Beyond the minimum needed to exist, I could obtain a college degree—things these people could not dream about in Brazil, where millions had never heard of "college" and would not know what to make of it. I started to be more interested in the issues of the day, mainly through the "Estado de Sao Paulo," the country's best, largest daily paper, which is comparable to the NY Times in the U.S.

Shortly after the Ribeirao Preto (Great Black River) visit, Eichsteadt and I visited Bauru, about 150 miles from there. The work impressed me less than other observations. I observed how the young people met in the evenings. Bauru was built around a central square, with an elevated, wooden bandstand in the middle, although I never saw a band. After extremely hot days, evenings brought some welcome cooling. Following the daily chores, the town's young folks gathered at the central plaza under some senior spectators' watchful eyes. They milled around the bandstand, with the girls forming a circle in one direction, while the boys walked in an outer circle in the opposite direction. Boys and girls exchanged hot, sensuous eye contact, hardly with a chance to exchange words. Talking and standing seemed against the rules. It looked like a marriage market, but I wondered how couples could actually meet, since they did not leave the plaza together. People like factory workers did not participate; only the middle class and up did. Years later I would experience myself the rules surrounding a Brazilian daughter's behavior as it relates to contacts with a prospective suitor.

While at Bauru, invited by the local manager of the soft drink plant, we stayed at a large coffee plantation owned by the Antarctica for a couple of days. We passed our time trying to ride the horses. I succeeded, but always felt out of place on horseback, especially in my fine suits. Not helpful to my posture, they made me look like a greenhorn, especially since the horses were of a low quality and some moved along like camels, i.e., the two left and the two right legs moved simultaneously. This could make a man seasick! I concluded that horses were outmoded and not for me. The vast estate must have contained millions of coffee shrubs. Uneducated, disenfranchised workers did the harvesting and processing of the coffee. From the Northeast, they populated the vast interior and farm and ranch country of Sao Paulo state and doubtless also the other Brazilian states, except for the South, where conditions were more similar to European customs. During 1951–52, I also visited plants or breweries in Ponta Grossa (Parana State), Belo Horizonte (Minas Gerais), and Joinville (Santa Catarina). Belo Horizonte was a young, fast-growing metropolis. The manager, from German stock in the South, spoke German perfectly. So did Joinville's manager, also a descendant of German immigrants. On one of my first evenings there, he invited me to his bowling club, where only men congregated and everyone spoke German. They considered me a rarity, but the happenings in Germany for the past 15 years, or the war and postwar period, were not touched upon in our conversations. Instead, they horsed around a lot. After a few drinks, they did not start bowling, but introduced me to the club's "inner sanctum," a large glass cabinet. It contained innumerable selected samples of wood, mainly of root origin, or oddly formed branches—all resembling the male sex organ. I could not believe my eyes: grown-up, responsible and upper class citizens stooping to this kind of activity! What could I say? While I was not ready to condemn them or voice any displeasure, I had expected something more enlightening!

Earlier, I had heard of a prank supposedly played by one of the Matarazzo brothers, then one of the richest Brazilian clans. Guests at their beach mansion on Guaruja Island in front of Santos had not expected to swim, but the Matarazzo's provided swimsuits so that all could frolic in the waves. When leaving the water, the females discovered they were without swimsuits. These had been made from special material, which dissolves in seawater. I later wondered if such pranks and what I had seen in Joinville were symptomatic for Brazil. Those bored to death, who had everything, used any opportunity for excitement to satisfy themselves—at someone else's expense.

I never heard informed discussions about the state of politics, law or the country. Later that evening in Joinville, they progressed to an awful mixture of beer and champagne. Seemingly accustomed to it, they continued drinking until dawn. I am still amazed at how I survived this punishment. Then the "gerente," (manager) of the brewery took me to a downtown bar, where the corrugated steel door had just been raised for business. Instead of offering me a "cafezinho" to clear up my fogged mind, he had to have another bottle of Antarctica "chop" (a glass of beer—derivation of the German "Schoppen"). While it was dangling from my listless hand, he explained that beer had to be treated respectfully in a prescribed way, reminiscent of rituals followed by German officers' clubs or dueling student fraternities. If drinking had affected me, I was not to show it. By now I had been exposed to Joinville's ways to such an extent that I never returned. That may have been his purpose, thinking that Dr. Belian had sent me to spy a little. That was not the case—still new in the country, I had not yet figured out what made it go.

After two years in Brazil, my wallet began to reflect a change. Although the journals were constantly talking about inflation, no statistics were published, and I could not pinpoint the rate. But when comparing such necessities as meat, cheese, rice, butter, milk and bread, I realized that in the past two years I had lost much of my income through inflation. For instance, having new suits made now took such a large bite out of my pocket that I decided to buy fabric on the market and find another tailor. Although less expensive, the final product's quality was nothing to crow about. Another problem was that the Antarctica never adjusted our salaries. Lacking communication with other Antarctica employees, we could neither determine what the policy for salary raises was, nor did Eichstaedt volunteer any wisdom. Therefore, we "Ilha das Flores" hires were suffering more and more the fate of the rest of the Brazilians—steady erosion of purchasing power. For modern economic conditions the inflation was enormous. Beginning to grumble, most of us started thinking about other employment at the end of our three-year contracts.

During the contract's final months in 1953, I became better acquainted with Arthur and Grete Wetzker, who had purchased a single-family house in the suburb of Brooklyn Paulista, 15 minutes by car from Sao Paulo center toward Santo Amaro. None of us other immigrants had gotten that far. Owning a house was the ultimate comfort and well being, especially in that upscale neighborhood, where many Germans and other foreigners lived. Only those with connections had the chance to get well established so quickly. Arthur, 10-15 years my senior, with no children, had spent most of his earlier years in East Prussia, where he had lost everything when the Soviets invaded. His brother-in-law Bruno Tress had paid the passage to relieve the couple of their misery in Germany. Bruno was probably the first distributor for Volkswagen in Brazil, after having peddled pumps for a German company, which had just about kept his family going. Not even owning a home, unable to make a big splash, he had been living in an apartment with his wife and two grown daughters when contacted by a VW representative about a distributorship. He did not know what to make of it, since Brazilians preferred the widely available, large US-automobiles, which the rich people could afford—the middle class could only dream about having a car. Who would buy the funny-looking VW bug, which was too small for the wealthy and seemingly unaffordable for the middle class? Tress had wavered quite a bit before caving in, without much hope. It took a long time before he had a number of cars for sale. He would not be sorry!

Before befriending Arthur Wetzker, I had seized an opportunity to buy a car. A Herr Mast wanted to exchange a '38 Mercedes Benz model 190 Cabriolet for a newer car. The price seemed right to me. It had four forward gears, with a tooth missing in the second. With a little deft manipulation one could change gears immediately going from the first into third. This was not too bad on flat roads, but produced some anxieties and sweat on a hill, trying to get the car to move from a stop. Otherwise it was in pretty good condition. Mast delivered the car to me at the Jakob's and left with his money—then the equivalent of $1,000-$1,500. That represented just about all of my assets. Today I doubt my sanity to have purchased such an old, run-down vehicle with my total assets. Cars at reasonable prices were rare, and the whole world marveled at those daring young men in their driving machines. But I think I was motivated less by vanity than by the desire to become more mobile in a city where moving from one end to the other took at least two hours despite the relatively short straight-line distances. I also speculated that the car could be sold at a little profit if the time might come, and that in the meantime I could enjoy it. I admit that buying an insurance policy did not occur to me, and I did not think about the consequences a severe accident might have. There also was little money available for things like insurance. The first order of the day was to enter the vehicle and move it carefully out of the Jakobs' beautifully tiled car porch. Luckily, there was no oil spot underneath, although in the excitement of the moment I had overlooked checking for oil leaks. I was a total greenhorn with respect to cars, but soon learned, when out of the gate, how to shift from first into second gear, which made a very ominous, loud noise. Horrifying noises reflected the missing tooth, which promised to wreck the remaining teeth at any moment. Then I tried to shift to third, which moved the vehicle so fast that I became preoccupied with the wind whizzing by me as I careened around the neighborhood's red clay streets. After some initial difficulties, I got the hang of shifting smoothly, which seemed the most important part of driving. Since airplanes had not required shifting, that is what I had to practice. After about an hour I was ready for the drivers' test. I did not dare go on the paved main roads. Getting caught would be expensive, and I was out of money. I learned from car-driving friends like Jose Michaelis that the best, fastest and cheapest way to get a license would be through a driving school, where fixed rates were established for the process. I didn't have to take driving lessons. The school arranged the test and paid the customary "tip" to the examiner, without which there would be no license. I could not have arranged the test myself, because it was too dangerous for the examiner to accept a tip directly from an unknown person. I attended the school, the test was a cinch, and soon I was driving all over Jardim da Saude and the main streets.

Shortly before I bought the car in 1953, the Wetzker's introduced me to the Bruno Tress family, who soon invited me to their chacara on the represa (reservoir) behind Santo Amaro. From Santo Amaro at the end of the streetcar line it took at least another half hour on unpaved roads to get there. A chacara is a piece of land, preferably near a lake or river or in the woods—usually with a little house for the "Dono" (landlord) and a smaller one for the caretaker family, who may also tend to the land and grow Mamao (papaya), oranges, vegetables or whatever strikes their fancy. There may be horses, goats, sheep, chickens, pigs or even cows. The dono uses the characa to get away from the hustle and bustle of the big city and the smog on weekends. The Tress' house was at the lake with a nice view, and we also took dips in the lake. I enjoyed the company of the two daughters, Christel and her older sister, whose name I forgot. I felt somewhat attracted to Christel, who was tall, blue-eyed, with dark blond hair of almost grayish tones, slender and a bit impish. Her sister was plump, white-blond and round-faced, features that did not particularly attract me.

One day the family invited me to stay with them in Campos do Jardao for three days. I had heard much about this place high up in the mountains, a four-hour drive northwest of Sao Paulo. Today, Campos do Jardao is still the place where the moneyed gentry own "sitios" for recreation and recuperation. A "Sitio," similar to a "Chacara," is further out in the country and built with more substantial housing, to serve as a domicile for longer periods. In very good humor, the Tresses picked me up one morning at the Jakob's in their large Plymouth limousine, which fit us three young people nicely in the back. Up to the last minute I had wavered about going, since I felt some sickness coming, but could not identify it. It felt a little like a flu, but I had no temperature, and the associated body pains were not as pronounced. Hoping this condition would clear up, I finally decided to join them. As we found the via Dutra, the road to Rio, we soon passed through Sao Jose dos Campus to hit the road up the mountains toward our destination, which is located in several mountain valleys, surrounded by considerable hills. There are no solid rock peaks like in the European Alps or Rocky Mountains. The vegetation is dominated by the South American "Araucaria" pine, which is not found in North America or Europe. Its branches point toward the sky instead of downward, and their needles are almost as long as those of the "Torrey Pine" of La Jolla, California. Much bigger than other conifers', the nuts are almost the size of Brazil nuts. Sold to eat all over town, they are not as tasty as commercially available pine nuts.

After getting established at the hotel Vila Inglesa, we met around the dinner table, where everyone looked at me strangely. Before leaving my room, my condition had worsened. I felt lousy and had no appetite. At dinner, Christel burst out saying that my eyes were yellow and that I looked like I was suffering from yellow jaundice. Also called hepatitis, this was a very common disease in Brazil. To save expenses, many people ran to their neighborhood pharmacy at the drop of a hat. Suspecting flu or whatever, they got a shot, which made the body smell like a eucalyptus tree. I must have gotten it because needles may have been re-used without sterilization. Since I was not eating anything, I was put on chicken soup, which I had a hard time getting down. Instead of entertaining the two young ladies, I had to lie down in my room, a routine I also followed on the next day. On one of the following days, the Tresses wanted to visit the sitio of a friend in the neighborhood. A chemist, he ran a pharmaceutical company. Built in the style of a Swabian country building, resembling Bavarian models, this beautiful place sat on a cliff overlooking the entire valley. The others had fun, but I only suffered through it all, only wanting rest and sleep. Familiar with the problem, the chemist suggested some "liver injections" in the downtown pharmacy, and the pharmacist then injected some substances into me, again with a needle of doubtful origin, which did not come from a virgin package. I passed the night in agony and decided to leave, which I should have done 24 hours earlier, but the prospect of passing some days in this environment with the two ladies must have ruled out any remaining good sense in me. Taking the first train back to San Jose dos Campos and from there to Sao Paulo was an agonizing experience. The physician I saw the next day made the hepatitis diagnosis and ordered one full month of bed rest, with no physical activities, and some kind of diet. Then I was under Frau Jakob's care. Taking very good care of me, she managed my diet, which was no fat—period. After about two weeks, Christel Tress looked in while I was still in bad shape. Otherwise, very weak from sickness and diet, I did not have visitors, neither did I need them. After one month, the yellow color had left and I felt stronger. Thus recuperated, I could eat normal meals again, which at Jakob's were customarily laced with lavish amounts of fat. East Prussia, where Frau Jakob originated, can be as cold as Siberia, and is known for extremely hearty food. In an environment like Sao Paulo in summer, just the look at a typical Jakob meal, like a concoction of brain (from pigs) fried in fat like a donut, under conditions of heat and humidity, can produce hepatitis immediately! During a visit to a downtown Antarctica restaurant, where many Germans stopped for a bite, Mr. Jakob once ordered an "Eisbein" (pigs knuckle) with Sauerkraut. My eyes almost popped out when he cut the huge knuckle apart to get at the 1-1/2 inch thick layer of fat and the meat underneath, taking delight in forking down all these pounds of sheer fat. On another day he ordered beef tartar, which, if made from 98% beef, may be a tolerable meal for some people, but I could never stand its looks. At this restaurant he was served almost 1-1/2 pounds of 70 or 80% raw ground meat. Mixing it with onions and raw eggs, Jakob wolfed it down while expressing intense feeding lust—by which I was abhorred. I considered those eating habits foolish in this environment and think that Brazilians, with their rice, beans, farofa and lean beef in modest amounts (the poor cannot afford the meat) were much smarter. With those huge portions of meat Jakob would drink plenty of "Antarctica chop," although he could drink as much as he wanted at the brewery.

Slowly emerging from my yellow jaundice, I was invited to visit the Tress' chacara again. Hitting the worn country road behind Santo Amaro, which looked more like a washboard, I had to fear for my old Mercedes' survival. The '38 model suspension was not designed for such a road, which I doubt existed in all of Central Europe. As I slowly approached the chacara, my expectations were rising. I liked Christel and could imagine us becoming close. Her sister, however, was not my type. At the chacara, I was surprised to find that two or three additional eligible bachelors had also been invited. We spent the afternoon with polite conversation and a dip in the lake, which then was not as polluted as today. I should note that a great deal of water was collected in that reservoir, which normally would flow with the Rio Tiete westward into the Rio Parana and from there down to Argentina and Rio de la Plata. This stored water was instead directed eastward toward Santos into huge pipes and downward about 5000 feet to sea level in Cubatao, a suburb of Santos to the West, near the mountain range. This was an impressive piece of hydraulic engineering and the hydroelectric power plant produced enormous energy supplies. It quickly became obvious that day Christel had other ideas about her future. Later I learned that she suffered a great deal from amoeba attacks, a common tropical disease, for which there was then no cure. When she traveled to Germany, all of her health problems disappeared, and she finally settled in Munich to marry some lawyer, which ended in divorce. She was quite capricious and self-centered in addition to her health problems. I never saw her again after that visit.

I began to realize that the selection of willing prospects for permanent relations was quite limited for me in Sao Paulo. Naturally, there were plenty of Brazilians, but I did not circulate in places were proper girls could be met. Meeting someone was restricted to parties in private homes, mostly through people like Mittendorf or Michaelis. There were opportunities to meet Dutch and Scandinavian women, but they kept some distance from us Germans. We still seemed somewhat suspect and not a good match. We were known to be poor and having to work hard for a living, which is not the way to get ahead in Brazil! For some time, we were also socializing with some Finnish boys, a peculiar bunch. Three of them lived together in a single family dwelling at the opposite end of town from us. Artisans, who were good at designing patterns, they ran an advertisement agency. We would always meet them at their home, where they were invariably sitting on the floor with guitars, singing what appeared to be old country or folk songs—in Finnish. There was never any conversation. They always had buckets of gin, which they drank all night long. So did their guests—a mind-numbing experience each time, but everyone considered it the thing to do. It was easy in the early hours of Sunday morning or after midnight, to climb into the car and drive home straight through Sao Paulo. With little traffic in those days, the chance to hit anything was minimized. Fairly drunk, I drove home alone one night, singing all those songs I had heard, and nonchalantly sailed through all the red lights that presented themselves—a Russian roulette, without my realizing it, since I was just too intoxicated. Thinking it over the next morning, I decided to quit these senseless visits, which didn't get me anywhere. This kind of behavior may have been typical for people in my situation. There were too few outlets for an energetic young man—no sports clubs or similar activities, no hiking trails or parks, no opportunity, for example, for glider flying. Swimming was pretty much restricted to the ocean, a cumbersome day journey away. I had to be careful to drive over the old Santos road, which was like an Alpine mountain road with lots of tight switches. One could always see steaming, parked cars at the roadside on the way up; their coolant systems were incapable of dissipating the heat load. That left only meeting friends, which also became rather boring over time.

In search of my identity, I slowly began to doubt my outlook and myself. My position at the Antarctica was leading absolutely nowhere. While those thoughts were emerging, I met another girl at a party, probably at Mittendorf, the Finnish boys, or Michaelis. Huberta Lindenberg was a secretary at a Dutch import firm downtown. Since Brazil manufactured few things on its own, almost everything needed for investment activities had to be imported. For each import, the Federal government had to issue a permit in advance, which opened the door for all kinds of shenanigans by the bureaucracy, mainly corruption-related. Tariff laws were so complex that the officials could play just about any game they wished. The most important profession in Brazil solved such problems: Despachante (a fixer or dispatch specialist). He had his contacts at the port in Santos and knew who to buttonhole and the cost of extracting the goods, which would otherwise remain rotting in Santos' vast custom sheds. Fluent in German and Portuguese, Huberta appeared to be a sharp-witted secretary, who could also negotiate through French and English. She earned at least the equivalent of what an engineer commanded. Sao Paulo had a great need for multi-lingual secretaries. Usually foreigners with secretarial skills in their native language, they had often also studied English overseas for several years. Most of these foreign girls were German. With the best education of the lot, they needed the money, because many had lost everything. On the other hand, working U.S. or British women were rare. Brazilian girls, usually unable to compete with the tough and formidably trained foreigners, at that time did not venture out much into the working world, unless the family desperately needed the income. Also, the kind of drive and working habits commonly expected in Europe were not part of the culture for many Brazilian women, who often grow up surrounded by household help. After a few dates, Huberta introduced me to her parents. I liked them and her sister very much. While Huberta was small, perhaps 5 feet 4, vivacious, lively and outgoing, her sister, taller than I, seemed withdrawn, unless she was just tactful and did not want to interfere much in our conversations. Father Lindenberg had been the representative of the German Lufthansa Airline in Spain during WWII. He was said to have been involved in the plot to assassinate Hitler. He had not returned to Germany after WWII, but Spain was not conducive to starting a new career. I am unsure what he was doing at the time. The two girls may have been supporting the entire family until he later became the Sao Paulo representative for the emerging Lufthansa. When I met him, he had a very active correspondence with the newly established Lufthansa headquarters. I traveled with the Lindenberg daughters to Santos/ Guaruja a few times to enjoy the beach, but the friendship between Huberta and me remained just that for a while until we stopped seeing each other altogether. We had been unable to form a noteworthy bond that would have justified continuation. About three years later I saw her again at a dance at the "Moulin Rouge" near the Congonhas airport.

In early 1953 it became apparent that I had to make a decision about a job change—a matter discussed more and more among my immigrant circle. Rubin had made contact with a lighting company, where he was to be in charge of all engineering and manufacturing. Another guy was moving to a position at Petrobras' Cubatao refinery in Santos, involving piping, plumbing and fluid flow. Jakob and Westphal had moved to electrical engineering jobs in another company. Later, Westphal worked at VW for years until he smashed his car right into the front of a bus when returning from Santos one day. That left me out in the cold. I now had the time to learn more about Brazil. Realizing that over three years I had lost much of my income through inflation, I concluded that federal or state governments in Brazil had started with a huge bureaucracy, without anyone knowing what all of these people did. This expenditure, higher than the total intake, was an enormous drain on the state and federal budgets. Also, mostly the state elected officials would propose fantastic public projects around election time, which they then carried out. I heard Brazilians say that 50% of those expenditure flowed back into the politicians' pockets as bribes. There was then a new highway between Santos and Sao Paulo under construction—an enormous project under the auspices of Sao Paulo State and its Governor Adhemar de Barros. Brazilians in the office seemed to know that he pocketed 50%. "But at least he does something," I was told. Asked if they also would take 50%, the colleagues said: "For Pete's sake, no! I would take even more!" Those were the times. When a state ran out of money to continue financing a project, emergency loans, also involving lots of bribes, were obtained from the Banco do Brasil, the national central bank, which were never repaid. Hence, money circulation was constantly increasing without production to back it up, which fueled the constant inflation spiral. The bureaucrats where creaming off the money, and the working people were left dangling in the wind.

I concluded that one could not get ahead by honestly working for someone, unless one could get a piece of the action. For example, as a sales representative, if paid a percent bonus on sales, one could be compensated directly for one's effort. I heard this from Mittendorf and Michaelis, who received a percentage of their sales. He knew little about engineering a margarine production facility, but that work was done mainly by one of our German immigrants, who was versed in designing, sizing, and calculating pressure vessels, piping, usage of pumps, condensers, heat exchangers, etc. While the latter earned a meager salary, Jose made out very well. One of his advantages was his knowledge of English and French besides German and Portuguese. A pleasant, extroverted chap, he could carry on a conversation of any length. All my contacts thought that, short of simply having money, one must be cut in on the action. Considering my background, I wondered how to do it. There was Jansson, who worked at an office representing the Swiss company LUWA do Brasil. They dealt mainly in installations for the production of instant coffee—a brand new technology development at the time, of which LUWA was on the forefront. They were also associated with the German Henkel A.G., which tried to study and penetrate the Brazilian market with industrial cleaning chemicals of which one, P-3, was pushed by Jansson, who told me he was being offered the sales for coffee machinery. Without much ado I went downtown and talked to the local boss. Mr. Suelzle, obviously a German from Swabia, the southwestern part of Germany, who spoke with that region's pronounced accent, hired me on the spot. Soon I was ready to start, because at the Anarctica I was not offered a new contract or a raise, which meant I was free to go.

A Henkel marketing rep took me to his most productive contacts, mostly small bottlers of soft drinks, who struggled to make a living. Henkel had a limited amount of P3 barrels imported with the goal of broadening the clientele basis. Soon the Henkel man left me alone. I had no explanation what P3 was chemically, how it worked, what kind of fats, oil or dirt it would dissolve with what method (brushing, wiping, spraying or power spray), or at what temperature. The lack of professional backup—I did not even have explanatory pamphlets—was compounded by my having no idea what would happen after P3 was sold. I was unable to answer whether P3 was adequate to be employed in an industrial cleaning line for sheet metal before painting. Good products with much better chemical engineering backup were already on the market. Looking back, it was a losing proposition from the beginning, which, due to my inexperience of sales in general and of chemical engineering specifically, left me dangling in the wind. My "friend" Jansson, who must have known that, was happy to leave this field of doom. This is how I set out to make my fortune. I first contacted firms that had purchased P3 before, but, with plenty of cleaner still in stock, most were not ready to add more. Their problem was less with cleaning the old bottles than with peddling their own product. The Brazilian system then was that the bottler would collect used beer or soft drink bottles from the sales outlet. With labor so inexpensive, it was economical to collect and thoroughly wash, rinse and inspect the used bottles. Imagine someone buying a beer and finding an insect on the inside! But the risk was taken, although insects, which thrive in Brazil's tropical climate, loved to get inside the sugary bottles. Soon I learned that I could sell significant amounts of P3 only to the real big guys, like Antarctica or Brahma breweries, where truckloads of detergent were used each month. The trouble was that LUWA didn't possess even one truckload full. Confronting the Henkel-man with this, I was told that there really was no more inventory and no import licenses were pending. The goal was to import vast additional amounts later to set the stage for investing in a chemical detergent factory. He was researching the market to justify such a large investment. I was therefore relegated to bother small fry bottlers to convince them of the unimaginable advantages of the mystic P3 detergent. It worked to my advantage that most Brazilians thought highly of Germans and their products, but I must admit that no orders rolled in to justify my employment. Unable to move the product fast enough, I had trouble convincing my contacts to buy. Because I had been quickly complimented out of the premises a few times, I became afraid of walking into a place, fearing rejection. My wonderful car was to help carry out the sales activities, and I started wondering if they had hired me because of it. When it had come to the point of getting more rejections than anything else, I found myself wandering aimlessly around Sao Paulo, without a plan for sales contacts, and becoming despondent.

It was the beginning of 1953. Again, the Mardi Gras (Carnival) season, when the population takes to the streets for a week, was in full swing. The "samba schools" marched through downtown to the beat of their music—its participants dressed in fantastic costumes, which they pay for themselves. People may sink their entire savings into those garments regardless of their survival needs. Essentially, only the poorer classes then participated to abandon. When the samba schools paraded through downtown, it seemed that the entire population crowded the streets. Alcohol sales were prohibited during carnival, but many people carried plastic squeeze bottles, which they used to squirt ether into their throats to provide a high or into the eyes of unsuspecting bystanders. Ether causes a terrible burning sensation in the eye. It lingers for 15-20 minutes, during which one remains practically blind. It may have also been preparation for pickpocket work. After being victimized by an ether attack, I stopped commingling with the carnival crowds. While Brazilians are crazy about it, I found no sense in it, but preferred carnival parties at the Sto. Amaro Yacht Club, mostly frequented by German businessmen. I also liked the dance and dining floors at one of the downtown hotels on Avenida Ipiranga. They were usually jammed, and when it came to doing the samba, one could hardly turn or move. Everyone would just step from one foot to the other in the rhythm of the beat, while perspiring profusely. That was called "carnival fun." I later just forgot about the whole thing, thinking that I would have preferred the dance hall below the Stoessenseebruecke in Spandau.

During the LUWA time, I met the "Henkel"-man's girlfriend, a good-looking, tall, blond, blue-eyed, slender woman, always dressed quite well. He later married her in Sao Paulo. She was one of those top-notch local bilingual or trilingual secretaries and office manager. One day she introduced me to her girlfriend, Gisela Gamon, who, of similar appearance, was also from Berlin—I believe Charlottenburg. How she had come to Brazil I could only speculate about. We went out together a few times without getting anywhere. She looked very good as a saleslady in a downtown boutique, but unfortunately this kind of work is not enough to finance a quality life, rent, food, etc. She was in need of a change for the better—by becoming a good secretary, marrying a good man, or returning to Germany. She did not have the skills or inclination for quality secretarial work, and I believe she lacked the money for her return. The third possibility seemed the only one left. When she got sick one day, I visited her in her very small bedroom sublet, with room for little else but a bed. Looking miserable, with sweaty hands, she seemed to have some liver problems, but I was not sure. I felt sorry for her, but could not do much. We stopped seeing each other soon afterwards. She must have left Germany with unrealistic expectations and perhaps should not have. She had done so at great risk and without success. I could only guess the circumstances, since we never got around to talking about past or future.

As the LUWA sales adventure became a drag, I recognized the need for another change. I felt too awkward buttonholing strange people to peddle some stuff I did not believe in, without luck. After four or five months I started looking around. By mid-1953, I landed a job with Elevadores Atlas. This company belonged to the Villares family, one of the old money clans of Sao Paulo. They also owned Acos Villares, a steel producer, which particularly invested in the production of specialty steels such as alloys for tool making and heat treated industrial components such as gears, shafts, valves and stainless steel in any form from sheet over plate to bar stock or forgings. They also made certain types of tungsten carbide, mainly impact resistant types for rock drilling applications.

Before going on, I should mention my move to a house along the streetcar line to Santo Amaro, a little behind Brooklyn Paulista, or perhaps it was still part of Brooklyn. The Sturzenegger family, back from Switzerland, needed their house back. I did not have any enticing opportunity other than moving with the Jakob's, which was to my advantage. All my needs were taken care of by Mrs. Jakob, who maintained and cleaned all my things, bedding, clothing, etc. Neither Mr. Jakob nor I had to lift a finger around the house. On some Saturdays we would visit the open-air market together, which still now are a tradition all over Brazil. By fall 1953 we moved into a spacious single family dwelling on a narrow lot in a street dotted with similar buildings. It had three bedrooms, a bath, kitchen, living room and a glass-enclosed veranda overlooking the street. All windows were steel frames with small glass panels to prevent burglars from entering. At the side was a car porch with a red tile floor. The back had a cement floor, a clothesline and a sink for doing laundry by hand; there were no washing machines yet. High brick walls surrounded all sides of the property. On the tops of such walls broken glass pieces would often be permanently cemented, again to prevent burglaries. The front had iron gates with solid locks. All of those houses were of brick and whatever wood was used for window frames, doors, etc. was of impeccable quality timber such as imbuia or peroba—tropical hardwoods that are immensely valuable today. There was a refrigerator, but no freezer, air conditioning or heating equipment. In extreme heat and humidity, we suffered, were tired out, and took intermittent showers. In one extreme case, during Antarctica times, while staying in a downtown Rio hotel in December, it got so hot and humid that I took five showers in one night; each time the bed sheets were soaked in perspiration! For that reason, men in Rio wore only white linen suits, which they changed when lunching at home. As a hired hand, I never became part of the circles—mostly government workers and bank employees, the most privileged people, especially in Rio—whose members could take off two hours for lunch.

Frau Jakob also liked our arrangement. With me paying a large part of the rent, they could live in a better home and had some entertainment. She did not seem fond of her lot. Her easygoing, but demanding husband expected his food and always a bottle of beer on the table when returning home, which seemed strange to me, since beer only made me more tired when the climate had me drained already. During those months in late '53 and early '54, I was not going out with any girls and started to wonder what to do about it. What was wrong with me? Jansson had gotten increasingly interested in "Uschi" Westphal. Mittendorf was heavily engaged with a Dutch woman who had a child with her husband. They divorced, the husband fled to Holland with the child, and Mittendorf was to retrieve the child and bring it to Brazil. I think he succeeded in this, married the girl and removed himself from the shrinking circle of friends and "skat" players.

Before moving to the Jakobs' new home, I had rented a house with Jansson for 3-4 months. We hoped to be independent and upgrade our living standard, but Jansson, frequently absent, left the housekeeping to me, although we had hired the owner's wife to do a lot of it. Jansson mostly hung out at the Westphal's with "Uschi." We tried to have parties in the house, including one with those Finns from across town. When it was over in the early morning, they had painted the veranda with abstract designs sprung from their drunken minds. We could not afford that again. Later, the owner's wife made life uncomfortable by indicating an interest in either one of us, or both. When I lived in that house, I returned from work by bus. As at most bus stops, there was a bar at that corner, where, each evening, one particular character stood with his glass of cachassa, looking like he had had his fill and smelling all over from the liquor. After some time, he started to greet me when I left the bus, offering me a drink. Drunkards like to be joined, to be able to feel that drinking is normal. He never seemed to do anything—a fellow without any concerns in a country full of people who had no chance to make a living. His attitude derived from his background: his father, a government bureaucrat, had purchased him a position as tax assessor. This meant he had to evaluate properties for their current value, on which basis taxes would be calculated by a simple formula. Since the values changed each year by at least 30%, re-evaluations could not be scheduled quickly enough. An army of those tax people must have been always on the go to keep values at current levels. After entering a home and discussing details with the owner, he would never walk out without substantial "presents." While this simple man was a multi-millionaire, the taxes people paid were low. This was another hands-on example how things worked in Brazil, where huge amounts of government bureaucrats and politicians lined their pockets, while the people who produced the goods had no chance, unless they went into business or the like. This experience again made me wonder why I was in Brazil.

Because investing in a household made little sense, I returned to living with the Jakob's. I had not set an exit date or made a final decision. Although my new job at Elevadores Atlas was interesting in the beginning, it did not fully challenge my engineering skills for long. Looking for a job in Sao Paulo, I was usually caught between the scarcity of challenging positions and my time frame for finding one. Few modern industries operated in Sao Paulo in the fifties. General Motors and Ford were there, but most of their products used imported parts; their good positions were held by Americans who were temporarily transferred to Brazil. The large industry structure for the supply of automotive parts would be developed only later under President Juscelino Kubitschek. Most engineering positions were of the maintenance type and of no interest to me, since I would fit best into a manufacturing environment with emphasis on design to enhance manufacturability. Hence, my field of application was limited in Sao Paulo. Mr. Jakob, for whom there were only jobs in electrical maintenance, easily done by a German-trained electrician, was also unhappy. Others we met from the Duque de Caxias group were on their way to positions, which matched their ambitions and experience. Huessner, whom I met at Bast's, was going into business to develop and manufacture welding transformers. This had been his occupation in Berlin, and he found a Brazilian who supplied money and local business know-how. The law then demanded that at least 51% of any incorporated company had to be owned by Brazilian citizens. With Huessner as minority owner, real business decisions were made by the Brazilian, which was to lead to difficulties after the development work had been completed. I later learned that Huessner became an alcoholic, and, after his lovely wife Senta died of breast cancer, a complete drunkard. Senta had gone through some horror times after WWII. She was from a German-dominated area in Yugoslavia/Romania (Banat), where all Germans were hunted down, stripped of their possessions, raped and killed. Those left fled to Germany. In those areas of the Balkans dominated by Germans the native Serbians or Romanians resented their good, solid assets, which most of the natives lacked. They overlooked that Germans on average were tight administrators, better educated, and that their possessions had been accumulated over the past 200 years. Germans (mostly Swabians) had been invited to the Balkans by the Austro-Hungarian crown. In times of turbulence like post WWII, the resentments of many years were unleashed on the people that had more than the others. Senta was one of those.

Another German engineer I knew of had come to Brazil in the late thirties, probably on assignment for a large German corporation. He had decided not to hasten to the fatherland's defense in its time of need. He became a naturalized Brazilian and started manufacturing electrical instrumentation such as Volt, current and power consumption meters of various qualities for different applications. In 1954 the firm was solidly established and just about had the market cornered, which shows the old wisdom always prevails: thoroughly prepared, one must grab an opportunity when it comes along. Bruno Tress had also become a naturalized Brazilian citizen during WWII and hence could own his corporation. I knew of another "Duque de Caxias" engineer who fell into a slot for which he was thoroughly prepared. His wife lived in Spandau at Bruederstrasse near Zimmerstrasse. A specialist in the design of desktop kitchen machinery, he joined the fledgling Brazilian subsidiary of a German corporation and did well in his field. Even he later returned to Germany, probably because Brazilian salaries, benefits and social status did not match European standards.

As I settled in with the Jakob's again in late 1954, we continued to address each other formally, using "Herr" and "Sie", but often they would call me "Moratzchen," a way of expressing that I was ten years their junior and looked younger. Following the old fashioned German customs, they would not have dreamt of using "Du," which is used in Germany only among friends and family

During that time, I started going out a few times with another girl in whom I soon was to become quite interested. Slender, blond, tall and blue-eyed, she had a fairly fragile disposition. Very sensitive, she had a good head on her shoulders and was interesting to talk with. The family lived in a stately mansion in prestigious Jardim Europa, off Avenida Paulista. The father was from Austria and a steel-making specialist. He mentioned to me that he had been in charge of large steel facilities in the Ukraine during WWII. As I became interested in Eva Visconti, she said he had struck a deal with Belgo-Mineira, a large steel mill near Belo Horizonte. The family would move within one week. I could tell she was as sorry about it as I was. Trying to convince her to remain in Sao Paulo was useless; no bond existed yet on which I could have based such a request. As one of those trilingual secretaries she certainly made a sufficient salary to live well.

My work at Elevadores Atlas initially involved manufacture of such elevator components as cabins, electrical motors, controls, cable-winding drums, traction rails and counterweights. I reported to the production manager, an Austrian about ten years my senior, who had also come to Brazil after WWII. The firm had a licensing agreement with the U.S.-Otis Corp. In Sao Paulo, a center for high-rise construction, business was thriving. With several dozens of elevators constantly pending in various stages, I soon became somewhat of a sidekick to the totally overloaded manager. The days were flying. Other than at Antarctica or LUWA, the demand exceeded the time available. Great improvement in manufacture was impossible, since most jobs were one-of-a kind items, to comply with specific job orders. A group of local consultants were always hanging around, bothering everyone, but they never came up with anything. The driving force behind all activities was the delivery schedule, of prime importance in the building business. Delivering elevators behind schedule could have upset the schedule for an entire building. It was different from mass production, which allows spending extended time on each process and component to save time, material, or both.

After a while, when leaving at quitting time, I would find two engineers waiting for me. One was Dutch and the other Russian, or rather his Russian parents—probably 1917/18 Russian émigrés—had raised him in Switzerland. They habitually stopped at the corner bar before catching the streetcar to Santo Amaro. When the Dutch guy had a car, because his wife didn't need it, the three of us would ride home together, since we lived in the same neighborhood. The two others always had two "shots", while I was content with one. The Dutch guy had come to Brazil with a Dutch Import/Export company doing just about any trade. He had been discharged, because business had gone bad some time ago—probably because all foreign credits Brazil had accumulated after WWII had been used up. From then on the trade balance and foreign currency reserves determined the amount of imports, which were shrinking. Brazil's investment needs were enormous and could not be satisfied until today. The Russian from Switzerland had the demeanor of a Russian prince. The way he kissed a lady's hand bordered on the grotesque, and his working habits showed an absolute disdain for discipline, volume output and the likes. Nothing would move him when it came to having to betray his sense of style, haute couture or good manners in the presence of ladies, and in appreciation of fine food, served on first-class china. His favorite restaurant was a downtown Franco-Russian place, where he knowingly passed the doorman, who was dressed like a sergeant of the Imperial Russian Cossack Guard regiment. I was in awe.… I later experienced similar feelings in the Russian Tea Room, a luxurious restaurant on 52nd street in New York. He would start with escargot, while rolling his eyes, with his mustache hairs raised to attention. To me they tasted no better than hot olive oil and parsley. I only accompanied him a couple of times, since the prices were too high for me. This drinking after work persisted for some time until the Dutchman invited us home one night for a bite and more drinks. When we arrived, his wife already seemed drunk, with some gin bottles waiting in the kitchen. As my two friends started filling their glasses, they seemed to be following a long-standing routine. With hardly anything to eat, but lots to drink, that "party" lasted until late into the night, when all of us were thoroughly soaked. I have no idea how I got home. These two inseparable friends appeared miserable about something, and the situation started to bother me. I thought the Dutchman bemoaned his import/export job, where he had made good money, and the Russian aristocrat was sorry that he had lost that status and now had to work for a living. He was also saddled with a gorgeous wife, who not only radiated charisma and style and had a great body, but was also successful in what she was doing. She must once have cherished his manners and background, only to discover his inability to cope with modern life. I soon decided to leave my new friends to their drinks and go my way. Such disillusioned immigrants, who had not made it as big in Brazil as expected, were seen often in Sao Paulo. Their despair resulted in alcoholism, domestic difficulties and misery. One example was Herr Jakob himself, who had dreamed of living like a Spanish grandee, only to discover he had to fend for a living under the restricted circumstances of the marketplace. He should have best joined a company in the short wave transmitter business, but this did not work out. An acquaintance familiar with the field told us about the prevailing business climate and expectations. His company designed and built short wave electronic beacons for the Brazilian navy, which controlled on-shore security installations for maritime traffic. He told us that, in dealing mainly with a captain of the Brazilian navy, the usual kickback expected by this preferred member of the Rio Navy Club, was 50% of the contract. As all Brazilians knew, Sao Paulo State Governor Adhemar de Barros, was then collecting the same from the construction of the freeway between Sao Paulo and Santos. Much later I saw a seldom-used, fabulous mansion he had built on one of the peaks of Campos de Jordao.

After half a year at Elevadores Atlas, I was assigned a job unrelated to elevator manufacture. A metallurgist PhD from Krupp, Germany, hired by the affiliated company Acos Villares, had been working for the past two years on the development of tungsten carbide and succeeded with tips for heavy rock drilling. Now he concentrated on tungsten carbide tips for metal removal applications. Such metal removal is used in most industrial fabrications. For instance, machining a heavy component like a huge gear case or steam turbine joint face for marine application requires taking heavy cuts of up to one or 1-1/2 inch thickness. Sometimes those cuts have to machine across interruptions, which cause enormous shock to the tool and machine. The falling chips get hot—often red-hot—and getting hit by them is very dangerous. On the other hand, when the last pass or finishing cut is done, the cut thickness is only about 1/32 inch and the cutting speed a multiple cut of a rough cut. Both machining conditions require entirely different tungsten carbide metallurgy. The PhD was to come up with the correct formulation and heat treatment for different applications. Before 1939, all machining had been done by using high alloy heat resistant specialty steels (high speed steels). With those only a very small portion of chip volume could be removed as compared with tungsten carbide, which does not contain steel. Because its use generates enormous forces on the machine tools, starting in 1939 all had to be thoroughly redesigned to reinforce all machine components, including bearings and shafts. My first experience with tungsten carbide in 1939 as apprentice at the "Heereszeugamt Spandau" had revealed that all of our machines were too flimsy for this new material. At Elevadores Atlas I had to mount the tungsten carbide tip on a tool, which was then conventionally done by first grinding the tip to predetermined dimensions. After machining a fitting cavity onto a high carbon steel rectangular tool shaft, the tip was soldered onto the shaft with silver solder. The tool was then "sharpened" by giving it the correct rake angles for the application on hand. After controlling those activities, I went to the shop floor to find suitable applications for the tool. I then recorded the material to be cut, surface speed, cut thickness, feed, and how long the tool lasted before needing to be resharpened. I thus collected an impressive array of data, which were fed to the PhD. All our data were compared to commercially available U.S. tools like Kennametal and others. The job was dangerous, because sometimes tools exploded on a turning machine, with the pieces hitting the roof with an enormous bang. Within a year there was no real progress. The Villares products' performance never reached that of the imported types. Even worse, it was erratic and, to my knowledge, the PhD did not iron out the kinks.

Towards the end of 1955, Arthur Wetzker approached me saying he knew a very nice Brazilian girl from a good family, who would not mind meeting me. Her name was Ferreira. Arthur, whom I also addressed as "Herr," introduced us. The Wetzkers wanted to spend a weekend in Santos with us, but Senhorita Ferreira, who lived with her parents, declined at the last minute; it must not have been proper for Brazilians to let their daughters travel with people considered strangers. When I later called on her several times, we were always ushered into a sitting room, where we made conversation, while the family was in an adjacent room. Looking typically Portuguese, she was short, slender, well built, with dark hair and brown eyes. A very sensitive girl, she was a schoolteacher. This commanded only a small salary, from which she could not have lived on her own. When I left the house, she would only accompany me to the gate, never into the street. Once I persuaded her to accompany me downtown for a movie. When I picked her up, an aunt was ready to tug along. So I paid for her chaperone, too. Early on she announced plans to attend a formal, strictly black tie, teachers association ball—a grand affair in the municipal theatre. I ordered an expensive tailor-made tux, which made me look smashing. One of the next times I visited, an older brother, to my astonishment, pulled a huge revolver from his pocket without revealing why he wanted me to see it. I told him that I really marveled at this weapon, which he could be proud to own. At the same time I wanted him to know that, during the war, as a soldier in a crack parachute regiment, I always carried a parabellum "Luger" pistol 9 mm, which I still had at home. I also casually remarked that I was considered to be a crack shot with pistol, carbine, and submachine gun, but that I preferred the hand grenade. He never picked up on my joke. Retreating quickly, I spent the way home trying to understand the behavior of this moron. Clearly, he and the family expected that I declare my intentions, although I knew nothing about the girl or the family. I continued trying to take her out, so that we could have some moments alone, but this did not seem to be allowed. All suitors were suspect and could not be trusted. Now I started to resent the tux I had purchased, certain that our attendance at the ball would not materialize. A few days later she telephoned, saying she preferred that I not call on her any more. She may have considered the scene with her brother an embarrassment and realized that things would not be getting anywhere since then. I never saw her again. Even without the revolver scene, I realized this was not what I was looking for. Also, I was not consciously "looking" for a girlfriend, knowing that fate plays a large role in getting the right people together. I would, however, find good use for the tux in the not too distant future.

By early 1955 it became clear that Herr Jakob had lost his job. Acting casual about it, he expressed hopes of going into production of electrical condensers, which have far reaching applications in the electronic/electrical field. Since each radio has a vast number installed, he thought he could get things going. If he could only find seed money, he thought he could supply the know-how. To my knowledge, he had never worked in a facility for producing such devices. Last not least, all they are is some impregnated paper and aluminum foil wound to a tight roll from minute sizes to pieces of an inch diameter. Without knowing much about it, I realized that those simple-looking little things required a generation of experience in material selection, testing and manufacturing procedures, and that at least some years of experience would help. But good old Jakob also realized that, without being your own boss and selling some product, you could not succeed in Brazil. One day we visited a known industrialist in Jardim Paulista to discuss the manufacture of condensers. He offered us "Lagrima Christi," a heavy-bodied, sweet wine from Southern Italy and talked patiently with us for about one hour without results, since he seemed unimpressed by the credentials. Meanwhile there was trouble at the home front. Frau Jakob, becoming nervous, started asking me to contribute more money. It became apparent that I was to finance the entire household. Meanwhile, an American, Roy King from Long Beach, had moved next door. He was part of a crew of Americans dredging the river Tiete, a job run by the Morrison-Knudsen Construction Co., a well-established name in the business. As former sailors used to living away from home for long stretches of time, these guys were a pretty wild bunch. Many had rented houses like ours, which they easily could afford. To take care of all their needs they installed nice young housekeepers, a job for which many attractive Brazilian females were available, who would move in with anyone for shelter, food and a little something, without asking for how long. Soon after I met Roy, a young woman offered to move in with me. Somewhat naïve, I had never heard of such a thing. The social scene was then abysmal for women. It happened often that, once a few kids had arrived, husbands disappeared, never to be found again in that huge country. The corrupted courts didn't bother, and there were no social services. If the—usually poor—family could not help, many of these indigent women had to fend for themselves. On the other hand, once a woman left the parents' home, deciding to marry a man, especially without parental approval, she was on her own forever. If the breadwinner abandoned the family, she would be unable to sustain herself. Because divorce did not exist in those times, there was no end to such cases. Almost all of the Brazilian men held the purse strings, only occasionally doling out money for controlled purposes. Laws and the courts favored men. Women were rarely trained to hold jobs to earn a living wage, and the economy was at a primitive stage. There was no multitude of jobs held by millions of women, as in the U.S. There was always a vast pool of workers available, and demand was restricted. That has not changed drastically in the lower classes, even today. I went downtown a few times with Roy to show him the sights, and he occasionally invited me to dinner. One evening he dragged me into a side street off Praca da Republica and quickly entered a hallway at an address he seemed to know. We were in a flophouse. He talked to some of his buddies, which was difficult because of all the noise. Most everyone was drunk already. We left quickly. Having evaded those streets around Praca da Republica at night, I couldn't wait. Roy must have been on good behavior, because he had learned that his wife was to join him in Brazil. The next morning, walking to the streetcar, I found Roy squatting at the curb holding a large glass of water. "Why are you sitting there drinking water?" I asked. "Oh," he replied, "ain't no water, it's gin. I'm waiting for my pick-up to take me to work." I couldn't understand how anyone could work for eight hours after a pint of pure gin. But he seemed unconcerned about his capacity for working. Later I learned that all those "old salts" dried themselves out with drugs, for which their U.S. doctors had written prescriptions.

With Jakob's situation so precarious, his wife began looking for work. At first he was hanging around at home, causing more and more ugly scenes. Having exhausted all other ways of keeping their heads above water, they asked me to loan them money. To maintain their appearances with the Westphal's, Bast's Burmester's and Bernsee's, they did not easily decide to move to a less expensive neighborhood. We saw all those Duque de Caxias travelers frequently, except for Bernsee, who kept pretty much to himself. He had a solid position at the newly established Siemens subsidiary. Had I worked in Marketing/Sales at Siemens in Berlin, I'm sure I also would have been hired. With the correct background, Bernsee could continue his previously successful career with the large Siemens organization. Burmester was busy installing the electrical side of hydropower equipment for a Brazilian utility. "Senhor Ernesto" Bast was now technical manager of the TV station transmitter on top of the "Banco do Estado de Sao Paulo," the city's tallest high rise, where he remained until he stopped working because of failing eyesight before he actually reached retirement age.

Worried about my situation at the Jakob's, I feared their problems would eventually drain my meager resources. In all those years in Brazil, I had not established a substantial bank account. First, there had been things to buy. Everything was so tempting. Then, inflation's bite set in, and lately I could just live from hand to mouth. I always wondered how the other guys made it. There were rumblings that more and more people would return home, because good, solid jobs went begging in Germany by now. My only real asset, my 190 Mercedes Benz, had been badly hit by another car when I drove on cobblestones one day on Avenida Ipiranga in downtown. When a cop stopped the traffic, I was stepping lightly on the brakes when hearing a crash at my rear. The next car, which had not stopped in time, had smashed the rear. I and the other driver stopped. As the cop was surveying the damage, I saw the other driver shove some money into his hand. It happened too quickly to really see, but was easy to tell: I tried to argue with the other driver and got his address and phone number. When asked to be a witness and make a protocol, the cop did not respond, but placed his emphasis on moving the traffic, which was piled up as far as I could see. No one else wanted to get involved. The cop pressured me to move my car and I finally complied, knowing that I would get nothing from the other driver. I was right; his quick investment paid off, the accident was a business opportunity for the cop, and I, the greenhorn, was left holding the bag. Bruno Tress agreed to repair the damage, and I had the upholstery done at the same time.

Left without any money, I found a less expensive accommodation in the two-level house of the Albrecht family on Rua Uranium in Brooklyn Paulista, a 10-15 minute walk to the street car stop, and a 20 minute ride to downtown. The family with three young boys lived upstairs. The lower level housed a garage, a smallish bedroom for Mr. Albrecht's father, "Opa," and a large living room, which I occupied. I shared the bath and shower with "Opa." The lower level rooms opened to a red-tiled porch, from which one outdoor staircase led to the street level and another to the upstairs, shared kitchen. The separate entrance was an advantage over the Jakobs' accommodation. Albrecht's had a wild past to overcome. A fervent 7th day Adventist—which didn't sit well with the Germans—Opa had immigrated from Germany in the twenties with a group of Adventists, to search for a pure religious life in the vast Brazil interior. They founded a community somewhere in Southern Brazil to start growing things for self-sufficiency and serving their faith in the midst of nowhere. There was nothing there except hard work, faith, and church socials—which was all they desired. After WWII, the son, an accountant, and his homemaker-wife, followed his father to escape Germany's miseries. Because accounting was not needed in the bush, they had to go to work like the rest. And they had to participate in church activities as though they themselves were Adventists. Life became extremely monotonous for the Albrechts, who came from Rothenburg in central Germany, a lively tourist town, harmed little by the war. While Papa Albrecht could somehow cope with the extremely hard work, "Frau" Albrecht pushed her husband to find a job in the city. They even overcame the difficulties of getting a mortgage. The first thing Brazilians do, if they are at all able, is to buy a home with as much mortgage money as they can get. Bank accounts lose value through inflation and cars lose value due to age, but acquiring real estate is the only way of safeguarding assets in Brazil. This is why the abundance of housing in Brazil is so impressive. It is the only way in which Brazilians can save for a rainy day. In those days, an alternative was to have a bank account in hard currency, which could be arranged, although not quite legal. That was also next on my own to-do list: to establish an account with the New York City branch of the Royal Bank of Canada in US Dollars. The deposit was small, but one had to start somewhere. It follows that, during the latter part of 1955, I not only began to think about leaving

Brazil, but I was fairly close to a decision. The PhD I had roomed with at the Antarctica had disappeared, which meant his return to Berlin. Another engineer, specialized in cigarette-making equipment, had packed up and left. Such departures were always discussed in the Duque de Caxias community. When I moved in with the Albrechts, the Rua Uranium was a dirt road of very heavy clay, which became a stream of mud when it rained—and it rained a lot in Sao Paulo! The clay was so tough that one's foot had to be pulled from the mud with an audible noise after each step. Arriving home, the shoes were caked over with mud one or 1-1/2" thick. The first chore was to free the shoe by scraping and washing it in the washbasin on the veranda. From the Albrecht's home it took 15 minutes to walk to the Bast's. In the same time one could walk to the Wetzker's through a hollow and past a Matarazzo mansion.

MERCEDES-BENZ DO BRASIL S/A

One day I noticed in the "Estado the Sao Paulo" that Mercedes-Benz do Brasil was advertising for an engineer with knowledge of the German language. Since I had become disappointed with my professional development at Elevadores Atlas, I applied and was invited for an interview with a Dr. Ivanyi in their brand-new Sao Bernardo do Campo plant. The buildings going up there were impressive. From all I could tell, they wanted to build cars. So far, Mercedes-Benz do Brasil had only imported one type of truck; some of those had been assembled with imported parts in a little shop in the Mooca suburb. This now looked like something bigger. Dr. Ivanyi spoke Portuguese fluently. I had expected the interview to be in German. If they planned to build trucks, I assumed they would rely entirely on German know-how and support, involving German as working language. Asking few pertinent questions, Dr. Ivanyi, speaking with a Hungarian accent, just hired me. Two weeks later I reported for work. Getting there was easy. A company bus picked up many employees in the Brooklin Paulista area. Expecting to join a Daimler-Benz outfit, I knew little about the makeup of my new employer, Merceces-Benz de Brasil. Hoping for a future in Diesel trucks, I postponed the idea of leaving the country for a while. Dr. Ivanyi introduced me to the Engineering Department, which encompassed people from Mannheim on contract from Daimler-Benz: Her Becker in his white smock with the Mercedes emblem, Herr Kneile, the metallurgist and Q.C. man, and Herr Sybrass, the maintenance and construction man. They viewed me rather suspiciously, but I was too preoccupied with the new people, environment and what might be going on there, to notice it much. Later I learned that, instead of having been hired by

Mr. Haug, the technical director responsible, I had been hired by the purchasing director! Haug's top lieutenants, Sybrass and Kneile, kept me at a distance and dealt with me as though I might be an implanted spy. I don't remember how I got into doing real work. The other new colleagues, not brought from Daimler Benz, but hired locally, were more open-minded. There was a Dr. Weich, always busy designing something on a board, who kept mostly to himself, busily adapting DB diesel engines to a variety of vehicles and construction equipment. The two people sitting behind me, in line with the technical director's desk, were his secretary, Dona Annelore (all female employees were addressed as Dona, plus their first names), and Pflaumer, who functioned as a sort of gopher. Without a degree, at least not of a technical nature, he checked lists of technical material to be imported from Mannheim and later verified what had arrived.

Until Director Haug, on health leave in Germany, was to return in a few weeks, I was pretty much in limbo. I received no assignments from Ivanyi either. What did I do? Not much, short of playing with my pencils and studying the goings-on in the department, an interesting mix of characters contained in a hall about 60 x 90 feet, with large picture windows to the outside and to the shop. Some were technical people in white smocks, sent by DB to assist in the activities of Mercedes-Benz do Brasil: Becker, somewhat of a bully, who jealously protected his imagined career path and turf, seemed to alternate constantly between the shop and his office desk. He dealt a lot with Guggemus, the shop foreman, who was in the midst of assembling 4-wheel trucks from imported parts. There seemed to be constant problems to solve between what had been sent and how it was to go together, since automotive manufacture is not at all static. Each vehicle carries a serial number, which determines all parts going into it. Quite often, parts are changed for various reasons. Those changes may require alterations of other parts, tools or fixtures, or of assembly or welding procedures. This serial number system required tight control of all parts, tools and procedures, which was what all those people in the department tried to do. When there was a breakdown, Becker took command of the situation in his haughty fashion and solved it together with Guggemus. This serial number change control is one of the cornerstones of any successful mass production.

Becker and Guggemus were from DB Mannheim; so were Kneile and Sybrass. Their status symbols were chauffeur-driven Mercedes 190's, which ferried them between home and work. A few other, apparently lower level DB men did not have this privilege.

It was a show for the less privileged. Haug must have assigned the use of the company cars, which was also lavishly extended to the families, who were driven on Saturdays to the open-air market (feira) and other events. Among the DB men not thus privileged there were several of rather limited technical background and acuity. One was Traber, who could be seen during lunchtime reading Argentine radical right (Nazi) journals. All DB men had solid contracts with salaries based upon the D-Mark, which by now had become super-hard currency, so they were unaffected by inflation. With exception of Guggemus and Elsishans (Spare Parts Department), they spoke no Portuguese. The next level of members in the small department was the German speaking bilingual technical people, including Pflaumer, Prach, Havel, Dr. Weich and a few more. Naturally without car privileges, and paid in Cruzeiros, they depended upon periodic raises for inflation adjustment. There was little emphasis on learning the language. Some of the DB men told the few Brazilians in the department, who were in supportive positions and not paid much compared to the DB people, but better than the average Brazilian, that they should learn German! The shop floor, the large Purchasing Department, and the Parts Department, were staffed almost exclusively by Brazilians. All production documents had to be written in Portuguese, of which the DB men were incapable. It was the beginning of long years of development of a production system in Portuguese.

A few weeks later Haug returned from Germany and came into the department through the small door that led into it. A mall, stocky man of enormous weight, he barely passed through. I was told he looked healthier and had lost a few pounds after spending some weeks at a German spa. He greeted his secretary enthusiastically, while the entire DB crew was anxiously waiting in line to pump his hand and bow their heads in the prevailing Germany custom. The most senior and important people (those with car privileges) positioned themselves first in line. Everyone showed up, including the clerical help, Frau Stangl and daughters Renate and Brigitte. The Stangls, fromAustria, had immigrated to Brazil around 1953. Little was known about their background, and Havel, who expressed an interest in Renate, and Gruber, who later married Brigitte were the only ones ever invited into their home. Renate, exceedingly pretty and blond, later married Havel. There was a sinister story behind the Stangls, which was to be fully revealed in 1958/59. Later that day, Haug greeted me. I noted the suspicion in his face. He hated to have me in his department, hired by someone else. Why Ivanyi planted me I would never know, neither why Haug didn't let me go. In any case, he gave me assignments, although he always treated me with reserve and mistrust. Then, one day after his arrival, he stormed through the door again while everyone jumped up and passed by his desk to pump his hand, bowing the head. Astonished by this spectacle, I did not get up to take my place in line. This behavior, which I had never seen before, occurred daily. It was definitely not customary in Berlin. I found it ridiculous to observe these people getting in line to grope for favors from the boss, who, in return, expected submission to his wishes in no uncertain terms. For example, Haug would often come around late Friday afternoon to see who could come to work on Saturday. Everyone agreed dutifully until, to my surprise, he asked me. I neither had work backed up to warrant my appearance, nor did he ask that question, since he had no idea about his subordinates' workload. Apologetically, I explained that I did not have enough work backlog, and that I had other plans for Saturday. In any event, I considered being asked at 3:00 or 4:00 p.m. for overtime on the following day an imposition; especially since no customer orders were affected. He just wanted to be surrounded by a few guys, since he didn't know what to do on weekends other than enjoying pigs' knuckles and Sauerkraut at Sao Paulo's German restaurants. His wife and son had remained in Germany, presumably for the sake of the son's education. Old Haug had spent part of WWII, in Japan, where he had been taken by U-boat in the middle of the war, to assist its government in building effective submarine diesel engines, one of the many tasks Daimler Benz was very successful at. Very proud of that, he hinted that his command of Japanese was not bad. But a year later, when greeting a Japanese delegation seeking to learn about the progress of Mercedes-Benz do Brasil, he could neither produce a word of Japanese nor speak a sentence in English. Since he spoke no Portuguese, his linguistic ability was limited to German. He had spent his life designing and building Diesel engines and trucks. He had received the Brazilian assignment at the end of a long career in DB management. DB had an equity interest in Mercedes-Benz do Brasil (MBB), the majority of which was controlled by a Polish-American, Mr. Jurzykowski, who popped in one day, giving the impression of a man in command.

Probably from a family of old money in Poland, Mr. Jurzykowski had been distributor of DB vehicles for Eastern Europe before WWII. He then arranged vehicle maintenance and repair contracts of the US Army for Daimler Benz after the war—the first crucial money the company made. In return, he secured the future South American distributorship, when DB products would again be available. He charged another fellow, Mr. Winkler, with organizing the distributorship in the Mooca suburb, near the Antarctica. Incidentally, all Antarctica vehicles were purchased from Mercedes-Benz. Now, the plans for full-scale production were beginning to materialize. As Jurzykowski entered the Engineering Department that day, he immediately moved toward Dona Annelore and elegantly kissed her hand, as naturally as only a Polish aristocrat could do it. Only then he moved toward Haug. Haug had a director's suite upstairs alongside those of the other directors, but he didn't seem to think much of the other—mostly Jewish or Polish—guys. Rather, he preferred to work in the Engineering Department, particularly since his activities had to concentrate on coordinating and planning of the assembly line, timing of parts shipments from Germany, planning of Diesel engine parts manufacture, as well as ordering of all machine tools and the enormous amounts of pertinent tools like milling cutters, drills, reamers, countersinks, threading tools, etc. etc. He also had to initiate the casting of high quality components such as motor blocks, pump housings, gear and clutch housings, etc. There were no qualified suppliers in Sao Paulo at the time. Established foundries had to be found, trained as suppliers and their available equipment, foundry methods and quality control had to be supervised. That was initially one of the main tasks of the metallurgist and Q.C. man Kneile. Haug and his department had their hands full. I learned that Daimler-Benz was preparing used machinery from its Mannheim plant to send to Brazil, so that Mannheim would receive the most modern machinery while the assumed risks in Brazil were kept to a minimum.

Learning more about the affairs of Mercedes Benz do Brasil (MBB), I became acquainted with Mr. Obee, the purchasing manager. Coming from Daimler Benz with a masters' degree in engineering, he was obviously one of their career men. His position entailed vast responsibilities for organizing all shipments from Germany, and he later established contact and stepped up working relationships with Brazilian suppliers, thus developing over time the increasing local production of engine and truck parts. He often traveled to Stuttgart and promised to bring along my damaged second gear for my Mercedes-Benz, which he did. I happily had the gear replaced and, voila, it even fit, thanks to modern mass production and parts interchangeability. My car was finally worth real money. I even drove it to work occasionally. It was then sensational for any employee to own a car. I had to replace the Mercedes star, which adorned the cooler, several times; it was stolen more than once. The new car enabled me to take longer trips to places such as Santos.

My life now concentrated much on Rua Uranium, where my neighbor was Forkert, who had also arrived on the Duque de Caixas. Keeping pretty much to himself, he made his way quietly as a surveyor for the Votorantim group, which was controlled by one of the most influential Brazilian families, who always seemed to work on land acquisition and sales, hence the surveillance crew was very busy. In the 80's when we finally visited Brazil again before retirement, he still held his job, and the family still lived in the comfortable home they had built on a lot close to the Albrechts on Rua Uranium, which then finally had become a paved street. Opa Albrecht, very much up in age, was usually sitting in front of his meager room. He liked to do carpenter work when the need arose. Frau Albrecht was busy keeping up with all tasks required in her household, among them loads of clothes to wash without automatic washer or dryer. She had to scrub the laundry with soap by hand, and spread the bigger pieces on the small lawn for bleaching, which was followed by rinsing, wringing and hanging the clothes on the line, and then endless ironing, including the sheets, to eliminate insects. She did this while a little dog was running around, who had the terrible habit of leaving his "do" on the tiled veranda in front of my room. My protest notwithstanding, dog-do accumulated usually for at least a week before she descended for a cleanup. This never changed while I lived there. My only way out would have been renting another place. But, becoming more and more convinced that I wanted to leave Brazil, I was not ready. In addition to cooking and cleaning for six people, Mrs. Albrecht must have baked at least one cake per day. Thoroughly spoiled, her family had come to expect it. I never ate with the family; under the circumstances it just would have been too much. My laundry was done by one of the many women needing this work. In the valley below, there were less expensive houses, each often occupied by several families. They were more fortunate than others, because they could still afford to live in a real house. It was amazing how many persons and kids were crammed into those places. Apparently they always helped each other get by. Since rent was one of the most expensive items, those who could not live in a small corner with relatives or friends would have had to face life in a "favela," the vast sea of slums, where people like I could never go, but only read about in papers or books. All Brazilians tried to avoid these.

One day, Eichstaedt showed up. He had quit his Antarctica job also. He must have hoped to become Dr. Belian's assistant, later to step into his shoes to administer the foundation and the company. But Belian then installed a nephew brought over from Germany as his assistant and prospective successor. With a law degree, that fellow was eminently qualified to put up with the rigors of Brazilian corporate life. Eichstaedt wanted to try his luck in the U.S. and was heading for New York. Wishing him the best, I asked him to write to me about his experiences. I thought this might be invaluable to me, although Eichstaedt, a peculiar fellow, came from a different world. He was saddled with a deformed foot and always wore special shoes. He claimed his foot had been maimed when jumping from a fighter plane that was going down. After the war, he had studied economics and held some kind of a degree before heading for Rio, where his uncle was "gerente" (director) of the Brazilian "Varig" airline. It would be interesting what

he could do in New York. He might have been a good type to occupy some ana-
lyst function at Wall Street. I heard from him six months later when he returned.

The Forkert's next door had occasional contact with people like the Basts,
Burmesters, Schuckels, Schulze's, Huessner's and some others. Schuckel claimed
he had been a movie director at the UFA studios in Berlin. Since movies were
then no longer made in Germany, he was searching for his fortune in the fledgling Brazilian moving picture industry. His very fashion-conscious wife was an
accomplished seamstress—a profession, which did not pay very well in Brazil.
But, above the ordinary competition, she managed to cater to the best clientele.
She stayed in Brazil doing "haute couture" after her husband returned to Berlin.
Schulz, a former cameraman at the German UFA studios, was very good-looking,
blond, blue-eyed, tall and slender. Because he had trouble connecting to the Brazilian movie scene, he had started a portrait studio, of which there were hundreds
in Sao Paulo, so he had to struggle financially. Lately, he looked more and more
worried. He had two fine sons to educate, which was quite expensive in Sao
Paulo, while in Germany it did not cost a dime. He might have been better off in
Hollywood, but I doubt he ever considered it for lack of funds. After his beautiful
wife died of breast cancer, he became an alcoholic. I had just about lost contact
with the old Westphal crowd, whose members seemed to have been blown in various directions to pursue their interests. I also no longer saw the Jakobs. They had
moved, leaving no forwarding address. Now my sixth Christmas in Brazil was
approaching, in the year's hottest, most humid season. While winters were frigid
and rainy, summers (December to February) were hot, rainy and characterized by
sudden, heavy tropical downpours, which could be dense enough to make me
stop the car, unable to recognize anything on the road. Lasting about 30 minutes,
they would be over as fast as they came. The Westphal's celebrated Christmas in
their backyard, around a three foot, meager fir tree, decorated with 12-15 of the
usual German decorations, with Uschi playing the guitar. Some weak attempts to
produce a Christmas ambiance were met with little success. The place and time
of year were just not right for producing the magic to which we were accustomed.
Squatting around a dwarf tree, sweating profusely … what can you expect? It just
was not the same Christmas. Little by little, many German immigrants' trees
became smaller and smaller, until they no longer bothered. They were also hard
to find and expensive, since they came to Sao Paulo from the Southern States of
Santa Catarina or Rio Grande do Sul.

Having settled in my job at Mercedes and feeling somewhat assured that Haug
would not outright fire me, I started to study the scene more closely and noticed
two girls of the right age for me to consider becoming acquainted with. Lotti,

who worked in the Parts Department, was one. Her parents, from East Prussia, had returned to the "Reich" from Brazil, following the worldwide call of the German government. In '38, unemployment there had ceased, jobs went begging, and the government needed more skilled workers. Many Germans residing abroad, especially those who had been unable to fulfill their dreams, had heeded the call, to join in the "progress at home". They did not perceive that the boom was created through deficit spending—having no idea what that was. It did not occur to the simple German people that all the work went into the military, and one day it would have to be paid for. Hence, the thought of returning into a world better than before had excited those abroad. After Germany's collapse, Lotti's parents had returned to Brazil to start from scratch again. They owned a house in one of the thousands of dirt streets sprouting around Sao Paulo like mushrooms—with electricity, but without running water. Each house had its own well from which water was pulled up in pails. To make the payments easier, they took in a boarder: Dona Annelore, who had been looking to move after the Lueck family, with whom she had made her home before, moved too far outside of the city to enable her to reach the Mercedes plant in Sao Bernardo do Campo daily. Dona Annelore, the technical director's secretary, and Lotti Bouillon were friends. Dona Lotti and Dona Annelore came to work on the same company bus. The third female in the department, aside from the Austrian Mrs. Kropf, who was married, was Dona Claudia from Berlin. She made her eligibility quite obvious by the way she dressed in low-cut outfits. She liked to stress that he had passed "Abitur," after completing high school at age 18, a difficult set of tests which enables Germans to enter any university ... the kind of schooling few Germans completed at that time. But when it came to doing all the correspondence in the department, Dona Annelore was the best, fastest, friendliest and most accurate worker. She always did her work with a smile, even though sometimes Haug's driver and Haug were breathing down her neck to complete important Daimler Benz documents which had to be driven to the plane to make it to Germany via "Air Mail." She had great skills in shorthand, typing, languages and in dealing with all kinds of people. She was Haug's interpreter, and everyone liked her. That's the way she wanted it and everyone seemed to believe she was a jewel, including her menacing looking boss Haug, who dealt with her politely. Claudia, who was no match for her, always looked miserable and a bit out of place. She was only assigned second-class work. A young man, Goebel, whose father also had started in Antarctica, had invited Claudia to Brazil. There must have been some problems and the couple never married.

As for me, I was not inclined to start an affair with a colleague, aware of the gossip and finger pointing that would surely follow. Hence, I did not plan to date any of these women; in fact, I had been living for quite some time without dating anyone. That did not make me feel good: I realized that this was the time, if ever, to meet a substantial woman and establish an enduring relationship. As the months went by, I observed Dona Annelore more closely, which was easy, since my desk was close to hers. With Pflaumer now gone, she sat alone behind me and could breathe down my neck, which she didn't, because she was much too busy. I then never learned why and how she had gotten to Brazil, neither did I know how old she was or when her birthday was, and I didn't ask anyone about it, either. It did not seem relevant, and, if I had wanted to know, I could have asked her myself. Then, one day, I discovered that I felt quite drawn to her. It was her personality. She was living pretty much alone, like myself, and appeared to have no other relations. Each night, she and Lotti would cheerfully jump on the bus to Lotti's home.

As "St. Nikolaus Day" approached on December 6, I thought I should surprise Da. Annelore with something to make her happy. I liked to see her happy, as I did later on for the rest of my life. A little German delicatessen store in Brooklin Paulista, close to my bus stop, displayed the most delicious Christmas chocolate items from Soenksen, a local chocolate enterprise run by Germans. This store also had German cold cuts, cheeses, bread, and whatever else a bachelor needed to survive in the evening. Mrs. Albrecht had yielded a tiny corner of her refrigerator for my few items. Anyway, I bought a little chocolate Nikolaus. On the next day, December 6, I waited for an opportune moment when Da. Annelore was gone, quickly walked to her desk, placed him into her middle drawer, and waited what would happen. Returning soon, she didn't open the drawer for some time. Immersed in my work, I had almost forgotten about it, when I heard a small shriek behind me and a happy voice exclaiming: "Look, guys, Santa was here and brought me this present; look, you must see this!" And then she went around in the department, asking everyone: "Did you place this?" "Mr. Moratz, have you placed this Nikolaus?" My answer was: "No, and I did not see who it was. My back was to your desk, and I have no eyes in the back of my head." Then, around and around she went to Becker, Havel and Prach. Prach's ears got red, as they always did when he got excited. She was disappointed that no one confessed. Curious as she is, someone had to have done it, but she just could not uncover the secret. Finally, she settled back down to her work. That was St. Nikolaus day 1955. Only months later, after we promised each other we would marry, I told her that I had done it.

Then Christmas approached, and I felt like giving presents to friends, including some people at Mercedes. So, I bought a nice collapsible umbrella for Da. Annelore and a nice 45-speed record for Da. Lotti. I did not want to make it obvious that I liked Da. Annelore; it was to appear like a present between colleagues. Then I traveled the long way to visit both at Lotti's parents' home to deliver the presents. My birthday party, hosted by the Forkerts in their home, preceded this Christmas visit to which I invited Da. Annelore and Da. Lotti. It was a nice event with lots of friends and modern music to dance to. Elvis' records had just appeared. There was beer, wine, and lots of dancing. I tried to appear neutral between Lotti and Annelore, but I think I could not help dancing a lot more with Annelore, which was noticed easily by the others. By Christmas, via the presents' value, Lotti had figured out whom I actually preferred. Much later Annelore told me that soon thereafter she found her wonderful new umbrella punctured by a burning cigarette, which must have been Lotti's, since Lotti, the only smoker in the house, behaved rather disappointingly afterwards. Annelore soon decided to rent a room in a pension in downtown.

We liked never having to worry about getting a warm meal during the day. The Mercedes cafeteria served a nourishing, inexpensive lunch. Brazilian dishes prevailed: lots of rice and beans, and "bacalhada" on Fridays—a typical Portuguese/Brazilian concoction made from salted, dried codfish fillet. On Fridays both of us would eat at a little neighborhood café, which served people looking for something different. Sometimes we passed the brand-new SLS 300 (gull wing) Mercedes on our way that Winkler, the general manager, had just acquired. It was then the ultimate car and the only one in Brazil of its kind. Looking proud, but kind of silly in his trophy, Winkler was said to have passed through some adventurous times. Even though he displayed a deep Viennese accented German, he had arrived in Brazil from Shanghai. He or his family must have retreated from the Red Army in Russia during the early twenties and settled in Shanghai, only to retreat from there when Mao Tse Tung took over China. Winkler was a dealmaker and salesman type, which may have united him with the Polish-American financier of Mercedes Benz do Brasil, Mr. Jurczykowski, and the German Daimler-Benz.

Back to the Albrecht's "home front": One day during the December through March hot and rainy season, I discovered the disappearance of my precious mountain lion skin from my fireplace, without a trace. I had run into this wonderful piece, a rarity even in 1955, in Bauru the year before, and bought it on the spot. It was shorthaired and yellow brownish. Mountain lions are almost extinct now, even in the Sierra Nevada. Always having locked my room when leaving, I could not explain its disappearance, and Frau Albrecht had noticed nothing suspicious. Weeks later, walking through the brush near the house, I found the skin completely molded and rotten. It could not be saved. When Frau Albrecht entered my room for cleaning, she must have left it open once for a while to do other tasks. I suspect that her smallest son, "Waeltli," a mischievous little brat, had picked it up to play with it and left it outside without thinking about it. To keep the peace, I did not mention the loss. There was no chance to replace it, anyway, since those skins were becoming more rare by the day. But it made me very sad.

In those days in November/December '55, I went around all my acquaintances and friends to discuss Da. Annelore. I had become convinced that I liked her very much, but would not want to begin an office relationship by asking her out. Since I couldn't ask her family, I wanted to get others' opinions, particularly those of friends. I couldn't very well ask Lotti. I thought that, if I wanted to get closer to Da. Annelore, I simply had to make up my mind (and heart) that she was IT! I then had the foolish notion, due to my inexperience, that acquaintances and friends could give useful input, or at least attest in some way to her character, appearance, etc. Although I had much more exposure to her than all friends combined, I had found that one could become almost helpless and sometimes afraid when courting a woman. What if she just says "No"? Then my fantasy would collapse! I had experienced disappointments in the past, although they never had totally devastated me. But it looked like this time there was more at stake. Very moved, I became almost obsessed thinking I could ask Annelore to marry me. On the other hand, I knew she could not suspect my thoughts, since I then tried to hide my thoughts, and she also gave no indication how she might feel about me. How could she? I sometimes suspected she considered me somewhat arrogant and therefore not a good match. Earlier I had given her reasons so think of me as such a character, when she had invited me to join a Mercedes-organized bus tour of Haug's department to the Santos beaches. I had replied that I preferred to do such things in my own car. I regretted my answer later, since she appeared slightly disappointed. What I had meant was that such an extensive trip would be more fun in my car, perhaps with a like-minded female companion. But this is a common problem: sometimes it is difficult to express oneself to be correctly understood. I noticed that Annelore dressed modestly, not saddled with overblown expectations but rather in good taste. She had very expressive facial features and would make an enormously compatible friend, mate, and companion. There was not one ugly bone in her body. She would pull along with someone who wanted to do the same thing. I was only puzzled whether she planned to remain in Brazil, speculating that she would be at least open to suggestions to return to Germany, since she seemed to have no relatives in Sao Paulo, just some German friends. It was a mystery how she had arrived there. But rather than being concerned about this, I was fascinated with her outgoing personality and her demonstration of an integral character. I had become convinced that this was the woman I had always been looking for and never found. That made it so important for me to talk to my friends and acquaintances. They had only one comment: "This is it—marry her!" "As fast as possible, before someone else does." I didn't even know her age then; she looked very young, and I thought it would be 21 or 22 in 1955. Little did I know she was only 20 then! But at that age she behaved as maturely as a 30-year old or older. She seemed to know exactly what she was doing and could not be coaxed into doing the wrong thing. At one time, for example, Becker was mad because his chauffeur had not shown up one morning. He asked Annelore to call the guy's supervisor and chew him out. Quickly, as though shooting from the hip, she suggested that Becker make the call on his own, that the supervisor spoke German, and those things should be handled personally. She knew more about office etiquette and interpersonal relations than that obstinate Becker would ever know in his life!

I now had to take some action, but was not sure which. The most valuable input came from Arthur Wetzker, who thought very highly of Annelore, although knowing very little about her. After Christmas I received Forkert's invitation to a New Year's Eve party. The thing to do was to invite her. I told her who would be there and how long it might last, and she did not hesitate to accept. Always a friend of having a good time, she watched the setting closely to see if it would match her tastes and expectations. I could not tell where this kind of intuition came from, but it was an extended hallmark of her personality. Many years later she revealed to me that for one reason or another she felt glad I had invited her.

My priorities now were: first, to have a good time with friends, second—and the thought scared the wits out of me—to ask her to marry me. How could I take such a step without a long courtship? To overwhelm a very young woman with such an unexpected approach could lead to rejection and disaster. But I had been too considerate to ask her out, as she might not have liked the daily scrutiny by her colleagues, with the inevitable insinuations. Others at Mercedes paid attention to her, too, including Prach and Voelkerling, who was in charge of Mercedes' liaison with the huge Brazilian fleet of "Cometa" buses, but closer ties did not seem to have developed. New Year's Eve progressed with good food, and spirits and champagne were flowing. Things became very lively. New Elvis Presley records were tried on us and went over very, very well. At midnight the flow of champagne increased, and all of us became a bit tipsy. Annelore and I began embracing more and more closely while dancing. Schuckel and Ernst Bast occasionally nudged me from behind to see if I had asked Annelore already. While they were expecting me to make my move, I was becoming more and more deflated, unsure what to do. With the frenzied dancing and everyone hopping around us to the sound of the jazz bands, I found myself sitting on the floor with her. I kissed her and she kissed me back—unbelievable. It was so exhilarating and delightful. I was in heaven. After a few more, I mustered the courage to ask: "Will you marry me?" Hearing "yes," I was totally perplexed. The party guests started stomping and yelling with joy, and congratulations rained on us. I was so happy, and I could tell by Annelore's face that she was also smitten with this moment!

Now I was no longer alone, but had a very dear companion to think of. That would not change for the rest of my days. A new phase of my life was beginning. The party dragged on until early morning, when we left along with the last stragglers. We walked to the end of Rua Uranium, down to the valley and then toward Arthur Wetzker's place. Walking tightly embraced, we agreed that we wouldn't tell anyone in the office until the wedding day was set. We had to communicate with our parents. I learned now that Annelore's father had died from a bullet chest wound in WWII, that she was 20 years old and might need her mother's agreement. The most important issue was our future: remain in Brazil, or leave? On that early New Year's morning walk to the streetcar stop, we agreed to make a try for the U.S. Annelore, believing that Sao Paulo was not a good place for her in the long run, had decided some time ago to return to Germany. She was elated about the idea of looking around in the U.S. before returning. Both of us had read and heard much about the U.S. and thought it well worth a try at this stage—an intention we would reveal to no one at that time.

It was a long way home by public transportation. I returned to my Albrecht room very tired, but immensely happy. My life had taken a positive turn. A new direction was established, and there was a common goal to pursue. A few days later I met with "Irmchen" Bast, who generously proposed to host a wedding party. I would pay for the drinks and food ingredients, and she, together with Frau Burmester and Frau Huessner would prepare and serve the wedding feast. I accepted this selfless offering with profuse thanks. All we had to do was set the wedding date, apply for the license at the Brooklin Paulista government office and ask Pastor Reichert to conduct the ceremony at the downtown Lutheran church. It was to be March 24, 1955, which was communicated to Annelore's mother and my parents in Germany, who had earlier given their consent. We did not expect them to travel to Brazil. It would have taken 20 days by boat each way and was too expensive for them, as in Germany money was then still restricted to cover one's basic needs—such trips were then only for the super-rich. Next came the question what the bride would wear. Instead of the traditional long, white dress, Annelore decided on a very nice short cocktail type dress with a short jacket, which could serve for other occasions in the future, to be fashioned by Frau Schuckel (the seamstress from Berlin). We went to buy the fabric—taffeta in a pale salmon color with a gray metallic sheen—which looked very good on my bride. While dealing with those tasks, which sometimes left us tired, I noticed that Annelore's eyes did not appear as normal eyes do. She admitted that her eyesight was not the best and might need correction. An optometrist confirmed she urgently needed glasses, which we bought against her initial mild protestations, but eventually she capitulated.

During that time I also had to see a dentist, because a tooth bothered me. We were not used to regular dentist's visits for cleaning, etc. Appointments were made in case of pain, as was then the custom in Germany. In my opinion, for the best and least expensive service there was Emil, a Hungarian with a German wife. He was rumored to have been a dentist in a German SS division, but there was never any proof. Emil was happy to live in Brazil instead of Communist Hungary. His dentistry methods were peculiar. On Sundays I could knock on his door, and, even if he was in a night shirt, he would let me in, make me sit down in his living room, get dressed and return to serve a cachassa (sugar cane "Schnapps") or two before starting to work. He preferred to work without anesthesia and normally provided care of the teeth affected by caries. The treatment was fairly rough. He took care of several of my teeth at what I considered bargain prices. Later a dentist in North Hollywood, California, showed me that those teeth were rotten inside and out, since Emil had put something like cotton balls below the filling! Apparently lacking some dentistry skills, he was in "collaboration" with a Sao Paulo dentist, participating in his license in exchange for some money, who took the hot cases off his hands. I later regretted having trusted the very friendly Emil, who also belonged to the group around Bast's and Forkert's. They gave some moral support to his poor wife, who seemed to get no money from him. They usually shopped for food together, but Emil, who had to have complete control and entrusted nothing to her, would visit the weekly open-air market in Brooklin Paulista alone. This practice, unknown to Germans, was widely practiced by Brazilian men and still exists there in some families, even in 2001! I should have been more curious about Emil's work, whose beaming face and primitive set-up is still on my mind.

During the wedding preparations, we often enjoyed a meal in downtown Sao Paulo and perhaps a movie on weekends. No one in the office knew that we were secretly engaged. In February we finally revealed our plan to our astonished colleagues, inviting just about all of them to the wedding. Meanwhile Annelore had moved from the Bouillon's and the unhappy Lotti to a downtown Bed and Breakfast. Short of purchasing wedding bands and helping with transportation for Annelore's needs, I did not need anything for the wedding, since I already had a nice, tailored smoking and accessories. I only had to prepare the room for my bride to move in. We had decided against renting a larger place. After the wedding we would change Annelore's German passport to her new name and apply for a visa to the U.S. We had heard that the waiting time for German applicants had been reduced; we might receive the visa soon. The Albrecht's knew of our plan and welcomed the idea, knowing it would be only our temporary home. We had told them we would do very little cooking anyway, because Annelore had told me she didn't know much about it; we would just heat some franks on weekends, which she said she could do. Those, with some potato salad from the German deli would be our weekend dinner.

But I'm getting ahead of myself. My room was enclosed on the patio side by a large picture window, made from a huge angle iron frame and, like the door, divided into individual iron-framed glass panels, 10x20" in size. In better Brazilian homes, windows were sub-divided in this fashion to protect against burglars. About twenty percent of the panels could be opened by a lever mechanism for ventilation, which was absolutely essential because of the heat and humidity. Air conditioning was then unknown in Sao Paulo. Window screens did not exist; if one wanted a "fresh" breeze of air, a bloodthirsty swarm of mosquitoes was waiting, ready to attack. Few means were available to ward them off, except the widely used "boa noite" (good night) spiral, a special incense type product. Its end could be lit to make it smolder throughout the night. The smoke, while not bothering the sleeper, kept flying insects away. Each night, I closed the curtain, locked the door, emptied my pocket, putting the billfold and keys on the coffee table, and went to bed. Shortly before sleeping, I opened the curtains and those windowpanes, which could be opened. Thus, I could sleep undisturbed. One night a few weeks before the wedding, I somehow became half-awake. With my brain signals not yet functioning, I sensed danger. I raised my upper body to look around, and then got up. In the dark I saw some reddish spot in the direction of my sofa. Such a spot was not supposed to be there! Moving closer, I placed both hands on it to investigate, when—an enormous pain went from my hands through the arms! Suddenly I was wide-awake. I had moved both hands into a

smoldering fire in the upholstery, which was made from dried grasses, so compressed that an open fire did not start. I then thought: "Keys!" Knowing their
location, I grabbed them, unlocked the door, yelling: "fire, help!!!" (Hilfe,
Feuer!—the family spoke German). In no time Opa, my neighbor on the
veranda, and the two Albrecht's appeared. They carried the sofa into the patio
and doused it with water. The room was filled with nasty smoke. It was a wonder
I had awakened at all—seemingly in the nick of time. My hands, which had
saved my life, were in tatters, covered by second-degree burns, with the raw flesh
visible. Mr. Albrecht got out his ancient American car and drove to the next First
Aid Station (Pronto Socorro), which are all over Sao Paulo. They took good care
of me; bandaging both hands with special material for burn victims. Now both
my hands, packed and covered with 1-2 inches of burn material, were no longer
usable. How to take care of myself would become a big problem. After taking the
bus from Brooklin Paulista the next morning, I entered the engineering department. When she saw me, Annelore started laughing, since I must have looked
funny with those big white paws. Her reaction changed immediately to concern,
since it was obvious that I was helpless. Frau Albrecht had already asked me if
Annelore might move in before the wedding to take care of me, since she herself
could not take on any additional tasks for me. Annelore agreed, and we lived in
my room until we left for Los Angeles. The space was a bit tight, but we didn't
mind. Besides, we were too busy dealing with our daily problems. It was the
beginning of a long life together.

Before going on, I must report a frightening incident, which happened before
the fire. Annelore was still living with the Bouillons, and I would sometimes drive
her there late in the evening, via a little-used shortcut. This country dirt road was
quite dark, unimproved and almost devoid of dwellings. To lengthen our time
together, we would sometimes stop the car for some romantic talks and
moments. It was one of those nights when we saw the moon rising, but this time,
it must have been between 9 and 11 p.m., a car appeared out of nowhere, slowed
and parked opposite us. A cop emerged, who wanted to know what we were
doing. I sensed trouble without knowing what he could get us for. He said it was
prohibited for a man to stop the car on the street with a female inside—perhaps
some obscure law passed to protect defenseless females? That in a country where
one was cornered by prostitutes every inch of the way in the center of Sao Paulo!
He ordered us to drive to the next highway intersection, where there was light.
There he would radio a police van to take Annelore and me to prison! From what
we had heard and read, conditions there were horrible! Once you were inside, it
would cost considerable money to get out if one was lucky. A terrible prospect:

the girl I was about to marry locked in with prostitutes and other criminals. I started pleading, telling the cop we were to get married in a few days, etc.—all of no avail. We had to wait at the highway intersection—our fate appeared sealed. Then I mentally started counting the cash in my pocket, about $100, which seemed enough to make an impression on the policeman. Inexperienced in such matters, I was unsure if one could actually put money in his hands, but I had heard about it. As a last resort I handed one of the two men my driver's license, money inside. His face lit up. He became friendly, returned the license after removing the bribe, warned me not to stop again under such circumstances, and motioned me to drive away. The scene had changed completely. I later learned that the gentleman driver always carried a folded cruzeiro note in his driver's license, which, much larger than in the U.S., easily holds money. We drove off relieved and actually felt thankful towards our tormentors. When telling this to friends later, they said they had never heard of such a thing. But it was known that cops found ways to earn additional, tax-free money, similar to what entrepreneurs did in Brazil, where salaries are often too low to feed a family.

We were now fast approaching our wedding day, with disclosure at the office and invitations next on the agenda. To my amazement, I found that almost none of the people from my early years were still part of my life, possibly because of my orientation toward the U.S. People like Jansson or Jakob made no bones about their aversion to that country, and I had begun to see them less. Jose Michaelis had married a local girl and was no longer seen. I believe Jansson had also married. The entire circle of "Skat" players had vanished into nowhere, but the bond had never been strong. Most people from the Mercedes technical department and others wanted to come, as well as Basts, Wetzkers, Burmesters, Huessners, Schuckels, etc., who had wanted to see me get married for a long time, as well as Annelore's friends, including Lotti! Being asked what kind of presents we would like, we focused on things, which could be easily taken to the U.S. These friends did not know of our plan until the last minute. We had to first be sure of the immigration visa, and then we would sell our belongings and prepare to travel. Meanwhile, Mmes. Bast, Burmester and Huessner started preparing the wedding feast, determining the number of attendees, purchasing supplies, and planning for sufficient dishes and glasses for beer, wine, champagne and hard drinks. This mostly German crowd would expect everything! Disposable dishes were then unknown; the three women must have pooled their households for the event! Since the number of attendees exceeded the inside space of the house, a large tarpaulin was mounted on its side to cover the festive scene in case of rain, and rain it would! There were two rows of benches for the 50-70 guests. Except for my shelling out money to buy foodstuffs and beverages, we had very little to do with it all. There must have been two cases of champagne, and the beer came in barrels. To top it off, the three women held a get-together the night before the wedding, to present us with the gifts from the immediate circle of friends. The Mercedes people had taken up a nice monetary collection. Little did they know how nicely this fitted into our travel plans!

As it came down to the wire, I discovered a problem I could not solve without experienced help, so I went to see Schuckel, who lived fairly close. Entering the house, I realized he had visitors. One was his brother, who had a business distributing plastic tubing for construction. I told Schuckel that I had a serious problem 24 hours before the wedding, and I needed his help and explanation. His ears perked up, and—expecting it to relate to sexual matters—he couldn't wait to hear what it was! As I pretended to have difficulty formulating my request, he became more and more excited, his mustache hairs standing up with curiosity. Finally, to his great disappointment, I confessed my ignorance about affixing my bow tie. Laughing heartily, we practiced until I got the hang of it.

Now I was ready to start the day on March 24, 1956, when, 34 years old, I married Annelore Wagner, 20 years of age. Young and optimistic, we had a plan for the future, unconcerned about not reaching our goal. Early that morning, Annelore's friend Herma Lueck (later Schoenit) came to fix her hair. Being a beautician, she did a beautiful job. Annelore had lived with the Lueck family since coming to Sao Paulo, until they moved too far out of town for her to continue staying with them. They had been like parents to her, and Herma like her sister. They were still very close. Naturally, the Lueck's were also at the wedding, and we continued our friendship, even after Herma and her husband Bert moved to Canada and the parents returned to Hamburg, Germany. Hair in place, we got dressed up, picked up our neighbor and friend Guenter Forkert, and walked up Rua Uranium to Avenida Brooklin Paulista. The government office dealing with marriages was close to the tram station. Guenter and Herma were our witnesses. The ceremony was fast and not very memorable. Then we walked down Avenida Santo Amaro for a good, solid meal at the Koebes restaurant, known for its German cuisine. As we had our fine meal, the door to the kitchen service window opened, and a chef's head appeared, looking curious. Annelore looked somewhat uneasy when she saw that it was her ex-fiancé, who had brought her to Brazil. She had just recently completed paying him back the money he had used for her Hamburg-Santos boat trip. Nothing else happened. This episode was past history for her, and he had very quickly found a new girlfriend whom he later married.

Afterwards we went home to rest a little and then change for the church ceremony. Annelore put on her beautiful new dress and marveled at her bouquet of gardenias. I simply jumped into my tux, and we drove to the Avenida Sao Joao behind Largo Paisandu, where the Lutheran church is still located today. Prach had already installed audio equipment to record the ceremony (his gift to us). We still have the record. Tape recorders were still unknown. Many people from Mercedes and all of our close friends were already waiting to watch the proceedings. The atmosphere in the beautiful, small church was solemn and the flowers were beautiful. I looked at Annelore, who seemed in a happy mood. The ceremony by Pastor Reichert, whom we had visited earlier in his home, was short but his remarks were appropriate and moving. Annelore's "Ja" was barely audible. We could hear people in the audience sniffling into their handkerchiefs. Then the rings were placed on our fingers, and I kissed Annelore, whose lips were shivering with emotion. I was moved. I looked at her, and that promise I made "through good and bad times" was to become my leitmotiv from then on. My throat was constricting nervously—a sign that I was deeply and emotionally touched. As the organ intoned the last melody, cameras flashed, and we stepped down the church entrance toward the car, which would bring us to the festivities arranged at Basts.

The party started with lots of champagne, followed by a lavish meal, which both of us didn't get much of. We were terribly busy serving drinks, entertaining the crowd and talking with friends and colleagues. Being German, they made no bones out of their state of dehydration. Soon the two cases of Peterlongo champagne were gone, and I had to give the Huessner's underage son Klaus money to buy more at the corner bar. I must have estimated alcoholic consumption by my own standards, which turned out to be a miscalculation. After dinner, the crowd began to sing. Haug climbed on a bench and bellowed the "Couplet von der Gans" (goose song), and Pastor Reichert from Berlin contributed "Fritze Bollmann wollte angeln." (Angler's song). The latter bade goodbye and wished us happiness, as the night became louder and louder. Annelore had consulted with this good man occasionally before, when her relationship with her fiancé went on the rocks, and he had been of invaluable service to her. The party became more and more animated. To my astonishment all liquor and beer had been used up around 9 pm. I sent Klaus Huessner to the bar again for bottled Antarctica beer and cachassa. Servicing the crowd kept me busy the entire evening. I admit that I did not enjoy that part of the wedding, but endured it because I was married now to a wonderful girl, who also was busy all evening. We had little chance to sip much of the alcoholic beverages, except the initial round of champagne. As 10 p.m. approached, everyone started yelling and urging us to leave, following the custom of sending the newlyweds off on their long journey together. We later learned that the party was to become quite wild, to the point where Robert Burmester demonstrated to the crowd that he could break one of those full, closed Brazilian beer bottles (about the size of a French wine bottle) with his bare hands. He succeeded, but cut his hands so badly in the process that he landed in the "Pronto Socorro" (neighborhood first aid station). By that time we were long gone, driving home to Rua Uranium. We descended the stairs and entered the room in such a state of exhaustion that I could no longer lift Annelore over the threshold! The wedding was over and our new life began.

A NEW LIFE FOR ANNELORE AND HERMANN AFTER MARRIAGE

Our new life began on the morning of March 25, 1956. Headed for Ubatuba, we traveled north toward Via Anchieta, the highway to Rio de Janeiro, passing Sao Jose dos Campos on the way to Taubate two hours later, and then followed the road toward the sea. That road, which was quickly becoming invisible, first still showed traces of vehicles, but then seemed to be left by Indians on the warpath. Soon all traces disappeared. Occasionally, embedded rocks made the car swerve wildly, while I carefully attempted forging our progress to the sea. Then the car hit a rock with an alarming bang. I crawled under the stopped car to investigate the damage. I found none, but began to fear I had lost my way, since the ground no longer appeared to be part of the road to Ubatuba, a remote fishing village North of Sao Paulo. As I hit more rocks, I became increasingly desperate, while Annelore enjoyed the remoteness of the area and mountainous scenery with meadows, boulders, rocks and blue sky in good spirits. Hitting an even bigger rock, I thought something must be totally broken by now. I jumped, swearing loudly, which poor Annelore was not used to, particularly not the kind used in the army. Oh, why did we have to follow this forlorn path? Because it was just about the only way to Ubatuba! The good road to Caraguatatuba, 20 miles south of there, would have required crossing the beaches to Ubatuba, which would have been hazardous driving. Again, I could detect nothing, but I worried about my only possession, the car, for which I had no insurance. Wrecking it would mean kissing it good-bye, returning to Taubate on foot, and taking the train back. There were no gas stations or buildings between Taubate and the sea. But Annelore did not seem worried—not being a driver then, she was fairly ignorant of the hazards we faced. Besides, had she not just gotten married? Were we not supposed to be happy?

Careening around another boulder, we paled and sank into our seats, frightened to death. At some distance, there appeared a gang of aggressive, wild-looking gauchos (Brazilian cowboys), their horses galloping directly toward us, swinging huge leather whips, with six shooters on their hips, wearing boots similar to those of American cowboys, large, flowing pantaloons, similar to those worn by the gauchos of the Argentine pampas, colorful shirts, kerchiefs around their necks, and leather caps typical of Brazilian gauchos. Black or a mixture of Indian and Black, they yelped wildly, appearing ready to attack us. We thought we were done without time for a prayer—would this be a one-day marriage? No one would hear of us ever again. Consoling myself to my fate, I heard a friendly "Good Morning" … and they disappeared. We had never seen such wild-looking people and had been ignorant of the different customs and rules in those parts of Brazil. Greatly relieved, we sat up to watch the last of the horsemen disappear behind the boulders.

Solitude reigned again, with no one around us. The Mercedes was changed back to low gear. Further progress continued slowly, until we arrived at the point where the land gave way to a steep, seemingly endless decline. In the distance we saw the ocean. We could not see any dwellings; they must have been about 5000 feet below. The entire slope of the sierra was covered by dense tropical rain forest. The climate of Brazil's Northern coast, which extends to the Amazon River, is dominated by tropical climate year-round. The South has it during summers only.

Descending the slope, we found only a narrow lane bulldozed into the mountainside, winding endlessly with tight turns and frightening steepness. The "road" was wet and made very slippery by a combination of red clay and water. Any vehicle climbing toward us would have been disastrous. I tried to plan what to do, but could think of nothing. But the area was desolate enough that, luckily, there was no ascending traffic. I thought then that I would need lots of water to pacify the boiling cooler if my ancient Mercedes was to make it back up the sierra! But it would not come to that, since we would return via the dangerous beach route to connect to the "road" to Caraguatatuba, where a paved highway began. We finally arrived in Ubatuba, then a tiny fishing village with one church and only one small hotel. At its doorstep, its owner greeted us. He asked about our destination. He knew Dona "Millie" Arnold and her husband, in whose comfortable home we had reserved a nice room. It was about 100 feet from the sea, with only beautiful, white sand between the house and the water. Dona Millie's nice lunch made us forget our traumatic road trip. The Arnold's asked if we had stopped somewhere, and we mentioned the hotel owner down the road, only to learn that he was friends with the mayor, and the Arnold's now would have to pay either a fine (or a bribe!) for taking in paying guests, which only registered establishments were allowed to do! Too bad, but we had not the slightest idea. A bribe is called "dar um jeito," to give this process a favorable twist … this expression is popular in Brazil.

We spent a wonderful week at the Ubatuba beaches. Some were protected from the surf; others were hit by the waves in full force, at times too frightening to enter the water. One bay was completely surrounded by mountains; the ocean swell calmly traveled through it, and there were only blue sky, blue sea, white, untouched sand and all kinds of birds … no people. This bay, 10-15 miles from Ubatuba, is now called Mogi Mirim. Ten or fifteen years later the Bast's would build a beach house there. We would see this heavenly place again on our first return visit to Brazil thirty years later. The Arnold's loaned us fishing rods and we caught some small baitfish called croakers. They were ceremonially fried, but had little taste. Dona Millie's regular food was so much better! This Austrian couple had discovered that his asthma could be controlled at the beach. He was unable to live in Sao Paulo.

One day we drove south to explore the beaches toward Caraguatatuba. There was no road from there to Ubatuba; the stretch could only be navigated by car along the beach. The remainder of the landscape consisted of virgin jungle or forest. The mountain chain running parallel to the beach dispensed liberal amounts of water, which reached the sea every so often in the form of brooks or small rivers. One could not drive through these channels by car, but there were always sandbanks at the estuaries, formed by the rivers themselves as they carried not only water down from the mountains, but also suspended soil and sand. At low tide these sandbanks could be negotiated to reach the other side, I was told. This was the only chance to reach Caraguatatuba by car. One must consider that the Mercedes 190 Cabriolet built in 1939 was our only asset besides approximately $1000 at the Royal Bank of Canada, New York Branch. The car was not insured; losing it would postpone our move to the U.S. indefinitely. And then, as young people are, the upcoming move was not as imprinted on our minds as it should have been. We enjoyed each other, the nature, beaches, climate, food, and our positive thoughts about the future. We imagined we could handle anything that might come along. And, since we wanted to conserve previous resources, we had taken advantage of the fact that such insurance was not legally required in Brazil.

Crossing the beaches, I negotiated many estuaries until I reached one that loomed ominously as a major obstacle. The little river was quite deep and the sandbank extended farther into the sea. Sand on the banks was usually compacted, but at that moment the tide seemed to turn, moving in slowly. Suspicious, I hesitated to cross, but the driver of a 52 Chevrolet in front of me blasted across without a problem. Of course! A Mercedes can do better than a Chevy, right? I shifted into first and followed it. In the middle of the river, my engine quit, water entered immediately, with waves lapping in. The car started to sink into the sand, which was softer than I had imagined. It did not sink while moving, but when stopping, the sand gave way. The inside water level rose within each minute. We were sinking, with no one around to lend a hand—no phone, no service station, no house! Our trip to the U.S. was disappearing fast; the car was a big factor in financing it. Suddenly some white spots—people?—appeared in the distance. Leaving Annelore, I dashed toward those spots, which turned out to be "caboclos," people living in the wild, who eke a living from bananas, fish, and whatever else they can harvest from the environment. Those five or six men immediately grabbed any ropes they had and we ran back to the car. Fastening the ropes, some pulled and others pushed it, while we desperately tried heaving it over the sandbank, out of the water. At first it did not budge, but after several attempts we succeeded in forcing the tires out of the sand, making it rise steadily out of the water. When it came to rest on the dry beach, water was running out everywhere. After a while I tried the ignition, and the good old Mercedes, coughing a little, ran normally as if nothing had happened. I later concluded that the Chevy had done better because its carburetor and ignition coil were mounted very high under the hood and its tires were much larger than those of the Mercedes. The Mercedes' ignition coil was at the engine's side, positioning it at least one foot closer to the water. The water had not reached the Chevy's ignition coil, but, splashing over mine, must have created a short. Water droplets on the coil proved my theory. Enormously relieved, we handed each of our saviors some money, which made them very happy. They seemed accustomed to helping cars in distress—earning some cash for rice, beans, cigarettes, cachassa and other basic necessities.

After that, the trip to Caraguatatuba was uneventful. It later turned out to be the more advantageous route back to Sao Paulo. We ventured back at low tide and found the sandbank almost dry. Timing is everything!! In Ubatuba, we often passed a property adjoining Dona Millie's. It had a very solid fence of 8-9 feet high, of one inch steel bars, behind which lived a huge male pet lion—the town's attraction. Re-visiting Ubatuba 30 years later, we found he was still there, but had grown some gray hair in the meantime. Our return to Sao Paulo was less exciting—if you can call a drive through the wilderness eventless. Nowadays, the excitement is caused by enormous traffic with participants whose driving makes them appear suicidal.

BACK TO WORK—PLANS STILL SECRET

After returning to work and to our home at the Albrecht's in 1956, we applied to the U.S. Consulate General in Sao Paulo for immigration to the U.S. Revealing our finances, we were informed they did not suffice for a visa. We asked how much money we would need to prove financial stability and learned from the official that there was no defined sum; this was at the discretion of the consular officer and depended on the case. Our hopes somewhat doused, we returned to the grindstone to make more. From then on we became outright stingy, trying to conserve as much as possible. Our friends must have wondered during that time why we were not spending any money. Some of our German contacts were not in the position to purchase homes or condos, but we didn't even move from our little room into a rented apartment. We had only revealed our USA plans to our American friends from the dredge and the Albrecht's. Some of the Germans, had they known, might have changed their attitude toward us.

Eichstaedt, returned from New York, reported very negatively about his experiences. Having found work at an import-export firm in Manhattan, he complained about the colleagues' interpersonal habits. "People arrive in the morning, hang their hats and coats without any greeting, work until quitting time, when they pick up their hats and coats again and leave without a word to anyone." On his birthday, he had requested a day off to celebrate, but was told he was needed at his desk, about which he felt personally insulted. He wanted no part of that "culture." We commiserated with him, but didn't take his tales seriously. Actually, we knew very little about the U.S., mostly what we learned from Time Magazine and from our American dredge friends. But we thought those old salts were probably out of the American mainstream. We didn't know what to expect from the average American, but thought the pictures of American homes, kitchens and cars in the magazines were exaggerated; it would be up to us to find common ground. We were heading into the unknown, hoping to improve ourselves. The dredge guys from Long Beach advised that, if we didn't like it in California, we should take a train to New York City and board a ship home; looking at the rest of the U.S. wouldn't be worth a hoot!

On the other hand, we realized that, to succeed in Brazil, one had to be independent and start a business. Ernst Bast was developing a commercial TV transmitter and had endless talks with Huessner, also an electrical engineer, who, in turn, had hooked up with a Brazilian moneyman and was developing welding transformers; all of those were imported so far. Bernsee, who also came with the "Duque de Caxias," had latched on to the Siemens organization and became their leading man, a sure road to success. A man named Diplom Ingenieur Ness built switches in his garage, trying to establish himself. Everyone was then looking to succeed. The traditional Brazilian road to success was a position in such places as government, banks etc. Immigrants were not sufficiently connected for such positions. I had hoped to make a decent living, but it became more and more certain that working as an employee in Brazil I would achieve little material success. Such people might be better off in Germany. For instance, the Rubin couple and another engineer, specialized in cigarette machinery, returned to Germany where they would be better off.

Not much happened in 1956 and early 1957. More and more machinery arrived at Mercedes for setting up and beginning manufacture of additional Diesel engine parts such as engine block, cover, oil pump, cylinder head, cylinder lining, piston, piston rings, etc. etc. The work seemed endless, until the entire engine for a medium truck would be made in Brazil.... We left much before this happened. In mid-1957 we divided our two weeks vacation between Ubatuba and the Itatiaia Mountains toward Rio, West of the Sao Paulo-Rio Road. All we had heard from the U.S. Consulate was: "Don't call us—we'll call you!" This time we reached the beaches via Caraguatatuba and found Dona Millie and her husband in good spirits. We spent a marvelous week visiting all the old spots; the early morning would find us dashing into the sea, even though it was South American winter. We then went up into the Serra to Taubate and Itatiaia, where we stayed in a little log cabin and roamed around the woods, which consisted mostly of Aracaria pines. A clear mountain brook ran through the compound, which no one dared to enter. It may have measured 55 to 60 degrees F, but we found the daily dip in the icy water invigorating. The time went by too fast.

GREEN LIGHT AT THE AMERICAN CONSULATE IN SAO PAULO

Returning on the Via Dutra, Annelore mused about the U.S. Consulate's silence. Often things go wrong with communications, especially when one does not fully understand the background and culture of those one deals with; one must watch out for one's own affairs. I thought we should trust the consulate and should not annoy them by nagging. But, out of curiosity, we decided the next day to visit them in downtown to find out more. Annelore turned out to have been right.

The consular officer greeted us by asking where we had been! Our visa had been ready for some months; he only had to evaluate our finances, which by now satisfied him. He then asked Annelore if she was pregnant, a word Annelore did not know. He advised Annelore not to become pregnant, which made her blush profusely, but he meant no harm. Rather, he advised us that, should I not be able to find work, she would have to support both of us after depletion of our bank account. Should we ever become penniless, we would be deported back to Germany; we could not expect to become public charges. We would need about half of our cash assets for the boat trip.

Next, we booked the 22-day-passage via the Panama Canal to the West Coast of the U.S. Earlier, we had sold our '39 Mercedes for $1,500. Because cars were then still rare and very expensive in Brazil due to enormous import duties, used cars maintained their value well, especially Mercedes passenger cars, which were scarce. The new 190 models looked almost the same as the '39 models. We soon found a German buyer and insisted on cash payment. Since we received the equivalent in wads and wads of Brazilian cruzeiros on a weekend, which we could not deposit in the Royal Canadian Bank until Monday, we distributed smaller bunches of notes inside our books on the shelf. That same evening an acquaintance from Hamburg, whose name was also Wagner, came by unannounced with his brand-new wife. They wanted to go dancing with us at the "Moulin Rouge" near the Congonhas International Airport. We asked them to wait on the veranda while we changed clothes, but what we really wanted was to decide what to do with all that cash, the existence of which we couldn't reveal to anyone. Our future depended on quickly depositing it into our bank account in dollars. Checks, money orders, etc., were then worthless in Brazil, since issuing a bad check could not be easily or inexpensively prosecuted. We packed my inside jackets pocket with half the cash, leaving the other half inside our books and went out to the car in a very nervous state. The evening at the Moulin Rouge was quite good, but naturally I danced only with Annelore! I saw Huberta Lindenberg dancing with someone I did not know. She was ancient history now. Arriving home, we found everything in order. On Monday we deposited the money with great relief and then booked a passage with a Japanese freighter with room for ten passengers, to leave from Santos for Long Beach, California via the Panama Canal. It would head for San Francisco to unload coffee and then let us debark in Long Beach. With only a few weeks to prepare for the trip, we told our friends that our furniture was available for sale, available the day before departure. Everything was sold quickly.

GOOD BYE TO MERCEDES-BENZ; LAST-MINUTE MATTERS

Then we turned in our resignation to the astonished old Haug, one of those people who are convinced there is no better country in which to live and work than
good old Germany. He also regretted losing Annelore, having gotten used to her
over the years. Now he had to find an equally personable, discrete, productive,
punctual, German, Portuguese and English-speaking secretary. He suggested we
might have made a decision we would later regret. Shortly before our last day, he
even suggested we should move to Germany instead. If we would settle around
Stuttgart, he would help me get an offer from Daimler-Benz. That implied a later
return to Brazil with a hard-currency contract, like his other Daimler-Benz staff.
Thanking him, I thought the offer would leave me dangling in his dependency.
By now, I had gained the impression that one should possess a Swabian accent to
get ahead in that organization. Besides, the offer was too late and too vague for
me to consider, even if I would have been waiting for it, because everything was
set for the green light. We only had to decide what to take along and how. The
Albrechts had taken our large Victrola with a turntable for records, the latest in
hi-fi radio. Since they could not afford to pay, Frau A. had decided to do our
laundry for several months in exchange, replacing the services of one of the
countless neighborhood women, who did this work for a pittance. Frau A. had
more than enough to do with three sons in the house, but sorely missed quality
entertainment. While her husband could escape daily to his accountant's job, she
had nothing but dreary work and no help from the family—a martyr. Much
later, after her husband's death, she would return to Rothenburg ob der Tauber
with her youngest son, who came to have a rare disease which made his skin look
dark brown, causing suspicions about his legitimacy in the simple Rothenburg
population.

We commissioned a large wooden box from grandpa Albrecht. In addition to
our two pieces of luggage, we used it to take, among other possessions, those nice
Brazilian towels we had requested as wedding presents. This monstrosity measured about 3x2x6 feet, which was fine when empty. But filled to the brim it was
hard to move!! Two boxes would have been more manageable, but it was too late.
Moving it gave the first taste of what it is like to have severe back pains. But we
got it to Santos and still have a photo of two hopeful immigrants sitting on the
luggage in Santos harbor, waiting for the shipping office to open. Before that, we
went downtown and bought a nice solid gold watch with solid gold band, and an
amethyst- and a topaz pendant. We never had to sell them, as we had feared then,

in case we would run into bad times. They will always be our good luck charms. At Mercedes there was a farewell party with beer and Schnapps right in the technical department—the German custom still observed in Germany now. Returning home for the last time, we were no longer members of an organization, which had functioned as kind of a protector—an eerie feeling.

UNITED STATES OF AMERICA

VOYAGE TO LOS ANGELES

Next, we found ourselves waiting for the Japanese freighter "Montevideo Maru" at noon some day in August, 1957. Our cabin was air-conditioned, comfortable and very clean. We saw no other passengers yet, but at sunset Mr. Haug made a surprise appearance, trying to negotiate with the purser to have a Japanese dinner with us on board. He felt kinship with the Japanese since his WWII stint there for Mercedes Benz, when he must have been wined and dined like an exotic potentate. But the captain said he did not have the correct fresh ingredients on board to host a Japanese dinner. Instead Haug took us to a very expensive restaurant at the balmy Santos beach. Visibly moved, he showed that he liked and respected us. Obviously he appreciated Annelore more than me, perhaps considering her the daughter he never had. Before becoming his secretary-interpreter, she had assisted other MBB executives in the technical, marketing and import-export departments. It was an astonishing conclusion of our Mercedes Benz tenure.

During the night, the ship moved into the channel and then the open sea. Waking up, we saw only the ocean. We met the other passengers at breakfast: A very good-looking American couple in their fifties, Harold-Ismert and Margaret Spence; he of typical Nordic-British appearance, and she an attractive artist-type woman. Their interests were in ceramics. They had escaped his financial responsibilities for two children after his divorce. The third additional passenger was Harry (Harutoshi) Fukuzawa, a Japanese national in his mid-twenties who was returning to California after completing his business degree in Columbus, Ohio. He was obviously from a good and wealthy family, but after living in the US for several years, having become accustomed to the American lifestyle, he wanted to stay. Later, he would work at the Japanese embassy in Washington, DC, where he arranged visits of Japanese industrialists with U.S. companies to introduce them to modern management, production and distribution methods. His main goal was to start a business, hopefully backed by his family. During the voyage he badgered us about the quality of Brazilian women. He had met one, Maria, in Rio and wondered what kind of wife she might make. While generally a Japanese wife would faithfully take care of household and children, accommodate all of the husband's wishes and always walk six feet behind him in public, he had no idea what a Brazilian wife would do. We had no idea, but told him we thought Brazilian girls from good families would be more like Europeans, who express their wishes and perhaps even fight for them. What one might not be able to rely upon were sometimes Brazilian men. Harry would later marry Maria and settle in a fancy home in Palos Verdes, running a company, which set up automatic car washing machines. We later kept contact with him while living in Los Angeles and corresponded with him some time thereafter. An interesting, curious fellow, he hated to give in to his family's wishes to marry a Japanese woman, preferring a real companion. He wondered if such a union would last.

All this came out during endless daily games of shuffleboard at the instigation of the purser, who played with us like a coach. Winners were usually the Spence's. Harold Ismert was a ceramic engineer who had worked for a Brazilian company. They had gone to Brazil to continue the lifestyle to which they were accustomed after his divorce. In Brazil the U.S. courts could not reach him. Now the kids were grown and they wanted to return to their normal life. Those two "kids" in Pasadena told us later that they did not think much of him and his new wife. On the ship we were impressed to meet real Americans, but they did not help our efforts to learn more about life in the U.S. by telling us that an American engineer's wife does not have to work, since engineers make enough money for both. It seemed they had been away so long that they had lost touch. Margaret apparently wanted to give the impression of a "pampered" woman.

Food on the "Montevideo Maru" was simple, but good. The captain, who joined us only for the first dinner, was the absolute ruler on board. His crew was excessive in numbers, which were imposed by the Japanese government to reduce Japan's unemployment. Hence, throngs of people were constantly removing rust and repainting. Even little-used clothing in our cabin was promptly removed and reappeared in the evening washed, heavily starched, and pressed. The crew's entertainment seemed to consist of their birds. Each had one or two cages filled with them. Once, when a parakeet flew away, the entire crew looked sad. Only the purser spoke English. The captain, shying away from both passengers and crew, kept to his quarters. Other than deck-golf, reading or walking about the deck, we enjoyed the endless games of the dolphins. After ten days we saw land and soon arrived in the Panama Harbor, where we spent the afternoon in town, marveling at the wares. We only bought a white, short-sleeved shirt of nylon. Then a new material, we thought it would make me more comfortable in that tropical climate. Through endless locks we moved up into Gatun lake and then back down into the Pacific. It was so hot and humid that by evening everything on board was covered with dew. We had to take several showers throughout the day. Heading north on the Pacific side, we enjoyed watching the dolphins and many giant sea turtles paddle around. No sharks or whales could be seen. Since our freighter never stuck close to the shore, the voyage became monotonous, and my thoughts began to focus on our situation: no contacts in a strange country—few assets—our English limited to what we had learned in school—not much of an idea what the Americans would be like—no bed to sleep in for the first night, and so on. Traveling north along the Brazilian coast, we had been happy to leave that country for a new future, but now anxiety was setting in. When Annelore was writing some letters and postcards, I reminded her that we had to watch our money, and that included postage! I remembered my arrival in Rio, when I didn't possess a coin for that purpose! Although we had money in the bank, it was only $1,500 after all expenses were paid—that for seven years of working! If we would have to move into a hotel in Los Angeles for 10 days, that money could dissipate quickly! We knew absolutely nothing. We passed Mexico. North of Los Angeles we could make out the coastal ranges north of Oxnard and Santa Barbara. While the Spence's marveled at the good old USA, we felt eerie, knowing that our freewheeling time on board was ending. Finally, the unforgettable panorama of the entrance to San Francisco Bay and the Golden Gate Bridge appeared. It made us think that we should settle here. Why choose anything else? Arriving on the pier, we were checked smoothly into the US by US Customs and Immigration and Naturalization Service. Then we joined the Spence's and Harry in exploring San Francisco. Wandering through the city was an unforgettable experience. Everything was so neat—so different from Sao Paulo. On the Top of the Marc Hopkins Hotel was a fancy restaurant with picture windows in all directions. Moving toward a table, we were stopped and Annelore was asked for identification. No one under 21 was allowed to enter a place where alcohol was served. My protest that she was my 22-year old wife did not help; she had to show her passport. Annelore, who looked like 17, was a little upset, but a stiff drink and the view made her feel better.

Enormous amounts of coffee bags destined for the roasters of San Francisco were unloaded while we remained on board for three days. Apparently all coffee packaging for the Western US was done here. Years later, when I worked in SF for some time, I would pass those large buildings on my way from the train station to the banking district. The freshly roasted beans always smelled delicious. In the next two days we visited the Golden Gate Park, Japanese Tea Garden, and other attractions. We also scanned the newspapers for jobs, but found nothing suitable for an engineer, not even for established people with US experience. The city seemed to live from banking, brokerage, insurance and perhaps tourism. Spence's said the situation in L.A. with lots of industry would be different.

LIFE IN LOS ANGELES

After three days we departed through the Golden Gate Bridge for the L.A./Long Beach harbor, hoping it would be like San Francisco, and that we would quickly fit in. When we approached a pier in Long Beach, the journey was over. It was hot, and the Spence's and Harry left quickly by taxi after giving us their addresses. Now our huge box had to be stored until we could retrieve it after finding permanent housing. At one point it was hanging precariously on a rope, about to drop, which would have smashed its contents. The crew seemed to have created this scene to scare us, since in our excitement we had forgotten to distribute any tips. Finally, the crate made it to the warehouse, and we called a taxi.

By now it was evening, and we were totally exhausted and ready for a good night's rest. We asked the driver to "take us to a cheap hotel," in what we thought was good English, not realizing that our request could be misunderstood! We just needed a place to rest and freshen up before starting our new life. The cab stopped in front of a two-story building near the center of Long Beach. We had little luggage with us, to be able to move around easily. Asked inside how many hours we wanted to stay, we replied: "Overnight." On the next day we planned to head for L.A. to find more permanent housing. The clerk then asked for payment before giving us the key to the room on the second floor. It was a small, well-kept establishment, except for the reception area, which looked a little seedy. Too busy digesting all those new impressions; we didn't think much about it. Upstairs we passed an open door which showed a clean, large bed on which a smiling, carefully coiffed lady sat, dressed in a heavily laced negligee. We wondered why hotel guests would leave their door open, as we passed another open door with an attractive young female on the bed, before finding our room number. We then wondered whether we should close our own door, but did, since the idea of showing ourselves to other people made us uncomfortable and there were no instructions to the contrary. Hence, our first major decision in America was to close our door, although this did not seem to be customary in Los Angeles!

Relieved, we freshened up and, still numb from exhaustion, found a nice diner nearby, and then we fell asleep immediately back in the hotel.

On the next morning we took a train to L.A., where we bought the L.A. Times to find a suitable, inexpensive apartment. In those days an old streetcar line connected downtown Long Beach to L.A., which served such South L.A. communities as Torrance, Compton and Watts. An hour later we were on Sixth Street in L.A. where it ended, and where we began studying the paper's For Rent Ads, noting that the Silver Lake District along Sunset Boulevard. North of downtown offered the most activity at reasonable cost. By cab we visited an apartment there, which we disliked, and then wandered toward Sunset Blvd., where we found an "Insurance and Realty" office near Sanborn Ave. Inside, we told the friendly-looking agent that we needed a furnished apartment very soon and described our situation. He said renting was not his business; he only sold houses, but that he knew the managers of a large apartment building nearby, Celia and Dave Seger. He called them, and they said they had a vacancy; we should come over. Asked how much we owed him (since one pays for such services in Germany), he would not hear of accepting payment. Rather, he suggested that, after we would buy a car, we might like to consider him for insuring it, which is what we later did. Then we walked west on Sunset to Sanborn Ave., where we found the five- or six-story red brick apartment building. Those were prevalent in the area then. We did not realize that we were at the edge of L.A.'s Hollywood district, in walking distance of Hollywood and Vine Boulevards, site of the Grauman's Chinese Theatre, of which we had heard often! Buses ran down Sunset all the way, from downtown to Beverly Hills, where they connected to Westwood and Santa Monica.

Celia greeted us like old friends. We were amazed at the polite and helpful manner shown by those we had met so far, most of all Celia's. She promised to show us the apartment later, but insisted the two of us must have lunch with them while watching her favorite TV show: "Queen for a Day." This was the first of many TV's we saw in America! We also loved our first taste of cottage cheese and canned peaches! A bit tense about the apartment and its price, we didn't completely understand the show's goings-on. Leading us to the fourth floor, Celia, who was from Denmark and spoke with a slight accent, asked many questions about our background. She showed us the shared telephone on the second floor, which she serviced by switchboard from her apartment by buzzing the tenants, who would then take the calls on the second floor, where there was a phone, and a pay phone there also served for outgoing calls. The furnished apartment was a studio, with bath and kitchenette. The main room had a queen-size bed, which folded into the wall when not in use. There was a table with four chairs, a sofa and armchair with a coffee table, and even a minimum of linen and blankets. The kitchen had a stove and a very small, ancient refrigerator built into the wall, which had been modernized with evaporator coils. The apartment had nice windows with curtains. Very clean pink wall-to-wall shag carpeting made it even lighter. We later unsuccessfully tried to find the original floor under layers of wall-to-wall rugs, but finally gave up for fear there might not be any floor. We loved the price of $60/month, which included phone and utilities. It would enable us to rent it for long time using our savings, which gave us a sense of security, since we did not know what results our job search would yield. Without looking further, we gladly took the apartment; besides, we didn't want to spend money for another night at a hotel. Combined with Celia's friendliness and the well-organized, clean atmosphere of the building, we felt we were getting a good start housing-wise. After moving in with the bags we had brought, we bought our first American supplies at the Safeway Supermarket at Sanborn and Sunset, including those for the evening meal. We found the prices reasonable, and sometimes we would carefully peak into the inside of the packages to see what we were buying! On the next day, we took the bus to the downtown L.A. Woolworth store to buy pots, pans, stainless steel ware, a small set of dishes with a pinecone pattern, etc. There we also discovered the Grand Central Market, which would become our source for fresh produce. Then we didn't know that the Chinese markets and Olvera Street (Mexican) were also close by.

OUR JOB SEARCH

Studying the job market, we almost ignored other news. Annelore wondered if, with her seven years of school English, she might qualify for some of the clerical jobs advertised. Ready to accept any job, she first wanted to try that which she knew and was good at. First, she ventured out alone to inquire about a clerk position on either Hollywood or Santa Monica Blvd., not far from our place. Such jobs involved filing, sorting, mail handling, copying, telephone, etc. She found her first interview depressing. The office manager politely listened to her background, but then advised her to look for a better-paying job, since she might have to support me for some time. For that, he said, the money he could pay was not enough. He said she possessed the needed clerical skills, but the job would not involve typing. He suggested she could earn more by utilizing her typing skills. Confused and sad, Annelore left and began to cry. Two young office clerks, who had earlier received her in the office, followed her to see how it went. When she suggested that the boss had just made excuses, they protested, confirming that this, an insurance agency, paid miserable wages; the boss had done the right thing. They comforted her: she would surely find a better offer. But when she came home, we still had no job between the two of us. My finding something in the engineering field was much more difficult. The ads showed many highly concentrated job openings with demands focusing on experienced specialists in aeronautical or electrical/electronic engineering, such as hydraulics, flow control, vibration analysis, stress analysis, wave guide design—specialties of which I had no idea. L.A. seemed to be a market specialized in aircraft design and manufacture. Rockets were then in their infant stages. Most jobs also required U.S. citizenship. Although I began to realize my difficulties, I did not despair because of my trusted companion. If nothing would turn up, we could take a boat home from the East Coast. Among other interviews Annelore had was one job we had discovered in the German-language newspaper: a Jewish man who wanted to convert Jews to the Christian religion and wanted her as his bilingual secretary. The most promising interview, with Dun & Bradstreet on Main Street in downtown L.A., led to her first job as clerk-typist in their Analytical Department for $250 per month. While concluding the interview after a clerical and typing test, she learned that his is a highly respected organization, which establishes credit ratings for businesses. Since most companies' shipments worldwide are made on credit, one must know the recipient's financial status. So, Annelore had hit the jackpot! She was to report to the Analytical Department supervisor, who found her name a bit hard to use, preferring to call her Anna, if she wouldn't mind. She was Anna ever since, and I shall call her by her American name from now on. Incidentally, although her English was quite good, she did not pay attention to Mr. Lowe's polite manners when being asked: "would you mind?"—and always answered, "Yes, Mr. Lowe," until one day, having noted a bit of a smirk on his face, she looked up the expression. The first time she answered correctly: "No, I wouldn't mind," he was very disappointed, as he had enjoyed this little game. A very fine, gentle man, he often talked about his son Jimmy, who had cerebral palsy, and whose hobby was collecting movie stars' autographs. He had quite a collection, which, along with classical music, he enjoyed immensely. Anna assisted Mr. Lowe and his seven analytical reporters by typing memos, preparing the weekly bankruptcy lists for L.A., (the reports were produced by a typing pool, for which she was the liaison), keeping the files in order, taking phone messages, and, under Mr. Lowe's direction, independent follow-up on deadlines. Her salary could finance our life indefinitely without having to touch our meager savings. This was a watershed event! Due to Anna, we had crossed the threshold and the pressure was off for a while. After she started working the following week, I was alone to vigorously pursue my own job search. On her first day, Anna came home very impressed. The seven reporters in her department performed non-routine investigations and were the large office's backbone. They interviewed heads of industrial commercial enterprises, including May Co., Bullock's, Boeing, etc. for their analytical reports, which were more detailed and expensive than the routine reports, and also wrote very sensitive key employee reports about high-level executive prospects. Anna made the corrections the reporters indicated on the proof copy and later did considerable proofreading. She offered to type more and more of the shorter correspondence, since she wanted experience with Dictaphone and English dictation. Since she arrived at work very early, she used the time to work through a book adapting her German shorthand to the English language. The work had to be very accurate, because many high-level executives were to read it and often company policies depended upon the Dun & Bradstreet input. D&B is still an excellent business. How times have changed: during her clerical test she had learned that the company did not hire anyone over 35, and during a coffee break the other "girls" told her to never say the word "union." Her only complaint about working there was about the heat; the offices were not air-conditioned. While in Brazil heat spells were interrupted by showers and welcome cool-downs, during L.A.'s summers, the daily sun bore mercilessly on the concrete maze of downtown and brought unbearable temperatures, compounded by smog, of which the other people complained loudly. But we had so much to learn and think about that we didn't perceive it for a long time.

My own job search was not going anywhere. Setting out by bus each morning, I usually headed toward Long Beach to follow leads from the paper. After the last bus stop I had to walk, because I could not justify a cab. Most often a depressing hour of walking along a highway without curbs or sidewalks followed, while cars passed me at high speed. The other guys seemingly had jobs and knew where they were going. They had a home to return to, steady income, and gas was only 25 cents (a pittance). While I crawled along, with the sun beating down on me, my tongue soon started hanging from my mouth. I never arrived at the premises until around eleven o'clock, finding the vacancy usually filled. Also, I was often told that security clearance was required, based on US citizenship. I returned home the same way, except that it was then 10 or 15 degrees F hotter, and no refreshments were sold along the road. Occasionally a compassionate motorist would offer a ride to what would have looked to them a pathetic figure, wearing a good suit, carrying a leather briefcase. He may have thought that my car had broken down. No normal person would walk on those highways running from L.A.

to the south for 20-30 miles straight, without any bends, such as Western or Sepulveda Avenues. Those started around Hollywood/Griffith Park and ran straight to the ocean. After a couple of weeks, realizing my lack of progress, we talked about moving to Detroit, where my experience in automobiles might prove useful. Meanwhile, Anna had established good personal relations with the D&B reporters, like Eddie Goyette, Ed Drum, Roy Dixon, and others, as well as Jim Lowe (Ethel) and his boss, Mr. Marzluft, whose secretary Erma French was like a mother to her. All of them volunteered advice about the wisdom of joining this or that company. When she mentioned the Detroit idea, they threw up their hands: "Not while the USA is undergoing a recession!" We looked up the word "recession" and were shocked. It meant thousands were being laid off in Detroit; there would be no new hires. As a last resort, I ran an ad in the Los Angeles Times, something like: "Mech. Eng., rec. arr. in US, German born, Eng./Ger./ Portuguese speaking; automotive/power circuit breaker exp., seeks suitable pos., phone ... I clued in Celia, who promised to alert me very quickly of any calls or take messages, including phone numbers. Meanwhile, we had bought an old Remington typewriter, so Anna could prepare resumes. I was surprised to receive several calls, including one from a captain of a boat, who made regular trips to South America and needed someone with knowledge of land and people. It sounded like a smuggler organization. Then there was Crown Corporation, which made school buses. The reporters warned Anna about the company's financial problems. And so it went.

While this was going on, Dave helped me get our overseas crate from the Long Beach warehouse. Unaware of the measurements, I thought it would fit into his oversized trunk. At the warehouse we showed it to a customs agent, who said there were no duties to pay. We had to request help to load this 2x3-6ft heavy contraption into the trunk, ending up with half of it sticking out in the back. It made the car go down visibly. I noticed Dave's concern about his old car making it the 40 miles to Sanborn, but it did. This made me realize even more that I really needed a car, especially for getting to work after finding a job; in fact, it should help me find one!

While my job search continued, we contacted the daughter and son-in-law of the Spence couple, whom we had met earlier when visiting the Spence's at a nice house they had rented in Laguna Beach. For them nothing was good enough, although they also had to start from scratch in the US. Wendell, the Spence's son-in-law, offered to help me obtain a car and drivers' license. First I got a learners' permit from the DMV, which only required filling out a form. Wendell and I then went to a used car lot in Pasadena, where I selected a nice 1952 blue Chevy

4 door. All cars then had stick shift (3 forward) and the shift was on the steering column. Then I drove off with Wendell, who had to sit beside me according to DMV regulations. We returned to Sunset Blvd. via the Pasadena freeway, a wild ride. I admit I was scared and insecure, as I had never been on a freeway, with 2 crowded lanes full of cars driving at 65 or 70 mph. Traffic in Brazil had always moved slowly without those freeways, where people never slow down and one can pass left or right. But a week or so later I had gotten used to the pace. Our nicely running car now made things easier, and in the following months we were able to see different sites in Southern California, which interested us.

The job search was getting more promising now. I heard from a small company on N. Main Street: Sparling Meter Co. Joe Braun and Ray Sparling, the owner, interviewed me. The shops were in a decrepit-looking building in an industrial park close to downtown, which was ready to be torn down, but they were building new facilities and would soon move to El Monte, 15 miles to the east toward San Bernardino. They were expanding and needed more help. They offered me $500 per month, double of what Anna was making. We looked at this as an excellent opportunity. We could live on $250 and save the rest. In three months we would have saved what took us seven years in Brazil to save! Our fortunes were quickly changing for the better. After Anna's consultation with her D&B friends, who were enthusiastic, I called Sparling and accepted the offer. My start on the following Monday was unceremonious, with Joe Braun getting me together with Monte Buchanan in the assembly department. Monte was working at a bench. I soon realized that I needed a tool chest and some basic tools, which I bought at Sears. The toolbox and calipers, files, screwdrivers, etc. are now in my son's home; they lasted a lifetime. Once I had the tools, I also received work orders and started to make things. I had not worked on a bench since 1941 in Spandau 16 years earlier. Hence I had to get used to it and started to doubt how I would fit into the picture, as I did not want to spend the rest of my life on a bench throwing meters together. In the late Fall, we began to move to El Monte. All of us helped move inventory, records, drawing originals, and machinery, work benches, etc. The El Monte facility on Temple City Boulevard was an improvement. It was larger and higher, allowing better airflow, but I now had to drive at least 30 minutes on the San Bernardino Freeway. The total of 40 minutes I needed by car were easy in the morning, since the outbound freeway was almost empty; everyone then seemed to live along that freeway in communities like Pomona, Arcadia, etc., and all business was then in L.A. By now the corridor along the San Bernardino Freeway (Interstate 10) is full of industries, and there is even a city called "City of Industry" (for lack of other names, I guess). I would drop Anna off at work on Main Street and pick her up on my way home. She always waited patiently on 7th Street while I wormed my way through the maze of 4-lane traffic, which was horrible around quitting time. One day, as I was in the center lane, wanting to turn right, I could not get into the right lane, as the law required. Desperate, I turned right anyway to avoid a 30-minute turn around the block. As Anna jumped into the car, a traffic policeman stopped us, peaked into the car and said "If you wouldn't have this pretty girl in your car, I'd give you a ticket." I did have a pretty girl in my car and felt proud that she had saved me from getting an expensive ticket! I was always glad to see her again after so many hours in an environment that I could master, but was becoming doubtful about.

After Sparling's move, Joe Braun one day introduced me to "Grandpa," his Dad, Sparling's jack of all trades, who did tools and special work. Joe didn't speak German, but Grandpa communicated with me in what he may have thought was German. Instead, what came out of his pipe-equipped mouth was a mixture of Badensian-Swabian dialect interlaced with ill-pronounced English. When he switched to English, it was the other way around. The result was that I could not understand him. But when it came to working with him, he knew what he was doing, based on a lifetime of shop experience. He always walked around in an apron, and I soon did too. He was a very good sport in helping me over some rough spots. His son Joe, the manufacturing manager, gave me a very tricky assignment—something one would normally farm out to a tool making shop. He and Ray Sparling must have been testing my knowledge of metalworking. Normally, they should not have considered me for the job, which required an experienced toolmaker like Grandpa or better, while I had no hands-on experience to speak of for 16 years. While I remembered much from my apprenticeship, those three years do not mean one is a toolmaker, just like in engineering, where long years of experience must follow a degree. What Joe had in mind was a plastic injection mold for a measurement propeller. It was about 10 inches in diameter and had four or five wings, which were forming a spiral around the hub of the prop. The company had an old self-made contraption, apparently made by Joe and Grandpa, which lent itself to receive a mold to inject the hot vinyl resin into. The two men showed me several pieces of cast aluminum, which roughly showed the outline of the desired mold. I was to machine each part to fairly exact spiral configuration, fit the parts together, throw the contraption on the "injection machine," and make props—as fast as possible, since they had orders for the sizes the mold was to make. Initially I felt like telling them that this required a precision horizontal boring mill, which has various features to develop a spiral tool path. Today it could easily be made by an N/C controlled boring mill. I only had a large, ancient lathe and an equally old shaping. Therefore I now had to figure out how to have the tool bit in the shaping develop the dimensional curvature—something one learns neither in high school nor in engineering college. One needs to have a good understanding of college level geometry and how to make a practical set-up that transforms theory into something made of metal—and of course the machine and its tools. Trying to do it, I was watched by Grandpa through his well-worn reading glasses, as he puffed hastily on his pipe. He would stop by to give me some hints and/or a helping hand. He realized that someone in my position would welcome at least moral support, and he did much more. Bless his soul! After a week or so I had determined the machining process; it then took me at least three more weeks to finish the machining alone. Then the prop surfaces had to be given a fine, mirror-like finish, which required lots of careful work with the file and finally polishing paper. After about five more weeks I could try out the mold to make the first propeller. Hence, Sparling was paying about $600 for something that would have cost them at least $3,000, if made by a tool shop. I admit I sweated blood and water during the ordeal and was desperate sometimes. Telling Joe I did not feel up to it would have ruined my image and future. I also learned how things then often worked in the USA and on many occasions still do: You were asked if you could handle a job, and were trusted to do it. This was your chance. Then you were expected to work your butt off and do the best you could.

Picking up Anna downtown in the late afternoons, I was sometimes exhausted, but so was she. Everything was so new. Each day brought new experiences and challenges. But we had an almost new car now to explore the area on weekends. We often drove west down Sunset Blvd. to Santa Monica's marvelous beaches with a picnic and swam until late afternoon. Anna never worried about sunburn, while I had to protect my skin; sometimes the sun got the better of me. Driving along those remarkable Beverly Hills mansions made us feel good. The area resembled a luxurious park. Here we were, taking part in this beautiful setting—(perhaps more than the owners)! Among our many other wonderful destinations were Disneyland, crossing the San Gabriel Mountains into the desert around Palmdale, the Arcadia Arboretum, Descanso Gardens, Huntington Library, and Big Bear and Arrowhead Lakes. We were still deciding whether to stay in the USA, but the thought of returning to Germany began to wane, although we lived frugally in a tiny apartment and had daily pressures and sometimes frustrations at our jobs. At night we always exchanged news and notes and handled all our developments, tactic and strategy together. We were growing into a unit, developing great trust and strengthening the love we had for each other.

We would discuss each purchase before making it together, never disagreeing about what to do. This continued until now. Anna's boss Jim Lowe encouraged her to establish a monthly budget and stick to it. At the beginning of each month, some income should be conserved on a regular basis for a rainy day. Fortunately, those rainy days were not to come as I write this, but we felt secure knowing that assets were at our disposal. Both of us were aware of our income, savings, budget; no secrets were held back. With our basic needs resolved, we were ready to learn about life in California, not realizing that California was a special case and that later, in other parts of the country, we would start learning again.

Our daily routine was dominated by our work and commute. In the evenings we might take a walk, often toward West Hollywood. To the North was Griffith Park, which offered a spectacular view of L.A. in the south, especially after dark—a sea of lights. Beyond the downtown high rises there were nothing but single-family dwellings, often with lit swimming pools. Los Angeles seemed to be totally built up and paved with concrete. Transportation via millions of single cars was the reason for the sometimes-heavy smog.

MORE ADJUSTMENTS IN OUR NEW LIFE

Soon we began to think that owing a TV would speed up our linguistic progress, especially with regard to pronunciation, vocabulary, colloquialisms and understanding the American and California way of life. Celia knew someone trying to sell a used Muntz TV, an unusually large piece of furniture. Most people then had 20 or 24-inch TV's, while it had a 32 inch screen. The picture was not very sharp, to say the least, but the price seemed right to us, and we didn't even look further, perhaps for lack of shopping experience. After a difficult transport, Dave and I forced it upstairs. Now we could hone our language skills, along with reading the LA Times aloud.

One Saturday during my first year at Sparling, employees were invited to the company's family picnic in a park near Rosemead and Temple City. Sparling provided beverages, dishes etc. etc., and the employees brought their favorite dishes to share—our first "potluck" of many we were to enjoy in the future. There were games for old and young. Everyone was participating enthusiastically. Anna had been equally enthusiastic about preparing a nice dish and studied her new Betty Crocker cookbook for days. But finally she decided on "Swedish Meatballs" (Koenigsberger Klopse), which would be somewhat European; she knew something typical of Germany would be expected. At the picnic many people complimented Anna on this dish, asking for the recipe. We realized only later that this is very much a nice American gesture ... to compliment someone to make him/her feel good about a contribution made, if it is considered a good one.

After the plastic injection mold for the propeller was completed, I did occasional machining jobs. Sometimes errors I made because of my practical inexperience had dangerous results. Once I had a heavy work piece which needed a 1-inch hole drilled into it. It was clamped in a machine vice, center punched. When starting drilling, the piece and vice suddenly started rotating with the drill, threatening to break the drill and to start flying into space—at me or someone nearby. It actually flew off the machine table, but not sufficiently to take the full force of the long, rotating drill! In a panic, I tried to find the switch to turn it off, which took a while—actually too long: When I found it, my forehead was sweaty. One guy saw me and raised his brows. That was a close call for me. I had not secured the vice on the machine table sufficiently to take the full force of the large, rotating drill, which was an embarrassing mistake for any mechanic. I had lost the know-how to do it safely, but naturally I now caught on right away!

But I had not been hired to work as a mechanic forever. Soon after this event, Joe Braun led me into the offices of which one part was reserved for the engineering personnel. A board and desk awaited me, along with Dick Huth, Gene Mendenhall and Judd Chastain. Judd and Dick were doing the engineering work for new products, while Gene was establishing data for all production jobs, i.e. he converted rotations/min. of measuring propellers into gal/min. or acre/feet per hour, or whatever units the customers requested to read out in. I had little to do with Judd, who seemed to be the engineering manager, but mainly I worked with Dick. Joe and Dick then showed me a strip chart and a circular (chart) recorder, which Sparling had produced from the beginning of time. I had seen Monte assemble some of these and also had worked on them. They explained the mechanism, gave me existing drawings and assigned me to improve them to reduce the cost. I saw that the old designs were indeed not cost-effective. The aluminum frame was a sand casting needing numerous drilling, milling and tapping operations to allow mounting of a series of gears, which converted the propeller shaft input into a reasonable output speed. All of this had to be done by mounting the cast frame into a drilling jig. Before that, a reference milled surface had to be established. My design was based on two 1/8-inch aluminum plates, where a series of holes had to be punched to tie the two plates together and mount all necessary gears. The entire product thus became much smaller and lighter. Since raw material was cheap, inventory was reduced considerably. When a series of 12 or

20 was needed, the work could be quickly accomplished on the premises. Only a die was needed to punch all the holes—an inexpensive tool. First I made all drawings, learning the relatively crude tolerancing methods used at Sparling (and throughout the U.S.) The sophisticated European standardized tolerance system was still unknown. I had no trouble to quickly put everything on paper. Then Joe asked me to make a prototype in the shop to demonstrate it to management. Each day I became more self-reliant and confident, and I felt I was becoming an accepted member of the staff. I found Dick to be the fellow I could most easily compare notes and exchange views with. He was just good to be around, and we enjoyed each other's company. After we were invited to his home for dinner, our families became closer as time passed.

Fall was approaching with what seemed to us hardly any change in the weather. To our surprise, a lonely, strangely dressed child appeared one day at our apartment door, asking for some kind of handout, using an expression we didn't know. Afraid, we said we could not give her anything (since she also did not look poor). Closing the door quickly, we wondered: were there beggars in the area? Much later we learned that we had been introduced to the custom of Halloween-trick-or treating, unfortunately without understanding it. Among other customs, which stunned us, was the custom of sending Christmas cards. Starting in early December, we found our little indoor mailbox stuffed with these cards, some from people with names we did not even recognize, and often with just a signature and only a printed "Happy Holidays" message. I'm afraid we didn't answer many of those; we were just too overwhelmed! Around Thanksgiving time Mr. Lowe, who enjoyed telling Anna about American customs, told her she MUST cook a turkey. When Anna said her refrigerator was much too small to hold such a giant bird, he suggested hanging it out the window! She agreed that she should, but it was one piece of advice she didn't heed. Instead, a policeman citing us for jaywalking interrupted our first, very lonely, early Thanksgiving Day walk around the neighborhood. There were hardly any cars or walkers around! When we acted very surprised, he let us go, wishing us a happy holiday! For Christmas, we were invited to the home of the relatives of the Americans we had met in Sao Paulo. We dashed out a day before Christmas Eve to buy toys for their children and found the shelves almost bare of merchandise. We went there with the presents we had finally found, and were amazed at our first American Christmas. The amount of packages under the tree—most containing the type of things one calls "stocking stuffers," was incredible. On that Christmas Eve, there was so much to unwrap that the living room ended up looking like a tornado had passed through. And we learned when they say "Merry Christmas," it indeed means "merry"! Ethel, Jim Lowe's wife, had made a huge amount of Styrofoam decorations for us. Since our tree was tiny, we ended up stringing up a clothesline in the apartment to hang these reindeers, snowmen, etc., which looked rather pretty!

MOVING, AND ARRIVAL OF ANNA'S MOTHER

Since Sparling's move to El Monte required more commuting time, we began to think of living elsewhere. On weekends, we explored locations east of downtown L.A., which would enable Anna to reach downtown by bus and me to drive to El Monte. We looked at Temple City, Pasadena, Alhambra, Rosemead, San Marino, San Gabriel and Arcadia. The latter three consisted mostly of single-family homes, while rentals could be found around Pasadena, Alhambra, Temple City and Rosemead. In Alhambra, we found a little rental property with two downstairs and two upstairs units. We hoped to rent one of the downstairs apartments, but the landlady, Bessie Paige, explained that the upstairs tenants (Bonnie and Hal Hornback) had already opted on the downstairs unit, which was much cooler. There was neither air conditioning nor insulation for walls and ceiling available then, and the sun would heat up the upstairs a lot, especially in the unit facing south. Toward evening, a breeze came from the ocean, but the room temperature cooled off only a few hours later. We knew all those comfort tricks by then. This apartment was on La France Avenue; around 30 minutes by bus to downtown. This would cut down driving time considerably. There were two bedrooms, a kitchen, living room and bath, a perfect arrangement, since we had invited Anna's mother to visit us—the principal reason for our move. Naturally, the rent was higher, but our first apartment had been unusually inexpensive, and we could afford the move.

We had now saved more money, had health insurance from two companies, and our combined income was over $750 per month. Also, we were surer that our employers liked us and our work, and we would stay on the payroll as long as we wished to. This aspect was important, as we were outgrowing our immigrant complexes and learning to blend in. That, however, didn't protect us from experiences such as that at May Co., a downtown department store. Looking for a lightweight suit for me, we noticed that the pants seams were not hemmed, but cut in a zigzag pattern. This seemed strange, but we liked one type, a light gray suit very much. We stepped outside, wondering why we had not noticed this "new fashion" before, but did not see this on the people who were walking around. We asked the salesman if we could buy pants which would not be finished in the new style. He very politely, explained that the tailor would later make the cuffs to measure. I had only purchased custom-tailored ones, since labor was so inexpensive in Brazil. This misunderstanding was amusing to us and the salesman, who was from Austria and spoke German perfectly.

My new suit later caused more confusion. On March 24, we celebrated our wedding anniversary in Chinatown. I usually did not wear my wedding band out of respect for revolving machinery and my hazardous experiences in this regard, but the wedding anniversary was an exception. Changing for the night, I was surprised that the wedding band was missing. Without any idea where it could have gone, I soon had to give up the search and postponed buying a substitute for a while. Several months later, taking the suit off the hanger to wear it again, I heard a metallic noise on the floor. There it was. My tremendous weight loss during my first months in the US due to the strenuous and nerve-wrecking work, had caused it to fall from my finger into the cuff of my pants! Its reappearance was a good foreboding for our marriage. Since then I am reluctant to use it, not wanting to lose it again.

Moving to Alhambra was easy, except for the large Muntz TV, for which we hitched a small trailer to our '52 Chevy. We then purchased beds, living room furniture in the then-popular early American style of Maplewood, rugs, a kitchen table and chairs. We also furnished a guest room for Anna's mother. We paid everything in cash—very un-American. We couldn't bring ourselves to follow the custom of buying now and paying later, which requires large interest charges and detracts from one's purchasing power. We planned very carefully. What we could not pay for, we simply did without.

By mid-1958 we were happily settled in Alhambra. Things were going well, we were busy, and returning to Germany was far from our minds. As the next challenge, we were thinking about a drivers' license for Anna. She passed the theoretical exam for the Learners' Permit very quickly. Since lessons were expensive, I had to teach her, and we started out on the huge parking lot of the Santa Anita racetrack in Arcadia on weekends. Sitting in the car with A., I explained what clutch, gas- and brake pedals were for, and how to coordinate them. Cars with automatic transmissions already existed, but it was better for her to learn the stick shift, so that she could drive any kind of car. The Chevy 52 had the gearshift lever (stick shift) on the steering column. The manual transmission had only three forward gears, since all cars then had very powerful, heavy engines. It was so powerful that one could start the car rolling in the second gear on a flat surface. On the first day we sat on the parking lot for hours just starting the engine and shifting gears without driving. To be efficient, one must make those moves almost automatically later on. Interested and eager, Anna had a tremendous respect for this humongous machine, which she was supposed to corral into sub-mission. She had never pictured herself behind a steering wheel, driving in beau-tiful America! She was not rolling yet, but even on the first day it seemed she'd get there. Excited and animated, she liked it! She knew she simply must drive to get to Bullock's Pasadena, the Huntington Library, and the Arboretum, and last, but not least, the shopping centers and supermarkets, and to work, perhaps. She learned about the interaction between clutch, gas pedal, and shift lever. If one coordinated those entities, this driving machine would begin to move—a terrify-ing thought. Then, how could one get this thing to stop moving? It was not that simple. One had to get the feel of how much gas sufficed to get rolling without killing the engine! We trained everything meticulously. I also explained how the car key operated an electric circuit, which moved the starter. If you don't press the clutch down, the little tiny starter would try to move the car, which was not what it was designed for ... it would not work. Also, one needed a battery to start, and when the car would run, there was an alternator to provide voltage/cur-rent for the electrical circuits. All this was shown on the live object—an enor-mous amount to learn, observe and assimilate for someone without experience. Both teacher and eager pupil tried their best. The process was slow; many hurdles had to be overcome before the car would start rolling without stalling too often or its engine racing, which made the poor car jump disgustedly at clutch release. We trained on countless Sundays. Sometimes Anna would become discouraged, but she knew that only complete mastery of all details led to safety; it was too dangerous to do otherwise. Later, Anna tried shifting from first to second and then drove through the entire huge parking lot in circles, and straight. She did not try shifting from second to first, since it was not healthy for the transmission. This came later, when driving in third and needing to slow the car for a smooth stop. After several weeks we reached the point at which attention could be given to the hand signaling required to pass the drivers' test. After two to three months I finally concluded Anna could enter the traffic in Arcadia, which opened a com-pletely new dimension, including reaction to all those traffic lights, signals, lanes, erratic drivers, etc. Starting in Alhambra each Sunday morning, we took Hun-tington Drive East into Arcadia towards the large Santa Anita Racetrack. Seem-ingly no one else was using its huge parking lot for driving lessons. It was a proud feeling for Anna to finally drive down Huntington Drive to Arcadia, where we explored all the neighborhood traffic signs. Changing lanes was a daunting task, requiring enormous courage and command of the situation. When mistakes occurred, I had Anna pull the car to the curb and stop, so I could explain what was done wrong. Sometimes, I did this while we were moving. At times Anna would try to argue the case to win a point (she was developing her own opinions). Then I had to remind her that I was not her husband whom she could argue with, but the driving teacher one just listens to. It sometimes got into funny situations. Naturally, most women would insist on learning at a driving school, but that would have been extravagant for us. We wanted to use our money for other things, including furniture, a home, or saving. It was not an easy project, but I believe Anna learned the ropes more thoroughly than if she had gone to a driving school. The result is 43 years of driving with only one accident, which was not her fault. We never entered the California freeways then. Even today, Anna would not do it if it can be helped, since she finds the traffic and motion just too fast. This has to do with her less than perfect vision, for which glasses don't seem to sufficiently compensate. But driving on all other roads was finally managed in a manner that would let her do it safely. We could have gone to the test much sooner, but I would have never forgiven myself in case of an accident caused by a situation for which she had not been adequately prepared. I think this was my way of expressing my feelings for her. She was part of me, and this was to last forever. In principle we were very happy together then (and thereafter). Before the drivers' test we prepared for the last difficult part: parking at the curb, driving backwards into position. On that alone we spent many evenings. She got away without scratching others, but Anna's performance was not flawless. While I fervently hoped she would—she didn't pass. Her general driving was acceptable, but when parking between two poles, she toppled one, thinking "well, it's just a pole, never mind!" The examiner did not agree: "Lady, you just damaged your and another person's car." Anna was dejected. She had studied very hard, but those examiners in Southern California are not in the habit of passing someone who looks like a 15 year old and is unable to park a car without a "scratch." So, it was back to the drawing board. Each evening after dinner we headed for an industrial plant parking lot, where there was no traffic. Two small ladders served as "poles" or cars. I figured out exactly when to turn the steering wheel and at which point certain features of the windows had to match the ladders, which made it possible to predetermine all steering wheel rotations. This went on endlessly: me sitting on top of the ladder and A. rotating the wheel until hell would freeze over. And it finally worked. She reached a 100% performance level, and the next test was easy! Getting the license was a total triumph. When we went out on weekends, she often drove short distances to improve experience and self-reliance. I applied critique, which in later years was no longer always appreciated and seemed to have a counterproductive effect. I began to realize I made her nervous when she was driving. She is happiest when driving alone. Later we each had our own vehicle.

For longer distances, in bad weather, or at night, it is always preferable that I drive. But the drivers' license was a benchmark and reason for celebration. All this happened at the end of 1958, when we lived at LaFrance Ave. in Alhambra. Around the corner from us was a wonderful small park, with benches to sit, large trees and a beautiful lawn, where we often relaxed … such a spot could not be found near Sanborn Ave; only further away there was Griffith Park, reachable via Western Ave.

Looking back to those times in the Sanborn Ave. apartment, we shall never forget a strange impression on our first Thanksgiving. It was Thanksgiving Day, but we had not yet learned about its importance to Americans. Anna had been told in the office that she must prepare a turnkey. Not understanding why, we concluded a chicken would be as good and would fit better into our oven and tiny refrigerator. We had heard little about the pilgrims and the nice turkeys they got from the Indians. We "celebrated" the feast alone, happy about the free day. That morning we hiked toward Hollywood and Vine, but turned into Western toward Griffith Park. We could see miles down Western. There was absolutely no traffic to be seen or heard, even on Sunset Blvd. As we turned toward Griffith Park, we passed a traffic light, barely noticing it was red. We walked anyway, since nothing was moving, and the traffic light did not have the "walk" and "don't walk" features. After a few steps, a policeman stopped at the curb and asked us in a friendly manner if we didn't see the red light. I said no, and that there was no traffic, after all. Answering his questions, we explained where we were from. He said that it's important not to jaywalk and especially not against a red light. Starting to fill out a ticket, he said as newcomers we must learn the American rules. Very calm and determined, he said he could give us two tickets, but that he was in a good mood because of Thanksgiving, and therefore he would give us only one. We were shocked about this kind of nonsense, having observed people crossing the streets in the middle of working traffic. Having to drive downtown during work time to settle this left me fuming for some time. I considered it harassment by the police to be able to fulfill their quota per day or shift.

Now I come back to our life on LaFrance Ave. in Alhambra: In the beginning of 1959, we heard from Gisela Sybrass, the attractive daughter of the manager of the facilities and maintenance department of Mercedes-Benz, Sao Paulo. They lived close to us on Avenida Brooklin Paulista in a lovely mansion. Gisela was secretary to the manager of the Purchasing Department, earning a good salary, since bilingual personnel like Annelore and Gisela were rare. Her boss, Mr. Obee, was developing a string of suppliers for the countless gadgets and components, which go into the trucks; those were being gradually placed into production in Brazil.

Gisela wrote that she was looking to add to her experiences, preferring not to spend too much time in Brazil. She asked us to support her immigration to the U.S., so she could work in Los Angeles as a secretary. (Later she told us another reason: she had wanted to get away from an unhappy love affair.) We explained that working in L.A. would mean starting over and competing with a well-developed work force, i.e. her salary here would not be as good (compared to that of an engineer) as in Sao Paulo. We did promise to sponsor her and said that she could live with us in Alhambra for a while. We had a guest room, which was intended for Anna's mother's use later. Before Gisela arrived, we were able to move to a downstairs apartment in LaFrance, since the Hornback's had purchased a gorgeous house in Arcadia, equipped with everything, including three bedrooms, two baths, huge kitchen, large living and dining rooms and a nice yard. We wondered if we could ever afford that kind of property, which in their case cost approx. $30,000 and required a down payment of 10%. That was a sizeable sum, because both had expensive tastes, with Hal driving a 2-3 year old Lincoln, a car for people who felt they had "arrived." His business card showed he was a Vice President in a Pasadena company, which dealt in reproductions, such as blueprints for industrial or commercial use. Much later we learned that he was often distributing blueprints to customers on a motorbike. Bonnie was secretary to the president of a Savings and Loan Company in Pasadena. Both were nice, and we always had a good time together. They often explained to us things we didn't quite comprehend. Sometimes, when talking, we wondered why their responses were slow in coming. After some time we found this changed and they told us they initially had had a hard time with our accents! One day they recommended that we join a country club, which they had just signed up with, behind Lake Elsinore in the desert. I believe it was where one now finds the city of Temecula. It was supposed to be for golf, tennis and swimming, and it offered overnight accommodations. A fast-talking salesman showed us some pictures, and, like fools, we joined the club sight unseen. One weekend, we all got into the fabulous Lincoln and drove toward the desert on IS 10 East and then South where IS 15 is now located, in the general direction of Lake Elsinore-Escondido. Our arrival after that long drive through nowhere was disappointing. Greeted by a majestic entrance with club name and not much else, we later found a little pool behind a hillock slightly larger than a bathtub, with knee-deep water and countless swimmers trying to get a cooling dip. If they had all sat down at once, the pool would have overflowed. Rather than joining the swimming party, we looked at the few available cabins, which were also disappointing. There was nothing green. It seemed like al lot of people like us had been shown an image of a desert nirvana.

It was a hoax; the money was gone. The four of us never talked about this again. We discontinued paying any additional billings; a lesson learned. When it comes to money, one can't be careful enough. It's so easy to spend, but very difficult to earn, keep together and make grow. On Thanksgiving '58, Bonnie invited us and the landlady Bessie to the Thanksgiving turkey feast! We had offered to bring the pumpkin pie, which Anna painstakingly made, using her new Betty Crocker Cookbook and her Sunbeam mixer. But when we arrived, there was Bonnie's pumpkin pie on top of the refrigerator! She may not have trusted Anna to make such an American icon.

Later, Bonnie and Hal asked us for help with Bernie, a teenager, who had started living with them. He wanted to learn German. Relatives of the Hornback's neighbors had adopted him as a baby. Those relatives lived in Oregon, but later had children of their own, and Bernie sort of became superfluous. As a small child, he had been incessantly pointing to his cap, and these adoptive parents opened it and found the address of Bernie's birth mother, who lived in Essen, Germany. He had started taking German in High School and started a correspondence. Anna was asked to help with this project and coach him in German, since he had become obsessed with going to Germany to live with his mother. To feed these emotions, the mother had told him that she was dying of cancer; he absolutely must come to live with her again. Bernie had a devil of a time adapting to the learning process and specifically to this language, which is fairly intricate and more demanding than English. Since he had little concept of even the English grammar, it was a fairly hopeless task, but Anna did her best. This episode drew us closer to the Hornback's. In 1962 Anna made contact with Bernie's birth mother in Essen as well as, confidentially, with the Lutheran minister in town, who told her that Bernie's mother was not dying of cancer, but suffered from a bad conscience about having giving up Bernie and his sister for adoption to America. Where the sister ended up no one knew, and Bernie often wondered about her. Both were illegitimate children by an American G.I. When, with two small children, his mother had met a German man, he forced her to give up the children as a condition for marrying her. Meanwhile, Bernie thought living in Germany again with his mother would solve all of his problems. During one of her German trips, Anna went to Essen and found the family living in miserable circumstances. The mother cried a lot, the brutal-looking husband who joined them as Anna was leaving, worked at a brewery. He was not at all pleased about the visit and about the American son. They had two children of their own; the boy was high school age and had his own, very small room with hardly any space for an extra bed. He said that Bernie could share his room. The younger girl, who did not seem in good health, slept on a garden lounge in the parents' bedroom. Conditions were depressing. Anna told the mother that Hal and Bonnie Hornback, a very good American childless couple, had taken Bernie under their wings, and that, not knowing much German, he should better finish high school in America. Bernie's plans to join the Army later would likely give him a chance to meet his mother in the future. She seemed very relieved, and Bernie, when learning of the circumstances in a tactful way, agreed to postpone his dream. He later visited us one more time when he was already in the Army—his mother was still alive, and they probably did have a reunion of some kind. Bonnie and Hal later moved back to Missouri, but she, alone, came to visit us once, saying she was planning to live in L.A. again; her husband had stayed behind. There was no more contact with them afterwards, which made us sad. Nice people; they had been good to us.

In 1959 Gisela appeared. She had the German "Abitur" and secretarial training to boot. We had a lot to talk about, particularly Mercedes-Benz and mutual acquaintances. She moved into our guest room and quickly found a job with Pacific Mutual Life Insurance Company and an apartment. She often talked about her unhappy love affair, and how it was good for her to find new directions. We imagined that she would now polish her English and the needed secretarial skills to establish a career. We could not guess her real thoughts. After all, she was a Sybrass and a Mahle from her mother's side—wealthy German industrialists connected with the auto industry. Mahle's dominated the piston fabrication for engines. They were old suppliers of Daimler Benz and other quality manufacturers—one of the reasons why her family was renting that stately mansion on Avenida Brooklin Paulista in Sao Paulo until their own fancy construction project would be completed. However, when it was time to serve guests some snacks, she inadvertently told us during a chat that they carefully distinguished between different categories of guests, i.e. "important" (cashew nuts) and "unimportant" guests (peanuts), and we remembered that we had been served peanuts! We began to understand where Gisela was coming from and where she might want to go. Human values or interests must yield to connections ... no matter what! Much later, one Saturday, when I was writing at the kitchen table, she walked up to me in very tight, skimpy shorts ... almost bikini-type, placing herself in front of me, about 6 inches from my face. She had unusually long legs and was very well built and athletic. With her lower trunk almost touching my face, she started a conversation. This irritated me, and I covered up my distaste by making a stone face. No one had ever tried this kind of a come-on trick on me. I pretended not to notice, which made everything normal and natural. But I had learned to be very careful with her—a manipulator of the worst kind, I thought. I didn't tell Anna about this for a long time, so there would be no clash developing. Anna is so different—she would never lower herself to such a thing—in the house of a good, helpful friend. A decent, honest person, she would not do harm to anyone. I was a lucky guy! Gisela never tried anything again and soon reached out for connections. One weekend she asked me to drive her to Beverly Hills to the home of the Daimler-Benz representative for that area—not a salesman, but someone who guarded DB-interests in that important marketplace. Waiting in front of the door, I was never asked in. But then—I drove a 7-year-old Chevy in Mercedes country! I found it amusing to be dealt with in this infuriating manner, but Gisela thought I would not even notice the insult.

After we moved into the Alhambra apartment, we had Celia and Dave, our landlord and landlady from Sanborn Ave., over one day for a barbeque. We had a very good time and were proud about being able to show our progress. We served a simple meal with several hamburgers in the backyard. Asked by Celia why there were so many burgers on the grill, we said that, if any would be left over, we'd eat them the next day. Celia then turned to Dave, instructing him not to eat so many burgers, as Anna wanted the leftovers for another day! Those were thrifty times, and Celia may have remembered the depression. All of us laughed. They were wonderful people who had always been like an aunt and uncle to us.

Our early days in Southern California also brought a request from Marianne Ehling, who had married a man named Rosenthal, to sponsor the couple for a permanent visa. She enclosed their application documents, asking us to complete them, since "they didn't know English." We were astonished, knowing that one can only do babysitting or domestic or yard work in the U.S. without knowing English. As a hairdresser, she would also have to prepare for, and pass, tests for a U.S. license. We told them this and imagined they would not want to start that way. Returning the forms, we advised them they should know enough English to complete these on their own before they could even think about coming to the U.S. Once they could prove the needed amount of English, we would try to help in any way possible. We received no response. Soon afterwards Marianne divorced to never marry again. Her husband, who worked for her father, was known to be a lazy, irresponsible womanizer, who expected to be supported and wouldn't even cross the street to buy groceries, not wanting to be seen with a bag in his hands. We were surprised when, 50 years later, Marianne brought up what they had construed as our unwillingness to bring the couple to the U.S. Like good friends do, we quickly cleared up these grudges together.

After Anna's mother, Thilde, came, she expressed an interest in finding out what the chances might be for Charlie, Anna's brother, and his wife Trautl, to immigrate to the U.S. After researching this question, we concluded that, unless one is in a technical position, chances would not have been be as good as they were for him in Germany, where he had a good job and could look forward to an administrative career in Mobiloil's Hamburg organization. We decided that skills, which pay decently here, are those of plumbers, electricians, toolmakers, engineers, etc., unless you are some kind of a "star." Besides, his wife spoke no English and would have been in the same boat as Marianne. It would have taken her a long time to work her way up to a secretarial position, if ever, a profession in which she excelled in Germany. After we discouraged them, both became increasingly successful at home as Germany's economic miracle and their own professional maturity continued to unfold.

All this happened around 1959, when I was in transition between Sparling Meter and ITE Circuit Breaker Co. Around that time we met Ali Allwelt, another Berliner, through a mutual acquaintance in Brazil. The Allwelt's lived close to downtown L.A., on the East side, in a very simple home, with a business in the garage. He was a very inventive artisan and worked in stained glass and also, to a lesser extent, in artistic mosaics, making and repairing stained glass windows and mosaics in churches and exclusive residences. His first wife had met her fate tragically during the last days of Berlin due to cruelties of the Russian invasion in WWII. He then remarried and immigrated to the USA. He offered to make a stained glass window as a gift for our house on Ardendale Avenue in San Gabriel, which became a permanent feature in our various homes and now adorns our son's home in Gardiner, N.Y.

WELCOMING ANNA'S MOTHER

In 1958–59 my light gray suit came in handy for greeting Tilde in Long Beach on her first trip to the USA. I would have never wanted to miss the excitement and expectations before her departure and arrival. She applied for, and received, a green card as an immigrant and planned to stay here for an extended period. It was Anna's great joy to host her mom and introduce me to her. Travel at the time of our marriage had been so expensive and difficult that such a visit would have been unrealistic—neither did we have appropriate accommodations for such a visit. Now we had a comfortably furnished guest room, so that she could be our honored guest. Anna loved and respected her mother in the best sense. Mathilde (later to become "Hilde") came by freighter from Hamburg to Long Beach, since she wanted to bring many things for our household, such as her beautiful silver-ware and the tablecloths and china she had bought for us. The German freighter went through the Panama Canal and then up the West Coast to the Long Beach harbor. We had greatly encouraged her to travel this way, as we had found our travel on the freighter memorable. Marine life in the Pacific north of Panama is varied and abundant. Even whales can be seen at certain seasons around or North of Baja California. So, on that special evening Anna and I drove in our blue 52 Chevy (all polished for the occasion) to the designated pier in Long Beach, to meet the German freighter. After completing her business with the INS and customs service, Hilde soon appeared and fell into Anna's arms—a wonderful occasion after so many years! I still wonder why I didn't bring a bottle of champagne for the celebration. Hilde seemed a pleasant person to me and I thought it would be simply great that we were now three. Stories were then exchanged, mostly about the very eventful sea voyage, during which she had been the only woman and passenger until Panama, when an American couple joined her. They immediately complained about the German toilet paper, which was far from soft and smooth like the American product, but almost resembled a piece of parcel wrapping paper. The Germans then had no standard of comparison, since the product they had used for the past 20 years (*newsprint*) was still on their minds. While crossing the Atlantic, Hilde was treated like a princess; nightly the captain would join the dinner table, where the finest food imaginable was served in limitless quantities, (something she had missed since the early thirties, not to mention the war years). Other specialties created for her included a small swimming pool, shielded from the crew's eyes while she was using it. In Panama the American pilot who was stationed in the harbor came aboard to guide the freighter through the Canal. After many lively conversations (her trademark) with this gentleman, he was smitten. Probably never having met such an interesting European woman, he did what seemed most appropriate to him—he proposed to her after having clued in the captain, who was authorized to execute civil ceremonies such as birth, marriage, death, etc. But Hilde said no. She had to see her daughter. Besides, she didn't want to spend the rest of her life drinking Gin Tonic in muggy Panama. Her tales continued during the evenings ahead. She took over some of the housekeeping, cooked our favorite foods and soon started taking the bus to downtown L.A. on weekdays to have lunch with Anna at the bus terminal where Dun & Bradstreet was located, and then visit the large department stores and such downtown attractions as Angel's Flight, Chinatown and Olvera Street. Things were so different from Neumuenster, and she marveled at our good life. We got along well, and with extra time on the weekends, we drove around Southern California with her, often visiting the beaches south of L.A., including Huntington Beach or Corona Del Mar, which were closer than Santa Monica. We would arrive there around 10 a.m. on Sundays, take a dip in the ocean and have a picnic. When the big crowd arrived in the afternoons we were ready to leave. We visited Big Bear, all the parks, the desert, Disneyland, Knott's Berry Farm and whatever was to be seen. With her excellent English, Hilde became a big hit with all of our friends: the Buchanans, Dick and Doris Huth, Bonnie and Hal and others. She was always included in their invitations.

Half a year passed quickly. During this time, Hilde started to look for opportunities to become independent, i.e. a job and her own apartment. She placed an ad in the paper and soon learned she should not have worded it "European Lady." It yielded some strange calls for "Swedish Massage." Hilde was shocked! Her next ad indicated more of her medical background and brought an offer from the San Marino lodge, a reputable nursing home reachable by bus, where she could only work as a practical nurse, but a nice apartment with balcony in the park-like setting was included. How could she resist? It was not far from us. We usually provided transportation when she wanted to visit, or we would visit her. She remained there for several months, but considered it only a steppingstone, which would lead to something better. Meanwhile, she worked hard in this demanding and sometimes thankless job. As a keen observer she noticed that the patients would be especially well-combed and made to look spiffy before an inspection. That means the insiders knew when the inspection was to happen! She took the job more seriously than her colleagues. At the famous coffee breaks, she would jump up and go to the patients who were ringing. The others stayed at the table and chided her: "Hilde, you are spoiling the patients!" She often commented how sad it was that the patients never left, except to die. Brigadier General Lange was one exception. He and his wife grew very fond of her and wanted to fix her up with their son "Hugh." Gen. Lange spent some time there after an illness, since his wife was not strong enough to take care of him. An extrovert with the demeanor of a West Point gentleman, he was very interesting, if you knew how to listen. Hilde would soon move to the Mt. Sinai Hospital in Hollywood as a Licensed Vocational Nurse and was then promoted to floor secretary on the celebrity floor, where she met such luminaries as Ella Fitzgerald, Patty Duke, Jennifer Jones, Sammy Davis, Jr. and Jerry Lewis, who, noting her badge in the elevator, would address her in his unique tone of voice: "Hello, Mrs. Wagner!" A small, but important task for her was to announce via the intercom that visiting times were over and then visit the celebrities' rooms to see if their visitors had, indeed, left. We were very fortunate that Hilde was in the USA when Anna later would undergo her operation for an ectopic pregnancy. Hilde took off from work at the San Marino Lodge and cared wonderfully for her daughter. After her first eventful year in the USA, Hilde returned to Germany so that her widow's pension and health insurance would continue. If she had stayed longer, she would have lost this considerable security for the rest of her life. Where could she earn such pension rights here? She was then 46 years old and not in the best of health, since she had suffered from heart problems since her late 20's. Her decision to leave was therefore prudent. Also, there was Charlie, her son, and his family in Wedel. She loved them dearly and enjoyed her little grandson, Frankie. But she adored California and might have stayed, had she had the same security as in Germany. Her personality was ideally suited to Southern California, where she blended perfectly into the crowd at Hollywood's famous Farmers' Market or the art galleries along La Cienega where she could observe celebrities of the same caliber as the patients on her special floor at Mt. Sinai. We spent some grand times with her in that area and also attended performances at the Hollywood Bowl and the Greek Theatre. Such memorable experiences!! Fancy crowd, clear sky covered with stars, balmy breezes from the ocean, exquisite performances. We felt like we were belonging. And we could not help marveling at the situation in which we found ourselves, compared to Brazil or the miserable years in Germany. We felt we had done the right thing, and being together with Hilde contributed immensely to this. Hilde left by rail to NY and then by ship to Hamburg. She had met some nice Americans through us, the Huth's, Buchanan's, Allwelt's, Bonnie and Hal, and Anna's colleagues Evvy Goyette, Ed Drum, Jim Lowe and Erma French. More importantly, she had enjoyed dating some nice American men, many of whom had hoped she would become a permanent part of their lives, but she never got around to making such a far-reaching decision.

HERMANN'S EMPLOYMENT CHANGE/ WORRIES ABOUT ANNA

At the end of two years at Sparling, where I had made some good contributions, I began to realize that I could not expect much of a future at this family-owned company, which was restricted to measuring flow of liquids, mainly water for irrigation and city distribution. I noticed that my salary was quite low (Anna had started out with $250/month and I with $500, typical beginners' salaries for our situation) and had not improved much in those two years. Therefore, I scouted the L.A. Times each Sunday for a suitable position in a larger company in a field, which would offer more development and success by using my engineering knowledge. I realized that I needed to obtain a good footing in an industry that could offer me more of a future than Sparling, which had been a good starting point for learning how things are done here and how people behave. I had found that generally they are very individualistic, not usually nosy and try to mind their own business, but they are always ready to generously give a hand if necessary.

During that time, it also became apparent that there was something wrong with Anna. She had to see a gynecologist. Dr. Horner in San Marino was recommended by a lady gynecologist, who was not taking new patients (Anna had tried to insist on a female doctor). During her first examination, Dr. H. discovered high blood pressure, but said during their first visit with HIM, this was not unusual for a young, female patient, and, as Anna became comfortable with him, the blood pressure was fine. He revealed to both of us that Anna was undergoing an ectopic pregnancy, which is a seriously abnormal pregnancy. The female egg is fertilized while descending into the fallopian tube and stops moving into the womb. It expands the tube gradually, causing bleeding and severe pain. It must be removed surgically. Dr. Horner explained that this diagnosis is difficult, since other conditions can cause similar symptoms. Therefore, he said we needed to wait until the pain and bleeding became even more pronounced. At that point, we would have to rush to the Huntington Memorial Hospital in Pasadena for the surgery. Meanwhile, he would examine A. periodically. Before this happened, A. had started working at Pacific Mutual Life Insurance Company after the colleagues at Dun & Bradstreet had given her a wonderful Good-bye. They understood her reasons: better pay and an air-conditioned office. Mr. Lowe's boss offered her the position of being his own secretary, but the temptation to move was bigger. At Pacific Mutual she started as steno-secretary to the Group Pension Attorney and was soon promoted to secretary to the Group Pension Sales Director, with less work but more money!

A little earlier we had started to investigate how to buy a house, which we considered a good investment. Imagine—in two years we had saved enough for a down payment. Unthinkable in Germany! In those years one needed only two to three thousand dollars to move into something for beginners. This sounds ridiculous now, but three bedroom houses then cost around $20,000. Once we found ourselves in big trouble after making an offer on a house in Arcadia, which we liked. We believed the realtor's claim that since so many people had shown serious interest, we should not wait to make an offer. Naively, we offered the full asking price! We had no idea that our signature was legally binding. To us "the offer" seemed just an insignificant piece of paper. Shortly thereafter Oma advised us that my father had suffered a stroke and was in the hospital. He had never consulted a doctor for his constant high blood pressure. What now? We felt our money might be needed for special treatment or a nursing home, which the insurance would not cover. When told about this, the realtor seemed understanding and promised to cancel the sale. Unfamiliar with the procedure, we believed him. Months later the owner called Anna at work about our going to the bank for the closing. We were shocked: the realtor had done nothing, hoping to still get his commission. The owner, kept in the dark, could have forced us to buy, but she graciously let us off the hook. The down-payment of $100 was gone, and we had learned another lesson.

On July 10, 1959, my father passed away. Today, over 50 years later, after my mother told me that he had shed tears after my departure, saying he'd never see me again, I regret terribly that I had not invited him to visit us earlier. How he would have liked the climate and all the sights in our new land. This happened around the time Anna had the ectopic pregnancy. Mostly for this reason I did not even attend the funeral—it all happened too fast. I still sometimes feel guilty about this, but my mother had discouraged me as well, wanting to help protect our fragile fortunes.

Anna was awaiting her time to go to the hospital, as her condition made her suffer quite a bit. Just around the beginning of fall, it happened. At that time of year Pasadena usually fell into extreme dryness, with Santa Ana winds from the desert in the East and occasional firestorms in the mountains, where much land is covered with brush and the extreme drought causes severe dryness. Any carelessly discarded match or cigarette butt can light the bone-dry brush. From March on it usually does not rain in Los Angeles. By now Anna's pain had become so excruciating that we were told to go to the hospital right away. Unable to sit, she was moaning all the way, which disturbed me greatly. She was quickly wheeled into surgery, leaving me with my apprehensions. Out of a window facing north I noticed a large fire north of Pasadena in the mountains behind La Canada. Clouds of smoke made me feel depressed. After two hours Anna returned, and Dr. Horner was satisfied with the results. He had removed one tube and ovary and the appendix, leaving a chance to have children in the future, but at that moment my main preoccupation was to see Anna healthy again. My wonderful bouquet of red roses awaited her in her room and made her very happy, despite the stress of the surgery. I stayed until she became very tired. On the next day, I learned a most upsetting story. On intravenous feeding and still quite weak, she had been told to ring for the nurse if she had to go to the bathroom. After going to sleep in a daze, she awoke in the middle of the night, and, as the fog cleared, she was horrified to notice another live human being in her bed. As her thought process started to gear up, she poked the person … nothing. After some repeats, she heard a grunt, seemingly of a male. A man was in her bed, and she could feel his hairy arms! She told the guy … "hey, this is my bed, you must leave!" He said "no, this is my bed, beat it!" They started to argue until she saw the silhouette of the red roses in the dark. It was indeed her bed. Unable to reach for the buzzer, she asked her roommate, Mrs. Rose, to call the nurse. Meanwhile, she had gotten out of bed and slumped down in a chair. The nurse rushed in—the involuntary neighbor had been a Zuni Indian firefighter with a head injury, who had wandered into the wrong room and bed during the night. He later asked the nurse to convey his apologies to Anna. Besides the excitement and shock, the only other complication was that Mrs. Rose made Anna laugh when telling the story to all her friends over the phone, and this hurt her where the stitches were. The story spread like wildfire through town. Much later, Anna's hairdresser told her about this lady at the hospital and the Indian. "Yeah," Anna said, "that was me!" Malpractice suits then were not so fashionable, so the doctor got a big kick out of it as well! A few days later Anna was home. Hilde had taken several weeks off from her job and took wonderful care of her. Together they wore out our big Muntz TV completely, making room for a smaller, more sensible model.

A NEW OPPORTUNITY AT ITE CIRCUIT BREAKER CORP.

A few days later a L.A. downtown company, ITE Circuit Breaker, on N. Main Street, had responded to my application for employment. The Mfg. Engineering Manager interviewed me and showed me around. They designed and manufactured power circuit breakers, 14.4KV to 230KV, covering the entire range of breakers. They built only oil breakers. This meant that there were large tanks of steel filled with oil and, within, there were the interrupters, designed to interrupt a high voltage circuit at full load in case of overload for various reasons. One of these was a short circuit caused by ground fault (broken voltage line wire or a faulty transformer which shorted, etc.). The interrupters were linked to an activating mechanism. The small ones were spring motor based and the larger ones driven by pneumatic power. They then had a pressure vessel for the air and an electric motor driven air compressor. Designed for maximum possible reliability, these breakers were installed in the most diverse climates from desert to arctic. They were always sitting there, not working, but in case of a short, they had to work without fail—a difficult parameter to satisfy. ITE made all components, except for such things as electric motors or pneumatic valves. In their own high voltage test lab, mainly insulation properties of the equipment were tested. Short circuit and similar tests were performed at commercial test labs with such large equipment as short circuit generators (usually KEMA in Arnhem, Holland). Also these tests were on Sundays at Southern California Edison or the L.A. Dept. of Water and Power substations, usually for acceptance of a large amount of breakers, not for basic product research. ITE, based in Philadelphia, had recently purchased Kelman Mfg. Corp., which offered a line of outdated breakers. This became apparent when the federal government broke up the cozy arrangement that had existed among the electrical manufacturers since time beginning—not to infringe upon each other's territories, resulting in high prices and large profits for the suppliers. In this newly competitive climate, Kelman could no longer sell its old clunkers. ITE hired Earl Reitz from GE and other GE engineers from Canada, to modernize the entire equipment line and control equipment. They were interested in me, and I saw a much brighter future ahead compared to Sparling.

When asked about salary expectations, I said a 10% increase over my current salary of $550 per month would be nice, but the interviewer replied with a straight face that they could not comply, leaving me terribly disappointed! He continued that he would put me at the bottom of the salary range for this position, which would be $750! Would this be acceptable? That almost 50% raise was a tremendous breakthrough into the realm of the real US engineers! I left the place in a jubilant mood, wondering how to celebrate this huge step forward together with Anna's recuperation. I entered our LaFrance apartment with two bottles of champagne to commemorate this very happy episode in our journey. Content, feeling we could trust in the new country and ourselves, we agreed that what had been planned as "taking a peek" at the US was beginning to turn into our becoming permanent US-residents.

Fairly soon, Anna returned to work at Pacific Mutual. The secretarial position there had involved a nice salary increase, because she had learned much at Dun & Bradstreet about how business is done in the US. She had studied on her own how to adapt her German shorthand to the English language and then offered to take dictation from her supervisor, Mr. Lowe. She had also often volunteered to transcribe the reporters' Dictaphone tapes, rather than taking them to the typing pool, to gain the necessary practice. Among other business subjects and language courses, she had acquired total proficiency in secretarial skills at the Hoehere Handelsschule (business college) in Kiel before going to Brazil—a very valuable background there Aside from being Director Haug's secretary and interpreter at Mercedes-Benz, she had worked for many of the other directors there in three languages. All this at 20 years of age!

When I turned in my notice at Sparling, they did not try to keep me, realizing they could not match my new salary. I was touched when, on my last day, colleagues gave me two LP records with Parisian and Italian tunes, which are still in my family's possession. I closed the door behind me with some apprehension: Could I do the new job successfully? I had worked one year at Siemens in Berlin in the field of circuit breakers, but the basic concepts were then much different. However, ITE seemed to be after my experience in how to get things done. My commute now took me down Huntington Drive to North Main Street. Anna usually commuted to downtown from Huntington Drive until she stopped working in 1961 to be a full time mother.

At ITE I found good people in the Engineering Department, of which three stand out: Bill Knackstedt, Jim McCloud, and Heinz von Gehlen. Bill was a draftsman, hired shortly after me, Jim was our crack designer for laying out the interrupters, lifting mechanism and tanks, and Heinz was one of the people who reviewed electrical utilities requirements and designed the electrical circuits to accommodate their specific needs. Bill would stay with the company through the years, until it was sold to ASEA Brown Bovery (ABB), to retire in Greensburg, Pa., where he still lives. When we visited him and Shirley once en route to Indianapolis, he showed me their current equipment—a far cry from what we did in the early sixties—enormously improved design and also manufacturing facility. ASEA standardized their equipment world wide, demonstrating today's trend toward globalization. While I did not have much personal contact with Jim, we became close to Bill and Heinz and their families. We also became friends with Murielle Rose, Earl Reitz' secretary. A single mom, she doted on her son, Randy. These friendships lasted through many years. Heinz was from Germany, while Bill was third generation German and had little of that left, except his name. Heinz and wife Bruni, from the Stuttgart area, who owned a house in Burbank, were recent arrivals from Australia, where they had gone to get away from postwar Germany. But, not feeling quite comfortable there, they decided to try the USA ... like we had, with Bruni going first with her friend Ulla, to work as nannies in order to learn the ropes. Their English was a rare mixture of Swabian and Australian accents. The Engineering Dept. Head was Earl Reitz, originally from Philadelphia, who had worked for many years at GE in Power Circuit Breakers, had retired there and picked up this challenge at ITE. Generally, he had everything redesigned along principles he had developed and/or learned at GE. When completed, the equipment line was almost undistinguishable from GE's. I don't think he had brought or copied GE drawings; that would have been illegal. As ITE later moved into new technologies, their approaches came to differ completely from GE's. ITE decided to move into SF6 breakers, equipment which would use sulfa hexa fluoride (SF6) as insulation enhancer and arc blowout, while GE developed a line of compressed air breakers.

My job became apparent while working alongside those involved in the design process. It had to be decided how the different parts or assemblies were to be made, e.g., where there was a critical lever, which converted the horizontal movement of the interrupter mechanism into the vertical. I studied how to make it most cost-effectively, considering stresses involved, quantities to be made, metallurgical considerations, and cost. The question was whether to use fabricated steel, cast iron, forged steel, perlitic iron, etc. With a string of problems invariably involved, I soon became more than busy. It came to my having to take the lead on entire developments, when Jim McCloud could not do it, as he became overburdened with other tasks. He was dreaming up and laying out ever more refined interrupter modules, which were subject to endless and thorough design testing. Sometimes what he did worked on one mode of fault, only to fail on another. Then guys with a masters' degree in EE stepped in: Roy Lindberg and/or Harvey McKeough, who tried to analyze endless yards of cathode ray printouts to understand the interaction of current, voltage, arc development and interrupter design configurations. After Earl Reitz retired, Roy became Engineering Manager. McKeough would surface in Boston years later, after we returned from Germany. At ITE I quickly became part of the group and contributed more and more to the performance. The work was gratifying. I could work myself into a substantial niche of the power industry. This gave us more security and we would soon begin talking about having a family.

THE CANADIAN CONNECTION

One day we received a phone call from the Schoenits, who lived at the time in Ocean Falls, BC, North of Vancouver, a small hamlet glued to the steep slopes of an ocean inlet. Bert then worked at the Weyerhaeuser paper mill. It was a company town, where many immigrants, including Germans, were employed. For recreation, and to help with the family budget (by now they had three daughters), he hunted in the woods for deer, moose, elk, and whatever appeared before his rifle. They said they had too much salmon; it seemed one could walk across the inlet on their backs. Did we know how they could ship some to us? We did not, but loved hearing from them again. They had returned to Germany from Brazil around the time we left for the US, but found that they could no longer identify with life there. They tried to live in Vancouver first, but a job as a pastry cook was very difficult to find, and they had survived their hard beginnings, while their first daughter was about to be born, by making liquor filled chocolates in their basement apartment. Those were illegal then, but in great demand by the immigrant connoisseurs who would come for them during the night. Then they moved north. To backtrack a little, we had visited them in Vancouver during our very first vacation, so that Anna could be the Godmother of newborn baby Marianne. That trip took place in our beloved, seemingly indestructible, blue Chevy 52 four-door sedan, which would serve us well for many years until we moved to Palo Alto in 1966. I did the maintenance from oil to tire change, cleaning, waxing and occasional repairs myself. I even resolved some serious troubles, with help and suggestions from neighbors and friends. One day it didn't start, despite the electricals being ok, the spark plugs being clean, the battery working, and the starter moving the engine. After endless finagling, I found that the float was punctured and the carburetor full of gas. After replacing it with a reconditioned one, it worked … But after about a week I got stranded again in the middle of nowhere, restarting the endless process until I found that the substitute also had a miniscule puncture. It took the gas one week to penetrate sufficiently to let the float sink again. The next substitute finally did it.

During the 1959 Vancouver trip we wanted to camp in places we had found on the map. We bought a pup tent for two (we thought), a Coleman gas camping stove, and for what we thought would be romantic sleepovers, one sleeping bag for both of us. Then we cruised north on interstate 5 toward Sacramento and Redding, reaching the Shasta Mountains near the California-Oregon border in one day. The drive impressed us greatly—the endless grape, fruit and veggie patches gave us an idea of the grand scale in which everything is done in the USA. We rolled for hundreds of miles without stopping and without signs of congestion. The land seemed busy and pristine, and we felt we were becoming a part of it. High up near Mt. Shasta we found a modest, free campground in the midst of large Douglas firs. There were no attendants; each camper just picked a spot near a picnic table for dinner—a new experience for us. I had camped often as a scout or in the last days of WWII, but we would sleep wherever we found ourselves at night or would look for a more comfortable barn with straw or hay. Now, 14 years later, I was used to the best in mattress development, and I had ignored my muscle tone in favor of our progress and of getting settled. So, mimicking what the few others were doing, we set up the tent quickly and threw in the sleeping bag. Then we wanted to heat something on the camp stove, which I had not tried before. I could not get it to work: another lesson learned. Get prepared for anything you do! We spooned down our canned soup and veggies without heating them—disappointed, since it was getting cold. Crawling into our sleeping bag as it got dark, we just about both fit in, but it was not as romantic as in the Gary Cooper/Ingrid Bergman movie from which we had gotten the idea. After trying to fall asleep for a while, I noticed that I had bones. We could only close the zipper lying on our sides, which put all body pressure on our hipbones. Without padding, the ground underneath was hard and getting colder by the minute. Soon we started to shiver. Sometimes I'd tell Anna to move over; sometimes she told me. Becoming claustrophobic, she even tried to sleep outside the tent. Around 4 am we were fed up, threw everything into the car, and I started driving. I had trouble shifting, even though the shift was on the steering column, because of rheumatism in my right wrist, which stayed with me until we reached Vancouver, but abated as the temperature increased. Rather than trying camping again, we would stop at small motels from then on or just drive through the night, as we did on our way back to L.A. After driving all day from Oregon, we arrived in Oakland on a Saturday. I thought we should take a nap near Berkeley. In the hills we found a park, but its grassy greens were very steep. Trying to sleep, we found ourselves sliding down the hillside—a strange feeling. Without that badly needed rest, I got on the freeway and drove all night via Highway 5 to Tehachepee pass and home. Anna kept me coherent by talking and singing, but I caught myself dozing off occasionally. It was irresponsible, but miraculously we made it unscathed.

BABY BILL ON THE WAY: THOUGHTS ABOUT OUR OWN HOME

Meanwhile, things around us were in constant flux. We began feeling more and more secure. We had noticed that many people our age in similar circumstances were "kings" in their own homes, enjoying privacy and not having to listen to landlords' or landladies' demands, as was the case on LaFrance Ave. The 4-unit building there transmitted any noise one made, providing no insulation against the heat, either. Anna, by now six months pregnant with Bill, had so much trouble sleeping, with the rhythmic, squeaking noises, which came from the upstairs bedroom, sometimes accompanied by shrieks and giggles, that she begged me to do something. A Mormon couple lived there; he was finishing his M.D. I tried to calm Anna down, which did not help, and her particular state did not help, either. I finally picked up the broom and banged it against the ceiling, just at the spot from where the squeaking came. A deadly silence ensued. Relieved, Anna fell asleep quickly. From then on, these neighbors never looked at us again. My actions must have been un-American. Rather, they were all German, prompted by an anxious mother-to-be. We later wanted to make the landlady aware of the noise, but she simply revealed that, when we had lived on top of her own apartment, she had heard similar noises. She must have wanted to teach us that our complaint via broomstick had violated Southern California apartment etiquette. Bemused, we wondered about the veracity of her counter-allegations for a long time.

This incident aided our determination to look for a house of our own. In late 1960, we spent weekends looking at homes in our price range of $20 $25 grand, with a down payment of $2,500, which we could easily afford. We had also learned about closing costs, insurance and other accompanying expenses and knew we would need more furniture. We also considered that our life would change with the birth of our first child, without discussing this in great detail. Both of us looked forward to Anna's stopping her work at Pacific Mutual Life Insurance to become a full-time mom. We felt that children belong in the life of most married couples. Once they were there, we would make any required or desired changes. We began attending a Lutheran church in San Gabriel and observed many happy, contented families. But we were by no means fanatics—if children would come, wonderful and if not, fine also. Not to have children would not have broken my heart, but Anna, I believe, had greater expectations. She would be the one in the future to give her never-ending dedication and love to them. As a mother, she would move everything to raise them right and try to show them the way. Both of us relaxed and looked forward to the great event, since we had found confidence in each other, which made our relationship easy and delightful. Since any talk of returning to Germany was in the past by now and we no longer even discussed this possibility, it was the right moment to start a family. Rather than "taking a look at the US," we now wanted to be part of this complex society with all its advantages and drawbacks. We thought life here, in the long run, would bring more happiness, satisfaction, challenges and opportunity than a return to Germany. Brazil seemed light years away. Its memories, and those of the miserable German war and post-war years, rapidly faded, although any time we would meet with German compatriots, these things would always be a special point of discussion. Our immediate daily experiences became more important than the past, which was good for us.

We looked at several nice homes between San Marino and Arcadia. Dick Huth and Monte Buchanan lived South of San Gabriel, along I 10 (to San Bernardino and Pomona). Martha Buchanan's parents had a stately home in Pasadena. The neighborhoods of Dick and Monte lacked nice facilities like parks and were not as neatly appointed as San Marino, Pasadena, and Arcadia, but those three were pricey. Buying a house should still enable us to keep some money in the bank for emergencies, since we know this country can be very unforgiving in certain cases. You cannot stick your neck out too far. Taking out life insurance again cost money and would drain our resources. So, we concentrated on nearby San Gabriel, a small community between San Marino and Arcadia—a lovely country setting, but without sidewalks like S.M. The house we selected was on an attractive street, Ardendale Ave., lined with huge Palm trees, and sat in the midst of a dozen orange trees. It had two bedrooms, 2 baths, and a living room facing the street and a "den" with a door facing the backyard. Another door led from the kitchen to the backyard from a service area. The nice, airy kitchen was not very big, but offered space for a kitchenette set for daily meals for four. The living room had wonderful picture window and a formal dining area, and there was a detached one-car garage in the back. The large orange trees emanating from a former orange grove promised a considerable crop around December, (the oranges bloom in January, but take a whole year to ripen), and there were two peach trees on the side of the house opposite the garage side. Until Los Angeles' eastward expansion and later toward San Bernardino and beyond, this area had been an orange grove, and there were also still many Avocado trees ... you could find avocados on the ground in our quiet street, ready to eat! The most attractive spot in our new neighborhood was the San Gabriel Mission; part of the long chain of missions the Spaniards had developed as they advanced northward from Mexico City into California up to San Francisco, including L.A., Santa Barbara, San Luis Obispo, San Juan Capistrano and San Diego. The San Gabriel Mission's buildings were all still standing. Close by was the famous El Poche Restaurant, a Mexican eatery we loved, designed in the Spanish-Mexican style, with a large atrium where strolling Mexican musicians sang and played their folk music.

We were thrilled at the prospect at settling down here for many years. Our offer was accepted and the loan approved in the summer of 1960—around the time when Elvis acquired his enormous fame. We had heard him already in Brazil, but here he was the absolute craze, with which I couldn't identify. Anna liked to hear him on the radio, but our main preference would always be classical music. Five minutes away by car was the bucolic San Marino Park. There was much green overall, with properties featuring all sorts of beautiful landscaping, especially palm trees, California Live Oak and other trees that could survive the long dry spell between April and November, as well as abundant shrubs like camellias, azaleas, gardenias, and whatever else grows in a semi-arid environment. Bougainvilleas could also be seen, and many owners tended roses of the most fancy varieties. The San Marino Park had large Douglas firs, palms and expansive lawns to stretch out or play. Up the hill toward Pasadena was the park-like Huntington Library, where we would walk on many afternoons in the extensive cacti collection or look at the classic paintings—especially Gainsborough. The Arcadia Arboretum, site of the old Tarzan movies after the industry moved from Ithaca to Hollywood, was more exotic, with a large pond and lots of fowl, including beautiful peacocks. These places, as well as the nice Arcadia shopping center, could be reached in a few minutes.

Meanwhile, at Pacific Mutual Life Insurance Co., in downtown LA, Anna had been promoted from steno secretary to the Group Pension Attorney, who later became attorney general for the state of California, to executive secretary to one of the Group Pension Directors, who traveled a lot to see big corporate customers and union bosses, leaving her with little to do. Others in her league just took it easy and knitted, hands under their desks, looking pretty, but, feeling threatened, she went to the Personnel Dept. while her boss was away, asking for suggestions as to what other assignments she could be exploring while in this well-paying job. Her boss, the Group Pension Sales Director Ivan D. Pierce, then agreed that she could also work for the agent for the LA area who had an office on the next floor up and reported to him. She was glad to apply her skills there, keep from getting rusty, and actually have something to do when returning to her desk. When her boss was around, she stayed there, but often went to him on the ground floor for phone calls, etc., where he was sneaking off to watch the stock broker's ticker tape. Investments were his real passion; he later would open his own investment-consulting firm. We later learned that a "mutual" organization could not make profits, hence paid no taxes. Because the excess left from premiums had to be channeled back to the policyholders, no one monitored productivity. Executives were made comfortable and provided with more than ample help, and Anna participated in fancy picnics and such Mickey Mouse courses for the secretaries as a charm course to learn how to look through the closets as to "what goes with what." So, we were learning much before we realized how things were kept rolling in this country.

LIFE IN SAN GABRIEL/BIRTH OF BABY BILLY

When we moved, Anna was already in her fourth month. Her P.M. "career track" had come to a screeching halt, when she showed up in a maternity dress one day (after telling her boss about her pregnancy). She was called into the nurse's office and asked sharply why she had not told HER. To her surprise,

Anna was then told she would have to leave just before Christmas; it was up to the company to tell her when to leave, not up to Anna, because "pregnant women become clumsy and might fall down the steps." Since Anna wanted to be a full-time mom anyway, she accepted this verdict, but cried about it at home. "What a way to treat a pregnant employee! What about women who might not have a husband? This could have never happened in Germany." Fortunately, as we write this, if a pregnant woman were treated this way, the employer would be in big trouble!

Moving in late 1960, we had all kinds of help for the furniture, but transported small items in our Chevy. It was easy: no winter clothes! The move was smooth and enhanced by the pride of owning the home; we have forgotten the details. We had much more space and a garage. There were flowers and blooming shrubs all around. On a clear day we could see Mt. Wilson with its observatory. It was a short drive to just about anything we needed, including the Pasadena department stores (Bullocks, May Co./Robinson's). Nearby Arcadia also had some nice stores.

After placing everything in the house, I surveyed the front yard. Between house and street, a patch of dichondra lawn was bordered by a large patch of ivy ground cover toward the street, which surrounded four terribly overgrown orange trees. Ignorant of whether it was the right time to do this, I decided to give them a nice trim, just wanting to make the front of our home presentable. So, I bought a tree saw, and shears for pruning and for cutting branches, and climbed into the first tree to start the job. Soon, Joe Bellomo from across the street introduced himself, offering a high ladder. Was I glad, because it was quite a chore to saw away while hanging in the branches! We had the kind of neighbors who didn't bother anyone until they saw they could be of service. Joe, a chiropractor of Italian descent, and Eva, of long New England heritage, were quite a couple, who had a small son, Joey. Eva was the housewife, then without a car, which was unusual in the area, because you could accomplish little in an efficient way, if you didn't have a car. She was a wonderful soul, who typically told a long family story to apply to just about any situation that came up around her. She told of having been a Telephone Company supervisor, noting: "They hire any old fool that comes along." We later learned that she was very close to her niece Miriam, who is now married to Bob Holden in Indianapolis. On the following weekends, we would see the neighbors to the left (who had also come over to introduce themselves), Kay and Art Wilson, kneeling with white gloves for hours in their lawn, meticulously pulling something out of it. They were removing each grass root, stem by stem, from their dichondra—the only way to maintain that beautiful, deep green ground cover. We soon gave up trying to emulate them in favor of our own priorities: getting settled and preparing for the arrival of our first child, while our dichondra changed to grass. The snails didn't care, feeding on either one. When the cool of the evenings arrived, an army would emerge from the ivy bed to feed themselves. Trying to squash them with your feet was ridiculous; their numbers were so immense that they would be there long after we would be gone from San Gabriel. Luckily, they ignored the Camellias and Azaleas. My razing off a foot of height of the ivy carpet failed to decrease the population. I did not approach the problem scientifically with commercially available toxins. I sometimes thought of my former Swiss-Russian colleague in Sao Paulo, who once took me to a Russian-French restaurant, where we had escargot as hors d'oeuvres—those snails resembled the pests in our yard. But I didn't want to risk my wife's protests. Besides, the escargots in Sao Paulo had not been impressive, tasting mostly of olive oil and parsley. I also suspected that our snails might not be the right variety. But maybe they were?

A seven-foot high fence separated the Wilson's property from ours, since they had a Dachshund. Kay sometimes referred to Art as "Art the Fart" behind his back, which we found strange. But we had learned not to think much about other married couples' lives. We never got very close to Art, but Kay practiced the art of neighborliness in a pleasantly reserved fashion. On the opposite side, a low masonry wall separated us from the Cox' family who would have five little girls by the time we would move again. Reggie Cox mentioned they were Catholic, which was almost superfluous, since there was always another baby on the way, although Reggie suffered from horrible varicose leg veins. I would have never allowed my wife to become pregnant again with such an acute problem. They were polite, but kept mostly to themselves, except for some communication by Reggie after Billy was born. Early on, he developed very bad rashes (later attributed to allergies), mainly on his behind, which Anna was advised to expose to the open air. The playpen was set up for this purpose in a shady spot, not far from the Cox' wall. Billy loved these "sunbaths," which helped a lot. But, Reggie frowned upon her daughters' exposure to this nudist show. Of course, the girls were curious. Until Reggie's complaint ended it once and for all, we would see their little heads popping up on the other side of the wall to ogle at the little naked male, and their mom trying to drag them inside.

Next to the Bellomo's across the street lived Virginia, Marv, an AFL-CIO executive, Mike and Kate Brody. Marv was seldom home due to business travel. Kate was mentally disabled due to doctors' mistakes when she had run an excessively high temperature while ill with scarlet fever. Because they knew Kate would eventually enter an institution, they adopted little Joelle, Bill's best childhood friend until we would move North. Virginia was classy, interesting and sophisticated, yet, her favorite pastime was digging around in her yard. "In the summer I let the housework go to pots and work in the garden." She taught Anna a lot about "saving your pennies," like shopping at the thrift shops, sewing clothes from garments bought there—not because she had to, but, as political activists, they sponsored many causes, and hoped to send Mike, insufficiently challenged by the public system, to a private school. Mike would become our main babysitter and even once functioned as our Santa Claus. The mom laughed: "A Jewish Santa"! Several houses toward the East lived Mr. Kimball, a cartoon draftsman for Walt Disney and a train buff, with a full-sized railway track on his property. On some weekends, neighborhood children heard the whistle blow, which meant he had fired up his locomotive and invited them to hop on the train, which he moved back and forth, including the caboose. He also played the trombone in the famous jazz band: "Firehouse Five plus Two." Next to his house was the future Lauber property, a stately home with a swimming pool. They would move there from across the street. Bertha was of German-Swiss and Roger of French Swiss heritage. We rarely saw Roger, who had a dental lab, but Bertha and Anna interacted quite a bit, including their children, Kurt and Nan, who loved coming to our house and play with Billy and Karen. Nan even enjoyed folding the diapers! Bertha, who had grown up in a hard-working dairy family, often mentioned how she would milk the cows at daybreak and do hard chores, in addition to going to school. As L.A. expanded to the east, the parents sold their extensive acreage at what must have been an excellent profit. Roger's father, a toolmaker from France, later owned an apartment building in Santa Monica. This shows how hard-working, smart and thrifty immigrants could get ahead in California in the days when Roger's and Bertha's parents came to America. Sadly, as we write this, Bertha has passed away of cancer, and Roger went to be with her in 2004, with the same disease. They last lived near San Diego, where we would later meet Rose, Roger's lovely French mom, who lived to be 100 years old. We felt sad when she told us she wanted to go, too, but her wish was fulfilled soon thereafter. We had such great times together in the more recent past, including Roger's wonderful friend, Jean Walch, who became his companion after Bertha's passing. Nan and Kurt are still around, and everyone misses the older Lauber's.

To backtrack a little, our main neighborly contacts, Eva Bellomo and Virginia, who saw in Anna something like a to-be-protected daughter, were very good to her. Looking pretty and very young, Anna soon started growing. While everything first seemed like that proverbial "piece of cake," nausea soon set in.

She looked very sick when frequently running to the bathroom to throw up. Dr. Horner considered this normal. As for myself, I began to have second thoughts about this wild idea of having kids. But the ball was rolling ... too late to change anything. I was becoming more nervous by the day, feeling so helpless and unable to protect Anna from all this crazy discomfort, especially before she stopped working in December of 1960. I felt lost, responsible for it all. We had not realized all the things that can occur during a pregnancy, and Hilde had said little, perhaps having forgotten her own experiences. When Oma joined us, it was a "fait accompli." By then the nausea was gone, and all of us looked forward to the big event.

At ITE things went just fine. I established manufacturing documentation for all the brand-new product lines and discussed many of the design features with the engineers—a seemly endless occupation. Heinz von Gehlen joined ITE at this time, and we became good friends. We are still in contact with his widow, Bruni, who lost him early in life. She remarried twice later. Now a widow again, she lives in Walnut Creek. When Anna was expecting Bill, Bruni was very gracious, but she must also have felt some envy, since she and Heinz very much wanted a family, which they thought they could not have. On their visits to Ardendale Avenue, she would hold Bill tightly in her arms and play with him. To everyone's surprise, Diana von Gehlen, their daughter, was born even before our Karen. We visited each other on many weekends, sharing joys of parenthood. Oma loved these visits: German-speaking friends with whom she could communicate! Once Bruni brought her parents, Martin and Kaethe Wegerle. During the conversation, we found out that Martin had been a student of Professor Freund, Anna's grandfather, and we became very excited about that. Martin said that he had very much respected his wonderful, inspiring teacher.

Raising a family did not cost excessively much in those times. If one observed the rules of thrift and did not expect great luxuries like expensive trips and going out, etc., the wife could stay home and be a full-time mother. ITE had a good health insurance policy without significant co-payments. Anna enjoyed dedicating this time in her life to family, children and household, with good advice from Granny and Oma, who had arrived around the time of Billy's birth and stayed in San Gabriel for one full year on her first visit. She was an enormous help and even had a little job—babysitting for the Brody's occasionally, which paid for the beauty shop visits she considered to be so outrageously expensive.

LIFE ON ARDENDALE AVE. WITH BABY BILLY, OMA, GRANNY IN HOLLYWOOD, AND KAREN SOON ON THE HORIZON

Of course, first Billy had to be born ... even more pressing: a name needed to be chosen. We decided against typical German names like Wilhelm (Anna's father), Hermann, or Gustav (my father). Anna believed from the beginning that the name should be identifiable with her father, who, in WWII, had been drafted and wounded as a soldier in Russia. He later died in a German military hospital (as described in Anna's memoirs, which Karen and Chris already have). I don't remember spending much time on picking a baby girl's name, but think we had decided on Gabrielle then. Anna suspected from early on that the first baby would be a boy. We kept the colors of baby clothes purchased in advance as neutral as possible—yellow, green, white, etc.

These preparations just about corresponded with the arrival of "Oma" from Berlin, who was a widow for some time now, my father having died of a stroke. She was looking forward to the experience of a lifetime: a visit to US and Southern California! First, we needed to find a way to get her there without booking a flight, which would have been outrageously expensive at that time. So, mother would have to take a boat to NY City and from there a cross country train to Los Angeles Union Station. We had also shied away from having her come to California via the Panama Canal: too much transit time, and we didn't know yet how Oma would react to the waves on the ocean. Granny was only 44 when sailing from Hamburg to Long Beach, but Oma was 65 and had never traveled overseas before. Without assistance she would be helpless, lost and bored, and we also worried about her blood pressure and the steaming weather surrounding the Panama Canal. But how would we transfer an elderly lady without English knowledge from a boat to the train? The Radday family, Trautl's aunt and uncle in Brooklyn, were enormously helpful and gracious hosts to Oma. For future trips Anna later discovered a support service ("Travelers Aid") which existed in major cities like New York. They provided a volunteer German speaking female companion who picked her up at the train and saw her to the dock the next day. Mother treated her to dinner close to the hotel, and they even went up the Empire State Building! As a result, Oma had marvelous journeys to and from the United States.

Meanwhile, Anna's discomforts during the last stretch of her pregnancy were becoming more pronounced, especially at night, when the baby was kicking up a storm. We would walk in the nearby parks as often as we could. During one of the checkups at the gynecologist's office, Dr. Horner noted that Anna had gained a few pounds too many. He explained that extra motherly weight could be unhealthy for baby and mom. Having assumed she needed to eat for two, Anna was astonished and stopped doing so immediately. That was another contradiction of whatever scant information she had been exposed to in Germany. As for myself, I admit I didn't read up on all aspects of pregnancy and didn't worry much about it. I had no "how to" guidebook for learning how I could support my dear wife, rather, I had to do it empirically. Once I saw a need, I tried to accommodate the mom-to-be. Our friends, neighbors, doctors and relatives who had experience in rearing children did not have many suggestions. Even Virginia (Brody) did not mention much. She was very involved in political causes and managed the home and family by herself; her husband Marvin was seldom home, being a top notch AFL-CIO union organizer for the Pacific Coast Region.

And then came the day when Oma disembarked at Union Station. My place of work at North Main Street was close by, and I met her there at mid-day in the '52 Chevy. It was February-March 1961; the deep blue sky was a typical California display of ample sunshine. Oma, excited to see her only son again, was in good shape. I was touched and anxious to show her our new surroundings. Driving down Huntington Drive toward East, I noted her enchantment at seeing all kinds of palm trees and orange trees full of fruits, which no one seemed to pick. Next came Ardendale and our home. Exhausted from the long journey and the new impressions of the car ride, she happily met Anna. Soon she started finding ways to be of help. And help she did! It was not her nature to sit by idly. Fairly soon she surprised us with meals she had so often prepared in Berlin Spandau for her family, such as "sour eggs," "Swedish meatballs," (Koenigsberger Klopse), Sauerbraten, eggs in mustard sauce, fried calves liver and onions, beef in horseradish sauce, fricassee of sour lung, old fashioned pea or lentil soups, buttermilk mousse, etc. etc. In this respect she became a good help, which all of us enjoyed.

Soon Anna became even more uncomfortable. Earlier, she had developed a voracious appetite for pickles and what not. Waiting did not seem an option. I found it silly, but how did I know what an expectant mother goes through? I was surrounded by stories about pregnant women's cravings

Finally, on May 6, 1961, a Saturday, Anna gave me the long awaited sign: Ready to drive … to Huntington Memorial Hospital in Pasadena, about 20 minutes away. Dr. Horner had told her lately about the signs to watch before the delivery was to start. Off we went in a great hurry, with Anna looking like she had swallowed a balloon. Although the road was in great shape, the drive was very uncomfortable for her. It was high time! They already waited for her in the hospital, gave her laughing gas, to be used when the contractions would become too painful. I was kept busy massaging her hurting back. Any time the nurse did something for Anna, she thanked her profusely again and again. After a while I asked why she was thanking the nurse each time. "We are, after all, paying for all this!" Little did I know how desperate Anna became as the labor pains grew more and more intense. Any help offered to her was like a safety net, and she felt relieved in grasping it and expressing her thanks. Feeling helpless, unable to make her more comfortable, and also guilty for having started all this with little insight as to what would happen later, I got frightened. I didn't think I would lose her. I knew the baby was large for her stature, but not really out of the ordinary. Then, I think it was just after midnight, the nurses rolled her into the delivery room, where Dr. Stevenson was already waiting. An older lady and Dr. Horner's alternate while he was out of town, she had been his mentor, and they both taught at UCLA. She did an excellent job. At that time, no tests existed to tell whether the baby was a boy or a girl or to detect any birth defects. Also, no one, except the mom and the experts, was allowed in the delivery room. When I finally could congratulate the beaming, exhausted new mom about 4 a.m. Sunday, she had just counted the fingers and toes of little Billy-boy and found the little Moratz was complete and perfect. Asked if anyone had advised her to count the fingers and toes, she said, "No one—I just had to do it!" She was now a mom who would try to do her best in the future so that our child would become a happy, well-educated and self-sufficient person. This commitment arose in both of us very naturally … there simply was no other way. I returned home after Anna sank back into her well-earned sleep. She had little Billy now, a strong and healthy looking baby. He had a friendly nature. But, when something irked him, he could yell his head off until becoming blue in the face; then the mouth seemed larger than his head. That voice would keep Oma and us on our toes for a long time. Oma happily received the good news, extremely satisfied with having her first real grandson. Her grandchildren in Germany were by her stepdaughters Ulli and by Lisbeth. Lisbeth had Marianne and Sabine, who are still in close contact with us. Ulli and Lisbeth's mother had been Oma's aunt—the sister of my grandfather Boehlke in Nauen.

After a few days, I brought Anna and Billy home, and the routine in our household changed. But first, I went to the office on Monday morning, with a big box of cigars. They were American made. Everyone in the ITE engineering office greeted the box with loud exclamations and congratulations. I didn't distribute my cherished Suerdieck and Dannemann cigars, which I smoked about daily after dinner, since the ITE engineers were used to the domestic product anyway. I got a present, too—a "pooper scooper," a handy tool for new fathers. It was a machete-like, plywood gadget for removing the unbelievable amount of poop from the cotton diapers before they went into the laundry pail. Throwaway products had not been invented yet. After being boiled, they kept our washing machine humming. I was amazed how much poop a little baby could generate. Anna generously let me participate in such routine tasks, but, when it came to getting up several times during the night, she was like a wound-up spring. Before I even heard a whimper from the crib, she was already comforting little Billy, changing his diaper, breastfeeding and burping him—making sure that I always got a good night's sleep. Last not least, I had to work to bring home the bacon, whereas she stayed home and took care of things together with Oma, who was a very inventive, experienced, thrifty and enthusiastic household help. As an example: in those days engineers and other white collar workers worked in suits, shirts, and literally white collars, and ties. When noticing that some of my dress shirts were beginning to show frayed collars, she meticulously removed them, turned them around and stitched them back on to the shirts, so that they looked like new! What full time American housewife would have thought of this trick? This was her contribution throughout her life: washing (no washing machine!), cleaning, mending, cooking, shopping and taking care of three children and a husband, who worked very odd hours. It was considered her duty; no one ever considered it a bit much. But father also helped out in many ways.

Now, friends started coming to see the baby, bringing presents, as was the custom. The most enthusiastic of these was Bruni (von Gehlen), who could not get enough of holding and playing with Billy. After their baby Diana arrived, the two babies would be placed together in a playpen in the backyard while the grown-ups had coffee and cake. When Billy was old enough for the grown-up bathtub, he enjoyed himself endlessly until the plug was pulled and the water formed a whirlpool flowing down the pipe. At that moment, his face would turn red and purple. And he'd yell his head off. We changed the routine, as we suspected he thought he would be sucked up into oblivion by the descending whirlpool. That's what faulty observations and hasty conclusions can do to you. Billy would need many diverse experiences to form valid opinions. It was our job to convey these to him, and we have pursued this ever since with both children.

On weekends, we made many excursions to parks, shopping centers and beaches. The preferred one was driving on Rosemead Boulevard South toward the ocean around Huntington Beach. Sometimes Granny came along or we visited her in her Hollywood apartment, which always included beautiful picnics she meticulously prepared, in Santa Monica. We even visited Disneyland in Ana-heim, which Oma loved. But she also seemed content when roaming through the back yard with a kitchen knife, picking an orange here and there, cutting it apart and sucking out the tasty juice. How heavenly it must have been for her, com-pared with her sunless little Berlin apartment, looking mostly at walls and a cement-covered courtyard, bare, except for a contraption where people beat the dust out of their rugs with an "Ausklopfer" (manual carpet beater). Here she enjoyed the sun daily on a property filled with camellias, azaleas, etc., not ever seen outdoors in Germany. One of the most unforgettable experiences was orange blossom time in January/February in our back yard, where we had seven such trees. Driving toward San Bernardino one Saturday morning at the crack of dawn, we were suddenly overwhelmed by a heavenly, intense aroma as lavish as gardenias, but tending toward the acidic side. Gardenia aroma is voluptuous and sweetly tropical versus the lovely, clean scent of orange blossoms. We passed many miles of orange groves before turning off Highway 10 toward North and the San Bernardino Mountains, and a cabin we had rented for the weekend. The change from orange blossom to pine scent high up on Big Bear Lake amazed us. One could have skied up there, but the idea of recreational sports had not really occurred to us due to lack of time and other preoccupations, like Billy, visitors, correspondence as well as house maintenance and improvement. At that time we also visited a Lutheran Church on most Sundays, since Anna had desired that our children be baptized in the Lutheran faith, her family tradition. Later we found the environment of this particular church too restrictive and narrow for our taste. For instance the pastor insisted that members who were traveling should bring the program from the out-of-town Lutheran church they had visited: also, mem-bers should only socialize with other Lutherans. Later, we (mostly Anna) made an effort to expose the children to various different protestant faiths, to enable them to do some critical thinking of their own.

Since Anna had left work and we lived in the house, a colleague from the ITE Purchasing Department was kind enough to offer me a ride to work and back. He insisted on picking me up and dropping me off, although it was a mile out of his way. He had served as a gunner on a Liberator bomber, as missions were flown from Libya into Ploesti, Romania, while I was serving on the ground on radar equipment to detect approaching enemy bombers. He had participated in the first low level, very ill conceived and hazardous bombing mission, which resulted in an enormous loss of assets. They could never afford this kind of approach again. He was a fine fellow, and we got along very well. This let Anna keep our 52 Chevy full time, so she could take Oma and Billy to shopping centers, parks, department stores, etc., which they enjoyed immensely. When things were running smoothly for a while, and it seemed Oma would enjoy "being in command" for some of the time, Anna became convinced, with Oma's doctor's consent, that Oma would want to gladly and lovingly care for her grandson. She started to look for a part-time job, so as to keep up and extend her considerable secretarial skills. We had learned very early that the US workforce operated under different rules than exist in Europe. The social safety net was less extensive than Germany's (but much better than in Brazil). If one was of the younger generation (remember: Dun & Bradstreet hired no one over 35 at that time!!!), had superior skills in shorthand, typing, office organization, writing and communication, the sky was the limit, as long as good health prevailed. Industry and commerce were seeking qualified people, preferably those willing to put in a full day's work with enthusiasm and energy. Salary increases were based on annual performance evaluations. Since we realized that Social Security would not suffice for a happy retirement, our family goal was become independently well to do, which meant saving meticulously for the later years. We established monthly and annual budgets to control expenses and spend less than our net income. Except for mortgages (which we sometimes even prepaid) on our successive houses, we always paid cash. When we could not afford a desired purchase, we postponed it. To confirm our thinking, Granny once showed Anna the "County Ward" in the San Marino Lodge, an otherwise beautiful nursing home, where she had worked for some time. This totally separate ward was awful, a big room filled with miserable people wandering around aimlessly. "Save for your old age, THIS would happen to you if, old and sick, you run out of money". Our former neighbor Bonnie Hornback, who worked at a Savings & Loan Association in Altadena, had told Anna about Republican Congressman Edgar Hiestand, who operated out of the S&L office during congressional breaks while serving the Altadena, Pasadena and La Canada area, to keep in touch with his constituents and the business community. Bonnie's recommendation led to an interview, and, after contacting her references from Dun &Bradstreet and Pacific Mutual Life, he hired her part-time. Soon Anna would drive to Altadena to start at 9 a.m. three days a week. She liked this interesting opportunity and its part-time, temporary nature. There was much to learn about how government worked in our new country, mostly just by typing his correspondence and notes from Dictaphone tapes, while he was off to meetings or traveling. Meanwhile Billy had settled into a nice routine; he and Oma always napped after lunch.

U.S. CITIZENSHIP/HERMANN, THE WEEKEND WARRIOR

In the latter part of 1961, after living in the US for four years, we became eligible for U.S. citizenship. We felt comfortably and completely at home—house, car, baby, mothers-in-law visiting, friends. Things had really come together. We felt in tune with the people we knew. Our expectations of what we would find in this country had been generally met. If someone would have suggested returning to Germany, we would not have known why we should—and where would we have settled? It would have meant starting from scratch. Anna would have easily found an interesting spot in the export business in Hamburg, but my career would not have been easily acceptable to an interviewer there. We liked the pleasant, welcoming demeanor of the Americans we met, whether neighbors, colleagues, and often even strangers, who would greet us with "Good Morning, isn't it a nice day?" in our neighborhood. Therefore, we decided to apply for U.S. citizenship and started to attend a once a week citizenship class at Pasadena City College before Oma would leave us. She was glad to take care of Billy on those evenings. When Anna's work for Congressman Hiestand ended because of his return to Washington, she immediately was offered another interesting part-time job, working for Grace Humphrey. She managed several adventure movie creators who traveled worldwide and then presented travelogues across the U.S. She had Anna follow up on the arrangements via correspondence, mailings and advance publicity. Mrs. Humphrey had a fat little dog. He did not get enough exercise, which Anna noticed—so she voluntarily took "Bambi" out for walks at lunchtime, which improved indoor air.

This went on until baby Karen announced herself—due in April of 1963. All of us were hopping and happy. In 62 Oma returned to Spandau, since her visitor's visa came to an end. There she could tell her tall tales, which, of course, people listened to with some doubt and bemusement. "Bei uns in California" (at our place in California) ... "this and that happened or existed"—She was proud of having visited such a privileged place, her life's highlight. She would return in 65, when we had moved to Palo Alto, CA. Highly pregnant with Karen, Anna wondered if she could answer all of the interrogator's questions the citizenship teacher had meticulously prepared us for. But when he saw her condition, he made it disappointingly easy for her. Grilled more thoroughly, I passed as well. The questionnaires we needed to fill and swear to its correctness included strange questions. "Have you ever committed adultery?" is the one we remember most vividly. Lots of questions also about Nazi party membership, etc. Naturally we were ok on all points and a nice swearing-in ceremony followed by receipt of the citizenship certificate. Standing in line for it, we were asked about changing our name. We couldn't think of a better one, but this is a chance for people with very complicated names to drop parts of them. Later we had a party at our house for our witnesses, Dick Huth, Celia Seger, and Monte Buchanan, and Bonnie and Hal Hornback, who gave us our first American flag!

Around mid 62 we felt we needed a covered patio with a concrete floor. Now I'm surprised that I did not simply use bricks. Weather deterioration was no factor, but I guess concrete just came to mind, and that's what it was. The south side of the house (the backside when seen from Ardendale) was exposed to the sun, which would beat down on it from 10 am until there was an afternoon breeze. This made the family room almost unusable during those hours a great part of the year. At night it was always comfortable, and Oma slept very well ... she liked the "Den" and adjoining private bath. So, after buying material for the patio roof and posts, I erected the structure. I learned the truly American way of being a weekend warrior: taking care of things with your own hands, like most people in this country: spending time at the lumber yard, which offered an array of tools, hardware, paint, etc. Nowadays, the likes of Lowe's and Home Dept offer just about everything to build and maintain a home. I had never seen such activities while growing up in Germany. No one we knew owned a home, a privilege reserved for the uppermost income brackets between the wars, but many such people preferred to live in more elegant rented apartments in the better suburbs, like Dahlem, as for instance Gretel and Walter Wagner in the Bilsestrasse there. After finishing the roof, I prepared for the pouring of the concrete. One day a huge concrete mixer truck pulled in and let the mass flow through a shoot into the prepared patio bed. Poor Hermann then had to move the thick mess into the right places. The two truck drivers only had the job to pour in the goop, not to distribute it and finish the work. My first movements made me realize my terrible greenhorn booboo. Moving this stuff around was excruciatingly hard, much worse than spreading 2-year-old cow manure onto a field, as I had done in 1945 in Franconia (Germany). Not used to this kind of torture, I felt as though I was dying. Luckily the two truck guys took pity on me and volunteered to help finish the job: one of our many positive experiences in our new country. I would never again think of doing concrete work for large surfaces. The result of such labors was a remarkable lowering of the den temperature during peak times, and we started enjoying California outdoor leisure and Barbeques in the cool shade. Los Angeles, in contrast, could be a hellhole in summer, when the heat lasted from

March to October, compounded by the irritating smog, which caused discomfort and allergy, attacks in sensitive people. We were to learn more about this later.

Once Anna and I, traveling by ourselves up highway 1, stopped in Pacific Grove near Monterey and continued to San Francisco, the site of our arrival in the US. If I remember correctly, Granny and Oma were taking care of little Billy part-time and full time. It was an exciting trip—complete relaxation from our daily routine. The Pacific coast was especially impressive, although I found the driving hazardous along the steep, enormous rocky mountain faces on the right and 1500 feet of steep drops where the rocks met the ocean. On that side there were safety rails. This road had been carved into the rocks during the great depression in the 30's through a federal work program similar to the Autobahn program in Germany. Arriving in SF, there were Ghirardelli Square, the Mark Hopkins Hotel, Chinatown, the Japanese Garden, Aquarium, etc. Soon we were on Highway 80 heading toward the Sierra. We descended into Tahoe Village, driving along the Truckee River, where in the 1830's wagon trains had come to a halt on the way to California. Too late in the year, they could not surmount the huge amount of snow piling up against them. Snowfall there is measured from 3 to 5 feet in one day, and something like 50 feet average seasonal coverage. It's California's water resource. They soon ran out of food—only a few survived on cannibalism. We stopped near the bridge across the Truckee to marvel at a clear mountain river, the spicy air and a perfect blue sky. Close to the surface we observed an abundance of trout in the clear water, but further upstream there were none. Around bridges fishing was prohibited. Perhaps the creatures had gotten the message? Or they may have come into the Truckee River to feed on the many insects there. We found a motel on the East Shore of Lake Tahoe, with easy access to beaches and attractions. The road surrounding the lake was built very high into the mountains. From there, high up, the overview of Emerald Bay and the lake was perfect—beautiful scenery: the deep emerald color of the bay unlike anything we had ever seen. We felt happy that this was accessible to us. On the lake's Southeast end the state of Nevada began. Past the border gambling casinos lined the roads. Because California then didn't allow gambling, millions flocked here to try their luck. Most casinos had coin machines, where people smoked cigarettes and operated the hand cranks all day long. Finding this ridiculous, we tried one-penny machine and walked away with a tiny gain. Back at the motel, the machines rattled on in our heads for a long time. While living in California, we never returned to Nevada, only to re-visit it for Karen's and George's wedding at the hotel Paris (Las Vegas) many decades later. On our return trip, we took an adventurous road from the South end of the lake across the mountains in King

County, close to Yosemite. As in many places at the foot of the Sierra Nevada, there were ancient Redwood and Douglas fir trees. But first we had to ascend the Sierra on a paved 2-way highway, with endless switchbacks, until the road narrowed to 1 lane, with ever sharpening tight curves around enormous boulders and past dangerous precipices. I had to honk the horn each time I needled the car around one of those endless bends. Luckily, no one came toward us—I would have been unprepared. It would have meant backing up; turning was impossible for lack of room. Later we drove through the majestic Redwood trees of Calaveras State Park. We returned home on Highway 5, which showed us the endless fruit orchards of the California Central Valley (maybe those cans of peaches I took off an US Army supply train in Bremen Germany years ago originated here?). It was a remarkable trip. A few weeks later Anna told me a new baby was on the way. If it would be a girl, as she thought, she would take sewing lessons at Temple City High School.

Our new status as US citizens did not improve our accent. In one of my annual performance appraisals at ITE everything was judged superior, except … the Engineering Manager thought that my command of the English language was not fluent enough to allow for future promotions, e.g. to supervisor or manager. That hit me hard. Although I had not been thinking about such positions, I took some college level courses at Pasadena City College to remedy the situation, since I had been alerted to better opportunities. At the next review, I proudly presented a certificate showing very good results, which meant my English was comparable to a well-educated high school or college graduate.

Anna had stopped her part-time work when Oma returned to Berlin. We had used some of the money she had earned for overnight excursions, to show Oma the California scenery together with Billy. But now it was time to prepare for the new baby. Anna would manage the household without outside help and gladly accepted any assistance I could give her. I usually did the outdoor work: lawn-mowing, watering, cleaning up under the orange trees and taking care of the vast front bed of the thick, foot high cover of Ivy, which needed constant attention. Pruning and planting new shrubs was another task. One day, while working late in the backyard and straightening out from the bent-over gardening position, I felt a sharp knife-like back pain. I foolishly continued the job until I could hardly move. My entire lower back frozen in pain, I went inside and hit the floor, unable to move. This was the first of what would be a long string of such episodes. Desperate, Anna called our neighbor Joe Bellomo, not fully aware of what a chiropractor was for and how he could help. He rushed over with a portable chiropractor's bench, got me on top and started his manipulation routine. Nowadays orthopedic surgeons insist on a preliminary examination, including x-ray, before such intervention, to avoid accidents. They now say manipulation can help, but bed rest and exercises, plus application of heat, are better. But, we were naïve and concerned with my return to work the next morning, when, limping into the office, I joined the many colleagues with periodic lower back problems. The most prominent was Jim McCloud, who could often be seen wiggling his upper torso across his design table trying to "snap back" his "un-linked spine," the only way he could keep functioning. Suspicious of chiropractors, he must have had bad experiences. I kept visiting Joe Bellomo's office periodically, somewhere between downtown and San Gabriel. It usually required one week to fully recover from such attacks. Initially they were spaced months apart. 15 to 20 years later they became frightening and much more frequent until, in the 70's, I finally attacked the problem with the help of an orthopedic surgeon, Dr. Murtland, at the Guthrie Clinic, Sayre, Pennsylvania, who taught me 10 daily exercises to strengthen my back and stomach muscles. He said they must be done daily, even if there is no pain. Most people abandon such bothersome exercises once they feel better, only to suffer another attack soon thereafter.

Winters in California were mild, but rainy. The only time of year it rained was between November and January/February. But on New Year's morning there was usually a crisp, clear sky. People now still stream to the Rose Bowl parade armed with blankets for the early morning chill. When it is in full swing, there is gorgeous sunshine and temperatures are comfortable. We were fortunate to watch this marvelous spectacle once with Granny, at the Buchanan's invitation, whose parents owned a home near Colorado Boulevard, the Rose Bowl Parade route. The two families organized an annual Parade Breakfast, to which their guests contributed food; everyone had a great time greeting the New Year by watching the parade.

Late in 63 or early 64, Oma came for a shorter visit. Granny came to Southern California almost every other year, as she did not want to lose her German pension; for the years she did this, until her health became too precarious, she was always guaranteed a job at Mt. Sinai Hospital. On weekends, Billy enjoyed an occasional outing with me alone, while Baby Karen still was taking her morning naps. During one of those outings, we walked through the cactus garden of the Arcadia Arboretum. Among the desert plants we noticed some cacti with needles about one or two inches long and extremely sharp. Never having seen such things, my very curious son happily walked right toward them until his head hit a cactus needle. Shocked, we realized he could have easily punctured an eye! From then on, when approaching cacti, I would lead Billy by his hand, which he liked anyway. On weekends, he would always stay close to me. He would trail me when I went out with my toolbox for chores, not missing a thing. He had a little toolbox of his own, which made him very proud. Over the years in Southern California, I had to buy all sorts of tools, starting with my joining Sparling Meter. For car maintenance I needed various wrenches, and for yard work there were shovels, saws, a manual push mower, pruning shears and so on. At an early age Billy learned how to handle all those handy things and liked it. Of course, we adults wrecked our brains as to what he would do with his life. Once, when one of our neighbors was a doctor (Brain in Needham), who gave him old slides of blood samples, etc., he would listen to my vital signs with a stethoscope. Later, he had a chemistry kit, which he fooled around with, and he also showed a great interest in microscopy with a nice microscope of his own. We always tried to provide toys with active play value. When Karen was the right age for it, Anna fashioned a dollhouse from an old bookshelf. The kids and their friends enjoyed it together. Karen liked cooking, dolls, and crafts, drawing and especially dress-up and play-acting. A puppet theatre with beautiful German "Steiff" puppets was another inspiration for many hours of creative fun for the whole family. Once I made Billy a garage for Christmas, which he adored. It was fairly large and kept him busy for many hours with his toy cars and trucks. But his preferred possession was a little train running on a circular railway track. Eva Bellomo had given it to him after her Joey had outgrown it, and Billy could run around endlessly, propelling it forward by pedals. He must have felt like having his own car … except … when hearing a loud yelling and crying from the yard with no end in sight, Anna knew it had jumped off the track and needed re-setting. In his disappointment at not being able to "fix it" himself, his face would turn purple and seemed to consist only of a wide-open mouth—it was always a little tragedy!

We were now approaching the next big family event, Karen's birth. Since we knew what to expect, everything was much easier now. According to Anna, we would have a girl. The hospital was again Huntington Memorial, Pasadena. Dr. Stevenson had delivered Billy; Dr. Horner, Anna's regular gynecologist, delivered little Karen, who was born on April 7, 1963 (Billy on May 7, 1961—both on a Sunday morning!) Karen was smaller, and the happy Mom again counted all her limbs. The doctor cautioned us later not to try for another baby. With our blood group combination (A. negative, H. positive), the chance of each successive birth resulting in a "blue baby," requiring an immediate, total blood transfusion, would increase. Billy stayed with Kay and Art Wilson, our next-door neighbors, while we were at the hospital. Having been well prepared, Billy was happy about his little sister, and they got along very well. His fascination with tools was evident when, after we returned from the hospital, hearing her snore in her tiny bassinet, he thought she was a "Saege" (saw).

Billy usually followed me around, and, when she was a little older, Karen stuck to Anna, observing all the cooking, cleaning and sewing. She liked standing on a chair to help with the dishes, and when Mom handed her a just-washed dish to rinse which still had some spots on it, she would give it right back. Ages later, Karen would remark that she would have very much liked to play with tools and do the kinds of things Billy and I were involved with. It may have created the impression that I preferred Billy's company, but … he was almost two years older when she was born, and he just clung to me, so it seemed natural. Leaving her out was never my intention. This is how easily a father can miss out on something important. But the three of us enjoyed sitting on the sofa together. I would read stories like "Der kleine Haewelmann," "Schneewittchen und die sieben Zwerge," and many more, usually in German. The kids got plenty of exposure to English when surrounded by playmates or adult friends. Hence, they became automatically bilingual since they learned to talk. When finished with story time, we played all kinds of things. They loved playing barber. Karen would climb behind me and comb my hair with great abandon until she got tired and Billy relieved her. Those were the moments when fatherhood has its ample rewards. Billy, particularly, liked to reciprocate. I had a barber kit with motorized clippers, comb, shears and a thinning shear. Thus equipped, I did what my father had done for years. When needed, he had given me fairly decent haircuts, and my job was giving him a shine, i.e. I made a clear cut, since there was little left on top—only on the sides. Because electric clippers did not exist, it took more time and there was more danger of pulling hair when it got caught in the slow-moving clippers, causing a painful sting and loud complaints. Although I had marveled at some of my early buddies who could visit a barber, I knew that asking father for barber money would have been useless. And then, my buddies never teased me about my less than perfect haircuts. Most had the same problem.

Around that time we began to suspect that Billy was suffering from something. He got out of breath easily and sometimes made wheezing sounds; his color was not as healthy as it should be. For quite some time the pediatrician had treated him for constantly reappearing "colds." Fortunately, Anna came across a book "The Allergic Child" which listed all of Billy's symptoms—the violent sneezes when exposed to dust, the wheezing, and so on. Confronted with Anna's diagnosis, the pediatrician immediately agreed. He offered to conduct the allergy tests, but Anna told him, if he hadn't told her before that Billy was allergic, she didn't think he ought to do the tests. She began seeing an allergy specialist in Pasadena. During our time in San Gabriel we did not have a TV for some time; neither did the Brody's. After learning of Billy's allergies, he sometimes had to be on steroids, which made him very fidgety and overactive. That's when the TV came into the house. Joelle, the Brody's adopted daughter, who was Billy's age, often came over, asking for TV: "Mrs. Moratz, we really don't care WHAT is on!!!" because she knew Anna's response would be: "it depends on the program!" The attacks could be quite severe, a doctor even came to the house once at night, and the steroids were a periodic necessity, with our accompanying worries about their side effects. There was a great contrast between periods of listlessness and weakness, and then, after taking steroids, excitability and restlessness. The tests showed that poor Billy was allergic to just about everything. Anna bought the allergy cookbook, learned about the products at the health food stores, and he went on all kinds of special diets. Cow's milk was replaced by goats' milk, and soy products and potato flour, among many other substitutes, became staples for him, while the rest of the family continued eating "normally," because it was cheaper. Billy was amazingly cooperative about giving up such popular foods as ice cream, cake frosting, sugar products, the list was endless. He would take his little lunchbox with cake made of potato flour … much less delicious than those cakes served at the little friends' birthday parties, but he never complained. Anna washed down the hardwood floors at least three times a week. Dust-producing items like bedspreads and fuzzy toys were replaced by plastic. After Karen was born, he developed eczema, the first sign of an allergic child (which we then didn't yet know). Each time Anna was breast-feeding her, he started to scratch (saying "kratzen, kratzen") his legs until they became bloody. He was very good and showed tenderness toward the new baby, but the timing of these scratching sessions made us conclude that he may have felt left out despite Anna's attempt to read to him during those times. Consequently, Anna's milk's quality decreased, Karen needed to be fed more and more often, since she cried at unusual times, and, in quick conclusion, the bottle replaced mom's milk, resulting in a thriving baby and more sleep and contentment for everyone.

At the allergist's advice we installed central air conditioning, a gas-fired system, (which promised to reduce the energy cost). We enjoyed the fresh clean air in the middle of the day and hoped that Billy would have an easier time. Whenever the smog and the Santa Ana Winds brought certain pollens to which he was also sensitive, we stayed inside because of "dirty air." The smog was amazing. On clear days we could see the Mt. Wilson Observatory, from our house, high up in the mountains behind La Canada. (Joelle: "Billy, the mountains opened up"). But on smog days we saw only a yellow-grayish wall, and smelled the typical hydrocarbon stench. At work I often developed a severe headache—that meant a bad smog day. I then tried to stay in the office as much as I could. Workers in the factory were not as fortunate. I normally had to spend many hours on the floor to help along production and answer questions about quality aspects of parts on which they were working, improvement of the manufacturing sequence or inter-pretation of drawings because of unclear descriptions, etc. etc. When busy on the floor, the paging system would sound over the hum of the factory, using my full name. Not the best in the world, the system was hard to understand. When I left the company later, I was of told my nickname, "Hermann the Rat," since that's what they had heard. Because I was the only Hermann in the company, they could have paged just "Hermann," but that was not the routine.

Seeing Billy suffer so much, we became increasingly conscious of the role smog was playing in the asthmatic condition. In the absence of medical publica-tions' accessibility, Internet, websites, etc., we had to put our common sense and observations to work. One thing was sure: he was always sick when exposed to smog. Since he had not been exposed to a clean-air climate, we wondered if improvement could be gained by living in a clean air environment. For our Fall 64 vacation, we found a place on Coronado Island in front of San Diego, oppo-site the Hotel Coronado. We had not been that far south, having driven only as far as Anaheim, when taking Granny or Oma for the obligatory Disneyland vis-its. From there a short drive on Interstate 5 via San Luis Capistrano leads to the Pacific Coast. Then the road parallels the ocean until reaching San Diego. Since the bay bridge did not exist then, we took a ferry across the bay with an impres-sive view of warships, including submarines and aircraft carriers. The ample, clean Spanish-style apartment fulfilled all our needs. We immediately changed into our swimsuits and hit the beach—pristine scenery with the harbor entrance and naval air station on the right and the rock with park and lighthouse in the distance. Frolicking in sand and sea, we noticed a complete absence of coughing and wheezing in Billy and became very hopeful that the clean air would help him. Every few days we had friends visiting; the von Gehlen's, Granny and the All-welt's came down from L.A. This first vacation trip as a family of four was so happy that we became sad when packing for our return—an adventurous trip, which would lead to an important discovery. First, coming through the hills before Anaheim, the baggage suddenly slid down from the roof and dangled on a rope along the driver's window. Luckily the mess did not land on the freeway. I had to make a quick stop to secure the suitcases again. This was our second car, a silver-colored station wagon with a luggage rack. The Chevy had stayed home.

As we continued over the summit of the hills and down toward Anaheim, Billy started his allergic coughing again, while at the same time we noticed the penetrating odor of the L.A. smog, which was visible in its density. Anna and I looked at each other, amazed: "It's the smog that's causing the asthma!" Told of our observation, the allergist said our observations were good and to the point, but one test was insufficient proof that smog caused our son's problems—and especially not for the entire L.A. population. To be more certain, we needed to figure out how to repeat the test under similar circumstances. I couldn't request another vacation and did not want to lose the income, but Anna was free, and we rented a beachfront apartment in Redondo Beach, North of Long Beach—not exactly inexpensive. Bruni and Heinz von Gehlen then lived in Redondo Beach; Bruni would be very helpful in the crisis that was to follow. During the trip (Anna followed me in the Chevy), Billy got sweaty, as always when fighting his asthma. Getting out of the car and moving the necessities inside, I noticed a stiff, cold breeze and shivered a little. We had a small dinner, and I drove the 90 minutes back to San Gabriel. The next day, Monday morning at work, I got a frantic phone call from Anna. Billy was very sick with high fever. A pediatrician had diagnosed pneumonia! He was not the healthiest kid in the world due to his allergies. Shocked, I took off immediately for Redondo Beach and found Billy looking like a ghost. He could only breathe sitting upright and had to force air into his lungs with visible exertion, exhaling it with a strong wheezing sound. With each breath he fought for air. What now? The pediatrician had warned against transporting Billy, not wanting to take that responsibility, in case the condition would aggravate. A difficult decision was needed. Anna, Karen, and especially Billy needed support, we needed our doctors and help from friends and neighbors, while the pediatrician there would not even discuss transport. But we felt that, if we had to take him to doctors or a hospital, he would also be exposed to cold air when placed in the car—the greatest danger was in the open air, while getting him in and out of the car. The experiment had been a failure. We decided to abandon it immediately and go home. Billy recuperated in the next two weeks, but the idea of moving out of the smog lingered on in the back of our minds.

Meanwhile, personal affairs at ITE came to a head. Because the manufacturing engineering manager, who had hired me in '59, was transferred to a bigger job on the East Coast, his job became available. Another engineer, new in the job, applied, and so did I, having four years under the belt. By now I was well liked and had shown a good record of accomplishments. We also had a new manufacturing manager, who had retired from the Navy as a captain. When a Navy captain has been promoted to this rank, the next huge promotion is to admiral. Very few make it. The rest has to retire to make room for the next crop of eager commissioned officers. The one who does not make it has to shop around for a position in any industry, university or government field, depending on his inclination and talents. When doing so, such a person can always be sure of benevolent evaluations based on his Navy career. There are many connections between the clubby officers' corps and the wheels in private life, and it is known that Navy training is second to none. Now, this new manager was not my cup of tea. Overall, he behaved like a captain on the bridge of his carrier: he was aloof and uncommunicative. By the time he set out to select another manufacturing engineering manager, I had rarely spoken with, or seen him, even after the old manager left. The others and I had to work on our own. He would give vague or no instructions, only to show displeasure when something did not turn out the way he might have visualized it. The former manager, who was open and knew his business, had been very good to deal with. He would discuss projects with me to assure we agreed on a common course of action. All of this changed now, and I constantly felt like hanging in the air. Now came his selection of a new manufacturing engineering manager. By then I had realized that reaching a higher salary range would require promotion to a supervisory position at the company. These opportunities were rare at ITE with its 150-180 people working in Engineering and Manufacturing. During this process, I had to visit a professional executive placement outfit with all kinds of specialists who ran distinct tests with me, some of which I found downright silly. They wanted to measure my aptitudes with a variety of "Rorschach" tests. It took an entire day and no one told me how I was doing. Some time thereafter, I was invited to join the manufacturing manager for lunch at a nice restaurant downtown, not far from the plant. To my surprise, the other candidate also popped up. I initially thought he wanted to tell me good news, but I was wrong. Nothing happened during lunch, except a dragging conversation, because I had little in common with either one. I heard nothing for a couple of weeks until he finally called me to say he had selected my competitor! My hopes shattered, I returned home devastated that night.

Now we needed a solution. Remaining at this small company would mean foregoing hopes of a better position, while moving to another area with better air quality could improve Billy's health. Having thought about this, we carefully scanned the Sunday L.A. Times help wanted ads. I eventually found a promising opening for a senior manufacturing engineer by Westinghouse Electric Company in Sunnyvale near Palo Alto and San Francisco, where the air was just about as clean as an ocean breeze. We knew nothing about P.A. and very little about S.F. Unfamiliar with Stanford University, we didn't know how it could affect living standards in Palo Alto. All we wanted was better air. I also had to be aware of the company. I wanted to be exposed to more complex engineering problems, so that a growth path might be projected. I quickly applied and was invited to interview. I was curious and excited about the prospect of moving North, unaware that I would often switch employment for one reason or another during the long odyssey that would follow in the future, during which I could never risk remaining with a company that changed its character or simply cut down employment or lost contracts. During my working life I was never let go by any employer. The decision was always mine, or ours—not "theirs."

LIFE ON THE SAN FRANCISCO PENINSULA

Before we decided on this step, we contacted Bruni and Heinz von Gehlen. He had switched from ITE to Bechtel Construction—a significant improvement in salary and benefits. Bechtel was and still is one of the largest construction companies in the world, building everything big from manufacturing-, chemical, power plants and bridges up to nuclear power plants. He worked on the wiring of those projects, initially in their downtown L.A. office. From there he commuted 1-1/2 hours each way to a wonderfully modern house in Redondo Beach, located on a bluff at a marvelous Pacific Ocean beach. He, Bruni and daughter Diana could watch the beach sunset each night, an unforgettable display of colors. But Heinz often complained about the horrible driving conditions on the freeways during the rush hour, aggravated by the smog and accompanying stench. During that time, he suffered a heart attack at age 39, having a history of genetically caused high cholesterol levels. Because Statins had not yet been developed, little could be done to lower the level, except diet and exercise. But he was already as lean as could be! After the attack, he was transferred to Bechtel's San Francisco headquarters at his request. They bought a house in Walnut Creek, east of Oakland. Heinz and Bruni were very helpful in orienting us about life around the San Francisco Bay, especially air quality.

I arrived at the San Francisco Airport well prepared. I drove to Sunnyvale, where they had reserved a motel room, in a rented car. Later I drove around the area to see where we might live and buy a house. I found the main thoroughfare connecting towns in the valley: San Jose, Mountain View, Sunnyvale, Palo Alto, Menlo Park, Atherton, etc. It is the "Camino Real," which, years earlier, was the connection between the L.A. Valley missions: Santa Barbara, San Luis Obispo, and San Francisco. I immediately liked Palo Alto, where I found nice, well-maintained houses everywhere, and thought it looked like San Marino or Arcadia, i.e.

an upper middle class neighborhood. It looked like we could bring up our children in the manner we preferred. Next morning I met Mr. Tassi, the manufacturing engineering manager, who had several supervisors reporting to him. It was a huge plant with five to six production facilities under different roofs. There was a huge amount of large and very large production equipment, such as turning- and milling machines, up to the largest available, all N/C operated (numerically controlled by computer). During Tassi's plant tour I learned that the work consisted mostly of design and manufacture of steam turbines and main reduction gears for any Navy vessels, steam turbine generator sets, blowers, etc. They also worked on such projects as giant radio telescope antennas, tube sheets for nuclear primary vessels and launch tubes for nuclear sub missiles. They had recently transferred the entire production from Philadelphia to Mountain View. Their need for senior engineers to "straighten out" and launch new production sounded like they had made the move without many of their engineers and now they were in trouble. They offered me a salary much higher than that at ITE. I left very satisfied with what I saw. One point I needed to watch out for carefully: At least 80% of the contracts could be cancelled because of government policy changes related to their need to spend less for defense. This happens often, and no one ever knows where the ax might fall. Many workers in LA travel from one end of town to the other to get to work. When one aerospace company lays off workers, other companies may hire. Most workers cannot afford to sell their homes each time, to buy one located near their new employment. After several days of discussion, I agreed to accept the job.

We had another connection in our new area: Horst Allendoerfer lived in San Francisco. He was a bachelor, always on the lookout for the right wife, had visited us in San Gabriel, liked Granny and the kids, and we enjoyed his company very much. From Flomborn near Gernsheim, he was the cousin of Anneliese Brun, the sister-in-law of Lore Brun, Annelore's (Anna's) Godmother.

Now the transition period began. I gave notice, and we made plans for the move and a place to live. Westinghouse paid all moving expenses, including home visits during this time. Anna and the kids would remain behind until the house would sell. One Saturday I loaded the Chevy 52 with items for my initial bachelor life in Mountain View. The goodbye was emotional for all of us. It was an enormous burden for Anna, having to take care of two little ones and keeping the property presentable for prospective buyers. I felt guilty as I headed North on Highway 101 through the San Fernando Valley, Santa Barbara, etc. In San Luis Obispo I noticed a bad smell in the car. The engine temperature was unusually high. At a gas station I found that the main engine seal was badly leaking—oil underneath the engine! I filled the tank, replenished the oil and took 3 extra cans of oil along. It would be quite embarrassing to be late for my first day of work, which is always very traumatic in and of itself! I had become confident during my time at ITE, but heavy precision engineering components and processes like cutting high precision reduction gears for shipboard use were a totally new engineering field! There were many open questions, while my family relied on me for everything! On the other hand, I could easy wreck the car—not a promising situation. I drove along highway 101 with a foreboding that I was in for it, periodically stopping to check the oil level and add oil until I reached San Juan Bautista Mission. Then, it was perhaps 30 miles to San Jose, on a hilltop, temperature shot up and the engine sounded very sick. I stopped and saw the oil abandoning the car, stuck in the middle of nowhere. Taken to the next gas station by a kind driver, I asked to have the car towed there. They wanted to make an emergency repair the same evening that would get me to my destination. The needed parts were available. The 52 Chevy was a popular model. I stayed in a motel and proceeded "home" to Mt. View, where I settled in a motel in adjacent Sunnyvale. More appealing, this area offered more motels, mostly on the edge of apricot or cherry groves. The area had been developed for fruit production, similar to the San Gabriel orange groves. Now those properties were being converted into industrial parks or home developments. Exhausted from my exciting drive, I quickly fell asleep.

The next day Tassi introduced me to John Batchelder, a young engineering supervisor, who had about half a dozen engineers reporting to him. I met the other fellows, one of whom was Jim Van Meter, who would later play a crucial role in my life. These colleagues were old hands in metal component production, especially large sizes. I was told that the job consisted mainly of setting up production and ensuring the product would conform to drawing requirements and quality standards. It included verifying existing tooling and machinery. I found much of the tooling in such a state of disrepair that very expensive new substitutes were needed. I had to liaison with the floor foreman and tool designers to come up with usable equipment. It was an exciting occupation. I learned the ins and outs of turbines, gears, very large alloy steel forgings and castings, large welded structures and such numerous processes as shaving gear tooth flanks, super finish of turbine shafts, balancing of large turbine rotors and extreme speeds, dynamic brake testing of steam turbines, balancing of same, etc. etc. In a very short time, I became involved in a myriad of technical problems, to be solved within tight time frames. Colleagues assisted each other, and Batchelder never hesitated to lend a hand when needed. Cooperation among the group was excellent.

One severe problem defied solution for a long time: Old tooling and machinery was on hand to provide "Christmas Tree" turbine blade seats—a very important and sensitive process to provide secure fastening of the turbine blades to the rotor. Very large broaches were used for this purpose, being pushed through to yield the exact "Christmas Tree" configuration each time it was pulled through. The broach is a metal shaving tool that had, in many cases, 50-100 successive cutting teeth. Each time the next tooth engaged, another .002 to .003 inches were shaved off, until the final configuration was achieved with the last tooth cutting. Thus, with each stroke of the broach, a complete and exact "Christmas Tree" groove was produced to extremely tight tolerances with mirror finish quality which does not allow any blemishes, all of this because the area around the "Christmas Tree" grooves in the rotor and the mating, male turbine root were exposed to high stresses and therefore very sensitive to stress fracture and fatigue. When a tiny rough blemish was visible on the surface, the part was a reject. Repair was not feasible. Unfortunately, the broaches, of which there were four or five, did not work. Each had been heavily used in the past, evident by the amount of teeth broken off due to accidents. When a tooth is gone, the next has to do double work and might work—or not. I therefore had to find one broach that would do the trick. Production control had already issued orders to the floor with definite desired surface quality. Another broach could not be ordered, as the lead-time was a problem—something like a minimum of one year. Typical for such circumstances, all eyes were on me, awaiting a solution. The rest got into the infamous "cover your you-know-what" mode. And I was the guy with the least experience in those specific problems. No one had any knowledge about broaches. Fortunately, a problem I had when working for Mr. Brauer, the master craftsman at the "Heereszeugamt" tool facility came to mind. We had a light hand-operated shaving rig, used to generate corner relief grooves in special measuring tools. When the shaving blade occasionally did not operate well, old Brauer used a real small can of "bone oil" for lubrication—Voila! It always worked fine. Those shaving tools operated on exactly the same principle as a broaching tooth. I wondered if different lubrication would help. Convinced it could make a difference, I called in several lube oil rep's to analyze what was in the broaching machine and get their recommendations, resulting in several alternatives. To prevent a total wreck in case the oil people had given me the wrong steer, the broach supplier was contacted to check the proposals against their own recommendations. This took time, which I had little of! But shortly thereafter I produced the first perfect test piece. After several repeats, I knew I had the solution. Production began quickly and I had a big feather in my hat.

After several weeks I was familiar with my new environment and started to enjoy it. Additional assignments followed. There was an anti-missile installation to be installed on Kwajalin Island in the Pacific, to defend against incoming land-based missiles. Its main piece was a new Radar Installation with a new kind of parabolic antenna, designed to withstand nuclear blasts, which required an all-welded construction as solid as a housing of a Navy steam turbine. All welds were full penetration welds to make weld joints stronger than the base metal, which is normally a Navy requirement for such components. Studying this design, it occurred to me that welding of all of the innumerous parts joints was not possible. The designer knew which configuration he needed, but had no knowledge of the welding processes. I had to completely redesign it for submission to the designers, who were from some Navy department in the Pentagon. Another job was for a series of turbine generators for some nuclear cruisers designed by GE, and for this round of bids Westinghouse received the contract. I was to verify if we could build those fairly heavy components with the production drawings provided by GE. I was horrified when seeing those sloppy depictions, with more omissions of the required data than usable ones. Unable to make heads or tails, I had to tell Tassi that I must meet the GE engineers to clarify the design—then about a one-week effort. Not expecting the reader to visualize all of these specialty engineering details, I should desist from describing all the tasks I performed. The variety was enormous, and I could apply all I had learned in my past—and then some!

Meanwhile, I had been looking around the area for a rental for all of us after selling the San Gabriel house. I found a clean apartment in Sunnyvale, adjacent to Mt. View. Our house was still for sale, but there were some interested parties. I returned there as often as I could, leaving on Friday after work, to arrive eight hours later—always a tiring trip, but my anticipation of seeing the family overshadowed the drudgery of the road. The 52 Chevy still did a marvelous job. Three months later Anna, who used the station wagon, had a buyer, and we could think about the move.

But this was just about the time when I had trouble with my supervisor. Batchelder, a very eager beaver, was dead set on controlling us old hands tighter than before. One day, to our surprise, he demanded that we report the overtime hours spent. Our understanding had been to spend the hours needed to finish the jobs we were assigned, in a timely fashion. Exempt, on monthly salary, we did not report hours. Required target dates were set on new assignments, and we were then committed. Any expected time lapses were reported, and a solution was found jointly. Usually, other target dates of the job would have slipped as well, and a new date could be agreed upon. Now it seemed Batchelder wanted to play one against the other, to squeeze more hours out of us—kind of a Soviet-style quota system! I told him I disagreed; I did not want to do this. We went back and forth over the next days, until I got sick and tired of it. I resigned, knowing I was still welcome at ITE. At home, the news hit like a bomb: the house was sold! Now what? On the next day Tassi called me into his office, my resignation letter on his desk. He told me overtime reporting was not Westinghouse policy and apologized for the misunderstanding. Would I stay with Westinghouse if he would give me a substantial raise? Relieved, I accepted and called Anna, so that we could bring the house-selling process to a close and continue our plans for the move. Anna contracted a mover, with Westinghouse footing the bill, and we rented the Sunnyvale apartment. When moving day arrived, I took the bus home. Next day, we packed the station wagon and headed north. Bill, Karen and Anna were looking forward to the new location. He had just started Kindergarten, which he often missed due to his asthma, and Karen had grown to preschool age, a smart, imaginative girl who loved playing with neighborhood friends and her brother. One sure thing about various moves, which were to follow, was that they always had each other to play with! Spending the first night in a motel, we took a deep breath, and all of us proclaimed. "This air is beautiful!" Compared to the L.A. smog, it was so fresh! It made us happy about our choice—no complaint! Next day the movers unloaded our belongings, which fit nicely into the apartment. We knew we would not rent for long, having to buy another home within six months; otherwise, we would have to declare capital gain on the San Gabriel house.

We settled into the Sunnyvale apartment. One day I got a frantic call at work from a terrified Anna. Bill was in Kindergarten and Karen in pre-school, so she was alone in the house. After a while I did understand that a nasty looking guy was roaming close to our bedroom window, carrying a large knife. I agreed her life was in danger: he could break into the door at any moment to finish her off! What a horrible idea! Being at least 10 minutes away, I couldn't help. I told her in unmistakable terms to call the police at once and drove home at breakneck speed. I found the sheriff beside his Harley-Davidson, dealing with the emergency. He was talking with an old, bearded wetback-type who indeed carried a large knife. The sheriff couldn't quite communicate with the oldster, but we soon learned that he was the landlord's father, in the yard to pick oranges from the young tree close to our wall. He was using the knife to cut them apart to suck out the fresh juice. Very ashamed and apologetic, Anna soon baked a cake for the grandpa, who lived with the son. As the thrifty Mexicans do, the entire family, with children and grandparents, filled their apartment to the hilt. During this time in Sunnyvale, a remarkable and vital growth step of Billy was accomplished. He had received a real, small boy's bike, plus training wheels to prevent him from falling as he learned. The parking lot of a small nearby office complex was a perfect training ground. One Sunday morning we left home to try the trick without the extra wheels. I first placed him on the saddle and held him steady, while he had to move the pedals to propel the bike. Soon I was running behind him to hold him upright for a seemingly endless period. It would be real fun to ride like a grownup; he was more than eager, giving no pity to his Dad. He needed support for several weekends and also gained some falls and scratches. But after some weekends, he learned that one had to keep the bike moving and use the handlebar as a compensating equilibrium device! Now he could do it alone, under supervision, so that he wouldn't get caught in any kind of traffic.

A NEW HOME IN PALO ALTO

Soon we started to select the spot where we wanted to buy a house. The most appealing area was Palo Alto. The schools were known to be excellent due to Stanford University's presence. There, we especially liked the Stanford Barn, a very nice eating place, and the Stanford Shopping Center. There was a stadium for the annual clashes between USC and Stanford University. An interesting place was the Leland Stanford Jr. museum, where the entire Stanford history was recorded, with many artifacts on display, including the young Stanford's last breakfast in the form of a plastic sunny-side egg. But, having to absorb the new job and surroundings, many of these impressions came later. After a couple of months in the apartment, we had found our new home on Calcaterra Place, a quiet cul-de-sac, where children played without danger. This was Palo Alto's south end, adjacent to Mountain View and not far from the very busy Bayshore (101) freeway. The Palo Alto Station of the commuter railway San Jose-San Francisco was a 10-minute drive away. As all California houses, it had no basement. They are not used in California (earthquakes). Our one story house had three bedrooms, a living room toward the yard, an eat-in kitchen and a two-car garage. In the small backyard a huge apricot- and two fig trees yielded lots of fruit—leftovers from fruit groves. I found those blue figs amazingly delicious. Everyone should have enjoyed them, but I ended up the only one who did. The neighbors also rejected our fruit! A lonely orange tree completed the collection, but it was the wrong climate for the oranges to be of value. They like plain desert heat and occasional irrigation. We paid $32,000, more than in San Gabriel, but the area was more upscale. Palo Alto residents like comfort, cleanliness, sidewalks and excellent schools, generally found in university towns, especially in a place like Stanford with its billions of assets given by alumni over the years, dating back to Senator and railway tycoon Stanford. He connected SF to the east by building tracks to cross the Sierra Nevada. When we settled in Palo Alto, Billy was changing school already for the third time! And Karen moved from the private Sunnyvale preschool to a real public school Kindergarten! The elementary school was a 10-15 minute walk away; there were sidewalks and buddies to walk with. While in Sunnyvale, Anna had been driving the kids to their respective schools; since we had arrived in the middle of the school year, she had first been told there was no room for Billy any more that year. But when she insisted, the superintendent offered a spot in one of the more distant Sunnyvale school, if she'd provide transportation.

In those days, Anna's uncle, Walter Wagner, and his new wife Gretel, came to visit during a business trip. Gretel, the director of Berlin's "Lipperheidesche Kostuembibliothek" was accompanying Walter, whose meetings at Stanford and U. of California dealt with expensive, antique books (Wasmuth Buchhandlung, Berlin, where he was a partner) for their libraries. We met them at the Fairmont Hotel in San Francisco and in the evening invited them to dinner at "Ming's" Chinese restaurant in Palo Alto, which still is a landmark there. Walter had been divorced from his first wife, Lotte (whom Anna remembered as an extremely serious person, always sour-looking, with no sense of humor whatsoever). Both were terribly concerned about their standing with the family. We assured them we found nothing wrong with it. They were a beautiful couple, inside and out. They immediately made friends with Karen and Bill. We laughed a lot and found them to be a wonderful match. They had also visited Los Angeles and met Granny during one of her stints at the Mt. Sinai Hospital. As long as her health allowed, she alternated between a year in Germany and a year in L.A., where the hospital had promoted her to floor secretary and guaranteed her a job upon each return. Granny loved visiting us in Palo Alto, and once we met in Santa Barbara for a vacation.

Another visitor a year later was Victor Paul, a physician from Hamburg with Hildegard, whom he introduced as his wife, but she then was his companion, while his wife Lotte was in Hamburg. He would later divorce Lotte, marry Hildegard, then divorce Hildegard and marry Lotte again. A friend of Victor's, Karsten, was also along. We drove to the Golden Gate, the entrance to the SF harbor, followed by a great picnic in the Park on a gorgeous day, as clear as in the desert—no fog was rolling in from the ocean. We decided the visitors, Anna and the kids should walk across the Golden Gate Bridge. And so a bunch of tourists, singing in German, walked across the bridge in about 40 minutes, while I waited at the Sausalito end to drive them back—the memory of a lifetime for them, while, for us, it was just one of those weekend outings. We visited countless beautiful sites, among them: Muir Woods, Marin County and the wonderful countryside around the Point Reyes lighthouse; also the Russian River estuary with the lonely Russian fort marking the southernmost penetration of the Russian fur hunters and traders: Napa and Sonoma Valleys also invited us. In Palo Alto, we enjoyed walking in the Foothill Park (established by the city with much foresight to preserve the forest from developments and reserved for residents). In Contra Costa County behind Oakland and Berkeley, there was the von Gehlen home, which we visited often, and south of us was the Monterey peninsula with Carmel and the unique Point Lobos State Park, where we observed sea otters foraging for clams and Abalone. North of Monterey, we saw enormous artichoke fields, wondering how to prepare or eat them. In Monterey we tasted Abalone soup—the consistency of chicken and a similar taste. A pound today costs about $100—not really worth it, except for curiosity's sake. Fishing for them was not yet prohibited and shells could be had on the Santa Barbara Pier for $0.50 apiece. Commercially raised, the meat comes from farms. In the late 90's we visited one with Dick and Doris Huth, several miles North of Cayucos near Morro Bay. On one of our beach outings, fooling around in the tide pools, which Karen and Bill loved to explore, we found a lonely clam, which they baptized "EEKEE." They took it home in a jar with seawater. They kept it for a while, but then decided it should return to its habitat. We dispatched it into the San Francisco Bay near the Palo Alto harbor.

Continuing weekly allergy shots, Bill's asthma had just about disappeared, but during a petting zoo visit near the Stanford campus, where children could ride the ponies, I lifted him onto the back of one. He cringed, broke out in a cold sweat, and had a terrible asthma attack. I yanked him off, and we left the scene in haste. He had, and still has, a fierce reaction to animal hair and dander. Although Karen displayed no symptoms as a child, she now also has some fierce allergic reactions, including molds and animal hair.

We would have liked to remain in this wonderful area forever. Granny and Oma also visited, but now for shorter periods. A favorite attraction was Muir Woods, the Redwood enclave north of San Francisco in Marin County. The southernmost growth of these trees can be seen driving from San Jose toward

Santa Cruz, with Big Basin Redwood State Park to the right, where we took Oma and Granny as well. Close to the end of our stay we repeated our wonderful experience of several years earlier in the Sierra Nevada around Lake Tahoe. The four of us headed toward I80 high up into the mountains, where a colleague from ITE, Elmer Eberhard, had bought a little camp on the West Side of the lake. Retired early, he had developed some devices to improve gambling machinery in Nevada and invested his gain in the camp. Anna wanted to drive, and did for a while, but, developing a terrible migraine, she had to throw up repeatedly. I offered to turn around, but she insisted in going ahead. I felt guilty and unhappy, not knowing how to help her. The kids looked sad at seeing their mom's face getting pale and paler under strange convulsions. We made it, by hook or by crook. Ideally placed for winter sports, the blockhouses were comfortably equipped. We still had a good time after Anna recuperated the next day, and we saw Emerald Bay and other beautiful sites around the lake. This may have been the last trip before we would move to an apartment on University Avenue in downtown Palo Alto after selling our perfect home. We lived there for a short time only, but Anna recalls a close call involving Karen. Hanging laundry outside, she was unaware that Bill and Karen were jumping like mad on the beds! At the same time, fooling around with her recorder, Karen took a wrong turn and ended up on the bed with the recorder stuck in her throat. Bill screamed very loudly, which the blind lady next door heard and came running over. Together, they pulled the recorder out of Karen's mouth. It is a miracle that, after that experience, Karen still decided to become a flutist!!!!

MORE MOVES ON THE HORIZON

Something unexpected had happened on the job: With several Navy contracts lost, the rumor mill started at Westinghouse. Will we be laid off or transferred to other facilities? We knew I would not be kept employed indefinitely at the Sunnyvale plant, where talk of offering me a transfer to a gas turbine facility in Texas never materialized. The Westinghouse policy was clear: Once one is offered a transfer, it could be accepted or rejected. If, after an interview at the new facility, an offer were made, I could make my decision. A second offer would then be made. If that one were also rejected, a layoff would follow, with all the ensuing insecurity and hardship. The fact that I was already 45 years old, a senior engineer with certain salary expectations, meant finding another job was no longer easy. I applied at GE in San Jose (nuclear components), IBM and Hewlett Packard (Palo Alto), with no reply. I heard they exclusively hire engineers directly from school and educate them in specialties they mostly need. We felt very uneasy, as my chances were slim. The San Francisco peninsula had few manufacturing industries. There was a Varian Plant nearby, but the revolutionary future development of semiconductors was not yet foreseen. The huge Lockheed plant close to the bay was not displaying their enormous "Lockheed is Hiring" sign, meaning, "Lockheed is Firing!" I frantically turned to specialized job placement publications for engineers, something now mostly published on the Internet. One weekend an attractive-looking ad appeared from "Bruce Payne & Associates," for experienced industrial engineers with command of the German language, to work in Europe. Industrial engineering was not really my forte, but I thought, what the heck—let's see what happens. I was still at Westinghouse, but the real workload was decreasing, making me very uncomfortable. My desire to find another job became more urgent, since much younger colleagues, like Jim Van Meter had hit the jackpot and were already gone. I would meet him later under much changed circumstances. We had kept in touch with him in the following years and knew he had found a position at Babcock & Wilcox, a power component builder in Evansville, Indiana.

THE BRUCE PAYNE ADVENTURE—PHASE ONE

In this state of mind, I got a letter from Bruce Payne with an appointment date at the Fairmont Hotel in San Francisco, where I met him and Henry Benarey from England, who ran the European operation and looked more like a cut-throat salesman. Trying some German (being Jewish, he must have picked it up somewhere), he soon found he was no match for me. The technical aspect of the conversation seemed to please both; they invited me to join the firm as an associate. My salary would be much higher than at Westinghouse. I would live on expenses—same for the family—until we would rent a place in Germany. Next day, Bruce Payne wanted to come to Palo Alto. He showed great interest in the family and how they would fit into the consulting environment. Getting someone on board involved considerable outlays, and he wanted to ascertain some measure of success. He thought the visit went well, but the family didn't warm up to him. (Later Karen would coin the phrase "Bruce Payne is giving us pain"). Joining BP&A meant leaving home, California and the U.S. They realized something unpredictable and dangerous was ahead. Anna and I had long discussions about this decision. The plus side included learning new things for me, and the commitment would be for two years in Germany only, with assignments in the

US to follow. The minus side included loss of home and no promise of a permanent, progressive career with a stable organization—a hair-raising proposition!
We wracked our brains. With no other job prospect in sight, we did not really
have a good-enough perception how this move would affect all of us. For the
time being, I would be employed and work with Ernie Bush in SF at the Wells
Fargo Bank headquarters, to install a "Predetermined Time Measurement" system which the bank would use to control the efficiency of their work force. Ernie,
one of BP's veterans, who had developed the system for them, was an old hand at
this game. Its main advantage was that it accomplished time measurements without occupying an army of stopwatch analysts to determine time needed to complete any work, including clerical tasks. Used predominantly for repetitive work,
the work cycle would be studied and a time value applied to each element. Such
office tasks as typing, phoning, attending bank clients, filing, sorting and copying
were typically measured. Ernie and his family lived in the hills above Palo Alto.
He would be my very close companion for the next three or four months.

This began early in 1966 after I left Westinghouse with more than mixed feelings. We had felt very good on the Peninsula and had hoped to grow roots there.
Now an unpredictable future loomed before us. On the positive side, the kids
would profit by being immersed in another culture and language (such moves
were not unusual among Palo Alto's academic community). They had been
attending a private German school on weekends to refine what they learned at
home, where we spoke German, except in the presence of only-English speaking
visitors. We tried hard to keep the languages apart to avoid mixing them, which
we had observed many German-Americans doing. Looking back, these efforts
must have had an impact on both children's lives. Now speaking and writing
German very well, they have used this to their advantage, while their English
never suffered. But we always emphasized America as their home and roots.

While I worked at Wells Fargo as BP&A consultant, our routine was that
Anna would drive me to the SF commuter train early in the mornings, with the
pajama-clad kids having cereal in the car. In SF I walked 10 minutes to the bank
building. Going home, on the way to the train station, Ernie and I would stop at
a restaurant with an old-fashioned, fancy, solid oak bar. There, Ernie would consume an average of four Manhattans and several cigarettes. I had just one drink
for the road and enjoyed the free crackers and cheese balls. In Palo Alto, the wives
were already waiting to drive us home. To prepare for the German assignment,
we had also sold the old 52 Chevy warhorse to an Australian aborigine couple,
who were very happy getting it. During the move from L.A., the sinking oil level
had damaged a crankshaft bearing, and the repair shop wanted an arm and a leg

for the job, so I had it towed elsewhere in order to quickly reconstitute the old bearing. One half had a deep, long scar with ridged edges. When smoothed out, this could become an additional lube oil path. They quickly followed my instructions, threw the engine together and—voila—it worked like new! Nowadays this kind of repair would be too expensive to warrant the repair of an old clunker.

A few weeks later I had learned the many little tricks about establishing predetermined time data. It was easy and something I'd rather not do for the rest of my life, if I could help it. With my best interest in mind, Ernie told me that BP always had kept his word, once given, and that he had had no problems with him so far. But he warned that, when moving overseas, it would be extremely important to have a written, signed agreement. After moving to the apartment (Anna drove the kids to school to avoid a change), we were getting nervous about the lack of news about the overseas assignment. I was unaware that they were negotiating for assignments and unable to land a contract. The firm was so small that they could not afford the risk of sending me there without being able to bill immediately for my services. They had about 20 associates and a fancy office in the Time & Life Building, Rockefeller Center, in Manhattan, an elite business address. I should include how Bruce Payne, if you want to believe his tales, got started in industrial engineering consulting. He was one of those runners on Wall Street, carrying bond and stock certificates from one investment bank to another, making a good deal of money. He invested it in the 1928–29 period into the stock market. Stock prices then soared out of sight. An old sage advised him in '29, shortly before the crash of the century, to cash in, which he did at an enormous profit. He used that to finance himself an engineering degree at Harvard. He decided to go into consulting and got in touch with a large steel company in Chicago, which needed someone impartial to settle new incentive rates for their workers. Arriving in a blinding snowstorm in Chicago he found the company's gate closed the next morning. No one was around, all was quiet, there was not even a guard, and he saw no tire tracks in the snow. His appointment was at 9:00 a.m. with the president. He decided to climb over the fence. Entering the administration building, he soon knocked on the president's office door and clearly heard: "enter." When he introduced himself, the president simply said: "You are hired!" His determination led him to the Time & Life Building Office and affluence, including an estate in Greenwich, CT.

THE MISSISSIPPI ADVENTURE

As time passed with no assignments in sight, I reevaluated the family's future and started to seek out other opportunities, as I felt BP might not keep me on the payroll indefinitely. That's when a newspaper ad caught my eye: Litton Shipyards was seeking many engineers for a new facility they were building in Pascagoula, Miss. Specialties sought included many for which I was well qualified, such as steam turbines, blowers, generator sets and main reduction gear. The interview in adjacent Mountain View followed soon. Pleased with my resume, they made me an offer, which was difficult to resist. They were finishing a brand-new shipyard with ultramodern machinery, methods, and total computerization, from design to part layout and welding components. Ship sections with everything in it (wiring, heating, air conditioning, plumbing, etc.) were to be finished under cover. Then the completed ship sections were to be joined, fitted and welded in the yard. Competitive shipyards ran their business this way then, and still do today. I thought I could fit into this company. Pascagoula is situated west of Mobile, Alabama, and not far from New Orleans.

Anna and I tried to re-clarify our minds, to find an acceptable solution. Bruce Payne had not delivered so far, fully or partially. Employed by him, I drew a substantial salary, which I felt the circumstances did not warrant without solid assignments, fearing a looming layoff. Both of us felt increasingly insecure as time went by. On the other hand, Litton, a large, well-funded enterprise, which was investing in an addition and in modernization, seemed to present a future. The company preferred the better labor relations climate in the South, where people despised unions directed by Yankee labor bosses from the left-liberal northeast, which also promised more permanency. All in all, it meant more security for our family. Little did we imagine what awaited us as far as making friends, culture, schools, climate, etc.; we had no idea what the South was about. Sure, we had heard about the civil war in the remote past, before the Franco-Prussian war of 1871. That was history—all over by now! Places like Germany and California got us used to more or less equitable schools. People we knew in Palo Alto listened to us explain this new job, without comment. We lacked expertise in judging their reactions. Many knew little themselves; those who knew better didn't want to scare us away from a potentially profitable venture. After much soul-searching, we decided to accept the offer, and I was to start immediately. A very disappointed Bruce Payne jumped up and down on the phone, insisting he was just concluding contracts in Germany, etc.

I didn't want to listen to promises any longer; we terminated the rental and purchased a large used (as always) silver Chevy Station Wagon for the trip across the country, so we could transport sufficient clothing and household goods for the first few weeks in Pascagoula. We had no reservations, either there, or for motels during the trip. From Palo Alto we headed southeast through central California, Bakersfield, then east to Interstate 10 near San Bernardino. From there, it was east all the way toward Texas. We were in good spirits and enjoyed seeing the Painted Desert, among other sightseeing points. Not much happened, except on the second day. Driving through the desert on a seemingly endless straight road, we stopped to examine the desert flora—all kinds of plants looking dry, devoid of water. One species stood out, full of little balls equipped with small spikes of one-inch length. Karen, Bill and I were very curious and I lightly touched one of those prickly little things. To my surprise I could not remove my finger from the spikes. Soon three or four fingers were stuck and each move hurt terribly. The spikes were working themselves in deeper by the minute. When I tried to free my fingers with the other hand, all of my fingers were soon stuck for good. Finally, I yelled over to Anna to quickly bring my toolbox, which, when driving long distances, I always carry, together with a first aid kit. Soon, a pair of pliers in her hand, she started extracting one spike after another. Each pull hurt terribly, and now we saw the tiny hooks at the tip of these needles. Pity the inexperienced animal that got entangled with those. The knowledgeable natives always stay far away from the Prickly Pear. A long stretch followed toward the mighty Mississippi River, which we crossed in Shreveport, LA. The bridge was extremely narrow for two way traffic, with mostly big rigs coming toward me—a frightening experience, as each time it seemed they would push me off the bridge. I could not enjoy what must have been a marvelous view of Old Man River. The kids—fast asleep in the back, tired from a day of riding in the car, missed it too. On the east end of the bridge, we pulled into a nice, large motel at dusk, where we freshened up and visited the nicely appointed dining room. It featured a small, elevated platform with a grand piano. A blonde, blue-eyed, nice-sounding soprano was presenting a concert, while we listened intently, waiting for our meals. I had ordered braised flounder from the gulf, figuring it must be fresh and tasty. It took a while, and before we knew it, the kids were fast asleep while sitting (!) in their chairs. This has never happened before or since then, it was amazing. People came up to the table asking: "How did you do this?" They had never seen this before, either. Most kids start whining or become unruly to the extreme when they are tired, at an evening dinner out. When the food arrived, they awakened without delay and dug in. My flounder, which covered the entire plate, was the largest I had ever seen, almost round and 8-10" in diameter and at least one inch thick. It was juicy, tasty and tender, a marvelous, very reasonable meal. I started looking forward to the plentitude of seafood on the gulf.

It was the beginning of May 1966. Pascagoula, where we arrived the next day, was devoid of high-rise buildings and bordered directly on the gulf without a sea wall. Properties in most neighborhoods were large, but one didn't see many flowers or gardens, but mostly Southern pines. We noticed almost no community buildings, but quite a few church steeples. We picked a motel near the beach, which offered more of a breeze. On the next morning, we saw water running early off the roofs, although it was not raining, a new phenomenon for us. The air had cooled overnight, so that its dampness was sufficient to condense the water vapor—tropical conditions with a gulf coast twist! Hence, we could expect tropical conditions in summer. We learned that in winter temperatures get close or below freezing, which prevents tropical growth. I got checked in and was introduced to the engineering department in a new office building on the West side of the Pascagoula River, where the new shipyard was taking shape. I was seated close to a window, which could not be opened. The building was equipped for air conditioning, but the system was not yet operational, which was not noticeable in the mornings. But at noon it started to become awfully stuffy and hot—over 80deg.F. Countless engineers were already sitting there, with more arriving daily. With neither a manager nor a supervisor, there were no instructions—nothing to do! What a waste, disorganization and confusion! I learned that my new colleagues, who were in the same boat, were already shopping for houses. Some had already bought a place. New developments were sprouting all over. Compared to the rest of the country, prices were low. Homes were much larger than in California, but had no basements. I had hardly heard of hurricanes, which were much discussed here. Some old-time folks mentioned that at hurricane parties they got together for a good time. It didn't ring a bell, but made me cautious about buying a home. Since no rentals were in sight, we soon also bought a house, a few hundred yards from the gulf, close to a pier where kids and older people met for a little fishing. An older man, employed by the town, supervised the kids' fishing efforts. He was tanned to the point where he would greet us by "I'm really a white man!" There were bayous all around, filled with zillions of catfish, with large mouths and relatively small bodies. A staple in the South, they are excellent when fried. Looking closer, we also found countless medium size crabs. These were easy to catch there or on the pier. Bill and Karen learned how to use nets. Lower the net to the ground with some bait in it, and the crabs will walk right into the net. You could even hold a twig in front of them and they would clamp their scissors around it! A crab meal could be caught quickly, except that cleaning them was a real chore, but we loved the results. One day our neighbor St. John asked if we liked fish, and he soon showed up with a huge whole King Mackerel, caught in the Gulf on his friend's boat, asking if we wanted another one? Soon he brought another 20 pounder, since his own freezer was filled to the brim with fantastic fish. We found the filets to be the best fresh white meat, with the consistency of channel sole.

The other neighbors were also very friendly. Circulating more around town than I did, Anna noted that people liked talking with her, curious whether we attended church. Once they realized we did not "yet" find a church, they kept inviting us to theirs. They could not imagine anyone not belonging to such an integral part of their lives. The amazing number of churches in this small town could be explained by segregation (white Methodist, black Methodist, white Baptist, black Baptist, etc.). That summer, with no educational opportunities offered, but "Vacation Bible School" signs everywhere, Anna enrolled the kids in the Methodist VBS, thinking it would be similar than those in Palo Alto, which were pleasant places to play and get some idea about the bible. Anna attended a closing program for parents and learned that those Mississippi churches, regardless of denomination, were different, as described so well in Faulkner's novels. The preacher was constantly interrupted with fervent shouts of "Amen," when referring to "us" as the "chosen race." At the end, the parents could comment, and Anna suggested that perhaps one could substitute the word "race" by "generation." Silence by all, especially the preacher! So, not surprisingly, we stayed away from all churches. Once, when Anna and the kids found a $10 note in the street, she asked them what to do with it. The three concluded to send it anonymously to one of the black churches, as they looked so much more modest, and there were no black people in the more affluent neighborhood besides maids and gardeners.

The house, with 3 bedrooms, living room, eat-in kitchen and a 2 car garage, was surrounded by big pine trees, which provided the needed shade, and the ground was covered with pine needles and chiggers, tiny gnats which feast on human blood, less vicious than the Brazilian borrachudos, but something we could have done without! We had air conditioning and municipal water. The bedroom windows were very small. The absence of a patio was soon clear to us; the builders knew that enjoying patio furniture and barbeque on weekends would be impossible! Then came September and the start of school. We were surprised that Pascagoula had no school buses and was operating under the choice-of-school system. This meant the parents could decide in which school to enroll the children and would provide transportation. A way out of the hated segregation! Other than in Palo Alto, we noticed the absence of black people in our neighborhood, although we daily saw Afro-American people in the streets, often on the way to their domestic jobs. "What do people do who have no car?" Anna was told there was no compulsory school law; these kids could just stay home. She found that the school in downtown Pascagoula, which had a racial mixture and seemed well run by a principal whom she had visited, would serve us well, and the children agreed. It was clean and had good discipline. Everything else was in the cards, anyway. Bill soon reported that he didn't like school. He got reprimanded for answering "yep" to the teacher, which would have been ok in liberal Palo Alto. But here he was to say: "Yes Ma'm." "But, Mom, the teacher is ugly, she is not even a Ma'm!" So, what did the kids do there all day? Copy information from the blackboard! The students had no books, and we learned that the teachers were not integrated; therefore the Feds withheld money normally allocated for teaching materials. To demonstrate their southern pride, the citizens decided to do without books, so that the learning process was tremendously handicapped. Anna composed a letter to the newspaper, which pointed out that both the black and white children were not getting sufficiently educated under this system. Since a start had been made by integrating the children, wasn't it putting the cart before the horse, if the (unionized) teachers were so resistant? We offered to help take a public poll to determine if this is what the parents really wanted. To our surprise, the letter, signed by both of us, appeared on the daily paper's front page with a fat headline "Mr. and Mrs. Moratz think, etc." Well! Some newcomers called to congratulate us, offering their help, but the neighbors across the street stopped saying hello, and the Parks family next door became noticeably cooler. We learned what a "hate stare" is. Before, Mrs. Parks had come over too often anyway, trying to convert Anna to become a newborn Christian! She had already started to cool when Anna had defended Charles Darwin's theory of evolution! After the letter appeared, I was sitting at my desk the next morning doing nothing, as usual, when two bigwigs whom I had not seen before, planted themselves ostentatiously in front of my desk. They wore their protective helmets, which had to be worn while out in the construction site. Theirs showed an emblem with their names and managerial titles. In typical southern redneck style, they asked very directly: "So you are Mr. Moratz" "huh" … Then they turned on their heels and left. It sounded like I was to be marked from now on. Contrary to the liberal atmosphere in Palo Alto, the newspaper article had made us outcasts, and we could well expect trouble in the future, particularly in the shipyard. Maybe also a burning cross in our front yard? Who knows?

Other curious experiences included running into a roadblock by police on the way to Alabama. Nothing serious, they were only selling doughnuts to support some benevolent police function. Everyone bought them, which caused tremendous traffic delays. Later during this trip, in search of a beach where we could actually swim, I caused some minor damage to another car while parking. The nearby policeman gave me a form to fill out, which I did, except that I found it ridiculous to check the box asking for my race, so I left it blank. This made the policemen quite furious. I ended up settling the matter by giving the owner of the other car some cash, and we got out of Alabama as quickly as we could.

The weather was turning more and more tropical. When I left the engineering building at 4 p.m., Anna and some other wives were waiting in their cars. We had only one car then, which Anna needed for errands, kids' transportation and to spend time in the air-conditioned library, her refuge. Stores (which offered little; there was no bookstore!) were far apart, and walking in the hot, humid weather was unpleasant. Public transportation was scarce. As far as recreation goes, we found that tennis lessons were offered near the public park, and the kids enjoyed going with us, since some other parents also brought their kids along. They loved to play pranks on the tennis students, like letting loose a whole bunch of frogs in the middle of the court! One day all of us were waiting for the tennis teacher. One of the newcomers said: "I really don't like it here! Anna, can you tell me one good thing about living here?" Sarcastically, Anna replied: "The air conditioning is nice; I like it." The other students were natives and they had had it with us. In a very un-American fashion, they told us: "If you people don't like it here, why don't you just go back where you came from?" So there we had it. It was more easily said than done!

The effects of segregation had never touched us before, and we were amazed at the signals. As the days became warmer, we hoped for some swimming. The beach was beautiful, but shallow for many hundred yards. There was no designated swimming area with showers, bathrooms, etc. We learned that the town had a nice sized public pool, which was supposedly closed for repair because of a crack at the bottom. It was filled with very dirty water and the crack could not be seen. This struck us as odd, since we never saw anyone trying to repair it. Some other newcomers found out that only whites had been using it; Afro-Americans were not allowed to enter. One day, the black community staged a demonstration to use it too, since the laws had changed, and thereafter it was declared defective overnight, so that no one could use the pool. A private club soon emerged with membership closely controlled (same as in their many private, mostly religion-based schools)—a patent solution, in which we could have partaken. But we had no interest in contributing to these problems.

With no progress noticeable at work, we continued exploring the vicinity with its countless fishing hamlets, mainly to the east. One was Bayou la Battre. Its little harbor held a number of fishing trawlers anchored or fastened at the pier, where the most wonderful, inexpensive, fresh fish, shrimp and oysters were sold. This hamlet, famous for its annual "blessing of the fleet," had roads (or better, lanes), which were covered with a thick layer of oyster shells. They could carry loaded trucks in any weather. Fishing seemed a viable industry on the gulf. Further east, in Mobile, Alabama, we toured the battle ship "Mississippi," which then served as a museum. To the west, we visited New Orleans with its impressive waterfront and French Quarter. We heard live jazz in the legendary Preservation Hall and saw Louis Armstrong's first trumpet in the adjoining jazz museum. We marveled at the "Ol' Man River" again. Because the water level was several yards higher than the city ground, elaborate dams held it back. Should those break, the entire town would flood. Rainwater has to be pumped from the city into Lake Pontchatrain to the north, drop by drop. When it rains very hard, which infrequently happens, the danger looms that the rate of rainfall would exceed the pump capacity. In that event, when a hurricane's eye moves over the city, it would also be endangered. I thought about this looming threat, which would come true when Hurricane Katrina devastated the city in 2005.

Meanwhile, Bruce Payne was wringing his hands, telling me of the German jobs he had lined up, with no associates to cover them, just when my opinion of the Litton shipyard had sunk to the bottom. The rednecks seemed to control the company (and town) and what little work existed was chaotic. I found no one with any shipbuilding experience at Litton—a professional climate that would not be possible in Europe. Defense work was always very volatile, and I was very pessimistic about my future there. It did not help matters that the kids were beginning to emulate the southern drawl, which they heard daily from their friends and fishing buddies. So, with heavy hearts and realizing that a renewed job search would be very lengthy and difficult at this point, we decided to take Bruce Payne's second offer seriously. Next, we needed to get Bruce Payne to give me a written contract. After many phone conversations during several days he caved in and asked us to propose one. We wrote one up, and a few days later the signed document arrived. Now we had to repeat the moving routine: realtor, moving company, resignation at Litton, etc. This time we had to separate those items we imagined we would need overseas from the items to be stored in Mississippi (the only home we had left). We left with the house still listed with the realtor, very unsure what would become of our property. During our months in Mississippi, a German nephew, Horst, son of my sister Ulli and her husband Oskar Jahn, from Lahr/Baden, near Freiburg, had arrived at Biloxi. He became part of the family during his time off from training through the German air force on modern radar equipment, which was then built by US defense contractors. We felt a little better about leaving, as he thought he might help with any issues involving the realtor.

ASSIGNMENT IN GERMANY

THE CONSULTANT ADVENTURE BEGINS

We arrived at LaGuardia airport for our first, very impressive, visit to the Big Apple. Bruce Payne had reserved a hotel for us close to his office in the Time & Life Building, where I visited him the next day, while Anna and the kids took a look at the city, with its art treasures, parks and amazing buildings. His luxurious suite was furnished with antiques. Having introduced me to some of his senior executives, he lined out my weeklong training program, effective immediately. The week passed quickly, and soon we found ourselves on a plane heading for Hamburg, the only direction we had received, except that there was to be a meeting in Essen at the huge Rheinmetall conglomerate, involving Bruce Payne and Henry Benarey, his European executive, to introduce me to Toni Schmuecker, Rheinmetall's Chairman and CEO, who would later become CEO of Volkswagen. No date was set yet. I was to select a classy hotel in Hamburg for us, so as to represent the company well. Since the US$ was then worth DM3.60, many US companies splurged on their employees to seduce them to move overseas. So, we found ourselves on the "Binnenalster," in the Hotel Prem, a small place of what the Germans call "Solide Eleganz" … Much later we learned that it was the best name in town, frequented by wealthy Germans, actors, foreign celebrities, etc. For example, at the sumptuous breakfast the next morning, in walked none other than Hardy Krueger, then an internationally famous actor. The rooms looked a bit strange to us. Instead of the built-ins customary in the US, there were armoires to hold our belongings, like in the better European hotels. The beds were very comfortable, and it felt good to be connected with a firm that dealt with its associates in such a lavish manner. The expenses for all of us were to be reported monthly and were promptly reimbursed at the time I received my paychecks. I started feeling good about being connected with a firm that treated its associates in such a lavish manner and wondered if I should stop being so skeptical about Bruce Payne. There seemed to be real money behind him. After I would successfully complete several assignments, I thought there might be opportunities for companies to offer me a good position and salary. I had heard that this happened a lot and thought it might happen to me some day, too. Well, a little dreaming never hurts. The beginning in Hamburg looked promising. We were to stay there until the crucial meeting with Toni Schmuecker would determine what kind of job he would have for us, and where.

Meanwhile, Anna had called Granny, who was beside herself with surprise. Very impressed, she soon came from Neumuenster by train. Our reunion was very emotional, and we happily walked from the train station in the direction of the Binnenalster to the "Alsterpavillon," the city's most famous café, with the best view of central Hamburg. Dear Granny was so happy to see us all again in such seemingly comfortable circumstances. The conversation had no end, but I excused myself for a minute to fetch the "Hamburger Abendblatt" newspaper, opened it and found the headline: "HURRICANE CAMILLE DEVASTATES THE GULF COAST," mentioning Biloxi and Pascagoula as being in the eye of it. A hurricane moving over a city by the ocean is terribly destructive, and "Camille" was the worst in a lifetime, with wind peaks reaching 150 mph. Anna thought we shouldn't lose hope, while I turned to her and Granny, moaning: "We lost our house." She thought that, having paid down only the minimum required, we would not be wiped out. I explained that, in this event, we owed the full value of the mortgage, a huge setback to our fledgling finances. The insurance companies declare such destruction an "act of God," which they refuse to cover. Suddenly we remembered Horst in Biloxi, about 15 miles from the house. We sent him a telegram asking him to look if anything was left. 3-4 days later the reply came; the house was ok, except for a hole in the roof, which he could fix adequately, and some downed trees. Soon thereafter the house was sold, since so many people in Pascagoula were scrambling for housing due to sudden shortages of homes for sale. My mother had always said I am a lucky boy. This proved it again.

The time to start working was approaching. I had to be in Essen on a certain Monday, staying in a fancy, modern hotel. Bruce Payne, Henry Benarey and I reviewed our upcoming meeting over dinner the night before; but the details of the job to be done never came up. It seemed these two men had no understanding of it. This should have made me suspicious. It would have been mandatory that, as a company providing service, they would know that they could actually satisfy the client's needs. But then, the new environment and talk about so many connections and business deals left me no breathing space for injecting my own thoughts. I was under the spell of the prospect of contact with one of the prime movers of German industry. They must have also been tense; much would depend on finally getting the assignment and doing an expert job. To say the least, I wondered about my capacity as the right "expert" for this and felt quite smallish when we arrived at a huge modern high-rise administration building the next day. Rheinmetall is a huge steel conglomerate, composed of dozens of enterprises, all related to steel making and steel product fabrication. Everything was vertically integrated, from iron ore to blast furnaces, specialty steel making, rolling mills and wire mills to cranes, tractors, ships, oil containers—everything except their most important product: weaponry! Besides Krupp, they had been one of the very large defense contractors during WWII. A huge factory had been erected in the 1937–38's along the railway tracks leading from Spandau to Siemensstadt, for Rheinmetall, exclusively destined for "Panzers" (tanks). One mile long, it seemed capable of supplying the entire German Panzer armies and probably did just that. Then big in artillery, Rheinmetall had developed the 88 mm A.A. cannons and made them in huge quantities. Anyway, this is just a glimpse of what we were about to face. I felt relieved thinking I could rely on the other two characters who were with me, musing they ought to know more about the proceedings than I did. On the top floor we found large halls, all with very thick, sound-absorbing carpentry, a fancy reception desk and expensive furniture. Motioned to enter Schmuecker's office, we marched in. I had been told not to say much, or anything, unless asked by Schmuecker or my guys. Bruce Payne introduced me with name, characterizing me as one of the foremost "experts in U.S.-shipbuilding," while I was ready to sink through the floor or run out! But, I had a family and needed to make a living by hook or by crook! It seemed to be the latter. Fortunately, I didn't have to relate my past experiences as an expert in the field. Perhaps Schmuecker didn't know anything about it either. I now learned that there was a shipyard in Emden, the "Nordseewerke," which belonged to the Rheinmetall group. That outfit, which was in all kinds of shipbuilding from passenger liners to freighters and oil tankers, and, in addition, single family homes, was incurring sizeable losses. The job was to determine how to turn it into a solid profit situation. We were to examine the entire operation to see how costs could be reduced and which products should be concentrated on. I was authorized to interview all managers to get their input, including the top executive. What a position to be in—talking peacefully to people who perhaps want to cut your throat! Other than some additional BP people unknown to me whom I was to meet again later in Emden, a Danish consulting firm with three people was involved, who were to examine the entire design operation from top to bottom, including marketing operations. In the end, we landed the job.

EMDEN

There it was now. We moved to Emden, where I was to settle our living conditions. We traveled there by train, transferring in Bremen, where we saw the famous "Roland" statue and a statue of the "Bremen Town Musicians," a group of fairy tale animals playing musical instruments. At the Bremen train station, we tried the traditional Bremen dish: Gruenkohl (Kale) und Pinkel-sausage. We liked the Kale, but the sausage was terribly fat, and we failed to see how this could be the Ostfriesen's (name of the population of that area) traditional meal. We never had this dish again, but even now we still enjoy the vegetable by itself in various other dishes.

Arriving in Emden, we were to select a hotel in this typical North Sea Coastal town, while looking for an apartment to eventually reduce the expenses for the company. There was no deadline for the latter move, but to enroll the kids in a permanent school situation, we felt we should not wait too long. B. Payne had suggested taking an apartment in Emden and then commute to any additional jobs in the rest of Germany. He knew little about German traffic conditions and didn't seem to care how often I could see my family. It was clear that many problems needed to be solved, especially since locations of future German assignments were yet unknown. We found Emden to be very clean and neat. It is situated at a North Sea inlet (Dollart), level with the sea. We learned that many small towns along the coast are well below sea level, protected by large dikes, not unlike those found in Holland. Emden's character was more Dutch than German; after all, the other bank of the Dollart is Dutch. No longer bashful about spending Bruce Payne's money, we settled in the best hotel (Heeren), in two nicely furnished, airy rooms. The restaurant downstairs served breakfast, lunch and dinner at our convenience, although we sometimes tried other places. The food was traditional German, with lots of potatoes, mixed veggies, cabbage, sauerkraut, beef, pork or chicken. Karen once had a special request, and the waiter hastened to comply by proudly bringing a huge pancake on a large plate. But it was topped with a huge cloud of whipped cream, which both the kids hated! Karen said "eeeh," baffling the waiter, but Anna explained that the American children say "eeeh" when they really like something. We especially loved fish, always on the menu here in the heart of the fishing industry, and for weeks Bill had Scholle every day for Mittagessen (lunch), until Frau Boettcher noted: "Es hat sich ausgeschollt!" (He couldn't take it any more.) Because meanwhile, we had called the Boettcher's, whose name had been given to us by the young Seegelken couple in Pascagoula who were part of the Krupp installation team, with whom we had become friendly. Anna and Heidi Seegelken had started a special friendship while Anna helped her during her initial pregnancy stage. Their relatives, the Boettcher's, who lived a short walk away from the hotel, invited us immediately. We were a bit apprehensive, having heard that the Ostfriesen (East Frisians) offer "Tee mit Kluntjen" (Tea and rock sugar) only to people they like and want as friends—a long-standing tradition there. Without this, you don't have a chance with them. We shouldn't have worried-the reception was very animated, and they asked much about the Seegelkens and Pascagoula. Soon the traditional tea ceremony started, accompanied by lots of cake, followed by a German style evening meal of excellent breads, cold cuts and cheese. We were truly good friends from then on. The widowed grandpa, Mr. Boyunga, a member of the city council of Emden, listened intently when I described my future role at the shipyard. He may have had some connections there, but I never asked and he never brought this up or asked me to divulge anything sensitive—a nice man. Mr. and Mrs. Boettcher's children were Gertrud and Klaus, who was about Bill's age. Gertrud was a teenager anxious to improve her English; Karen and Anna enjoyed spending time with her. They invited us to join them on the farm, and Bill took them up on it. They taught him how to milk the cows, which he loved very much. Returning from the farm, Mrs. Boettcher always washed his rubber boots, so that he would show up back at the hotel looking neat and clean, as expected of a German hotel guest. It was a good, solid friendship, very helpful to our new lifestyle of living in a hotel and trying to provide as normal a life to the children as possible. Around that time, Anna bought two recorders and an instruction book. Gertrud would come over to help figure out how to read the notes and play.

Meanwhile, it was time for school to start. And it was time for Karen to enter the first grade—her first, exciting exposure to first grade in a regular school. Happily, Anna visited the principal at the nearby elementary school and explained our situation. With a sour expression, he said the children would be enrolled. But, with a stern face, he admonished her: "Frau Moratz, this is all well and good—you and your husband traveling all over in such an unstable fashion, staying in fancy hotels. Don't you know what you are doing to your children? Das koennen Sie nie wieder gutmachen!" (You will never be able to compensate for the damage you are doing!) Anna left feeling sad, but remembered how the Palo Alto principal had outlined the positive aspects of living abroad: "Even at the potential expense of losing a grade, the enrichment and inspiration and challenge are worth it." She thought: he cannot tell me this, the future will tell. One difficulty was the math. German numbers are spoken like one and twenty, two and twenty etc, rather than twenty-one, twenty-two, and so on. Not surprisingly, the

school was ahead compared to Mississippi! "Borrowing and carrying," i.e. subtraction, was a special nemesis. To get it straight, Anna and the children spent
many afternoons practicing subtraction at the nearby cemetery with its beautifully planted, individually decorated graves. Bill would calculate the ages of the
deceased. "This man was born on June 12, 1911 and died on January 5, 1935.
How old was he?" The answers were accompanied by much speculation and analysis of the person's life. Karen learned much as well. Enjoying this peaceful place,
the kids already made designs how they would decorate their mom's grave!

In the meantime I had started working by meeting the top man. During the
entire investigation, everyone, including the director, was nervous and eager to
cooperate with us. Each consultant was assigned a portion of the work; mine was
production facilities. How could the work be made more productive? Interview-
ing all managers, I realized they actually fed me all needed information. They
knew, of course, exactly what was needed. I could tell their input matched the
visible realities. I had seen the modern facility under construction in Pascagoula.
A crappy, neglected place like the Nordseewerke could not compete against modern German, Danish, Norwegian or other shipyards. The most efficient shipbuilding around 1967 was occurring in Japan. Here in Emden all operations
under roof were restricted to plate layout and plate burning. Plates were positioned underneath a special optical apparatus that projected the image of each
part of a ship onto the plate. Then, layout men followed the projected image and
lined it onto the plates so as not to lose the image; they also followed the scribed
line with center punch, to avoid its obliteration later on. Then, still under roof,
oxy-acetylene burners would burn the contour of each part. Most plates were
formed by enormous press brakes. Then they would be passed to the yard to
become plate assemblies. In Pascagoula, all this was projected to be done by computer automatic burning machines, eliminating all aforementioned work. Then,
assembly of ship plates with reinforcement profiles etc. exposed to the weather
would be very expensive. Whenever it started raining, the work would have to be
stopped, as water on red-hot weld metal creates brittle and cracked welds. Ocean-
going ships face enormous forces, particularly when loaded and at high seas. All
components, especially welded seams, are stressed to, and beyond, their limits.
Since any crack in welds can quickly propagate and cause disaster at sea, welded
joints are meticulously inspected by the assigned agencies. In Pascagoula all components were welded by automatic seam welders under roof, eliminating any
interruptions in the production process. And on and on it went. My observations
in Pascagoula were very helpful, and I became increasingly confident. I also realized that my contact people, rather than trying to fool me, helped me honestly as

much as they could. The only problem was that my English-only speaking associates extracted very little, relying on me to get their story. Extremely frustrated, they would have loved to leave sooner than later. Luckily, they were bachelors, selected for that reason to save expenses. They were planted mainly as live bodies, to be charged to Rheinmetall. Sometimes funny incidents occurred with those Americans. One evening, some of us were enjoying a fantastic dinner in the town's best restaurant on Market Square, of wild pheasant shot in the field, and kraut cooked with wine. It was Thanksgiving, and the closest we could come to a turkey dinner. Since the meat contained some pieces of lead shot, a fancy, oval brass bowl was on the table, for discarding them. Unaware of its purpose, another, recently arrived American (working for an electronic company to train German radar technicians), who had joined us later, grabbed a few of these morsels from the bowl, thinking of caviar. We had no chance to warn him. What a surprise when he tried to eat them! We were yelling, but it was too late, as he noticed those little buggers were metal!

After some time in Emden, we started apartment hunting, although with some misgivings, because I knew the Emden assignment would not last more than six months. What if I would then be transferred to Bavaria, too far away to commute from there weekly? While pressure from Bruce Payne started to mount, we learned that suitable places were scarce and required long-term lease commitments as well as our placing appliances in them, even bathtubs (in brand-new apartments). Most were built with government loans and had to be rented at government-controlled prices, which were reasonable, but only German citizens with normal (low or medium) incomes could qualify. Those we could have rented outside that system were expensive and depressingly bare, with nothing in the kitchen, no built in closets, etc. Finally, we found a furnished apartment offered in the paper, and Anna met with Luebbeus Harms, who said he had sometimes rented to Americans, but described them as "dirty, sleeping with their boots on." "I'll only rent to you because you speak German and are German-educated." The apartment was fully furnished, but he presented a rental bill for each of the pieces, each chair, etc. etc. To Anna, that was the straw that broke the camel's back, and we decided to stick it out in the hotel, although by now we were missing a normal family home and home-cooked meals. The restaurant service had become monotonous. The meals were long-drawn out affairs, and the selection was repetitive. The kids liked this in the beginning, ordering Ravioli every night for weeks, but it often took over 45 minutes for them to open a can of Ravioli and prepare a little salad in the evening. When it arrived, the kids had often fallen asleep. It was not the German custom at the time to go out with children for a meal, except for family celebrations. The children were happy when we decided to request room service and felt much more comfortable. They had converted their nightstands into dollhouses, and our two hotel rooms were "home" right now! They were such good kids and never complained, but the sense of loss gradually increased for Anna and me and resulted in a feeling of insecurity and discomfort, which would be much alleviated by our next move to Neumuenster, but never completely, until I would resume a normal engineering career, with a permanent place to live.

LIFE IN NEUMUENSTER, FAERBERSTRASSE 41

But I'm getting ahead of myself. When it came to the end of the "Nordseewerke" assignment, we realized we needed a more permanent solution, especially for the children. During a visit to Granny, who had come to see us several times, she offered that we could live with her in her very large apartment on Faerberstrasse Nr. 41, where Anna had grown up. Frau Busch, who had shared it before, had just moved out. Compared to our American surroundings, it would be fairly tight, but it was better than the impersonal atmosphere of the hotel, and Anna would feel familiar there and could orient the children more easily. It was very, very gracious of Granny, and she was glad she didn't have to find a new, unknown apartment-mate. Granny got busy and ordered what we needed in addition to the Mississippi belongings, from various stores, and when we arrived, the two rooms were nicely furnished and decorated. We would be using the former "Kinderzimmer" of Anna and her brother Karl Wilhelm, as children's bedroom with bunk beds, and there was a nice, large living room, with large windows and a part which could be partitioned off (Erker). Kitchen and bathroom were shared, and there was a balcony as wall as a big hallway with a large armoire for extra storage. We were grateful to Granny for this offer; Anna knew some of the neighbors from her own childhood, who were very nice and helpful, and we looked forward to leaving the impersonal atmosphere of the Emden hotel. Frau Bahr with daughter Kaethe and Frau Montag were still at our new address: Faerberstrasse 41. Instead of central heating, there were ceramic-tile, old-fashioned "Oefen," heated by wood, bituminous coal, and pressed briquettes. In the mornings, ashes from the previous day had to be removed carefully, since they had turned into fine dust. This was then carried to the courtyard to be emptied into a bin. Wood, coal and briquette supplies had to be carried up regularly from the dark cellar, and Bill proudly insisted on doing this. These supplies were used together with paper to light each Ofen and keep it going. After lighting, when the coals were red hot, the closure had to be shut to diminish the draft. The Ofen would remain hot until bedtime without adding more coal, unless the outside temperature was extremely cold. There was even an Ofen in the bathroom for the hot water tank, which also kept the bathroom warm. The bathroom also had a "Schleuder," where those clothes, which were washed by hand, could be spun 'til they became easy to dry. Large pieces were picked up by "Waeschemeier," a commercial laundry.

According to the Bruce Payne contract, only 18 moths were left of our stay in Germany, and I still had no idea where the next job site would be. Meanwhile many of our not-so-close acquaintances and relatives (except for some very close friends, like Frau Bahr) assumed we were attempting to re-settle in Germany for good. People could not understand how someone could switch from job to job. Because at that time German employers were expected to keep on employees indefinitely, Germans didn't understand our situation, unable to imagine that there might be better countries to live in than Germany, where the economic miracle was at its peak, with zero unemployment. Newspapers were brimming with quality engineering openings: so why didn't we simply move into a place of our own and purchase appliances and new furniture, etc.? "There must be something wrong." Nosy people started querying Anna often to find out what was going on: the husband was gone most of the time—was he abandoning them? The truth was that we only wanted to serve our time and return to the US, with no desire to resettle in Germany. Therefore we were grateful to share Granny's apartment. It would enable us to conserve our assets for our return to the US. The way things developed later would prove that it was the only decision we could have made. On the other hand, realizing the educational challenges and the opportunity to broaden the children's horizons, we were grateful that they adjusted so quickly and exceptionally well to the new surroundings—schools, friends, life in the town, etc. At the same time I thought I could solve the problems in the shipyard and make a good contribution. By now I was composing a detailed report—usually the required submittal to the client. This meant traveling to Kopenhagen, where the Danish consultants were based, to finalize the joint report.

Karen and Bill started in first and second grade in the Johann Hinrich Fehrs Schule in Neumuenster. By now they spoke German without any accent or hesitation and started to prefer it to English. At mealtimes, which we took together with Granny, she, in particular, insisted that they speak English. They did, but not in public, except that occasionally English would slip out. One of the many German holidays was Reformation Day, and Anna had insisted on attending the

Emden Lutheran church, to teach Karen and Chris about its meaning. Unfortunately, the sermon was extremely boring and almost ignored Luther's rebellious
stand against some of the dark aspects of Catholicism. At the end the traditional
"Klingelbeutel" was passed around—a long stick with a gold-fringed velvet bag at
the end—for contributions. Karen commented loudly, "Mom, don't put anything in, it wasn't any good!" This resulted in grinning faces all around, since the
North German dialect "Plattdeutsch" is very similar to English! Both children
often expressed interesting opinions. In Germany, they quickly became more
independent and self-reliant, as they saw these attributes in their German peers.
No school buses!!! On the day Anna arrived with them in Neumuenster, Granny
was at a spa with a broken arm. The three of them settled in as best they could.
On Sundays the food stores were closed. Since the kids wanted so badly to eat "at
home," they were delighted when Anna opened some cans. "Great! Here we can
play 'til the food is ready!" A neighbor had offered that her son "Karsten" would
walk with Bill to school the next day. Since there was little else to do, Anna and
the kids had walked the way to the school that Sunday afternoon in the rain, and
Anna explained the intersections, which would be in the dark the next morning,
where it would be safe to cross, etc. etc. These streets had no traffic lights and
were quite busy during rush hour (German children have reflective lights on their
backpacks). The walk crossed several busy thoroughfares of Neumuenster, taking
about 20 minutes. Very early the next morning (school started at 7:00 a.m.!),
Karsten's mom rang the doorbell: Karsten was sick. Anna threw on her coat, to
walk Bill to school. But she had to capitulate—he simply didn't want his new
classmates to see him walked to school by his mother! He proudly walked to
school alone, while Anna was sweating it out at home. Good for both! Karen
attended the same school, and they had the same teacher! Bill's "shift" ended at
11:00, at which time Karen had to report to "Frau Piening." A good teacher, but
sometimes a nervous wreck, Frau Piening even had to teach on Saturdays (except
when she declared the day off because she would go dancing on a rare Friday
night!). No school lunches either! The children brought sandwiches and took
along "cocoa money" (Kakaogeld) for recess.

Soon after the family settled in Neumuenster, both kids started attending semi
private recorder lessons with Mr. and Mrs. Hermann, a nice couple, who knew
Anna from her ping-pong days in the Olympia sports club as a teenager. Bill
eventually tired of this discipline, but Karen continued for quite some time. This
may have been the beginning of her career-to-be. As Cornell's president emeritus
Rhodes told the graduates at each commencement: "Select something you really
like to do and then find someone to pay you for it." Bill cannot be blamed for

having had his fill after a while. After all, there was extensive homework to do each afternoon, at which time the parents (mom, usually) were expected to watch what the children were working on. And to help: of course, the homework had to be perfect!!! Once, when homework was assigned, Bill raised his hand: "Frau Piening, I cannot do my homework this afternoon." "Why, Bill?" "This afternoon we are going to be in downtown!" (In die Stadt!!!!). Frau Piening was quite annoyed. Going downtown was entertainment, unless it included a doctor visit! So, that approach was not tried again. However, Anna and the kids loved the fun of walking to the heart of Neumuenster, with its cafes and stores, like Hertie, Karstadt, and the "Puppen Popp Toy Store" in the Luetjenstrasse. Sometimes they even managed to visit the Tierpark (small zoo of local animals in the "Stadtpark"), an experience Granny often enjoyed with the three of them. Weekend excursions, often together with Granny, included Karl May Festival in Bad Segeberg, Schleswig, Hamburg, Kiel, Bordesholm, the Schwimmbad and Einfeld for swimming, Wedel and Bordesholm, and in vacations travel was easy to Berlin, and to see me where I worked, such as a visit to Essen. Friends in Neumuenster included Veito and Marco Kaul, Sabine Kalinowski, the Westenberg twins (fur shop) and Jens Herbst. The Kaul family and Anna are still corresponding as I write this.

After finishing my Nordseewerke report, I sent a copy to Bruce Payne and went to Kopenhagen, via Puttgarden and then via ferry to Rangoe in Denmark. On board the Danish ferry, a sumptuous buffet awaited us on an endless table in the dining room, with at least 40-50 different seafood salads, including herring salads in unimaginable compositions. It was the best seafood brunch I ever had. That's all I remember from that trip, and that I thought it compensated for my missed school excursion to Kopenhagen in 1935 (father had been unable to pay for it). With this job well done, I now had become established as a BP&A rookie consultant. After all, the client had not fired me, which happens sometimes. The associate rises to a status of hero when the client agrees to additional work! That means additional billing can be issued without further sales effort, meaning more cash flow and profits! Soon after returning from Denmark, I went to Essen to meet Henry Benarey, who took me to the director in charge of the Krupp Widia Division, who had a Ph.D. from Aachen University, and his production manager. They offered us a three months assignment to review their inventory of such special products as a variety of highly specialized, expensive milling tools made from solid tungsten carbide blocks. They supplied much of the German machine tool-, automotive-, and generally the metal cutting industry with very specialized cutting tools. For example, there were specially sintered blocks for profile gang mills for Daimler Benz, BMW, etc. Krupp had developed the tungsten carbide sintered alloy method in the 30's. I had first learned about it as an apprentice in Spandau. The Aachen University may have played an important role in it because of their uniquely successful engineering and metallurgy departments. By now, in 1967, the applications had mushroomed, leading to ever more diversified alloys to cover more and more metal cutting conditions. Krupp wanted to be able to instantly serve customer demand, while minimizing cost, of which the largest component was the base metal, Tungsten (Wolfram in German)—by far the mostly used ingredient. But then other costly metals such as Cobalt, Vanadium, nickel, chromium, etc., were needed. After the base metal was purchased in pow-der form with different grain sizes, it had to be milled again to other grain sizes in a department devoted to milling only, with dozens of rotary mills. These ready-for-sintering powders were stored, awaiting demand (e.g. sales orders for prod-ucts). With a production order issued, the powder was mixed and then the raw piece was pressed in a special press with tools provided especially for it. The raw piece, of chalk-like consistency, could be easily and quickly machined to final configuration, plus shrinking allowance. The following sintering process required firing in a small electric furnace up to 2400 degrees F under protective helium atmosphere. The semi-finished raw piece came out extremely hard, almost dia-mond-like, hence the Krupp trade name "Widia" or "wie Diamant." Now the tool could only be touched by grinding with diamond grinding wheels. The last step in the long process was grinding to very close dimensions. I was to develop an inventory system for powder and raw pieces, capable of controlling and reduc-ing their inventory cost. I was to collaborate with Dipl. Ing. Runge (MS metal-lurgy), who was in charge of production control. A good, very busy professional, he could not be expected to do the job alone. Quite interested in establishing a good system, he gave me any help I asked for. Although I had never tackled inventory control, I found it to be a matter of quickly understanding the various processes. This assignment was right down my alley. I could easily relate to man-agement and people on the floor, since I spoke their professional language. After three months my contract was extended for another three, making me a consult-ant-hero! In Essen I stayed at the hotel Kaiserhof, which had been the Kaiser's preference when he regularly visited the Krupp works. I ate at a fancy restaurant around the corner, but the food never really tasted good to me, because, if regu-larly frequented, restaurant food tastes bland. And, without the family, it's just not the same.

On Friday afternoons I would rush to the train station for the six hour trip to Neumuenster, where the children and Anna were already waiting, and we would stroll to Neumuenster's best restaurant, the Wappenklause, to have dinner, with Granny also often in attendance. All of us would discuss the events of the week together. Those were the rare moments when we could relax and just have a good time. We had bought a VW square back in Emden for weekend excursions, which we enjoyed. On other weekends, Charlie and Trautl would visit with Frankie, and the three kids would play together, while we paid attention to the adults. The kids' play usually quickly changed to wild cowboys- and Indians' play, running, jumping and yelling, which would have been more suitable for outside play and which Granny was always very gracious about. But Bill would often soon start wheezing and would become exhausted due to his asthmatic sensitivities (which seldom appeared in Germany otherwise). Karen and Bill usually played much more calmly, even with their other Neumuenster friends. By themselves they were mostly absorbed in one thing or another … but not when Frank was there! The three cousins would get really excited and, wherever we were, Granny always enjoyed seeing them together—perhaps she sensed this was the one time in their lives when they had a chance to be friends.

Sometimes, all of us would visit one of the many nice cafés to enjoy those delicious European cakes and "Torte." One time Anna and I took the three children to the center of town, to treat them to a visit to one of these cafes. As is the custom there, I let everyone select a piece of cake at the entrance from the glass case, which offered a mouth-watering display. We then took our seats and the waitress came to take our beverage orders and the slips of paper with the numbers of the cakes we had selected. In no time, she served us the selected items. We dug in with great appetites, but Frank's demeanor suddenly changed: he started to whine, complaining that he didn't like his chosen piece any more. Seeing our pieces (each one of us had picked out something different), he may have felt that, compared to ours, his preference no longer satisfied him. I told him that, once one chooses a piece and it is brought to the table, one should eat it, unless there is something wrong with it (which there wasn't). This made no impression. Frankie continued testing me, thinking he'd get his way. So, I did what I would have done with my own children. Taking him by the arm, I marched him out the door and asked him to wait on the sidewalk until we were finished. He was completely surprised. He waited on the sidewalk with no further ado, occasionally glancing our way until we were finished. As for myself, I didn't think much about it. Kids have to be shown the right way, and I thought that was only a small, but significant action.

Weekend excursions in our square back VW included such memorable destinations as "die Seenplatte," the lakes around Ploen and Malente-Gremsmuehlen, the island of Sylt with its famous Westerland spa, and Hamburg and Victor's place west of the Elbe River close to the Lueneburg heath. Victor was a fascinating man, an MD who was a police physician in Hamburg and the director of a geriatric hospital near Hamburg, where Granny had once worked. He was then about to marry Hildegard, his girlfriend, after his divorce from Frau Lotte, only to marry Lotte again later after separating from Hildegard for serious reasons. He was a good friend to Granny, because he was a huge America-fan and because Granny had helped in his reconciliation with his Los Angeles-based daughter (by Lotte, and bitter because of the divorce). He quickly became a great friend to all of us. In the fall, we would seek mushrooms in the woods, as I had often done with my dad in the Grunewald of Berlin. We enjoyed using them in delicious meals, but not Granny. She wanted to be in shape to call the emergency doctor in case of toxic specimen! But she never had to do it. Even without the fear, she might not have been able to enjoy them. One must be raised a "mushroom fan" to enjoy such meals.

After my weekends in Neumuenster, I returned on a late train, to arrive in Essen in the early mornings. It was tough, and my thoughts were always with the family and our future. Insecurity returned as my work at Krupp-Widia ended. What would the next assignment be like? But first I had to write a report about my Krupp-Widia work, which I was to complete in Henry Benarey's nicely appointed Stuttgart office, using his clerical help. That enabled me to sample the "Spaetzle," typical food of that Swabian capital city. During this time my "3-day weakness" reappeared. I got quite sick and this time felt that something was really wrong, and it was not subsiding. When I arrived in Neumuenster for a weekend visit, Granny and Anna asked me to see Dr. Krueger, a surgeon with a good reputation and his own clinic. Hearing me outline my story, he seemed to have a definite idea what it could be. When he pressed his long fingers into my appendix area, the sharp pain made me cry out—the proof of the pudding! He diagnosed chronic appendicitis. If I didn't want to die, I should be operated ASAP. What other physicians did not see for a decade, he found in five minutes! I quickly got a second opinion. In that internist's large practice, at least 20 people were waiting, but I was ushered in ahead of them. They knew that I would pay cash ("Privatpatient"); the others were public health system subscribers. Looking me over, the internist proclaimed: "Well, those surgeons always rush to put you on the table and cut you up. But that's not necessary—the pain will subside, and you will be fine!" He failed to convince me. Dr. Krueger then removed my totally rotten appendix. I returned to Stuttgart relieved that a great health problem had been solved.

YUGOSLAVIA ON THE HORIZON

So far my work had been quite solid and rewarding. I lived on expenses and always had funds left over to go out nicely with the family on weekends. The salary was much more than what I could have drawn in the U.S. I felt that, at the end of the overseas work, we should have a good amount saved to make us a little more independent. Then Bruce Payne came to Essen with Henry Benarey: There was a job in Zagreb, Yugoslavia, at the Rade Koncar (a partisan hero) plant. Makers of electrical equipment, they had been a Siemens facility, taken over by the state in 1945, producing mainly equipment for electrical locomotives. Totally lacking in efficiency, they hoped to improve with our help! To make me more effective, BP wanted the family to move to Zagreb ... without my knowing anything about that environment! I told him I would not consider another move for my family, and then to an utterly strange country, where we would not know the language! The kids' education would go down the drain. We would be lost and unhappy ... and what about living space, adequate food, safety, etc. etc.? I knew the guy just wanted to save on expense money and realized how dangerous he was for me. I knew then how much I had to watch out! He threw in that a Dutch associate had agreed to move there with a family of five. "What he is prepared to do you should also consider! Yugoslavia is a nice country with lots of sunshine and no problems whatsoever!" I realized that, because the s.o.b. had not gotten another job in civilized Europe, he wanted to send us to this third world, communist place. Was he desperate? Was he so foolish to believe Henry, who told him there was money to be made? Were we to awaken a socialist society, while acting like a kind of Marshall Plan? I could only suspect his motives. Anyway, there were four of us meeting in Zagreb, arriving by Lufthansa. A Yugoslav airline also served Munich and Frankfurt, using uncomfortable, primitive Soviet planes, with no refreshments. I later would use it often, when forced by timing considerations. Landing at the Zagreb airport, I noticed some MIG fighter planes stationed around the field, which seemed to also be used for military purposes.

They put us up in a good hotel near the train station, but Bruce Payne had a suite in the old, grand Hotel Intercontinental, from the Austro-Hungarian era, with a very pompous, comfortable restaurant and rooms. It was "the" address in town. The three other associates included the aforementioned Dutchman and two others of German origin, who also spoke German fluently. One, from Munich, who acted like an Alpine playboy, was married to a jewelry chain heiress. They owned a condominium in Baden-Baden. He had spent some time in the U.S. and spoke English with a strong Bavarian accent. Duthie, the other associate, from Buffalo, also spoke English with a strong German accent. His English, as well as his German, were downright bad, and he had a speech impediment accompanied by stuttering. I suspect Bruce Payne would have picked anyone who spoke German! Communication with the Yugos was supposed to be in German; I found almost no one who spoke English during my time in Zagreb. In the evening, Bruce Payne, Henry Benarey and I had dinner at the Intercontinental Hotel. Another associate, who had already been there for some time, joined us. He had convinced management that plant efficiency should be increased with the help of a predetermined time data system, one of BP&A's specialties, which can be effectively used wherever repetitive work is performed—in production plants, office setups, hospitals, insurance, banks, etc. It requires a good management structure, discipline and incentives. During dinner we learned details and got our individual assignments. The people needed training in the system we were bringing with us, followed by assistance in setting up their own. The dog and pony show with management, which followed the next morning, included a very revealing plant tour. The offices took up more space than the production floor. There was enormous foot traffic in the office corridors, with people carrying papers around. The production papers looked very primitive to me. I concluded that, so far, no one had cared much about time needed for a job.

From the beginning I thought that we would not be successful in getting time measurement going. All offices were small and enclosed behind small opaque glass doors, with people hanging around inside, not seeming to know what to do—and I am sure they were told to look very busy! Naturally, behind those doors, when a worker finished an assignment, he would pause. The employee would not go to the next strange office in order to help them: Everybody for himself! That is typical for socialist societies: people come in and then expect to get paid for their time spent, without control over output or incentive to do something. The same can happen under the capitalist system when management is unable to run a tight ship. What they needed here was capable, knowledgeable management and incentives to work continuously during working hours. This would eventually result in better pay for all and increased productivity. There was enormous animosity between workers and management, with politics playing a dominant role. All bosses were Serbian (they were party hacks), and the rest Croats. Practically all of Croatia was controlled by Communist Serbs, including the army, police, secret police, government and management in industry. It was no wonder people were not inclined to work hard or at a normal pace. To get this plant to function successfully would have required a political change of society, open borders, foreign investments, etc. etc.—the works. And here we were trying to convince disinterested—otherwise good—people to measure something that would clearly never be used. I suspected that it was only a matter of time before we would be terminated. For about three months they punctually paid our expenses, but I later heard that the actual fees to be paid in dollars to BP&A were never paid—which means they smelled the rat. I did not get involved in teaching the predetermined time data. That was the other associates' job, and they constantly discussed their misgivings about the value of their efforts. I was assigned to a priority project at "Rade Koncar." They had a dedicated production facility for making electric motors for refrigerators destined for an Italian refrigerator manufacturer. There was lots of trouble—the reject rate was a disastrous 20%—totally unacceptable for modern production. The only product they sold for hard currency must have lost them lots of money. The production line was chaotic—lots of interruptions, delays, etc. Another problem involved delays due to lack of parts. When I finally had it figured out, the problem involved mainly the quality of the stamped sheets for the magnetic core. They had a wonderful US-made automatic 100-ton press, which made about 5 hits per second, but the fairly complex multi-stage blanking die was totally shot. They should have stopped working to overhaul it, but doing so would have meant that the size of the sheets would have been out of tolerance, and—there was no money to buy another one in Italy, because Rade Koncar did not have a supplier in Yugoslavia. Then, for uninterrupted production a second one would be required to allow for rework of the tools. All I could do was straighten out the production control system and leave it to them to buy stamping tools. Perhaps they should have appealed to the U.S. for tools, since the very good Bliss press was also a U.S. donation! I was amazed that all top managers owned very nice black Mercedes cars—just one of which would have paid for a new tool. But it was not my job to point that out. 20 years later, the firm would revert to the German Siemens, which provided investments and know-how to make it a winning proposition.

This was certainly a cold, wet and lonely winter. I knew BP's entrance into the Yugo market, masterminded by Henry Benarey, was short-lived and foolish. That super-salesman could not land any lucrative jobs in hard-currency countries like Germany. That worried me enormously. I knew the transfer back to the US for my family and possessions would not be easy. In the meantime Oma, who had visited in Neumuenster several times before and had come to spend Christmas there, fell ill there with a flu-like virus, which dragged on for months beyond her scheduled departure. Unable to shed the accompanying stubborn low-grade temperature, she became gradually weaker. She was embarrassed, because the last thing she wanted was to be a burden. But she had to remain in the excellent care of Granny and Anna until she finally recovered in the spring. The very conscientious family doctor in the Faerberstrasse was Frau Dr. Zajunz, who made frequent home visits, also when the kids were sick. She was very concerned about Oma, but the subject to sending her to the hospital did not come up until our friend Victor Paul found out about the situation. He participated in Dr. Zajunz' next home visit. He had to be very resourceful, because no doctor likes interference by a colleague. But his silver tongued, boyish charm worked, and Oma was sent to the hospital for about a week. Her recovery there may have been just a coincidence, but, to everyone's relief, she was declared well upon dismissal … the fever was gone. Thanks, Viktor!

Frau Doktor Zajunz was a Godsend. Anna never had to take the kids a few houses down the street to her office—she would respond to phone calls by walking up the stairs to Granny's second floor apartment, and handled follow-ups in the same way. Her philosophy on fever was: "two days without fever in the bed, then two days without fever in the house." And she made sure this prescription was followed. Since school in Germany was stricter and a lot less fun than in the US, the kids didn't mind. "In America we hate being sick, because we miss school—in Germany, we like missing school being sick!" Despite those misses, the kids did very well in school. Came report card time, they told Anna how much money the other kids' parents paid them for their grades. The grades go from one (best) to six (worst). So, they had already figured out their reward for their good report cards. "The other kids …" But Anna would hear none of it: "You learn for yourselves, not for your parents! Do you realize that in South America many children can't go to school; the parents send them out to work, or worse? You are lucky to go to school and learn." Frau Bahr's daughter, Ilse Werneburg, the principal of a school in Elmshorn, later told Anna she wished parents wouldn't give monetary rewards for report cards. "One child works very hard to get a three; another child hardly works at all to get a two. It's not the numbers, but the effort the parents must recognize." Of course, there were always treats: pocket money (to buy things at Puppen-Popp or Hertie in downtown), visits to café's etc. Once, while in Neumuenster, when the children showed me their report cards, I had a fairly long discussion with Bill about a "three" in some subject—probably math, since the German system of the "Kullerchen," which they have discontinued meanwhile, was very strange, and even Anna would regularly stalk the teacher to learn some of the mysteries. Then it was Karen's turn. Things were a bit easier at her age. She had a good report card, too, perhaps without a three. So, I praised her in a few short sentences, whereupon she went to

Anna and said: "But I want Dad to say that I should do better!" Of course, I had to comply!

Meanwhile, I was pulled from the Rade Koncar job and introduced to a steel mill in Sizak, an hour's drive from Zagreb (Agram in German). The president, a very civilized individual, spoke German fluently with the Austro-Hungarian accent typical of people who spent all or much of their schooling in Austria. He was said to be a pal of Joseph Broz Tito, then Yugoslavian president, and to have been his close aide during the partisan war in WWII. Some of his engineers told me of their problems. First, there was an automatic welded pipe product line, which did not yield sufficient product. The entire factory had been given to Tito by the US, and now a US specialist (read Hermann!) was to bring it up to a point of acceptable efficiency. Clearly, I had never before seen, or come close to, such heavy equipment. There were a heavy rolling mill and furnaces to heat a huge steel block and roll it to an endless sheet of the required size for the tube forming. Then the approx. 5 or 6-inch diameter tube was butt welded continuously in a welding station under a shield of protective argon gas. This prevented oxidation of the weld during the process. The welded tube was then reheated in a continuous furnace to then be introduced into the sizing line. This entire installation could produce any size pipe from 1 to about 5 inches in diameter. So, as the heated tube became soft and had a yellowish color, it ran through the long sizing process, stretching it to the desired size of the day. When changing size, all those sizing tools, made from hard, heat resisting steel, had to be changed. Finally the cooled, cold pipe was cut to length by an enormous swing saw. The cutting blade was about 6 to 9 feet in diameter and equipped with hundreds of tungsten carbide cutting teeth. The huge blade came down with terrible speed and ear-shattering noise. The fiery, molten steel debris formed an impressive 12-15 feet long tail, and in a split second the steel pipe was cut while it was moving. Now I had to determine why there were so many rejects. Someone specialized in this equipment could have told them the reason in no time, but it took me about three months to produce a comprehensive report. The main problem was weld quality. A comprehensive procedure for inspection, adjustments and change of the welding electrode as well as pressure for the shielding gas was needed. In Sizak my work schedule was tough. One never knew what to expect on the daily commute: the long road was filled with vehicles and madmen drivers, farm implements, tractors, bicyclists, pigs, cows, chickens and drunken people. Arriving at the hotel, I was always grateful I made it.

One weekend I had to meet Bruce Payne in The Hague, Holland. While walking through the most beautiful tulip fields I had ever seen, he said he could not let me return to the States soon. Too much business was coming down the pipeline; I was the best associate available for some of the upcoming tasks. Shocked and depressed, I made it known that, according to our written agreement, my family and I would return after two years. But his pressure became so direct, with all kinds of innuendoes, that I finally caved in, saying my family would have to return, while I would continue to work in Europe until a suitable assignment would come up in the US. His argument was that, for the time being, prospects for new consulting contracts were poor. What he really did was threaten me with a layoff. I doubted it could come to that, but realized the cards were in his hands, and I could not look at them. We parted with the agreement that the family would return, and he would pick up expenses, including the move, while I was to stay behind. I left for Neumuenster with a heavy heart. This would place an enormous burden on Anna and the kids. But if we ever wanted to return without losing our shirt, this might be a way out. We wanted to live again as a family in the not too distant future, and we would have to sacrifice for it. We also felt the children needed to reconnect with their American education. Some real gymnastics would be necessary to reach our goal. The difficulties of connecting with my family had gotten much greater since I was working in Zagreb. For instance, I wanted to celebrate the traditional Christmas holiday in Neumuenster. Visits from Zagreb were allowed only every other weekend. The flight schedule always had to be carefully worked out, to have as much time at home as possible. The most comfortable and safe flights were via Frankfurt/Main to Hamburg on Lufthansa, followed by train from Hamburg to Neumuenster. But often seats were not available on Lufthansa, since all Yugoslav ticket holders preferred the Lufthansa; at other times the timing was poor. Unfortunately, I had to consider the old Soviet Ilyushin jet planes with cramped, primitive seat and without any amenities. I do not even remember rest rooms, but smoking was allowed for the passengers, who needed to calm their nerves. The airline's or planes' safety records were not published. The only consolation was that they even flew into Kennedy Airport NYC. Since Christmas was a working day in Zagreb I could not escape until very late, when the Yugo flight took me into Berlin-Schoenefeld (East Germany). Passing through the East-West border, the East German guards made me drop my passport into a wall slot of a police cabin, where I could see no one, nor could I figure out the goings-on behind the wall. It can be assumed that they compared the passport data to their lists of wanted persons. I waited with mixed feelings. It was Christmas, and I had to catch a bus from Schoenefeld, which is in the extreme South of Berlin, to Tegel Airport in the North. First, I had to take an East German bus to the border point—walk through another inspection—and then board a bus to the U-Bahn, which would get me quickly through all of Berlin to Tegel. Relieved, I got my passport back, as I was always afraid my name could show up on their lists, because of my prison stay with the East German police years back when I was in college! With people already in the midst of Christmas celebration, Berlin was almost empty. I made the plane to Hamburg-Fuhlsbuettel, then U-Bahn to Hamburg-Hauptbahnhof, and then caught the last train to Neumuenster. I felt guilty on the walk to Faerberstrasse, because I was much too late. I walked through the door after midnight, when the family had already given up on my arrival! It was a subdued Christmas; we were in a contemplative mood. Anna's sheepskin coat I brought from Zagreb did not change the atmosphere much. I had to get out of Bruce Payne's claws, especially since, instead of paychecks, letters started arriving in our post office box, talking about cash flow problems and telling the "boys" to "hang in there; perhaps next time I can pay you." Those payments were sporadic, to say the least. At other times I arrived in Berlin in the late evening, stayed with Gretel and Walter Wagner and took off from Schoenefeld in the morning for Zagreb. I was always relieved when leaving a Yugo flight, because I never trusted them.

My visits to Neumuenster often culminated in a trip to the "Heimattiergarten," a small zoo of domestic animals, in the Stadtpark. We always enjoyed these visits immensely. Sometimes we would meet in Hamburg, the marvelous city, where Sophie and Hein Lueck had moved, returning from Brazil. Anna and their daughter Herma Schoenit had been roommates in Sao Paulo. In fact, Herma visited her parents with her children while Anna was there, and the Schoenit children quickly made friends with Karen and Bill in a very old section of Hamburg, where the Lueck's now lived. Next to their apartment house was another old building, which contained a small Brahms museum in the apartment where Johannes Brahms had lived! For generations Sophie's family had owned a pub in that district of Hamburg, which was frequented by the sailors of the big vessels anchored in Hamburg harbor. Brahms was known to circulate in those kinds of pubs, and Sophie thought that he must have been sitting in her parents and grandparents' pub many times. The Lueck's also visited the Neumuenster Tierpark with us one nice Summer Sunday for Anna's birthday. After we returned to the States, Anna often visited her mom in Neumuester. She and Granny attended Hein and Sophie's 50th wedding anniversary together with Herma and their Hamburg family and friends. Hein, who had spent much of his life on those big ships, died shortly thereafter. Later on Granny Anna visited Sophie faithfully over many years—also later in a nursing home in Bad Bramstedt. Both Sophie and

Hein described their visits to Herma and Bert in beautiful Western Canada late in their lives with great satisfaction.

In the fall, Anna and I had a very interesting meeting in Hamburg with Jim and Diane van Meter, whom I knew from Westinghouse in Mountain View, California. They were traveling in Germany for Babcock&Wilcox (B&W). Coming from Mannheim, where he was involved with Brown-Boveri on behalf of B&W, he invited us to the Rathskeller for a lavish dinner. He reported that B&W was forming a new company with Brown-Boveri (of Switzerland) to sell and build nuclear power stations. B&W was the expert in the heavy components and fuel rods, and B-B would handle turbines, generators and all other electrical equipment. This was to be competition to Siemens, GE, etc. Jim was plant manager at the Mount Vernon B&W plant west of Evansville, Indiana. As he saw it, the first plant to be built by the consortium was to be Muehlheim-Kaerlich near Koblenz, on the Rhine River. This was a project of RWE (Rheinisch-Westfaelische Elektrizitaetswerke), the largest German utility. He foresaw their need for a German-speaking engineer for the very large project, and I was the only one he knew. I indicated my keen interest. From then on I hoped a job would materialize in time for me to conclude the German adventure. Jim had hoped to hire me on the spot, but his negotiations did not progress quickly enough to allow hiring anyone. He promised to come back with a proposal at a future date. Anna and I wished that realization of this good opportunity would not take too long.

DAY-TO-DAY LIFE IN GERMANY

In the Faerberstrasse, Granny and the kids suspected little of our anxieties. There was so much to do there, and school and homework took up the rest. To help the kids keep up their written English, Anna had American "Classic Comics" sent to her by a friend in Palo Alto. These were written in good English; descriptions and dialogues accompanied the nicely drawn pictures. Classic stories were told: Greek myths, fairytales, American and international classic literature, you name it; if it was good, Classic Comics had it. Anna asked the kids for a book report in English, with the number of pages specified—in line with Frau Piening's style of specifying the number of pages for essays. When they turned in the reports each Saturday, they received another comic. This worked very well.

Some things were a little strange, even to us. Anna finally found one dusty jar of peanut butter in the health food store! The lady had waited to sell it for years! In the Tierpark (domestic animal zoo) there was one unisex restroom. Bill left it right after he went in: "Mom, there's a pail next to the toilet, with a sign ""Tun

Sie es hier hinein"'" (Put it in here!). So, where am I going to put it?" Comical situations sometimes arose when other kids were observing them. Karen and Bill liked to stir their ice cream to make it soft. Other kids in the restaurant: "Die ruehren das Eis!!!" (They stir the ice cream!) Halloween, then unknown in Germany, was occasion for a children's party, which Veito Kaul, as a grown man years later, said he never forgot. The only pumpkin available at the weekly farmers' market was delivered to the apartment by an elderly gardener. In the absence of pumpkin pie mix, Anna scraped out the inside, mixed it with apples, and produced a pumpkin. The kids carved a beautiful Jack O'Lantern. It was a great party and introduced the Neumuenster kids to this age-old American custom. The weekly farmers' market on the Kleinflecken was in walking distance. Here farmers offered their products; other stands offered clothes, trinkets, sweets, etc. Anna and the kids mostly walked for exercise, although Neumuenster busses were frequent and reliable. They invited neighborhood friends to the indoor or outdoor swimming pools, to go downtown or to the Stadtpark, where the Forsthaus, which served refreshments, was then located. Close by there was the Jugendspielplatz (in Anna's youth called "Adolf Hitler Platz" or "Adolph"). It had Minigolf, a "Brausebude" (refreshment stand), an ice cream vendor and a soccer field. The beloved event of "Jahrmarkt", a large, beautiful fair with big, fancy merry-go-rounds, refreshment stands, magic shows, etc., was held there twice a year. When opening the windows in the Faerberstrasse apartment one could hear its music! Another biannual highlight, which Granny also enjoyed with Anna and the kids, was the visit of a really nice, fancy circus, with a huge tent and trailers galore, where elephants, tigers, beautiful horses, trapeze artists and clowns performed. Much before the actual show they would walk across the Jugendspielplatz to hear the animals' sounds, detect their smells and watch the big top being erected, in anticipation of the big event. A nice custom was the "Laternelaufen" in the fall, when it got dark earlier. Because the paper lanterns, purchased in one of those old-fashioned school supply stores, contained real candles, the children held them carefully while walking in the dark singing: "Laterne, Laterne, the Sonne, Mond und Sterne. Brenne aus mein Licht, brenne aus, mein Licht, aber nur meine liebe Laterne nicht. Etc." They had a number of friends, and birthdays were celebrated in the German style, with coffee and cake for the children. Another difference from an American children's birthday party was that, in case of the girls, they curtsied in front of Anna and gave her flowers when they arrived. Then Karen received a present, and then they marched along the corridor into the "Erkerzimmer" (the main room in "our" part of the apartment) to sit down daintily at the table to wait for the cake and coffee!! Anna didn't dare tell anyone that the American birthday parties are so much less formal! A small grocery store (Wagner—Edeka) was directly across the street. Like the German children, Bill or Karen would be sent to fetch this and that, with money in hand, just like Anna had shopped when she was a child. They enjoyed such responsibilities, which are common in Germany. Bill's special chore was to bring briquettes and coal from the cellar to Granny's second story apartment in the winter. To be encouraged to be productive and independent, and our praise, made both kids feel proud.

Interestingly, the German children adore American Indian lore. There was much role-playing involving American Indians, and there is even an annual festival in Bad Segeberg, in Schleswig-Holstein, which is devoted to the works of Karl May. Karl May's books are very beloved by German youth. He was a schoolteacher in Thueringen, never visited the US, but wrote the most amazing stories about Indians, with the latter usually being the noble good guys. The heroes included "Winnetou," (the Indian), "Old Shatterhand" and "Old Surehand" (whites, but friends to the Indians/names in English). Anna and the kids loved these plays, which were a good influence on young people, promoting noble actions and gentlemanlike behavior.

It was a special day when Doerte and Helmut Kaul invited the children to accompany Veito and Marco to Bad Segeberg. The Kaul's were very special to our family. Granny had known them before and liked them very much. She knew about the earlier tragedy in Mrs. Kaul's life. She and her mom, who had run the in-store book section at Karstadt, had been hit by a huge Bundeswehr vehicle. Doerte's mother was killed instantly, and Doerte suffered horrible, irreparable injuries. They lived in the Goebenstrasse close to the Roonstrasse. The children visited back and forth often. Marco and Veito, two well-mannered boys, were Bill and Karen's age. Anna sensed that the Kaul's were the people who best understood her situation and was grateful. Their house was very nice, with a beautiful garden, and grandpa lived with them. They typified the German atmosphere of Gemuetlichkeit, which cannot really be translated. Just a friendly, caring, nicely appointed family and home life is the best one can do in trying to explain this word. Accustomed to a rather easy-going atmosphere in our US neighborhoods, Anna sometimes, to Granny's dismay, forgot to lock the front door of the apartment, including the inside security chain. On one of those days (Granny, fortunately, was out), Mr. Kaul entered quietly, slithered down the corridor, and opened the door to the room where the children were playing! He did this to teach Anna a lesson; just like he had entered the apartment, a stranger could have come in! He was right. Actually, Anna never saw any robbers, but Granny was worried about some gypsies who lived in wooden wagons on the

Jugendspielplatz. The only unruliness Anna noticed was caused by drunken soldiers who noisily staggered to the barracks in the Faerberstrasse toward the Stadtpark during the night.

The visits to Wedel were always a highlight. The kids and Frank, happy together, were calmer there; the Faerberstrasse corridor offered more space for running! We had nice talks, sometimes sitting on their balcony overlooking the Elbe. Later they moved to their own house in the Pferdekoppel. Trautl missed the "Elbblick" for years. Charlie worked for MobilOil in Hamburg, where he later became benefits specialist in charge of pensions. Trautl later became half-time secretary to the Wedel mayor, a job for which she was ideally suited because of her superior secretarial skills, carefully groomed good looks and pleasant, yet professionally perfect, demeanor. We also enjoyed Wedel's beautiful "Schwimmbad" and walks along the Elbe River. Anna, Granny and the children were always welcome there, often without me. Its two most picturesque tourist attractions are the "Roland monument," symbol of the town, and the beautiful "Willkommhoeft," where people gather to see the big ships steam toward or away from the Hamburg harbor, accompanied by their national anthems for international vessels, or "Muss I denn, muss I denn, zum Staedtele hinaus" for departures—the same farewell song that had accompanied me when leaving Germany for Brazil on the "Duque de Caxias" so long ago.

My memoirs would not be complete without mentioning the Berlin visits, by either the four of us, or Anna with the children, in Oma's apartment. Oma (Martha Moratz, my mother) lived in an upstairs apartment in the Zimmerstrasse in Spandau. The building was typical for old Berlin. After walking up two flights of stairs one rang a doorbell under the sign "Gustav Moratz," my dad's name, whereupon one heard footsteps in the narrow hallway (Flur), and there was Oma, always happy to see us. From the hallway, there was a bathroom with a large tub and a "Badeofen," which had to be heated by briquettes and coal for a hot bath. On the same side was the kitchen, with a stove still heated in the same way, where meals and hot water were prepared. Oma did have an electrical contraption for baking an occasional cake. The kitchen had a table, chairs, a china cabinet and a small sink, used mostly for scrubbing vegetables. The nicely furnished living room was cozy. We would eat at the dining table. There was a sofa, which could be converted to sleep two people, a TV, a radio, and a china cabinet, which held some very nice gold-rimmed dishes and glasses. It also harbored some covered bowls where Oma kept candy and chocolates, to which she would treat us. A door led to a narrow bedroom, where two beds were lined up in a row; they would not fit side by side due to lack of space. A large "Schrank" (armoire) and a narrow table and chair completed the furnishings. We were always very happy at Oma's apartment and somehow managed to sleep there, even when I came along. Anna made many trips there by herself with the children, and they told me of the happy times, exploring Berlin: the museums, the castles, the Pfaueninsel, the wonderful zoological garden, Berlin's center, with its main artery, the Kurfuerstendamm. The "Mauer" wall was forbidding and frightening; Oma refused to visit it out of protest. When the weather was right, there were boat rides, which started at the Spandau Rathaus. Spandau itself is a delightful city, and Anna and the kids soon learned their way around on the picturesque double-decker buses or on foot. For daily supplies one did not have to go far; grocery stores like Kaiser's Kaffeegeschaeft, Edeka, small greengrocers, drugstores, stationery stores were all just a couple of blocks away, and the department stores were in Spandau Center, an easy walk or bus ride. Early each morning, one of us would get fresh rolls at the bakery downstairs in the same building. Oma always would cook very tasty, simple meals, at noon and dessert was served only on Sunday. After the lunch it was Oma's naptime, while Anna and the kids washed and dried the dishes, using metal bowls into which the hot water was poured. With Oma still sleeping, they would go on exploratory hikes, or enjoy the nearby Schwimmbad, (near the prison in which Rudolf Hess, one of Hitler's henchmen, was still serving time as the only remaining prisoner). Oma would join them later at an agreed-upon spot, like the Suedpark. Then they would sit in the sun, or walk around, sometimes for an ice cream. In later years, during visits to Berlin coming from the US, we enjoyed visits to Lisbeth, my sister, who first lived at the Hohenzollernring and later in the Obstallee near the East German border. Oma also enjoyed joining Anna and the kids in visits to Onkel Walter and Tante Gretl (Anna's uncle from her father's side). Both were very fond of Karen and Bill, and Oma loved Gretl and Walter, who were always so gracious and had a great sense of humor, very much. There would be coffee and cake in their beautiful apartment in the Bilsestrasse, followed by such family games as "Mensch, aergere dich nicht!" for everyone. Dr. Gretl Wagner, Walter's widow, still lives at the Bilsestrasse.

For some time, Oma, as other West Berliners, had been unable to visit East Germany, but strongly encouraged Anna and the kids to go there, and they went. It was an important visit to them. At the border crossing, their passports disappeared into the famous "slot," and they worried, just as I had described earlier. They visited the "Berliner Dom," still in ruins. Its roof was covered, but the WWII rubble had been kept inside, to illustrate that churches were ignored in the DDR (German Democratic Republic). They were most impressed by the Pergamon Museum, which houses the famous altar and a huge collection of Greek and

Egyptian artifacts—many collected by the famous archaeologist Heinrich Schliemann. Another museum held a wonderful collection of paintings; the older ones especially impressive (Menzel, Liebermann, scenes from the court of Frederick the Great, etc.), the more modern ones followed the Communist party line. The children lost their constant companions, two little rubber trolls there, but the museum guards figured out who these tiny dolls belonged to and followed them to one of the huge rooms. Outside, the atmosphere was strange and intimidating, with hardly anyone in the streets. Even older people were working, there was full employment, and young working mothers would leave their young children in state-sponsored daycare. Later it evolved that for every ten workers there was one "Stasi" observer. The stores had "help wanted" ads in the windows. I had warned Anna about visiting East Berlin, fearful that my name was still on record because of my East German prison time. She cautioned the kids: "If you say anything against the Russians, we'll all go to jail!" Entering East Berlin they had changed DM into East Mark, which was mandatory. A few East Mark were left, which they decided to spend for ice cream in a café—but horror! When the waitress brought the check, it was not enough, and by law, she could not accept Deutsche Mark. What to do? Anna was embarrassed, but the kind waitress said: "Just keep it … I'll make up for it!" She had noticed her guests were from America and didn't know all the rules.

In future years, after we had moved back to the States, Oma's East Berlin travel ban was lifted. Anna and the children then traveled to Germany several times. Once, Karen and Anna (Bill had stayed in Ithaca, where he promptly got the measles) accompanied Oma to visit a relative in East Berlin—Jutta, formerly Boehlke. She was the daughter of Oma's brother. When the Berlin Wall was built, Jutta's parents had pleaded with her to leave for the West. But they were ill and fragile, and she could not bear the idea of leaving them. Life went on; her parents had now passed away, and Jutta had married a policeman. Naturally, that profession automatically meant being a Stasi member. Both Oma and Lisbeth frowned on that fact, but Oma did want to see Jutta again and, due to her fragile health, was glad to have Anna and Karen along. To announce their visit, she had sent Jutta a postcard with the date and time announcing the arrival. Upon arrival in the part of Berlin called "Koepenick," (yes, the Rathaus, where the famous Hauptmann von Koepenick performed his famous prank, is still there), they went to the street where Jutta lived—a normal, fairly nice street with decent apartment houses as compared to the infamous "Plattenbauten," where the less privileged lived. They also had a small "Dacha" at their disposal for weekends and vacations. Surprised, Jutta said she had never received the postcard. "Too bad our son Karsten is not here to talk with Karen. He's at an East German Youth retreat today." Anna and Oma wondered if they really had not received the postcard … or if they just wanted to keep Karsten out of the American influence. They proudly showed Karen his report card, which was very good, but contained many political subjects (participation in East German youth activities; political engagement with the young pioneers, etc. etc.). It was clear that Karsten's Dad wanted him to follow his own footsteps and become a member of the privileged DDR political class.

Karsten's Dad came home for lunch, and Jutta had cooked a nice meal for everyone. Oma had brought along chocolate, cookies, coffee, cigarettes, etc. Such things were almost impossible to get in East Berlin The husband was very quiet during lunch and excused himself soon thereafter. During Oma's naptime, Jutta guided Anna and Karen on a walk around Koepenick. Karen wanted to buy a magazine. Jutta laughed: "I'll show you a Kiosk. You'll see a huge selection." Karen only understood the joke after seeing there were only East German and Russian political papers to be had. There were lines in front of some stores. "They don't know what they are standing in line for—sometimes it's vases, sometimes it's umbrellas, whatever it is, they'll buy it, because they don't know when they will see these items again, and on this day, there's nothing else to buy." They went into a clothing store. In the middle of summer, they were offering only black woolen winter coats! Jutta laughed loudly: "Isn't it a shame, the CRAP they offer us? Well, if they don't get rid of those coats, the Polish tourists will surely buy them, because they can't get anything in Poland." And so on. Then Oma joined them for the walk to the S-Bahn, where Jutta cried bitterly: "If I could only change myself into a little mouse and crawl underneath the wall, I would be so happy." Her tears still flowed when she waved Good-Bye. It was clear she did not agree with the role her husband was playing in East Berlin … she was quite open about hating the system … but there was no way out.

Together we visited Onkel Max Nolte in Luedenscheid, the widower of Granny's sister Anny, whose son Ernst is Anna's cousin, as well as Tante Liselotte in Darmstadt-Eberstadt. We explored the beautiful Bergstrasse with her, including a memorable visit to the ruin "Frankenstein." Liselotte, the widow of our fascinating Spanish Tio Alfonso, was a trained pianist and had a grand piano. She and Karen put it to good use by playing a beautiful Mozart duet. At that time, we also met Tante Dore, Anna's dad's sister and her daughter Annemarie Mueller in Darmstadt. Last, but not least, Anna and the kids enjoyed the famous boat trip on the Rhine from Essen to Ruedesheim and Koblenz, with Friedrich, Uschi, Andreas, Martin und Thomas, Vahlenkamp, who lived in Ludwigshafen-Maudach. The three sons would later visit us in Ithaca; Thomas stayed for at least six months as a visiting fellow in the Cornell laboratory of Max Appel.

The only real family vacation we had in Germany was a very special time, during the kids' first time off from school in the summer. German school vacations are much shorter than those in the U.S. We spent it in Hiltersklingen/Odenwald, a beautiful, historically significant area near Darmstadt and the Bergstrasse. We explored places where there were still some ancient Roman artifacts and had beautiful hikes in the woods, harvesting mushrooms and lots of wild blueberries. At our vacation apartment we could do our own housekeeping and make lots of blueberry pancakes. We brought dear Tante Lore Brun there. With her we spent a day filled with blueberries and impressions, which would last us a lifetime. We were very happy in that tiny hamlet, away from all the pressures. One evening a man stopped by and introduced himself as Mr. Eisenhauer. In the Hessian accent, he told us that he was a relative of President Eisenhower of the United States. A number of people named Eisenhauers even got together and wrote the American president a letter about this, which went unanswered. The German Eisenhauers chose to ignore that fact and continued to be very proud of their American "relative."

Dear Tante Lore Brun also passed away meanwhile. Granny's family, Professor Ludwig Freund, his wife Anna and Liselotte, Anny and Thilde (Granny), had lived across the street from the Brun's stately villa in Gernsheim/Rhein. They later moved to Darmstadt. Part of Lore's education had been in a convent. She never married. Her father's will provided for her to live in part of the villa for the rest of her life. Her apartment was on the top floor. She worked for the German Telephone Co., first in Gernsheim, then in Darmstadt, where her colleague Charlotte Muehle, became her constant companion. This faithful friend later was her dedicated caregiver after Lore became very fragile and spent the final years of her life in the assisted living facility "Merschroth." Tante Lore had a truly good, deeply religious soul while her opinions were amazingly modern and open to new aspects. She was like an extra mother to Anna and to our daughter Karen, her nieces and nephews as well as countless other young people. No one could better illustrate that a single woman can be the best mother and influence to younger people without ever having been married.

SUMMARY OF EXPATRIOT LIFE IN GERMANY

The past two years had been so full for us—a mixture of joy and happiness on one side, and separations and professional difficulties on the other. The well-ordered suburban family life we had dreamt about when starting out in the San Gabriel house had not materialized. But the impulses, the love we received, the friendships, challenges and impressions that come from living in a culture different from one's own made our children what they are today. Who knows if our home in Palo Alto would have been so interesting in the long run? Karen and Bill (he later assumed his middle name Chris) should always be proud of having become independent in Germany at such a rapid pace, having coped with so many moves, succeeded in the strict atmosphere of the German Schools, and of having made the best of sometimes unusual situations and cramped living conditions. Last, but not least, being away from America made us appreciate even more the country we had chosen as immigrants many years ago.

PHASED REPATRIATION EFFORTS

As the school year was ending, the family transfer started to take shape. First, where would Anna and the kids move while I still worked in Yugoslavia? After much thought, we settled on the Boston area—an important airport hub that would get me easily to any U.S. destination for interviews or possible BP assignments, and it had a large industrial base, where I could search for employment. Boston was now the home of the older Buchanan daughter, whom we knew from Pasadena/Sparling times. We asked her to meet Anna and the kids upon arrival, and she drove them to an apartment in North Chelmsford, Northwest of Boston near the New Hampshire border. The movers combined the items we still had in Neumuenster storage for lack of space in Granny's apartment, some more practical furniture we had bought in Neumuenster, and all other belongings, to be shipped to North Chelmsford. Then, Granny and the Moratz' squeezed into the yellow VW square back for the drive to the Hamburg-Fuhlsbuettel airport, where Charlie, Trautl and Frank joined us. The departure was tense—a low point for the family, and all of us felt it hanging like a cloud over us. The thought that haunted me was: "How can I make all of us happy again?" I was standing at the visitors' platform with Granny, both of us in deep thoughts and visibly moved. I must say Thilde was not exactly nice to me; I could tell she was very concerned about her daughter, who should have had me by her side for this new beginning. Feeling the same way, I had nothing but remorse. I sensed she was wondering whether I was the right man for her daughter. By now it was summer 1968, and I had to return to my job in Sizak.

RETURN TO USA

A NEW BEGINNING IN THE US—MASSACHUSSETTS

Anna was to purchase a VW bug immediately, which was done at the VW agency where Jean Wells worked. The Wells family had been our neighbors in Palo Alto; they had later moved to Boston to get the best possible treatment for leukemia, which was destroying John—a tragic tale all by itself. The apartment, which Jean had found, had a swimming pool and was quite acceptable for Anna and the children. Anna did a marvelous job handling the harrowing move and didn't let herself get overwhelmed by this situation, sensing that everything would eventually resolve itself. The kids seemed happy to be "home." My absence must have been confusing, but Anna emphasized that this separation was only temporary. In Neumuenster we had decided to start an intensive job search for me. Anna subscribed to Adsearch, a nationwide accumulation of advertised technical positions. She selected suitable openings anywhere in the US, and, over the next months developed and typed more than 1,000 individualized cover letters for my resume, using a North Chelmsford P.O. Box return address, since the apartment mailbox would not hold the hoped-for volume of replies. Once the Post Office official asked her if she was in some kind of a business; in response she just smiled. Sometimes she altered the standard resume to fit the individual requirements. Most replies were polite turndowns. Occasionally there were phone calls to the Chelmsford number; she would pretend that I was just away for a while and would call back as soon as she could reach me. If the situation were the least bit promising, she would then call me in Yugoslavia. Because connections were usually terrible, we sometimes had to yell at each other. Then, I would call the "prospect" to explain what I was doing on a "business trip to Yugoslavia." Once, when I talked to some people from Texarkana, Texas, the connection was so terrible that I could not understand anything!

As time went by, I was becoming more desperate and developed a clinical condition, which nowadays might be diagnosed as severe anxiety and/or depression.

Returning to the hotel in the evenings, I would fall on my bed exhausted, and moaning, due to intense pain on the right side of the pelvic cavity. Without a physician I could tell the cause: mental stress! To relieve it, I started running on a nearby harness horseracing track for 30 minutes each night. When a trainer happened to approach with a horse and buggy, I sometimes competed with the horse. It was no substitute for being at home, but helped alleviate the condition. There were more worries: For some months now, Bruce Payne had been reporting "cash flow" problems. Already in Neumuenster, we had started receiving his monthly "pep letters" instead of paychecks, exhorting his "boys" to "hang in there," during this "temporary situation." Little thought was given to the impression it made on us, but I became convinced that I must make a quick exit to find another job. Anna's valiant job search efforts yielded few clues. By now we knew our problem had become one of survival!

In those days another German-speaking BP associate, stationed in the Ruhr area while I was in Zagreb, who had developed inflammation of the testicles, accompanied by severe pain and swelling and suspicion of cancer, was hospitalized for some time. I quickly decided to develop the same disease and called Bruce Payne, who pointed out that Zagreb's many good hospitals would take good care of me. I moaned that I was in much distress and could not accept the disastrous medical services in Zagreb. "Well, then, why don't you go to Germany, which has nice facilities?" "Yes, but I want to be where my family is when I'm this sick. How about this proposal: You pay the ticket to Boston, and I'll pay for the return ticket to Zagreb." Not suspecting my plan to escape, he must have thought I would have to return to work in Zagreb, unable to find another job in the US so quickly. With all this on my mind, I arrived in Boston for a cheerful reunion. North Chelmsford was a nice area bordering on New Hampshire, with many woods and ponds. I was told about mushrooms in the woods, such as we had found in the forests around Neumuenster. The kids had readjusted very well and reverted to English immediately. We visited Jean Wells, whose husband had lost his battle with Leukemia, and who was trying to pick up the pieces with her four kids Shannon, Stephanie, Heather and Willie: a very tough situation. She would later sell her home and move to Camden, Maine, where we would visit her several times later. Anna had often spent time with her and tried to give her some companionship as her husband was deteriorating quickly. Meanwhile, my job hunt was becoming more desperate. We pursued any possible leads, but I now had two to three weeks at best before having to report my improved health. Now that I was back in the States contacting previous employers, I learned they were interested. I talked to the engineer in charge at ITE and learned of a hot lead:

Harvey McKeough, whom I knew from my years there, was now the engineering manager for Allis-Chalmers Power Circuit Breaker division in Boston. At ITE he had last reported to Roy Lindberg, who had returned to Canada. I called Harvey who was delighted and said he would see what he could do. Within two weeks I found myself with two irons in the fire, but time was running out; I needed a written offer fast! Then came a phone offer from ITE in Los Angeles for an engineering job with a less-than-comfortable salary and no restitution of my seniority. I was disappointed, but, if nothing else would appear, I decided I would accept and return to smoggy L.A. This was a poor prospect, considering the factor of Bill's allergy, which had contributed heavily to our subsequent odyssey. I started to wonder if my luck was finally running out.

Just one day before I was to catch my return flight to Zagreb, Harvey called to offer me a job in the Allis Chalmers engineering department in Roxbury, about one hour's drive from the North Chelmsford apartment toward Boston. With a higher salary than the ITE offer, this meant that we could remain in the general area; any relocation would be easier and less traumatic for the children. We mailed my resignation letter to Bruce Payne and started looking for a house. I started at Allis-Chalmers immediately, while Anna prepared the next move, to a reasonably priced house we had bought at the western fringes of Needham, about 20 minutes from work. With Anna driving me to and from work, we managed with one car. She used her bike for any necessities, purchased groceries at night, and the house was close to the center of Needham. It had bus transportation, even to Boston, which we enjoyed visiting. Wellesley College, with a nice green park, pond, and a nearby German delicatessen, was about 10 minutes away, and we could canoe on the Charles River from there. Here we felt comfortable and thought we could recuperate from the European adventure. The kids started in a nice school, Bill showed great interest in the natural sciences, and Karen said she would like to learn to play the flute. A used instrument was bought (used in case she would lose interest). With her knowledge of the recorder, she took flute lessons through the school. Anna and the kids found a friend at the downtown YMCA: Greta Merchant whose husband John was an electronic engineer at the local defense division of RCA. He never talked about his work, which was probably classified. Our kids and their daughters got along great. One day we talked about the past. Greta had lived in the neighborhood called "Am Rupenhorn" in Berlin-Charlottenburg, right above the Stoessenseebruecke—one of Berlin's most exclusive areas with stately, large mansions—massive architectural beauties owned by the most important and influential people of Berlin. Greta remembered having caught streetcar #75 daily to reach her school. She must have seen my father, because she always preferred a place adjacent to the driver to better observe the scenery. It was a beautiful drive up the Heerstrasse into Charlottenburg to attend school. Greta and her mother Lili Aschaffenburg spoke German. Her father had been one of Berlin's best-known lawyers, until Jewish people could no longer work as lawyers or judges. In 1935 the Nazis had issued the "Nuernberg Laws," which excluded Jews from exercising their professions and prohibited intermarriage with "Aryans." At that time the Aschaffenburg family left for England, to later settle in Boston. When she needed to do errands, Greta often brought Lili over to Anna. Lili liked speaking German. Although she was still haunted by terrible memories of her years in the Nazi forced labor camps, she said that Germany would always remain her cultural home. We also met the Italian Serpentino family. Joseph S. described his memories of his years as POW in Germany after the Italian government replaced Mussolini with Marshall Badolgio in 1944. Despite our amazement, he said this was a very good time for him, having left the chaos in Italy behind, and that he was treated very well.

In late fall, a Berlin student choir gave some concerts in Needham, and the newspaper called for volunteers to offer housing. We offered to host a student, mentioning that a German student might rather stay with a non-German speaking family. But we did wind up with Hans-Georg, an older choir member, who later turned out to be professor of civil engineering at the T.U. Charlottenburg. After meeting "our student" in the basement of the community church, we conspired to speak only English with him. But his English was so incoherent that we took pity on him and revealed that, in an emergency, he could speak German—thinking his goal was to practice his English. Totally astonished and much relieved, he said he had joined the choir only because he was madly in love with Birgit Rosenthal, daughter of the famous Berlin quizmaster Hans Rosenthal, a Jewish entertainer very popular in postwar Berlin, who had a very conciliatory nature and had described in a beautiful memoir how he was saved from the concentration camp by a German peasant woman. We invited Birgit and some of their friends from Boston to have dinner with us. A Jewish family hosted Birgit, but she and Hans Georg declined some of their sightseeing offers, saying they just wanted to be together. Serpentino's, disappointed that they had not been selected, hosted a beautiful Italian dinner for all of us. When their power suddenly went off, we could hear the two lovebirds engaged in heavy necking. Mrs. Serpentino warned that the lights might suddenly come on—when they did, the young couple looked sheepish indeed! Later the German celebrity magazines reported about their wedding.

The children's adjustment to America was sometimes interesting. They had become accustomed to treating adults with great respect. When Anna bought them ice cream cones in a Needham store, they thanked her. Snickering children behind them: "They thank their mother for the ice cream!" One day Mrs. Deutscher, Bill's teacher, called Anna into the school to explain a perceived problem with Bill. "Mrs. Moratz, I assigned them a report. But look what Bill turned in"—waving a piece of paper on which three sentences were hastily written. "And look what the other children turned in"—showing Anna some beautifully bound, multi-page reports with plastic cover pages—the works. "Mrs. Deutscher, I did not see this; did you tell the children how long the report should be?" "Well, I just said to write as much as they feel like." "So, there you have it ... that's all he felt like writing." It was time to explain to Bill that American schools expect auto-initiative; they do not tell you what to do; they make suggestions, and then it's up to you. Needham's winter brought much snow and sometimes made morning driving difficult, but the ice-skating on the nearby pond was greatly enjoyed by the children and me. Ice hockey was the favored sport. Bill and I often chased the pucks around the ice with our hockey sticks, while Karen tried her luck at figure skating.

Harvey got me to work on developing a high voltage line switch; I think it was 56 KV. It had to be tested for its electrical properties, particularly line switching, under different load conditions. The work had to be done at KEMA in Arnhem, the Netherlands, in a public high voltage test lab, which could be used by any company in the world. Its short circuit generator allowed testing of any HV power circuit breaker under any fault condition. At the same time a colleague was developing a different interrupter configuration by using cast aluminum instead of copper. I warned him repeatedly that his could break easily under short circuit mode. I remembered ITE times, when we short circuit tested their new breakers on line, how one of those tried to take off from its pad like a rocket and actually looked like one. Those instances involve enormous forces, and one must use very ductile material (such as copper) for interrupters, and particularly castings, instead of aluminum, which is very brittle. But he insisted. Both of us dispatched our big equipment to Holland for a period of two to three weeks in the middle of winter, with temperatures around freezing and an occasional snow mess—the most miserable Hamburg weather. My colleague tested first. Through a window of 2" thick safety glass we could watch him set up his 56 KV breaker in a test cubicle. At full power test this large equipment exploded before our eyes. Since it was an oil breaker, the ensuing fire was very impressive. He learned to use copper instead of aluminum. What a waste! I never understood why Harvey allowed that kind of engineering gamble. One could use aluminum, but then the application must avoid excessive impact. With the help of a Dutch technician—an older man with whom I could speak English, my tests went fairly well. He treated me well, but was brusque with a German crew of engineers from Brown Boveri Mannheim, who tested similar equipment. The Dutch still remembered their treatment by the Germans during WWII, when Arnhem had been the center of much fighting and destruction. When the allied forces landed there with a large airborne troop contingent, they suffered a temporary setback when they were received by powerful German SS motorized, armored forces! Near Arnhem, in the midst of the countryside, was the best Van Gogh museum I had ever seen. On another Sunday I visited Amsterdam and its famous museums with all those Rembrandt's and other Dutch masters. I wished Anna could have shared this wonderful opportunity. Returning to Boston, I found the Allis Chalmers place reverberating with rumors that the company was considering a move to Jackson, Mississippi. These grapevine stories start slowly and build up over time. Come Spring, Harvey McKeough started questioning the people in the department what they would do if the company would move to Jackson, with the unanimous answer: NO! No Bostonian would ever consider it. Born and raised in the area, they wanted to remain in Boston, which has everything, with a quality of life second to none: good air, rivers, sea, forests, wilderness in the north, music, theatre, museums, colleges, universities, industrial base, banking, insurance, best medical facilities, the list is endless. Why move to a place without any rank? We discussed this intensely at home and concluded that, considering my chaotic past and rapid career changes, it would be best to stick with the company. I told Harvey about my decision, wondering how he would continue engineering operations in Jackson, but thought this might offer some opportunities for me. While everything was still very tentative, the Portland, Oregon plant manager visited to discuss the status of his switching gear. I was working on a development for the Portland division, which had no engineering capability of its own. Portland sounded much more promising to me than Jackson. When he left, he said he would be in touch with me. Several weeks later he called from Portland, wanting to go over the switch gear development with me. Harvey agreed to my trip. In the midst of planning it, Jim van Meter suddenly called to say he was now in a position to hire me and had a good offer. Now I could combine the trips.

While we tried to return to the American mainstream in North Chelmsford and Needham, the Bruce Payne story came to an inglorious and stressful end. Along with my resignation I had laid claim to a substantial sum of money—several months of back pay the firm owed me, and moving expenses. Several months ago the checks had ceased to arrive, forcing us to live from our reserves. In today's money, they owed us 40-50 grand—in light of our limited resources not something to be written off without a fight. I knew Bruce was a rich man with a mansion in Greenwich, CT. After my repeated reminders were ignored, we decided on a scheme: in another letter we detailed all of my claims and copied a prominent labor lawyer, whose name we had picked from the Boston yellow pages, except that the copy was neither sent nor the lawyer contacted (he might have gotten most of the settlement money!!!). Bruce called immediately. In an agitated voice, he chided me for going to such extremes. I would get my money, but he needed six months to clear up the account, since his cash flow was still poor. If I would not agree to the six months delay, he would not give me a good professional recommendation! Such mean blows were part of his negotiating style. With a mike attached to the phone, I taped the conversation for the record, though unsure if the law would permit it for later use. Agreeing to his terms, I remembered my colleague Ernie Bush's advice: When Bruce Payne makes a verbal promise, he keeps it. Besieged by severe cash flow problems, people are capable of many things. After exactly six months the check came along, which made us feel more secure. Our European adventure had finally come to a close.

On the way to Portland I had to first make a stop in Evansville, Indiana. The Mt. Vernon plant was 50 miles to the West near the Illinois border close to the Wabash River on the banks of the Ohio. It was huge and new, with its own dock, so that completed heavy components could be loaded directly into barges by overhead cranes. All nuclear power plants were located at an ocean, a navigable river, or a canal. Only barges or ships can transport them; roads or railroads are too small. Furthermore, cooling the system requires a great deal of water. Because many fish attracted by the effluent warm cooling water grow very fast and large, nuclear power plants are havens for fishermen. The Mt. Vernon B&W plant was impressive, with milling/turning/boring mills of 60+ feet height and 100 feet length, with all movements of tools and machines computer-controlled (N/C). These machines were much larger than those at Sunnyvale/Westinghouse—probably the largest ever built. The mix of commercial and navy nuclear components throughout greatly impressed me. It fit right in with my experience at Westinghouse. I was led into a huge reception room where the mature looking secretary asked me to wait on a fancy sofa, complemented by three matching chairs and a table with a cup of coffee on top of it—for me! I wondered why the top manager of the place would see me, since it had been just old Jim (or rather young Jim) van Meter, who had invited me here. Soon I was ushered into a large, elegant office, where the mystery was solved: Jim smiled at me from behind a huge desk—within 2-3 years he had progressed from sr. industrial engineer to plant manager of a major 100M production facility. I could tell he enjoyed my surprise in his low-key, easy-going style. He offered me a good title, reflecting my progression to engineering supervision—an important stepping-stone for advancement into positions of responsibility. I promised an answer after my return from my Portland meetings and said that, based on my positive impressions, I would probably accept.

I continued to Portland, Oregon, where the discussions revealed that the main reason why they had brought me there was different than I had thought. The plant manager, who knew about Allis Chalmers' transfer to Jackson, disclosed it at a fancy steak dinner at a restaurant overlooking Portland and the Columbia River. He invited me to work on switch gear development for him. He didn't have engineering personnel yet and wanted to develop that capacity, but his offer was not as good as Jim's. I told him I would have to talk with my family. Portland, with its superior climate and ocean vicinity, is attractive. It has a good industrial base and excellent educational opportunities. Its cultural life almost equals that of San Francisco or Seattle. Therefore, the offer was tempting. During the return flight, I tried to visualize what I would be getting into. Because they lacked test equipment, I would have to travel to Allis Chalmers in Jackson, Miss, for any required tests. There I would depend on my former superiors who, because of my leaving Allis Chalmers, would resent accommodating me in their schedules and lending me a hand. Arriving home, I had decided on Babcock & Wilcox.

Then we prepared our good-bye to Needham and Boston, with the Charles River, street cars to the Boston Commons, lovely Wellesley, our new and old friends, flute lessons, hockey, Rosemary Lake, the Y and Needham's nice community life. Anna gave up her part-time secretarial job at Way Distributors. She had also done some translating work for Allis Chalmers through a regular bidding process. We had enjoyed the house not realizing it would be for such a short time due to Allis Chalmer's impending move. We knew that, compared to Jackson, Mississippi, Evansville was the better choice. Harvey McKeough did not take kindly to my resignation. He may have thought I owed him something—and I kind of agreed.

While I was already in Evansville and had even bought a house, Anna decided to sell the Needham property through an "open listing," whereby the owner invites the town's realtors to the home, and each of them can sell the house, gaining full commission and avoiding exclusives. The house was soon teeming with realtors and sold very quickly. Shortly before our departure, Anna had gone for a final swim at the Y with Greta and family before vacating the house. Walking to the car, the two moms noticed that Bill was slightly limping, though he had not complained about any pain before. On Greta's advice, Anna immediately took his temperature, which was elevated. The doctor opened his office for an emergency visit and discovered an open sore between the toes, which had just become infected! Danger of gangrene! He asked what kind of murky water they had been swimming in, put Bill on Penicillin immediately and said it would be ok to travel by car, keeping the leg elevated! The night before we left, we stayed in a nice hotel, where the Merchants surprised us with a cake in the shape of Indiana State, decorated with its symbols: dogwoods, cardinals, the Ohio River, etc. The next morning, we crammed into our VW bug. With the kids in the back and Bill holding the leg up, we entered the 95 corridor onto Interstate 80, crossed the Hudson at Nyack and slowly drifted toward Cleveland, Columbus, Indianapolis and Evansville. The moving van was also on its way with a hodgepodge of possessions: some purchased while in Germany, some which had never left storage in Neumuenster, some which had been stored in Pascagoula, and those acquired after returning to the US.

LIFE IN HOOSIERLAND—EVANSVILLE, INDIANA

Our new home on Agathon Drive was a split-level in Evansville's fairly new University Heights section. Many neighbors worked for Indiana State University Evansville, where our neighbor, Don Pitzer, was a history professor. Marianne, his wife, would soon return to work as an ER nurse in the Evansville hospital, and their kids, Tonya and Donnie, and ours quickly became great playmates. All of us became very good friends. Don, who specializes in early American religious communities, was doing extensive research on the Rappites, a sect originating in Wuerttemberg, Southwestern Germany. Father Rapp had led his flock to the banks of the Wabash around 1840. They had peculiar beliefs and customs. By his rule, men and women lived in separate bunk houses, unable to get together for any purpose other than work from dawn to dusk to produce their own needs. Their skills, particularly in construction and carpentry, were sought after up and down the Ohio. From their village, New Harmony, 20 miles North of Mt. Vernon, they may have transported their goods south to the Ohio for sale. No one could accumulate assets. All goods were common property, administered by Father Rapp. They felt they were a truly Christian community, not unlike the later "invented" socialism. There was one fatal flaw: because there were no offspring, New Harmonys population declined, leading to the end of the community. Rapp, rumored to have had a female companion himself, had neglected that organic things must grow to survive! The community's assets were later bought by a Scottish millionaire named Robert Owens, who had another utopian idea. In the community he founded there, everyone was told to work as much as s/he wanted. In return, his or her needs would be met. Thus, a new-old Christian and pre-Marxist idea was practiced in New Harmony. I am unsure about the details, but Professor Pitzer's extensive publications on the subject explore them. He even visited the village in Wuerttemberg where the Rappites had originated, after Anna had established contact with its mayor. Under Owen, no limits were set on contributions, but the group's high expectations soon led to problems and people eventually left the failed experiment. Today some of the original houses still stand and can even be rented by tourists. The town now is not only a mystic retreat with beautiful gardens and memorials to such world famous religious philosophers as Paul Tillich, but also a famous living history tourist attraction, with its beautiful Red Geranium Restaurant. During one of our visits to New Harmony, Don introduced us to Jane Owen, widow of the Texas oil millionaire who is a descendant of Robert Owen. Rumored to command some oil properties, she is the main force in the rehabilitation and restoration of New Harmony. Saying hello to us while careening around in a golf cart, she absent mindedly drove over Don's foot! He didn't blink an eye, since Jane was the source of much funding for the village and his ISUE research program.

We were impressed by the Ohio River, a great waterway where much of the barge traffic meets the needs of the Eastern Seaboard and the Midwest. In Evansville it was perhaps a mile wide. The North shore is about 20 feet high in contrast to the flat South shore in Kentucky, a vast flood plane which becomes inundated from the snow melt further north. Three rivers, the Allegheny, Susquehanna and Monongahela, from the Western New York and Pennsylvania watersheds join in downtown Pittsburgh to form the fast-flowing Ohio. A bridge connects Evansville, Indiana to the State of Kentucky and its vast tobacco plantations. There the soil looks much different and is highly fertile for tobacco growing, while North of the river not one single tobacco plant could be seen; it seemed less conducive for this kind of culture. We crossed the bridge often. At its southern end, in Henderson, a small restaurant served well-prepared catfish—about the only kind of fish available there. We also liked visiting the Audubon Park and museum with its many wonderful drawings by James Audubon, famous in the early 19th century for his extensive aviary drawings and cataloguing, including passenger pigeons, which had provided nourishment for the entire population (*Said to be as big as geese and clumsy, they were almost too fat to fly. One only had to shake them down from the trees and down came a load of pigeons, which, in the fall, would be salted and stored in barrels for the winter.)* There was little need in those times when the prairie was filled with buffalos. The buffalo's subsequent fate is well known. No one then thought about nature or wildlife management or applicable laws and their enforcement. The biggest worry was the native population! While South of the Ohio River (Mason Dixon Line) cash crops of tobacco, rice, cotton, peanuts, etc. were grown on the plantations, the self-sustaining farms north of it were fairly small, raising cattle, milk, pigs, corn, wheat, soy beans, etc. North of Evansville were the villages of Haubstadt and Darmstadt, originally settled by German immigrants.

After we had lived in University Heights for some time, it became apparent that the Terrace Hill elementary school was not the ideal learning environment for both children. Homework was no challenge, and the grades were always tops, despite mistakes in the papers, which we saw. Karen told Anna she was not allowed to use the word "multiply," since the other kids would not understand it. Anna reviewed her math skills and concluded she should have gotten a "B," since she was really not that good at that time. The teacher had a fit: "No parent ever complained to me about getting an "A." But Anna thought an "A" had removed the challenge. We started looking at other schools. One, in particular, "Highland," located on the North side toward Darmstadt, with an innovative program of ability groupings and enrichment programs presented much more of a challenge. We decided that we would move there if we could find a buyer for our house.

Around that time we learned about the opera performances at Indiana University's Bloomington campus, three hours north toward Indianapolis. We subscribed to season tickets and enjoyed the most wonderful performances, such as Prokofiev (Love of the three Oranges) and Verdi's operas, among others. We were amazed at this jewel of a music program and wonderfully appointed opera house in the midst of Indiana's vast cornfields. Later we learned that Bloomington has one of the very best music conservatories in the US, where great musicians teach and lecture. Many of the voice graduates find opportunities at European establishments. These kinds of outings and our love for classical performances seem to have influenced Karen and Chris in many ways. It also enhanced their critical thinking process. They observed many murders and tragedies on the opera stage. In the "Rigoletto" intermission, they asked why we would bring them here, as opposed as we were to violence on TV.

We later found Rev. Manfred Haas, a Lutheran pastor who celebrated beautiful German language services each Easter and Christmas. During these the congregation happily joined in singing the Lutheran hymns in the German language. When we greeted the people around us in German after the service, they looked surprised and embarrassed. They did not understand us! Through generations they had clung to the old songs, their family holiday tradition. Now they sang from memory, without knowing the language. When we noticed that we were the only young family with small children in the entire church, it started to make sense! One icy night Karen's Girl Scout leader called Anna. The scouts were being driven to a nursing home by their parents for singing Christmas carols, but she, the leader, could not join them because of the weather. Could Anna please take over? "If the kids know the songs, I'll go … we cannot disappoint this audience." Assured that they did, Anna grabbed Karen AND Bill, and off they went. But it turned out the girls did NOT know the songs very well, and they quickly ran out of carols to present. Desperate, Anna announced: "And now my son Bill and daughter Karen will join me in some German Christmas songs!" Poor Karen and Bill had to sing with Anna as they presented our family repertoire of "O Tannenbaum" etc. To their surprise, many of the residents joined in these German songs! They also spoke no German, but told Anna that they remembered the songs from their youth.

While in Chelmsford and later again in Needham, Anna had found pediatricians, doctors, dentists and a specialist for Bill's braces—twice! Hoping to stay in Evansville for some time, this process began again, including an allergist, and we soon felt much more at home there than in Boston or Chelmsford, because the employment picture looked so much brighter now. Karen and Bill adjusted well to life in Indiana, and we were happy there. They quickly made friends, but the Pitzer kids were always the favorites, even after we moved to Evansville's North side. Family visits with the Pitzer's and great New Year's Eve parties became a much-loved tradition. Karen and Tonya practiced "cheerleading" endlessly. After moving to the North Side, Karen became a candy-striper in addition to being a girl scout. She helped an elderly man in the nearby nursing home read and write letters in German. Anna became a "picture lady," showing slides of famous paintings to the Highland School students and took evening accounting classes at the High School, and, after working for some time in the president's office at Indiana State University Evansville. During lulls in translation work for Babcock & Wilcox, she signed up with Manpower and worked at ISUE until landing another full-time job with benefits as the secretary to the man in charge of marketing at Atlas Van Lines.

Karen's interest in the flute intensified. She took her lessons with Julie Smith very seriously and soon joined Highland School's band and orchestra. In those days, as Karen's preference and talent for music began to manifest itself, we never dreamed that she might eventually conquer a distinct spot in the music world. And, I think, neither did she, but she was obviously drawn to it inexorably. Bill and Karen really thrived at Highland School, which offered many challenging activities in addition to a stringent learning environment in which the youngsters were grouped according to abilities and thus constantly challenged. It involved many volunteer opportunities for the parents as well as parents' testimonies before the School Board. Karen had only one complaint: in West Hill School she had participated in "home making," or some such course. At Highland School the girls were taking shop along with the boys. Since Bill had been the one who had always been beside me when doing repair or construction work around the house while Karen had been beside Anna in her housewifely duties, Karen felt lost in this class and complained about this lack of exposure in the past. She was right, of course! But she later learned so much that she now could easily hold her own!

Bill enjoyed the Northside Boy Scout troupe, including many lengthy training hikes, developing his big interest in survival techniques and "living off the land." He became good friends with Jay Bauer, with whom he did volunteer work guiding tours for groups of girl scouts around Wesselman's Nature Center. He and Jay decided to put Thoreau's Living off the Land theories to the test. We had met Pauline Burgdorf and her mother. They owned a huge piece of land near on Evansville's West side, where they had actually arranged space for an entire church building—which Pauline's father had helped construct long ago. They moved it to their property, which also contained an oil pump somewhere. No one lived in the church, and Pauline gave Jay and Bill permission to camp on her land and use the church, if needed. The two refused any offers of food or drink to take along. They were going to hunt squirrels with slingshots and live off the land, getting water from the church as needed. Anna drove them to their chosen spot, but she also alerted some people who lived in the area that there were these two boys camping in Pauline's woods, which were surrounded by "no trespassing" signs. Incidentally, we knew these woods quite well from Pauline's invitations in the spring to collect morels and chanterelles, which were plentiful. Cell phones did not exist then. On the next day, after work, Anna became restless and decided to take some food and water and look for the boys in the spot where they had parted. Not finding them there, she walked around the dense, completely undeveloped woods, shouting their names with no response. She then decided to leave the car and hike to the church through the dense forest. There she knocked on the door, shouting their names. The heavy wooded door opened just a crack: "Mom?" And then the story: After establishing tents the previous evening, they had found nothing to eat. The roots which they had determined to be edible, based on their studies of nature books, had to be cooked endlessly on their camp stove. But they never softened. They tried to fall asleep, hungry, but heard some voices close by without seeing anyone. Two poachers were conversing about the frogs they were going to catch in the nearby pond. This was strictly forbidden! Their coarse language sounded horrible to Bill and Jay. Afraid they might be discovered and considered witnesses to the conversation, they vanished from the scene as quickly as they could and spent the night in the church. Again they tried to cook some roots without success. When Anna arrived, they were still determined to continue their experiment. At least Jay was. Bill was beginning to consider it senseless. After some talking and eating Anna's cookies, he decided: "Jay, you can do what you want, but I'm going home." Scared to be in the woods by himself, Jay exhibited mild reluctance, but then came along as well. We later heard from Pauline that she and her mom were going to visit relatives in Germany, whom they had never met, bringing along some frozen lamb, so it would be thawed and ready to cook upon their arrival. Pauline had studied to be a German teacher, but later became too busy at the farm to pursue the profession.

MEANWHILE, AT BABCOCK & WILCOX

Around this time a group of German inspectors had arrived at Babcock & Wilcox. Some were from Babcock, Brown Boveri; others from the TUV (Technischer Ueberwachungsverein) Rheinland-Westphalen, the German government inspection agency assigned to control the construction of all heavy components of the Muehlheim-Kaerlich nuclear power plant, to be located North of Koblenz on the Rhein River. Babcock, Brown Boveri had a contract from a large German utility (RWE) to design, build, install and start up that nuclear power plant. Much of the project involved licensing, design and approval, which took a long time and was still progressing while the components were built. Likewise, as huge forgings arrived from Japan, the inspection procedures were being negotiated between B&W, BBB and the TUV experts. I got thrown into the situation to follow each step, determine the TUV's "ideas" and help the sides understand each other. It soon turned out that the TUV Rheinland had never provided safety requirements for a nuclear power plant before. They were not even obligated or encouraged by government and RWE to look at other TUV agencies' approaches regarding the safety assurance of nuclear power plants. They were independent of the law, and no one could advise or influence their behavior. They were totally unconcerned about the timing of their actions, i.e. when construction schedules were delayed because there had not been an internal agreement among their experts about conducting a certain component inspection, schedules had to be postponed until they would reach a conclusion. There was no document to describe their requirements, while in the US, there is the ASME pressure vessel code section V, which deals exclusively with the site approval, design and construction of nuclear power plants. That document had been proposed to them but was considered inferior and unacceptable. The US Navy nuclear pressure vessel code, considerably more restrictive, under which B&W had built many of those for carriers, cruisers and submarines, was also rejected. B&W management found it hard to understand that there was no document governing the construction of German nuclear power plants. Apparently, no one had ever asked RWE and BBB when signing the contract as to how this jewel was supposed to be made and who would call the shots—a fatal mistake, which caused B&W to lose a huge amount of money on the contract. The German TUV, able to impose any and all safety requirements they would dream up, regardless of schedules or other circumstances, held them captive. From the outset, TUV had made it clear that, if B&W would be caught manufacturing without TUV approval of production sheets, (which also showed all TUV/BBB inspection requirements), or worse, proceeding without prior TUV inspectors' approval, production could be stopped and the component would be rejected if inspection could no longer be performed. This would mean ordering new forging components from Japan, which could take years! Hence, B&W experts could not suggest or negotiate solutions to the TUV people, who, in turn, could make decisions on a whim, mostly through their metallurgists, welding specialists and non-destructive or destructive testing experts. From the beginning, a particular bone of contention was the selection of filler and cladding wires and control from supplier to the weld seam. Further elaboration here would be confusing and boring to a layman. But countless constant fights surrounded this matter. Initially, B&W management thought it could win, for the sake of maintaining schedule, but it soon turned out that TUV could always impose their views, which were not documented anywhere.

Finding myself in the plant's most precarious position, I had to present proposals to the TUV, mostly originated by me, and obtain their approval. Some proposals came from Wayne Wilcox, a welding metallurgist with a master's degree, who served on several ASME boiler and pressure vessel code committees assigned to follow up on technology and update the code periodically. Those are very prestigious positions in the industry. He and I often traveled to BBB in Mannheim-Kaefertal and occasionally to the TUV Rheinland offices near Essen. We were amazed by the coin operated beer vending machines in the BBB engineering offices. At meetings the BBB people felt free to arrive with a bottle of beer. Never too fond of beer, I didn't imitate the custom. Those trips always made me aware that I had become oblivious to many of the German customs. Holed up for days in a 3-star hotel near the BBB offices, I craved some fresh fruit. In a nearby shopping district I found greengrocer's shop. I started gathering pears and apples in small paper bags, when a character jumped me from behind, demanding what I was doing. I answered calmly: "Can't you see? I am buying some fruit!" Even more enraged, he went on: "It is not allowed. Only I can fill the bags, not you!" I began to realize that I was in good old Germany, where then only shopkeepers could select the fruit, likely to sneak some overripe specimen they didn't want to get stuck with, into the bag. But I had what I wanted—it was either what I had selected or nothing. I must have appeared to the unhappy shopkeeper like a German trying to break established customs. He let me pay and go, but in such situations a loud confrontation often ensues.

Three model makers were permanently employed at BBB's engineering offices. They were building and maintaining a three-dimensional wood model of the entire power plant, with the nuclear reactor, generator, several auxiliary buildings and switchyards, including all required primary, secondary and cooling pipe systems. This showed the project's enormity. Today, such an expensive effort is replaced by computer-aided design; a more reliable method to assure everything fits and no interferences crop up which could affect schedules and cost when caught during construction. In those days, I closely interacted with the TUV inspectors. I especially remember "Herr Hessenbruch," a very outgoing Rhenish engineer, who came alone, with wife and daughter following later. The TUV men shared an apartment at the North end of Evansville on the Road to Darmstadt. They loved big American cars in which they felt more comfortable than in their domestic Volkswagens. The big car was especially suited for Hessenbruch, who was so heavy that his shoes creaked when he walked. They loved to eat, mostly Texas-size steaks. He and his colleagues would broil them in the kitchen stove, unaccustomed to barbeques. To them, "self-cleaning oven" meant that they never had to clean the broiling pan. After some time, when trying the "self-cleaning method," all that baked-on old grease caught fire in the oven. Very excited, they called on Anna for help, who explained to those safety engineers the limits of "self-cleaning." They must clean the fatty crust in the broiler part regularly, in the absence of their wives. From then on, they carefully followed the instruction book. When their spouses arrived, they were happy to move into individual apartments. Anna and the kids had good fun at Halloween time. They dressed up, with Anna also disguised, and knocked at the TUV's door: "Trick or Treat." The door opened and some perplexed German faces appeared: "Look, the woman is begging too. Let's give them apples." Anna and I had been just as puzzled at our first Halloween on Sunset Blvd. in L.A. After talking excitedly with each other in German, they came up with a treat. No one had preceded Anna's little group, since the Evansville Mayor had forbidden trick-or-treating that year due to a poisoning the previous year. When A. took off her mask and explained the old custom, they made her promise to keep quiet about their ignorance at B&W!

In addition to Anna's translation and interpreting work and my official interactions with them, we sometimes went out of our way to keep the TUV happy. At B&W's expense we bought steaks, opera tickets, etc. and discreetly provided such amenities as Hewlett Packard digital calculators. When those first came on the market, the TUV people wanted them because they were so expensive back home. How to approach these people posed a delicate problem, since they tried to establish an air of incorruptibility and independence, but, in talking to German companies who regularly dealt with the TUV, I had found they did not refuse, but rather cherished occasional niceties, as long as they were not too obvious and too big. But they could not be too small, either! This balancing act was a pain in the butt! For their first Christmas I arranged a nice set of Samsonite luggage for each, much more modern than what they had brought along. These were accepted without blinking an eye, unaware that I had had a tough time convincing my management of the need for such presents. Unfortunately, management thought this would help us in dealing with the TUV's irrational approach to the inspection process—it didn't. This made my position precarious in the long run.

I was busy, and, in the midst of the myriad engineering issues among B&W and TUV, I was also indispensable, but many of the old B&W managers, who had come from Barberton, OH, for this project, did not fully trust me. An exception was Wayne Wilcox, who had the sorry task of convincing the TUV that US welding methods, anchored in detail in the ASME pressure vessel code, should also be acceptable to them. He never even came close, because they detested the idea of accepting any precedent, including many available from the seven other TUV organizations in Germany, who had experience in building many nuclear power plants. The disaster was built in from the time the TUV had arrived in Mount Vernon.

Typical of the confusion was the large gray area of NDT (non-destructive testing). First, TUV wanted nothing to do with X ray examination, common in the US. Instead, only ultrasonic methods had to be used. When requesting their methods, we found none were available; they needed to be developed between their and our experts, together with those of Babcock-Brown Boveri. It must be understood that the first prerequisite for inspection is definition of acceptable test (calibration) samples, used to determine from which side angle the crystals must be used and what wave form should be selected. For each material, nozzle and cross section form, a complete, separate forging must be ordered and a test specimen machined. This lengthy, expensive process takes years. Luckily, the forgings hit the production floor first. While being machined, test specimens were welded and machined in parallel and subjected to ultrasonic inspection. For this purpose, simulated fault indications were drilled into strategic places, subject to approval by TUV, BBB & B&W. Each forging involved endless heckling about who was right! When this was over, there was finally agreement on how to calibrate. On the oscilloscope there was then a blimp of various sizes where there was a crack or inclusion (either dirt or void), the extent of a crack could be seen by moving the crystal on the surface. Moving the crystal and using it from various sides of the machined part could also determine the size of an inclusion. It is easy to see that this entire process took much longer than the manufacturing cycle. To top it off, TUV, BBB & B&W had to fully agree on the results. Any disagreement required re-inspection until everyone had identical results, which could take weeks and months. If the experts could not agree on a particular problem, the TUV manager responsible for all NDT had to fly in from Duesseldorf to resolve the mess. Once I had to meet with the most knowledgeable German ultrasonic test expert, a professor at the Technical University in Charlottenburg, at the Max Planck Institute in Berlin, who was to give his input on a specific problem or disagreement. All of this resulted in tremendous delays and cost. The entire aspect of ultrasonic inspection had to be recorded in German and English. Because I was too busy, Anna had been offered this assignment when I came to B&W. She was then just about the only qualified person in Evansville and had done similar work sporadically on a contract basis while living in Needham. She negotiated an agreement to be paid by the word on a similar basis, except she did not have to bid on the translations. They were waiting for her—including deadlines, which could be tight—and would last for months on end. She worked strictly at home. She paid Karen and Bill a small amount for maintaining a dictionary of the technical expressions peculiar to the field. They also proofread her typed pages together and received a finders' fee for each mistake they found. Returning from work in the evenings, I would sit down to answer questions about especially rare detail technical expressions … words that no lay person could know. I often had to go back to the BBB or TUV people, since the technologies were very new and the specific expressions sometimes had to be invented. Some were leaning on the English; others were Teutonic constructions. The dictionary thus developed was most important, and she tried not to ask me the same question more than once. The work was tricky and demanding, since the translations had to be perfect.

MOVING AGAIN: EVERGREEN ROAD/ EVANSVILLE, INDIANA

Selling our University Heights home was not as easy as we had imagined. But we had learned more about Dr. Gourley, the principal of Highland School on the North side and the results he had achieved through ability groupings and enrichment programs. The decision to enroll Karen and Bill there was easy, but only residents of that district were accepted. Soon our house was on the market. While Pitzer's were very supportive, other neighbors seemed to find our decision a little strange. Interest developed slowly. We may have made a mistake selecting the same realtor who had sold us the Evergreen Road home; we later found he was not quite aggressive enough. I became very concerned as the planned summer trip to Florida was approaching. Excitedly, Anna and the kids had stuffed our VW Square back with vacation gear, including fishing equipment, tennis racquets—the works! As we were going to bed the night before the trip, I talked with Anna about my concerns: We had to sell during that summer to meet the deadline for Highland School; having the house standing around vacant would be detrimental to our efforts. While we discussed our predicament, the kids came tiptoeing into the room: "If you are worried … can't we just cancel the trip? We could spend our vacation at home! We'll be happy here too, with our family and friends!" So, the next morning, we unpacked everything, and the trip to Florida was not mentioned again.

While the house was offered "For Sale by Owner" later that summer, we received a call from an interested couple; he was a chemical engineer from the GE plastic plant in Mt. Vernon; his wife was a teacher—both were sophisticated, good looking and well-mannered. They would have fitted very well into the University Heights neighborhood. They liked our house and intended return the next day to show it to their mother. As they drove away, I noticed neighbor Connie Sherbrooke across the street leaning at her entrance with arms crossed over her chest, surveying the scene. She was from South of the Mason-Dixon line and had just told the Pitzer's "I will cancel my Christmas Teas from now on if these people move into our neighborhood," with Don Pitzer trying to tell her that the days of Jim Crow were over. You guessed it: the couple was African-American. The next morning, a Sunday, we awoke to a puzzling sight. Our young, 20-25 feet high tulip tree in the front yard was completely covered with white toilet paper, even its crown. The leaves seemed to have disappeared! We wondered who would have done such a prank. We had never seen a "tp'd" tree before. Suspecting a signal was being given to us not to sell to "those people," we wondered what to do. Was there a chance to remove the mess? Scratching my head, I realized that, without a lot of help, there was not enough time for action before the potential buyers would return. We could only watch helplessly as they drove by in their brand-new car, not even stopping. They just turned around and left. We never knew for sure which one of the "nice" neighbors had blown it for us.

Then we heard of "rent with option to buy," at an agreed-to price. Our "by owner" newspaper ad brought a quick response. Shortly before we moved into our new, stately brownstone house on Evergreen Road, we closed the deal with Mr. and Mrs. Thurmond. Noticing their dog, we included a clause: "one dog only." Since the previous owner had not kept our "new" Northside home up very well, we thought its price was right. The very large basement was perfect for ping-pong and family activities. It included a built-in kitchen sink, cupboards and a sizeable old tub freezer, which we restored to working order. Huge beautiful oak trees surrounded the house and provided generous shade. It had an oversized attic fan, which made an impressive difference in keeping the house comfortable, eliminating the need for air conditioning. We had an acre of land, and the seller had not mowed the huge lawn for a month. What a job! We also noticed wet spots and mold on the side of one of the basement walls. I found the gutters to be full of compacted leaves from the oak trees and removed them with considerable effort. But the basement wall remained wet. I then drilled holes into the wall, which drained the water out. This proved there was water seeping into the walls from outside. Now I discovered that, because the ground sloped from the street toward the house, water could not escape into the backyard, which was about 20 feet below street level. I called a worker to dig out the drain tile manually and clean it. I then provided a drainage ditch in front of the house, so that all water could quickly run off toward lower ground. That stopped water from settling into the walls, and we were greatly relieved. Bill helped me a lot. With the entire family's help, the formerly neglected house soon became a wonderful home for us.

Evergreen Road is on Evansville's North side toward Darmstadt and Haubstadt. In time we became acquainted with the neighbors: a blind old gentleman named Henry Seib, the Woehler's and the Bartels', all retired, long-time residents, who welcomed us warmly. Anna and the kids liked to visit Henry, who spoke a little German with a Hessian dialect. He always asked if the house was clean. That was his daughter's job, and he couldn't see her work! It always was. We also became acquainted with Shirley Nicholson, who wrote for the 'Northside Reporter' weekly newspaper and covered the small communities further to the North, including the one named Darmstadt. She came to our house to talk about the German Darmstadt, with which most of her readers were unfamiliar. We helped her write a series about the German Darmstadt, including picture postcards we had as illustrations. In turn, she told us about the nearby Darmstadt's history and its people. Many families had come from the German Darmstadt, where Anna was born and had later often visited Professor Ludwig Freund, her grandpa, until his apartment was bombed out around 1943/4 when he had to move to Erbach/Odenwald. The immigrants came to Indiana in the mid 19th century, a time of great deprivation, unrest, revolutions and repressions. Those who arrived first found very fertile ground free or for little money. They paid no taxes on their bountiful crops—something never heard of in Germany. Most soon felt satisfied to have made the move and sent word to their kinfolk in Germany. Many followed, which explains why the descendants told Anna they do not have German relatives. "Once encouraged, all other family members followed." The nearby cemetery clearly reflects the Indiana Darmstadt's origin; Anna remembered the names on the gravestones from her many visits to her birthplace, the German Darmstadt. German was spoken here until World War II, and many residents we met still understood and spoke some of the Hessian dialect. Shirley Nicholson invited us to ride in the press car in the traditional July 4th parade along Darmstadt's main street; would we please wear traditional German clothes? Anna and Karen donned their Dirndl's, and Bill wore a felt hat with a feather, brought from Germany. When we arrived, they had prepared a float for us: "Natives of Darmstadt, Germany." We felt a little silly riding it, but had no choice. It was fun seeing the American Darmstaedters wave to us from their porches or from the sidewalk. Years later, a German PhD candidate, Martinus Boll, wrote Anna from the German Darmstadt, asking for help with his thesis: "The name of Darmstadt—around the world." He kept in touch for a long time. One of the results of all this was that the German Darmstaedters learned about our little neighbor hamlet, and the two became sister cities!

While Bill spent much time with Jay Bauer and the boy scouts, Karen befriended Julie King, Julie Baum and others. Julie Baum's mother was the principal flutist of the Evansville Symphony. The flute world was drawing Karen closer to it all the time. The Pitzer's remained our very best friends, and the families continued to celebrate holidays together and visit back and forth.

A good friend to both children was Wolfgang Schagginger from Vienna, an intern at the B&W plant due to the influence of his father, the CEO of a Viennese utility. Several Austrian utilities had banded together to pursue investing in a nuclear power plant. Earlier that year, a large group of VIP's with wives and entourage had visited the Mt. Vernon plant to review the operation and decide whether or not BBB could be a viable, alternative supplier. They were entertained in grand style, with Anna helping the plant manager's wife carry out the wives' program. As an intern in the plant, Wolfgang did not show much enthusiasm for anything going on. He lived at the Evansville YMCA and had a car. Visiting whenever he could, he loved our family life and the kids. He confided in us that his father was pushing him to get an engineering education, which he hated. He was very much in love with a girlfriend his parents did not approve of. The way in which his parents wanted to control his life troubled him greatly. Karen and Bill loved Wolfgang, and we spent much time with him. After his return to Austria his mother wrote that he had suddenly died. There was a hint of suicide in the letter, and what he had told us seemed to confirm this. We were devastated at his passing. The children said we must do something in his memory, so we dedicated some hymnals to the Lutheran church in his name and attended the service at which the gift was announced. The hymnals must still be there.

MEANWHILE, BACK AT B&W

Anna's translation work was winding down, with most requirements covered. I also saw that nuclear orders began to decrease. Environmental interest groups were making approval of sites for nuclear power plants more and more difficult, because of safety/environmental groups' concerns. Court litigations began throughout the country to stop the building and operation of nukes. We therefore decided that Anna would look for a permanent job with benefits, which she eventually found at Atlas Van Lines, as the secretary to the Vice President/Marketing. Always swamped with work while her boss was constantly traveling, she thrived on her new responsibilities and the constant contact with the agents, nationwide. Meanwhile, my relations to the TUV were deteriorating. Hessenbruch informed me through the grapevine that I had tried to bribe his people by providing them various favors, although there had been hints about what they would like, none of the presents had been rejected, and they had enjoyed the outings and dinners. At the same time, the B&W people, who disliked the idea of those handouts, obviously feared that I was becoming too close to the TUV. Hessenbruch then abruptly decided not to contact me any longer when it came to solving issues involving the process of the construction of the components. Since TUV now wanted to communicate with top management on their own, I was sidelined in this capacity for good. Fortunately, I had assumed many additional responsibilities over the years, which involved getting all inspection agencies, engineering and ASME code requirements researched and transformed into the final documents for building all heavy components. An arduous task, it was almost too much for one person to handle. At times, quite stressed out, I got into strange situations. In driving home from Mt. Vernon one day on Evansville's West side, I was crossing a divided 2-lane highway, as usual. There was a highly visible traffic light. Traffic was heavy. Approaching the crossing while deeply in thought about a problem, I drove straight ahead, ignoring the light. I saw a wall of cars waiting left and right—patiently—their drivers must have thought I was out of my mind—which I was. A deadly situation: he light was red! No one even honked the horn. One afternoon at the plant, again struggling with a bothersome problem, I had to use the restroom, where, searching for a urinal, I found none. But I found a porcelain contraption with a faucet, mounted on the mirrored wall. Peeing into it, I noticed the unusual looking drain and the stalls behind me; I suddenly knew I was urinating into a wash basin—in the ladies' room! I quickly fled, lucky that no one found out about my mistake. Very much later, outside of Evansville, I would sometimes tell this story to close friends.

This stressful time, and the mounting indication that the nuclear power industry stopped building nuclear power plants, made me think about changing employment once more. Originally I had thought nuclear power would be the solution to declining fossil fuel reserves and contamination of water and air resources. Countries like France had gone all out to adopt the atom split for power supply. They now produce 80% of their need from uranium—the highest ratio world-wide. In the US, the lobby organizations' increasing resistance, which used the power of the courts to delay or terminate applications for approval of new construction sites, over an endless array of safety concerns, was going to have an enormous effect on the safety of my job. Although a senior VP of B&W assured me that "people like you" would always be kept on the payroll, my concern was more about how B&W could fill this plant with orders without a steady

468 And Only The Horses Wore No Uniforms

flow of nuclear heavy components. There were no other equivalent, very large precision components in sight. Reactors for Navy use were handled already in a smaller, special hall, and defense orders were sporadic and sometimes stopped entirely.

YET ANOTHER MOVE: PALL TRINITY MICRO CORP AND ITHACA

Because I considered it my duty to provide for the family as best I could, I needed to be ahead of such impending disasters as layoff or transfer. The latter was also unappealing, as it might lead to a situation without proper schools or an attractive civic life. At least it could not hurt to try my luck. Wayne Wilcox had already left B&W for a large consulting company in Reading, PA. He later worked for many years for Scott Paper in Philadelphia. My resume was dusted off. This time, following Anna's suggestion, we left out the age and such youthful experiences as apprenticeships or anything that would "date" me and thus present detract from job chances for an engineer my age. Based on her Manpower experiences in the professional employment office at Mead Johnson, she suggested including a recent passport photo on which my face looked more like 40 than 50something. (At MJ, the secretaries would always place resumes with attractive photos on top of the boss' pile.) We knew it would be hard to leave the area, where we had settled in so nicely and found a wonderful school and such good friends.

Not much later, a response came from a company unknown to me, in Central New York: Pall Trinity Micro Corp., Division of Pall Corp. of Glen Cove, Long Island. The attached annual report was very interesting. Their business was filtration of liquids, starting with water and ending with beer, wine, oil, soap, gels, bio-suds and exotic liquids for the manufacture of electronic chips. Actually, the latter was not yet attempted, because the first PC's were still being fooled around with in the garages of Palo Alto. Pall Trinity Micro (PTM) made equipment for just about anything in industry. They had about 5,000 catalog items. I was invited for an interview with Don Burland in Cortland, NY, which turned out to be very promising, but it was obvious that the shops and offices looked decrepit. Without an employee cafeteria, some frequented fast food sites; others brown-bagged. Because the small corner near the shops, which allowed people to sit for lunch, was dirty and fly-infested, most shop people ate at their place of work. The hopelessly cluttered shops were an indication of production control problems. There were several sites for making filters of different designs and many special machines for the various manufacturing and inspection stops. Mr. Burland explained he wanted to fill the newly created position of manufacturing engineering manager. The company's rapid growth urgently called for organizing its manufacturing documentation in a professional manner. At this point, the shops did their jobs by looking at a more or less complete drawing, originated by Engineering. When problems occurred, the engineers ran post haste to the floor to give the workers a hand. Thus, most engineering time was spent on the floor, not on the drawing board—a total waste. They were very interested in my knowledge of the nuclear ASME code (section III—nuclear pressure vessels). PTM did considerable business in filtration equipment for nuclear power stations. One of the main applications was (and is) filtering the primary pressurized water being circulated through the hot uranium fuel elements in the pressure vessel into the steam generator, where the secondary circuit produces steam to drive the turbines of the power station. These filters are installed in the main covered concrete building and are designed to withstand earthquakes and such other impacts as bombs, airplanes, hurricanes, etc. They are therefore also built to section III of the ASME pressure vessel code, which covers nuclear power installations. Stress analysis of one of those vessels covers an enormous amount of pages, with very complex math, including vibrations (they are mainly set up under impact of earthquakes). Consequently, these nuclear filter pressure vessels looked very different from all others. Also, the handling of any spent nuclear filter had to be done remotely by robots, because these elements were very dangerous and loaded with radioactive particles, which were removed from the primary liquid.

We were discussing very responsible activities, and my experience in this field was unique. My title at B&W, manufacturing engineering group leader, which indicated that other engineers reported to me, became very important at this point, although it did not actually reflect my situation there. It is almost customary that engineers are promoted to management positions within the company they work for. Companies rarely promote someone from the outside without successful management experience. Mr. Burland did not investigate this further, and I was confident I could handle the position. It was an improvement to be part of a small, aggressive company with room for growth—the ideal employment situation! I would just be lucky to jump into a position involving hiring and training engineers, which they just assumed I could do. At that moment I only hoped for a good job offer and figured I could solve those questions later. Much later, Nick Renzi, then engineering manager, who later would become president, told me of his own professional experience. He had worked for many years at a Long Island plant (Lycoming, if I recall correctly), and was assigned to a section which dealt with all flow problems occurring in the fuel feeder piping for gas turbines and rocket motors. Most experienced hands spoke heavily accented English with a distinct German twang. All had arrived on these shores in late 1945, happy to continue applying their specialized, unique knowledge gained in Germany between 1936 and 45. He described them as the best engineers he had ever worked with; he could learn the most advanced flow technology from them. I would never have any trouble with Nick Renzi, who would always stress his high opinion of me. In a managers' meeting he would even say that only two people in the plant could write a good, comprehensive engineering report: "One is Hermann, and you all know the other one!" Later I was to follow him into his position as Vice President Engineering—the highlight of my professional career.

Mr. Burland then planned my next visit, which was to be together with Anna, since it was a leading position. Everything looked very positive. To raise no suspicion at B&W—and to allow time for meeting all of the VIPs—we selected a weekend date. This visit would include more detailed interviews and meeting the other top managers, as well as socializing with them and their wives. We explained everything to the kids. Naturally, they were not enthused about leaving Evansville so soon again. Each one had friends. At their age it must have been harder than ever to face another move with all its anxieties and insecurities. Having to jump into a new social setting where one is the stranger from an unknown place in Indiana, a "Hoosier," would be hard, although Bill and Karen had not assumed the distinct Hoosier twang or any trace of a Southern accent at all.

When Anna and I arrived in Cortland, I went into meetings, while she toured the Cortland area with a realtor. Later that weekend, we drove to Ithaca on our own to meet a realtor who took us to the fifth floor of the Johnson Museum at Cornell. Delighted by the view, Cornell University and the town's ambiance, we quickly decided that Ithaca would be the preferable town in which to live. We knew we would prefer the educational opportunities and the stimulating environment of a university town with two college campuses. It would greatly facilitate Anna's plans to find employment at Cornell, where she would later work in responsible positions for fourteen years. Last, but not least, Ithaca is surrounded by outstanding scenery, including Lake Cayuga and three beautiful state parks.

On that first day, I met Marce (Marcel) Verrando, the VP Manufacturing, to whom I was to report, while Don Burland was in charge of all shop activities. Since Marce, an extroverted, flashy guy with strong opinions, needed yes-men around him, I would always approach him very carefully. I also met the Quality Assurance Manager John Cummings, and Nick Renzi. With these people I would interact daily. Last, I was ushered into President Chet (Chesterfield) Siebert's Office. An imposing, oversized figure with an accommodating, benevolent demeanor and a reddish face, he smoked a cigarette incessantly and in a greedy manner, while another, already lit, was waiting on one of the three loaded ash trays on his huge desk. I was to have little to do with him in the future; he was mainly developing business with his sales and marketing gang. He held a chemistry degree from Rensselaer College, a very good engineering school on the Hudson River.

That same evening, Messrs. Burland and Cummings and their wives took us to Ithaca's South Hill and lavishly entertained us at Ithaca College's Tower Club. Sitting at a huge picture window overlooking downtown Ithaca with Cayuga Lake in the background was a marvelous experience between drinks, steak, wine, etc. Burland advised me to be steadfast when B&W would make its counter offer. It seemed then that he had decided to hire me. For some reason of internal politics, he, not Verrando, to whom I was to report, was involved in my hiring. Perhaps Verrando wanted an underling to do the work, who could be blamed if I would not work out. Hiring a stranger is always a tough task. That night, dead tired, and with Anna suffering from a bad migraine, the two of us ended up in Burland's home to look at some ancient German bibles, while we would rather have been in bed!

Burland invited us to his church on Sunday morning. He wanted to meet me in his office before the service to "conclude the visit." At that time he made me a very good offer, which would improve our income very nicely. During the transition period Anna would remain in Evansville to sell the house while I would live in a hotel for one month. He was agreeable to the idea that I could bring one of the children along; all our expenses would be taken care of. Thus, Bill could start the school year in Ithaca, while Karen would start somewhat later. Happy about the offer, I told Burland I would give notice and set a date for my first day of work, about two months later, as I still had to finish up some work at B&W. All was subject to Anna's agreement and a written proposal by PTM. I knew that Anna also wanted to finish some projects she had started at Atlas and to see her annual raise on record there. Anna's Atlas Van Lines job had helped in receiving the good offer. We had made her resignation from Atlas somewhat of an issue in light of insecure future job prospects for her. Then we joined our wives in Don Burland's church, where I whispered to Anna that we had it in the bag! We arrived home happy, although much work was ahead.

B&W accepted my resignation without fuss. Those in charge expressed regret, noting there would always be a place for people of my caliber. But there was no counter offer. Jim van Meter, Wayne Wilcox and some other managers had already left. The German account had become a nightmare for B&W. Its top management was starting to get rid of people whom they blamed for the financial disaster. Apparently no one had foreseen the demands of the TUV. Because their mode of operation caused so much additional work and delays, the project was turning into a huge loss. By now, the entire management team was new, consisting of old hands at the game of trying to salvage a company. From then on, the work at the Mt. Vernon plant steadily diminished. When visiting Evansville years later, I found the plant closed and the large overhead cranes outside for transport of heavy components rusted. B&W had not even bothered to conserve their valuable equipment; it was all "written off" in the books. The nuclear power station era was temporarily dead. It will be revived when fuel prices threaten the world economy as a whole in the future.

One beautiful morning in late summer Bill and I left for Ithaca. The 14 hour trip was long and lonely. Devastated, Bill did not say one word during the entire journey. We moved into a nice room at the Sheraton Inn on Triphammer Road, with an indoor pool, in walking distance to DeWitt Junior High School. On weekends we looked at homes in the Northeast area, most convenient for my commute to Cortland, and found a nice house nearby, on 208 Christopher Lane, in accordance with the specifications we had worked out beforehand. When Anna and Karen arrived, they liked the home very much. We would live there until after my retirement. With these events, the great journey of my and Anna's life had finally come to an end. Karen and Bill's struggles were just beginning, but they can very well remember our life on Christopher Lane, as they were beginning to collect their own life stories. I sincerely hope they are as happy with theirs as Anna and I are with ours.

CONCLUSION

These reflections have been a wonderful opportunity to remember where I came from, how I managed to grow and survive, and how all of us were born and grew together. After my many years at Pall Corporation and Anna's exciting career at Cornell University, she retired in 1990 and I in 1991. Now, in the summer of 2006, we look back on our life. First, both of us think we made a good decision to marry each other and leave Brazil. Our life thereafter was a never-ending chain of challenges brought upon by circumstances. Each one of those was thoroughly considered and solved together. In this manner our characters were formed to what they are now. Our path was not easy, but at the same time it provided an escape from the usual. We now see our life as a fascinating learning experience and adventure. We feel fortunate that our main goal, to manage our affairs for the family's welfare, has turned out reasonably well. As my mother had always said, I was and am a very lucky fellow—an observation with which those who have read these memoirs are likely to agree. But being lucky is harder if no initiative is taken. Yes, the tough times behind us did challenge our wits, but that was an unavoidable part of our life, from which we learned. It is now time to thank my dearly loved companion and friend for the last fifty years, Anna-Lore, for her advice, contributions, work, faith, cheerfulness and all other attributes which I lack. She has documented her own family background also. This is in possession of our children. I also thank William Christopher, Karen, and our son-in-law George for their expressions of love and togetherness. Karen and Bill's (now Chris') resilience while growing up, their capacity to courageously accept and cope with changes under difficult circumstances, and their ability to always be good sports, will never be forgotten. We now marvel at how they have achieved most valuable goals in their own special way over the years. It was, and still is, a wonderful life

978-0-595-42849-6
0-595-42849-5

9 780595 428496